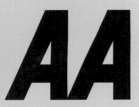

BIG ROAD ATLAS BRITAIN

Atlas contents

Map pages	inside front cover
Route planning	***II–XVI***
Route planner	*II–V*
London district	*VI–VII*
Restricted junctions	*VIII*
Smart motorways	*IX*
Caravan and camping sites in Britain	*X–XI*
Traffic signs and road markings	*XII–XIII*
Channel hopping and the Isle of Wight	*XIV–XV*
Scotland, North Sea and Irish Sea ferries	*XVI*
Atlas symbols	**1**
Road maps 1:190,000 scale	**2–112**
Channel Islands 1:135,000 scale	6–7
Isle of Man 1:190,000 scale	60
Skye & The Small Isles 1:340,000 scale	100
Western Isles 1:703,000 scale	106
Orkney and Shetland Islands 1:709,000 scale	106

Ferry ports

Aberdeen Harbour	*XVI*	Heysham Harbour	*XVI*	Plymouth, Port of	*XIV*
Calais	*XIV*	Holyhead Harbour	*XVI*	Poole, Port of	*XIV*
Channel Tunnel	*XV*	Hull, Port of	*XVI*	Port of Tyne	*XVI*
Dover, Port of	*XV*	Liverpool Docks	*XVI*	Portsmouth Harbour	*XIV*
Fishguard Harbour	*XVI*	Newhaven Harbour	*XV*	Southampton, Port of	*XIV*
Harwich International Port	*XVI*	Pembroke Dock	*XVI*		

Tourist sites with satnav friendly postcodes	**113**
Ireland road maps 1:1 million scale	**114–115**

Town plans

Aberdeen	99	Glasgow	118	Norwich	120
Aberystwyth	32	Great Yarmouth	51	Nottingham	120
Bath	116	Harrogate	118	Oxford	120
Birmingham	116	Inverness	118	Peterborough	121
Blackpool	116	Ipswich	119	Plymouth	121
Bradford	116	Kingston upon Hull	119	Portsmouth	121
Bristol	116	Leeds	119	Salisbury	121
Cambridge	116	Leicester	119	Sheffield	121
Canterbury	117	Lincoln	119	Southampton	121
Cardiff	117	Liverpool	54	Southend-on-Sea	23
Chester	117	Llandudno	53	Stratford-upon-Avon	122
Coventry	117	London	119	Sunderland	71
Derby	117	Manchester	120	Swansea	122
Dundee	117	Middlesbrough	71	Swindon	122
Durham	118	Milton Keynes	120	Wolverhampton	122
Edinburgh	118	Newcastle upon Tyne	120	Worcester	122
Exeter	118	Newquay	3	York	122

Index to place names	**123–144**
County, administrative area map	123
Distances and journey times	**inside back cover**

Scale 1:190,000
or 3 miles to 1 inch

27th edition June 2017

Original edition printed 1991.

Cartography: All cartography in this atlas edited, designed and produced by the Mapping Services Department of AA Publishing (A05504).

Publisher's Notes: Published by AA Publishing (a trading name of AA Media Limited, whose registered office is Fanum House, Basing View, Basingstoke, Hampshire RG21 4EA, UK. Registered number 06112600).

ISBN: 978 0 7495 7855 8 (spiral bound)
ISBN: 978 0 7495 7854 1 (paperback)

A CIP catalogue record for this book is available from The British Library.

The publishers would welcome information to correct any errors or omissions and to keep this atlas up to date. Please write to the Atlas Editor, AA Publishing, The Automobile Association, Fanum House, Basing View, Basingstoke, Hampshire RG21 4EA, UK.
E-mail: *roadatlasfeedback@theaa.com*

Acknowledgements: AA Publishing would like to thank the following for their assistance in producing this atlas:
Crematoria data provided by the Cremation Society of Great Britain. Cadw, English Heritage, Forestry Commission, Historic Scotland, Johnsons, National Trust and National Trust for Scotland, RSPB, The Wildlife Trust, Scottish Natural Heritage, Natural England, The Countryside Council for Wales (road maps). Award winning beaches from 'Blue Flag' and 'Keep Scotland Beautiful' (summer 2016 data): for latest information visit *www.blueflag.org* and *www.keepscotlandbeautiful.org*

Printer: Printed in Italy by G. Canale & C. S.p.A.

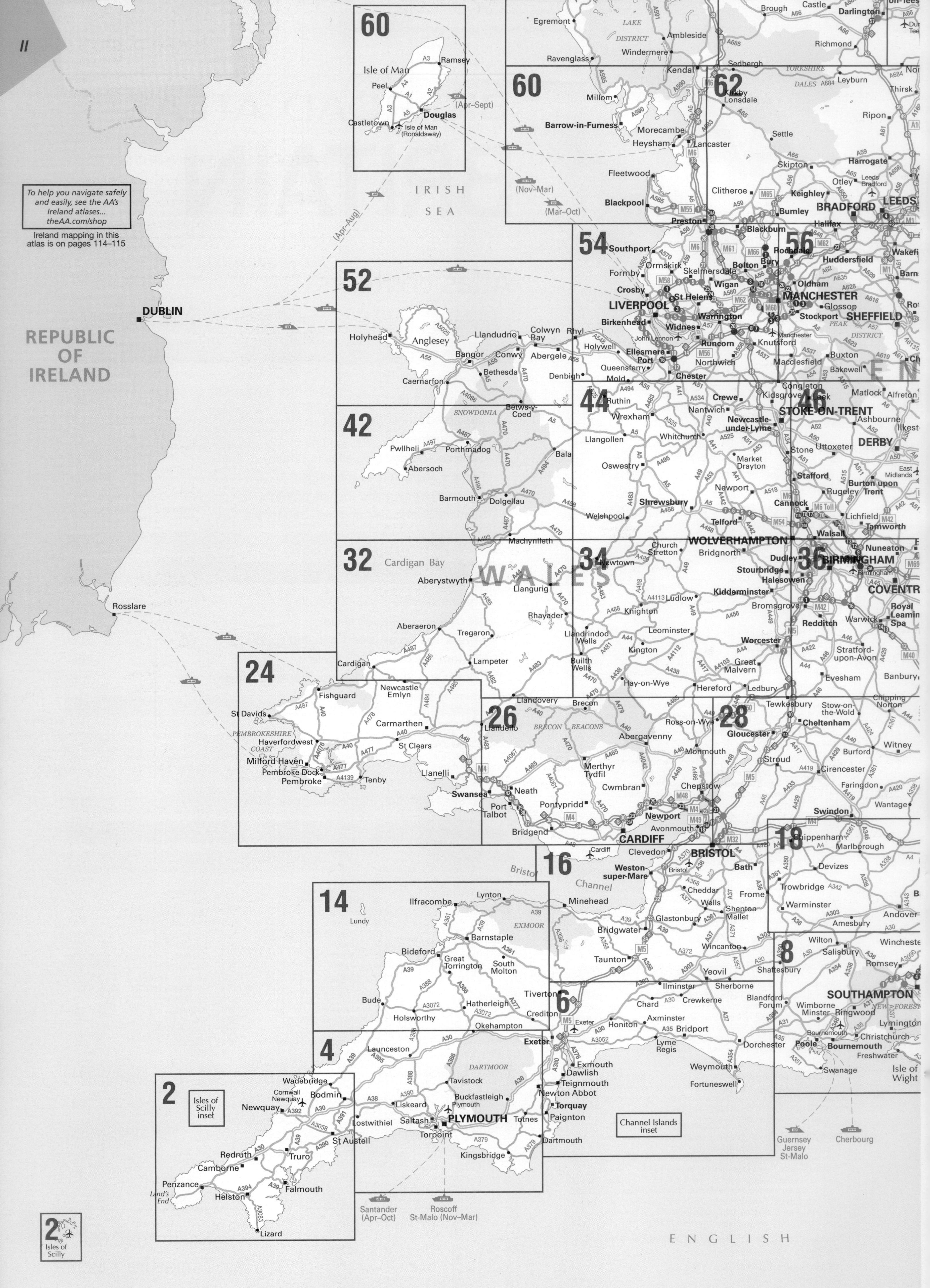

To help you navigate safely and easily, see the AA's Ireland atlases... theAA.com/shop
Ireland mapping in this atlas is on pages 114–115
REPUBLIC OF IRELAND
DUBLIN
Rosslare
IRISH SEA
Isle of Man
Ramsey
Peel
Douglas
Castletown
Isle of Man (Ronaldsway)
(Apr–Sept)
(Apr–Aug)
(Nov–Mar)
(Mar–Oct)
60
62
54
56
52
44
46
42
32
34
36
24
26
28
16
18
14
8
6
4
2
Keswick
Egremont
LAKE DISTRICT
Ambleside
Windermere
Ravenglass
Kendal
Sedbergh
Kirkby Lonsdale
Millom
Barrow-in-Furness
Morecambe
Heysham
Lancaster
Fleetwood
Blackpool
Preston
Clitheroe
Burnley
Keighley
BRADFORD
LEEDS
Halifax
Huddersfield
Barnard Castle
Brough
Darlington
Stockton-on-Tees
Richmond
YORKSHIRE DALES
Leyburn
Thirsk
Ripon
Settle
Skipton
Harrogate
Otley
Southport
Ormskirk
Formby
Crosby
LIVERPOOL
Birkenhead
St Helens
Skelmersdale
Wigan
Bolton
Bury
Rochdale
Blackburn
Oldham
MANCHESTER
Glossop
Stockport
SHEFFIELD
Warrington
Widnes
Runcorn
Knutsford
Ellesmere Port
Chester
Northwich
Macclesfield
Buxton
Bakewell
Holyhead
Anglesey
Llandudno
Colwyn Bay
Rhyl
Bangor
Conwy
Abergele
Holywell
Bethesda
Denbigh
Queensferry
Mold
Caernarfon
SNOWDONIA
Betws-y-Coed
Ruthin
Wrexham
Crewe
Nantwich
Congleton
Kidsgrove
Leek
STOKE-ON-TRENT
Newcastle-under-Lyme
Matlock
Alfreton
Ashbourne
DERBY
Pwllheli
Porthmadog
Abersoch
Bala
Llangollen
Whitchurch
Oswestry
Market Drayton
Stone
Uttoxeter
Stafford
Barmouth
Dolgellau
Newport
Shrewsbury
Telford
Welshpool
Cannock
Rugeley
Burton upon Trent
Lichfield
Tamworth
Walsall
Machynlleth
WOLVERHAMPTON
Bridgnorth
Church Stretton
Newtown
Dudley
BIRMINGHAM
Nuneaton
COVENTRY
Cardigan Bay
Aberystwyth
WALES
Llangurig
Stourbridge
Halesowen
Kidderminster
Ludlow
Knighton
Rhayader
Bromsgrove
Redditch
Warwick
Royal Leamington Spa
Aberaeron
Tregaron
Llandrindod Wells
Leominster
Kington
Worcester
Stratford-upon-Avon
Cardigan
Lampeter
Builth Wells
Hay-on-Wye
Great Malvern
Evesham
Banbury
Fishguard
Newcastle Emlyn
Hereford
Ledbury
Tewkesbury
St Davids
Llandovery
Brecon
Cheltenham
Stow-on-the-Wold
Chipping Norton
PEMBROKESHIRE COAST
Carmarthen
BRECON BEACONS
Ross-on-Wye
Gloucester
Haverfordwest
St Clears
Llandeilo
Abergavenny
Monmouth
Stroud
Burford
Witney
Milford Haven
Pembroke Dock
Pembroke
Tenby
Llanelli
Merthyr Tydfil
Cirencester
Faringdon
Swansea
Neath
Port Talbot
Cwmbran
Chepstow
Pontypridd
Newport
Swindon
Wantage
Bridgend
CARDIFF
Avonmouth
BRISTOL
Chippenham
Marlborough
Clevedon
Weston-super-Mare
Bath
Devizes
Bristol Channel
Cheddar
Wells
Frome
Trowbridge
Warminster
Andover
Lundy
Ilfracombe
Lynton
EXMOOR
Minehead
Glastonbury
Shepton Mallet
Barnstaple
Bridgwater
Amesbury
Bideford
Great Torrington
South Molton
Taunton
Wincanton
Wilton
Salisbury
Winchester
Romsey
Shaftesbury
Yeovil
Sherborne
Bude
Hatherleigh
Tiverton
Ilminster
Crewkerne
Chard
SOUTHAMPTON
Holsworthy
Crediton
Exeter
Honiton
Axminster
Blandford Forum
Wimborne Minster
Ringwood
NEW FOREST
Lymington
Okehampton
Bridport
Lyme Regis
Christchurch
Bournemouth
Poole
Launceston
DARTMOOR
Exmouth
Dorchester
Freshwater
Dawlish
Weymouth
Swanage
Isle of Wight
Tavistock
Teignmouth
Fortuneswell
Newton Abbot
Wadebridge
Bodmin
Buckfastleigh
Torquay
Isles of Scilly inset
Newquay
Cornwall Newquay
Liskeard
Plymouth
Paignton
Lostwithiel
Saltash
PLYMOUTH
Totnes
Channel Islands inset
Torpoint
St Austell
Dartmouth
Redruth
Truro
Kingsbridge
Guernsey Jersey St-Malo
Cherbourg
Camborne
Penzance
Land's End
Helston
Falmouth
Lizard
Santander (Apr-Oct)
Roscoff St-Malo (Nov-Mar)
Isles of Scilly
ENGLISH

EMERGENCY DIVERSION ROUTES

In an emergency it may be necessary to close a section of motorway or other main road to traffic, so a temporary sign may advise drivers to follow a diversion route. To help drivers navigate the route, black symbols on yellow patches may be permanently displayed on existing direction signs, including motorway signs. Symbols may also be used on separate signs with yellow backgrounds.

For further information see *theaa.com/motoring_advice/general-advice/emergency-diversion-routes.html*

FERRY INFORMATION

Information on ferry routes and operators can be found on pages *XIV–XVI*.

Motorway	
Toll motorway	
Primary route dual carriageway	
Primary route single carriageway	
Other A road	
Vehicle ferry	or V
Fast vehicle ferry or catamaran	
National Park	
98	Atlas page number

0	10	20	30 miles
0	10	20	30	40 kilometres

To help you navigate safely and easily, see the AA's France and Europe atlases...
theAA.com/shop

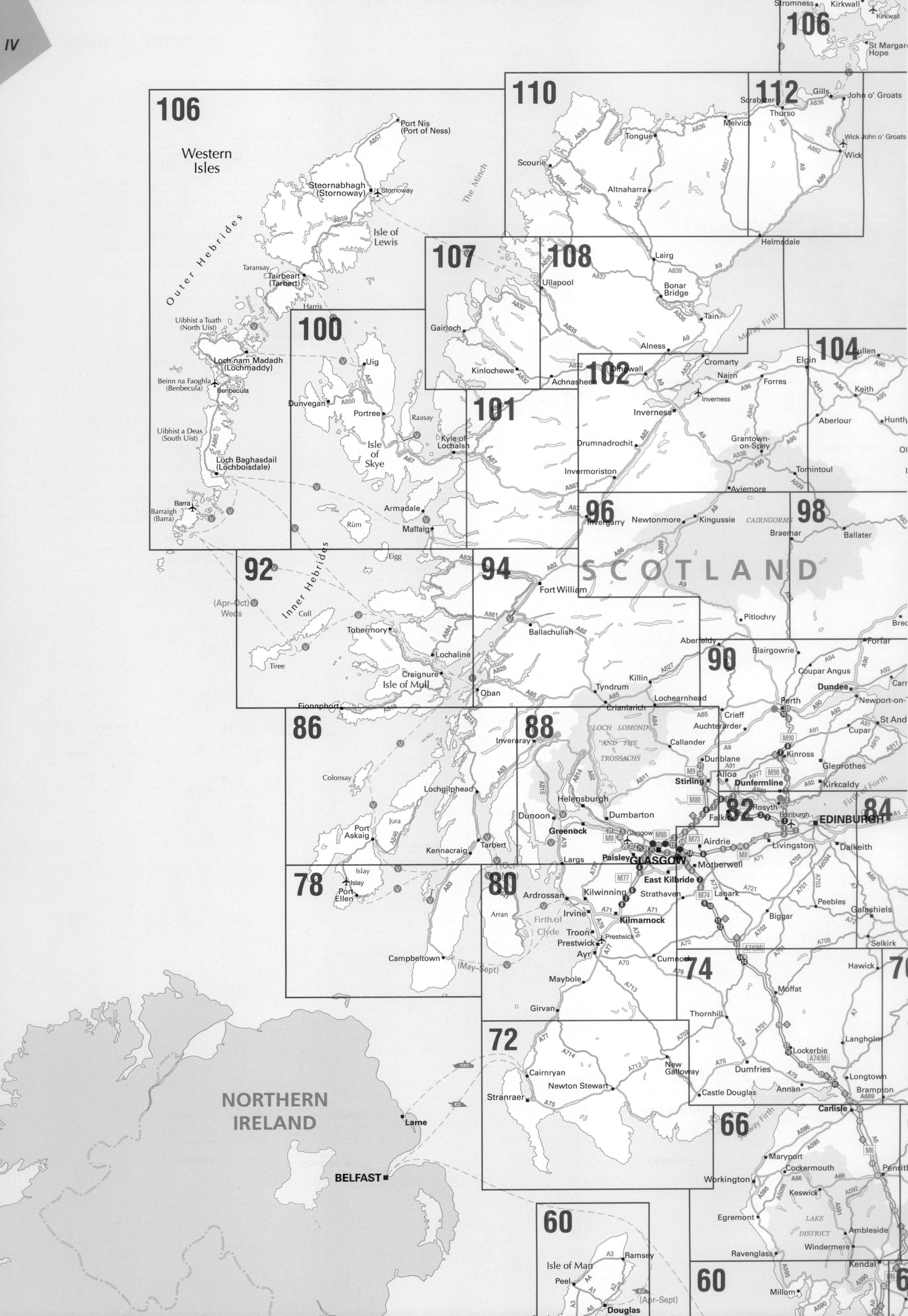

106
Western Isles

106

110

112

107

108

100

104

102

101

96

98

SCOTLAND

92

94

90

86

88

82

84

78

80

74

70

NORTHERN IRELAND

72

66

60

60

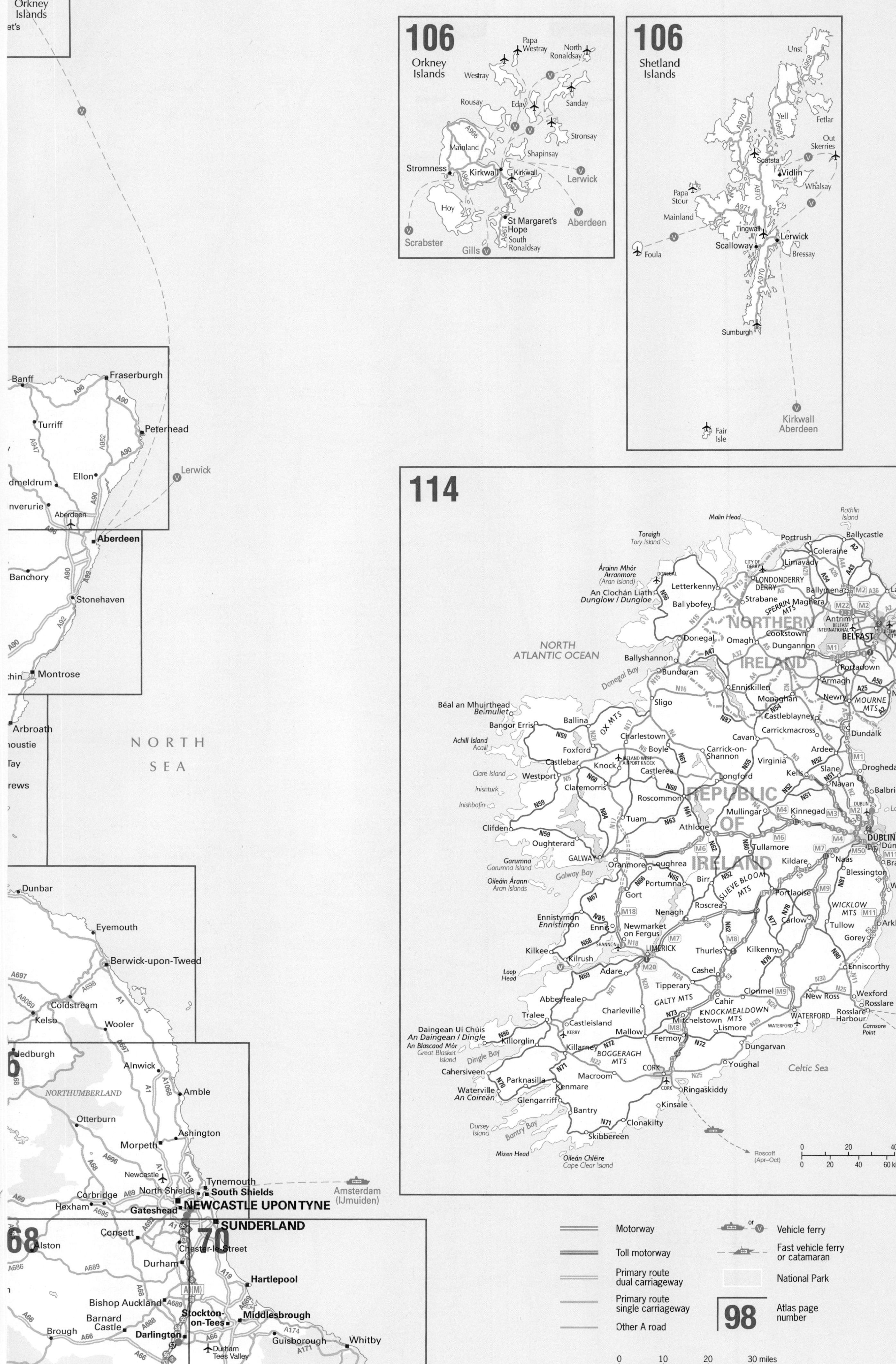
106
Orkney Islands
Papa Westray
North Ronaldsay
Westray
Rousay
Eday
Sanday
Stronsay
Mainland
Shapinsay
Stromness
Kirkwall
Lerwick
Hoy
St Margaret's Hope
South Ronaldsay
Aberdeen
Scrabster
Gills
106
Shetland Islands
Unst
Yell
Fetlar
Out Skerries
Scatsta
Vidlin
Whalsay
Papa Stour
Mainland
Tingwall
Lerwick
Scalloway
Bressay
Foula
Sumburgh
Fair Isle
Kirkwall
Aberdeen
114
Malin Head
Rathlin Island
Portrush
Ballycastle
Coleraine
Limavady
LONDONDERRY DERRY
Letterkenny
Ballymena
Larne
Strabane
Ballybofey
An Clochán Liath
Dunglow / Dungloe
NORTHERN IRELAND
Antrim
Cookstown
BELFAST
Bangor
Newtownards
Omagh
Dungannon
Donegal
NORTH ATLANTIC OCEAN
Ballyshannon
Bundoran
Enniskillen
Portadown
Armagh
Portaferry
Downpatrick
Sligo
Monaghan
Newry
MOURNE MTS
Newcastle
Béal an Mhuirthead
Belmullet
Bangor Erris
Ballina
OX MTS
Castleblayney
Carrickmacross
Dundalk
IRISH SEA
Achill Island
Charlestown
Foxford
Boyle
Cavan
Castlebar
Knock
Carrick-on-Shannon
Virginia
Ardee
Westport
Castlerea
Kells
Slane
Drogheda
Claremorris
Longford
Navan
Balbriggan
REPUBLIC OF IRELAND
Roscommon
Mullingar
Kinnegad
Tuam
Athlone
Clifden
DUBLIN
Dún Laoghaire
Oughterard
Tullamore
Bray
GALWAY
Oranmore
Loughrea
Kildare
Naas
Blessington
Galway Bay
Portumna
Birr
SLIEVE BLOOM MTS
Wicklow
Gort
Portlaoise
Roscrea
Nenagh
WICKLOW MTS
Ennistymon
Ennis
Newmarket on Fergus
Carlow
Tullow
Arklow
Gorey
Kilkee
Kilrush
LIMERICK
Thurles
Kilkenny
Adare
Cashel
Enniscorthy
Loop Head
Tipperary
GALTY MTS
Abbeyfeale
Cahir
Clonmel
Wexford
New Ross
Rosslare
Tralee
Charleville
Castleisland
KNOCKMEALDOWN MTS
WATERFORD
Rosslare Harbour
Mitchelstown
Lismore
Killorglin
Mallow
Fermoy
Dungarvan
Killarney
BOGGERAGH MTS
Celtic Sea
Cahersiveen
Macroom
CORK
Youghal
Parknasilla
Kenmare
Ringaskiddy
Waterville
An Coireán
Glengarriff
Kinsale
Bantry
Bantry Bay
Clonakilty
Skibbereen
Mizen Head
Oileán Chléire
Cape Clear Island
0 20 40 miles
0 20 40 60 kilometres
Banff
Fraserburgh
Turriff
Peterhead
Ellon
Lerwick
Aberdeen
Banchory
Stonehaven
Montrose
Arbroath
NORTH SEA
Dunbar
Eyemouth
Berwick-upon-Tweed
Coldstream
Kelso
Wooler
Jedburgh
Alnwick
Amble
NORTHUMBERLAND
Otterburn
Ashington
Morpeth
Tynemouth
South Shields
North Shields
Corbridge
Hexham
Gateshead
NEWCASTLE UPON TYNE
Amsterdam (IJmuiden)
SUNDERLAND
Consett
Alston
Chester-le-Street
Durham
Hartlepool
Bishop Auckland
Stockton-on-Tees
Middlesbrough
Barnard Castle
Brough
Darlington
Guisborough
Whitby
Durham Tees Valley
NORTH YORK MOORS
Richmond
Sedbergh
YORKSHIRE DALES
Leyburn
Northallerton
Scarborough
Thirsk
Pickering
Helmsley
Filey
Kirkby Lonsdale
Ripon
Easingwold
Malton
Motorway
Toll motorway
Primary route dual carriageway
Primary route single carriageway
Other A road
Vehicle ferry
Fast vehicle ferry or catamaran
National Park
98
Atlas page number
0 10 20 30 miles
0 10 20 30 40 kilometres

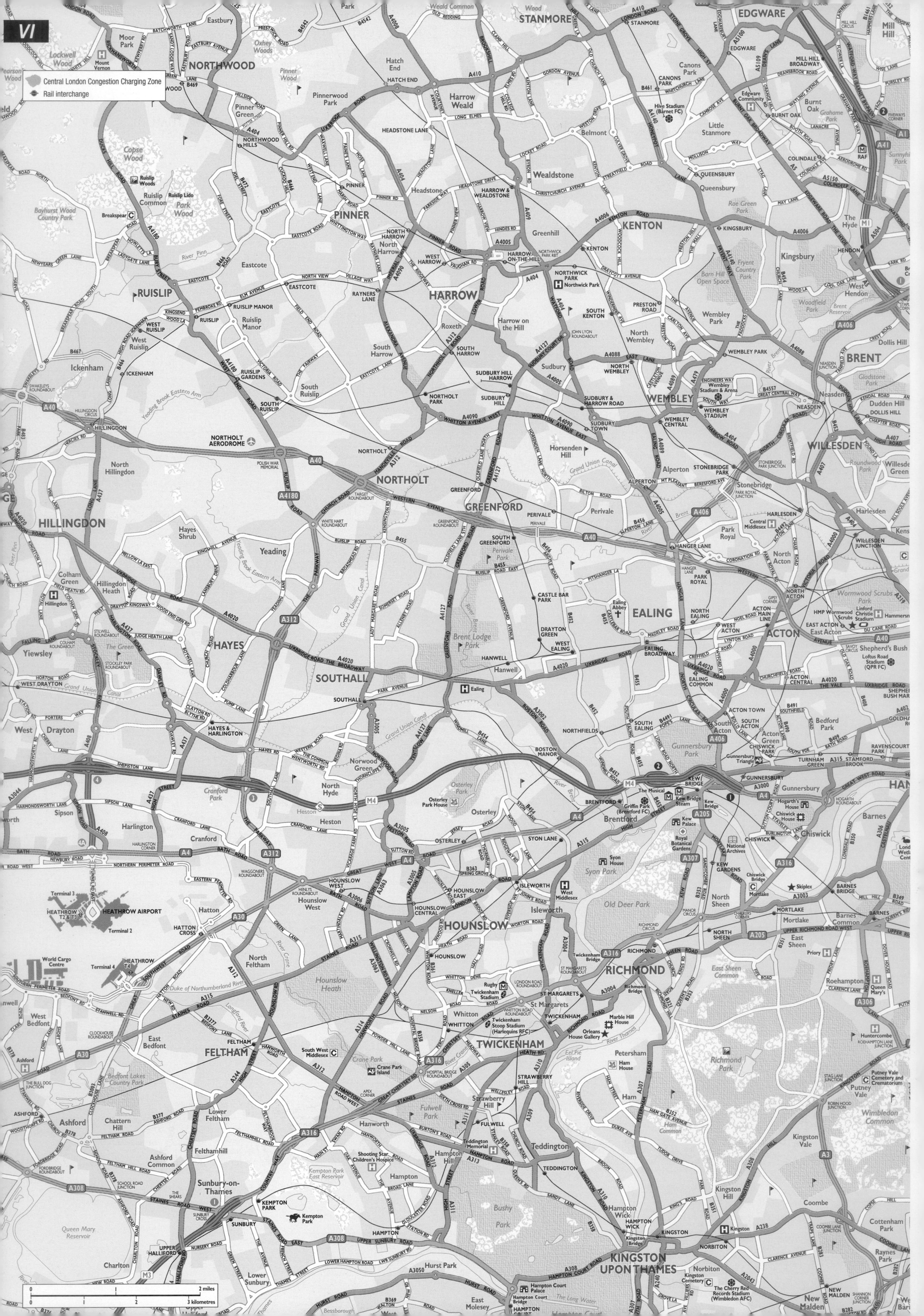
VI
Central London Congestion Charging Zone
Rail interchange
STANMORE
EDGWARE
NORTHWOOD
Harrow Weald
Canons Park
Hatch End
Pinnerwood Park
Mill Hill
Burnt Oak
Little Stanmore
Belmont
Wealdstone
Queensbury
Colindale
Headstone
PINNER
Ruislip Common
KENTON
Kingsbury
Greenhill
Eastcote
RUISLIP
HARROW
Wembley Park
Roxeth
Harrow on the Hill
North Wembley
Ruislip Manor
West Ruislip
Ickenham
South Harrow
South Ruislip
Sudbury
WEMBLEY
BRENT
Neasden
WILLESDEN
HILLINGDON
North Hillingdon
NORTHOLT
GREENFORD
Perivale
Alperton
Stonebridge
Harlesden
Hayes Shrub
Yeading
Park Royal
North Acton
EALING
ACTON
Colham Green
Hillingdon Heath
HAYES
Yiewsley
SOUTHALL
Hanwell
Brent Lodge Park
West Drayton
Drayton
West
HAYES & HARLINGTON
Norwood Green
North Hyde
Heston
Cranford
Harlington
Sipson
Osterley
BRENTFORD
Gunnersbury
Chiswick
Barnes
Kew Gardens
HEATHROW AIRPORT
Terminal 2
Terminal 3
Terminal 4
Hatton
Hounslow West
HOUNSLOW
Isleworth
Syon Park
Old Deer Park
North Sheen
East Sheen
Mortlake
RICHMOND
North Feltham
Hounslow Heath
St Margarets
TWICKENHAM
Whitton
West Bedfont
East Bedfont
FELTHAM
Ashford
Chattern Hill
Lower Feltham
Hanworth
Fulwell Park
Strawberry Hill
Teddington
Petersham
Ham
Richmond Park
Roehampton
Putney Vale
Wimbledon Common
Kingston Vale
Kingston Hill
Coombe
Ashford Common
Sunbury-on-Thames
Hampton
Hampton Hill
Hampton Wick
Bushy Park
Queen Mary Reservoir
Charlton
Upper Halliford
Lower Sunbury
Hurst Park
East Molesey
KINGSTON UPON THAMES
Norbiton
New Malden
Cottenham Park
Raynes Park
2 miles
3 kilometres

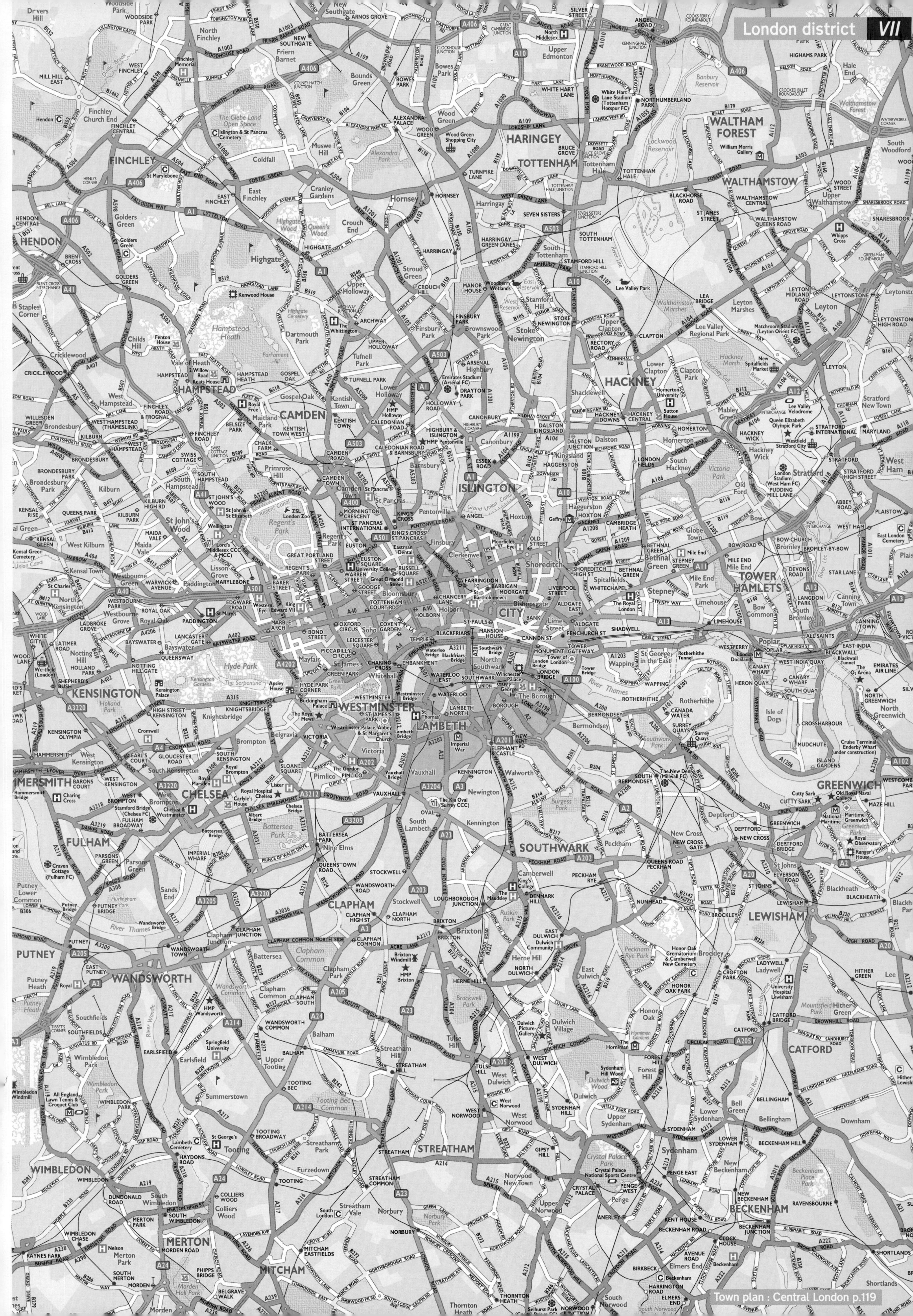

HENDON
FINCHLEY
HARINGEY
TOTTENHAM
WALTHAM FOREST
WALTHAMSTOW
HAMPSTEAD
CAMDEN
HACKNEY
ISLINGTON
KENSINGTON
WESTMINSTER
CITY
TOWER HAMLETS
LAMBETH
CHELSEA
FULHAM
GREENWICH
SOUTHWARK
CLAPHAM
LEWISHAM
PUTNEY
WANDSWORTH
CATFORD
STREATHAM
WIMBLEDON
BECKENHAM
MERTON
MITCHAM
Highgate
Hampstead Heath
Regent's Park
Hyde Park
River Thames
Battersea Park
Shoreditch
Stratford
Canary Wharf
Isle of Dogs
Brixton
Peckham
Dulwich
Crystal Palace
Sydenham

Town plan : Central London p.119

Restricted junctions

Motorway and Primary Route junctions which have access or exit restrictions are shown on the map pages thus:

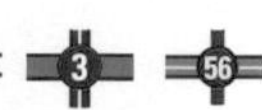

M1 London - Leeds

Junction	Northbound	Southbound
2	Access only from A1 (northbound)	Exit only to A1 (southbound)
4	Access only from A41 (northbound)	Exit only to A41 (southbound)
6A	Access only from M25 (no link from A405)	Exit only to M25 (no link from A405)
7	Access only from A414	Exit only to A414
17	Exit only to M45	Access only from M45
19	Exit only to M6 (northbound)	Access only from A14 (southbound)
21A	Exit only, no access	Access only, no exit
23A	Access only from A42	No restriction
24A	Access only, no exit	Access only, no exit
35A	Access only, no exit	Exit only, no access
43	Exit only to M621	Access only from M621
48	Exit only to A1(M) (northbound)	Access only from A1(M) (southbound)

M2 Rochester - Faversham

Junction	Westbound	Eastbound
1	No exit to A2 (eastbound)	No access from A2 (westbound)

M3 Sunbury - Southampton

Junction	Northeastbound	Southwestbound
8	Access only from A303, no exit	Exit only to A303, no access
10	Exit only, no access	Access only, no exit
14	Access from M27 only, no exit	No access to M27 (westbound)

M4 London - South Wales

Junction	Westbound	Eastbound
1	Access only from A4 (westbound)	Exit only to A4 (eastbound)
2	Access only from A4 (westbound)	Access only from A4 (eastbound)
21	Exit only to M48	Access only from M48
23	Access only from M48	Exit only to M48
25	Exit only, no access	Access only, no exit
25A	Exit only, no access	Access only, no exit
29	Exit only to A48(M)	Access only from A48(M)
38	Access only, no exit	No restriction
39	Access only, no exit	Access only or exit
42	Exit only to A483	Access only from A483

M5 Birmingham - Exeter

Junction	Northeastbound	Southwestbound
10	Access only, no exit	Exit only, no access
11A	Access only from A417 (westbound)	Exit only to A417 (eastbound)
18A	Exit only to M49	Access only from M49
18	Exit only, no access	Access only, no exit

M6 Toll Motorway

Junction	Northwestbound	Southeastbound
T1	Access only, no exit	No access or exit
T2	No access or exit	Exit only, no access
T5	Access only, no exit	Exit only to A5148 (northbound), no access
T7	Exit only, no access	Access only, no exit
T8	Exit only, no access	Access only, no exit

M6 Rugby - Carlisle

Junction	Northbound	Southbound
3A	Exit only to M6 Toll	Access only from M6 Toll
4	Exit only to M42 (southbound) & A446	Exit only to A446
4A	Access only from M42 (southbound)	Exit only to M42
5	Exit only, no access	Access only, no exit
10A	Exit only to M54	Access only from M54
11A	Access only from M6 Toll	Exit only to M6 Toll
with M56 (jct 20A)	No restriction	Access only from M56 (eastbound)
20	Exit only to M56 (westbound)	Access only from M56 (eastbound)
24	Access only, no exit	Exit only, no access
25	Access only, no exit	Exit only, no access
30	Access only from M61	Exit only to M61
31A	Access only, no exit	Exit only, no access
45	Exit only, no access	Access only, no exit

M8 Edinburgh - Bishopton

Junction	Westbound	Eastbound
6	Exit only, no access	Access only, no exit
6A	Access only, no exit	Exit only, no access
7	Access only, no exit	Exit only, no access
7A	Exit only, no access	Access only from A725 (northbound), no exit
8	No access from M73 (southbound) or from A8 (eastbound) & A89	No exit to M73 (northbound) or to A8 (westbound) & A89
9	Access only, no exit	Exit only, no access
13	Access only from M80 (southbound)	Exit only to M80 (northbound)
14	Access only, no exit	Exit only, no access
16	Exit only to A804	Access only from A879
17	Exit only to A82	No restriction
18	Access only from A82 (eastbound)	Exit only to A814
19	No access from A814 (westbound)	Exit only to A814 (westbound)
20	Exit only, no access	Access only, no exit
21	Access only, no exit	Exit only to A8
22	Exit only to M77 (southbound)	Access only from M77 (northbound)
23	Exit only to B768	Access only from B768
25	No access or exit from or to A8	No access or exit from or to A8
25A	Exit only, no access	Access only, no exit
28	Access only, no exit	Exit only, no access
28A	Exit only to A737	Access only from A737

M9 Edinburgh - Dunblane

Junction	Northwestbound	Southeastbound
2	Access only, no exit	Exit only, no access
3	Access only, no exit	Exit only, no access
6	Access only, no exit	Exit only to A905
8	Exit only to M876 (southwestbound)	Access only from M876 (northeastbound)

M11 London - Cambridge

Junction	Northbound	Southbound
4	Access only from A406 (eastbound)	Exit only to A406
5	Access only, no exit	Exit only, no access

(M11 continued)

Junction		
8A	Exit only, no access	No direct access, use jct 8
9	Exit only to A11	Access only from A11
13	Exit only, no access	Access only, no exit
14	Exit only, no access	Access only, no exit

M20 Swanley - Folkestone

Junction	Northwestbound	Southeastbound
2	Staggered junction; follow signs - access only	Staggered junction; follow signs - exit only
3	Exit only to M26 (westbound)	Access only from M26 (eastbound)
5	Access only from A20	For access follow signs - exit only to A20
6	No restriction	For exit follow signs
11A	Access only, no exit	Exit only, no access

M23 Hooley - Crawley

Junction	Northbound	Southbound
7	Exit only to A23 (northbound)	Access only from A23 (southbound)
10A	Access only, no exit	Exit only, no access

M25 London Orbital Motorway

Junction	Clockwise	Anticlockwise
1B	No direct access, use slip road to jct 2	Access only, no exit
	Exit only	
5	No exit to M26 (eastbound)	No access from M26
19	Exit only, no access	Access only, no exit
21	Access only from M1 (southbound)	Access only from M1 (southbound)
	Exit only to M1 (northbound)	Exit only to M1 (northbound)
31	No exit (use slip road via jct 30), access only	No access (use slip road via jct 30), exit only

M26 Sevenoaks - Wrotham

Junction	Westbound	Eastbound
with M25 (jct 5)	Exit only to clockwise M25 (westbound)	Access only from anticlockwise M25
with M20 (jct 3)	Access only from M20 (northwestbound)	Exit only to M20 (southeastbound)

M27 Cadnam - Portsmouth

Junction	Northbound	Southbound
4	Staggered junction; follow signs - access only from M3 (southbound). Exit only to M3 (northbound)	Staggered junction; follow signs - access only from M3 (southbound). Exit only to M3 (northbound)
10	Exit only, no access	Access only, no exit
12	Staggered junction; follow signs - exit only to M275 (southbound)	Staggered junction; follow signs - access only from M275 (northbound)

M40 London - Birmingham

Junction	Northwestbound	Southeastbound
3	Exit only, no access	Access only, no exit
7	Exit only, no access	Access only, no exit
8	Exit only to M40/A40	Access only from M40/A40
13	Exit only, no access	Access only, no exit
14	Access only, no exit	Exit only, no access
16	Access only, no exit	Exit only, no access

M42 Bromsgrove - Measham

Junction	Northeastbound	Southwestbound
1	Access only, no exit	Exit only, no access
7	Exit only to M6 (northwestbound)	Access only from M6 (northwestbound)
7A	Exit only to M6 (southeastbound)	No access or exit
8	Access only from M6 (southeastbound)	Exit only to M6 (northwestbound)

M45 Coventry - M1

Junction	Westbound	Eastbound
Dunchurch (unnumbered)	Access only from A45	Exit only, no access
with M1 (jct 17)	Access only from M1 (northbound)	Exit only to M1 (southbound)

M48 Chepstow

Junction	Westbound	Eastbound
21	Access only from M4	Exit only to M4 (eastbound)
23	No exit to M4	No access from M4 (westbound)

M53 Mersey Tunnel - Chester

Junction	Northbound	Southbound
11	Access only from M56 (westbound)	Access only from M56 (westbound)
	Exit only to M56 (eastbound)	Exit only to M56 (eastbound)

M54 Telford - Birmingham

Junction	Westbound	Eastbound
with M6 (jct 10A)	Access only from M6 (northbound)	Exit only to M6 (southbound)

M56 Chester - Manchester

Junction	Westbound	Eastbound
1	Access only from M60 (westbound)	Exit only to M60 (eastbound) & A34 (northbound)
2	Exit only, no access	Access only, no exit
3	Access only, no exit	Exit only, no access
4	Exit only, no access	Access only, no exit
7	Exit only, no access	No restriction
8	Access only, no exit	No access or exit
9	No exit to M6 (northbound)	No access from M6 (northbound)
15	Exit only to M53	Access only from M53
16	No access or exit	No restriction

M57 Liverpool Outer Ring Road

Junction	Northwestbound	Southeastbound
3	Exit only, no access	Access only, no exit
5	Access only from A580 (westbound)	Exit only, no access

M58 Liverpool - Wigan

Junction	Westbound	Eastbound
1	Exit only, no access	Access only, no exit

M60 Manchester Orbital

Junction	Clockwise	Anticlockwise
2	Access only, no exit	Exit only, no access
3	No access from M56	Access only from A34 (northbound)
4	Access only from A34 (northbound). Exit only to M56	Access only from M56 (eastbound). Exit only to A34 (southbound)
5	Access and exit only from and to A5103 (northbound)	Access and exit only from and to A5103 (southbound)
7	No direct access, use slip road to jct 8. Exit only to A56	No exit, use jct 8
14	Access from A580 (eastbound)	Exit only to A580 (westbound)
16	Access only, no exit	Exit only, no access
20	Exit only, no access	Access only, no exit
22	No restriction	Access only, no exit
25	Access only, no exit	No restriction
26	No restriction	Exit only, no access
27	Access only, no exit	Exit only, no access

M61 Manchester - Preston

Junction	Northwestbound	Southeastbound
3	No access or exit	Access only from A34 (northbound)
with M6 (jct 30)	Exit only to M6 (northbound)	Access only from M6 (southbound)

M62 Liverpool - Kingston upon Hull

Junction	Westbound	Eastbound
23	Access only, no exit	Exit only, no access
32A	No access to A1(M) (southbound)	No restriction

M65 Preston - Colne

Junction	Northeastbound	Southwestbound
9	Access only, no exit	Exit only, no access
11	Access only, no exit	Exit only, no access

M66 Bury

Junction	Northbound	Southbound
with A56	Exit only to A56 (northbound)	Access only from A56 (southbound)
1	Exit only, no access	Access only, no exit

M67 Hyde Bypass

Junction	Westbound	Eastbound
1	Access only, no exit	Exit only, no access
2	Access only, no exit	Access only, no exit
3	Exit only, no access	No restriction

M69 Coventry - Leicester

Junction	Northbound	Southbound
2	Access only, no exit	Exit only, no access

M73 East of Glasgow

Junction	Northbound	Southbound
1	No exit to A74 & A721	No exit to A74 & A721
2	No access from A89. No access from A89 (eastbound)	No access from or exit to A89. No exit to M8 (westbound)

M74 and A74(M) Glasgow - Gretna

Junction	Northbound	Southbound
3	Exit only, no access	Access only, no exit
3A	Access only, no exit	Exit only, no access
4	No access from A74 & A721	Access only, no exit to A74 & A721
7	Access only, no exit	Exit only, no access
9	No access or exit	Exit only, no access
10	No restriction	Access only, no exit
11	Access only, no exit	Exit only, no access
12	Exit only, no access	Access only, no exit
18	Exit only, no access	Access only, no exit

M77 Glasgow - Kilmarnock

Junction	Northbound	Southbound
with M8 (jct 22)	Exit only to M8 (westbound)	No access from M8 (eastbound)
4	Access only, no exit	Exit only, no access
6	Access only, no exit	Exit only, no access
7	Access only, no exit	No restriction
8	Access only, no exit	Exit only, no access

M80 Glasgow - Stirling

Junction	Northbound	Southbound
4A	Exit only, no access	Access only, no exit
6A	Access only, no exit	Exit only, no access
8	Exit only to M876 (northeastbound)	Access only from M876 (southwestbound)

M90 Edinburgh - Perth

Junction	Northbound	Southbound
1	No exit, access only	Exit only to A90 (eastbound)
2A	Exit only to A92 (eastbound)	Access only from A92 (westbound)
7	Access only, no exit	Exit only, no access
8	Exit only, no access	Access only, no exit
10	No access from A912. No exit to A912 (southbound)	No access from A912. No exit to A912

M180 Doncaster - Grimsby

Junction	Westbound	Eastbound
1	Access only, no exit	Exit only, no access

M606 Bradford Spur

Junction	Northbound	Southbound
2	Exit only, no access	No restriction

M621 Leeds - M1

Junction	Clockwise	Anticlockwise
2A	Access only, no exit	No restriction
4	No exit or access	No restriction
5	Access only, no exit	Exit only, no access
6	Exit only, no access	Access only, no exit
with M1 (jct 43)	Exit only to M1 (southbound)	Access only from M1 (northbound)

M876 Bonnybridge - Kincardine Bridge

Junction	Northeastbound	Southwestbound
with M80 (jct 5)	Access only from M80 (northeastbound)	Exit only to M80 (southwestbound)
with M9 (jct 8)	Exit only (eastbound)	Access only from M9 (westbound)

A1(M) South Mimms - Baldock

Junction	Northbound	Southbound
2	Exit only, no access	Access only, no exit
3	Access only, no exit	No access or exit
5	Access only, no exit	No access or exit

A1(M) Pontefract - Bedale

Junction	Northbound	Southbound
41	No access to M62 (eastbound)	No restriction
43	Access only from M1 (northbound)	Exit only to M1 (southbound)

A1(M) Scotch Corner - Newcastle upon Tyne

Junction	Northbound	Southbound
57	Exit only to A66(M) (eastbound)	Access only from A66(M) (westbound)
65	No access to A194(M) & A1 (northbound)	No exit to A194(M) & A1 (southbound)

A3(M) Horndean - Havant

Junction	Northbound	Southbound
1	Access only from A3	Exit only to A3
4	Exit only, no access	Access only, no exit

A38(M) Birmingham, Victoria Road (Park Circus)

Junction	Northbound	Southbound
with B4132	No exit	No access

A48(M) Cardiff Spur

Junction	Westbound	Eastbound
29	Access only from M4 (westbound)	Exit only to M4 (eastbound)
29A	Exit only to A48 (westbound)	Access only from A48 (eastbound)

A57(M) Manchester, Brook Street (A34)

Junction	Westbound	Eastbound
with A34	No exit	No access

A58(M) Leeds, Park Lane and Westgate

Junction	Northbound	Southbound
with A58	No restriction	No access

A64(M) Leeds, Clay Pit Lane (A58)

Junction	Westbound	Eastbound
with A58	No exit (to Clay Pit Lane)	No access (from Clay Pit Lane)

A66(M) Darlington Spur

Junction	Westbound	Eastbound
with A1(M) (jct 57)	Exit only to A1(M) (southbound)	Access only from A1(M) (northbound)

A74(M) Gretna - Abington

Junction	Northbound	Southbound
18	Exit only, no access	No exit

A194(M) Newcastle upon Tyne

Junction	Northbound	Southbound
with A1(M) (jct 65)	Access only from A1(M) (northbound)	Exit only to A1(M) (southbound)

A12 M25 - Ipswich

Junction	Northeastbound	Southwestbound
13	Access only, no exit	No restriction
14	Exit only, no access	Access only, no exit
20A	Access only, no exit	Exit only, no access
20B	Exit only, no access	Access only, no exit
21	No restriction	Exit only, no access
23	Exit only, no access	Access only, no exit
24	Access only, no exit	Exit only, no access
27	Access only, no exit	Access only, no exit
Dedham & Stratford St Mary (unnumbered)	Exit only	Access only

A14 M1 - Felixstowe

Junction	Westbound	Eastbound
with M1/M6 (jct 19)	No exit to M1 or M6 and M1 (northbound)	Access only from M6 and M1 (southbound)
4	Exit only, no access	Access only, no exit
31	Exit only to M11 (for London)	Access only, no exit
31A	Access only to A14 (eastbound)	Access only, no exit
34	Access only, no exit	Exit only, no access
36	Exit only to A11, access only from A1303	Access only from A11
38	Access only from A11	Exit only to A11
39	Exit only to A11	Access only from A11
61	Access only, no exit	Exit only, no access

A55 Holyhead - Chester

Junction	Westbound	Eastbound
8A	Access only, no exit	Exit only, no access
23A	Access only, no exit	Exit only, no access
24A	Exit only, no access	Access only, no exit
27A	No restriction	No access or exit
33A	Access only, no exit	No access or exit
33B	Exit only, no access	Access only, no exit
36A	Exit only to A5104	Access only from A5104

Since Britain's first motorway (the Preston Bypass) opened in 1958, motorways have changed significantly. A vast increase in car journeys over the last 60 years has meant that motorways quickly filled to capacity. To combat this, the recent development of smart motorways uses technology to monitor and actively manage traffic flow and congestion.

How they work

Smart motorways utilise various active traffic management methods, monitored through a regional traffic control centre:

- Traffic flow is monitored using CCTV
- Speed limits are changed to smooth traffic flow and reduce stop-start driving
- Capacity of the motorway can be increased by either temporarily or permanently opening the hard shoulder to traffic
- Warning signs and messages alert drivers to hazards and traffic jams ahead
- Lanes can be closed in the case of an accident or emergency by displaying a red X sign

- Emergency refuge areas are located regularly along the motorway where there is no hard shoulder available

The map shows the main motorway network with the three different types of smart motorway in operation or planned to open over the next five years:

Controlled motorway
Variable speed limits without hard shoulder (the hard shoulder is used in emergencies only)

Hard shoulder running
Variable speed limits with part-time hard shoulder (the hard shoulder is open to traffic at busy times when signs permit)

All lane running
Variable speed limits with hard shoulder as permanent running lane (there is no hard shoulder); this is standard for all new motorway schemes since 2013

Standard motorway

Quick tips

- Never drive in a lane closed by a red X

- Keep to the speed limit shown on the gantries
- A solid white line indicates the hard shoulder – do not drive in it unless directed or in the case of an emergency
- A broken white line indicates a normal running lane
- Exit the smart motorway where possible if your vehicle is in difficulty. In an emergency, move onto the hard shoulder where there is one, or the nearest emergency refuge area
- Put on your hazard lights if you break down

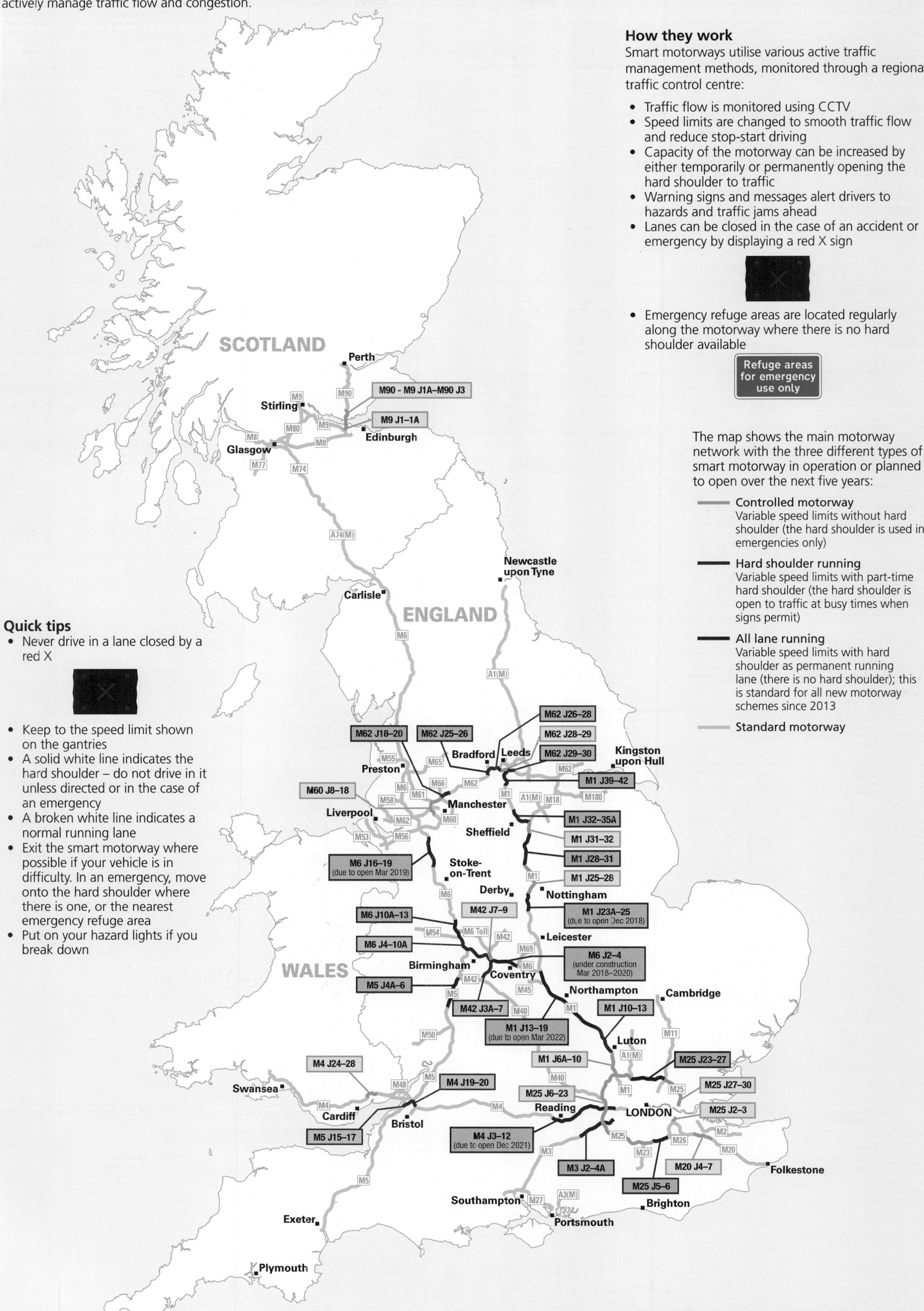

Smart motorways (*Intelligent Transport Systems* in Scotland) are the responsibility of Highways England, Transport Scotland and Transport for Wales

Caravan and camping sites in Britain

These pages list the top 300 AA-inspected Caravan and Camping (C & C) sites in the Pennant rating scheme. **Five Pennant Premier sites are shown in green, Four Pennant sites are shown in blue.**
Listings include addresses, telephone numbers and websites together with page and grid references to locate the sites in the atlas. The total number of touring pitches is also included for each site, together with the type of pitch available. The following abbreviations are used: **C = Caravan CV = Campervan T = Tent**
To find out more about the AA's Pennant rating scheme and other rated caravan and camping sites not included on these pages please visit ***theAA.com***

ENGLAND

Alders Caravan Park
Home Farm, Alne, York
YO61 1RY
Tel: 01347 838722 64 C6
alderscaravanpark.co.uk
Total Pitches: 87 (C, CV & T)

Andrewshayes Holiday Park
Dalwood, Axminster
EX13 7DY
Tel: 01404 831225 6 H5
andrewshayes.co.uk
Total Pitches: 150 (C, CV & T)

Apple Tree Park C & C Site
A38, Claypits, Stonehouse
GL10 3AL
Tel: 01452 742362 28 E6
appletreepark.co.uk
Total Pitches: 65 (C, CV & T)

Appuldurcombe Gardens Holiday Park
Appuldurcombe Road, Wroxall, Isle of Wight
PO38 3EP
Tel: 01983 852597 9 Q12
appuldurcombegardens.co.uk
Total Pitches: 130 (C, CV & T)

Atlantic Bays Holiday Park
St Merryn, Padstow
PL28 8PY
Tel: 01841 520855 3 M2
atlanticbaysholidaypark.co.uk
Total Pitches: 70 (C, CV & T)

Ayr Holiday Park
St Ives, Cornwall
TR26 1EJ
Tel: 01736 795855 2 E8
ayrholidaypark.co.uk
Total Pitches: 40 (C, CV & T)

Back of Beyond Touring Park
234 Ringwood Road, St Leonards, Dorset
BH24 2SB
Tel: 01202 876968 8 F8
backofbeyondtouringpark.co.uk
Total Pitches: 80 (C, CV & T)

Bagwell Farm Touring Park
Knights in the Bottom, Chickerell, Weymouth
DT3 4EA
Tel: 01305 782575 7 R8
bagwellfarm.co.uk
Total Pitches: 320 (C, CV & T)

Bardsea Leisure Park
Priory Road, Ulverston
LA12 9QE
Tel: 01229 584712 61 P4
bardsealeisure.co.uk
Total Pitches: 83 (C & CV)

Barlings Country Holiday Park
Barlings Lane, Langworth
LN3 5DF
Tel: 01522 753200 58 J11
barlingscountrypark.co.uk
Total Pitches: 84 (C, CV & T)

Barn Farm Campsite
Barn Farm, Birchover, Matlock
DE4 2BL
Tel: 01629 650245 46 H1
barnfarmcamping.com
Total Pitches: 62 (C, CV & T)

Bath Chew Valley Caravan Park
Ham Lane, Bishop Sutton
BS39 5TZ
Tel: 01275 332127 17 Q5
bathchewvalley.co.uk
Total Pitches: 45 (C, CV & T)

Bay View Holiday Park
Bolton le Sands, Carnforth
LA5 9TN
Tel: 01524 732854 61 T6
holgates.co.uk
Total Pitches: 100 (C, CV & T)

Beaconsfield Farm Caravan Park
Battlefield, Shrewsbury
SY4 4AA
Tel: 01939 210370 45 M10
beaconsfieldholidaypark.co.uk
Total Pitches: 60 (C & CV)

Beech Croft Farm
Beech Croft, Blackwell in the Peak, Buxton
SK17 9TQ
Tel: 01298 85330 56 H12
beechcroftfarm.co.uk
Total Pitches: 30 (C, CV & T)

Bellingham C & C Club Site
Brown Rigg, Bellingham
NE48 2JY
Tel: 01434 220175 76 G9
campingandcaravanningclub.co.uk/bellingham
Total Pitches: 64 (C, CV & T)

Beverley Parks C & C Park
Goodrington Road, Paignton
TQ4 7JE
Tel: 01803 661961 6 A13
beverley-holidays.co.uk
Total Pitches: 172 (C, CV & T)

Bingham Grange Touring & Camping Park
Melplash, Bridport
DT6 3TT
Tel: 01308 488234 7 N5
binghamgrange.co.uk
Total Pitches: 150 (C, CV & T)

Blackmore Vale C & C Park
Sherborne Causeway, Shaftesbury
SP7 9PX
Tel: 01747 851523 8 A4
blackmorevalecaravanpark.co.uk
Total Pitches: 13 (C, CV & T)

Blue Rose Caravan Country Park
Star Carr Lane, Brandesburton
YO25 8RU
Tel: 01964 543366 65 Q10
bluerosepark.com
Total Pitches: 58 (C & CV)

Briarfields Motel & Touring Park
Gloucester Road, Cheltenham
GL51 0SX
Tel: 01242 235324 28 H3
briarfields.net
Total Pitches: 72 (C, CV & T)

Broadhembury C & C Park
Steeds Lane, Kingsnorth, Ashford
TN26 1NQ
Tel: 01233 620859 12 K8
broadhembury.co.uk
Total Pitches: 110 (C, CV & T)

Brokerswood Country Park
Brokerswood, Westbury
BA13 4EH
Tel: 01373 822238 18 B10
brokerswoodcountrypark.co.uk
Total Pitches: 69 (C, CV & T)

Brompton Caravan Park
Brompton-on-Swale, Richmond
DL10 7EZ
Tel: 01748 824629 69 Q12
bromptoncaravanpark.co.uk
Total Pitches: 177 (C, CV & T)

Budemeadows Touring Park
Widemouth Bay, Bude
EX23 0NA
Tel: 01288 361646 14 F12
budemeadows.com
Total Pitches: 145 (C, CV & T)

Burrowhayes Farm C & C Site & Riding Stables
West Luccombe, Porlock, Minehead
TA24 8HT
Tel: 01643 862463 15 U3
burrowhayes.co.uk
Total Pitches: 120 (C, CV & T)

Burton Constable Holiday Park & Arboretum
Old Lodges, Sproatley, Hull
HU11 4LJ
Tel: 01964 562508 65 R12
burtonconstable.co.uk
Total Pitches: 105 (C, CV & T)

Cakes & Ale
Abbey Lane, Theberton, Leiston
IP16 4TE
Tel: 01728 831655 41 R8
cakesandale.co.uk
Total Pitches: 55 (C, CV & T)

Calloose C & C Park
Leedstown, Hayle
TR27 5ET
Tel: 01736 850431 2 F10
calloose.co.uk
Total Pitches: 109 (C, CV & T)

Camping Caradon Touring Park
Trelawne, Looe
PL13 2NA
Tel: 01503 272388 4 G10
campingcaradon.co.uk
Total Pitches: 75 (C, CV & T)

Capesthorne Hall
Congleton Road, Siddington, Macclesfield
SK11 9JY
Tel: 01625 861221 55 T12
capesthorne.com
Total Pitches: 50 (C & CV)

Carlyon Bay C & C Park
Bethesda, Cypress Avenue, Carlyon Bay
PL25 3RE
Tel: 01726 812735 3 R6
carlyonbay.net
Total Pitches: 180 (C, CV & T)

Carnon Downs C & C Park
Carnon Downs, Truro
TR3 6JJ
Tel: 01872 862283 3 L8
carnon-downs-caravanpark.co.uk
Total Pitches: 150 (C, CV & T)

Carvynick Country Club
Summercourt, Newquay
TR8 5AF
Tel: 01872 510716 3 M5
carvynick.co.uk
Total Pitches: 47 (C & CV)

Castlerigg Hall C & C Park
Castlerigg Hall, Keswick
CA12 4TE
Tel: 017687 74499 67 L8
castlerigg.co.uk
Total Pitches: 68 (C, CV & T)

Cayton Village Caravan Park
Mill Lane, Cayton Bay, Scarborough
YO11 3NN
Tel: 01723 583171 65 P3
caytontouring.co.uk
Total Pitches: 310 (C, CV & T)

Charris C & C Park
Candy's Lane, Corfe Mullen, Wimborne
BH21 3EF
Tel: 01202 885970 8 D9
charris.co.uk
Total Pitches: 45 (C, CV & T)

Cheddar Mendip Heights C & C Club Site
Townsend, Priddy, Wells
BA5 3BP
Tel: 01749 870241 17 P6
campingandcaravanningclub.co.uk/cheddar
Total Pitches: 90 (C, CV & T)

Chy Carne Holiday Park
Kuggar, Ruan Minor, Helston
TR12 7LX
Tel: 01326 290200 2 J13
chycarne.co.uk
Total Pitches: 30 (C, CV & T)

Clippesby Hall
Hall Lane, Clippesby, Great Yarmouth
NR29 3BL
Tel: 01493 367800 51 R11
clippesby.com
Total Pitches: 120 (C, CV & T)

Cofton Country Holidays
Starcross, Dawlish
EX6 8RP
Tel: 01626 890111 6 C8
coftonholidays.co.uk
Total Pitches: 450 (C, CV & T)

Concierge Camping
Ratham Estate, Ratham Lane, West Ashling, Chichester
PO18 8DL
Tel: 01243 573118 10 C9
conciergecamping.co.uk
Total Pitches: 15 (C, CV & T)

Concierge Glamping
Ratham Estate, Ratham Lane, West Ashling, Chichester
PO18 8DL
Tel: 01243 573118 10 C9
conciergecamping.co.uk
Total Pitches: 4 (T)

Coombe Touring Park
Race Plain, Netherhampton, Salisbury
SP2 8PN
Tel: 01722 328451 8 F3
coombecaravanpark.co.uk
Total Pitches: 50 (C, CV & T)

Corfe Castle C & C Club Site
Bucknowle, Wareham
BH20 5PQ
Tel: 01929 480280 8 C12
campingandcaravanningclub.co.uk/corfecastle
Total Pitches: 80 (C, CV & T)

Cornish Farm Touring Park
Shoreditch, Taunton
TA3 7BS
Tel: 01823 327746 16 H12
cornishfarm.com
Total Pitches: 50 (C, CV & T)

Cosawes Park
Perranarworthal, Truro
TR3 7QS
Tel: 01872 863724 2 K9
cosawestouringandcamping.co.uk
Total Pitches: 59 (C, CV & T)

Cote Ghyll C & C Park
Osmotherley, Northallerton
DL6 3AH
Tel: 01609 883425 70 G13
coteghyll.com
Total Pitches: 77 (C, CV & T)

Country View Holiday Park
Sand Road, Sand Bay, Weston-super-Mare
BS22 9UJ
Tel: 01934 627595 16 K4
cvhp.co.uk
Total Pitches: 190 (C, CV & T)

Crafty Camping
Woodland Workshop, Yonder Hill, Holditch
TA20 4NL
Tel: 01460 221102 6 K4
mallinson.co.uk
Total Pitches: 8 (T)

Crealy Meadows C & C Park
Sidmouth Road, Clyst St Mary, Exeter
EX5 1DR
Tel: 01395 234888 6 D6
crealymeadows.co.uk
Total Pitches: 120 (C, CV & T)

Crows Nest Caravan Park
Gristhorpe, Filey
YO14 9PS
Tel: 01723 582206 65 P3
crowsnestcaravanpark.com
Total Pitches: 49 (C, CV & T)

Dell Touring Park
Beyton Road, Thurston, Bury St Edmunds
IP31 3RB
Tel: 01359 270121 40 F8
thedellcaravanpark.co.uk
Total Pitches: 50 (C, CV & T)

Dolbeare Park C & C
St Ive Road, Landrake, Saltash
PL12 5AF
Tel: 01752 851332 4 K8
dolbeare.co.uk
Total Pitches: 60 (C, CV & T)

Dornafield
Dornafield Farm, Two Mile Oak, Newton Abbot
TQ12 6DD
Tel: 01803 812732 5 U7
dornafield.com
Total Pitches: 135 (C, CV & T)

Dorset Country Holidays
Sherborne Causeway, Shaftesbury
SP7 9PX
Tel: 01747 851523 8 A4
blackmorevalecaravanandcampingpark.co.uk
Total Pitches: 7 (T)

East Fleet Farm Touring Park
Chickerell, Weymouth
DT3 4DW
Tel: 01305 785768 7 R9
eastfleet.co.uk
Total Pitches: 400 (C, CV & T)

Eden Valley Holiday Park
Lanlivery, Nr Lostwithiel
PL30 5BU
Tel: 01208 872277 3 R5
edenvalleyholidaypark.co.uk
Total Pitches: 56 (C, CV & T)

Eskdale C & C Club Site
Boot, Holmrook
CA19 1TH
Tel: 019467 23253 66 J12
campingandcaravanningclub.co.uk/eskdale
Total Pitches: 100 (CV & T)

Exe Valley Caravan Site
Mill House, Bridgetown, Dulverton
TA22 9JR
Tel: 01643 851432 16 B10
exevalleycamping.co.uk
Total Pitches: 48 (C, CV & T)

Fields End Water Caravan Park & Fishery
Benwick Road, Doddington, March
PE15 0TY
Tel: 01354 740199 39 N2
fieldsendcaravans.co.uk
Total Pitches: 52 (C, CV & T)

Flusco Wood
Flusco, Penrith
CA11 0JB
Tel: 017684 80020 67 Q7
fluscowood.co.uk
Total Pitches: 36 (C & CV)

Globe Vale Holiday Park
Radnor, Redruth
TR16 4BH
Tel: 01209 891183 2 J8
globevale.co.uk
Total Pitches: 138 (C, CV & T)

Golden Cap Holiday Park
Seatown, Chideock, Bridport
DT6 6JX
Tel: 01308 422139 7 M6
wdlh.co.uk
Total Pitches: 108 (C, CV & T)

Golden Square C & C Park
Oswaldkirk, Helmsley
YO62 5YQ
Tel: 01439 788269 64 E4
goldensquarecaravanpark.com
Total Pitches: 129 (C, CV & T)

Goosewood Holiday Park
Sutton-on-the-Forest, York
YO61 1ET
Tel: 01347 810829 64 D7
flowerofmay.com
Total Pitches: 100 (C & CV)

Green Acres Caravan Park
High Knells, Houghton, Carlisle
CA6 4JW
Tel: 01228 675418 75 T13
caravanpark-cumbria.com
Total Pitches: 35 (C, CV & T)

Greenacres Touring Park
Haywards Lane, Chelston, Wellington
TA21 9PH
Tel: 01823 652844 16 G12
greenacres-wellington.co.uk
Total Pitches: 40 (C & CV)

Greenhill Farm C & C Park
Greenhill Farm, New Road, Landford, Salisbury
SP5 2AZ
Tel: 01794 324117 8 K5
greenhillfarm.co.uk
Total Pitches: 160 (C, CV & T)

Greenhill Leisure Park
Greenhill Farm, Station Road, Bletchingdon, Oxford
OX5 3BQ
Tel: 01869 351600 29 U4
greenhill-leisure-park.co.uk
Total Pitches: 92 (C, CV & T)

Grouse Hill Caravan Park
Flask Bungalow Farm, Fylingdales, Robin Hood's Bay
YO22 4QH
Tel: 01947 880543 71 R12
grousehill.co.uk
Total Pitches: 175 (C, CV & T)

Gunvenna Holiday Park
St Minver, Wadebridge
PL27 6QN
Tel: 01208 862405 4 B5
gunvenna.com
Total Pitches: 75 (C, CV & T)

Gwithian Farm Campsite
Gwithian Farm, Gwithian, Hayle
TR27 5BX
Tel: 01736 753127 2 F8
gwithianfarm.co.uk
Total Pitches: 87 (C, CV & T)

Harbury Fields
Harbury Fields Farm, Harbury, Nr Leamington Spa
CV33 9JN
Tel: 01926 612457 37 L8
harburyfields.co.uk
Total Pitches: 59 (C & CV)

Haw Wood Farm Caravan Park
Hinton, Saxmundham
IP17 3QT
Tel: 01502 359550 41 R6
hawwoodfarm.co.uk
Total Pitches: 60 (C, CV & T)

Heathfield Farm Camping
Heathfield Road, Freshwater, Isle of Wight
PO40 9SH
Tel: 01983 407822 9 L11
heathfieldcamping.co.uk
Total Pitches: 75 (C, CV & T)

Heathland Beach Caravan Park
London Road, Kessingland
NR33 7PJ
Tel: 01502 740337 41 T3
heathlandbeach.co.uk
Total Pitches: 63 (C, CV & T)

Hele Valley Holiday Park
Hele Bay, Ilfracombe
EX34 9RD
Tel: 01271 862460 15 M3
helevalley.co.uk
Total Pitches: 50 (C, CV & T)

Hendra Holiday Park
Newquay
TR8 4NY
Tel: 01637 875778 3 L4
hendra-holidays.com
Total Pitches: 548 (C, CV & T)

Herding Hill Farm
Shield Hill, Haltwhistle
NE49 9NW
Tel: 01434 320175 76 E12
herdinghillfarm.co.uk
Total Pitches: 22 (C, CV & T)

Herding Hill Farm Glamping Site
Shield Hill, Haltwhistle
NE49 9NW
Tel: 01434 320175 76 E12
herdinghillfarm.co.uk
Total Pitches: 24 (T)

Hidden Valley Park
West Down, Braunton, Ilfracombe
EX34 8NU
Tel: 01271 813837 15 M4
hiddenvalleypark.com
Total Pitches: 100 (C, CV & T)

High Moor Farm Park
Skipton Road, Harrogate
HG3 2LT
Tel: 01423 563637 63 Q8
highmoorfarmpark.co.uk
Total Pitches: 320 (C & CV)

Highfield Farm Touring Park
Long Road, Comberton, Cambridge
CB23 7DG
Tel: 01223 262308 39 N9
highfieldfarmtouringpark.co.uk
Total Pitches: 120 (C, CV & T)

Highlands End Holiday Park
Eype, Bridport, Dorset
DT6 6AR
Tel: 01308 422139 7 N6
wdlh.co.uk
Total Pitches: 195 (C, CV & T)

Hill Cottage Farm C & C Park
Sandleheath Road, Alderholt, Fordingbridge
SP6 3EG
Tel: 01425 650513 8 G6
hillcottagefarmcampingandcaravanpark.co.uk
Total Pitches: 95 (C, CV & T)

Hill Farm Caravan Park
Branches Lane, Sherfield English, Romsey
SO51 6FH
Tel: 01794 340402 8 K4
hillfarmpark.com
Total Pitches: 100 (C, CV & T)

Hill of Oaks & Blakeholme
Windermere
LA12 8NR
Tel: 015395 31578 61 R2
hillofoaks.co.uk
Total Pitches: 43 (C & CV)

Hillside Caravan Park
Canvas Farm, Moor Road, Knayton, Thirsk
YO7 4BR
Tel: 01845 537349 63 U2
hillsidecaravanpark.co.uk
Total Pitches: 50 (C & CV)

Hollins Farm C & C
Far Arnside, Carnforth
LA5 0SL
Tel: 01524 701767 61 S4
holgates.co.uk
Total Pitches: 12 (C, CV & T)

Holmans Wood Holiday Park
Harcombe Cross, Chudleigh
TQ13 0DZ
Tel: 01626 853785 6 A8
holmanswood.co.uk
Total Pitches: 73 (C, CV & T)

Honeybridge Park
Honeybridge Lane, Dial Post, Horsham
RH13 8NX
Tel: 01403 710923 10 K7
honeybridgepark.co.uk
Total Pitches: 130 (C, CV & T)

Hurley Riverside Park
Park Office, Hurley, Nr Maidenhead
SL6 5NE
Tel: 01628 824493 20 D6
hurleyriversidepark.co.uk
Total Pitches: 200 (C, CV & T)

Hylton Caravan Park
Eden Street, Silloth
CA7 4AY
Tel: 016973 31707 66 H2
stanwix.com
Total Pitches: 90 (C, CV & T)

Island Lodge C & C Site
Stumpy Post Cross, Kingsbridge
TQ7 4BL
Tel: 01548 852956 5 S11
islandlodgesite.co.uk
Total Pitches: 30 (C, CV & T)

Isle of Avalon Touring Caravan Park
Godney Road, Glastonbury
BA6 9AF
Tel: 01458 833618 17 N9
avaloncaravanpark.co.uk
Total Pitches: 120 (C, CV & T)

Jacobs Mount Caravan Park
Jacobs Mount, Stepney Road, Scarborough
YO12 5NL
Tel: 01723 361178 65 N2
jacobsmount.com
Total Pitches: 156 (C, CV & T)

Jasmine Caravan Park
Cross Lane, Snainton, Scarborough
YO13 9BE
Tel: 01723 859240 65 L3
jasminepark.co.uk
Total Pitches: 68 (C, CV & T)

Juliot's Well Holiday Park
Camelford, Cornwall
PL32 9RF
Tel: 01840 213302 4 D4
southwestholidayparks.co.uk/parks/juliots-well
Total Pitches: 39 (C, CV & T)

Kenneggy Cove Holiday Park
Higher Kenneggy, Rosudgeon, Penzance
TR20 9AU
Tel: 01736 763453 2 F11
kenneggycove.co.uk
Total Pitches: 40 (C, CV & T)

Kings Down Tail C & C Park
Salcombe Regis, Sidmouth
EX10 0PD
Tel: 01297 680313 6 G6
kingsdowntail.co.uk
Total Pitches: 80 (C, CV & T)

King's Lynn C & C Park
New Road, North Runcton, King's Lynn
PE33 0RA
Tel: 01553 840004 49 T10
kl-cc.co.uk
Total Pitches: 150 (C, CV & T)

Kits Coty Glamping
84 Collingwood Road, Kits Coty Estate, Aylesford
ME20 7ER
Tel: 01634 685862 12 D3
kitscotyglamping.co.uk
Total Pitches: 4 (T)

Kneps Farm Holiday Park
River Road, Stanah, Thornton-Cleveleys, Blackpool
FY5 5LR
Tel: 01253 823632 61 R11
knepsfarm.co.uk
Total Pitches: 40 (C & CV)

Knight Stainforth Hall Caravan & Campsite
Stainforth, Settle
BD24 0DP
Tel: 01729 822200 62 G6
knightstainforth.co.uk
Total Pitches: 100 (C, CV & T)

Ladycross Plantation Caravan Park
Egton, Whitby
YO21 1UA
Tel: 01947 895502 71 P11
ladycrossplantation.co.uk
Total Pitches: 130 (C, CV & T)

Lady's Mile Holiday Park
Dawlish, Devon
EX7 0LX
Tel: 01626 863411 6 C9
ladysmile.co.uk
Total Pitches: 570 (C, CV & T)

Lamb Cottage Caravan Park
Dalefords Lane, Whitegate, Northwich
CW8 2BN
Tel: 01606 882302 55 P13
lambcottage.co.uk
Total Pitches: 45 (C & CV)

Langstone Manor C & C Park
Moortown, Tavistock
PL19 9JZ
Tel: 01822 613371 5 N6
langstone-manor.co.uk
Total Pitches: 40 (C, CV & T)

Lanyon Holiday Park
Loscombe Lane, Four Lanes, Redruth
TR16 6LP
Tel: 01209 313474 2 H9
lanyonholidaypark.co.uk
Total Pitches: 25 (C, CV & T)

Lebberston Touring Park
Filey Road, Lebberston, Scarborough
YO11 3PE
Tel: 01723 585723 65 P3
lebberstontouring.co.uk
Total Pitches: 125 (C & CV)

Lee Valley Campsite
Sewardstone Road, Chingford, London
E4 7RA
Tel: 020 8529 5689 21 Q3
visitleevalley.org.uk/wheretostay
Total Pitches: 81 (C, CV & T)

Lickpenny Caravan Site
Lickpenny Lane, Tansley, Matlock
DE4 5GF
Tel: 01629 583040 46 K2
lickpennycaravanpark.co.uk
Total Pitches: 80 (C & CV)

Lime Tree Park
Dukes Drive, Buxton
SK17 9RP
Tel: 01298 22988 56 G12
limetreeparkbuxton.com
Total Pitches: 106 (C, CV & T)

Lincoln Farm Park Oxfordshire
High Street, Standlake
OX29 7RH
Tel: 01865 300239 29 S7
lincolnfarmpark.co.uk
Total Pitches: 90 (C, CV & T)

Long Acres Touring Park
Station Road, Old Leake, Boston
PE22 9RF
Tel: 01205 871555 49 N3
long-acres.co.uk
Total Pitches: 40 (C, CV & T)

Longnor Wood Holiday Park
Newtown, Longnor, Nr Buxton
SK17 0NG
Tel: 01298 83648 56 G14
longnorwood.co.uk
Total Pitches: 47 (C, CV & T)

Lower Polladras Touring Park
Carleen, Breage, Helston
TR13 9NX
Tel: 01736 762220 2 G10
lower-polladras.co.uk
Total Pitches: 39 (C, CV & T)

Lowther Holiday Park
Eamont Bridge, Penrith
CA10 2JB
Tel: 01768 863631 67 R7
lowther-holidaypark.co.uk
Total Pitches: 180 (C, CV & T)

Manor Farm Holiday Centre
Charmouth, Bridport
DT6 6QL
Tel: 01297 560226 7 L6
manorfarmholidaycentre.co.uk
Total Pitches: 400 (C, CV & T)

Manor Wood Country Caravan Park
Manor Wood, Coddington, Chester
CH3 9EN
Tel: 01829 782990 45 L2
cheshire-caravan-sites.co.uk
Total Pitches: 45 (C, CV & T)

Mayfield Park
Cheltenham Road, Cirencester
GL7 7BH
Tel: 01285 831301 28 K6
mayfieldpark.co.uk
Total Pitches: 105 (C, CV & T)

Meadowbank Holidays
Stour Way, Christchurch
BH23 2PQ
Tel: 01202 483597 8 G10
meadowbank-holidays.co.uk
Total Pitches: 41 (C & CV)

Middlewick Farm
Wick Lane, Glastonbury
BA6 8JW
Tel: 01458 832351 17 P9
middlewickholidaycottages.co.uk
Total Pitches: 3 (T)

Middlewood Farm Holiday Park
Middlewood Lane, Fylingthorpe, Robin Hood's Bay, Whitby
YO22 4UF
Tel: 01947 880414 71 R12
middlewoodfarm.com
Total Pitches: 100 (C, CV & T)

Minnows Touring Park
Holbrook Lane, Sampford Peverell
EX16 7EN
Tel: 01884 821770 16 D13
minnowstouringpark.co.uk
Total Pitches: 59 (C, CV & T)

Moon & Sixpence
Newbourn Road, Waldringfield, Woodbridge
IP12 4PP
Tel: 01473 736650 41 N11
moonandsixpence.eu
Total Pitches: 50 (C & CV)

Moor Lodge Park
Blackmoor Lane, Bardsey, Leeds
LS17 9DZ
Tel: 01937 572424 63 T11
moorlodgecaravanpark.co.uk
Total Pitches: 12 (C & CV)

Moss Wood Caravan Park
Crimbles Lane, Cockerham
LA2 0ES
Tel: 01524 791041 61 T10
mosswood.co.uk
Total Pitches: 25 (C, CV & T)

Naburn Lock Caravan Park
Naburn
YO19 4RU
Tel: 01904 728697 64 E10
naburnlock.co.uk
Total Pitches: 100 (C, CV & T)

New Lodge Farm C & C Site
New Lodge Farm, Bulwick, Corby
NN17 3DU
Tel: 01780 450493 38 E1
newlodgefarm.com
Total Pitches: 72 (C, CV & T)

Newberry Valley Park
Woodlands, Combe Martin
EX34 0AT
Tel: 01271 882334 15 N3
newberryvalleypark.co.uk
Total Pitches: 110 (C, CV & T)

Newlands Holidays
Charmouth, Bridport
DT6 6RB
Tel: 01297 560259 7 L6
newlandsholidays.co.uk
Total Pitches: 240 (C, CV & T)

Newperran Holiday Park
Rejerrah, Newquay
TR8 5QJ
Tel: 01872 572407 2 K6
newperran.co.uk
Total Pitches: 357 (C, CV & T)

Ninham Country Holidays
Ninham, Shanklin, Isle of Wight
PO37 7PL
Tel: 01983 864243 9 R12
ninham-holidays.co.uk
Total Pitches: 135 (C, CV & T)

North Morte Farm C & C Park
North Morte Road, Mortehoe, Woolacombe
EX34 7EG
Tel: 01271 870381 15 L3
northmortefarm.co.uk
Total Pitches: 180 (C, CV & T)

Northam Farm Caravan & Touring Park
Brean, Burnham-on-Sea
TA8 2SE
Tel: 01278 751244 16 K5
northamfarm.co.uk
Total Pitches: 350 (C, CV & T)

Oakdown Country Holiday Park
Gatedown Lane, Weston, Sidmouth
EX10 0PT
Tel: 01297 680387 6 G6
oakdown.co.uk
Total Pitches: 150 (C, CV & T)

Old Hall Caravan Park
Capernwray, Carnforth
LA6 1AD
Tel: 01524 733276 61 U5
oldhallcaravanpark.co.uk
Total Pitches: 38 (C & CV)

Orchard Park
Frampton Lane, Hubbert's Bridge, Boston
PE20 3QU
Tel: 01205 290328 49 L5
orchardpark.co.uk
Total Pitches: 87 (C, CV & T)

Ord House Country Park
East Ord, Berwick-upon-Tweed
TD15 2NS
Tel: 01289 305288 85 P8
ordhouse.co.uk
Total Pitches: 79 (C, CV & T)

Oxon Hall Touring Park
Welshpool Road, Shrewsbury
SY3 5FB
Tel: 01743 340868 45 L11
morris-leisure.co.uk
Total Pitches: 105 (C, CV & T)

Padstow Touring Park
Padstow
PL28 8LE
Tel: 01841 532061 3 N2
padstowtouringpark.co.uk
Total Pitches: 150 (C, CV & T)

Park Cliffe C & C Estate
Birks Road, Tower Wood, Windermere
LA23 3PG
Tel: 015395 31344 61 R1
parkcliffe.co.uk
Total Pitches: 60 (C, CV & T)

Parkers Farm Holiday Park
Higher Mead Farm, Ashburton, Devon
TQ13 7LJ
Tel: 01364 654869 — 5 T6
parkersfarmholidays.co.uk
Total Pitches: 100 (C, CV & T)

Parkland C & C Site
Sorley Green Cross, Kingsbridge
TQ7 4AF
Tel: 01548 852723 — 5 S11
parklandsite.co.uk
Total Pitches: 50 (C, CV & T)

Penrose Holiday Park
Goonhavern, Truro
TR4 9QF
Tel: 01872 573185 — 2 K6
penroseholidaypark.co.uk
Total Pitches: 110 (C, CV & T)

Pentire Haven Holiday Park
Stibb Road, Kilkhampton, Bude
EX23 9QY
Tel: 01288 321601 — 14 F10
pentirehaven.co.uk
Total Pitches: 120 (C, CV & T)

Petwood Caravan Park
Off Stixwould Road, Woodhall Spa
LN10 6QH
Tel: 01526 354799 — 59 L14
petwoodcaravanpark.com
Total Pitches: 98 (C, CV & T)

Polmanter Touring Park
Halsetown, St Ives
TR26 3LX
Tel: 01736 795640 — 2 E9
polmanter.co.uk
Total Pitches: 270 (C, CV & T)

Porlock Caravan Park
Porlock, Minehead
TA24 8ND
Tel: 01643 862269 — 15 U3
porlockcaravanpark.co.uk
Total Pitches: 40 (C, CV & T)

Porthtowan Tourist Park
Mile Hill, Porthtowan, Truro
TR4 8TY
Tel: 01209 890256 — 2 H7
porthtowantouristpark.co.uk
Total Pitches: 80 (C, CV & T)

Quantock Orchard Caravan Park
Flaxpool, Crowcombe, Taunton
TA4 4AW
Tel: 01984 618618 — 16 F9
quantock-orchard.co.uk
Total Pitches: 60 (C, CV & T)

Ranch Caravan Park
Station Road, Honeybourne, Evesham
WR11 7PR
Tel: 01386 830744 — 36 F12
ranch.co.uk
Total Pitches: 120 (C, CV & T)

Riddings Wood C & C Park
Bullock Lane, Riddings, Alfreton
DE55 4BP
Tel: 01773 605160 — 47 M3
riddingswoodcaravanandcamping.co.uk
Total Pitches: 75 (C, CV & T)

Ripley Caravan Park
Knaresborough Road, Ripley, Harrogate
HG3 3AU
Tel: 01423 770050 — 63 R7
ripleycaravanpark.com
Total Pitches: 60 (C, CV & T)

River Dart Country Park
Holne Park, Ashburton
TQ13 7NP
Tel: 01364 652511 — 5 S7
riverdart.co.uk
Total Pitches: 170 (C, CV & T)

River Valley Holiday Park
London Apprentice, St Austell
PL26 7AP
Tel: 01726 73533 — 3 Q6
rivervalleyholidaypark.co.uk
Total Pitches: 45 (C, CV & T)

Riverside C & C Park
Marsh Lane, North Molton Road,
South Molton
EX36 3HQ
Tel: 01769 579269 — 15 R7
exmoorriverside.co.uk
Total Pitches: 58 (C, CV & T)

Riverside Caravan Park
High Bentham, Lancaster
LA2 7FJ
Tel: 015242 61272 — 62 D6
riversidecaravanpark.co.uk
Total Pitches: 61 (C & CV)

Riverside Caravan Park
Leigham Manor Drive, Marsh Mills,
Plymouth
PL6 8LL
Tel: 01752 344122 — 5 N9
riversidecaravanpark.com
Total Pitches: 259 (C, CV & T)

**Riverside Meadows
Country Caravan Park**
Ure Bank Top, Ripon
HG4 1JD
Tel: 01765 602964 — 63 S5
flowerofmay.com
Total Pitches: 80 (C, CV & T)

Robin Hood C & C Park
Green Dyke Lane, Slingsby
YO62 4AP
Tel: 01653 628391 — 64 G5
robinhoodcaravanpark.co.uk
Total Pitches: 32 (C, CV & T)

Rose Farm Touring & Camping Park
Stepshort, Belton, Nr Great Yarmouth
NR31 9JS
Tel: 01493 780896 — 51 S13
rosefarmtouringpark.co.uk
Total Pitches: 145 (C, CV & T)

Rosedale C & C Park
Rosedale Abbey, Pickering
YO18 8SA
Tel: 01751 417272 — 71 M13
flowerofmay.com
Total Pitches: 100 (C, CV & T)

Ross Park
Park Hill Farm, Ipplepen, Newton Abbot
TQ12 5TT
Tel: 01803 812983 — 5 U7
rossparkcaravanpark.co.uk
Total Pitches: 110 (C, CV & T)

Rudding Holiday Park
Follifoot, Harrogate
HG3 1JH
Tel: 01423 870439 — 63 S9
ruddingholiday.co.uk
Total Pitches: 86 (C, CV & T)

Run Cottage Touring Park
Alderton Road, Hollesley, Woodbridge
IP12 3RQ
Tel: 01394 411309 — 41 Q12
runcottage.co.uk
Total Pitches: 45 (C, CV & T)

Rutland C & C
Park Lane, Greetham, Oakham
LE15 7FN
Tel: 01572 813520 — 48 D11
rutlandcaravanandcamping.co.uk
Total Pitches: 130 (C, CV & T)

St Helens Caravan Park
Wykeham, Scarborough
YO13 9QD
Tel: 01723 862771 — 65 M3
sthelenscaravanpark.co.uk
Total Pitches: 250 (C, CV & T)

St Mabyn Holiday Park
Longstone Road, St Mabyn, Wadebridge
PL30 3BY
Tel: 01208 841677 — 3 R2
stmabynholidaypark.co.uk
Total Pitches: 120 (C, CV & T)

Sandy Balls Holiday Village
Sandy Balls Estate Ltd, Godshill,
Fordingbridge
SP6 2JZ
Tel: 0844 693 1336 — 8 H6
sandyballs.co.uk
Total Pitches: 225 (C, CV & T)

Seaview International Holiday Park
Boswinger, Mevagissey
PL26 6LL
Tel: 01726 843425 — 3 P8
seaviewinternational.com
Total Pitches: 201 (C, CV & T)

Severn Gorge Park
Bridgnorth Road, Tweedale, Telford
TF7 4JB
Tel: 01952 684789 — 45 R12
severngorgepark.co.uk
Total Pitches: 12 (C & CV)

Shamba Holidays
East Moors Lane, St Leonards, Ringwood
BH24 2SB
Tel: 01202 873302 — 8 G8
shambaholidays.co.uk
Total Pitches: 150 (C, CV & T)

Shrubbery Touring Park
Rousdon, Lyme Regis
DT7 3XW
Tel: 01297 442227 — 6 J6
shrubberypark.co.uk
Total Pitches: 120 (C, CV & T)

Silverbow Park
Perranwell, Goonhavern
TR4 9NX
Tel: 01872 572347 — 2 K6
silverbowpark.co.uk
Total Pitches: 90 (C, CV & T)

Silverdale Caravan Park
Middlebarrow Plain, Cove Road,
Silverdale, Nr Carnforth
LA5 0SH
Tel: 01524 701508 — 61 T4
holgates.co.uk
Total Pitches: 80 (C, CV & T)

Skelwith Fold Caravan Park
Ambleside, Cumbria
LA22 0HX
Tel: 015394 32277 — 67 N12
skelwith.com
Total Pitches: 150 (C & CV)

Somers Wood Caravan Park
Somers Road, Meriden
CV7 7PL
Tel: 01676 522978 — 36 H4
somerswood.co.uk
Total Pitches: 48 (C & CV)

South Lytchett Manor C & C Park
Dorchester Road, Lytchett Minster, Poole
BH16 6JB
Tel: 01202 622577 — 8 D10
southlytchettmanor.co.uk
Total Pitches: 150 (C, CV & T)

South Meadows Caravan Park
South Road, Belford
NE70 7DP
Tel: 01668 213326 — 85 S12
southmeadows.co.uk
Total Pitches: 83 (C, CV & T)

Stanmore Hall Touring Park
Stourbridge Road, Bridgnorth
WV15 6DT
Tel: 01746 761761 — 35 R2
morris-leisure.co.uk
Total Pitches: 129 (C, CV & T)

Stowford Farm Meadows
Berry Down, Combe Martin
EX34 0PW
Tel: 01271 882476 — 15 N4
stowford.co.uk
Total Pitches: 700 (C, CV & T)

Stroud Hill Park
Fen Road, Pidley, St Ives
PE28 3DE
Tel: 01487 741333 — 39 M5
stroudhillpark.co.uk
Total Pitches: 60 (C, CV & T)

Sumners Ponds Fishery & Campsite
Chapel Road, Barns Green, Horsham
RH13 0PR
Tel: 01403 732539 — 10 J5
sumnersponds.co.uk
Total Pitches: 86 (C, CV & T)

Sun Valley Resort
Pentewan Road, St Austell
PL26 6DJ
Tel: 01726 843266 — 3 Q7
sunvalleyresort.co.uk
Total Pitches: 29 (C, CV & T)

Swiss Farm Touring & Camping
Marlow Road, Henley-on-Thames
RG9 2HY
Tel: 01491 573419 — 20 C6
swissfarmcamping.co.uk
Total Pitches: 140 (C, CV & T)

Tanner Farm Touring C & C Park
Tanner Farm, Goudhurst Road, Marden
TN12 9ND
Tel: 01622 832399 — 12 D7
tannerfarmpark.co.uk
Total Pitches: 120 (C, CV & T)

Tattershall Lakes Country Park
Sleaford Road, Tattershall
LN4 4LR
Tel: 01526 348800 — 48 K2
tattershall-lakes.com
Total Pitches: 186 (C, CV & T)

Tehidy Holiday Park
Harris Mill, Illogan, Portreath
TR16 4JQ
Tel: 01209 216489 — 2 H8
tehidy.co.uk
Total Pitches: 18 (C, CV & T)

Teversal C & C Club Site
Silverhill Lane, Teversal
NG17 3JJ
Tel: 01623 551838 — 47 N1
campingandcaravanningclub.co.uk/teversal
Total Pitches: 126 (C, CV & T)

The Inside Park
Down House Estate, Blandford Forum
DT11 9AD
Tel: 01258 453719 — 8 B8
theinsidepark.co.uk
Total Pitches: 125 (C, CV & T)

The Laurels Holiday Park
Padstow Road, Whitecross,
Wadebridge
PL27 7JQ
Tel: 01209 313474 — 3 P2
thelaurelsholidaypark.co.uk
Total Pitches: 30 (C, CV & T)

The Old Brick Kilns
Little Barney Lane, Barney, Fakenham
NR21 0NL
Tel: 01328 878305 — 50 H7
old-brick-kilns.co.uk
Total Pitches: 65 (C, CV & T)

The Old Oaks Touring Park
Wick Farm, Wick, Glastonbury
BA6 8JS
Tel: 01458 831437 — 17 P9
theoldoaks.co.uk
Total Pitches: 98 (C, CV & T)

The Orchards Holiday Caravan Park
Main Road, Newbridge, Yarmouth,
Isle of Wight
PO41 0TS
Tel: 01983 531331 — 9 N11
orchards-holiday-park.co.uk
Total Pitches: 160 (C, CV & T)

The Quiet Site
Ullswater, Watermillock
CA11 0LS
Tel: 07768 727016 — 67 P8
thequietsite.co.uk
Total Pitches: 100 (C, CV & T)

The Ranch Caravan Park
Cliffe Common, Selby
YO8 6PA
Tel: 01757 638984 — 64 F13
theranchcaravanpark.co.uk
Total Pitches: 44 (C, CV & T)

Treago Farm Caravan Site
Crantock, Newquay
TR8 5QS
Tel: 01637 830277 — 2 K4
treagofarm.co.uk
Total Pitches: 90 (C, CV & T)

Tregoad Park
St Martin, Looe
PL13 1PB
Tel: 01503 262718 — 4 H9
tregoadpark.co.uk
Total Pitches: 200 (C, CV & T)

Treloy Touring Park
Newquay
TR8 4JN
Tel: 01637 872063 — 3 M4
treloy.co.uk
Total Pitches: 223 (C, CV & T)

Trencreek Holiday Park
Hillcrest, Higher Trencreek, Newquay
TR8 4NS
Tel: 01637 874210 — 3 L4
trencreekholidaypark.co.uk
Total Pitches: 194 (C, CV & T)

Trethem Mill Touring Park
St Just-in-Roseland, Nr St Mawes, Truro
TR2 5JF
Tel: 01872 580504 — 3 M9
trethem.com
Total Pitches: 84 (C, CV & T)

Trevalgan Touring Park
Trevalgan, St Ives
TR26 3BJ
Tel: 01736 791892 — 2 D9
trevalgantouringpark.co.uk
Total Pitches: 135 (C, CV & T)

Trevella Park
Crantock, Newquay
TR8 5EW
Tel: 01637 830308 — 3 L5
trevella.co.uk
Total Pitches: 165 (C, CV & T)

Trevornick
Holywell Bay, Newquay
TR8 5PW
Tel: 01637 830531 — 2 K5
trevornick.co.uk
Total Pitches: 688 (C, CV & T)

Truro C & C Park
Truro
TR4 8QN
Tel: 01872 560274 — 2 K7
trurocaravanandcampingpark.co.uk
Total Pitches: 51 (C, CV & T)

Tudor C & C
Shepherds Patch, Slimbridge, Gloucester
GL2 7BP
Tel: 01453 890483 — 28 D7
tudorcaravanpark.com
Total Pitches: 75 (C, CV & T)

Two Mills Touring Park
Yarmouth Road, North Walsham
NR28 9NA
Tel: 01692 405829 — 51 N8
twomills.co.uk
Total Pitches: 81 (C, CV & T)

Ulwell Cottage Caravan Park
Ulwell Cottage, Ulwell, Swanage
BH19 3DG
Tel: 01929 422823 — 8 E12
ulwellcottagepark.co.uk
Total Pitches: 77 (C, CV & T)

Vale of Pickering Caravan Park
Carr House Farm, Allerston, Pickering
YO18 7PQ
Tel: 01723 859280 — 64 K3
valeofpickering.co.uk
Total Pitches: 120 (C, CV & T)

Wagtail Country Park
Cliff Lane, Marston, Grantham
NG32 2HU
Tel: 01400 251955 — 48 C5
wagtailcountrypark.co.uk
Total Pitches: 76 (C & CV)

Warcombe Farm C & C Park
Station Road, Mortehoe,
Woolacombe
EX34 7EJ
Tel: 01271 870690 — 15 L3
warcombefarm.co.uk
Total Pitches: 250 (C, CV & T)

Wareham Forest Tourist Park
North Trigon, Wareham
BH20 7NZ
Tel: 01929 551393 — 8 B10
warehamforest.co.uk
Total Pitches: 200 (C, CV & T)

Waren C & C Park
Waren Mill, Bamburgh
NE70 7EE
Tel: 01668 214366 — 85 T12
meadowhead.co.uk
Total Pitches: 150 (C, CV & T)

Watergate Bay Touring Park
Watergate Bay, Tregurrian
TR8 4AD
Tel: 01637 860387 — 3 M3
watergatebaytouringpark.co.uk
Total Pitches: 171 (C, CV & T)

Waterrow Touring Park
Wiveliscombe, Taunton
TA4 2AZ
Tel: 01984 623464 — 16 E11
waterrowpark.co.uk
Total Pitches: 44 (C, CV & T)

Wayfarers C & C Park
Relubbus Lane, St Hilary, Penzance
TR20 9EF
Tel: 01736 763326 — 2 F10
wayfarerspark.co.uk
Total Pitches: 32 (C, CV & T)

Wells Touring Park
Haybridge, Wells
BA5 1AJ
Tel: 01749 676869 — 17 P7
wellstouringpark.co.uk
Total Pitches: 72 (C, CV & T)

Wheathill Touring Park
Wheathill, Bridgnorth
WV16 6QT
Tel: 01584 823456 — 35 P4
wheathillpark.co.uk
Total Pitches: 25 (C & T)

Whitefield Forest Touring Park
Brading Road, Ryde,
Isle of Wight
PO33 1QL
Tel: 01983 617069 — 9 S11
whitefieldforest.co.uk
Total Pitches: 90 (C, CV & T)

Widdicombe Farm Touring Park
Marldon, Paignton
TQ3 1ST
Tel: 01803 558325 — 5 V8
widdicombefarm.co.uk
Total Pitches: 180 (C, CV & T)

Widemouth Fields C & C Park
Park Farm, Poundstock, Bude
EX23 0NA
Tel: 01288 361351 — 14 F12
peterbullresorts.co.uk/widemouth-fields
Total Pitches: 156 (C, CV & T)

Wight Glamping Holidays
Everland, Long Lane, Newport, Isle of Wight
PO30 2NW
Tel: 01983 532507 — 9 Q11
wightglampingholidays.co.uk
Total Pitches: 4 (T)

Wild Rose Park
Ormside, Appleby-in-Westmorland
CA16 6EJ
Tel: 017683 51077 — 68 E9
harrisonholidayhomes.co.uk
Total Pitches: 226 (C & T)

Wilksworth Farm Caravan Park
Cranborne Road, Wimborne Minster
BH21 4HW
Tel: 01202 885467 — 8 E8
wilksworthfarmcaravanpark.co.uk
Total Pitches: 85 (C, CV & T)

Willowbank Holiday Home & Touring Park
Coastal Road, Ainsdale, Southport
PR8 3ST
Tel: 01704 571566 — 54 H4
willowbankcp.co.uk
Total Pitches: 87 (C & CV)

Wolds View Touring Park
115 Brigg Road, Caistor
LN7 6RX
Tel: 01472 851099 — 58 K6
woldsviewtouringpark.co.uk
Total Pitches: 60 (C, CV & T)

Wood Farm C & C Park
Axminster Road, Charmouth
DT6 6BT
Tel: 01297 560697 — 7 L6
woodfarm.co.uk
Total Pitches: 175 (C, CV & T)

Wooda Farm Holiday Park
Poughill, Bude
EX23 9HJ
Tel: 01288 352069 — 14 F11
wooda.co.uk
Total Pitches: 200 (C, CV & T)

Woodclose Caravan Park
High Casterton, Kirkby Lonsdale
LA6 2SE
Tel: 015242 71597 — 62 C4
woodclosepark.com
Total Pitches: 22 (C, CV & T)

Woodhall Country Park
Stixwould Road, Woodhall Spa
LN10 6UJ
Tel: 01526 353710 — 59 L14
woodhallcountrypark.co.uk
Total Pitches: 115 (C, CV & T)

Woodland Springs Adult Touring Park
Venton, Drewsteignton
EX6 6PG
Tel: 01647 231695 — 5 R2
woodlandsprings.co.uk
Total Pitches: 81 (C, CV & T)

Woodlands Grove C & C Park
Blackawton, Dartmouth
TQ9 7DQ
Tel: 01803 712598 — 5 U10
woodlands-caravanpark.com
Total Pitches: 350 (C, CV & T)

Woodovis Park
Gulworthy, Tavistock
PL19 8NY
Tel: 01822 832968 — 5 L6
woodovis.com
Total Pitches: 50 (C, CV & T)

Yeatheridge Farm Caravan Park
East Worlington, Crediton
EX17 4TN
Tel: 01884 860330 — 15 S10
yeatheridge.co.uk
Total Pitches: 103 (C, CV & T)

SCOTLAND

Aviemore Glamping
Aviemore Inn, Grampian Avenue, Aviemore
PH22 1RW
Tel: 01479 810717 — 103 N13
aviemoreglamping.com
Total Pitches: 4 (T)

Banff Links Caravan Park
Inverboyndie, Banff
AB45 2JJ
Tel: 01261 812228 — 104 K3
banfflinkscaravanpark.co.uk
Total Pitches: 55 (C, CV & T)

Beecraigs C & C Site
Beecraigs Country Park, The Visitor Centre,
Linlithgow
EH49 6PL
Tel: 01506 844516 — 82 K4
beecraigs.com
Total Pitches: 36 (C, CV & T)

Blair Castle Caravan Park
Blair Atholl, Pitlochry
PH18 5SR
Tel: 01796 481263 — 97 P10
blaircastlecaravanpark.co.uk
Total Pitches: 226 (C, CV & T)

Brighouse Bay Holiday Park
Brighouse Bay, Borgue, Kirkcudbright
DG6 4TS
Tel: 01557 870267 — 73 Q10
gillespie-leisure.co.uk
Total Pitches: 190 (C, CV & T)

Cairnsmill Holiday Park
Largo Road, St Andrews
KY16 8NN
Tel: 01334 473604 — 91 Q9
cairnsmill.co.uk
Total Pitches: 62 (C, CV & T)

Craigtoun Meadows Holiday Park
Mount Melville, St Andrews
KY16 8PQ
Tel: 01334 475959 — 91 Q8
craigtounmeadows.com
Total Pitches: 56 (C, CV & T)

Gart Caravan Park
The Gart, Callander
FK17 8LE
Tel: 01877 330002 — 89 P4
theholidaypark.co.uk
Total Pitches: 128 (C & CV)

Glen Nevis C & C Park
Glen Nevis, Fort William
PH33 6SX
Tel: 01397 702191 — 94 G4
glen-nevis.co.uk
Total Pitches: 380 (C, CV & T)

Glenearly Caravan Park
Dalbeattie
DG5 4NE
Tel: 01556 611393 — 74 F13
glenearlycaravanpark.co.uk
Total Pitches: 39 (C, CV & T)

Hoddom Castle Caravan Park
Hoddom, Lockerbie
DG11 1AS
Tel: 01576 300251 — 75 N11
hoddomcastle.co.uk
Total Pitches: 200 (C, CV & T)

Huntly Castle Caravan Park
The Meadow, Huntly
AB54 4UJ
Tel: 01466 794999 — 104 G7
huntlycastle.co.uk
Total Pitches: 90 (C, CV & T)

Linnhe Lochside Holidays
Corpach, Fort William
PH33 7NL
Tel: 01397 772376 — 94 F3
linnhe-lochside-holidays.co.uk
Total Pitches: 85 (C, CV & T)

Loch Ken Holiday Park
Parton, Castle Douglas
DG7 3NE
Tel: 01644 470282 — 73 R5
lochkenholidaypark.co.uk
Total Pitches: 40 (C, CV & T)

Loch Shin Wigwams
Forge Cottage, Achfrish, Shinness, Lairg
IV27 4DN
Tel: 01549 402936 — 108 K2
Total Pitches: 2 (T)

Lomond Woods Holiday Park
Old Luss Road, Balloch, Loch Lomond
G83 8QP
Tel: 01389 755000 — 88 J9
holiday-parks.co.uk
Total Pitches: 115 (C & CV)

Milton of Fonab Caravan Park
Bridge Road, Pitlochry
PH16 5NA
Tel: 01796 472882 — 97 Q10
fonab.co.uk
Total Pitches: 154 (C, CV & T)

River Tilt Caravan Park
Blair Atholl, Pitlochry
PH18 5TE
Tel: 01796 481467 — 97 P10
rivertiltpark.co.uk
Total Pitches: 30 (C, CV & T)

Runach Arainn
The Old Manse, Kilmory, Isle of Arran
KA27 8PH
Tel: 01770 870515 — 80 D8
runacharainn.com
Total Pitches: 3 (T)

Sands of Luce Holiday Park
Sands of Luce, Sandhead, Stranraer
DG9 9JN
Tel: 01776 830456 — 72 E9
sandsofluceholidaypark.co.uk
Total Pitches: 80 (C, CV & T)

Seaward Caravan Park
Dhoon Bay, Kirkcudbright
DG6 4TJ
Tel: 01557 870267 — 73 R10
gillespie-leisure.co.uk
Total Pitches: 22 (C, CV & T)

Shieling Holidays
Craignure, Isle of Mull
PA65 6AY
Tel: 01680 812496 — 93 S11
shielingholidays.co.uk
Total Pitches: 90 (C, CV & T)

Silver Sands Holiday Park
Covesea, West Beach, Lossiemouth
IV31 6SP
Tel: 01343 813262 — 103 V1
silver-sands.co.uk
Total Pitches: 140 (C, CV & T)

Skye C & C Club Site
Loch Greshornish, Borve, Arnisort,
Edinbane, Isle of Skye
IV51 9PS
Tel: 01470 582230 — 100 c4
campingandcaravanningclub.co.uk/skye
Total Pitches: 105 (C, CV & T)

Strathfillan Wigwam Village
Auchtertyre Farm, Tyndrum, Crianlarich
FK20 8RU
Tel: 01838 400251 — 95 M13
wigwamholidays.com
Total Pitches: 23 (T)

Thurston Manor Leisure Park
Innerwick, Dunbar
EH42 1SA
Tel: 01368 840643 — 84 J4
thurstonmanor.co.uk
Total Pitches: 120 (C & CV)

Trossachs Holiday Park
Aberfoyle
FK8 3SA
Tel: 01877 382614 — 89 M6
trossachsholidays.co.uk
Total Pitches: 66 (C, CV & T)

Witches Craig C & C Park
Blairlogie, Stirling
FK9 5PX
Tel: 01786 474947 — 89 T6
witchescraig.co.uk
Total Pitches: 60 (C, CV & T)

WALES

Bron Derw Touring Caravan Park
Llanrwst
LL26 0YT
Tel: 01492 640494 — 53 N10
bronderw-wales.co.uk
Total Pitches: 48 (C & CV)

Bron-Y-Wendon Caravan Park
Wern Road, Llanddulas, Colwyn Bay
LL22 8HG
Tel: 01492 512903 — 53 R7
northwales-holidays.co.uk
Total Pitches: 130 (C & CV)

Bryn Gloch C & C Park
Betws Garmon, Caernarfon
LL54 7YY
Tel: 01286 650216 — 52 H11
campwales.co.uk
Total Pitches: 160 (C, CV & T)

Caerfai Bay Caravan & Tent Park
Caerfai Bay, St Davids, Haverfordwest
SA62 6QT
Tel: 01437 720274 — 24 C6
caerfaibay.co.uk
Total Pitches: 106 (C, CV & T)

Cenarth Falls Holiday Park
Cenarth, Newcastle Emlyn
SA38 9JS
Tel: 01239 710345 — 32 E12
cenarth-holipark.co.uk
Total Pitches: 56 (C, CV & T)

Daisy Bank Caravan Park
Snead, Montgomery
SY15 6EB
Tel: 01588 620471 — 34 H2
daisy-bank.co.uk
Total Pitches: 38 (C, CV & T)

Deucoch Touring & Camping Park
Sarn Bach, Abersoch
LL53 7LD
Tel: 01758 713293 — 42 F8
deucoch.com
Total Pitches: 70 (C, CV & T)

Dinlle Caravan Park
Dinas Dinlle, Caernarfon
LL54 5TW
Tel: 01286 830324 — 52 F11
thornleyleisure.co.uk
Total Pitches: 175 (C, CV & T)

Eisteddfa
Eisteddfa Lodge, Pentrefelin, Criccieth
LL52 0PT
Tel: 01766 522696 — 42 K6
eisteddfapark.co.uk
Total Pitches: 100 (C, CV & T)

Erwlon C & C Park
Brecon Road, Llandovery
SA20 0RD
Tel: 01550 721021 — 33 Q14
erwlon.co.uk
Total Pitches: 75 (C, CV & T)

Fforest Fields C & C Park
Hundred House, Builth Wells
LD1 5RT
Tel: 01982 570406 — 34 D10
fforestfields.co.uk
Total Pitches: 120 (C, CV & T)

Hendre Mynach Touring C & C Park
Llanaber Road, Barmouth
LL42 1YR
Tel: 01341 280262 — 43 M10
hendremynach.co.uk
Total Pitches: 240 (C, CV & T)

Home Farm Caravan Park
Marian-Glas, Isle of Anglesey
LL73 8PH
Tel: 01248 410614 — 52 G6
homefarm-anglesey.co.uk
Total Pitches: 102 (C, CV & T)

Islawrffordd Caravan Park
Tal-y-bont, Barmouth
LL43 2AQ
Tel: 01341 247269 — 43 L9
islawrffordd.co.uk
Total Pitches: 105 (C, CV & T)

Llys Derwen C & C Site
Ffordd Bryngwyn, Llanrug, Caernarfon
LL55 4RD
Tel: 01286 673322 — 52 H10
llysderwen.co.uk
Total Pitches: 20 (C, CV & T)

Moelfryn C & C Park
Ty-Cefn, Pant-y-Bwlch, Newcastle Emlyn
SA38 9JE
Tel: 01559 371231 — 25 P3
moelfryncaravanpark.co.uk
Total Pitches: 25 (C, CV & T)

Pencelli Castle C & C Park
Pencelli, Brecon
LD3 7LX
Tel: 01874 665451 — 26 K3
pencelli-castle.com
Total Pitches: 80 (C, CV & T)

Penhein Glamping
Penhein, Llanvair Discoed, Chepstow
NP16 6RB
Tel: 01633 400581 — 27 T9
penhein.co.uk
Total Pitches: 6 (T)

Penisar Mynydd Caravan Park
Caerwys Road, Rhuallt, St Asaph
LL17 0TY
Tel: 01745 582227 — 54 C11
penisarmynydd.co.uk
Total Pitches: 71 (C, CV & T)

Plas Farm Caravan Park
Betws-yn-Rhos, Abergele
LL22 8AU
Tel: 01492 680254 — 53 Q8
plasfarmcaravanpark.co.uk
Total Pitches: 54 (C, CV & T)

Plassey Holiday Park
The Plassey, Eyton, Wrexham
LL13 0SP
Tel: 01978 780277 — 44 H4
plassey.com
Total Pitches: 90 (C, CV & T)

Pont Kemys C & C Park
Chainbridge, Abergavenny
NP7 9DS
Tel: 01873 880688 — 27 Q6
pontkemys.com
Total Pitches: 65 (C, CV & T)

Red Kite Touring Park
Van Road, Llanidloes
SY18 6NG
Tel: 01686 412122 — 33 T3
redkitetouringpark.co.uk
Total Pitches: 66 (C & CV)

River View Touring Park
The Dingle, Llanedi, Pontarddulais
SA4 0FH
Tel: 01635 844876 — 25 U9
riverviewtouringpark.com
Total Pitches: 60 (C, CV & T)

Riverside Camping
Seiont Nurseries, Pont Rug, Caernarfon
LL55 2BB
Tel: 01286 678781 — 52 H10
riversidecamping.co.uk
Total Pitches: 73 (C, CV & T)

St David's Park
Red Wharf Bay, Pentraeth, Isle of Anglesey
LL75 8RJ
Tel: 01248 852341 — 52 H6
stdavidspark.com
Total Pitches: 52 (C & CV)

The Little Yurt Meadow
Bay Tree Barns, Mill Road, Bronington
SY13 3HJ
Tel: 01948 780136 — 45 L6
thelittleyurtmeadow.co.uk
Total Pitches: 3 (T)

Trawsdir Touring C & C Park
Llanaber, Barmouth
LL42 1RR
Tel: 01341 280999 — 43 L10
barmouthholidays.co.uk
Total Pitches: 70 (C, CV & T)

Trefalun Park
Devonshire Drive, St Florence, Tenby
SA70 8RD
Tel: 01646 651514 — 24 J10
trefalunpark.co.uk
Total Pitches: 90 (C, CV & T)

Tyddyn Isaf Caravan Park
Lligwy Bay, Dulas, Isle of Anglesey
LL70 9PQ
Tel: 01248 410203 — 52 G5
tyddynisaf.co.uk
Total Pitches: 80 (C, CV & T)

White Tower Caravan Park
Llandwrog, Caernarfon
LL54 5UH
Tel: 01286 830649 — 52 G11
whitetowerpark.co.uk
Total Pitches: 52 (C & CV)

CHANNEL ISLANDS

Beuvelande Camp Site
Beuvelande, St Martin, Jersey
JE3 6EZ
Tel: 01534 853575 — 7 e2
campingjersey.com
Total Pitches: 150 (C, CV & T)

Durrell Wildlife Camp
Les Augres Manor, La Profonde Rue,
Trinity, Jersey
JE3 5BP
Tel: 01534 860095 — 7 e2
durrell.org/camp
Total Pitches: 12 (T)

Fauxquets Valley Campsite
Castel, Guernsey
GY5 7QL
Tel: 01481 255460 — 6 d3
fauxquets.co.uk
Total Pitches: 120 (C, CV & T)

Rozel Camping Park
Summerville Farm, St Martin, Jersey
JE3 6AX
Tel: 01534 855200 — 7 f2
rozelcamping.co.uk
Total Pitches: 100 (C, CV & T)

Traffic signs and road markings

Traffic signs

Signs giving orders

Signs with red circles are mostly prohibitive. Plates below signs qualify their message.

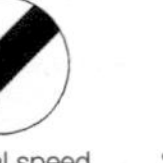

 Entry to 20mph zone

 End of 20mph zone

 Maximum speed

 National speed limit applies

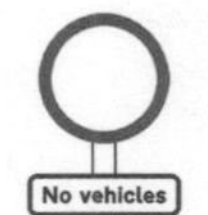

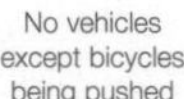

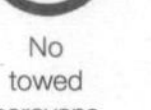

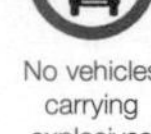

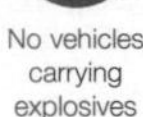

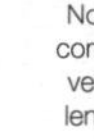

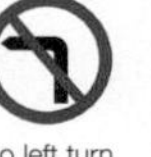

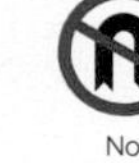

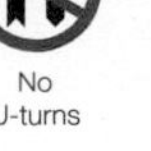

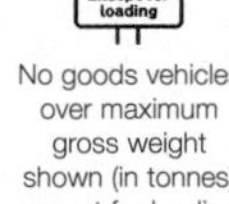

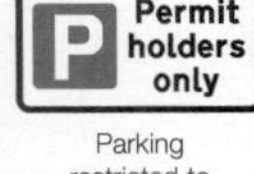

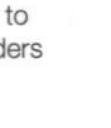

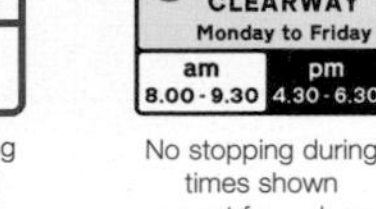

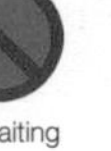

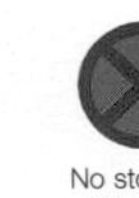

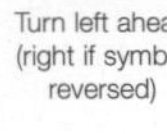

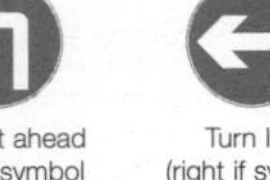

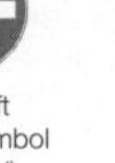

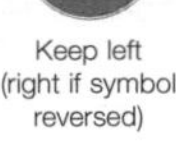

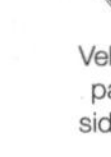

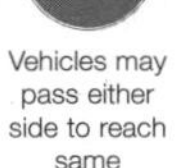

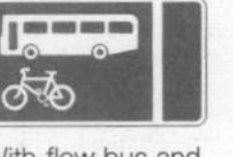

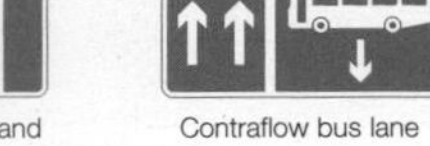

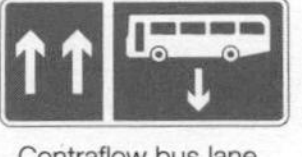

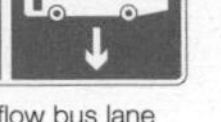

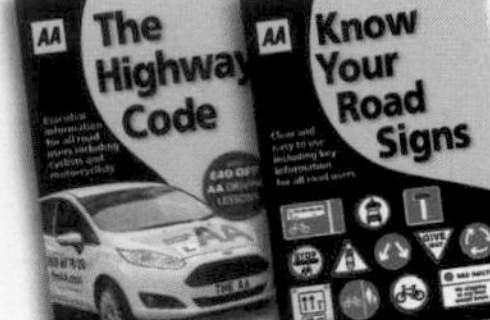

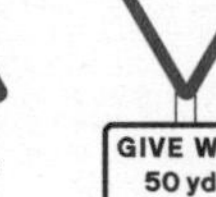

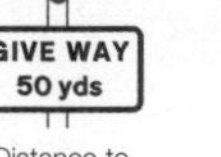

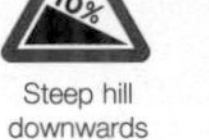

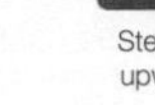

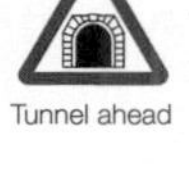

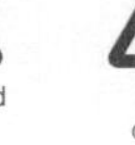

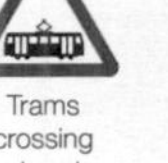

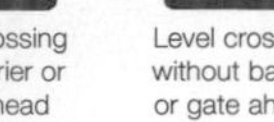

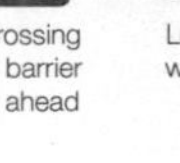

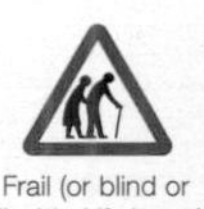

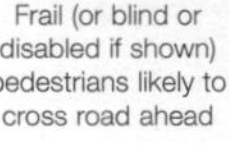

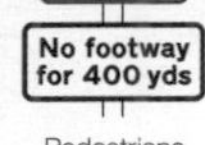

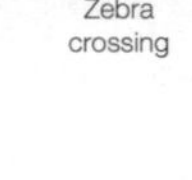

 School crossing patrol

 Stop and give way

 Give way to traffic on major road

 Manually operated temporary STOP and GO signs

 No entry for vehicular traffic

No vehicles except bicycles being pushed

No cycling

No motor vehicles

No buses (over 8 passenger seats)

No overtaking

No towed caravans

No vehicles carrying explosives

No vehicle or combination of vehicles over length shown

No vehicles over height shown

No vehicles over width shown

Give way to oncoming vehicles

No right turn

No left turn

No U-turns

No goods vehicles over maximum gross weight shown (in tonnes) except for loading and unloading

Give priority to vehicles from opposite direction

WEAK BRIDGE 18T m g w No vehicles over maximum gross weight shown (in tonnes)

Permit holders only Parking restricted to permit holders

RED ROUTE No stopping at any time except buses No stopping during period indicated except for buses

URBAN CLEARWAY Monday to Friday am 8.00 - 9.30 pm 4.30 - 6.30 No stopping during times shown except for as long as necessary to set down or pick up passengers

No waiting

No stopping (Clearway)

Signs with blue circles but no red border mostly give positive instruction.

Ahead only

Turn left ahead (right if symbol reversed)

Turn left (right if symbol reversed)

Keep left (right if symbol reversed)

Vehicles may pass either side to reach same destination

Mini-roundabout (roundabout circulation – give way to vehicles from the immediate right)

Route to be used by pedal cycles only

Segregated pedal cycle and pedestrian route

Minimum speed

End of minimum speed

Only Buses and cycles only

Only Trams only

Pedestrian crossing point over tramway

One-way traffic (note: compare circular 'Ahead only' sign)

With-flow bus and cycle lane

Contraflow bus lane

With-flow pedal cycle lane

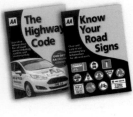

Note: The signs shown in this road atlas are those most commonly in use and are not all drawn to the same scale. In Scotland and Wales bilingual versions of some signs are used, showing both English and Gaelic or Welsh spellings. Some older designs of signs may still be seen on the roads. A comprehensive explanation of the signing system illustrating the vast majority of road signs can be found in the AA's handbook Know Your Road Signs. Where there is a reference to a rule number, this refers to The Highway Code. Both these publications are on sale at theaa.com/shop and booksellers.

Warning signs

Mostly triangular

 STOP 100 yds Distance to 'STOP' line ahead

Dual carriageway ends

Road narrows on right (left if symbol reversed)

Road narrows on both sides

GIVE WAY 50 yds Distance to 'Give Way' line ahead

Crossroads

Junction on bend ahead

T-junction with priority over vehicles from the right

Staggered junction

Traffic merging from left ahead

The priority through route is indicated by the broader line.

Double bend first to left (symbol may be reversed)

Bend to right (or left if symbol reversed)

Roundabout

Uneven road

REDUCE SPEED NOW Plate below some signs

Two-way traffic crosses one-way road

Two-way traffic straight ahead

Opening or swing bridge ahead

Low-flying aircraft or sudden aircraft noise

Falling or fallen rocks

Traffic signals not in use

Traffic signals

Slippery road

Steep hill downwards

Steep hill upwards

Gradients may be shown as a ratio i.e. 20% = 1:5

Tunnel ahead

Trams crossing ahead

Level crossing with barrier or gate ahead

Level crossing without barrier or gate ahead

Level crossing without barrier

Patrol School crossing patrol ahead (some signs have amber lights which flash when crossings are in use)

Frail (or blind or disabled if shown) pedestrians likely to cross road ahead

No footway for 400 yds Pedestrians in road ahead

Zebra crossing

Safe height 16'-6" Overhead electric cable; plate indicates maximum height of vehicles which can pass safely

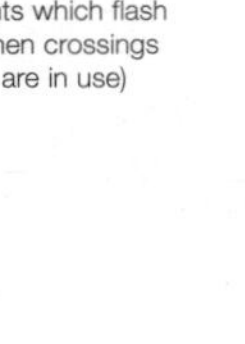

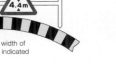

 Available width of headroom indicated

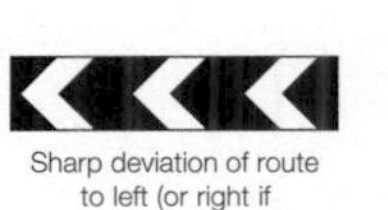

Sharp deviation of route to left (or right if chevrons reversed)

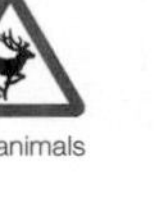

STOP when lights show Light signals ahead at level crossing, airfield or bridge

Red Green STOP Clear IF NO LIGHT - PHONE CROSSING OPERATOR Miniature warning lights at level crossings

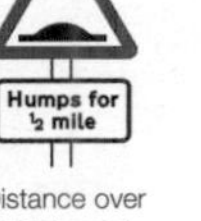

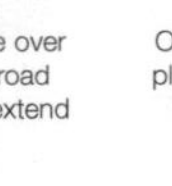

Cattle

Wild animals

Wild horses or ponies

Accompanied horses or ponies

Cycle route ahead

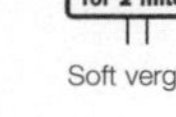

Ice Risk of ice

Queues likely Traffic queues likely ahead

Humps for ½ mile Distance over which road humps extend

Hidden dip Other danger; plate indicates nature of danger

Soft verges for 2 miles Soft verges

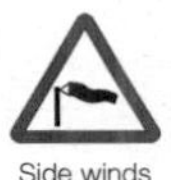

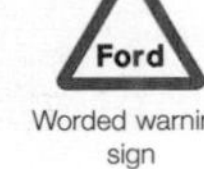

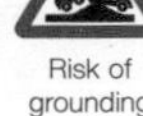

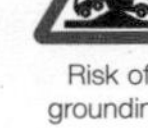

Side winds

Hump bridge

Ford Worded warning sign

Quayside or river bank

Risk of grounding

Direction signs

Mostly rectangular

Signs on motorways – blue backgrounds

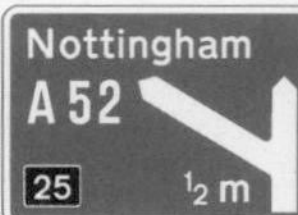

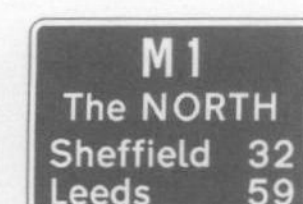

 Nottingham 23 M1 At a junction leading directly into a motorway (junction number may be shown on a black background)

Nottingham A 52 25 ½ m On approaches to junctions (junction number on black background)

M1 The NORTH Sheffield 32 Leeds 59 Route confirmatory sign after junction

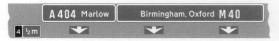

 A 404 Marlow Birmingham, Oxford M 40 4 ½ m Downward pointing arrows mean 'Get in lane' The left-hand lane leads to a different destination from the other lanes.

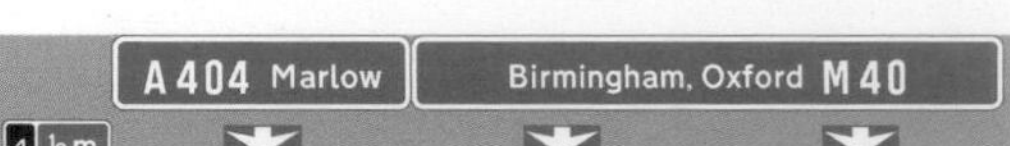

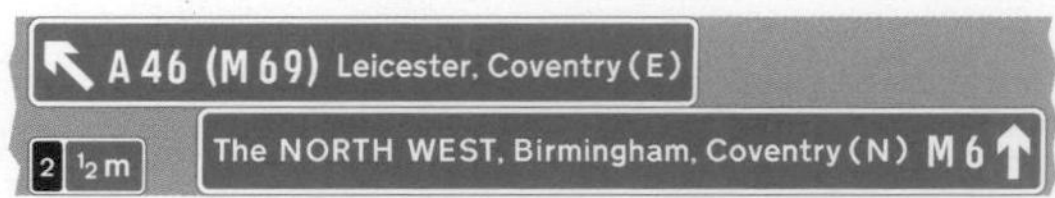

 A 46 (M 69) Leicester, Coventry (E) 2 ½ m The NORTH WEST, Birmingham, Coventry (N) M 6 The panel with the inclined arrow indicates the destinations which can be reached by leaving the motorway at the next junction

Signs on primary routes - green backgrounds

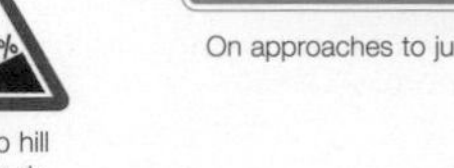

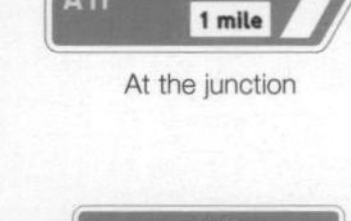

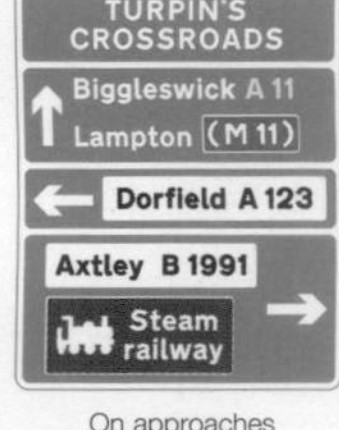

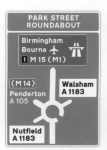

 PARK STREET ROUNDABOUT Birmingham Bourne 1 M 15 (M1) (M 14) Penderton A 105 Walsham A 1183 Nutfield A 1183 On approaches to junctions

Lampton Axtley A 11 1 mile At the junction

A 46 The SOUTH Nottingham 17 Leicester 32 (M 1 South) 35 Route confirmatory sign after junction

TURPIN'S CROSSROADS Biggleswick A 11 Lampton (M 11) Dorfield A 123 Axtley B 1991 Steam railway On approaches to junctions

Swansea Abertawe A 483 On approach to a junction in Wales (bilingual)

Blue panels indicate that the motorway starts at the junction ahead. Motorways shown in brackets can also be reached along the route indicated. White panels indicate local or non-primary routes leading from the junction ahead. Brown panels show the route to tourist attractions. The name of the junction may be shown at the top of the sign. The aircraft symbol indicates the route to an airport. A symbol may be included to warn of a hazard or restriction along that route.

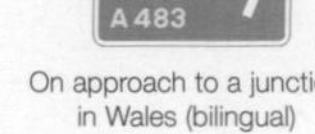

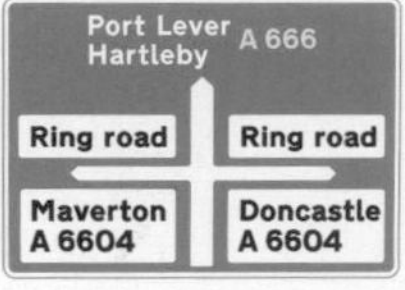

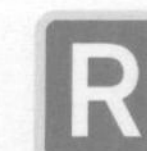

Port Lever Hartleby A 666 Ring road Ring road Maverton A 6604 Doncastle A 6604 Primary route forming part of a ring road

R

Signs on non-primary and local routes - black borders

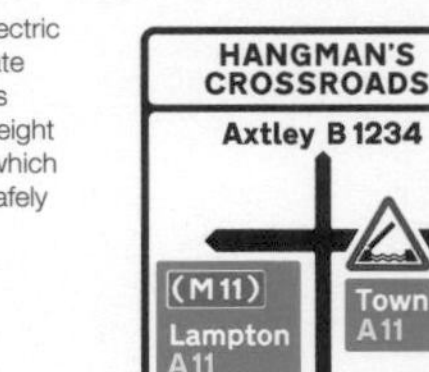

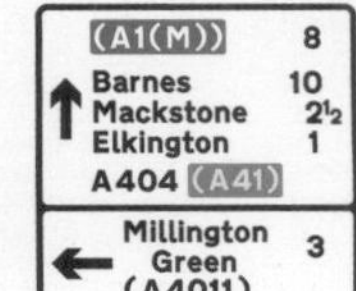

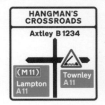

 HANGMAN'S CROSSROADS Axtley B 1234 (M 11) Lampton A 11 Townley A 11 On approaches to junctions

(A1(M)) 8 Barnes 10 Mackstone 2½ Elkington 1 A404 (A 41) Millington Green (A 4011) 3

Market Walborough B 486 7 At the junction

WC Direction to toilets with access for the disabled

Green panels indicate that the primary route starts at the junction ahead. Route numbers on a blue background show the direction to a motorway. Route numbers on a green background show the direction to a primary route.

Other direction signs

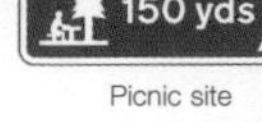

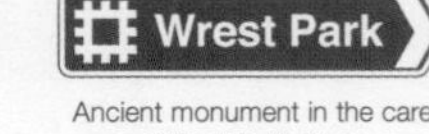

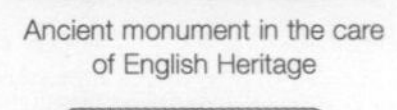

150 yds Picnic site

Wrest Park Ancient monument in the care of English Heritage

Saturday only Direction to a car park

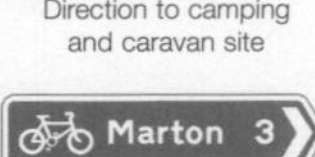

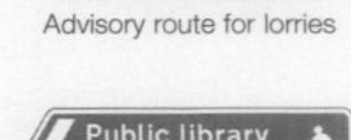

Zoo Tourist attraction

300 yds Direction to camping and caravan site

(A 33) (M 1) Advisory route for lorries

4 Route for pedal cycles forming part of a network

Marton 3 Recommended route for pedal cycles to place shown

Public library Council offices Route for pedestrians

Emergency diversion routes

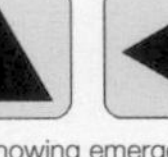

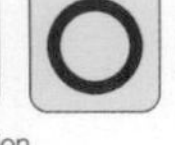

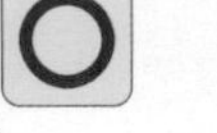

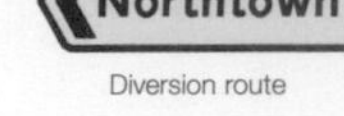

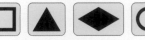

 Symbols showing emergency diversion route for motorway and other main road traffic

Northtown Diversion route

In an emergency it may be necessary to close a section of motorway or other main road to traffic, so a temporary sign may advise drivers to follow a diversion route. To help drivers navigate the route, black symbols on yellow patches may be permanently displayed on existing direction signs, including motorway signs. Symbols may also be used on separate signs with yellow backgrounds.

For further information see www.theaa.com/motoring_advice/general-advice/emergency-diversion-routes.html

Information signs

All rectangular

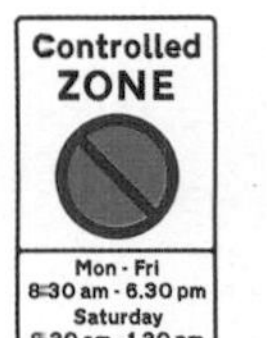

Entrance to controlled parking zone

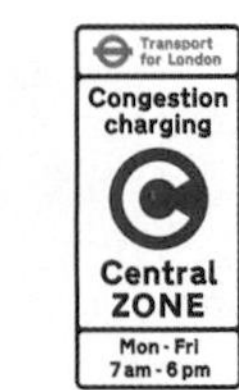

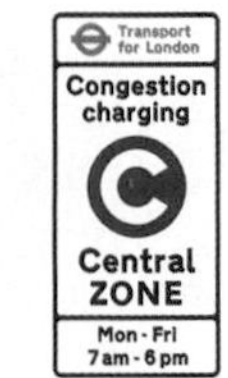

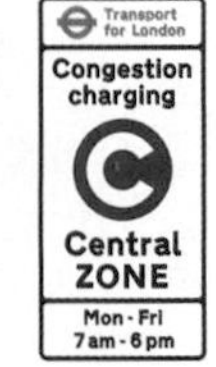

Entrance to congestion charging zone

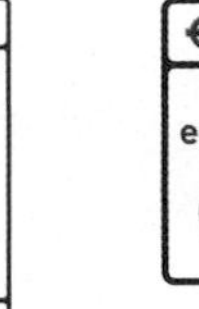

Greater London Low Emission Zone (LEZ)

Advance warning of restriction or prohibition ahead

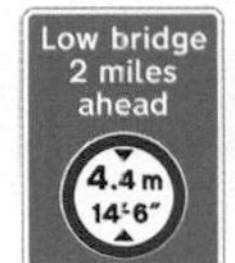

Parking place for solo motorcycles

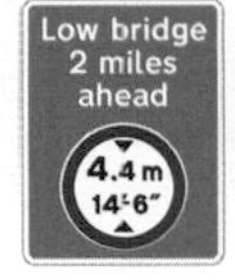

With-flow bus lane ahead which pedal cycles and taxis may also use

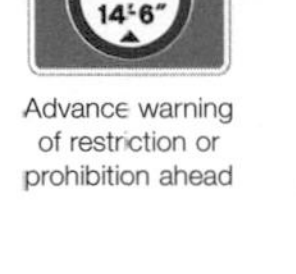

Lane designated for use by high occupancy vehicles (HOV) – see rule 142

Vehicles permitted to use an HOV lane ahead

End of motorway

Start of motorway and point from which motorway regulations apply

Appropriate traffic lanes at junction ahead

Traffic on the main carriageway coming from right has priority over joining traffic

Additional traffic joining from left ahead. Traffic on main carriageway has priority over joining traffic from right hand lane of slip road.

Traffic in right hand lane of slip road joining the main carriageway has priority over left hand lane

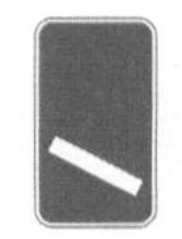

'Countdown' markers at exit from motorway (each bar represents 100 yards to the exit). Green-backed markers may be used on primary routes and white-backed markers with black bars on other routes. At approaches to concealed level crossings white-backed markers with red bars may be used. Although these will be erected at equal distances the bars do not represent 100 yard intervals.

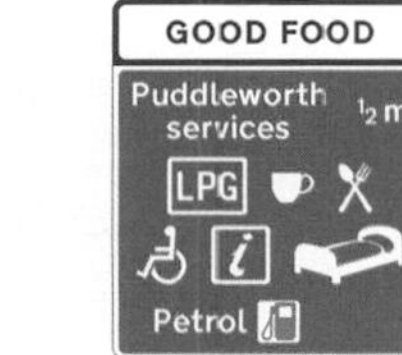

GOOD FOOD Puddleworth services LPG Petrol
Motorway service area sign showing the operator's name

Priority over oncoming vehicles — Traffic has priority over oncoming vehicles

Hospital ahead with Accident and Emergency facilities

Tourist information point

No through road for vehicles

Recommended route for pedal cycles

Home Zone Entry*

Area in which cameras are used to enforce traffic regulations

Bus lane on road at junction ahead

*Home Zone Entry – You are entering an area where people could be using the whole street for a range of activities. You should drive slowly and carefully and be prepared to stop to allow people time to move out of the way.

Roadworks signs

Road works

Loose chippings

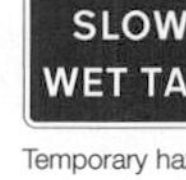

Temporary hazard at roadworks

Temporary lane closure (the number and position of arrows and red bars may be varied according to lanes open and closed)

 Slow-moving or stationary works vehicle blocking a traffic lane. Pass in the direction shown by the arrow.

Mandatory speed limit ahead

Roadworks 1 mile ahead

End of roadworks and any temporary restrictions including speed limits

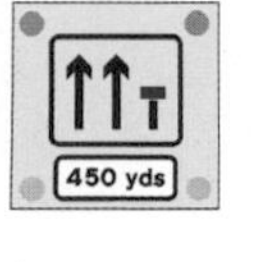

Signs used on the back of slow-moving or stationary vehicles warning of a lane closed ahead by a works vehicle. There are no cones on the road.

450 yds

Lane restrictions at roadworks ahead

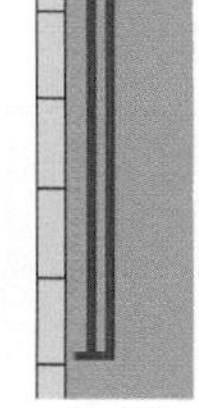

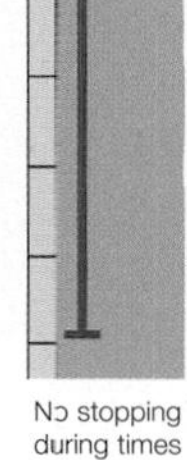

One lane crossover at contraflow roadworks

Road markings

Across the carriageway

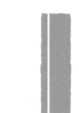

Stop line at signals or police control

Stop line at 'Stop' sign

Stop line for pedestrians at a level crossing

Give way to traffic on major road (can also be used at mini roundabouts)

Give way to traffic from the right at a roundabout

Give way to traffic from the right at a mini-roundabout

Along the carriageway

Edge line

Centre line See Rule 127

Hazard warning line See Rule 127

Double white lines See Rules 128 and 129

See Rule 130

Lane line See Rule 131

Along the edge of the carriageway

Waiting restrictions

Waiting restrictions indicated by yellow lines apply to the carriageway, pavement and verge. You may stop to load or unload (unless there are also loading restrictions as described below) or while passengers board or alight. Double yellow lines mean no waiting at any time, unless there are signs that specifically indicate seasonal restrictions. The times at which the restrictions apply for other road markings are shown on nearby plates or on entry signs to controlled parking zones. If no days are shown on the signs, the restrictions are in force every day including Sundays and Bank Holidays. White bay markings and upright signs (see below) indicate where parking is allowed.

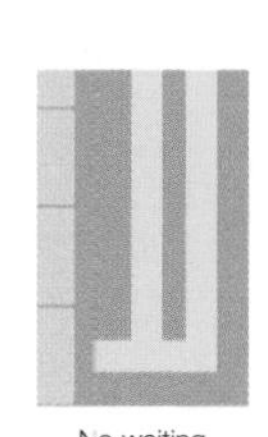

No waiting at any time

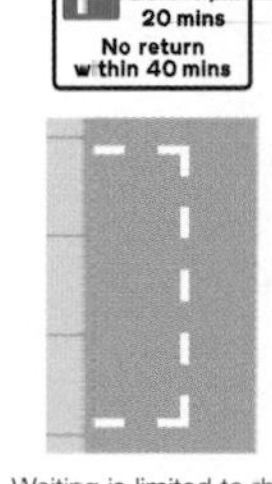

No waiting during times shown on sign

Waiting is limited to the duration specified during the days and times shown

Red Route stopping controls

Red lines are used on some roads instead of yellow lines. In London the double and single red lines used on Red Routes indicate that stopping to park, load/unload or to board and alight from a vehicle (except for a licensed taxi or if you hold a Blue Badge) is prohibited. The red lines apply to the carriageway, pavement and verge. The times that the red line prohibitions apply are shown on nearby signs, but the double red line ALWAYS means no stopping at any time. On Red Routes you may stop to park, load/unload in specially marked boxes and adjacent signs specify the times and purposes and duration allowed. A box MARKED IN RED indicates that it may only be available for the purpose specified for part of the day (e.g. between busy peak periods). A box MARKED IN WHITE means that it is available throughout the day.

RED AND SINGLE YELLOW LINES CAN ONLY GIVE A GUIDE TO THE RESTRICTIONS AND CONTROLS IN FORCE AND SIGNS, NEARBY OR AT A ZONE ENTRY, MUST BE CONSULTED.

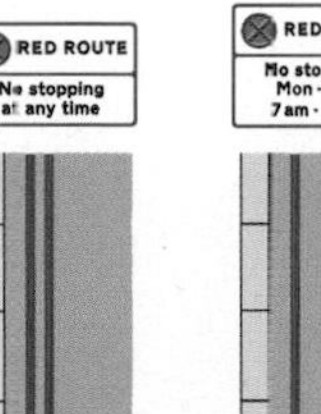

No stopping at any time

No stopping during times shown on sign

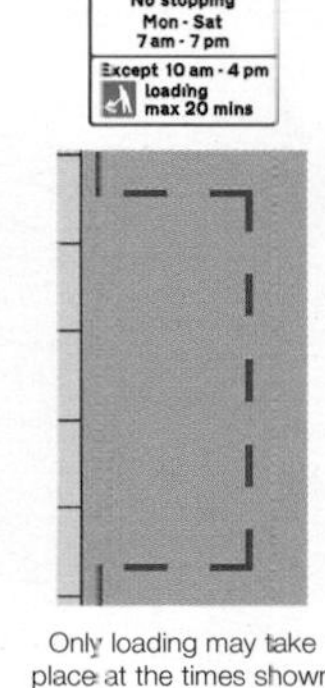

Parking is limited to the duration specified during the days and times shown

Only loading may take place at the times shown for up to a maximum duration of 20 mins

On the kerb or at the edge of the carriageway

Loading restrictions on roads other than Red Routes

Yellow marks on the kerb or at the edge of the carriageway indicate that loading or unloading is prohibited at the times shown on the nearby black and white plates. You may stop while passengers board or alight. If no days are indicated on the signs the restrictions are in force every day including Sundays and Bank Holidays.

ALWAYS CHECK THE TIMES SHOWN ON THE PLATES.

Lengths of road reserved for vehicles loading and unloading are indicated by a white 'bay' marking with the words 'Loading Only' and a sign with the white on blue 'trolley' symbol. This sign also shows whether loading and unloading is restricted to goods vehicles and the times at which the bay can be used. If no times or days are shown it may be used at any time. Vehicles may not park here if they are not loading or unloading.

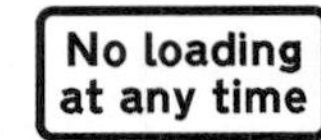

No loading or unloading at any time

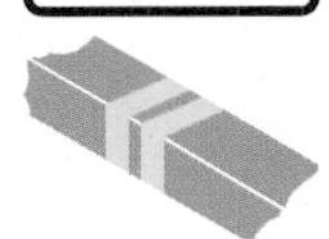

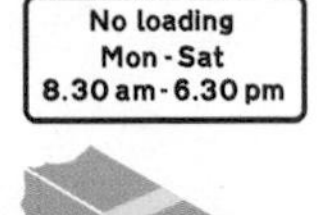

No loading or unloading at the times shown

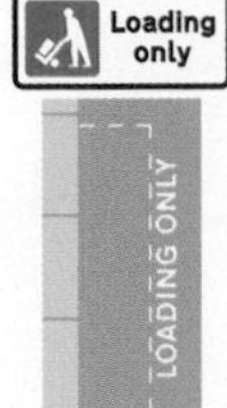

Loading bay

Other road markings

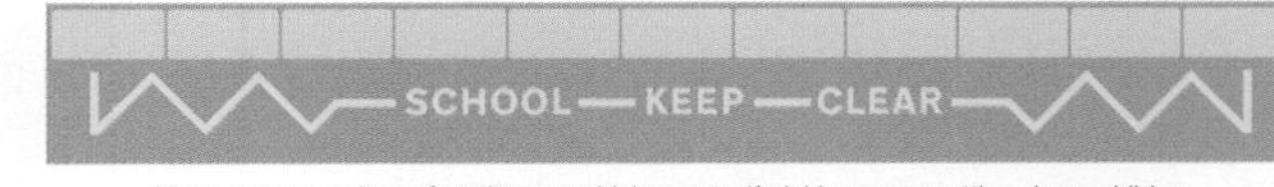

SCHOOL — KEEP — CLEAR
Keep entrance clear of stationary vehicles, even if picking up or setting down children

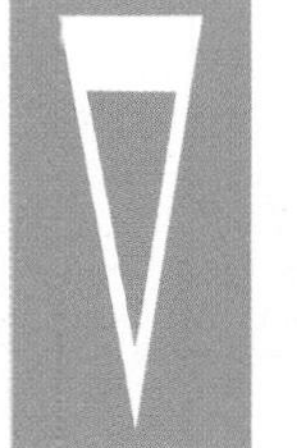

Warning of 'Give Way' just ahead

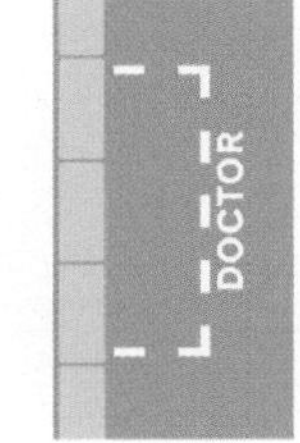

Parking space reserved for vehicles named

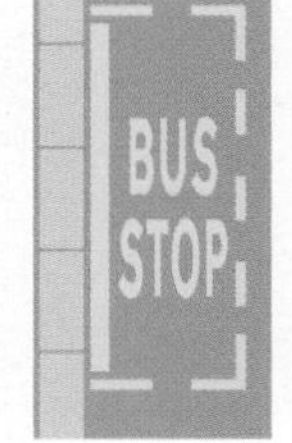

BUS STOP See Rule 243

BUS LANE See Rule 141

Box junction – See Rule 174

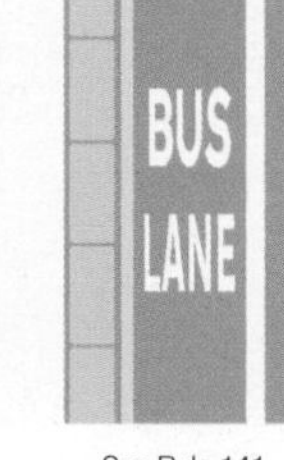

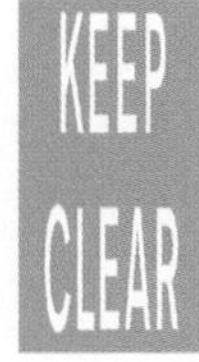

KEEP CLEAR Do not block that part of the carriageway indicated

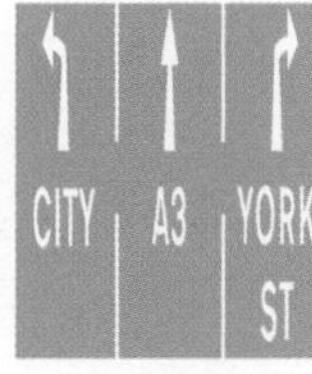

Indication of traffic lanes

Light signals controlling traffic

Traffic Light Signals

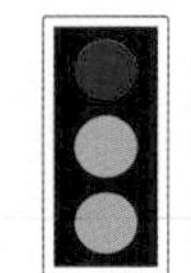

RED means 'Stop'. Wait behind the stop line on the carriageway.

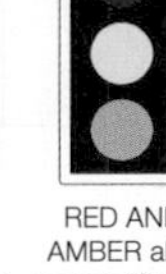

RED AND AMBER also means 'Stop'. Do not pass through or start until GREEN shows.

GREEN means you may go on if the way is clear. Take special care if you intend to turn left or right and give way to pedestrians who are crossing.

AMBER means 'Stop' at the stop line. You may go on only if the AMBER appears after you have crossed the stop line or are so close to it that to pull up might cause an accident.

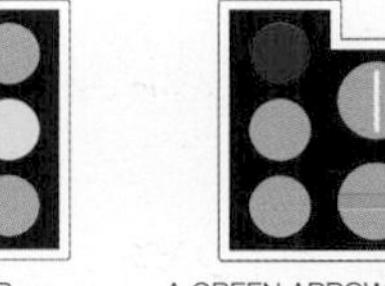

A GREEN ARROW may be provided in addition to the full green signal if movement in a certain direction is allowed before or after the full green phase. If the way is clear you may go but only in the direction shown by the arrow. You may do this whatever other lights may be showing. White light signals may be provided for trams.

Flashing red lights

Alternately flashing red lights mean YOU MUST STOP

At level crossings, lifting bridges, airfields, fire stations, etc.

Motorway signals

You MUST NOT proceed further in this lane

Change lane

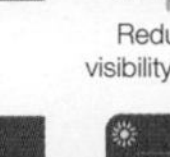

Reduced visibility ahead

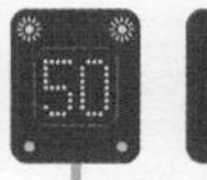

Lane ahead closed

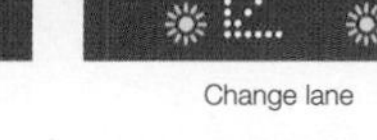

Temporary maximum speed advised and information message

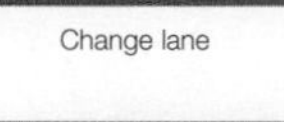

Leave motorway at next exit

Temporary maximum speed advised

End of restriction

Lane control signals

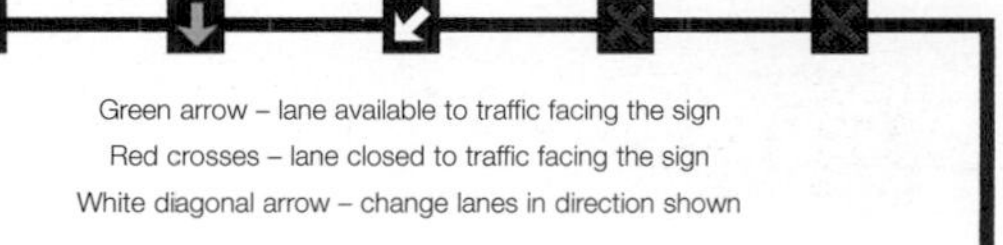

Green arrow – lane available to traffic facing the sign
Red crosses – lane closed to traffic facing the sign
White diagonal arrow – change lanes in direction shown

Channel hopping and the Isle of Wight

For business or pleasure, hopping on a ferry across to France, the Channel Islands or Isle of Wight has never been easier.

The vehicle ferry services listed in the table give you all the options, together with detailed port plans to help you navigate to and from the ferry terminals. Simply choose your preferred route, not forgetting the fast sailings (see 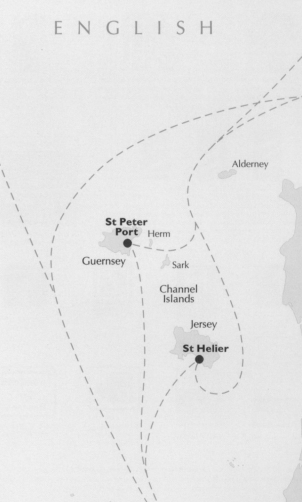). Bon voyage!

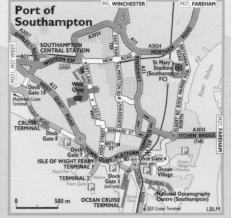

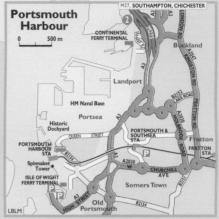

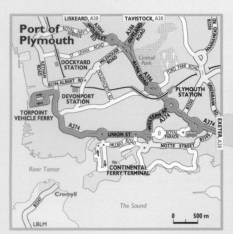

ENGLISH CHANNEL AND ISLE OF WIGHT FERRY CROSSINGS

From	To	Journey time	Operator website
Dover	Calais	1 hr 30 mins	dfdsseaways.co.uk
Dover	Calais	1 hr 30 mins	poferries.com
Dover	Dunkirk	2 hrs	dfdsseaways.co.uk
Folkestone	Calais (Coquelles)	35 mins	eurotunnel.com
Lymington	Yarmouth (IOW)	40 mins	wightlink.co.uk
Newhaven	Dieppe	4 hrs	dfdsseaways.co.uk
Plymouth	Roscoff	6–8 hrs	brittany-ferries.co.uk
Plymouth	St-Malo	10 hrs 15 mins (Nov–Mar)	brittany-ferries.co.uk
Poole	Cherbourg	4 hrs 15 mins	brittany-ferries.co.uk
Poole	Guernsey	3 hrs	condorferries.co.uk
Poole	Jersey	4 hrs 30 mins	condorferries.co.uk
Poole	St-Malo	7–12 hrs (via Channel Is.)	condorferries.co.uk
Portsmouth	Caen (Ouistreham)	6–7 hrs	brittany-ferries.co.uk
Portsmouth	Cherbourg	3 hrs (May–Aug)	brittany-ferries.co.uk
Portsmouth	Cherbourg	5 hrs 30 mins (May–Aug)	condorferries.co.uk
Portsmouth	Fishbourne (IOW)	45 mins	wightlink.co.uk
Portsmouth	Guernsey	7 hrs	condorferries.co.uk
Portsmouth	Jersey	8–11 hrs	condorferries.co.uk
Portsmouth	Le Havre	8 hrs (Jan–Oct)	brittany-ferries.co.uk
Portsmouth	St-Malo	9–11 hrs	brittany-ferries.co.uk
Southampton	East Cowes (IOW)	60 mins	redfunnel.co.uk

The information listed is provided as a guide only, as services are liable to change at short notice. Services shown are for vehicle ferries only, operated by conventional ferry unless indicated as a fast ferry service (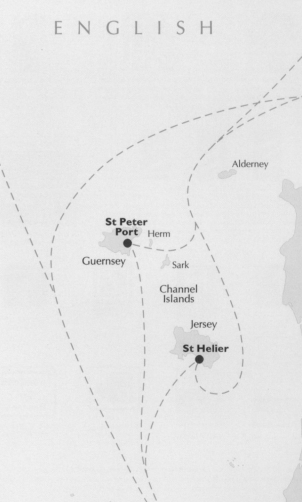). Please check sailings before planning your journey.

Travelling further afield? For ferry services to Northern Spain see *brittany-ferries.co.uk*.

ENGLISH

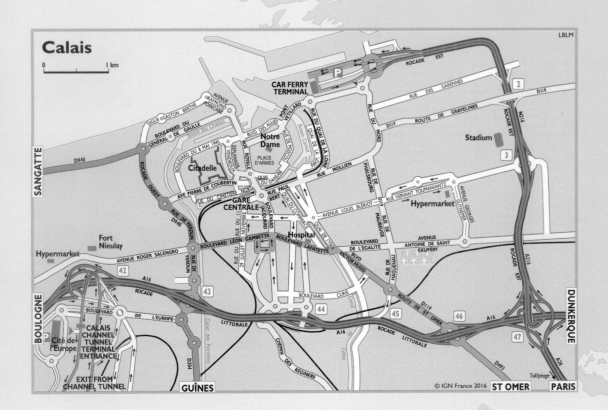

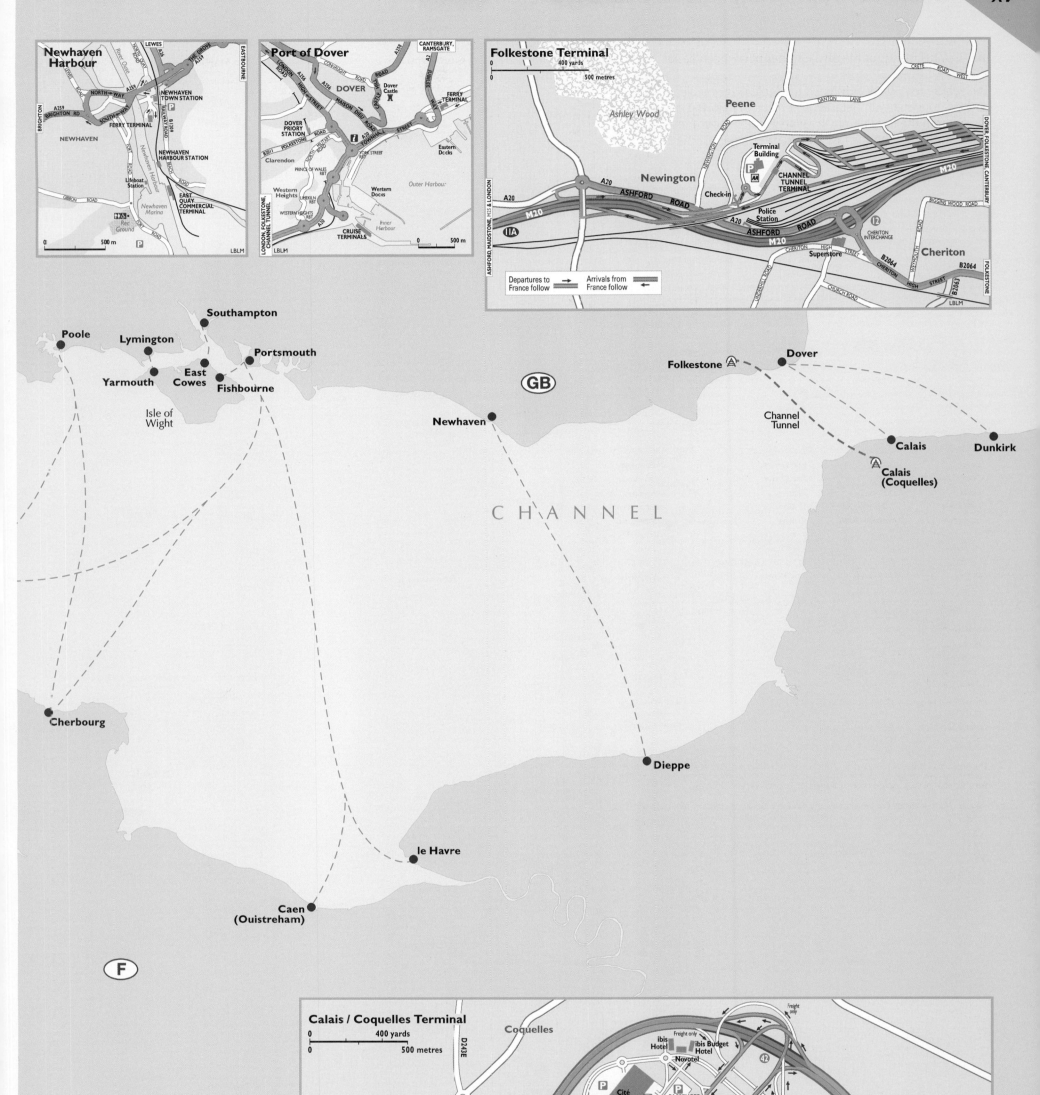

Newhaven Harbour

LEWES
THE DROVE
EASTBOURNE
NORTH WAY
NEWHAVEN TOWN STATION
P
FERRY TERMINAL
SOUTH WAY
A259 BRIGHTON RD
BRIGHTON
NEWHAVEN
A26 A259
River Ouse
A259
A259
NEWHAVEN HARBOUR STATION
Lifeboat Station
Newhaven Harbour
EAST QUAY COMMERCIAL TERMINAL
Newhaven Marina
GIBBON ROAD
Rec Ground
P
0   500 m
LBLM

Port of Dover

CANTERBURY, RAMSGATE
A256
CONNAUGHT ROAD
A258
CASTLE STREET
DOVER
Dover Castle
FERRY TERMINAL
LONDON A2
A256
MAISON DIEU ROAD
Eastern Docks
DOVER PRIORY STATION
FOLKESTONE ROAD
PRINCE OF WALES RBT
YORK STREET
DOUGLAS ROAD
Clarendon
Western Heights
WESTERN HEIGHTS RBT
A20
LIMEKILN RBT
Western Docks
Outer Harbour
Inner Harbour
CRUISE TERMINALS
LONDON, FOLKESTONE, CHANNEL TUNNEL
0   500 m
LBLM

Folkestone Terminal

0   400 yards
0   500 metres
Ashley Wood
Peene
CRETE ROAD WEST
DANTON LANE
CRETE ROAD EAST
Newington
Terminal Building
P
AA
CHANNEL TUNNEL TERMINAL
DOVER, FOLKESTONE, CANTERBURY
M20
A20
ASHFORD ROAD
Check-in
Police Station
A20
M20
11A
ASHFORD, MAIDSTONE, M13 & LONDON
ASHFORD ROAD
CHERITON HIGH STREET
M20
Superstore
CHERITON
12
CHERITON INTERCHANGE
BIGGINS WOOD ROAD
B2064
Cheriton
B2064
B2064
FOLKESTONE
CHURCH ROAD
LBLM

Departures to France follow →
Arrivals from France follow ←

Poole
Lymington
Southampton
Yarmouth
East Cowes
Fishbourne
Portsmouth
Isle of Wight
GB
Newhaven
Folkestone
Dover
Channel Tunnel
Calais
Dunkirk
Calais (Coquelles)

C H A N N E L

Cherbourg
Dieppe
le Havre
Caen (Ouistreham)

F

Calais / Coquelles Terminal

0   400 yards
0   500 metres
Coquelles
D243E
Freight only
ibis Hotel
ibis Budget Hotel
Novotel
Freight only
Cité Europe
P
P
P
PASSENGER TERMINAL
P
Petrol Station
12
Check-in
Frontier Controls
A16 (E402) ROCADE LITTORALE
BOULEVARD DE L'EUROPE
Freight only
BOULEVARD DE LA CÔTE D'OPALE
A16 (E402) ROCADE LITTORALE
CALAIS
BOULOGNE
11
BOULEVARD DE L'EUROPE
13
DUNKIRK, A16 (PARIS)
D304
HGV Fuel Station
Eurotunnel Administration Headquarters
Freight Terminal
Parc d'activites les Terrasses
Arrivals Platforms
Departure Platforms
Freight only
Freight only
Freight only
Departures to England follow →
Arrivals from England follow ←
LBLM

Scotland, North Sea and Irish Sea ferries

SCOTLAND FERRIES

From	To	Journey time	Operator website
Scottish Islands/west coast of Scotland			
Gourock	Dunoon	20 mins	western-ferries.co.uk
Glenelg	Skye	20 mins (Easter–Oct)	skyeferry.co.uk
Numerous and varied sailings from the west coast of Scotland to Scottish islands are provided by Caledonian MacBrayne. Please visit calmac.co.uk for all ferry information, including those of other operators.			
Orkney Islands			
Aberdeen	Kirkwall	6 hrs	northlinkferries.co.uk
Gills	St Margaret's Hope	1 hr	pentlandferries.co.uk
Scrabster	Stromness	1 hr 30 mins	northlinkferries.co.uk
Lerwick	Kirkwall	5 hrs 30 mins	northlinkferries.co.uk
Inter-island services are operated by Orkney Ferries. Please see orkneyferries.co.uk for details.			
Shetland Islands			
Aberdeen	Lerwick	12 hrs 30 mins	northlinkferries.co.uk
Kirkwall	Lerwick	7 hrs 45 mins	northlinkferries.co.uk
Inter-island services are operated by Shetland Island Council Ferries. Please see shetland.gov.uk/ferries for details.			

Please note that some smaller island services are day dependent and reservations are required for some routes. Book and confirm sailing schedules by contacting the operator.

NORTH SEA FERRY CROSSINGS

From	To	Journey time	Operator website
Harwich	Hook of Holland	7–8 hrs	stenaline.co.uk
Kingston upon Hull	Rotterdam (Europoort)	10 hrs 45 mins	poferries.com
Kingston upon Hull	Zeebrugge	13 hrs 15 mins	poferries.com
Newcastle upon Tyne	Amsterdam (IJmuiden)	15 hrs 30 mins	dfdsseaways.co.uk

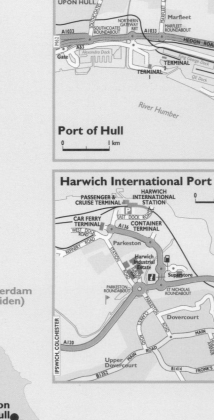

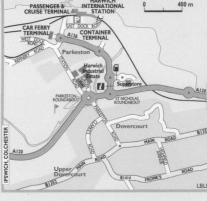

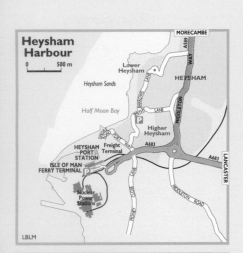

Heysham Harbour

Liverpool Docks

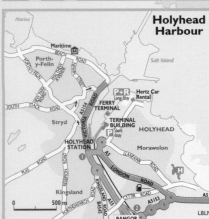

Holyhead Harbour

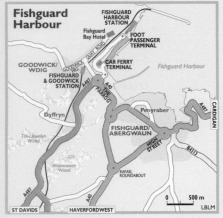

Fishguard Harbour

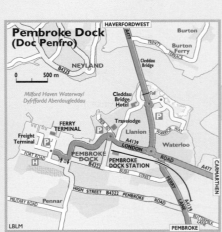

Pembroke Dock (Doc Penfro)

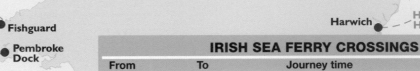

IRISH SEA FERRY CROSSINGS

From	To	Journey time	Operator website
Cairnryan	Belfast	2 hrs 15 mins 🚢	stenaline.co.uk
Cairnryan	Larne	2 hrs	poferries.com
Douglas	Belfast	2 hrs 45 mins (April–Sept) 🚢	steam-packet.com
Douglas	Dublin	2 hrs 55 mins (April–Aug) 🚢	steam-packet.com
Fishguard	Rosslare	3 hrs 30 mins – 4 hrs	stenaline.co.uk
Heysham	Douglas	3 hrs 30 mins	steam-packet.com
Holyhead	Dublin	1 hr 50 mins 🚢	irishferries.com
Holyhead	Dublin	3 hrs 30 mins	irishferries.com
Holyhead	Dublin	3 hrs 30 mins	stenaline.co.uk
Liverpool	Douglas	2 hrs 45 mins (Mar–Oct) 🚢	steam-packet.com
Liverpool	Dublin	7 hrs 30 mins – 8 hrs 30 mins	poferries.com
Liverpool (Birkenhead)	Belfast	8 hrs	stenaline.co.uk
Liverpool (Birkenhead)	Douglas	4 hrs 15 mins (Nov–Mar) 🚢	steam-packet.com
Pembroke Dock	Rosslare	4 hrs	irishferries.com

The information listed is provided as a guide only, as services are liable to change at short notice. Services shown are for vehicle ferries only, operated by conventional ferry unless indicated as a fast ferry service (🚢). Please check sailings before planning your journey.

Motoring information

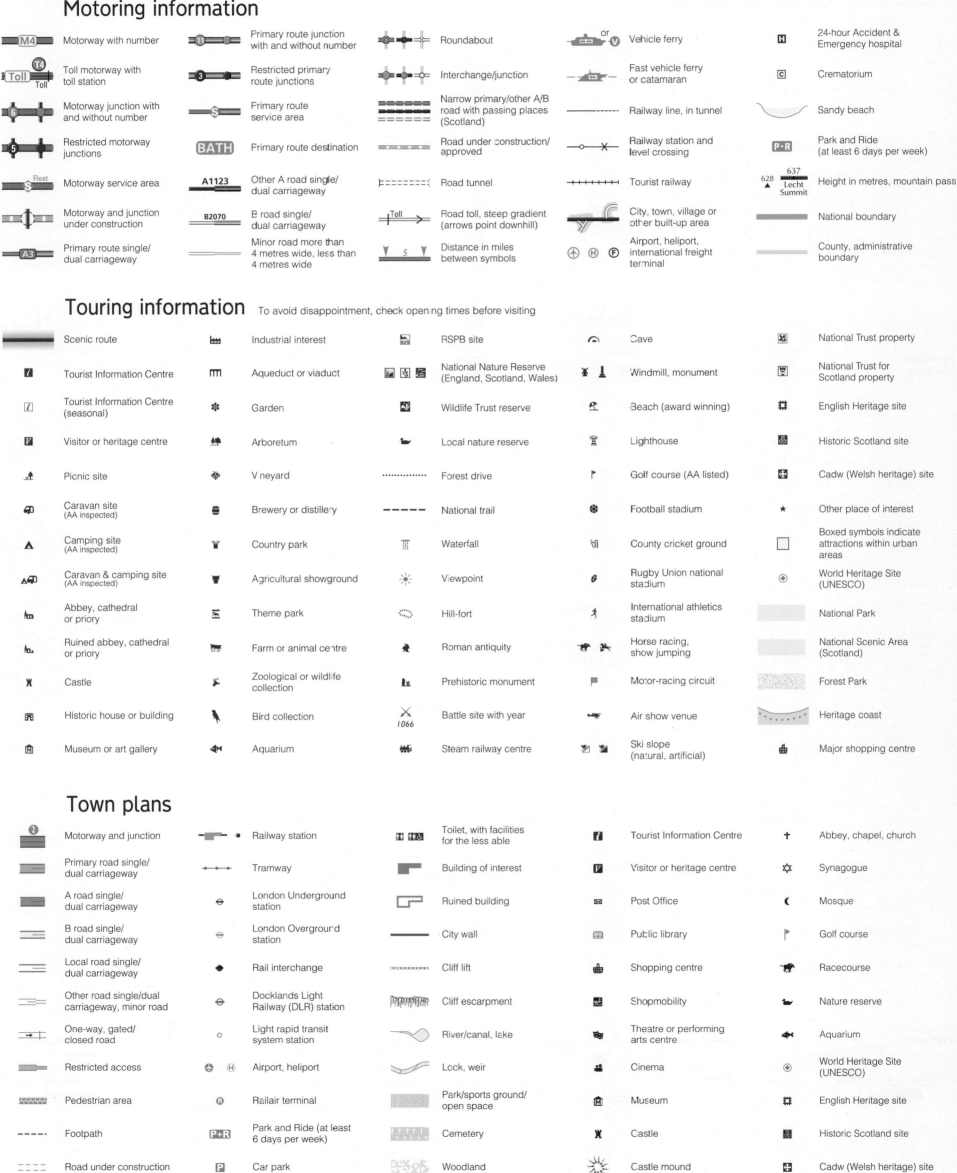

M4	Motorway with number	1	Primary route junction with and without number		Roundabout	or V	Vehicle ferry	H	24-hour Accident & Emergency hospital
Toll	Toll motorway with toll station	3	Restricted primary route junctions		Interchange/junction		Fast vehicle ferry or catamaran	C	Crematorium
6	Motorway junction with and without number	S	Primary route service area		Narrow primary/other A/B road with passing places (Scotland)		Railway line, in tunnel		Sandy beach
5	Restricted motorway junctions	BATH	Primary route destination		Road under construction/ approved		Railway station and level crossing	P·R	Park and Ride (at least 6 days per week)
Fleet S	Motorway service area	A1123	Other A road single/ dual carriageway		Road tunnel		Tourist railway	628 ▲ 637 Lecht Summit	Height in metres, mountain pass
	Motorway and junction under construction	B2070	B road single/ dual carriageway	Toll	Road toll, steep gradient (arrows point downhill)		City, town, village or other built-up area		National boundary
A3	Primary route single/ dual carriageway		Minor road more than 4 metres wide, less than 4 metres wide	5	Distance in miles between symbols	✈ H F	Airport, heliport, international freight terminal		County, administrative boundary

Touring information To avoid disappointment, check opening times before visiting

	Scenic route		Industrial interest		RSPB site		Cave		National Trust property
i	Tourist Information Centre		Aqueduct or viaduct		National Nature Reserve (England, Scotland, Wales)		Windmill, monument		National Trust for Scotland property
i	Tourist Information Centre (seasonal)		Garden		Wildlife Trust reserve		Beach (award winning)		English Heritage site
V	Visitor or heritage centre		Arboretum		Local nature reserve		Lighthouse		Historic Scotland site
	Picnic site		Vineyard		Forest drive		Golf course (AA listed)		Cadw (Welsh heritage) site
	Caravan site (AA inspected)		Brewery or distillery		National trail		Football stadium	★	Other place of interest
▲	Camping site (AA inspected)		Country park		Waterfall		County cricket ground	☐	Boxed symbols indicate attractions within urban areas
	Caravan & camping site (AA inspected)		Agricultural showground		Viewpoint		Rugby Union national stadium		World Heritage Site (UNESCO)
	Abbey, cathedral or priory		Theme park		Hill-fort		International athletics stadium		National Park
	Ruined abbey, cathedral or priory		Farm or animal centre		Roman antiquity		Horse racing, show jumping		National Scenic Area (Scotland)
	Castle		Zoological or wildlife collection		Prehistoric monument		Motor-racing circuit		Forest Park
	Historic house or building		Bird collection	✕ 1066	Battle site with year		Air show venue		Heritage coast
M	Museum or art gallery		Aquarium		Steam railway centre		Ski slope (natural, artificial)		Major shopping centre

Town plans

2	Motorway and junction		Railway station		Toilet, with facilities for the less able	i	Tourist Information Centre	†	Abbey, chapel, church
	Primary road single/ dual carriageway		Tramway		Building of interest	V	Visitor or heritage centre	✡	Synagogue
	A road single/ dual carriageway		London Underground station		Ruined building		Post Office	☾	Mosque
	B road single/ dual carriageway		London Overground station		City wall		Public library		Golf course
	Local road single/ dual carriageway		Rail interchange		Cliff lift		Shopping centre		Racecourse
	Other road single/dual carriageway, minor road		Docklands Light Railway (DLR) station		Cliff escarpment		Shopmobility		Nature reserve
	One-way, gated/ closed road	○	Light rapid transit system station		River/canal, lake		Theatre or performing arts centre		Aquarium
	Restricted access	✈ H	Airport, heliport		Lock, weir		Cinema		World Heritage Site (UNESCO)
	Pedestrian area	R	Railair terminal		Park/sports ground/ open space	M	Museum		English Heritage site
	Footpath	P+R	Park and Ride (at least 6 days per week)		Cemetery		Castle		Historic Scotland site
	Road under construction	P	Car park		Woodland		Castle mound		Cadw (Welsh heritage) site
	Road tunnel		Bus/coach station		Built-up area	•	Monument, statue		National Trust site
	Level crossing	H H	24-hour Accident & Emergency hospital, other hospital		Beach		Viewpoint		National Trust for Scotland site

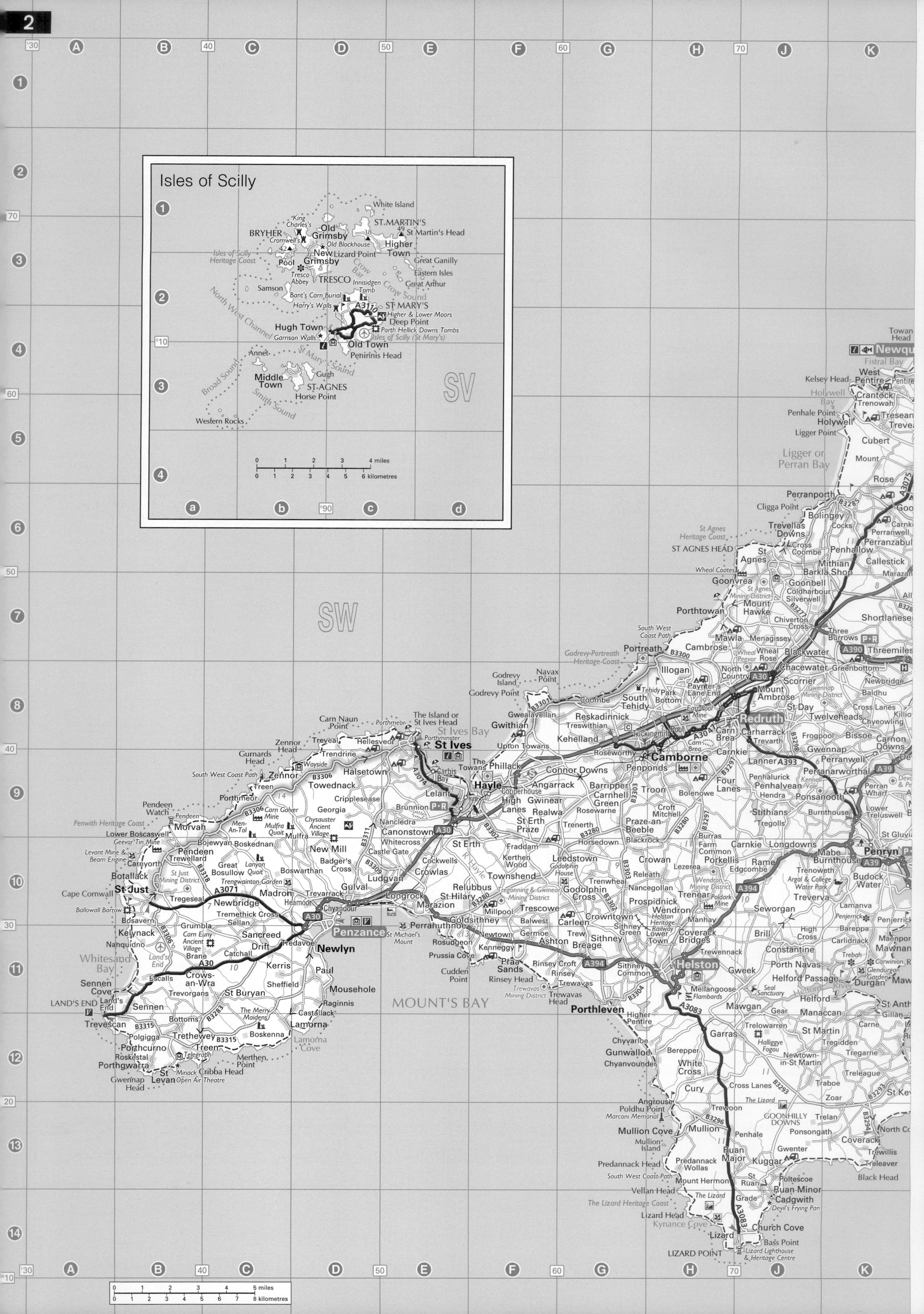
Isles of Scilly
St Ives
Penzance
Newlyn
Hayle
Camborne
Redruth
Helston
Porthleven
St Just
MOUNT'S BAY
St Ives Bay
LIZARD POINT
LAND'S END
SW
SV

Padstow Bay
Pentire Point
Stepper Point
Trevose Head
Constantine Bay
Padstow
Wadebridge
St Columb Major
Bodmin
BODMIN MOOR
Brown Willy
Jamaica Inn
Colliford Lake
Liskeard
Lostwithiel
St Austell
St Austell Bay
Fowey
Gribbin Head
Polperro
Looe
Looe Bay
Mevagissey
Mevagissey Bay
Dodman Point
Veryan Bay
Gerrans Bay
St Mawes
Falmouth
Falmouth Bay
Truro
Newquay
Watergate Bay
Eden Project
Lost Gardens of Heligan
Lanhydrock
Restormel Castle
Camel Valley
Bodmin & Wenford Railway
SX
The Roseland Heritage Coast
Gribbin Head - Polperro Heritage Coast
South West Coast Path
Newquay
Newquay Bay
Fistral Beach
Towan Beach
Great Western Beach
Tolcarne Beach
Newquay Station
Newquay Zoo
Trenance Leisure Park
Trenance Holiday Park
Gannel Road
Trevemper Road
Edgcumbe Ave
Hilgrove Road
St Columb Minor
Redruth, Bodmin

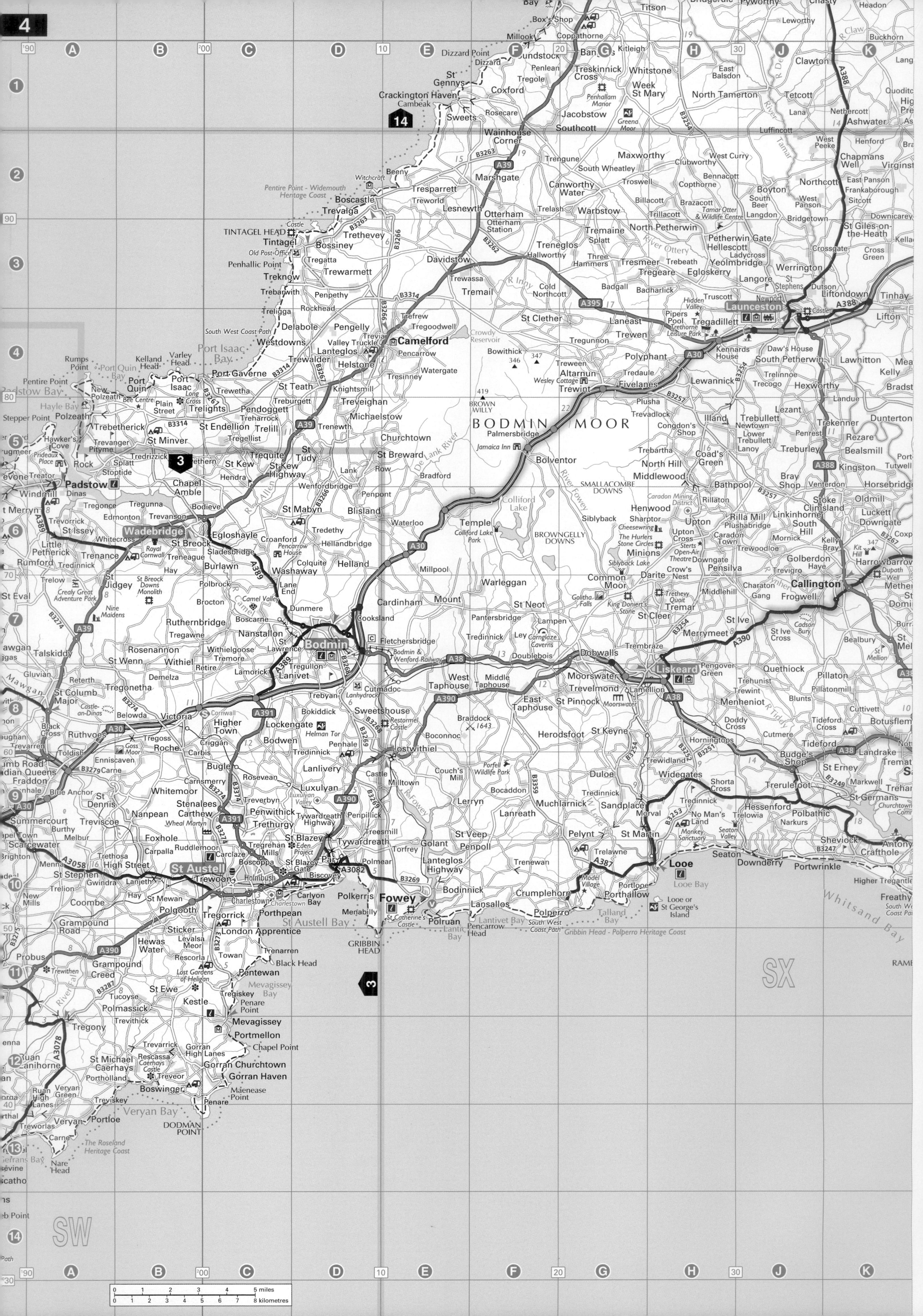

A
B
C
D
E
F
G
H
J
K
1
2
3
4
5
6
7
8
9
10
11
12
13
14
Titson
Pyworthy
Chasty
Headon
Lewworthy
Box's Shop
Millook
Coppathorne
Buckhorn
Dizzard Point
Dizzard
Bangors
Kitleigh
Penlean
Treskinnick Cross
Whitstone
East Balsdon
Clawton
St Gennys
Tregole
Week St Mary
Quoditch
Crackington Haven
Cambeak
Coxford
Penhallam Manor
North Tamerton
Tetcott
Netherscott
Sweets
Rosecare
Jacobstow
Greena Moor
Lana
Ashwater
Wainhouse Corner
Southcott
Luffincott
Henford
Trengune
Maxworthy
West Curry
West Peeke
Chapmans Well
Virginstow
Beeny
Clubworthy
South Wheatley
Bennacott
Witchcraft
Marshgate
Canworthy Water
Troswell
Copthorne
Boyton
Northcott
East Panson
Frankaborough
Pentire Point - Widemouth Heritage Coast
Trespasrett
Boscastle
Treworld
South Beer
West Panson
Sitcott
Trevalga
Lesnewth
Billacott
Brazacott
Otterham
Otterham Station
Trelash
Warbstow
Trillacott
Tamar Otter & Wildlife Centre
Langdon
Bridgetown
Downicarey
Castle
TINTAGEL HEAD
Tintagel
Trethevey
Tremaine
North Petherwin
Petherwin Gate
Hellescott
St Giles-on-the-Heath
Old Post Office
Bossiney
Splatt
River Ottery
Crossgate
Cross Green
Penhallic Point
Tregatta
Davidstow
Treneglos
Hallworthy
Three Hammers
Tresmeer
Trebeath
Ladycross
Yeolmbridge
Werrington
Trewarmett
Treknow
Tregeare
Egloskerry
Langore
St Stephens
Trewassa
Trebarwith
Tremail
Cold Northcott
Badgall
Badharlick
Truscott
Dutson
Penpethy
Liftondown
Tinhay
Rockhead
Trefrew
Hidden Valley
Newport
Launceston
Lifton
Treligga
Delabole
Pengelly
Tregoodwell
Crowdy Reservoir
St Clether
Laneast
Pipers Pool
Tregadillett
Trethorne Leisure Park
South West Coast Path
Westdowns
Valley Truckle
Trevia
Camelford
Trewen
Kennards House
Daw's House
Port Isaac Bay
Trewalder
Lanteglos
Bowithick
Tregunnon
South Petherwin
Lawhitton
Rumps Point
Kelland Head
Varley Head
Helstone
Pencarrow
Treween
Polyphant
Trelinnoe
Port Quin Bay
Port Gaverne
Tresinney
Watergate
Altarnun
Wesley Cottage
Tredaule
Lewannick
Trecogo
Hexworthy
Kelly
Pentire Point
Port Quin
Port Isaac
St Teath
Knightsmill
Trewint
Fivelanes
Padstow Bay
New Polzeath
Long Cross
Trewetha
Treburgett
Treveighan
Plusha
Landue
Hayle Bay
Bee Centre
Plain Street
Trelights
Pendoggett
Michaelstow
Brown Willy
Trevadlock
Lezant
Stepper Point
Polzeath
Treharrock
Congdon's Shop
Illand
Trebullett
Newtown
Trekenner
Dunterton
Trebetherick
St Endellion
Trelill
Trenewth
Bodmin Moor
Palmersbridge
Lower Trebullett
Penrest
Rezare
Hawker's Cove
Trevanger
St Minver
Tregellist
Churchtown
Jamaica Inn
Lanoy
Treburley
Bealsmill
Pityme
Trebartha
Coad's Green
Prideaux Place
Rock
Tredrizzick
St Tudy
St Breward
Bolventor
North Hill
Splatt
Stoptide
St Kew
Trequite
St Kew Highway
Lank
Row
Bradford
Middlewood
Bray Shop
Venterdon
Kingston
Tutwell
Treator
Hendra
Smallacombe Downs
Bathpool
Horsebridge
Padstow
Chapel Amble
Wenfordbridge
Caradon Mining District
Rillaton
Stoke Climsland
Windmill
Dinas
Penpont
Henwood
Oldmill
St Merryn
Tregonce
Tregunna
Bodieve
St Mabyn
Blisland
Colliford Lake
Sharptor
Rilla Mill
Linkinhorne
Luckett
Trevorrick
Edmonton
Trevanson
Waterloo
Temple
Siblyback
Upton
Plushabridge
South Hill
Downgate
St Issey
Wadebridge
Tredethy
Colliford Lake Park
Cheesewring
Whitecross
Egloshayle
Croanford
Browngelly Downs
The Hurlers Stone Circles
Upton Cross
Caradon Town
Mornick
Kelly Bray
Little Petherick
St Breock
Pencarrow House
Hellandbridge
Minions
Sterts Open-Air Theatre
Trewoodloe
Kit Hill
Royal Cornwall
Sladesbridge
Trenance
Treneague
Colquite
Helland
Downgate
Golberdon
Harrowbarrow
Rumford
Tredinnick
Burlawn
Washaway
Millpool
Siblyback Lake
Crow's Nest
Pensilva
Haye
Trevigro
Dupath Well
Hay
Darite
Trelow
St Jidgey
St Breock Downs Monolith
Polbrock
Lane End
Warleggan
Common Moor
Callington
Crealy Great Adventure Park
Trethevy Quoit
Middlehill
Charaton
Metherell
Brocton
Camel Valley
Golitha Falls
Frogwell
St Eval
Cardinham
Mount
St Neot
King Doniert's Stone
Tremar
Gang
Nine Maidens
Dunmere
Cooksland
Pantersbridge
Lampen
St Cleer
Boscarne
St Ive
Cadson Bury
Ruthernbridge
Nanstallon
Tredinnick
Ley
Carnglaze Caverns
Merrymeet
St Ive Cross
Bealbury
St Mellion
Tregawne
Fletchersbridge
Talskiddy
Rosenannon
Withielgoose
St Lawrence
Bodmin
Doublebois
Dobwalls
Trembraze
Bodmin & Wenford Railway
Tremore
Quethiock
St Wenn
Withiel
Retire
Lamorick
Tregullon
Lanivet
Moorswater
Liskeard
Pengover Green
Pillaton
Gluvian
West Taphouse
Middle Taphouse
Trehunist
Pillatonmill
Reterth
Demelza
Trevelmond
Lamellion
Trewint
Tregonetha
Cutmadoc
St Columb Major
Lanhydrock
East Taphouse
St Pinnock
Moorswater
Menheniot
Blunts
Castle-an-Dinas
Belowda
Trebyan
Sweetshouse
Restormel Castle
Braddock
Cuttivett
Victoria
Bokiddick
Doddy Cross
Botusfleming
Black Cross
Ruthvoes
Higher Town
Lockengate
Helman Tor
Boconnoc
Herodsfoot
St Keyne
Tideford Cross
Tregoss
Goss Moor
Criggan
Bodwen
Penhale
Cutmere
Roche
Hornincltops
Tideford
Trevarren
Toldish
Carbis
Tredinnick
Lostwithiel
Budge's Shop
Landrake
Enniscaven
Trewidland
Trematon
Indian Queens
Carne
Bugle
Lanlivery
Couch's Mill
Porfell Wildlife Park
Duloe
Widegates
St Erney
Fraddon
Carnsmerry
Rosevean
Castle
Milltown
Shorta Cross
Markwell
Blue Anchor
St Dennis
Whitemoor
Luxulyan
Luxulyan Valley
Bocaddon
Trerulefoot
St Germans
Stenalees
Treverbyn
Lerryn
Tredinnick
Tredinnick
Hessenford
Summercourt
Nanpean
Carthew
Penwithick
Tywardreath Highway
Penpillick
Lanreath
Muchlarnick
Sandplace
Morval
No Man's Land
Trelowia
Polbathic
Burthy
Treviscoe
Wheal Martyn
Trethurgy
Monkey Sanctuary
Narkurs
Melbur
St Blazey
Treesmill
St Veep
Pelynt
St Martin
Seaton Valley
Scarcewater
Foxhole
Tregrehan Mills
Eden Project
Tywardreath
Golant
Penpoll
Trelawne
Sheviock
Antony
Trethosa
Carpalla
Ruddlemoor
Carclaze
St Blazey Gate
Par
Torfrey
Lanteglos Highway
Seaton
Crafthole
High Street
St Austell
Boscoppa
Polmear
Trenewan
Looe
Downderry
Portwrinkle
St Stephen
Trewoon
Holmbush
Biscovey
Looe Bay
Higher Tregantle
Gwindra
Lanjeth
Tregantle
Trelion
Hay
St Mewan
Charlestown
Carlyon Bay
Polkerris
Fowey
Bodinnick
Crumplehorn
Model Village
Portlooe
Porthallow
Looe or St George's Island
Freathy
Whitsand Bay
South West Coast Path
New Mills
Coombe
Polgooth
Tregorrick
Porthpean
Menabilly
St Catherine's Castle
Polruan
Lansallos
Polperro
Talland Bay
Grampound Road
Sticker
St Austell Bay
London Apprentice
Lantic Bay
Pencarrow Head
Lantivet Bay
Gribbin Head - Polperro Heritage Coast
Hewas Water
Levalsa Meor
Gribbin Head
Probus
Trewithen
Grampound
Rescorla
Trenarren
Black Head
SX
Rame
Creed
Lost Gardens of Heligan
Pentewan
Mevagissey Bay
St Ewe
Tregiskey
Tucoyse
Kestle
Penare Point
Polmassick
Trevithick
Mevagissey
Tregony
Portmellon
Trevarrick
Gorran High Lanes
Chapel Point
Ruan Lanihorne
St Michael Caerhays
Rescassa
Caerhays Castle
Gorran Churchtown
Treveor
Gorran Haven
Portholland
Boswinger
Maenease Point
Ruan High Lanes
Veryan Green
Treviskey
Penare
Veryan Bay
Veryan
Portloe
Dodman Point
Treworlas
Carne
The Roseland Heritage Coast
Gerrans Bay
Nare Head
SW
A39
A30
A38
A389
A390
A391
A3058
A3078
A3082
A387
A388
A395
B3263
B3266
B3314
B3267
B3254
B3257
B3274
B3268
B3269
B3252
B3253
B3251
B3249
B3247
B3359
B3287
B3273
B3279
B3262
14
3
0 1 2 3 4 5 miles
0 1 2 3 4 5 6 7 8 kilometres

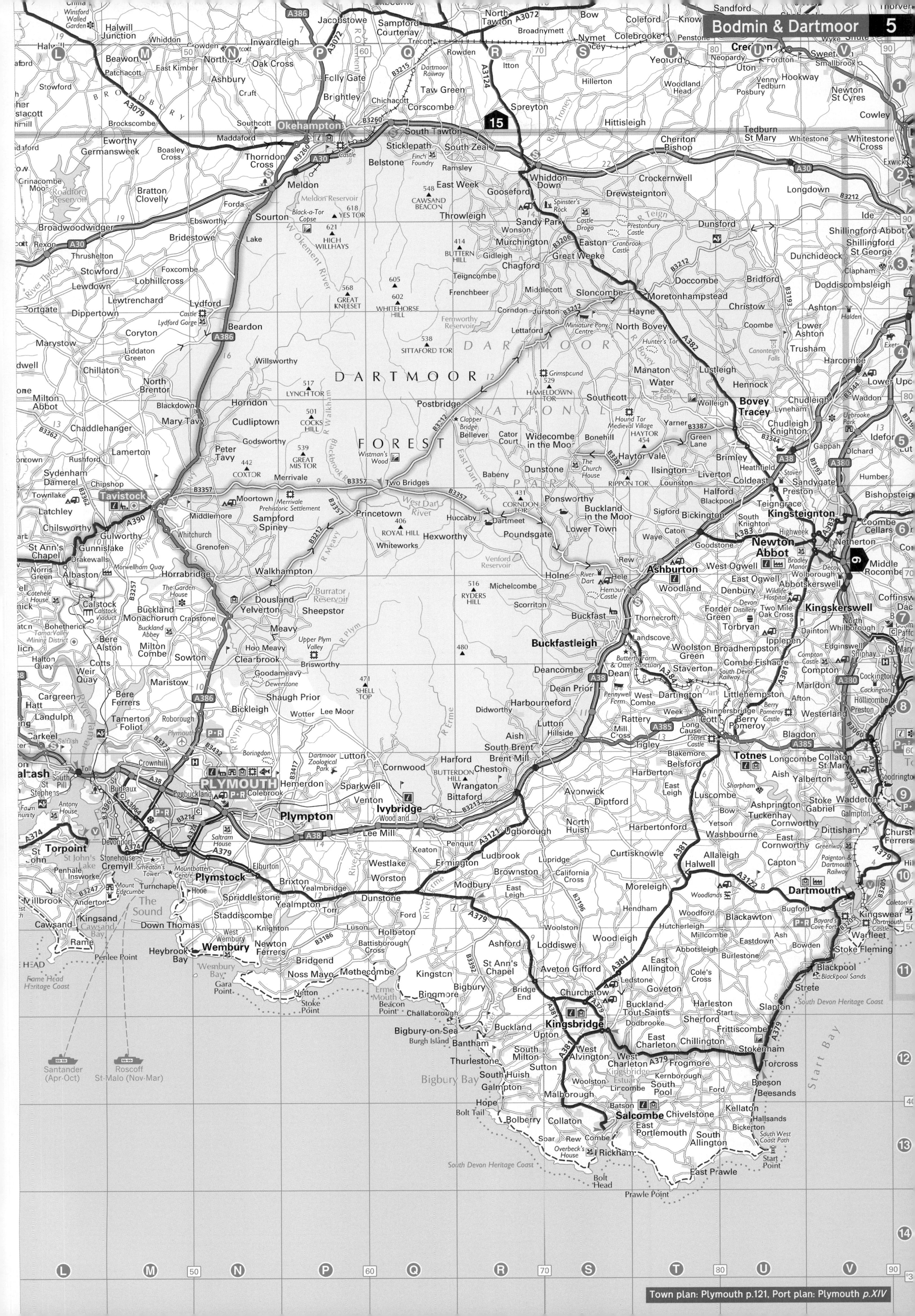

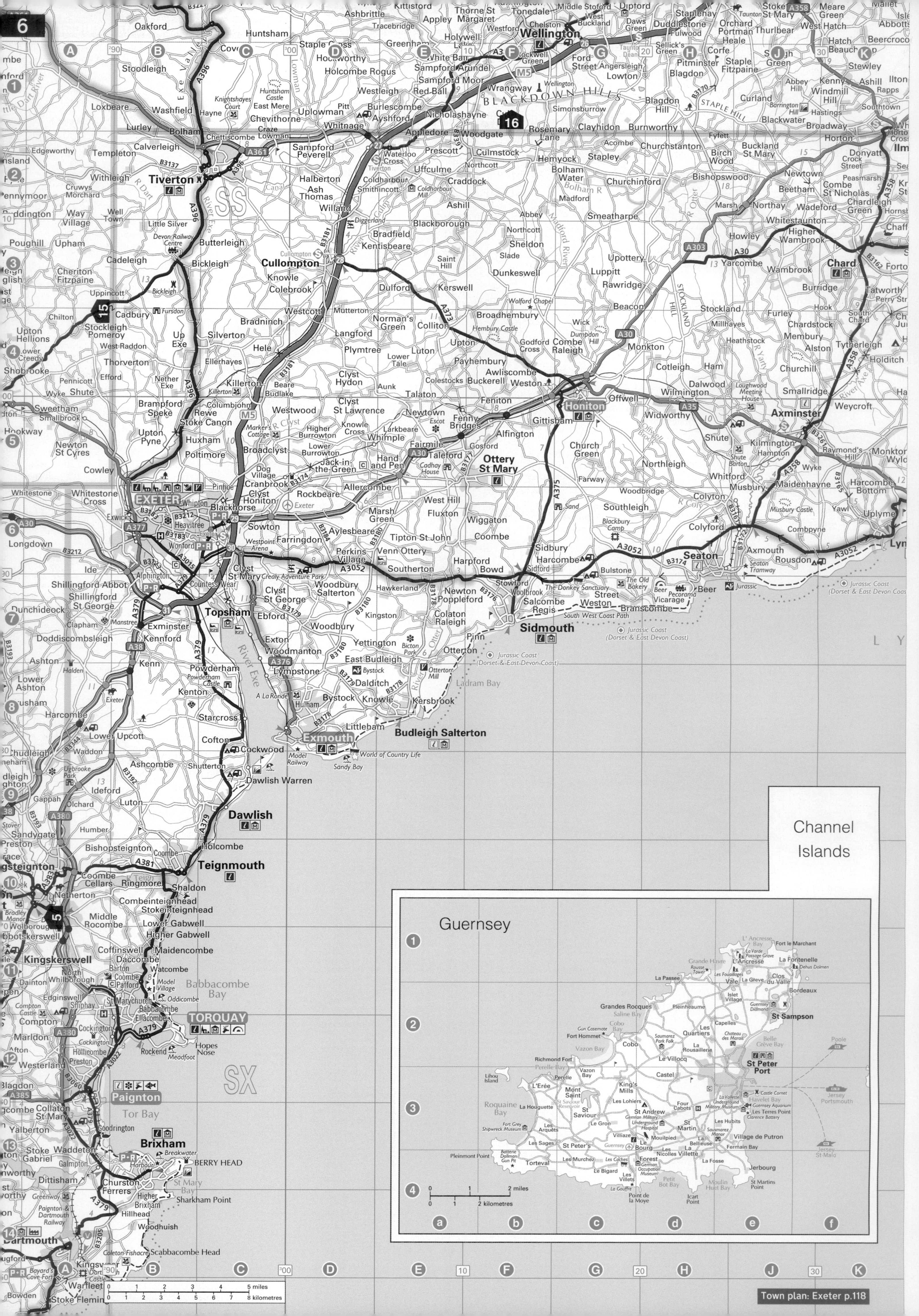
Wellington
BLACKDOWN HILLS
Tiverton
Cullompton
Honiton
Chard
Axminster
Ottery St Mary
EXETER
Topsham
Sidmouth
Seaton
Exmouth
Budleigh Salterton
Dawlish
Teignmouth
TORQUAY
Paignton
Brixham
Dartmouth
Kingskerswell
Babbacombe Bay
Tor Bay
Ladram Bay
Lyme Bay
Dawlish Warren
BERRY HEAD
Sharkham Point
Scabbacombe Head
Hopes Nose
River Exe
South West Coast Path
Jurassic Coast (Dorset & East Devon Coast)
SS
SX
Channel Islands
Guernsey
St Peter Port
St Sampson
Vale
Castel
St Saviour
St Andrew
St Martin
Torteval
Forest
St Peter's
L'Ancresse Bay
Fort le Marchant
La Fontenelle
Grande Havre
Bordeaux
Grandes Rocques
Cobo
Vazon Bay
Perelle
L'Erée
Lihou Island
Rocquaine Bay
Pleinmont Point
Le Gouffre
Icart Point
Jerbourg
Fermain Bay
Village de Putron
Les Hubits
Belle Grève Bay
Poole
Jersey Portsmouth
Jersey St-Malo
2 miles
2 kilometres
5 miles
8 kilometres

Town plan: Exeter p.118

Yeovil
Sherborne
Martock
Crewkerne
Bridport
Dorchester
Weymouth
Fortuneswell
Sturminster Newton
Blandford Forum
Portland
Portland Bill
Portland Harbour
Chesil Beach
West Bay
Lyme Bay
Stalbridge
Beaminster
Maiden Newton
Cerne Abbas
Abbotsbury
Charmouth
Chideock
Puddletown
Wool
Milborne St Andrew
Bere Regis
Lulworth Camp
West Lulworth
Durdle Door
Ringstead Bay
Weymouth Bay
Jurassic Coast (Dorset & East Devon Coast)
South West Coast Path
Cerne Giant
Maiden Castle
Hardy Monument
Eggardon Hill
Golden Cap
Bulbarrow Hill
Sea Life Tower
Nothe Fort
Portland Castle
Castletown
Easton
Weston
Southwell
Wyke Regis
Preston
Osmington
Poxwell
Upwey
Broadwey
Chickerell
Charminster
Poundbury
Winterborne Monkton
Martinstown
Stinsford
Athelhampton
Tolpuddle
Moreton
Crossways
Owermoigne
East Chaldon (Chaldon Herring)
Lulworth Castle
Winfrith Newburgh
Langton Herring
Portesham
Swyre
Burton Bradstock
West Bexington
Litton Cheney
Long Bredy
Kingston Russell
Winterbourne Abbas
Winterbourne Steepleton
Toller Porcorum
Frampton
Sydling St Nicholas
Piddletrenthide
Alton Pancras
Buckland Newton
Minterne Magna
Melbury Osmond
Yetminster
Bradford Abbas
Milborne Port
Henstridge
Hinton St Mary
Okeford Fitzpaine
Shillingstone
Child Okeford
Winterborne Stickland
Winterborne Kingston
Ibberton
Woolland
Mappowder
Hazelbury Bryan
Lydlinch
Bishop's Caundle
Holwell
Longburton
Folke
Thornford
Lillington
Chetnole
Leigh
Stockwood
Halstock
Corscombe
South Perrott
North Perrott
Misterton
Hardington Mandeville
East Coker
West Coker
Montacute
Stoke sub Hamdon
Norton sub Hamdon
South Petherton
Merriott
Broadwindsor
Drimpton
Thorncombe
Marshwood
Pilsdon
Netherbury
Powerstock
Loders
Uploders
Askerswell
Symondsbury
Whitchurch Canonicorum
Morcombelake
Walditch
Bothenhampton
Shipton Gorge
Chilcombe
Puncknowle
Littlebredy
Seatown
Eype
Allington
Lyme Regis
A30
A35
A37
A352
A354
A356
A357
A3030
A3066
A303
A3088
SY
17
8
Jersey
St Helier
St Aubin
St Brelade
Gorey
St Ouen's Bay
St Aubin's Bay
Royal Bay of Grouville
Grosnez Point
Plemont Point
Sorel Point
Ronez Point
Belle Hougue Point
La Colombière
Vicard Point
Bouley Bay
Rozel
La Coupe Point
Nez du Guet
Fliquet Bay
Verclut Point
St Martin
St Catherine's Bay
Archirondel
Fauldouet
Mont Orgueil
Grouville
La Rocque
La Rocque Point
Plat Rocque Point
Le Hocq
Le Bourg
Pontac
Le Croc
St Clement's Bay
Green Island
Samarès Manor
St Clement
Longueville
Fort Regent
Elizabeth Castle
Noirmont Command Bunker
Portelet Bay
Point La Fret
Point La Moye
Corbière
Corbière Point
La Pulente
St Brelade's Bay
Belcroute Bay
Beaumont
Millbrook
Les Quennevais
St Peter
St Lawrence
Trois Bois
Six Rues
St Mary
St Ouen
L'Etacq
Leoville
Millais
La Greve de Lecq
Rouge Nez
Portinfer
Plemont
Ville la Bas
Les Landes
St John
Fremont Point
Hautes Croix
Trinity
Carrefour
Becquet Vincent
Grand Chemins
Five Oaks
La Hougue Bie
Maufant
Queen's Valley Reservoir
Bellozanne Valley
St Saviour
Vallée des Vaux
Swiss Valley
Waterworks Valley
St Peter's Valley
Mourier Valley
Greve de Lecq Valley
Channel Islands Military Museum
Jersey War Tunnels
Durrell Wildlife Park
Hamptonne Country Life Museum
Le Moulin de Quetivel
Le Moulin de Tesson
Jersey Lavender Farm
Guernsey, Poole
Guernsey, Portsmouth
St-Malo
0 1 2 miles
0 1 2 kilometres
0 10 mls
0 20 km
Alderney
St Anne
Guernsey
St Peter Port
Herm
Sark
Jersey
St Helier
France

Longleat Forest
Shear Cross
Sutton Veny
Knook
Upton Lovell
Codford St Peter
Winterbourne Stoke
West Amesbury
Amesbury
Solstice Park
Cholderton
Grateley
Pottle Street
Longbridge Deverill
Tytherington
Corton
Yarnbury Castle
Normanton
Newton Tony
Palestine
Hill Deverill
Brixton Deverill
Boyton
Sherrington
Codford St Mary
Fisherton de la Mere
Berwick St James
Wilsford
Lake
Allington
Boscombe
Over Wallop
BRIMSDOWN HILL
Stockton
Deptford
Steeple Langford
Overstreet
Upper Woodford
Great Durnford
Monkton Deverill
Bapton
Wylye
Stapleford
Netton
Idmiston
Jack's Bush
Kingston Deverill
Norton Ferris
Hanging Langford
Langford Lakes
Little Langford
Middle Woodford
Heale
High Post
Porton
Kilmington Street
Pertwood
Salterton
Winterbourne Dauntsey
Gomeldon
Lopcombe Corner
Great Wishford
Stoford
Lower Woodford
Winterbourne Gunner
KEYSLEY DOWN
Chicklade
South Newton
Little Durnford
Winterbourne Earls
Figsbury Ring
Hurdcott
Middle Winterslow
East Winterslow
Whiteshoot Hill
Old Sarum
Firsdown
Stourton
West Knoyle
Berwick St Leonard
Fonthill Bishop
Farmer Giles Farmstead
Teffont Magna
Dinton Park & Philipps House
Baverstock
Barford St Martin
Ditchampton
Wilton
Stratford sub Castle
Ford
Paul's Dene
Winterslow
The Common
Mere
Wolverton
Burton
Upton
Hindon
Ridge
Chilmark
Dinton
Fonthill Gifford
Teffont Evias
Quidhampton
Laverstock
Pitton
West Winterslow
The Green
East Knoyle
Barrow Street
Holloway
Tisbury
Lower Chicksgrove
Burcombe
Bulbridge
Bemerton
Old Deanery
Salisbury
Farley
West Tytherley
East Tytherley
Huntingford
Milton on Stour
Tuckingmill
Upper Chicksgrove
Newtown
Fovant
Compton Chamberlayne
Netherhampton
Harnham
East Harnham
Sedgehill
East Hatch
West Hatch
Sutton Mandeville
Regimental Badges (chalk hill carvings)
Chiselbury
Stratford Tony
Coombe Bissett
Odstock
Britford
Alderbury
East Grimstead
North End
Semley
Ansty
Swallowcliffe
Whaddon
West Dean
East Dean
Locke
Gillingham
Ham Common
Motcombe
Old Wardour Castle
Donhead St Andrew
Donhead St Mary
Fyfield Bavant
Broad Chalke
Bishopstone
Homington
Nunton
Bodenham
West Grimstead
Dean Hill
Knap Corner
West End
Ebbesborne Wake
Mount Sorrel
Stoke Farthing
Croucheston
Charlton All Saints
Pepperbox Hill
Whiteparish
Enmore Green
Ivy Cross
Shaftesbury
Ludwell
Alvediston
Bowerchalke
Cowesfield Green
East Stour
Stour Row
West Stour
Stour Provost
Guy's Marsh
Cann
Cann Common
Charlton
Berwick St John
Woodminton
Downton
Redlynch
Newton
Sherfield English
Todber
Margaret Marsh
West Melbury
Melbury Abbas
Cobley
Martin Drove End
WHITSBURY DOWN
Wick
Morgan's Vale
Langley Wood
Moorside
Hartgrove
Compton Abbas
Fontmell & Melbury Downs
Ashmore
Tollard Royal
Garston Wood
New Town
Woodyates
Deanland
East Martin
Martin
Whitsbury
BREAMORE DOWN
Breamore
Woodfalls
Lover
Plaitford
East Orchard
Woodbridge
Fontmell Down
Dean End
Martin Down
Tidpit
Upper Street
North Street
North Charford
Hamptworth
Landford
Bedchester
West Orchard
Woodcutts
Sixpenny Handley
Pentridge
Rockbourne
Outwick
Breamore
Hale
Canada
Bramshaw Commons
Fontmell Magna
Larmer Tree
Tollard Farnham
Dean
Farnham
North End
Rockbourne Villa
Lower Burgate
Upper Burgate
Hale Purlieu
Woodgreen
Nomansland
Furzley
Hinton St Mary
Manston
Sutton Waldron
CRANBORNE CHASE
New Town
Minchington
Boveridge
Damerham
South End
Godshill
Bramshaw
Newbridge
Fontmell Parva
Iwerne Minster
Stubhampton
Gussage St Andrew
Monkton Up Wimborne
Bellows Cross
Sandleheath
Fordingbridge
Brook Hill
Hammoon
Gold Hill
Tarrant Gunville
Chettle
Cashmoor
Cranborne
Cranborne Manor
Alderholt
Stuckton
Bickton
Blissford
Frogham
Fritham
Brook
Upper Canterton
Childe Okeford
Hambledon Hill
Shroton
Iwerne Courtney
Chettle House
Gussage St Michael
Wimborne St Giles
Cripplestyle
Hyde
Hungerford
Rufus Stone
Stoney Cross
Okeford Fitzpaine
Little Hanford
Hanford
Tarrant Hinton
Church & Earthworks
Edmondsham
Dorset Heavy Horse Farm Park
Harbridge Green
North Gorley
Shillingstone
HOD HILL
Long Crichel
Gussage All Saints
Knowlton
Romford
South Gorley
Furzey
Minstead
Newtown
Belchalwell
Ash
Stourpaine
Pimperne
Tarrant Launceston
Tarrant Monkton
Moor Crichel
Verwood
Harbridge
Ibsley
Ibsley Common
Mockbeggar
Linwood
Rockford Common
Belchalwell Street
Durweston
Turnworth
Bryanston
Royal Signals
Blandford Camp
Tarrant Rawston
Manswood
New Town
Woodlands
Horton
Whitmore
Ellingham
Rockford
Emery Down
Blashford
North Poulner
Linford
Bank
Blandford Forum
Witchampton
Chalbury
Uppington
Chalbury Common
Crab Orchard
Mannington
Three Legged Cross
Ringwood
Poulner
Shobley
Picket Post
Bulbarrow Hill
Winterborne Houghton
Blandford St Mary
Littleton
Langton Long Blandford
Tarrant Rushton
Hinton Martell
Gaunt's Common
Holt Heath
Moors Valley
Ashley Heath
Hightown
Burley Street
NATIONAL
Rhinefield Ornamental Drive
Winterborne Stickland
Charlton on the Hill
Charlton Marshall
Tarrant Keyneston
Stanbridge
Lower Mannington
Ashley
Liberty's Owl, Raptor & Reptile Centre
Crow
Burley Lawn
Winterborne Clenston
Thornicombe
Tarrant Crawford
Badbury Rings
Honeybrook
Pig Oak
Holt
Holt Heath
St Leonards
St Ives
Moortown
Kingston Great Common
MARKWAY HILL
Brockenhurst
Higher Whatcombe
Spetisbury
Kingston Lacy
Clapgate
Furzehill
Broom Hill
West Moors
Avon Heath
Kingston
North Kingston
Burley
Milton Abbas
Lower Whatcombe
Shapwick
Abbott Street
Hillbutts
Merry Field Hill
Pilford
Colehill
Canford Bottom
Ferndown
FOXBURY HILL
Bisterne
Sandford
Winterborne Whitechurch
Sturminster Marshall
Pamphill
Stapehill
Trickett's Cross
North Ripley
Thorney Hill
Sway
Almer
Wimborne Minster
Leigh Park
Knoll
Hampreston
Lower Street
Oakley
Ripley
Wootton
Battramsley Cross
Winterborne Kingston
Winterborne Tomson
Winterborne Zelston
Combe Almer
Sleight
Ashington
Merley
Canford Magna
Longham
Dudsbury
East Parley
Bournemouth Aviation
Hurn
Avon
Bransgore
North Bockhampton
Neacroft
Bashley
Tiptoe
Milborne St Andrew
Anderson
West Morden
Morden
Corfe Mullen
Bearwood
Knighton
Kinson
West Parley
Parley Green
Ensbury
Red Hill
Adventure Wonderland
Sopley
Mid Bockhampton
Godwinscroft
Beckley
Sammy Miller Motorcycle
Upper Pennington
Bere Regis
Newport
Broadstone
West Howe
Cudnell
East Howe
Moordown
Throop
Winkton
South Bockhampton
Burton
Hinton Admiral
Hinton
New Milton
Hordle
Tolpuddle
Bloxworth
East Morden
Lytchett Matravers
Upton Heath
Canford Heath
Wallisdown
Talbot Village
Winton
Walkford
Ashley
Pennington
Everton
Affpuddle
Turners Puddle
East Bloxworth
Post Green
Creekmoor
Newtown
Highcliffe
Highcliffe Castle
Barton-on-Sea
Downton
Briantspuddle
Throop
Sherford
Slepe
Upton
Branksome
Pokesdown
Tuckton
Iford
Christchurch
Mudeford
Lytchett Minster
Castle
Wick
Morden Bog
Organford
Hamworthy
Lower Hamworthy
Parkstone
Westbourne
Branksome Park
Boscombe
Southbourne
Christchurch Bay
Milford on Sea
Clouds Hill
Holton Heath
Lilliput
BOURNEMOUTH
Hengistbury Head
HENGISTBURY HEAD
Moreton
Bovington Camp
Tank
Sandford
POOLE
Canford Cliffs
Poole Harbour
Winfrith
Bovington
Monkey World
Northport
Arne
Brownsea Island
East Burton
Stokeford
Binnegar
Worgret
Wareham
Sandbanks
POOLE BAY
Giddy Green
Bindon
East Stoke
Stoborough
Ridge
Toll
Alum Bay
Wool
West Holme
East Holme
Stoborough Green
Stoborough Heath
Purbeck Heritage Coast
THE NEEDLES
East Knighton
Winfrith Newburgh
Coombe Keynes
Hartland Moor
Studland Beach
Studland Bay
ISLE OF PURBECK
The Blue Pool
Creech
East Lulworth
East Creech
Corfe Castle
Studland
THE FORELAND
East Chaldon (Chaldon Herring)
HALDON DOWN
Lulworth Castle
Lulworth Camp
Purbeck Hills
Swanage Railway
Ballard Point
Cherbourg
West Lulworth
Lulworth Cove
BINDON HILL
Durdle Door
Tyneham
Steeple
Church Knowle
Harman's Cross
Ulwell
Swanage Bay
Worbarrow Bay
Purbeck Marine
Kimmeridge
Kingston
Herston
Swanage
Kimmeridge Bay
South West Coast Path
Langton Matravers
Acton
Durlston
DURLSTON HEAD
Guernsey
Jersey
St-Malo
Jurassic Coast (Dorset & East Devon Coast)
Chapman's Pool
Worth Matravers
Anvil Point
ST ALDHELM'S OR ST ALBAN'S HEAD
0 1 2 3 4 5 miles
0 1 2 3 4 5 6 7 8 kilometres

Town plan: Salisbury p.121, Port plan: Poole p.XIV

Winchester
Kings Worthy
New Alresford
Four Marks
Alton
Whitehill & Bordon
Liss
Petersfield
Romsey
North Baddesley
Chandler's Ford
EASTLEIGH
Bishop's Waltham
Hedge End
West End
Botley
Wickham
Totton
SOUTHAMPTON
Lyndhurst
Hythe
Fawley
Netley
Hamble-le-Rice
FAREHAM
Portchester
WATERLOOVILLE
Horndean
Denmead
HAVANT
Emsworth
Southbourne
GOSPORT
Southsea
PORTSMOUTH
Lee-on-the-Solent
Stubbington
Hayling Island
South Hayling
Beaulieu
Lymington
Cowes
East Cowes
Ryde
Newport
Yarmouth
Freshwater
Brading
Bembridge
Sandown
Shanklin
Ventnor
ISLE OF WIGHT
THE SOLENT
SPITHEAD
Cherbourg (May-Aug)
Guernsey
Jersey
St-Malo
Caen (Ouistreham)
Cherbourg (May-Aug)
Le Havre (Jan-Oct)
Bilbao (Jan-Oct)
Santander (Jan-Oct)

Aldershot
Odiham
Farnham
Haslemere
Godalming
Milford
GUILDFORD
Shalford
Dorking
Cranleigh
Alton
Whitehill & Bordon
Liphook
Liss
Petersfield
Midhurst
Petworth
Pulborough
Billingshurst
Storrington
Steyning
Arundel
Chichester
HAVANT
Emsworth
Southbourne
Littlehampton
Rustington
Angmering
Lancing
Sompting
WORTHING
Middleton-on-Sea
BOGNOR REGIS
Selsey
SELSEY BILL
South Hayling
Hayling Bay
Chichester Harbour
Bracklesham Bay
Pagham Harbour
Haslemere
Hindhead
Grayshott
Headley
Kingsley
Selborne
Chawton
Wisborough Green
Kirdford
Loxwood
Rudgwick
Slinfold
Warnham
Alfold
Dunsfold
Chiddingfold
Northchapel
Plaistow
Fernhurst
Lurgashall
Graffham
Singleton
West Dean
Charlton
East Dean
Upwaltham
Slindon
Fontwell
Barnham
Yapton
Felpham
Westergate
Tangmere
Boxgrove
Lavant
Bosham
Fishbourne
West Wittering
East Wittering
Bracklesham
Earnley
Birdham
Sidlesham
Pagham
Church Norton
Rowland's Castle
Compton
Harting
Elsted
Trotton
Rogate
Stedham
Easebourne
Cocking
Heyshott
Duncton
Sutton
Bignor
Amberley
Washington
Findon
Ferring
East Preston
Climping
Ford
Lyminster
SOUTH DOWNS NATIONAL PARK
SU
SZ
A3
A31
A272
A283
A286
A285
A29
A24
A27
A259
A281
A325
A287
A32
0 1 2 3 4 5 miles
0 1 2 3 4 5 6 7 8 kilometres

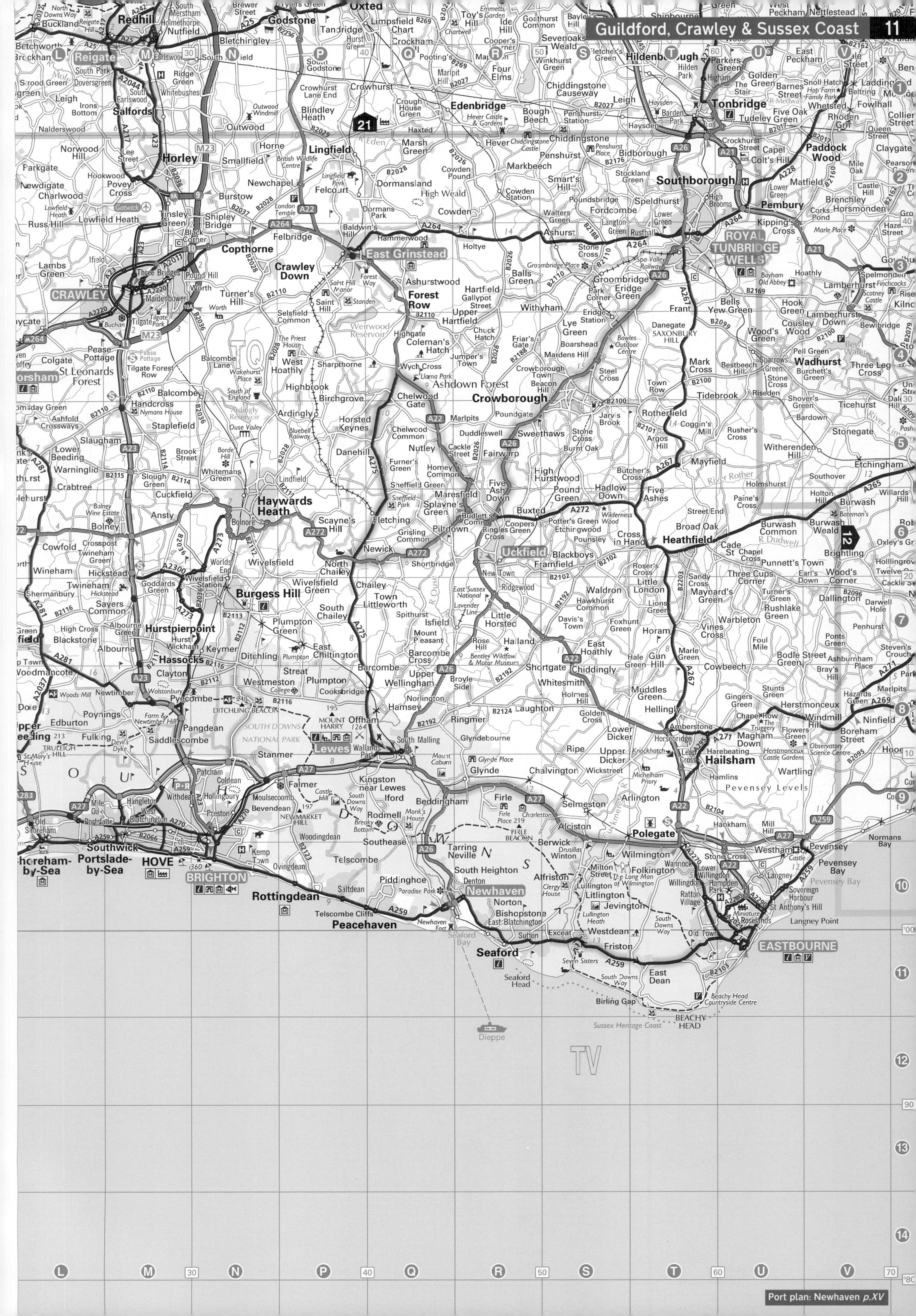
Redhill
Reigate
Godstone
Oxted
Salfords
Horley
Lingfield
Edenbridge
Tonbridge
Hildenborough
Southborough
Paddock Wood
Pembury
Gatwick
Crawley
Copthorne
East Grinstead
Crawley Down
Forest Row
Royal Tunbridge Wells
Groombridge
Frant
Wadhurst
Crowborough
Ashdown Forest
Haywards Heath
Burgess Hill
Hurstpierpoint
Hassocks
Uckfield
Heathfield
Mayfield
Hailsham
Lewes
Polegate
Brighton
Hove
Shoreham-by-Sea
Portslade-by-Sea
Southwick
Rottingdean
Peacehaven
Newhaven
Seaford
Eastbourne
Pevensey
Pevensey Bay
Beachy Head
Seaford Bay
Dieppe
South Downs National Park
Sussex Heritage Coast
TQ
TV

Port plan: Newhaven p.XV

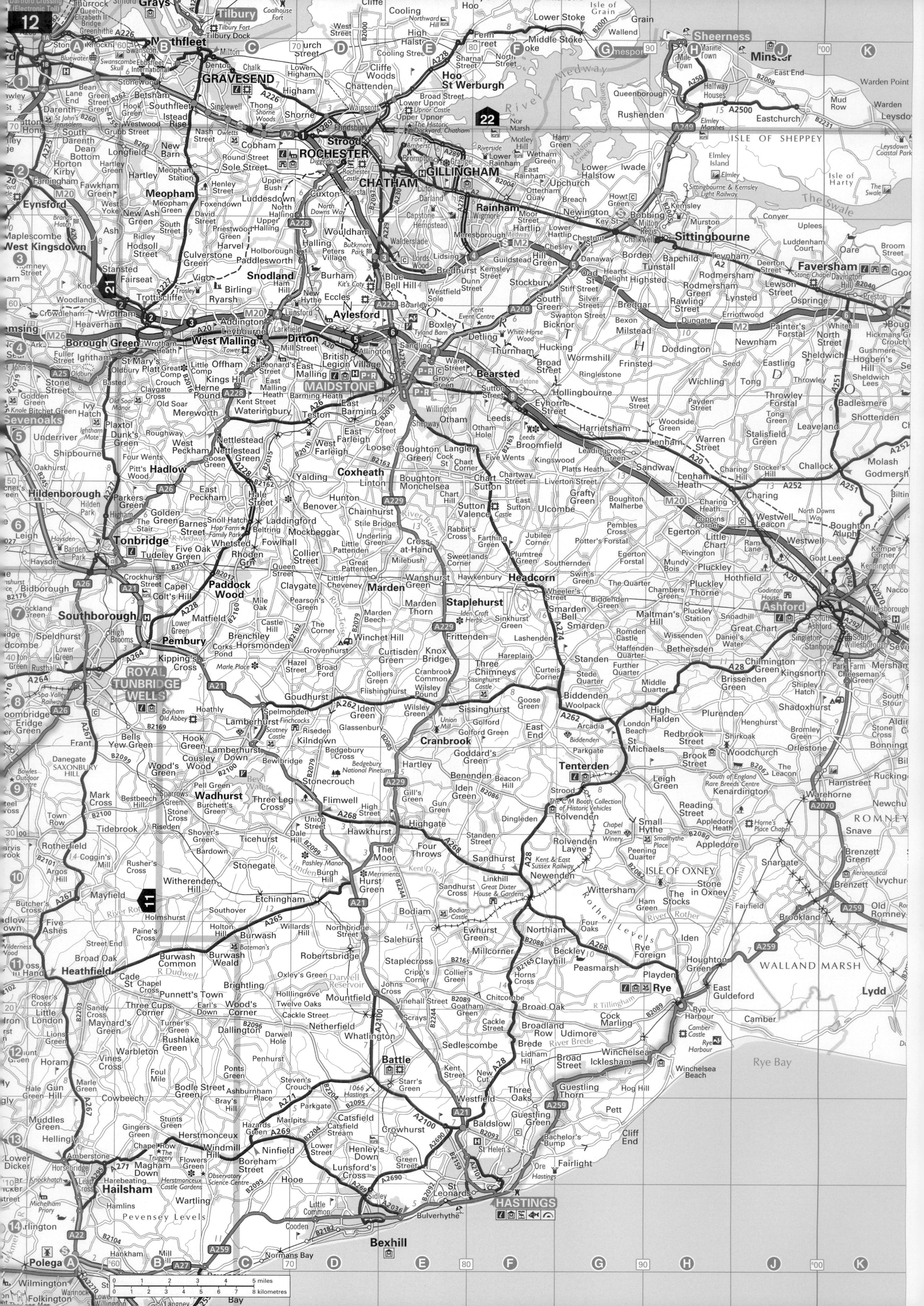
Grays
Tilbury
Northfleet
GRAVESEND
Cliffe
Cooling
Hoo
Isle of Grain
Grain
Lower Stoke
Middle Stoke
Sheerness
Minster
East End
Warden Point
Queenborough
Halfway Houses
Mud Row
Warden
Leysdown
Rushenden
Eastchurch
ISLE OF SHEPPEY
River Medway
Hoo St Werburgh
Higham
Shorne
Strood
ROCHESTER
CHATHAM
GILLINGHAM
Rainham
Cobham
Meopham
Eynsford
Swanley
Dartford
Farningham
West Kingsdown
Fawkham Green
Hartley
New Ash Green
Ash
Snodland
Aylesford
Ditton
West Malling
Borough Green
Wrotham
Kemsing
Otford
Sevenoaks
Ightham
Offham
Kings Hill
MAIDSTONE
Bearsted
Boxley
Detling
Hollingbourne
Leeds
Harrietsham
Lenham
Charing
Sittingbourne
Milton Regis
Bobbing
Iwade
Newington
Upchurch
Teynham
Faversham
Oare
The Swale
Doddington
Boughton Aluph
Ashford
Kingsnorth
Tonbridge
Hildenborough
Hadlow
Paddock Wood
Southborough
ROYAL TUNBRIDGE WELLS
Pembury
Matfield
Brenchley
Horsmonden
Lamberhurst
Goudhurst
Marden
Staplehurst
Headcorn
Coxheath
Yalding
Linton
Sutton Valence
Biddenden
Tenterden
Cranbrook
Hawkhurst
Sissinghurst
Benenden
Rolvenden
Wadhurst
Ticehurst
Frant
Mayfield
Heathfield
Burwash
Etchingham
Robertsbridge
Bodiam
Northiam
Rye
Winchelsea
Camber
Rye Bay
Lydd
Brookland
Brenzett
Appledore
Hamstreet
Romney
Ivychurch
WALLAND MARSH
Battle
Hailsham
Herstmonceux
Ninfield
Bexhill
HASTINGS
St Leonards
Fairlight
Polegate
Pevensey Levels
Wilmington
Folkington
Westfield
Sedlescombe
Isle of Oxney
Wittersham
Peasmarsh
Beckley
Icklesham
Cliff End
Guestling Thorn
Dallington
Netherfield
Crowhurst
Catsfield
Whatlington
Mountfield
M2
M20
M25
M26
A2
A20
A21
A26
A28
A229
A249
A259
A262
A268
A274
A2070
0 1 2 3 4 5 miles
0 1 2 3 4 5 6 7 8 kilometres

Folkestone Terminal
Departures to France follow
Arrivals from France follow
Calais / Coquelles Terminal
Departures to England follow
Arrivals from England follow
STRAIT OF DOVER

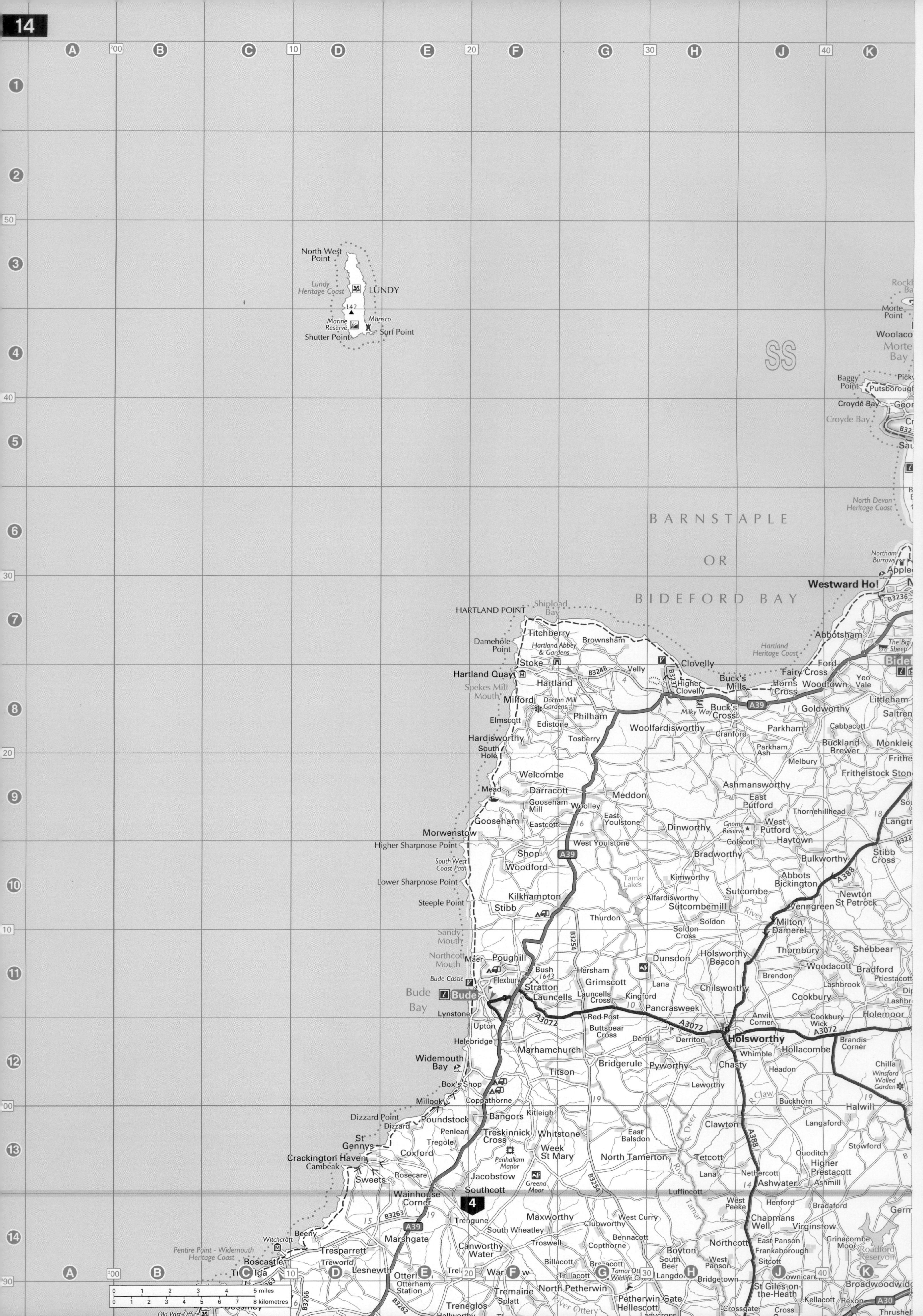

A B C D E F G H J K

1
2
50
3

North West
Point

Lundy
Heritage Coast   LUNDY

142

Marine   Marisco
Reserve
Shutter Point   Surf Point

4

SS

Rockl
Ba

Morte
Point

Woolaco
Morte
Bay

Baggy   Picky
Point   Putsborough
Croyde Bay   Geor
Croyde Bay   Cr

40

5

Sau

North Devon
Heritage Coast

6

B A R N S T A P L E

Northam
Burrows   Apple

O R

30

Westward Ho!   N

B I D E F O R D   B A Y

7

HARTLAND POINT   Shipload
Bay
Damehole   Titchberry   Brownsham   Hartland
Point   Hartland Abbey   Heritage Coast   Abbotsham
& Gardens   Ford
Stoke   Velly   Clovelly   Fairy Cross   Bide
Hartland Quay   B3248   Higher   Buck's   Yeo
Clovelly   Mills   Horns   Woodtown   Vale
Spekes Mill   Hartland   4   Buck's   Cross   Littleham
Mouth   Cross   Goldworthy   Saltren
Milford   Docton Mill
Gardens   Philham   Woolfardisworthy   Cranford   Parkham   Cabbacott   Monkle
Elmscott   Edistone   Tosberry   Parkham   Buckland   Frith
Hardisworthy   Ash   Brewer
South   Melbury   Frithelstock Ston
Hole   Welcombe   Ashmansworthy
Darracott   Meddon   East

8

20

9

Mead   Gooseham   Woolley   Putford   Thornehillhead   So
Mill   East   West   Langt
Gooseham   Eastcott   16   Youlstone   Dinworthy   Gnome   Putford   B32
Morwenstow   West Youlstone   Reserve   Colscott   Haytown
Higher Sharpnose Point   Shop   A39   Bradworthy   Stibb
South West   Woodford   Bulkworthy   Cross
Coast Path   Kimworthy   Abbots
Lower Sharpnose Point   Alfardisworthy   Sutcombe   Bickington   Newton
Steeple Point   Kilkhampton   Sutcombemill   Venngreen   St Petrock
Stibb   Thurdon   Soldon   Milton
10   Tamar   Soldon   Damerel
Lakes   Holsworthy   Thornbury   Shebbear
Sandy   Cross   Beacon   Woodacott
Mouth   Maer   Poughill   Dunsdon   Brendon   Bradford
Northcott   Bush   Hersham   Lana   Lashbrook   Priestacott
Mouth   1643   Grimscott   Chilsworthy   Cookbury   Di
Bude Castle   Flexbury   Stratton   Launcells   Kingford   Cookbury   Lashb
Bude   Launcells   Cross   Pancrasweek   Anvil   Wick   Holemoor
Bude   Lynstone   Red Post   10   Corner
Bay   Upton   Cookbury   Brandis
Buttsbear   Derril   Derriton   Holsworthy   Corner
Helebridge   A3072   Cross   A3072
Marhamchurch   Bridgerule   Pyworthy   Chasty   Hollacombe
Widemouth   Titson   Leworthy   Headon   Chilla
Bay   Winsford
Box's Shop   Whimble   Walled
Millook   Coppathorne   Buckhorn   Garden
Dizzard Point   Bangors   Kitleigh   Halwill
Dizzard   Poundstock   Clawton   Langaford
St   Penlean   Treskinnick   Whitstone   East   A388   Quoditch   Stowford
Gennys   Tregole   Cross   Balsdon   Tetcott   Higher
Crackington Haven   Coxford   Week   North Tamerton   Lana   Prestacott   Ashmill
Cambeak   Penhallam   St Mary   Nethercott   Cross
Sweets   Rosecare   Manor   Greena   Boyton   West   Henford   Bradford
Jacobstow   Moor   Peeke   Chapmans   Virginstow
Wainhouse   Southcott   Luffincott   Well
Corner   Maxworthy   West Curry   East Panson   Grinacombe
Trengune   South Wheatley   Clubworthy   Northcott   Moor   Roadford
Beeny   Canworthy   Troswell   Copthorne   Frankaborough   Reservoir
Witchcraft   Marshgate   Water   Billacott   Bra   West   Sitcott   Cross
Boscastle   Treworld   Trel   War   w   Tremaine   South   Langdon   Bridgetown   St Giles-on-   Cross
Ti   lga   Otterl   North Petherwin   Beer   Downicare   the-Heath
Otterham   Petherwin   Kellacott   Broadwoodwid
Station   Tremaine   Gate   Thrushel

10   11   12   13   14

Pentire Point - Widemouth
Heritage Coast
Old Post Office

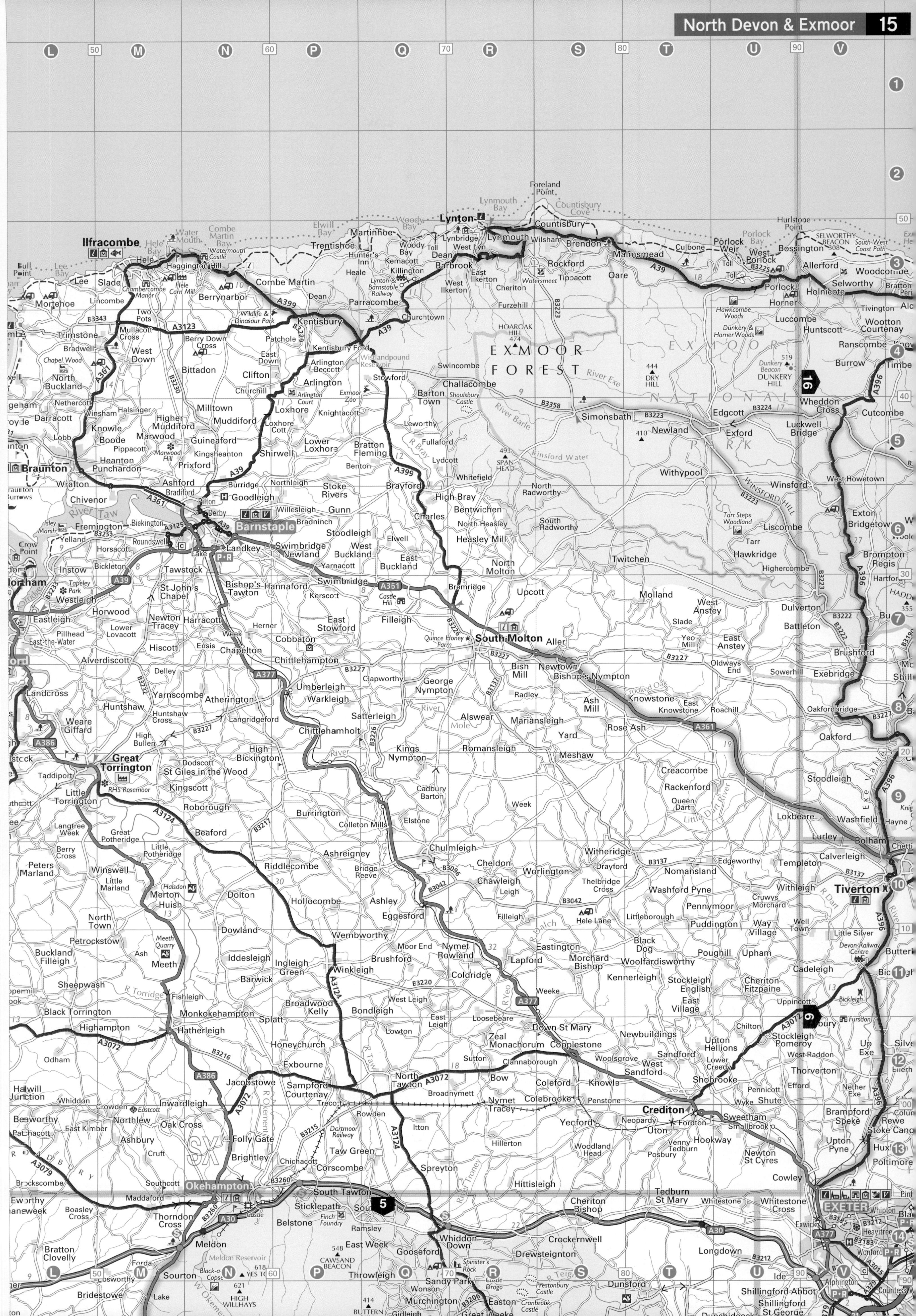
Foreland Point
Lynmouth Bay
Countisbury Cove
Lynton
Lynmouth
Countisbury
Hurlstone Point
Porlock Bay
Porlock Weir
Porlock
West Porlock
Bossington
Selworthy Beacon
South West Coast Path
Ilfracombe
Hele Bay
Hele
Water Mouth
Combe Martin Bay
Watermouth Castle
Haggington Hill
Combe Martin
Elwill Bay
Woody Bay
Martinhoe
Trentishoe
Hunter's Inn
Heale
Kemacott
Killington
Lynton & Barnstaple Railway
Lynbridge
West Lyn
Barbrook
Dean
East Ilkerton
West Ilkerton
Cheriton
Wilsham
Brendon
Rockford
Watersmeet
Tippacott
Malmsmead
Oare
Culbone
Allerford
Woodcombe
Selworthy
Holnicote
Horner
Luccombe
Tivington
Wootton Courtenay
Huntscott
Hawkcombe Woods
Dunkery & Horner Woods
Bull Point
Lee Bay
Lee
Slade
Mortehoe
Lincombe
Chambercombe Manor
Hele Corn Mill
Berrynarbor
Wildlife & Dinosaur Park
Kentisbury
Parracombe
Churchtown
Furzehill
Hoaroak Hill 474
Exmoor Forest
Exmoor National Park
Two Pots
Mullacott Cross
Trimstone
Bradwell
Chapel Wood
West Down
Berry Down Cross
Patchole
Kentisbury Ford
Woolacombe
North Buckland
East Down
Bittadon
Arlington Beccott
Arlington
Arlington Court
Exmoor Zoo
Wistlandpound Reservoir
Stowford
Swincombe
Challacombe
Shoulsbury Castle
Barton Town
Dry Hill 444
Dunkery Beacon 519
Dunkery Hill
Ranscombe
Burrow
Timberscombe
Clifton
Churchill
Loxhore
Loxhore Cott
Knightacott
Milltown
Muddiford
Higher Muddiford
Halsinger
Winsham
Nethercott
Darracott
Knowle
Boode
Marwood
Marwood Hill
Guineaford
Kingsheanton
Pippacott
Lobb
Heanton Punchardon
Prixford
Shirwell
Lower Loxhore
Bratton Fleming
Benton
Leworthy
Fullaford
Lydcott
River Barle
Simonsbath
Newland
Exford
Edgcott
Wheddon Cross
Cutcombe
Luckwell Bridge
Kinsford Water
Span Head 493
Whitefield
North Radworthy
Withypool
Winsford
Winsford Hill
West Howetown
Braunton
Wrafton
Braunton Burrows
Chivenor
Ashford
Bradiford
Pilton
Burridge
Northleigh
Goodleigh
Stoke Rivers
Brayford
High Bray
Bentwichen
North Heasley
Heasley Mill
South Radworthy
Tarr Steps Woodland
Tarr
Liscombe
Exton
Bridgetown
River Taw
Fremington
Bickington
Isley Marsh
Yelland
Crow Point
Horsacott
Roundswell
Barnstaple
Derby
Willesleigh
Gunn
Bradninch
Stoodleigh
West Buckland
Elwell
Charles
Landkey
Swimbridge Newland
Lake
East Buckland
North Molton
Twitchen
Hawkridge
Highercombe
Brompton Regis
Instow
Bickleton
Tawstock
Yarnacott
Swimbridge
Bremridge
Northam
Tapeley Park
Westleigh
St John's Chapel
Bishop's Tawton
Hannaford
Kerscott
Castle Hill
Filleigh
Upcott
Molland
West Anstey
Dulverton
Battleton
Hartford
Eastleigh
Horwood
Lower Lovacott
Newton Tracey
Harracott
Herner
Cobbaton
East Stowford
Slade
Yeo Mill
East Anstey
Pillhead
East-the-Water
Hiscott
Ensis
Week
Chapelton
Quince Honey Farm
South Molton
Aller
Bish Mill
Newtown
Bishop's Nympton
Oldways End
Brushford
Exebridge
Sowerhill
Alverdiscott
Delley
Chittlehampton
Clapworthy
George Nympton
Crooked Oak
Knowstone
East Knowstone
Roachill
Oakfordbridge
Landcross
Yarnscombe
Atherington
Umberleigh
Warkleigh
Radley
Ash Mill
Huntshaw
Huntshaw Cross
Langridgeford
Satterleigh
River Mole
Alswear
Mariansleigh
Rose Ash
Weare Giffard
High Bullen
Chittlehamholt
Yard
Oakford
Great Torrington
Dodscott
St Giles in the Wood
High Bickington
Kings Nympton
Romansleigh
Meshaw
Taddiport
RHS Rosemoor
Little Torrington
Kingscott
Cadbury Barton
Creacombe
Rackenford
Stoodleigh
Queen Dart
Little Dart River
Exe Valley
Roborough
Burrington
Week
Loxbeare
Washfield
Langtree Week
Great Potheridge
Beaford
Colleton Mills
Elstone
Lurley
Bolham
Little Potheridge
Berry Cross
Chulmleigh
Ashreigney
Witheridge
Drayford
Edgeworthy
Templeton
Calverleigh
Peters Marland
Winswell
Little Marland
Riddlecombe
Bridge Reeve
Cheldon
Worlington
Nomansland
Chawleigh
Leigh
Thelbridge Cross
Washford Pyne
Withleigh
Tiverton
Halsdon
Merton
Huish
Dolton
Hollocombe
Ashley
Eggesford
Filleigh
Hele Lane
Littleborough
Pennymoor
Cruwys Morchard
Puddington
Way Village
Well Town
North Town
Little Silver
Dowland
Wembworthy
Petrockstow
Meeth Quarry
Moor End
Nymet Rowland
Eastington
Black Dog
Poughill
Upham
Devon Railway Centre
Buckland Filleigh
Ash
Meeth
Iddesleigh
Ingleigh Green
Brushford
Lapford
Morchard Bishop
Woolfardisworthy
Cadeleigh
Bickleigh
Sheepwash
Barwick
Winkleigh
Coldridge
Kennerleigh
Stockleigh English
Cheriton Fitzpaine
River Torridge
Fishleigh
Broadwood Kelly
West Leigh
Bondleigh
Weeke
East Village
Uppincott
Black Torrington
Monkokehampton
Splatt
River Yeo
Fursdon
Highampton
Hatherleigh
Lowton
East Leigh
Loosebeare
Down St Mary
Chilton
Stockleigh Pomeroy
Up Exe
Odham
Honeychurch
Zeal Monachorum
Copplestone
Newbuildings
Upton Hellions
West Raddon
Exbourne
Sutton
Clannaborough
Woolsgrove
Sandford
West Sandford
Lower Creedy
Thorverton
Halwill Junction
Jacobstowe
Sampford Courtenay
North Tawton
Broadnymett
Bow
Coleford
Knowle
Shobrooke
Pennicott
Efford
Nether Exe
Whiddon
Crowden
Eastcott
Inwardleigh
River Okement
Trecott
Nymet Tracey
Colebrooke
Penstone
Crediton
Wyke
Shute
Beaworthy
Northlew
Oak Cross
Rowden
Dartmoor Railway
Itton
Yeoford
Neopardy
Uton
Fordton
Sweetham
Smallbrook
Brampford Speke
Rewe
Patchacott
East Kimber
Ashbury
Folly Gate
Hillerton
Woodland Head
Venny Tedburn
Hookway
Posbury
Upton Pyne
Stoke Canon
Cruft
Brightley
Taw Green
Newton St Cyres
Huxham
Poltimore
Granite Way
Brockscombe
Southcott
Okehampton
Chichacott
Corscombe
Spreyton
River Troney
Hittisleigh
Cowley
Tedburn St Mary
Whitestone
Whitestone Cross
Exeter
Whipton
Heavitree
Wonford
Exwick
Ewworthy
Maddaford
South Tawton
Sticklepath
South Zeal
Cheriton Bishop
Boasley Cross
Thorndon Cross
Okehampton Castle
Finch Foundry
Belstone
Ramsley
Whiddon Down
Crockernwell
Meldon
Meldon Reservoir
Bratton Clovelly
East Week
Cawsand Beacon 548
Gooseford
Drewsteignton
Longdown
Forda
Sourton
Black-a-Tor Copse
Yes Tor 618
High Willhays 621
Throwleigh
Spinster's Rock
Castle Drogo
Prestonbury Castle
River Teign
Dunsford
Ide
Alphington
Countess Wear
Shillingford Abbot
Shillingford St George
Germansweek
Lewdown
Bridestowe
Lake
West Okement
Buttern 414
Wonson
Sandy Park
Murchington
Gidleigh
Easton
Cranbrook Castle
Great Weeke
Roadford
Broadbury
SX

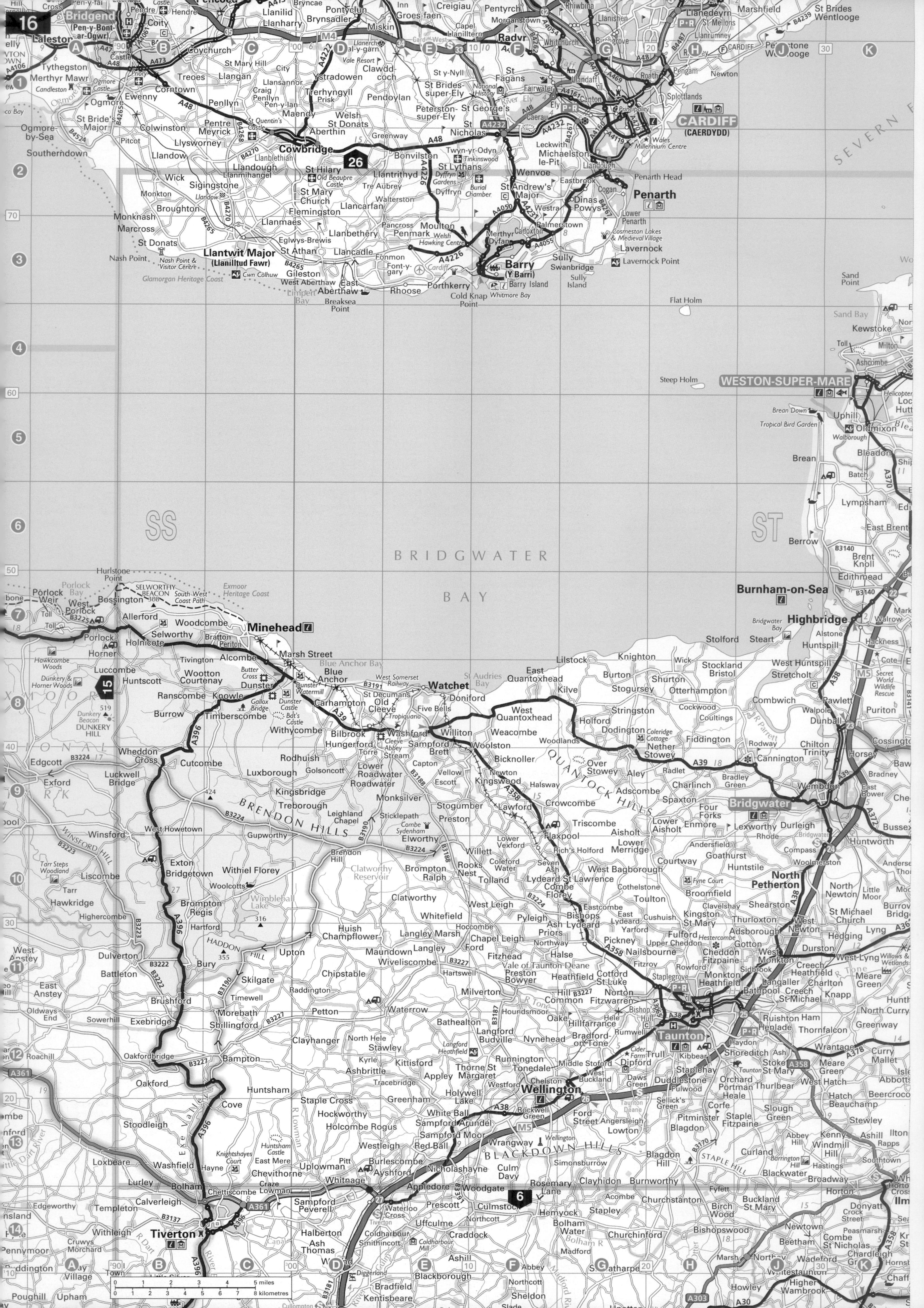

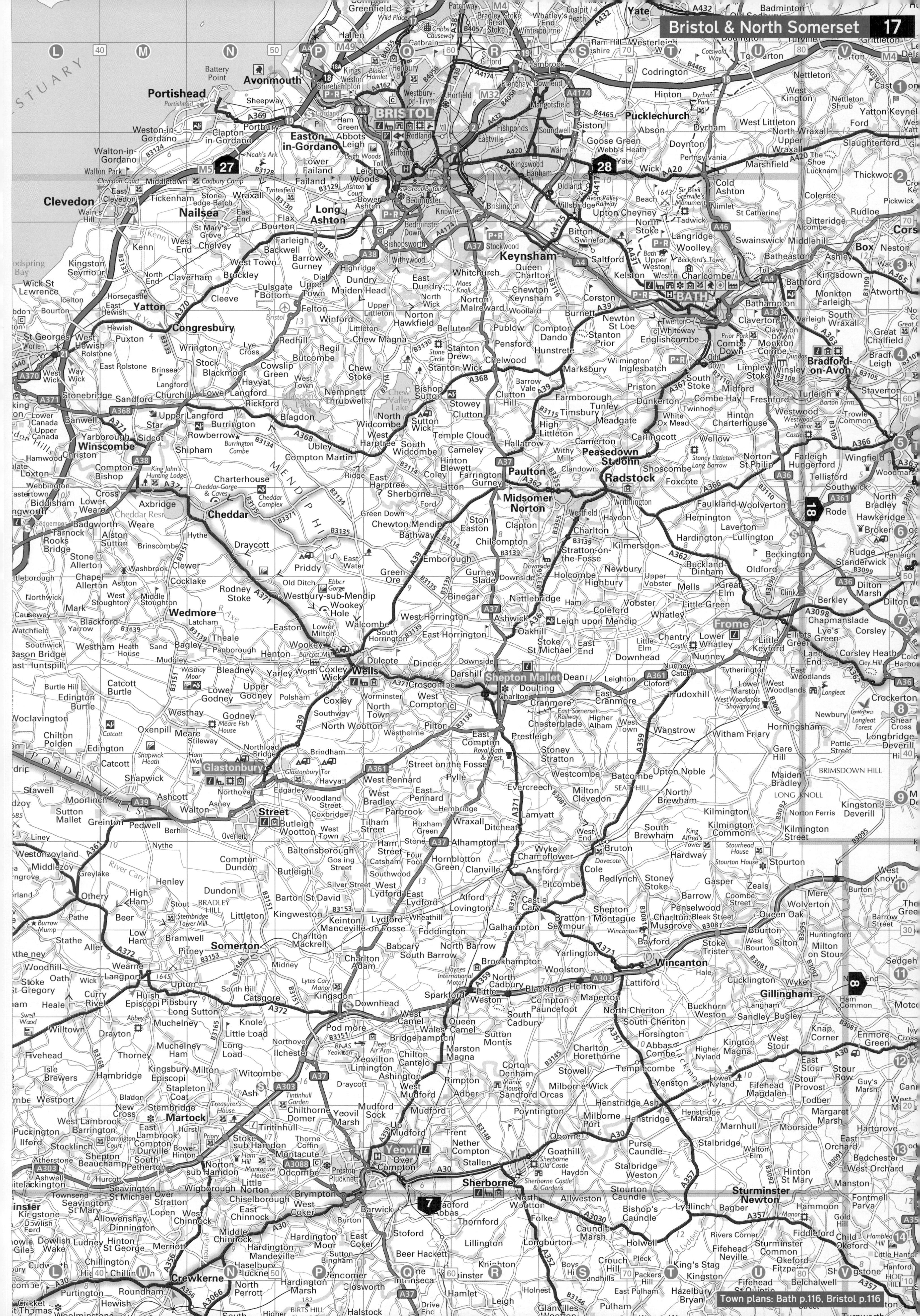
Avonmouth
Portishead
Clevedon
Nailsea
BRISTOL
Keynsham
BATH
Yatton
Congresbury
Cheddar
Wedmore
Wells
Glastonbury
Street
Shepton Mallet
Frome
Radstock
Midsomer Norton
Paulton
Bradford-on-Avon
Somerton
Martock
Yeovil
Sherborne
Wincanton
Gillingham
Crewkerne
Sturminster Newton
Pucklechurch
Yate
Long Ashton
MENDIP HILLS
POLDEN HILLS

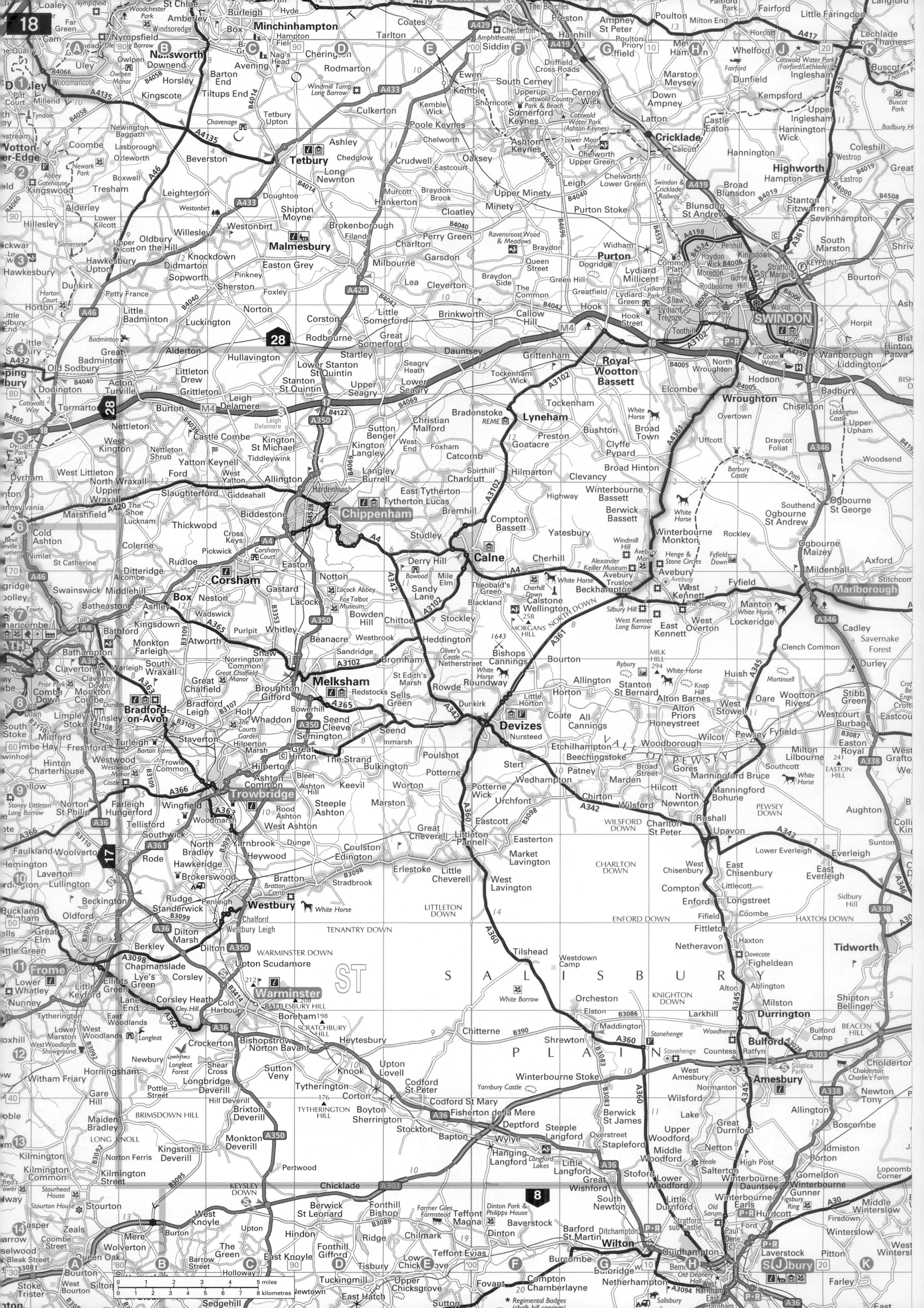
28
8
17
Nailsworth
Minchinhampton
Tetbury
Malmesbury
Cricklade
Highworth
SWINDON
Royal Wootton Bassett
Wroughton
Lyneham
Purton
Chippenham
Calne
Corsham
Box
Melksham
Bradford-on-Avon
Trowbridge
Devizes
Marlborough
Westbury
Warminster
Frome
Pewsey
Tidworth
Durrington
Bulford
Amesbury
Wilton
Salisbury
VALE OF PEWSEY
SALISBURY PLAIN
M4
A419
A429
A46
A4
A350
A361
A342
A345
A360
A36
A303
A338
0 1 2 3 4 5 miles
0 1 2 3 4 5 6 7 8 kilometres

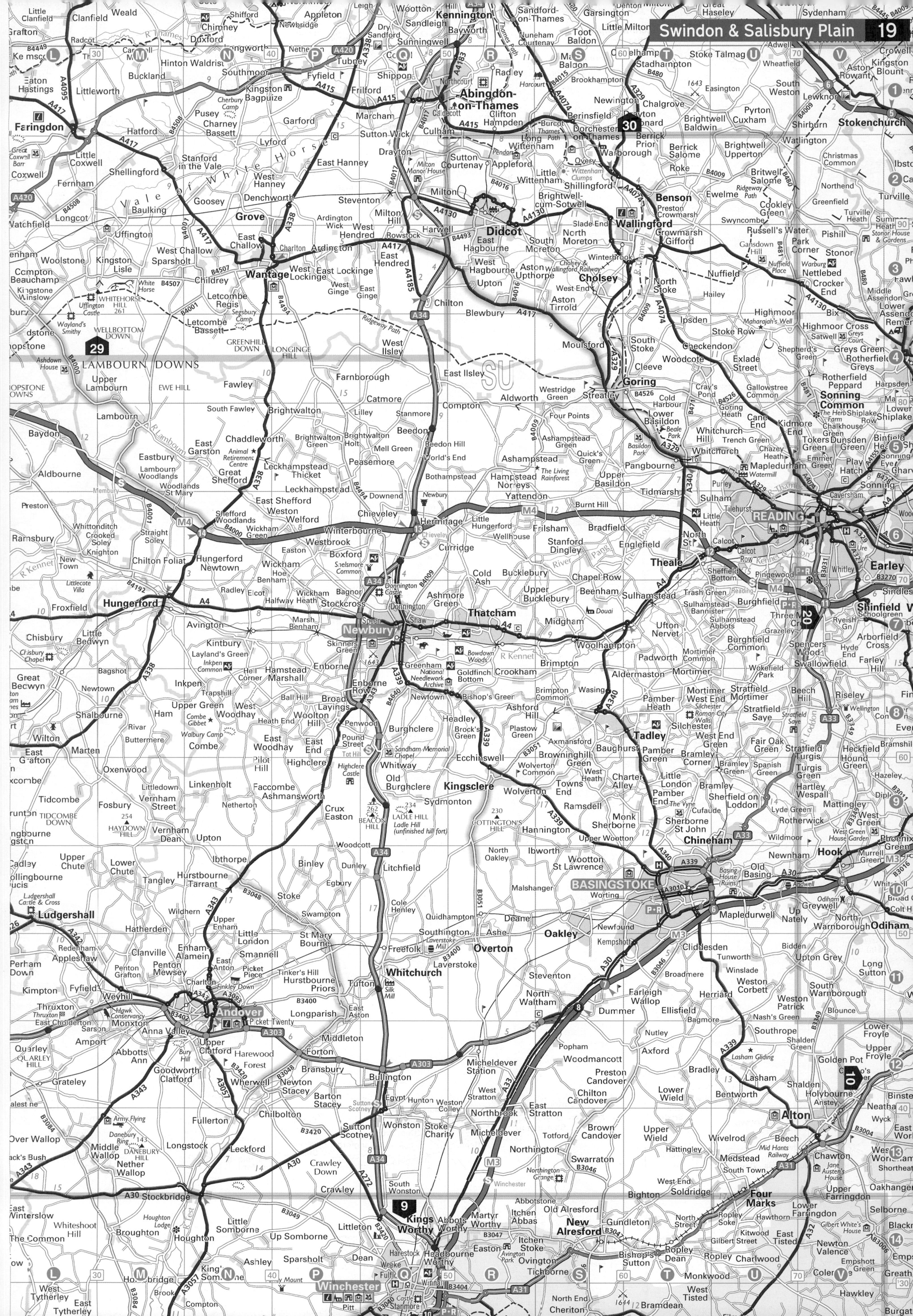

Swindon & Salisbury Plain
19
Faringdon
Abingdon-on-Thames
Kennington
Didcot
Wallingford
Benson
Cholsey
Goring
Streatley
Pangbourne
Grove
Wantage
Lambourn
LAMBOURN DOWNS
Hungerford
Newbury
Thatcham
Theale
READING
Earley
Shinfield
Tadley
Kingsclere
BASINGSTOKE
Chineham
Hook
Odiham
Oakley
Overton
Whitchurch
Andover
Ludgershall
Alton
Four Marks
New Alresford
Kings Worthy
Winchester
Stokenchurch
Sonning Common
Vale of White Horse
29
30
20
10
9
L
M
N
P
Q
R
S
T
U
V
SU

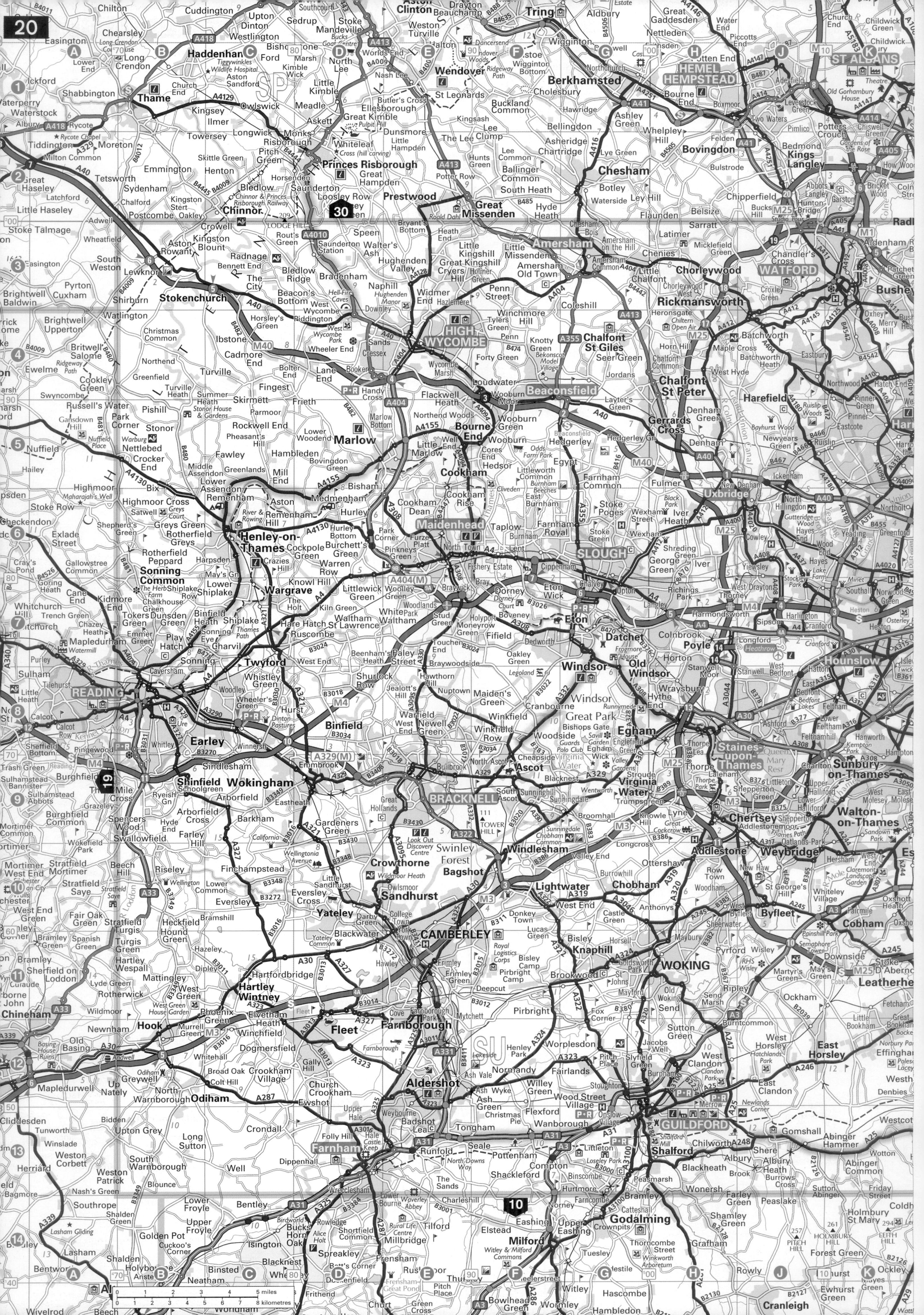
Chilton
Cuddington
Upton
Dinton
Westlington
Haddenham
Long Crendon
Thame
Shabbington
Tiddington
Milton Common
Great Haseley
Little Haseley
Stoke Talmage
Chearsley
Kingsey
Towersey
Ilmer
Longwick
Monks Risborough
Princes Risborough
Whiteleaf
Dunsmore
Great Kimble
Little Kimble
Ellesborough
Wendover
Halton
Weston Turville
Aston Clinton
Drayton Beauchamp
Tring
Aldbury
Wigginton
Berkhamsted
Cholesbury
Buckland Common
Bellingdon
Chesham
Asheridge
Chartridge
Lye Green
Bovingdon
Kings Langley
Hemel Hempstead
Bourne End
Potten End
Nettleden
Great Gaddesden
Water End
Piccotts End
St Albans
Chipperfield
Bucks Hill
Flaunden
Belsize
Sarratt
Latimer
Chenies
Chorleywood
Watford
Rickmansworth
Croxley Green
Bushey
Chandler's Cross
Aldenham
Mill End
Chalfont St Giles
Chalfont St Peter
Seer Green
Jordans
Beaconsfield
Gerrards Cross
Denham
Harefield
Ickenham
Uxbridge
Hillingdon
Iver
Slough
Langley
Datchet
Windsor
Old Windsor
Eton
Eton Wick
Dorney
Burnham
Farnham Royal
Stoke Poges
Wexham
Fulmer
Hedgerley
Taplow
Maidenhead
Cookham
Cookham Dean
Bourne End
Marlow
Little Marlow
Wooburn
Flackwell Heath
Loudwater
High Wycombe
Hazlemere
Penn
Tylers Green
Knotty Green
Coleshill
Amersham
Amersham Old Town
Little Missenden
Great Missenden
Prestwood
Hughenden Valley
Naphill
Speen
Lacey Green
Saunderton
Bledlow
Bledlow Ridge
Chinnor
Crowell
Kingston Blount
Aston Rowant
Lewknor
Stokenchurch
Radnage
Ibstone
Christmas Common
Watlington
Northend
Turville
Fingest
Frieth
Skirmett
Hambleden
Fawley
Medmenham
Hurley
Bisham
Remenham
Henley-on-Thames
Wargrave
Twyford
Sonning
Sonning Common
Caversham
Reading
Earley
Woodley
Winnersh
Wokingham
Shinfield
Arborfield
Finchampstead
Crowthorne
Sandhurst
Yateley
Camberley
Bagshot
Windlesham
Lightwater
Chobham
Bracknell
Binfield
Ascot
Sunningdale
Virginia Water
Egham
Staines-upon-Thames
Sunbury-on-Thames
Chertsey
Addlestone
Weybridge
Walton-on-Thames
Byfleet
Cobham
Woking
Knaphill
Bisley
Pirbright
Farnborough
Fleet
Aldershot
Hook
Hartley Wintney
Odiham
Crookham Village
Church Crookham
Farnham
Tongham
Seale
Puttenham
Compton
Guildford
Shalford
Chilworth
Godalming
Milford
Elstead
Tilford
Frensham
Bentley
Upper Froyle
Lower Froyle
Binsted
Alton
Basingstoke
Old Basing
Chineham
Sherfield on Loddon
Bramley
Stratfield Saye
Mortimer
Burghfield
Mapledurham
Purley
Pangbourne
Tilehurst
Whitchurch
Goring
Cane End
Kidmore End
Nettlebed
Nuffield
Ewelme
Britwell Salome
Brightwell Baldwin
Cuxham
Pyrton
Shirburn
West Horsley
East Horsley
Ripley
Send
Worplesdon
Normandy
Ash
Leatherhead
Gomshall
Shere
Albury
Wonersh
Bramley
Cranleigh
Ewhurst
Hascombe
Witley
Churt
Rowledge
Headley
Lasham
Herriard
Long Sutton
Crondall
Ewshot
Heathrow
Hounslow
Poyle
Colnbrook
Stanwell
Ashford
Feltham
Shepperton
Thorpe
Wraysbury
M4
M40
M25
M3
A404(M)
A329(M)
30
19
10
0 1 2 3 4 5 miles
0 1 2 3 4 5 6 7 8 kilometres

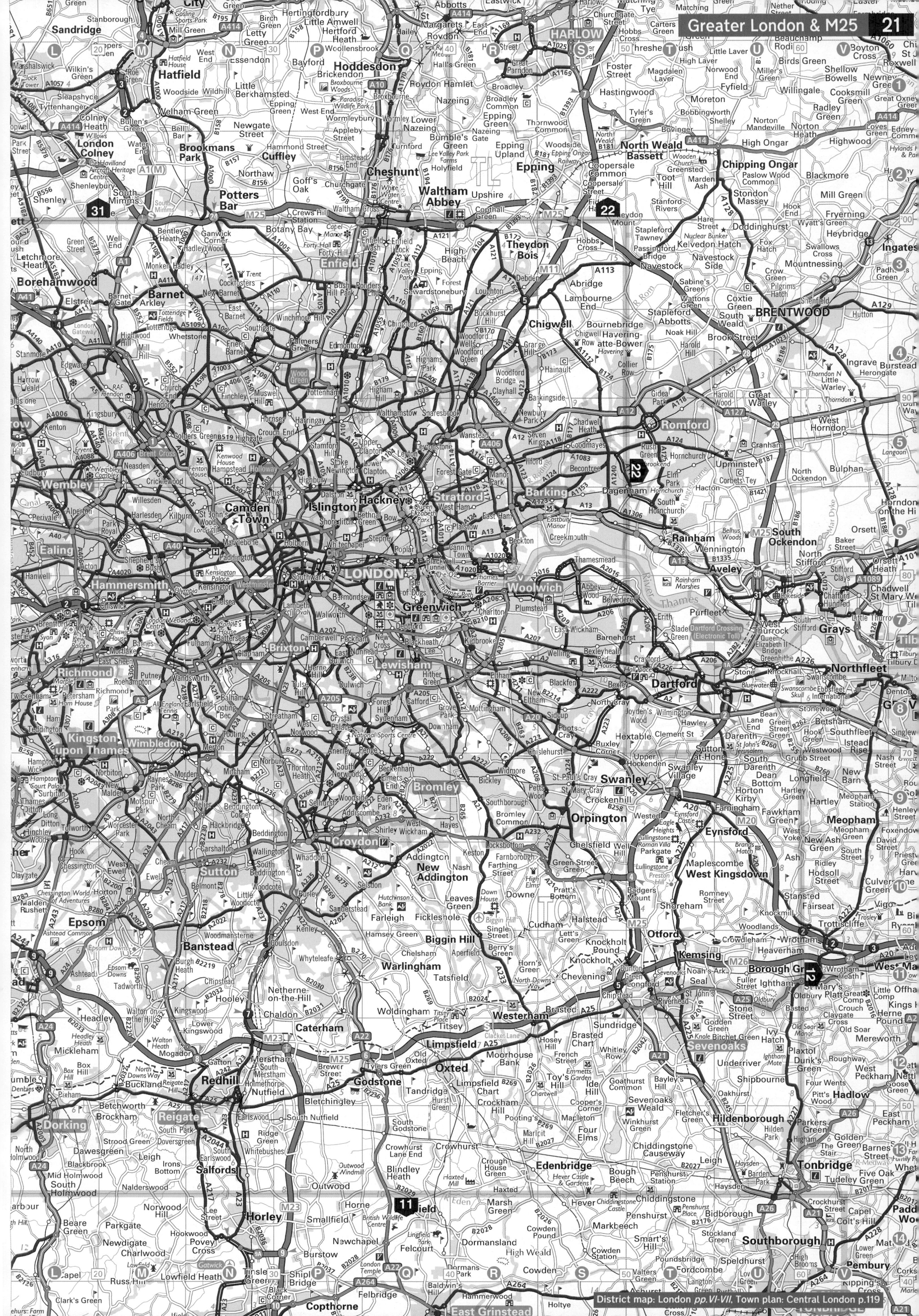

Buntingford
Bishop's Stortford
Stansted Mountfitchet
Sawbridgeworth
HARLOW
Ware
Hoddesdon
Cheshunt
Waltham Abbey
Epping
North Weald Bassett
Chipping Ongar
Theydon Bois
Chigwell
Great Dunmow
Thaxted
Braintree
Great Notley
Coggeshall
Halstead
Sible Hedingham
Witham
Hatfield Peverel
CHELMSFORD
Writtle
Danbury
South Woodham Ferrers
Ingatestone
BRENTWOOD
Billericay
Wickford
BASILDON
Rayleigh
Hockley
Hadleigh
South Benfleet
Canvey Island
Stanford le Hope
Romford
Grays
Tilbury
Aveley
South Ockendon
Rainham
Barking
Stratford
Hackney
LONDON
Greenwich
Woolwich
Lewisham
Bromley
Croydon
Orpington
Swanley
Dartford
Northfleet
GRAVESEND
ROCHESTER
Strood
CHATHAM
GILLINGHAM
Hoo St Werburgh
HOO PENINSULA
THAMES
THE RODINGS
LONDON GATEWAY TERMINAL
Dartford Crossing (Electronic Toll)
Eynsford
West Kingsdown
Meopham
Newport
Saffron Walden
M11
M25
M20
A12
A13
A127
A130
A120
TL
0 1 2 3 4 5 miles
0 1 2 3 4 5 6 7 8 kilometres

Harwich International Port
Southend-on-Sea
Colchester
Clacton-on-Sea
Southend-on-Sea
Harwich
Manningtree
Wivenhoe
Brightlingsea
West Mersea
Mersea Island
Walton-on-the-Naze
Frinton-on-Sea
Jaywick
St Osyth
Tiptree
Maldon
Tollesbury
Bradwell-on-Sea
Southminster
Burnham-on-Crouch
Rochford
Shoeburyness
Foulness Island
River Blackwater
River Crouch
River Stour
Felixstowe
Hook of Holland
Pennyhole Bay
Sheerness
Minster
Isle of Sheppey
Sittingbourne
Whitstable
Herne Bay
Margate
Isle of Thanet
TM
TQ
TR
Estuary

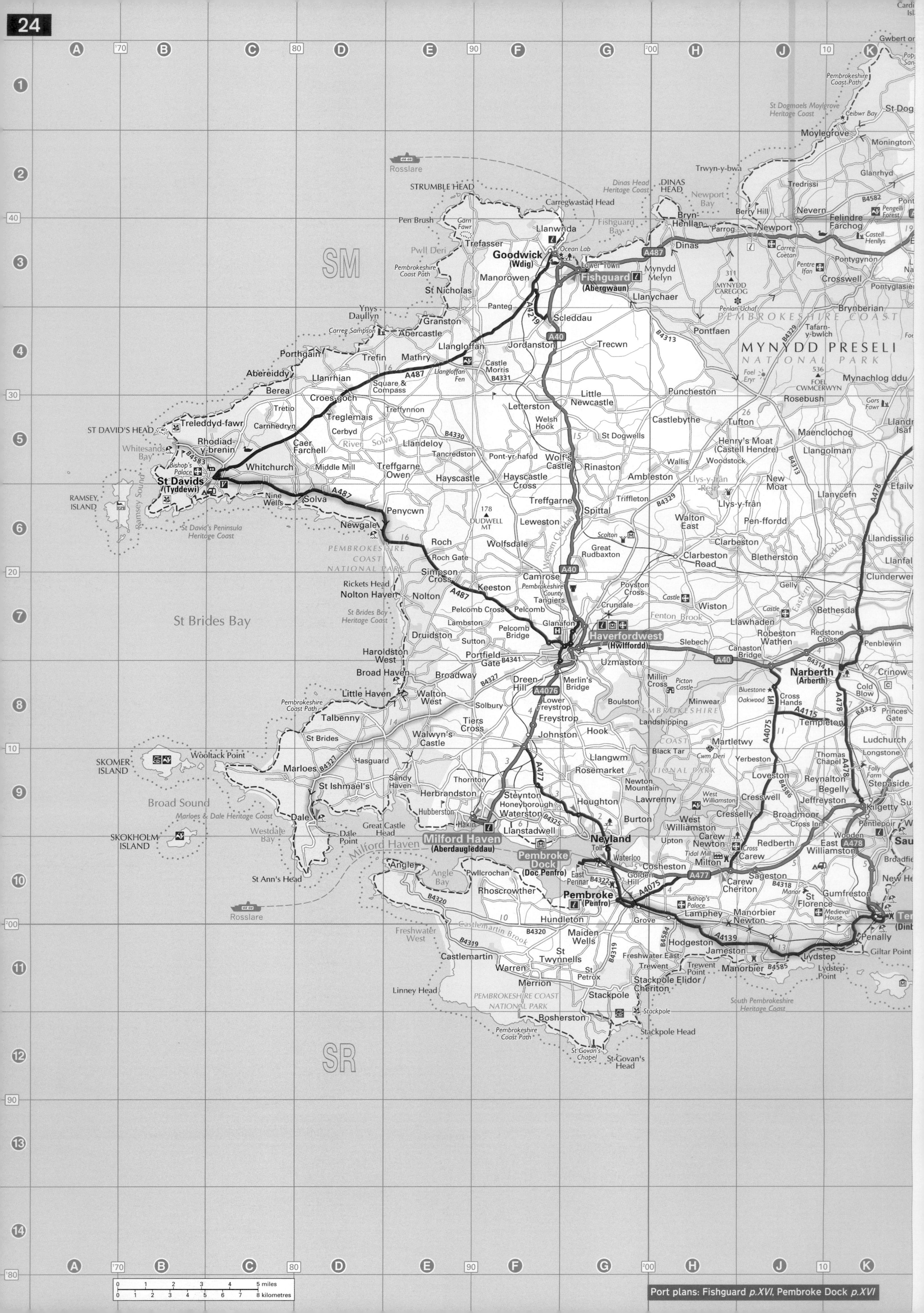
A
B
C
D
E
F
G
H
J
K
70
80
90
00
10
40
30
20
10
00
90
80
1
2
3
4
5
6
7
8
9
10
11
12
13
14
SM
SR
Rosslare
STRUMBLE HEAD
Carregwastad Head
Pen Brush
Garn Fawr
Trefasser
Pwll Deri
Pembrokeshire Coast Path
Llanwnda
Ocean Lab
Goodwick
(Wdig)
Lower Town
Fishguard
(Abergwaun)
Fishguard Bay
Manorowen
St Nicholas
Panteg
Scleddau
Dinas Head Heritage Coast
DINAS HEAD
Newport Bay
Bryn-Henllan
Dinas
Parrog
Newport
Trwyn-y-bwa
Berry Hill
Nevern
Felindre Farchog
Castell Henllys
Carreg Coetan
Mynydd Melyn
Llanychaer
311
MYNYDD CAREGOG
Pentre Ifan
Crosswell
Pontygynon
Pontyglasier
Brynberian
Tafarn-y-bwlch
Penlan Uchaf
PEMBROKESHIRE COAST
MYNYDD PRESELI
NATIONAL PARK
Pontfaen
Foel Eryr
536
FOEL CWMCERWYN
Mynachlog ddu
Rosebush
Gors Fawr
Gwbert on Sea
Pembrokeshire Coast Path
St Dogmaels Moylgrove Heritage Coast
Ceibwr Bay
St Dogmaels
Moylegrove
Monington
Glanrhyd
Tredrissi
B4582
Pengelli Forest
Ynys Daullyn
Granston
Carreg Sampson
Abercastle
Llangloffan
Jordanston
Trecwn
B4313
B4329
Porthgain
Trefin
Mathry
Castle Morris
B4331
Llangloffan Fen
Abereiddy
Llanrhian
A487
Square & Compass
Berea
Croes-goch
Tretio
Treglemais
Cerbyd
Treffynnon
Letterston
Little Newcastle
Puncheston
Carnhedryn
Treleddyd-fawr
ST DAVID'S HEAD
Whitesands Bay
Rhodiad-y-brenin
Caer Farchell
River Solva
Llandeloy
B4330
Welsh Hook
St Dogwells
Castlebythe
Tufton
Henry's Moat (Castell Hendre)
Maenclochog
Llangolman
Whitchurch
Middle Mill
Tancredston
Pont-yr-hafod
Wolf's Castle
Rinaston
Wallis
Woodstock
B4583
Bishop's Palace
St Davids
(Tyddewi)
Treffgarne Owen
Hayscastle
Hayscastle Cross
Ambleston
Llys-y-frân Resr
Llys-y-frân
New Moat
Llanycefn
RAMSEY ISLAND
Ramsey Sound
Nine Wells
Solva
A487
Penycwn
Treffgarne
Triffleton
Spittal
Walton East
Pen-ffordd
St David's Peninsula Heritage Coast
Newgale
178
DUDWELL MT
Leweston
Western Cleddau
Scolton
Clarbeston
Great Rudbaxton
Clarbeston Road
Bletherston
Roch
Wolfsdale
PEMBROKESHIRE COAST NATIONAL PARK
Roch Gate
Simpson Cross
Rickets Head
Nolton Haven
Nolton
Keeston
Camrose
Pembrokeshire County Tangiers
A40
Poyston Cross
Crundale
Castle
Wiston
Gelly
Eastern Cleddau
St Brides Bay
St Brides Bay Heritage Coast
Pelcomb Cross
Pelcomb
Fenton Brook
Llawhaden
Castle
Bethesda
Lambston
Glanafon
Druidston
Sutton
Pelcomb Bridge
Haverfordwest
(Hwlffordd)
Slebech
Robeston Wathen
Redstone Cross
Penblewin
Haroldston West
Portfield Gate
B4341
Uzmaston
Canaston Bridge
A40
B4314
Narberth
(Arberth)
Crinow
Broad Haven
Broadway
B4327
Dreen Hill
Merlin's Bridge
Millin Cross
Picton Castle
Bluestone
Oakwood
Cross Hands
Cold Blow
Little Haven
Walton West
A4076
Lower Freystrop
Boulston
Minwear
A4115
Templeton
B4315
Princes Gate
Pembrokeshire Coast Path
Talbenny
Solbury
Freystrop
PEMBROKESHIRE
Landshipping
A478
Tiers Cross
Johnston
Hook
COAST
Martletwy
Ludchurch
St Brides
Walwyn's Castle
Black Tar
Cwm Deri
Yerbeston
A4075
Thomas Chapel
Longstone
Wooltack Point
SKOMER ISLAND
Marloes
B4327
Hasguard
Llangwm
Rosemarket
NATIONAL PARK
Loveston
Folly Farm
Reynalton
Stepaside
St Ishmael's
Sandy Haven
Thornton
Newton Mountain
Begelly
Herbrandston
Steynton
Honeyborough
Lawrenny
West Williamston
Cresswell
Jeffreyston
Kilgetty
Broad Sound
Marloes & Dale Heritage Coast
Hubberston
Waterston
B4325
Houghton
Cresselly
Broadmoor
Dale
Hakin
Llanstadwell
Burton
West Williamston
Cross Inn
Pentlepoir
SKOKHOLM ISLAND
Westdale Bay
Dale Point
Great Castle Head
Milford Haven
(Aberdaugleddau)
Neyland
Upton
Carew Newton
Redberth
East Williamston
Wooden
A478
Saundersfoot
Milford Haven
Toll
Tidal Mill
Cross
Pembroke Dock
(Doc Penfro)
Waterloo
Cosheston
Milton
Carew
Broadfield
St Ann's Head
Angle
Angle Bay
Pwllcrochan
East Pennar
B4322
Golden Hill
A477
Sageston
New Hedges
Rosslare
Rhoscrowther
Pembroke
(Penfro)
A4075
Carew Cheriton
B4318
Manor
Gumfreston
St Florence
B4320
Bishop's Palace
Lamphey
Medieval House
Hundleton
Grove
Manorbier Newton
Tenby
(Dinbych-y-pysgod)
Castlemartin Brook
B4320
Freshwater West
B4319
Maiden Wells
B4584
Hodgeston
A4139
Penally
Castlemartin
St Twynnells
B4319
Freshwater East
Jameston
Lydstep
Giltar Point
Warren
St Petrox
Trewent
Trewent Point
Manorbier
B4585
Lydstep Point
Linney Head
Merrion
Stackpole Elidor / Cheriton
PEMBROKESHIRE COAST NATIONAL PARK
Stackpole
South Pembrokeshire Heritage Coast
Stackpole
Bosherston
Pembrokeshire Coast Path
Stackpole Head
St Govan's Chapel
St Govan's Head
0 1 2 3 4 5 miles
0 1 2 3 4 5 6 7 8 kilometres

Port plans: Fishguard p.XVI, Pembroke Dock p.XVI

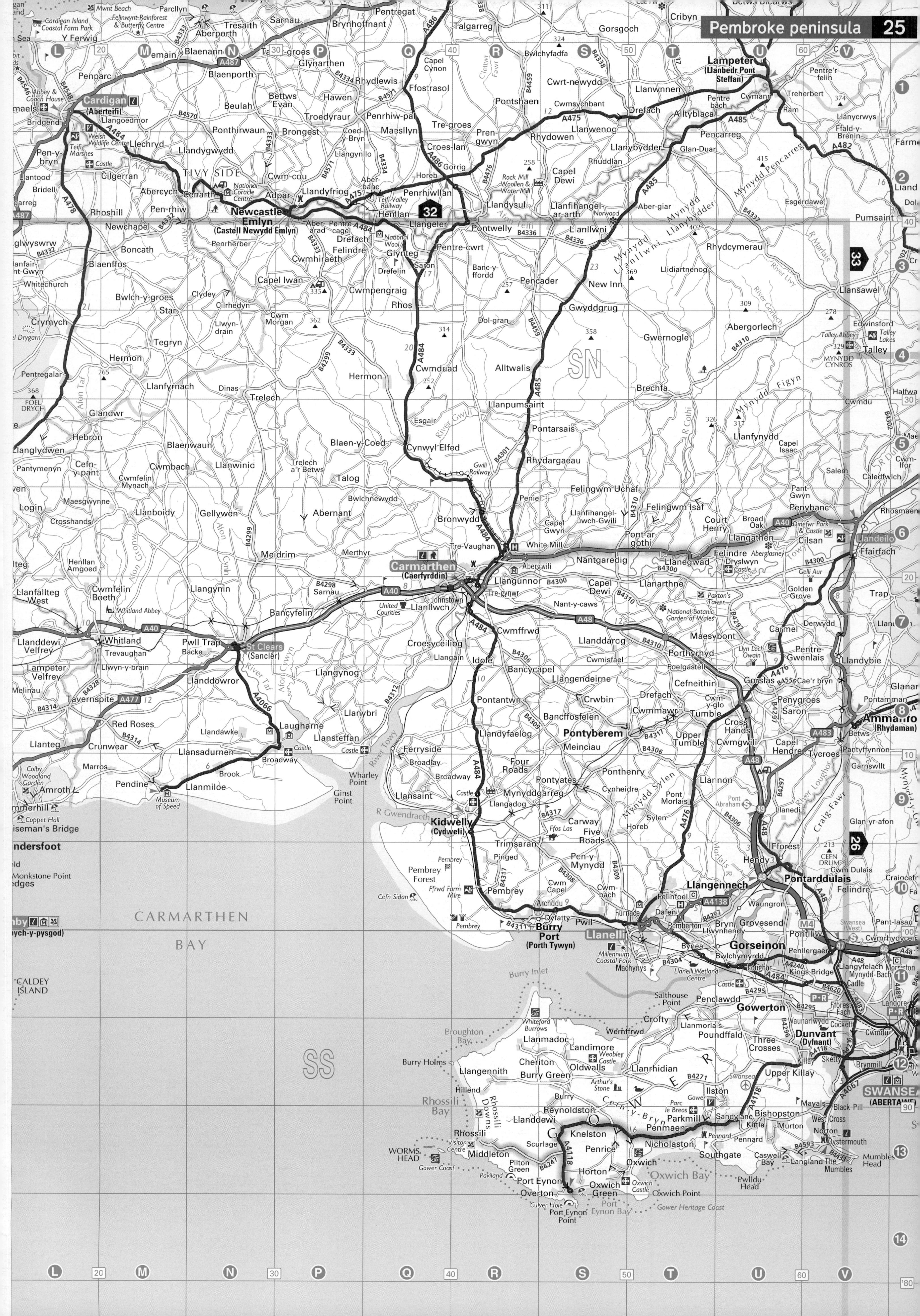
Cardigan
(Aberteifi)
Newcastle Emlyn
(Castell Newydd Emlyn)
Lampeter
(Llanbedr Pont Steffan)
Carmarthen
(Caerfyrddin)
St Clears
(Sanclêr)
Kidwelly
(Cydweli)
Llanelli
Burry Port
(Porth Tywyn)
Gorseinon
Pontarddulais
Gowerton
Dunvant
(Dyfnant)
Llandeilo
Ammanford
(Rhydaman)
SWANSEA
(ABERTAWE)
Llangennech
Pontyberem
Whitland
Laugharne
Pendine
Llansteffan
Ferryside
Llansaint
Pembrey
Trimsaran
Mynyddygarreg
Cross Hands
Tumble
Llandybie
Ffairfach
Llanarthne
Nantgaredig
Llangunnor
Cwmffrwd
Idole
Bronwydd
Cynwyl Elfed
Llanpumsaint
Alltwalis
Cwmduad
Gwyddgrug
New Inn
Pencader
Llandysul
Brechfa
Abergorlech
Talley
Llansawel
Aberporth
Tresaith
Blaenporth
Llechryd
Cilgerran
Cenarth
Adpar
Henllan
Llangeler
Pentre-cwrt
Saron
Rhos
Cwmpengraig
Capel Iwan
Boncath
Newchapel
Crymych
Hermon
Llanfyrnach
Trelech
Blaenwaun
Llanwinic
Talog
Abernant
Meidrim
Llangynin
Bancyfelin
Llanboidy
Gellywen
Llanddowror
Red Roses
Tavernspite
Crunwear
Llansadurnen
Llanmiloe
Amroth
Llanteg
Rhossili
Llangennith
Llanmadoc
Cheriton
Burry Green
Llanrhidian
Oldwalls
Landimore
Reynoldston
Knelston
Penrice
Horton
Oxwich
Port Eynon
Nicholaston
Penmaen
Parkmill
Southgate
Bishopston
Kittle
Murton
Mumbles
Mumbles Head
Ilston
Three Crosses
Upper Killay
Killay
Penclawdd
Crofty
Pontlliw
Pontardulais
Hendy
Felindre
CARMARTHEN BAY
CALDEY ISLAND
Worms Head
Rhossili Bay
Port Eynon Bay
Oxwich Bay
Burry Inlet
Gower Heritage Coast
Gower
SN
SS

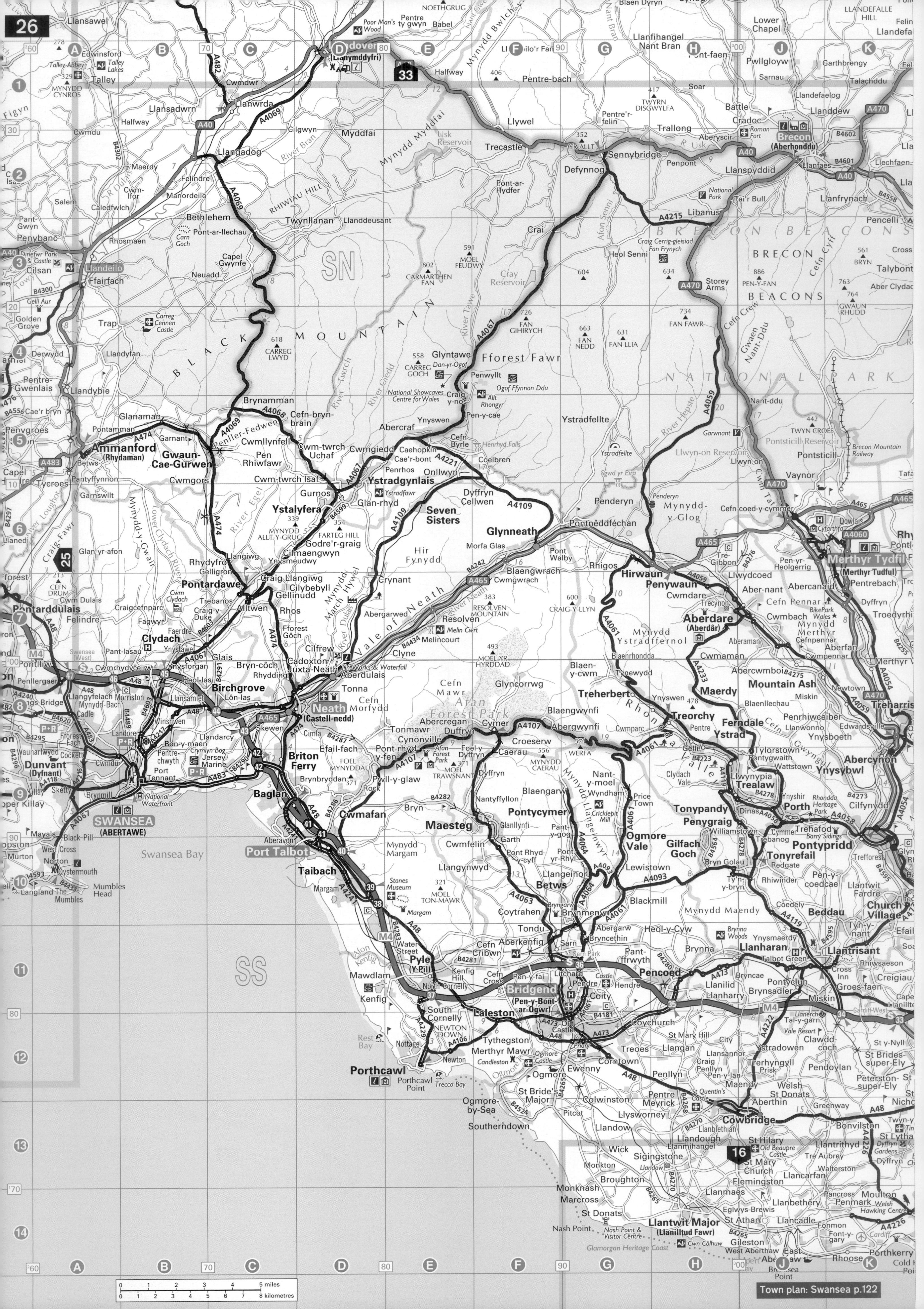
Llansawel
Edwinsford
Talley Abbey
Talley Lakes
Talley
MYNYDD CYNROS
Llandovery (Llanymddyfri)
Poor Man's Wood
Pentre ty gwyn
Babel
NOETHGRUG
Halfway
Pentre-bach
Llanfihangel Nant Bran
Pont-faen
Lower Chapel
Pwllgloyw
Garthbrengy
Sarnau
Talachddu
LLANDEFALLE HILL
Llandefalle
Cwmdwr
Llanwrda
Llansadwrn
Halfway
Cwmdu
Cilgwyn
Myddfai
Mynydd Myddfai
Usk Reservoir
Trecastle
Llywel
TWYRN DISGWYLFA
Pentre'r-felin
Trallong
Battle
Cradoc
Aberyscir
Roman Fort
Brecon (Aberhonddu)
Llandefaelog
Llanddew
Llangadog
Sennybridge
Defynnog
Penpont
Llanspyddid
Llanfaes
Llechfaen
Maerdy
Felindre
Manordeilo
Cwm-Ifor
Salem
Caledfwlch
RHIWIAU HILL
Pont-ar-Hydfer
National Park
Tai'r Bull
Llanfrynach
Bethlehem
Pont-ar-llechau
Carn Goch
Twynllanan
Llanddeusant
Libanus
Pencelli
Pant-Gwyn
Penybanc
Rhosmaen
Crai
Craig Cerrig-gleisiad Fan Frynych
Heol Senni
BRECON BEACONS
Dinefwr Park & Castle
Llandeilo
Cilsan
Ffairfach
Capel Gwynfe
Neuadd
SN
MOEL FEUDWY
CARMARTHEN FAN
Cray Reservoir
PEN-Y-FAN
Storey Arms
Talybont
Aber Clydach
GWAUN RHUDD
Gelli Aur
Golden Grove
Trap
Carreg Cennen Castle
BLACK MOUNTAIN
CARREG LWYD
FAN GIHIRYCH
FAN NEDD
FAN LLIA
FAN FAWR
Cefn Crew
Gwaen Nant-Ddu
Derwydd
Llandyfan
CARREG GOCH
Dan-yr-Ogof
Glyntawe
Fforest Fawr
Penwyllt
Ogof Ffynnon Ddu
Allt Rhongyr
NATIONAL PARK
Pentre-Gwenlais
Llandybie
National Showcaves Centre for Wales
Craig-y-nos
Pen-y-cae
Nant-ddu
Cae'r bryn
Penygroes
Glanaman
Brynamman
Cefn-bryn-brain
Penller-Fedwen
Ystradfellte
Ynyswen
Abercraf
TWYN CROES
Pontsticill Reservoir
Brecon Mountain Railway
Pontamman
Ammanford (Rhydaman)
Garnant
Gwaun-Cae-Gurwen
Cwmllynfell
Cwm-twrch Uchaf
Cwmgiedd
Caehopkin
Cae'r-bont
Cefn Byrle
Henrhyd Falls
Coelbren
Garwnant
Llwyn-on Reservoir
Pontsticill
Betws
Pantyffynnon
Pen Rhiwfawr
Cwmgors
Cwm-twrch Isaf
Penrhos
Onllwyn
Ystradgynlais
Ystradfawr
Sgwd yr Eira
Vaynor
Capel
Tycroes
Garnswllt
Gurnos
Glan-rhyd
Dyffryn Cellwen
Penderyn
Mynydd-y Glog
Cefn-coed-y-cymmer
Dowlais
Cyfarthfa
Ystalyfera
Seven Sisters
MYNYDD ALLT-Y-GRUG
FARTEG HILL
Godre'r-graig
Glynneath
Pontneddfechan
Llanedi
Craig-Fawr
Glan-yr-afon
Mynydd-y-Gwair
Lower Clydach River
River Egel
Cilmaengwyn
Ynysmeudwy
Hir Fynydd
Morfa Glas
Pont Walby
Rhigos
Hirwaun
Penywaun
Tre-Gibbon
Llwydcoed
Pen-yr-Heolgerrig
Merthyr Tydfil (Merthyr Tudful)
Pentrebach
CEFN DRUM
Cwm Dulais
Pontarddulais
Felindre
Rhydyfro
Gelligron
Pontardawe
Llangiwg
Craig Llangiwg
Cilybebyll
Gellinudd
Mynydd March Hywel
Crynant
Blaengwrach
Cwmgwrach
Aber-nant
Abercanaid
Cwm Clydach
Trebanos
Craig-y-Duke
Craigcefnparc
Alltwen
Rhos
Abergarwed
Vale of Neath
RESOLVEN MOUNTAIN
Resolven
CRAIG-Y-LLYN
Cwmdare
Trecynon
Aberdare (Aberdâr)
Cefn Pennar
Cwmbach
BikePark Wales
Dyffryn
Troedyrhiw
Fagwyr
Faerdre
Clydach
Ynystawe
Fforest Goch
Melin Cwrt
Melincourt
Mynydd Ystradffernol
Mynydd Merthyr
Cefnpennar
Aberfan
Pant-lasau
Glais
Bryn-côch
Cilfrew
Cadoxton
Juxta-Neath
Clyne
MOEL YR HYRDDAD
Blaen-y-cwm
Blaenrhondda
Aberaman
Cwmaman
Abercwmboi
Merthyr Vale
Pontlliw
Penllergaer
Cwmrhydyceirw
Ynysforgan
Heol-las
Birchgrove
Rhydding
Aberdulais
Tonna
Tyn Works & Waterfall
Glyncorrwg
Cefn Mawr
Afan Forest Park
Tynewydd
Treherbert
Ynyswen
Mountain Ash
Miskin
Newtown
Llangyfelach
Morriston
Mynydd-Bach
Cadle
Llansamlet
Lôn-las
Neath (Castell-nedd)
Cefn Morfydd
Abercregan
Duffryn
Cymer
Blaengwynfi
Abergwynfi
Rhondda
Treorchy
Blaenllechau
Penrhiwceiber
Treharris
Winshwen
Skewen
Cimla
Tonmawr
Cynonville
Croeserw
Cwmparc
Pentre
Ferndale
Ystrad
Llanwonno
Edwardsville
Ynysboeth
Landore
Bon-y-maen
Llandarcy
Crymlyn Bog
Pentre-chwyth
Jersey Marine
Efail-fach
Briton Ferry
Pont-rhyd-y-fen
Afan Forest Park
Foel-y-Dyffryn
Caerau
MYNYDD CAERAU
WERFA
Gelli
Tylorstown
Pontygwaith
Wattstown
Abercynon
Ynysybwl
Dunvant (Dyfnant)
Cockett
Cwmdu
Fforest Fach
Waunarlwydd
Port Tennant
FOEL MYNYDDAU
Brynbryddan
Pwll-y-glaw
Rock
MOEL TRAWSNANT
Dyffryn
Nant-y-moel
Wyndham
Clydach Vale
Llwynypia
Trealaw
Killay
Sketty
Brynmill
National Waterfront
Baglan
Cwmafan
Bryn
Nantyffyllon
Blaengarw
Pontycymer
Cricklepit Mill
Price Town
Tonypandy
Penygraig
Dinas
Porth
Ynyshir
Rhondda Heritage Park
Cilfynydd
SWANSEA (ABERTAWE)
Mayals
Black Pill
West Cross
Norton
Oystermouth
Swansea Bay
Aberavon
Port Talbot
Maesteg
Glanllynfi
Garth
Pant-y-gog
Ogmore Vale
Gilfach Goch
Williamstown
Trebanog
Trehafod
Barry Sidings
Cymmer
Pontypridd
Trefforest
Murton
Mumbles Head
Langland
The Mumbles
Mynydd Margam
Cwmfelin
Pont Rhyd-y-cyff
Pont-yr-Rhyl
Lewistown
Bryn Golau
Tonyrefail
Redgate
Taibach
Margam
Stones Museum
MOEL TON-MAWR
Llangynwyd
Llangeinor
Betws
Tyn-y-bryn
Rhiwinder
Pen-y-coedcae
Llantwit Fardre
Coedely
Beddau
Church Village
Coytrahen
Bryngarw
Brynmenyn
Blackmill
Mynydd Maendy
Tondu
Aberkenfig
Sarn
Abergarw
Bryncethin
Heol-y-Cyw
Brynna Woods
Ynysmaerdy
Tyn-y-nant
Efail Isaf
SS
Water Street
Pyle (Y Pil)
Kenfig Hill
Cefn Cribwr
Sarn Park
Pant-y-ffrwyth
Brynna
Llanharan
Talbot Green
Llantrisant
Rhiwsaeson
Creigiau
Mawdlam
Kenfig
North Cornelly
Cefn Cross
Pen-y-fai
Litchard
Pendre
Castle
Hendre
Pencoed
Llanilid
Llanharry
Brynsadler
Pontyclun
Cross Inn
Groes-faen
Miskin
Bridgend (Pen-y-Bont-ar-Ogwr)
Coity
South Cornelly
Laleston
Oldcastle
Coychurch
Llanerch
Tal-y-garn
Vale Resort
Cardiff West
Newton Down
Tythegston
St Mary Hill
Treoes
Llangan
City
Llansannor
Ystradowen
Clawdd-coch
St y-Nyll
Rest Bay
Nottage
Merthyr Mawr
Candleston
Ogmore Castle
Ewenny
Corntown
Craig Penllyn
Pen-y-lan
Trerhyngyll
Prisk
Pendoylan
St Brides-super-Ely
Newton
Porthcawl
Porthcawl Point
Trecco Bay
Ogmore
St Bride's Major
Penllyn
Maendy
Welsh St Donats
Peterston-super-Ely
Ogmore-by-Sea
Pitcot
Colwinston
Pentre Meyrick
St Quentin's Castle
Aberthin
Cowbridge
Greenway
Southerndown
Llysworney
Llandow
Llanblethian
Bonvilston
Twyn-yr-odyn
Wick
Llandough
Llanmihangel
Sigingstone
St Hilary
Old Beaupre Castle
Llantrithyd
St Lythans
Dyffryn Gardens
Monkton
Llandow
Broughton
St Mary Church
Flemingston
Llancarfan
Tre Aubrey
Walterston
Monknash
Marcross
Llanmaes
Pancross
Penmark
Llanbethery
Moulton
Welsh Hawking Centre
St Donats
Nash Point
Nash Point & Visitor Centre
Llantwit Major (Llanilltud Fawr)
Eglwys-Brewis
St Athan
Llancadle
Fonmon
Font-y-gary
Cwn Colhuw
Gileston
West Aberthaw
East Aberthaw
Rhoose
Rhoose Point
Porthkerry
Glamorgan Heritage Coast
A40
A482
A4069
A4300
B4302
A483
A476
A474
A4068
A474
A4067
A4109
A4221
B4599
A4221
A465
B4242
A4059
A470
A4215
A4061
A4233
A4119
A4058
A4093
A4064
A4063
A4107
B4282
A48
M4
A4241
B4283
A4229
A4106
B4281
A473
A4061
A4222
A4226
B4270
B4265
B4268
A4054
B4275
B4278
B4273
B4595
B4601
B4602
B4558
Town plan: Swansea p.122
0 1 2 3 4 5 miles
0 1 2 3 4 5 6 7 8 kilometres

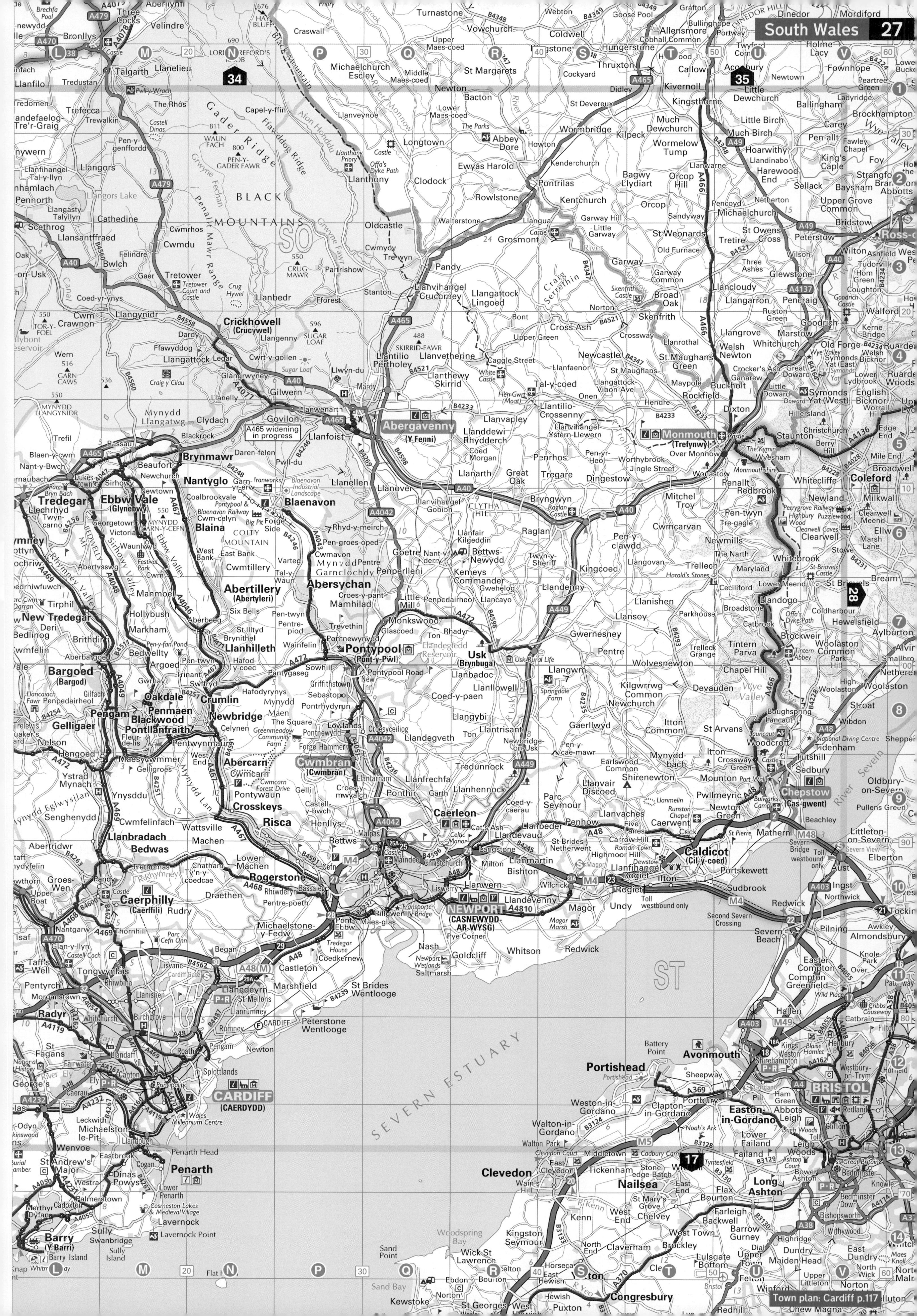

BLACK MOUNTAINS
Gader Ridge
Ffawddog Ridge
Black Mountain
SO
ST
SEVERN ESTUARY
Talgarth
Llanelieu
Hay Bluff
Craswall
Turnastone
Vowchurch
Michaelchurch Escley
St Margarets
Longtown
Abbey Dore
Clodock
Ewyas Harold
Pontrilas
Kentchurch
Grosmont
Kilpeck
Wormbridge
Much Dewchurch
Wormelow Tump
Little Dewchurch
Holme Lacy
Fownhope
Ross-on-Wye
Llangors
Llangors Lake
Bwlch
Tretower
Crickhowell (Crucywel)
Llangynidr
Llangattock
Llanbedr
Partrishow
Llanvihangel Crucorney
Llangattock Lingoed
Skenfrith
Garway
St Weonards
Llangarron
Goodrich
Welsh Bicknor
Symonds Yat (East)
Symonds Yat (West)
Gilwern
Govilon
Clydach
Abergavenny (Y Fenni)
Llanfoist
Llantilio Pertholey
Llanvetherine
White Castle
Llantilio-Crossenny
Llanvapley
Rockfield
Monmouth (Trefynwy)
Dixton
Staunton
Coleford
Brynmawr
Nantyglo
Blaenavon
Beaufort
Ebbw Vale (Glynebwy)
Tredegar
Blaina
Abertillery (Abertyleri)
Abersychan
Llanover
Raglan
Dingestow
Mitchel Troy
Trellech
Tintern Parva
Llandogo
St Briavels
Pontypool (Pont-y-Pŵl)
Usk (Brynbuga)
Llangybi
Cwmbran (Cwmbran)
Crumlin
Newbridge
Oakdale
Blackwood
Pengam
Bargoed (Bargod)
Gelligaer
New Tredegar
Abercarn
Crosskeys
Risca
Caerleon
Newport (Casnewydd-ar-Wysg)
Rogerstone
Bedwas
Llanbradach
Caerphilly (Caerffili)
Magor
Undy
Caldicot (Cil-y-coed)
Chepstow (Cas-gwent)
Tidenham
Mathern
Portskewett
Sudbrook
Severn Beach
Pilning
Almondsbury
Nash
Goldcliff
Whitson
Redwick
Peterstone Wentlooge
St Brides Wentlooge
Marshfield
Castleton
Cardiff (Caerdydd)
Llandaff
St Fagans
Radyr
Penarth
Barry (Y Barri)
Barry Island
Sully
Lavernock
Dinas Powys
Portishead
Avonmouth
Clevedon
Nailsea
Portbury
Easton-in-Gordano
Long Ashton
Bristol
Congresbury
Kewstoke
Sand Bay
Sand Point
Woodspring Bay
Flat Holm
Second Severn Crossing
Toll westbound only
A465 widening in progress
M4
M5
M48
M49
A40
A48
A449
A466
A4042
A470

Town plan: Cardiff p.117

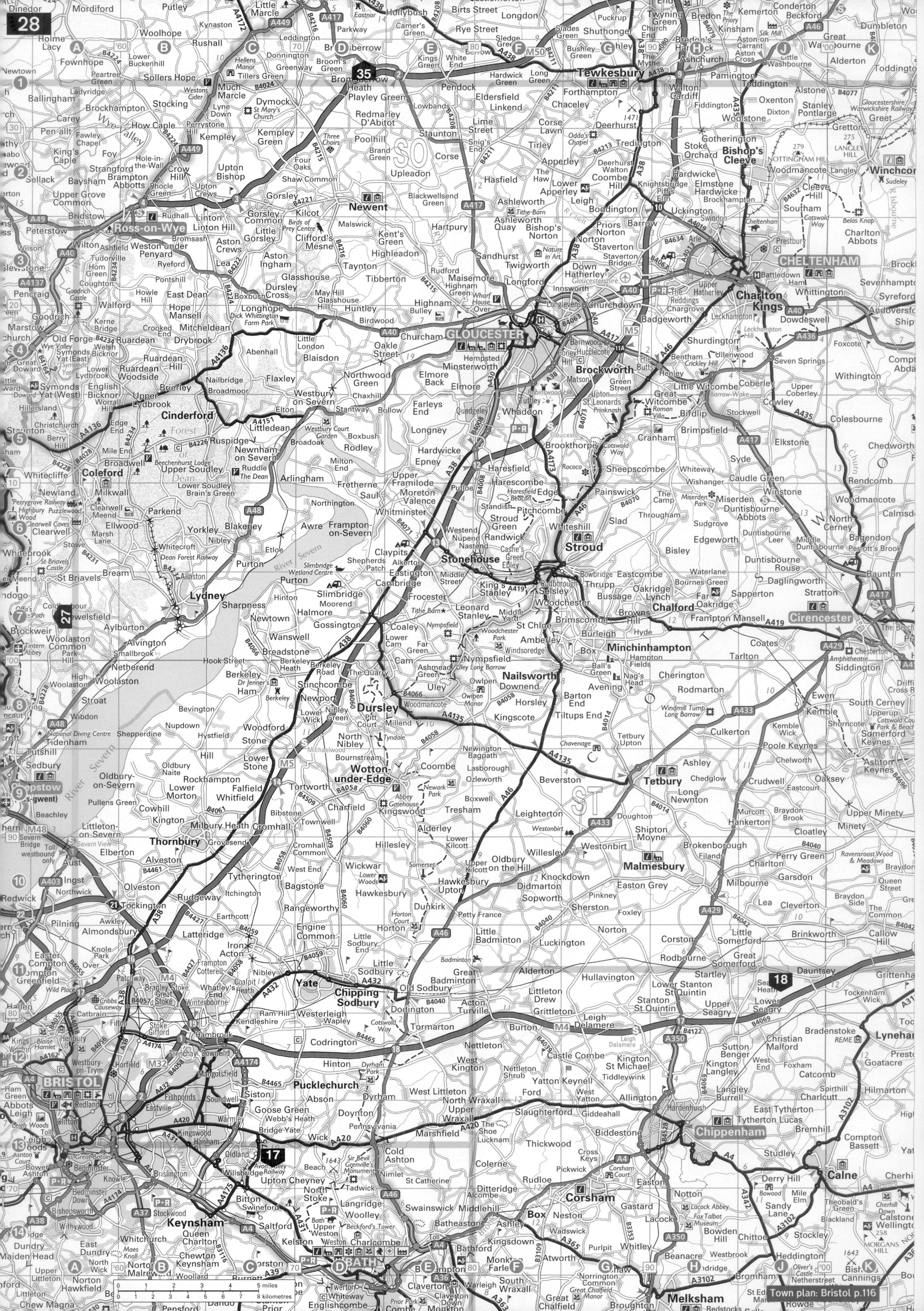

35
27
18
17
Tewkesbury
Bishop's Cleeve
CHELTENHAM
Charlton Kings
Winchcombe
Newent
Ross-on-Wye
GLOUCESTER
Brockworth
Cinderford
Coleford
Lydney
Stonehouse
Stroud
Nailsworth
Minchinhampton
Chalford
Cirencester
Dursley
Wotton-under-Edge
Tetbury
Malmesbury
Thornbury
Chepstow
Yate
Chipping Sodbury
BRISTOL
Keynsham
BATH
Corsham
Chippenham
Calne
Melksham
Ledbury
Upton Bishop
Mitcheldean
Newnham on Severn
Sharpness
Berkeley
Frampton-on-Severn
Painswick
Bisley
Sapperton
Kemble
Badminton
Marshfield
Pucklechurch
Box
Lacock
Hullavington
Sherston
Didmarton
Leighterton
River Severn
Forest of Dean
Cotswold Way
M4
M5
M32
M48
M50
A38
A46
A417
A419
A429
A433
A4135
A40
A48
A449
A4136
A420
A4
A350
SO
ST
0 1 2 3 4 5 miles
0 1 2 3 4 5 6 7 8 kilometres

Town plan: Bristol p.116

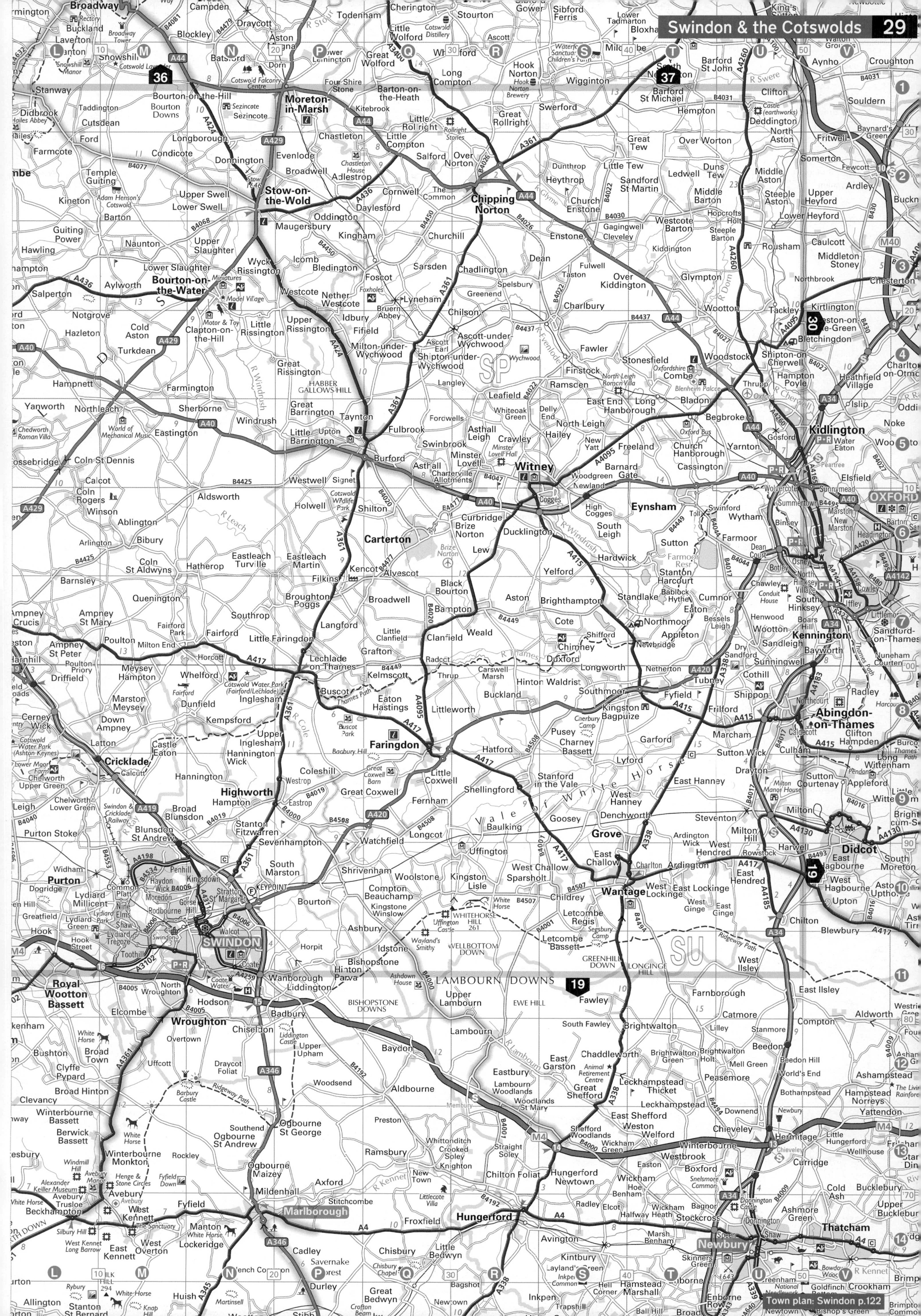
Broadway
Moreton-in-Marsh
Stow-on-the-Wold
Chipping Norton
Bourton-on-the-Water
Burford
Witney
Carterton
Eynsham
Kidlington
OXFORD
Abingdon-on-Thames
Kennington
Faringdon
Highworth
Cricklade
SWINDON
Royal Wootton Bassett
Wroughton
Wantage
Grove
Didcot
Marlborough
Hungerford
Newbury
Thatcham
LAMBOURN DOWNS
Vale of White Horse
SP
SU
36
37
30
19

Town plan: Swindon p.122

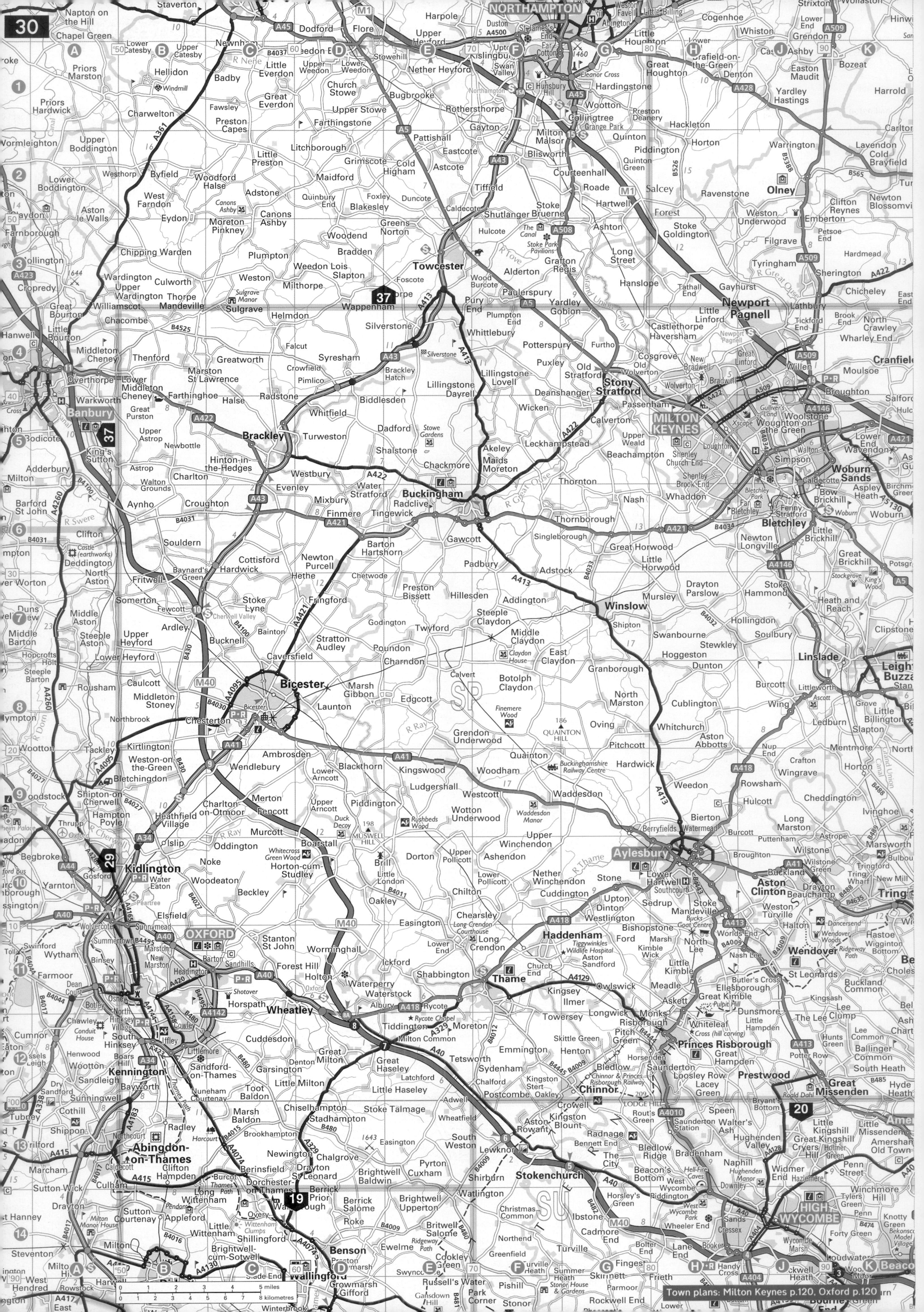
NORTHAMPTON
Napton on the Hill
Staverton
Chapel Green
Lower Catesby
Upper Catesby
Newnham
Dodford
Flore
Harpole
Duston
Cogenhoe
Strixton
Priors Marston
Hellidon
Badby
Little Everdon
Upper Weedon
Lower Weedon
Stowehill
Nether Heyford
Upper Heyford
Kislingbury
Swan Valley
Hunsbury Hill
Hardingstone
Great Houghton
Little Houghton
Brafield-on-the-Green
Denton
Whiston
Lower End
Grendon
Easton Maudit
Bozeat
Yardley Hastings
Harrold
Priors Hardwick
Charwelton
Fawsley
Preston Capes
Great Everdon
Church Stowe
Upper Stowe
Bugbrooke
Rothersthorpe
Wootton
Collingtree
Grange Park
Preston Deanery
Hackleton
Farthingstone
Gayton
Milton Malsor
Quinton
Horton
Warrington
Lavendon
Cold Brayfield
Wormleighton
Upper Boddington
Litchborough
Pattishall
Eastcote
Blisworth
Piddington
Quinton Green
Olney
Lower Boddington
Westhorp
Byfield
Little Preston
Grimscote
Cold Higham
Astcote
Courteenhall
Woodford Halse
Maidford
Tiffield
Roade
Salcey
Ravenstone
Clifton Reynes
Newton Blossomville
Aston le Walls
West Farndon
Adstone
Quinbury End
Foxley
Duncote
Caldecote
Stoke Bruerne
Hartwell
Weston Underwood
Emberton
Claydon
Canons Ashby
Eydon
Blakesley
Shutlanger
Forest
Stoke Goldington
Petsoe End
Farnborough
Moreton Pinkney
Greens Norton
Hulcote
Ashton
Filgrave
Woodend
Bradden
Long Street
Chipping Warden
Plumpton
Towcester
Alderton
Grafton Regis
Tyringham
Hardmead
Mollington
Wardington
Upper Wardington
Culworth
Thorpe Mandeville
Weston
Weedon Lois
Slapton
Milthorpe
Foscote
Wood Burcote
Paulerspury
Hanslope
Tathall End
Gayhurst
Sherington
Chicheley
Cropredy
Sulgrave
Williamscot
Helmdon
Wappenham
Pury End
Plumpton End
Yardley Gobion
Little Linford
Newport Pagnell
Lathbury
Great Bourton
Little Bourton
Chacombe
Silverstone
Whittlebury
Potterspury
Castlethorpe
Haversham
Tickford End
Brook End
North Crawley
Hanwell
Middleton Cheney
Falcut
Syresham
Crowfield
Furtho
Cosgrove
Great Linford
Wharley End
Cranfield
Thenford
Greatworth
Pimlico
Brackley Hatch
Lillingstone Lovell
Old Stratford
New Bradwell
Willen
Moulsoe
Overthorpe
Marston St Lawrence
Lillingstone Dayrell
Stony Stratford
Deanshanger
Wolverton
Bradwell
Broughton
Banbury
Warkworth
Lower Middleton Cheney
Farthinghoe
Halse
Radstone
Biddlesden
Wicken
Passenham
Great Purston
Whitfield
Calverton
MILTON KEYNES
Woolstone
Woughton on the Green
Upper Astrop
Brackley
Turweston
Dadford
Stowe Gardens
Leckhampstead
Upper Weald
Loughton
Bodicote
Newbottle
Akeley
Shenley Church End
Wavendon
King's Sutton
Hinton-in-the-Hedges
Shalstone
Maids Moreton
Beachampton
Simpson
Adderbury
Astrop
Charlton
Westbury
Chackmore
Thornton
Shenley Brook End
Woburn Sands
Walton Grounds
Evenley
Water Stratford
Buckingham
Caldecotte
Aspley Heath
Barford St John
Aynho
Croughton
Mixbury
Radclive
Nash
Whaddon
Bletchley Park
Bow Brickhill
Woburn
Finmere
Tingewick
Thornborough
Fenny Stratford
Bletchley
Clifton
Souldern
Barton Hartshorn
Gawcott
Singleborough
Newton Longville
Little Brickhill
Deddington
Cottisford
Newton Purcell
Great Horwood
Great Brickhill
Castle (earthworks)
North Aston
Fritwell
Baynard's Green
Hardwick
Hethe
Chetwode
Padbury
Adstock
Little Horwood
Stockgrove
King's Wood
Duns Tew
Somerton
Preston Bissett
Hillesden
Drayton Parslow
Stoke Hammond
Heath and Reach
Stoke Lyne
Fringford
Addington
Mursley
Winslow
Middle Aston
Fewcott
Cherwell Valley
Steeple Claydon
Middle Barton
Steeple Aston
Ardley
Bainton
Godington
Twyford
Middle Claydon
Shipton
Hollingdon
Upper Heyford
Stratton Audley
Poundon
Claydon House
East Claydon
Swanbourne
Soulbury
Clipstone
Hopcrofts Holt
Bucknell
Caversfield
Charndon
Stewkley
Linslade
Lower Heyford
Hoggeston
Dunton
Steeple Barton
Granborough
Leighton Buzzard
Caulcott
Bicester
Calvert
Botolph Claydon
Burcott
Rousham
Marsh Gibbon
Littleworth
Ascott
Middleton Stoney
Launton
Edgcott
Finemere Wood
North Marston
Cublington
Grove
Little Billington
Wing
Northbrook
Chesterton
Grendon Underwood
QUAINTON HILL
Oving
Whitchurch
Ledburn
Slapton
Wootton
Tackley
Kirtlington
Aston Abbotts
Pitchcott
Nup End
Mentmore
Weston-on-the-Green
Ambrosden
Blackthorn
Kingswood
Quainton
Buckinghamshire Railway Centre
Hardwick
Crafton
Wendlebury
Lower Arncott
Woodham
Rowsham
Wingrave
Bletchingdon
Ludgershall
Weedon
Horton
Shipton-on-Cherwell
Westcott
Waddesdon
Cheddington
Woodstock
Merton
Hampton Poyle
Heathfield Village
Charlton-on-Otmoor
Fencott
Upper Arncott
Piddington
Wotton Underwood
Waddesdon Manor
Hulcott
Ivinghoe
Thrupp
Murcott
Duck Decoy
MUSWELL HILL
Rushbeds Wood
Long Marston
Bierton
Berryfields
Watermead
Burcott
Puttenham
Marsworth
Islip
Oddington
Boarstall
Whitecross Green Wood
Upper Winchendon
Astrope
Begbroke
Kidlington
Noke
Brill
Dorton
Upper Pollicott
Ashendon
Aylesbury
Broughton
Wilstone
Bulbourne
Water Eaton
Woodeaton
Horton-cum-Studley
Little London
Lower Pollicott
Nether Winchendon
Stone
Lower Hartwell
Southcourt
Buckland
Aston Clinton
Tring Wharf
New Mill
Tring
Yarnton
Beckley
Oakley
Chilton
Cuddington
Dinton
Sedrup
Stoke Mandeville
Drayton Beauchamp
Gosford
Elsfield
Upton
Westlington
Weston Turville
Wolvercote
Sunnymead
Easington
Chearsley
Long Crendon Courthouse
Haddenham
Bishopstone
Marsh
Bucks Goat Centre
Halton
Dancersend
Hastoe
Wigginton
OXFORD
Stanton St John
Lower End
Long Crendon
Tiggywinkles Wildlife Hospital
Aston Sandford
Ford
Kimble Wick
North Lee
Wendover
Wendover Woods
Summertown
Swinford
Wytham
Marston
Worminghall
Wigginton Bottom
Binsey
New Marston
Barton
Sandhills
Forest Hill
Ickford
Shabbington
Thame
Church End
Little Kimble
Nash Lee
Ridgeway Path
Headington
Holton
Waterperry
Meadle
Butler's Cross
St Leonards
Cholesbury
Farmoor
Dean Court
Shotover
Waterstock
Kingsey
Owlswick
Ellesborough
Buckland Common
Botley
Horspath
Wheatley
Albury
Rycote
Ilmer
Askett
Great Kimble
Kingsash
Osney
North Hinksey Village
Cowley
Rycote Chapel
Towersey
Longwick
Monks Risborough
Pulpit Hill
Dunsmore
Lee Clump
Chawley
Conduit House
Iffley
Tiddington
Moreton
Little Hampden
The Lee
Cumnor
South Hinksey
Milton Common
Skittle Green
Pitch Green
Whiteleaf Cross (hill carving)
Hunts Green
Lee Common
Boars Hill
Littlemore
Cuddesdon
Great Milton
Tetsworth
Emmington
Henton
Horsenden
Princes Risborough
Ballinger Common
Henwood
Wootton
Sandford-on-Thames
Denton
Great Haseley
Sydenham
Bledlow
Saunderton
Great Hampden
Potter Row
Kennington
Sandleigh
Garsington
Latchford
Chinnor & Princes Risborough Railway
Loosley Row
Lacey Green
Prestwood
South Heath
Dry Sandford
Bayworth
Nuneham Courtenay
Toot Baldon
Little Milton
Little Haseley
Chalford
Kingston Stert
Chinnor
Oakley
Great Missenden
Hyde Heath
Sunningwell
Postcombe
LODGE HILL
Cothill
Marsh Baldon
Chiselhampton
Stadhampton
Stoke Talmage
Adwell
Crowell
Roald Dahl
Bryant's Bottom
Tubney
Radley
Wheatfield
Aston Rowant
Kingston Blount
Rout's Green
Saunderton Station
Speen
Walter's Ash
Little Kingshill
Little Missenden
Amersham
Shippon
Northcourt
Harcourt
Brookhampton
Easington
South Weston
Radnage
Bennett End
Hughenden Valley
Great Kingshill
Holmer Green
Old Town
Abingdon-on-Thames
Marcham
Caldecott
Newington
Chalgrove
Lewknor
Stokenchurch
The City
Bledlow Ridge
Bradenham
Naphill
Cryers Hill
Culham
Clifton Hampden
Berinsfield
Drayton St Leonard
Brightwell Baldwin
Pyrton
Cuxham
Shirburn
Beacon's Bottom
Hell-Fire Caves
Hughenden Manor
Widmer End
Penn Street
Hazlemere
Sutton Wick
Long Wittenham
Burcot
Thames Path
Dorchester-on-Thames
Berrick Prior
Berrick Salome
Brightwell Upperton
Watlington
Horsley's Green
West Wycombe
Piddington
Downley
Winchmore Hill
Tylers Hill
Drayton
Pendon
Sutton Courtenay
Appleford
Overy
Warborough
Roke
Christmas Common
Ibstone
West Wycombe Park
Wheeler End
Sands
HIGH WYCOMBE
Cressex
Knotty Green
Milton Manor House
Little Wittenham
Wittenham Clumps
Shillingford
Britwell Salome
Northend
Cadmore End
Forty Green
Beaconsfield Model Village
Milton
Brightwell-cum-Sotwell
Benson
Preston Crowmarsh
Ewelme
Ridgeway Path
Cookley Green
Greenfield
Turville
Bolter End
Lane End
Booker
Wycombe Marsh
Loudwater
Steventon
Turville Heath
Fingest
Handy Cross
Cockwell Heath
Wooburn
Beacon
West Hendred
Rowstock
Harwell
Slade End
Wallingford
Crowmarsh Gifford
Swyncombe
Russell's Water
Park Corner
Pishill
Summer Heath
Stonor House & Gardens
Skirmett
Frieth
Parmoor
Rockwell End
Stonor
Gangsdown Hill
Winterbrook
East Hendred
SP
SU
0 1 2 3 4 5 miles
0 1 2 3 4 5 6 7 8 kilometres

Town plans: Milton Keynes p.120, Oxford p.120

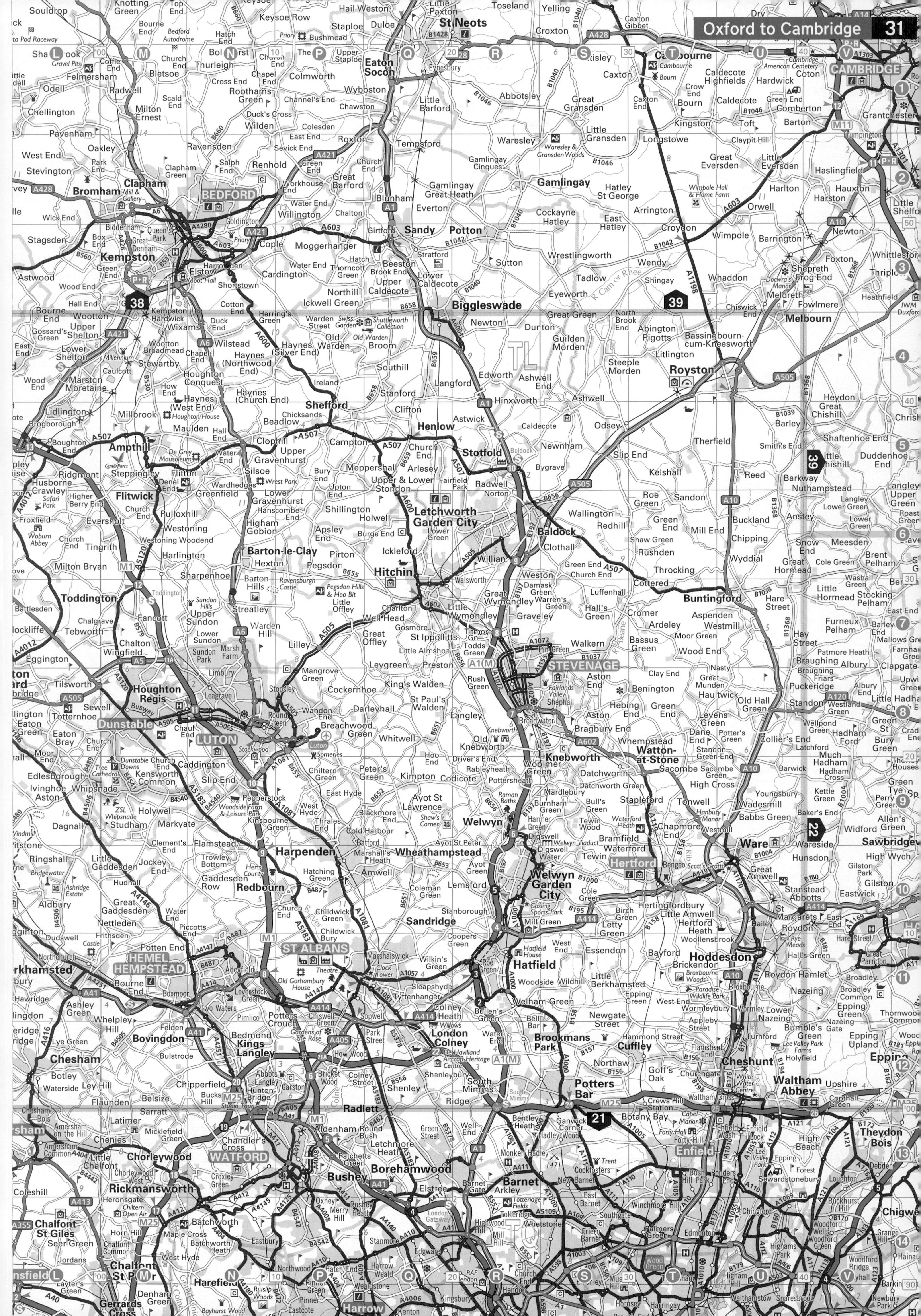

St Neots
Eaton Socon
Caxton Gibbet
Cambourne
CAMBRIDGE
BEDFORD
Bromham
Clapham
Kempston
Sandy
Potton
Gamlingay
Biggleswade
Royston
Melbourn
Shefford
Henlow
Stotfold
Ampthill
Flitwick
Letchworth Garden City
Baldock
Hitchin
Barton-le-Clay
Toddington
Buntingford
Houghton Regis
Dunstable
LUTON
STEVENAGE
Knebworth
Watton-at-Stone
Welwyn
Harpenden
Wheathampstead
Redbourn
Welwyn Garden City
Hertford
Ware
Sawbridgeworth
Hatfield
Hoddesdon
ST ALBANS
HEMEL HEMPSTEAD
Berkhamsted
Chesham
Bovingdon
Kings Langley
London Colney
Brookmans Park
Cuffley
Cheshunt
Waltham Abbey
Potters Bar
Radlett
WATFORD
Chorleywood
Rickmansworth
Borehamwood
Bushey
Barnet
Enfield
Theydon Bois
Epping
Chalfont St Giles
Chalfont St Peter
Harefield
Harrow

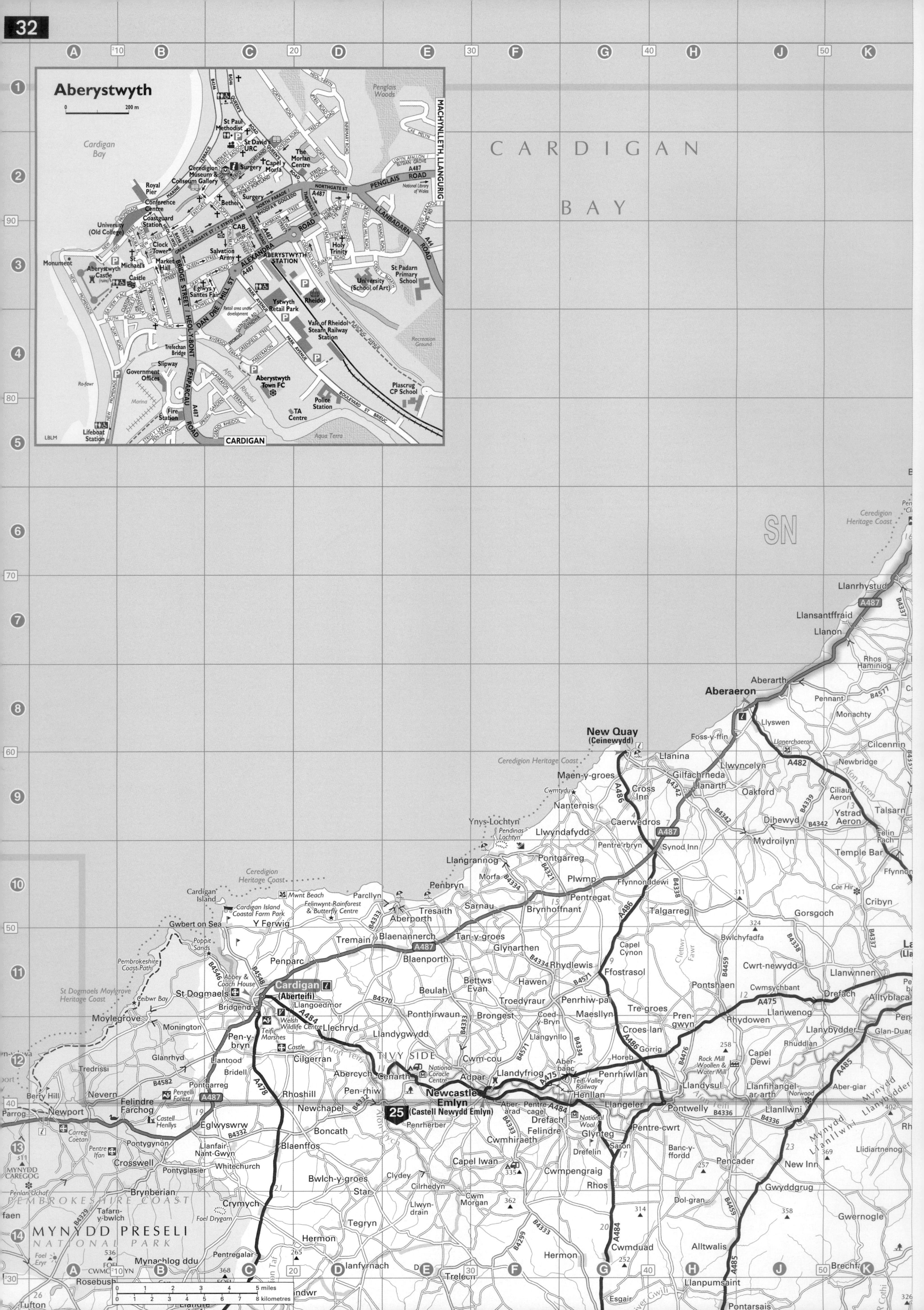
Aberystwyth
CARDIGAN BAY
SN
Aberaeron
New Quay (Ceinewydd)
Cardigan (Aberteifi)
Newcastle Emlyn
St Dogmaels
Newport
Moylegrove
Aberporth
Llangrannog
Llanarth
Llanon
Llansantffraid
Llanrhystud
Synod Inn
Llandysul
Henllan
Cenarth
Crymych
Boncath
Eglwyswrw
Cwmduad
Llanybydder
Pencader
Alltwalis
Brechfa
MYNYDD PRESELI
PEMBROKESHIRE COAST NATIONAL PARK
Ceredigion Heritage Coast
25 (Castell Newydd Emlyn)
A487
A484
A486
A475
A478
A485
A482
0 1 2 3 4 5 miles
0 1 2 3 4 5 6 7 8 kilometres

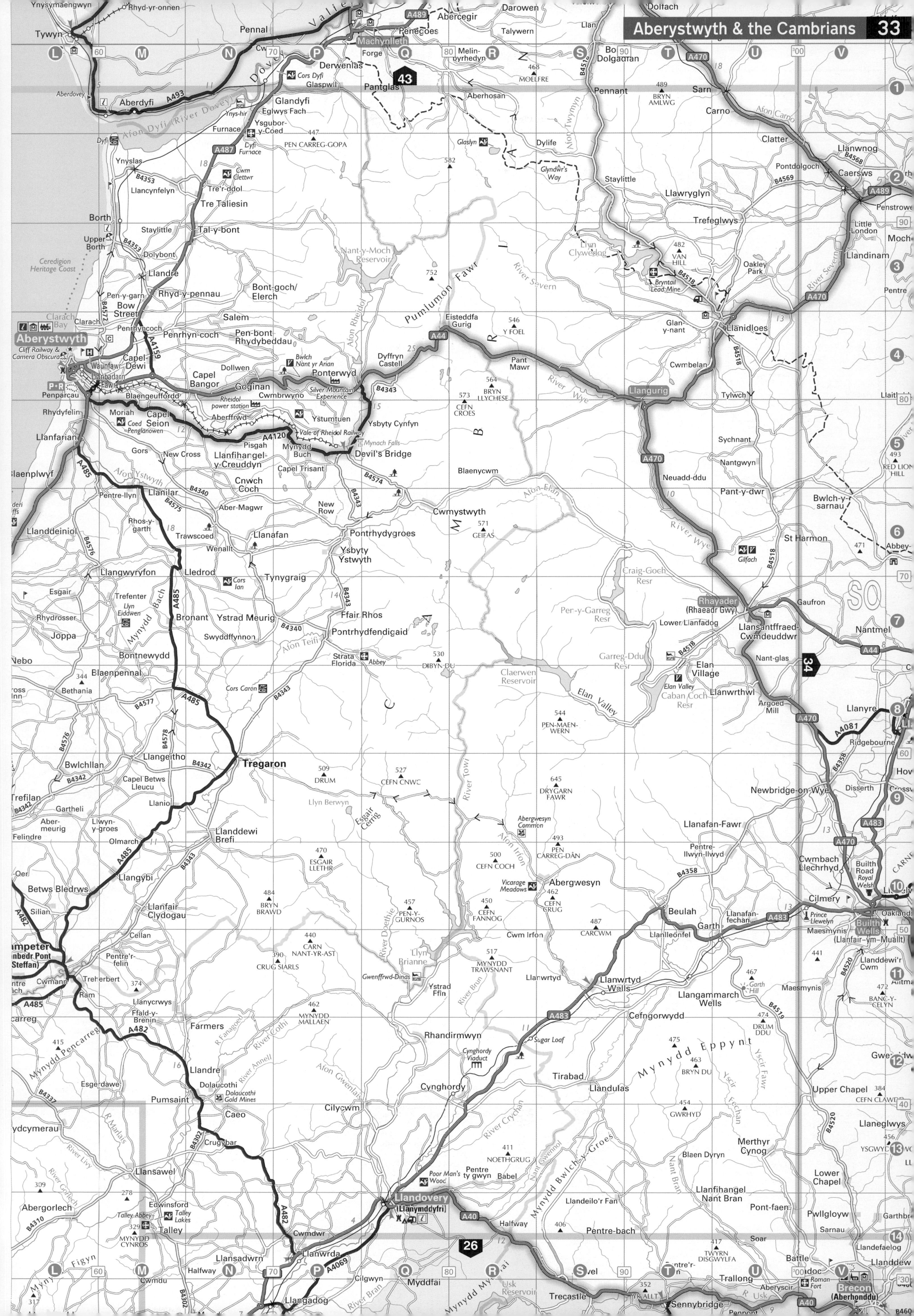
Aberystwyth
Machynlleth
Aberdyfi
Borth
Tal-y-bont
Bow Street
Llanidloes
Llangurig
Devil's Bridge
Pontrhydfendigaid
Rhayader
(Rhaeadr Gwy)
Elan Village
Tregaron
Lampeter
Llanddewi Brefi
Abergwesyn
Beulah
Builth Wells
(Llanfair-ym-Muallt)
Llanwrtyd Wells
Llangammarch Wells
Llandovery
(Llanymddyfri)
Brecon
(Aberhonddu)
Sennybridge
Llangadog
Pumsaint
Talley
Cynghordy
Rhandirmwyn
Ystrad Ffin
Llyn Brianne
Claerwen Reservoir
Nant-y-Moch Reservoir
Pumlumon Fawr
Mynydd Eppynt
Elan Valley
River Wye
River Severn
Ponterwyd
Ysbyty Ystwyth
Pontrhydygroes
Cwmystwyth
Strata Florida
Newbridge-on-Wye
Llanafan-Fawr
St Harmon
Carno
Caersws
Llanwnog
Trefeglwys
Llanbrynmair
Dylife
Staylittle
Llanfarian
Llanilar
Lledrod
Bronant
Llangeitho
Llanybydder
Cwrt-y-Cadno
Caeo
Llansawel
Crugybar
Llanwrda
Myddfai
Trecastle
Llangynidr
Merthyr Cynog
Upper Chapel
Llandeilo'r Fan
Pentre-bach
Tirabad
Llandulas
Garth
Cilmery
A44
A470
A483
A485
A487
A4120
A482
A40
43
34
26

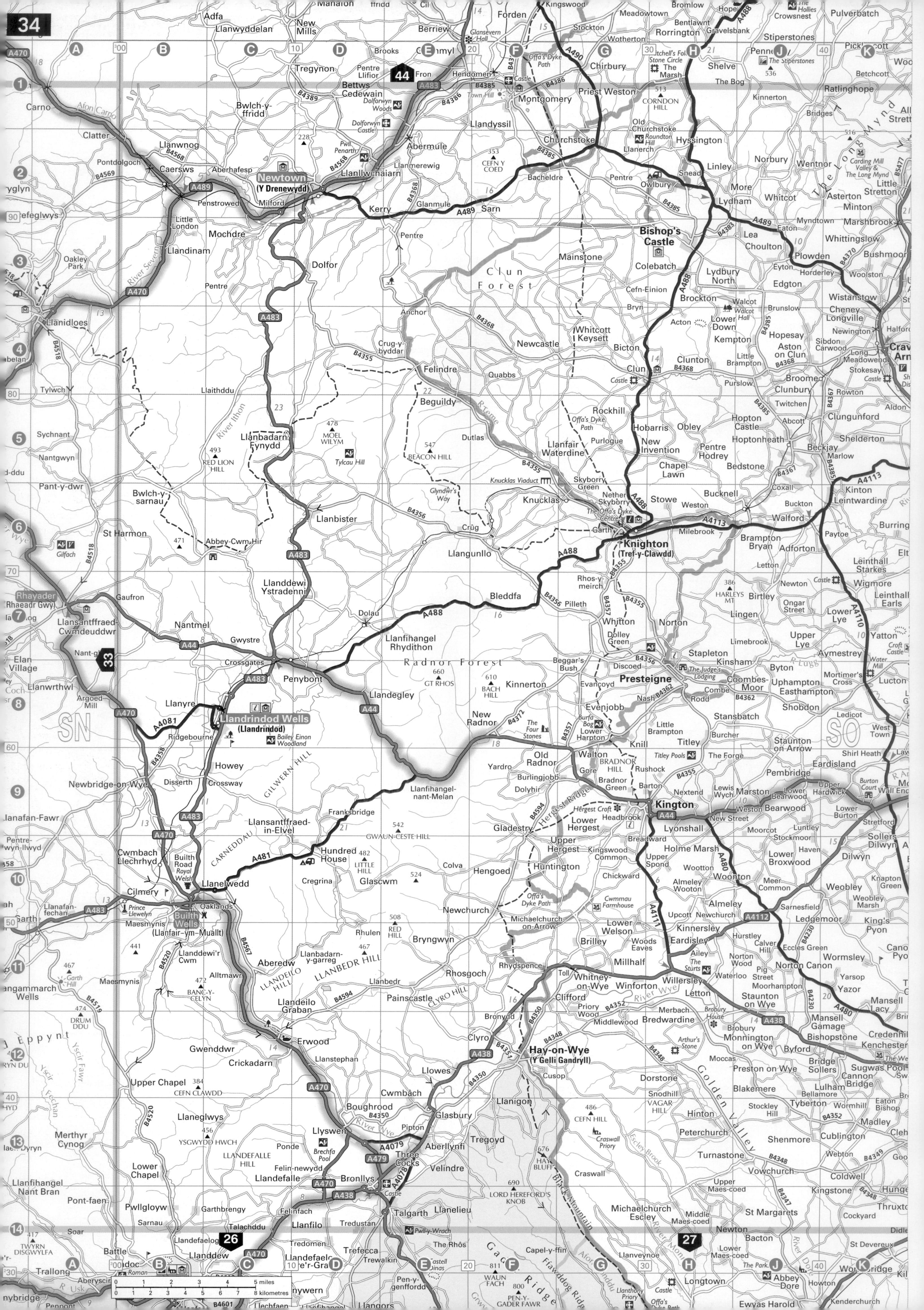
Adfa
Llanwyddelan
New Mills
Berriew
Forden
Kingswood
Meadowtown
Bromlow
Bentlawnt
Gravelsbank
Rorrington
Hope
Crowsnest
Pulverbatch
Glansevern Hall
Stockton
Wotherton
Stiperstones
Tregynon
Pentre Llifior
Brooks
Fron
Hendomen
Chirbury
Shelve
The Stiperstones
The Bog
Betchcott
Carno
Afon Carno
Bettws Cedewain
Dolforwyn Woods
Dolforwyn Castle
Montgomery
Priest Weston
Corndon Hill
Ratlinghope
Bwlch-y-ffridd
Town Hill
Kinnerton
Bridges
Clatter
Llandyssil
Old Churchstoke
Roundton Hill
Churchstoke
Hyssington
The Long Mynd
Llanwnog
Pontdolgoch
Caersws
Aberhafesp
Newtown (Y Drenewydd)
Pwll Penarth
Abermule
Llanmerewig
Cefn y Coed
Llanerch
Norbury
Wentnor
Carding Mill Valley & The Long Mynd
Linley
Bacheldre
Pentre
Owlbury
Snead
More
Whitcot
Asterton
Little Stretton
Minton
Penstrowed
Milford
Llanllwchaiarn
Glanmule
Kerry
Sarn
Lydham
Myndtown
Marshbrook
Little London
Mochdre
Pentre
Bishop's Castle
Lea
Eaton
Choulton
Whittingslow
Plowden
Bushmoor
Llandinam
Oakley Park
River Severn
Dolfor
Mainstone
Colebatch
Lydbury North
Eyton
Horderley
Woolston
Clun Forest
Edgton
Llanidloes
Pentre
Anchor
Cefn-Einion
Brockton
Walcot
Wistanstow
Brunslow
Cheney Longville
Bryn
Acton
Lower Down
Newington
Halford
Craven Arms
Whitcott Keysett
Kempton
Hopesay
Aston on Clun
Sibdon Carwood
Crug-y-byddar
Newcastle
Bicton
Clunton
Little Brampton
Long Meadowend
Stokesay Castle
Felindre
Quabbs
Clun Castle
Purslow
Broome
Clunbury
Tylwch
Llaithddu
Rowton
Beguildy
Rockhill
Twitchen
Aldon
Hopton Castle
Abcott
Clungunford
Sychnant
Llanbadarn Fynydd
River Ithon
Moel Wilym
Beacon Hill
Dutlas
River Teme
Offa's Dyke Path
Hobarris
Obley
Hoptonheath
Shelderton
Nantgwyn
Red Lion Hill
Tylcau Hill
Llanfair Waterdine
Purlogue
New Invention
Pentre Hodrey
Beckjay
Marlow
Bedstone
Chapel Lawn
Knucklas Viaduct
Skyborry Green
Pant-y-dwr
Glyndŵr's Way
Bwlch-y-sarnau
Knucklas
Nether Skyborry
Stowe
Bucknell
Coxall
Buckton
Kinton
Leintwardine
Llanbister
Weston
Walford
Burrington
St Harmon
Gilfach
Abbey-Cwm-Hir
Crûg
Garth
Knighton (Tref-y-Clawdd)
Milebrook
Brampton Bryan
Paytoe
Adforton
Llangunllo
Letton
Leinthall Starkes
Rhayader (Rhaeadr Gwy)
Gaufron
Llanddewi Ystradenni
Rhos-y-meirch
Pilleth
Harley's Mt
Birtley
Newton
Wigmore
Leinthall Earls
Llansantffraed-Cwmdeuddwr
Nantmel
Bleddfa
Whitton
Ongar Street
Lingen
Lower Lye
Elan Village
Gwystre
Dolau
Llanfihangel Rhydithon
Dolley Green
Norton
Limebrook
Upper Lye
Yatton
Aymestrey
Croft Castle
Crossgates
Penybont
Radnor Forest
Gt Rhos
Bach Hill
Beggar's Bush
Discoed
Stapleton
The Judge's Lodging
Kinsham
Byton
River Lugg
Mortimer's Cross
Lucton
Llanwrthwl
Argoed Mill
Llanyre
Llandegley
Kinnerton
Presteigne
Evancoyd
Nash
Rodd
Coombes-Moor
Combe
Uphampton
Easthampton
Llandrindod Wells (Llandrindod)
Ridgebourne
Bailey Einon Woodland
New Radnor
The Four Stones
Burfa Bog
Evenjobb
Lower Harpton
Little Brampton
Stansbatch
Shobdon
Ledicot
Knill
Titley
Burcher
Staunton on Arrow
West Town
Howey
Gilwern Hill
Old Radnor
Yardro
Walton
Titley Pools
The Forge
Shirl Heath
Eardisland
Newbridge-on-Wye
Disserth
Crossway
Burlingjobb
Bradnor Hill
Rushock
Gore
Bradnor Green
Pembridge
Dolyhir
Barton
Nextend
Lewis Wych
Marston
Lower Bearwood
Upper Hardwick
Burton Court
Wall End
Llanafan-Fawr
Llanfihangel-nant-Melan
Franksbridge
Hergest Ridge
Hergest Croft
Headbrook
Kington
Weston
Bearwood
Lower Burton
Llansantffraed-in-Elvel
Gladestry
Lower Hergest
New Street
Lyonshall
Moorcot
Luntley
Stretford
Gwaun-Ceste Hill
Carneddau
Upper Hergest
Breadward
Stockmoor
Sollers Dilwyn
Pentre-Ty-wyn-llwyd
Cwmbach Llechrhyd
Builth Road
Royal Welsh
Hundred House
Little Hill
Colva
Kingswood Common
Holme Marsh
Haven
Lower Broxwood
Dilwyn
Hengoed
Huntington
Upper Spond
Wootton
Chickward
Almeley Wooton
Woonton
Meer Common
Weobley
Knapton Green
Llanelwedd
Cregrina
Glascwm
Cilmery
Prince Llewelyn
Oaklands
Offa's Dyke Path
Cwmmau Farmhouse
Almeley
Sarnesfield
Weobley Marsh
Llanafan-fechan
Maesmynis
Builth Wells (Llanfair-ym-Muallt)
Newchurch
Michaelchurch-on-Arrow
Upcott
Newchurch
Kinnersley
Ledgemoor
King's Pyon
Garth
Red Hill
Rhulen
Bryngwyn
Lower Welson
Brilley
Woods Eaves
Eardisley
Hurstley
Calver Hill
Eccles Green
Canon Pyon
Llanddewi'r Cwm
Aberedw
Llanbadarn-y-garreg
Llanbedr Hill
Rhosgoch
Rhydspence
Millhalf
Ailey
The Sturts
Norton Wood
Pig Street
Norton Canon
Wormsley
Llangammarch Wells
Garth Hill
Maesmynis
Alltmawr
Bang-y-Celyn
Llandeilo Hill
Llanbedr
Toll
Whitney-on-Wye
Winforton
Willersley
Waterloo
Moorhampton
Yarsop
Yazor
Drum Ddu
Llandeilo Graban
Painscastle
Clyro Hill
Clifford
Priory Wood
Letton
River Wye
Staunton on Wye
Mansell Lacy
Bronydd
Merbach
Bredwardine
Brobury House
Mansell Gamage
Bishopstone
Credenhill
Mynydd Eppynt
Erwood
Clyro
Middlewood
Brobury
Monnington on Wye
Byford
Kenchester
Gwenddwr
Crickadarn
Llanstephan
Hay-on-Wye (Y Gelli Gandryll)
Arthur's Stone
Moccas
Preston on Wye
Bridge Sollers
Sugwas Pool
The Weir
Cusop
Dorstone
Cannon Bridge
Upper Chapel
Cefn Clawdd
Llowes
Snodhill
Vagar Hill
Golden Valley
Blakemere
Lulham
Bellamore
Eaton Bishop
Cwmbach
Boughrood
Llanigon
Hinton
Stockley Hill
Tyberton
Wormhill
Llaneglwys
Glasbury
Cefn Hill
Madley
Ysgwydd Hwch
Llyswen
River Wye
Pipton
Tregoyd
Craswall Priory
Escley Brook
Peterchurch
Cublington
Shenmore
Merthyr Cynog
Ponde
Brechfa Pool
Aberllynfi
Three Cocks
Turnastone
Webton
Llandefalle Hill
Felin-newydd
Velindre
Hay Bluff
Craswall
Vowchurch
Coldwell
Lower Chapel
Llandefalle
Bronllys
Bronllys Castle
Lord Hereford's Knob
Black Mountain
Upper Maes-coed
Kingstone
Llanfihangel Nant Bran
Pont-faen
Pwllgloyw
Garthbrengy
Felinfach
Talgarth
Llanelieu
Michaelchurch Escley
Middle Maes-coed
St Margarets
Cockyard
Thruxton
Sarnau
Llanfilo
Tredustan
Pwll-y-Wrach
Newton
Soar
Talachddu
Llandefaelog
Tredomen
Trefecca
The Rhôs
Bacton
St Devereux
Twyn Disgwylfa
Llanddew
Llandefaelo
Trewalkin
Capel-y-ffin
Llanveynoe
Lower Maes-coed
River Dore
Battle
Trallong
Aberyscir
Roman Fort
Castell Dinas
Gader Ridge
Afon Honddu
The Park
Abbey Dore
Wormbridge
River Usk
Waun Fach
Pen-y-genffordd
Llangors
Pen-y-Gader Fawr
Longtown
Llanthony Priory
Longtown Castle
Offa's Dyke Path
Ewyas Harold
Kenderchurch
Howton
Penpont
Llechfaen
SN
SO
0 1 2 3 4 5 miles
0 1 2 3 4 5 6 7 8 kilometres

44
33
26
27

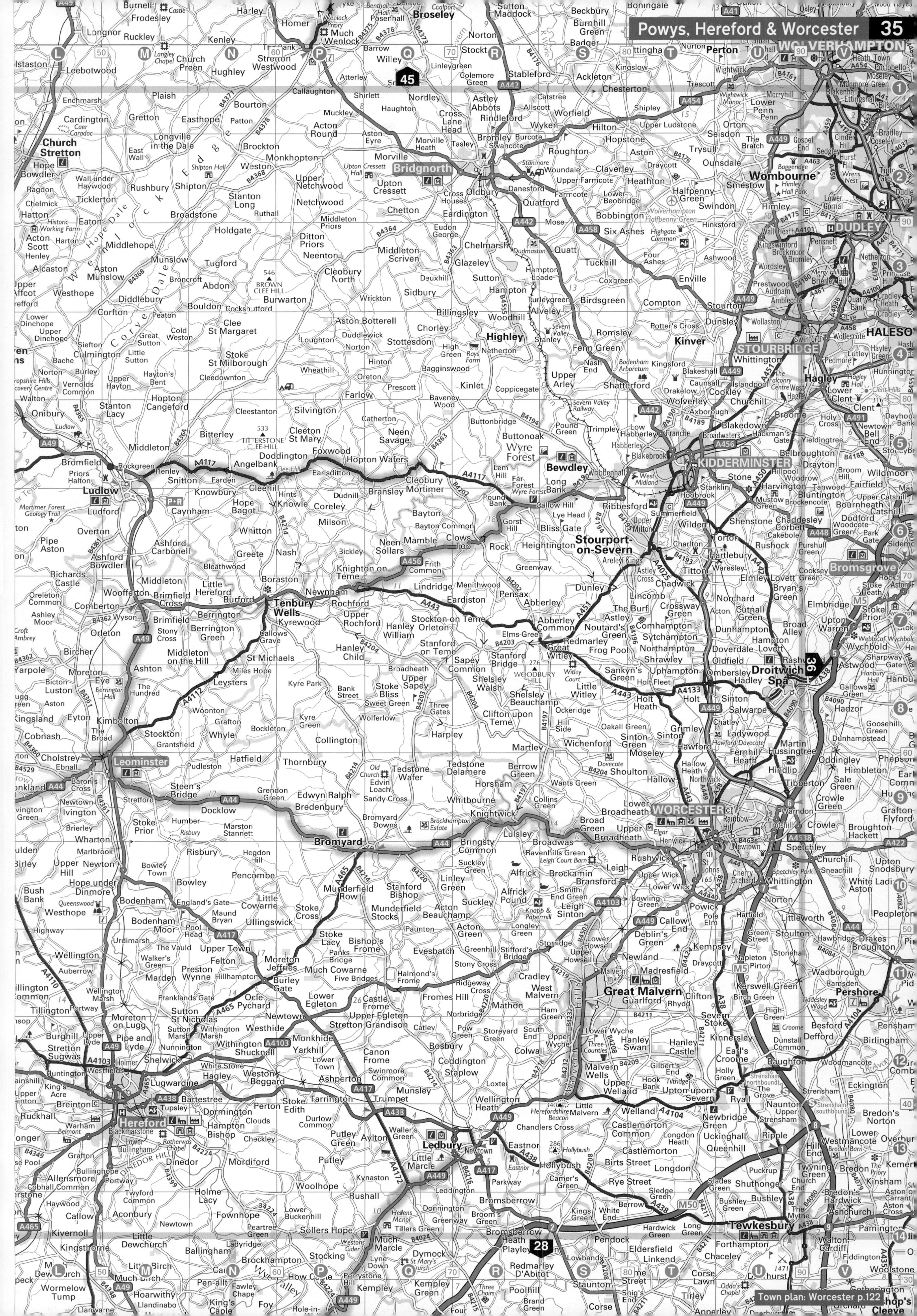
Church Stretton
Bridgnorth
Broseley
Much Wenlock
Wolverhampton
Wombourne
Dudley
Stourbridge
Kinver
Highley
Bewdley
Kidderminster
Stourport-on-Severn
Bromsgrove
Hagley
Ludlow
Tenbury Wells
Leominster
Droitwich Spa
Worcester
Bromyard
Great Malvern
Pershore
Hereford
Ledbury
Tewkesbury
Wyre Forest
A49
A44
A4103
A438
A449
A442
A456
A4117
A443
A465
A417
M5
M50

Town plan: Worcester p.122

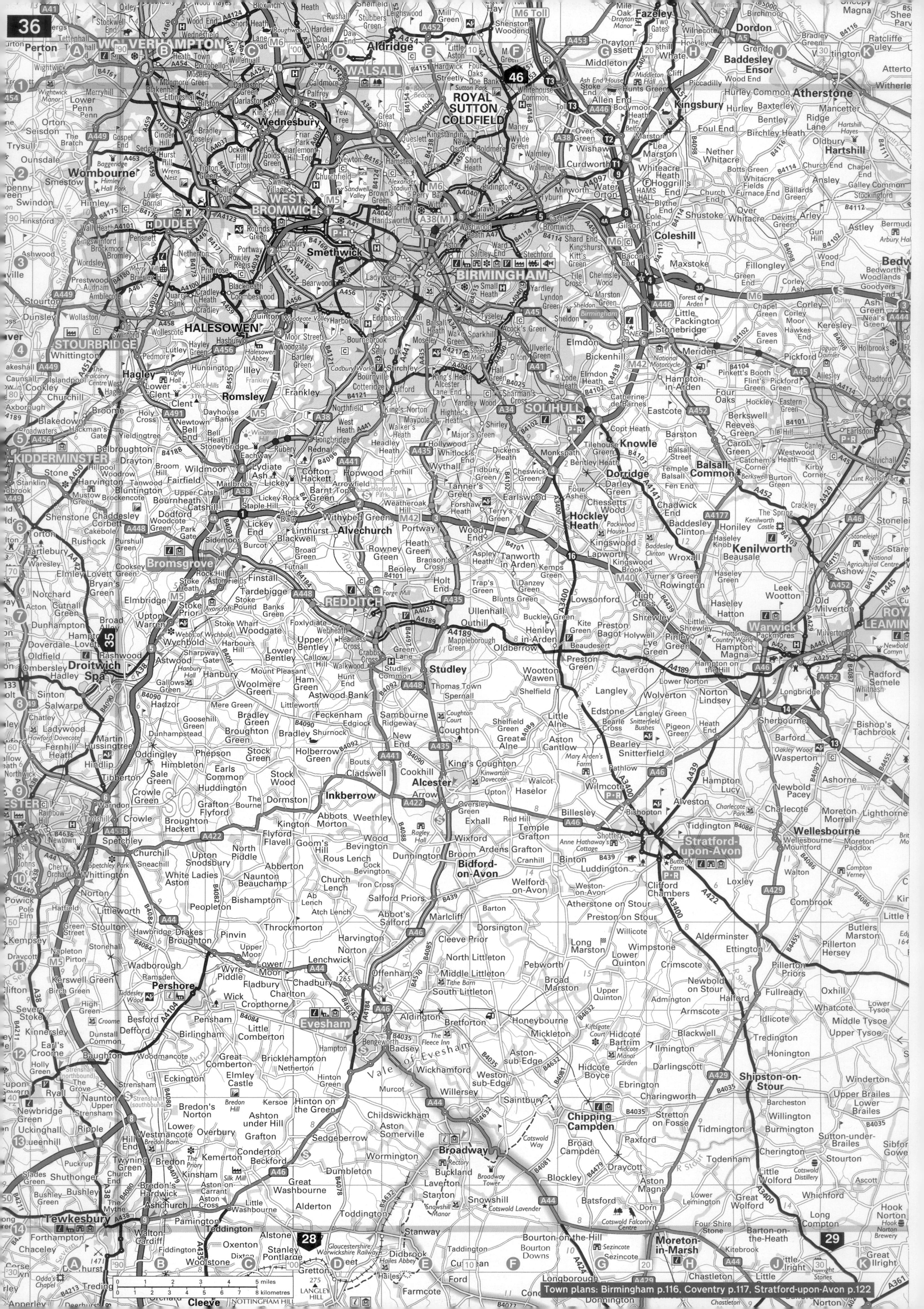

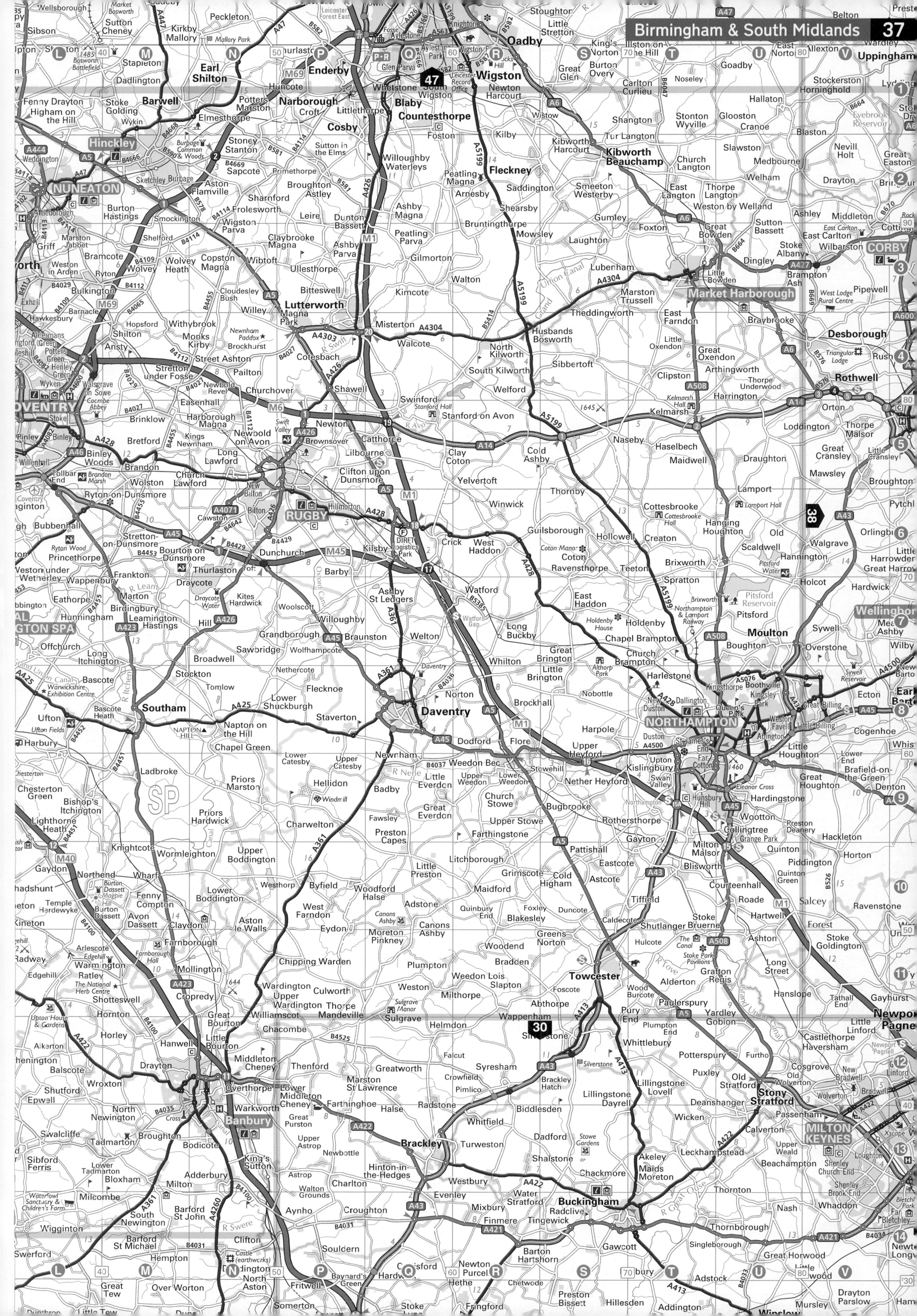
Oadby
Wigston
Enderby
Earl Shilton
Barwell
Hinckley
NUNEATON
Narborough
Blaby
Countesthorpe
Cosby
Kibworth Beauchamp
Fleckney
Lutterworth
Market Harborough
Desborough
Rothwell
CORBY
RUGBY
Daventry
NORTHAMPTON
Moulton
Southam
Towcester
Brackley
Buckingham
Banbury
Stony Stratford
MILTON KEYNES
Uppingham
M1
M6
M45
M40
M69
A5
A14
A45
A43
A422
A361
A5199
A4304
A508
A6
A421
A413
SP
38
47
30

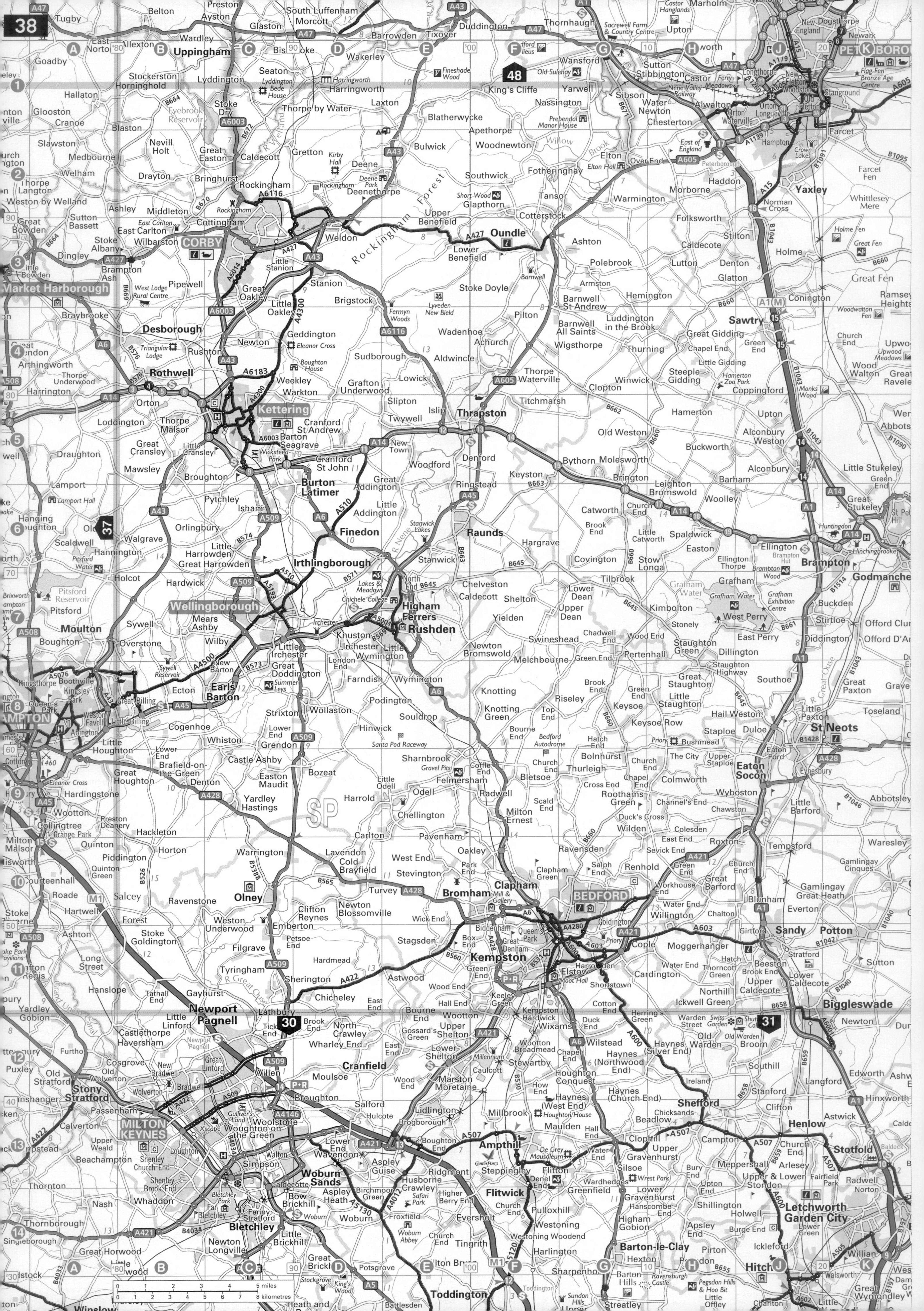
A47
Tugby
Belton
Preston
Ayston
South Luffenham
Morcott
Glaston
A43
Duddington
Thornhaugh
A47
Castor Hanglands
Marholm
Sacrewell Farm & Country Centre
Upton
New England
Dogsthorpe
Newark
PETERBOROUGH
East Norton
Allexton
Wardley
Uppingham
Bisbrooke
Barrowden
Tixover
Wakerley
Wittering
Wansford
Sutton
Stibbington
Castor
Longthorpe
Flag Fen Bronze Age Centre
Goadby
Stockerston
Horninghold
Lyddington
Seaton
Harringworth
Fineshade Wood
King's Cliffe
Old Sulehay
Yarwell
Sibson
Water Newton
Alwalton
Orton Waterville
Orton Longueville
Stanground
Hallaton
Lyddington Bede House
Eyebrook Reservoir
Stoke Dry
Thorpe by Water
Laxton
Nassington
Prebendal Manor House
Chesterton
Glooston
Cranoe
Blaston
A6003
Blatherwycke
Apethorpe
East of England
Hampton
Farcet
Slawston
Medbourne
Nevill Holt
Great Easton
Caldecott
Gretton
Kirby Hall
Deene
Bulwick
Woodnewton
Willow Brook
Elton
Elton Hall
Over End
Peterborough
Crown Lakes
Welham
Drayton
Bringhurst
Rockingham
Deene Park
Deenethorpe
Southwick
Fotheringhay
Haddon
Farcet Fen
Thorpe Langton
Weston by Welland
A6116
Rockingham Forest
Short Wood
Glapthorn
Tansor
Warmington
Morborne
Norman Cross
Yaxley
Great Bowden
Sutton Bassett
Ashley
Middleton
East Carlton
Cottingham
Upper Benefield
Weldon
Cotterstock
Folksworth
Whittlesey Mere
Stoke Albany
Wilbarston
CORBY
A427
Oundle
Ashton
Stilton
Holme Fen
Dingley
Brampton Ash
Little Bowden
Market Harborough
Little Stanion
Lower Benefield
Polebrook
Caldecote
Holme
Great Fen
West Lodge Rural Centre
Pipewell
Great Oakley
Stanion
Barnwell
Stoke Doyle
Armston
Lutton
Denton
Glatton
Great Fen
Little Oakley
A4300
Brigstock
Fermyn Woods
Lyveden New Bield
Barnwell St Andrew
Hemington
Conington
Ramsey Heights
Braybrooke
Desborough
A6003
Geddington
Eleanor Cross
Pilton
Barnwell All Saints
Luddington in the Brook
Sawtry
A1(M)
Woodwalton Fen
Arthingworth
Triangular Lodge
Rushton
Newton
Wadenhoe
Achurch
Wigsthorpe
Great Gidding
Chapel End
Green End
Church End
Upwood
Upwood Meadows
Rothwell
Boughton House
Sudborough
Aldwincle
Thurning
Little Gidding
Wood Walton
Thorpe Underwood
Harrington
A14
A6183
Weekley
Warkton
Grafton Underwood
Lowick
Thorpe Waterville
Winwick
Clopton
Steeple Gidding
Hamerton Zoo Park
Coppingford
Monks Wood
Great Raveley
Orton
Kettering
Slipton
Islip
Thrapston
Titchmarsh
Loddington
Thorpe Malsor
Cranford St Andrew
Twywell
Hamerton
Upton
Great Cransley
Little Cransley
A6003
Barton Seagrave
Wicksteed Park
Cranford St John
New Town
Denford
Old Weston
Alconbury Weston
Abbots Ripton
Draughton
Mawsley
Broughton
Burton Latimer
Great Addington
Woodford
Keyston
Bythorn
Molesworth
Brington
Buckworth
Alconbury
Little Stukeley
Lamport
Lamport Hall
Pytchley
Isham
Ringstead
Leighton Bromswold
Barham
Woolley
Great Stukeley
Hanging Houghton
Orlingbury
A509
A6
A510
Little Addington
A45
Catworth
Church End
A14
Huntingdon
Scaldwell
Walgrave
Hannington
Little Harrowden
Finedon
Stanwick Lakes
Raunds
Hargrave
Brook End
Little Catworth
Spaldwick
Ellington
Brampton
Pitsford Water
Great Harrowden
Irthlingborough
Stanwick
Covington
Stow Longa
Easton
Ellington Thorpe
Brampton Hut
Brampton Wood
Holcot
Hardwick
B571
Lakes & Meadows
North End
Chelveston
Caldecott
Shelton
Tilbrook
Grafham Water
Grafham
Godmanchester
Pitsford Reservoir
Brixworth
Pitsford
Wellingborough
Chichele College
Higham Ferrers
Rushden
Lower Dean
Upper Dean
Kimbolton
Grafham Exhibition Centre
Buckden
Moulton
Sywell
Mears Ashby
Irchester
Yielden
Stonely
West Perry
Stirtloe
Offord Cluny
Offord D'Arcy
Boughton
Overstone
Wilby
Knuston
Little Irchester
Chadwell End
Wood End
Swineshead
East Perry
Diddington
Newton Bromswold
Pertenhall
Staughton Green
Dillington
Sywell Reservoir
New Barton
Great Doddington
London End
Wymington
Melchbourne
Green End
Staughton Highway
Kingsthorpe
Boothville
Kingsley Park
A4500
Earls Barton
Summer Leys
Farndish
Brook End
Great Staughton
Southoe
Great Paxton
NORTHAMPTON
Weston Favell
Little Billing
Ecton
A45
Strixton
Wollaston
Podington
Knotting
Riseley
Little Staughton
Keysoe
Hail Weston
Little Paxton
Toseland
Abington
Cogenhoe
Lower End
Souldrop
Knotting Green
Top End
Keysoe Row
Staploe
Duloe
St Neots
Whiston
Grendon
Hinwick
Bourne End
Bedford Autodrome
Hatch End
Priory
Bushmead
Little Houghton
Lower End
Brafield-on-the-Green
Castle Ashby
Santa Pod Raceway
Sharnbrook
Gravel Pits
Coffle End
Church End
Bolnhurst
Thurleigh
Church End
The City
Upper Staploe
Eaton Ford
Eaton Socon
Eynesbury
Great Houghton
Denton
Easton Maudit
Bozeat
Felmersham
Bletsoe
Colmworth
Eleanor Cross
Hardingstone
A428
Yardley Hastings
Little Odell
Harrold
Odell
Radwell
Cross End
Chapel End
Roothams Green
Wyboston
Abbotsley
Wootton
Chellington
Milton Ernest
Scald End
Channel's End
Chawston
Little Barford
Collingtree
Preston Deanery
Hackleton
SP
Carlton
Pavenham
Duck's Cross
Wilden
Colesden
Milton Malsor
Quinton
Grange Park
Horton
Warrington
Lavendon
Oakley
East End
Sevick End
Roxton
Tempsford
Waresley
Piddington
Cold Brayfield
West End
Park End
Ravensden
Salph End
Renhold
Church End
Gamlingay Cinques
Quinton Green
Stevington
Clapham Green
Great Barford
Courteenhall
Roade
Salcey
Ravenstone
Olney
Turvey
A428
Bromham
Clapham
BEDFORD
Workhouse End
Blunham
Gamlingay
Great Heath
Hartwell
Forest
Clifton Reynes
Newton Blossomville
Mill & Gallery
Water End
Willington
Chalton
Everton
Stoke Bruerne
Weston Underwood
Emberton
Wick End
Biddenham
Goldington
A603
Girtford
Sandy
Potton
Ashton
Stoke Goldington
Petsoe End
Stagsden
Box End
Queen's Park
Priory
Cople
Moggerhanger
Long Street
Filgrave
Great Denham
Kempston
Hatch
Thorncote Green
Stratford
Beeston
Sutton
Grafton Regis
Tyringham
Hardmead
Green End
Elstow
Water End
Brook End
Lower Caldecote
Hanslope
Sherington
Astwood
Wood End
Harrowden
Cardington
Upper Caldecote
Tathall End
Gayhurst
Chicheley
Shortstown
Northill
Yardley Gobion
Newport Pagnell
Lathbury
East End
Hall End
Keeley Green
Cotton End
Ickwell Green
Biggleswade
Little Linford
Tickford End
Brook End
North Crawley
Bourne End
Wootton
Kempston Hardwick
Herring's Green
Warden Street
Swiss Garden
Shuttleworth Collection
Newton
Castlethorpe
Haversham
Newport Pagnell
Gossard's Green
Upper Shelton
Wixams
Duck End
Old Warden
Broom
Wharley End
East End
Lower Shelton
A421
Wootton Broadmead
Wilstead
Haynes (Silver End)
Furtho
Great Linford
Cranfield
Millennium
Chapel End
Haynes (Northwood End)
Southill
Cosgrove
New Bradwell
Willen
Caulcott
Stewartby
Houghton Conquest
Edworth
Puxley
Old Stratford
Old Wolverton
Bradwell
Moulsoe
Wood End
Marston Moretaine
Ireland
Langford
Stony Stratford
Wolverton
P+R
Broughton
How End
Haynes (West End)
Haynes (Church End)
Shefford
Stanford
Hinxworth
Passenham
A422
A509
A4146
Salford
Hulcote
Lidlington
Millbrook
Houghton House
Chicksands
Beadlow
Clifton
Henlow
Astwick
Calverton
MILTON KEYNES
Gulliver's Land
Xscape
Woolstone
Wavendon Gate
Woughton on the Green
Brogborough
Maulden
Hall End
Upper Weald
Loughton
Walton
Lower End
Wavendon
A421
Boughton End
A507
Ampthill
Clophill
Upper Gravenhurst
Campton
Stotfold
Beachampton
Shenley Church End
Simpson
Aspley Guise
De Grey Mausoleum
Water End
Silsoe
Meppershall
Arlesey
Shenley Brook End
Caldecotte
Woburn Sands
Husborne Crawley
Ridgmont
Steppingley
Flitton
Wardhedges
Wrest Park
Upper & Lower Stondon
Fairfield Park
Radwell
Thornton
Bletchley Park
Bow Brickhill
Aspley Heath
Birchmoor Green
Safari Park
Higher Berry End
Flitwick
Denel End
Greenfield
Lower Gravenhurst
Hanscombe End
Shillington
Holwell
Letchworth Garden City
Norton
Nash
Whaddon
Far Bletchley
Fenny Stratford
Woburn
Froxfield
Church End
Pulloxhill
Higham Gobion
Thornborough
Bletchley
Little Brickhill
Woburn Abbey
Eversholt
Westoning
Apsley End
Burge End
Lower Green
Singleborough
Newton Longville
Church End
Tingrith
Westoning Woodend
Barton-le-Clay
Ickleford
Great Horwood
Little Horwood
Great Brickhill
Potsgrove
Milton Bryan
Harlington
Pirton
Hexton
Hitchin
Willian
Stockgrove
King's Wood
Sharpenhoe
Barton Hills
Ravensburgh Castle
Pegsdon Hills & Hoo Bit
Offley
Walsworth
Great Wymondley
Toddington
Sundon Hills
Streatley
Little Wymondley
Winslow
Heath and Reach
Battlesden
Charlton
A1
A6
A5
M1
A600
A428
A45
A509
A5130
A4012
A421
B4034
A507
A505
A602
31
30
48
37
0 1 2 3 4 5 miles
0 1 2 3 4 5 6 7 8 kilometres

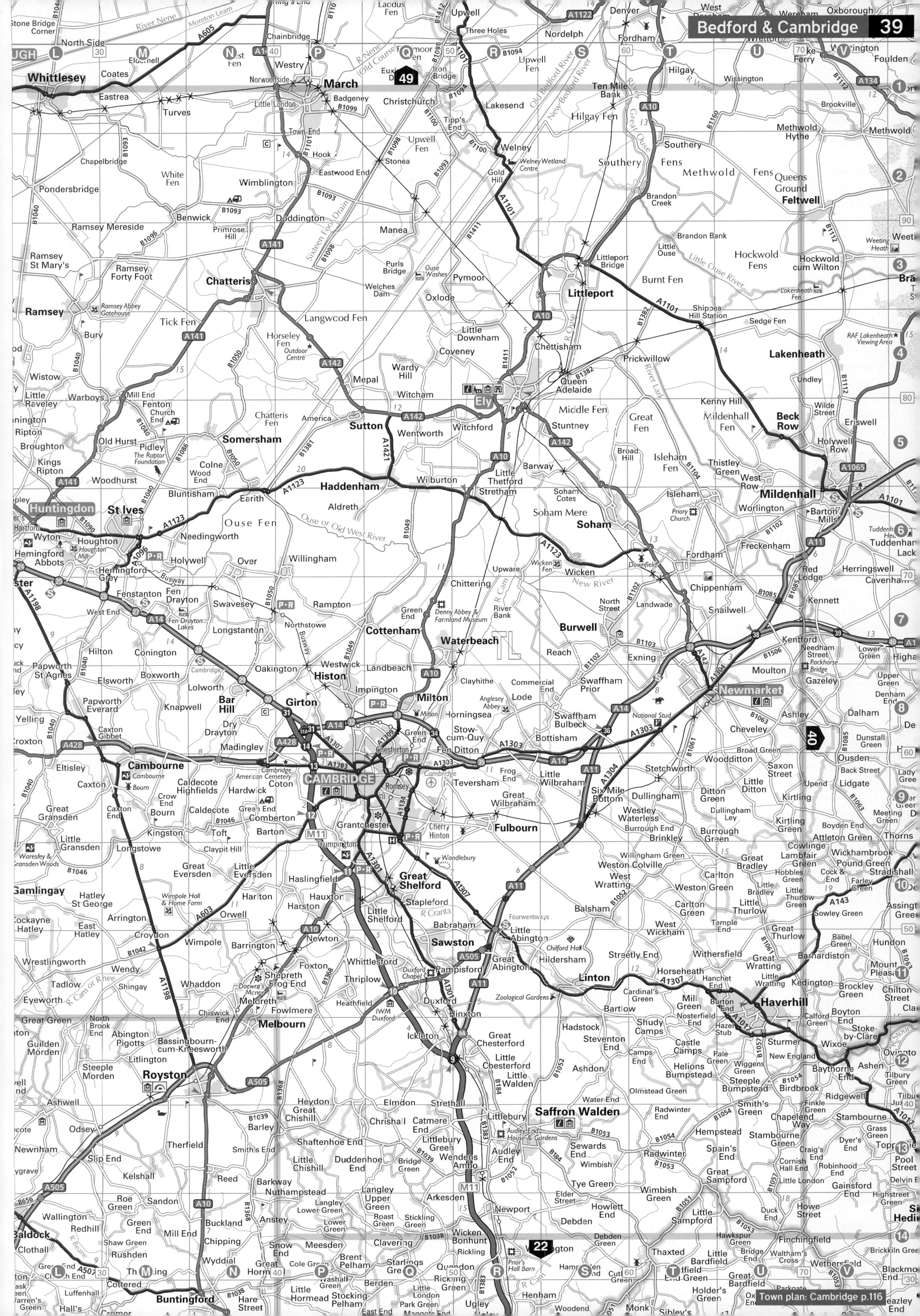

Whittlesey
March
Chatteris
Ramsey
Huntingdon
St Ives
Somersham
Haddenham
Sutton
Ely
Littleport
Soham
Mildenhall
Lakenheath
Feltwell
Burwell
Newmarket
Cottenham
Waterbeach
Histon
Girton
Milton
CAMBRIDGE
Cambourne
Bar Hill
Fulbourn
Great Shelford
Sawston
Linton
Haverhill
Melbourn
Royston
Saffron Walden
Buntingford
Baldock
Gamlingay
Welney
Manea
Chettisham
Prickwillow
Fordham
Chippenham
Kentford
Bottisham
Swaffham Bulbeck
Swaffham Prior
Teversham
Grantchester
Trumpington
Harston
Duxford
Ickleton
Great Chesterford
Littlebury
Audley End
Newport
Balsham
Horseheath
Steeple Bumpstead
Thaxted
Great Sampford
Barley
Therfield
Bassingbourn-cum-Kneesworth
Meldreth
Shepreth
Orwell
Harlton
Comberton
Madingley
Longstanton
Swavesey
Over
Willingham
Rampton
Oakington
Impington
Landbeach
Stretham
Wilburton
Witchford
Mepal
Earith
Bluntisham
Warboys
Pidley
Hemingford Grey
Hemingford Abbots
Houghton
Wyton
Fenstanton
Hilton
Papworth Everard
Elsworth
Caxton
Eltisley
Great Gransden
Longstowe
Toft
Kingston
Bourn
Arrington
Croydon
Wimpole
Barrington
Foxton
Fowlmere
Thriplow
Whittlesford
Pampisford
Babraham
Stapleford
Hauxton
Haslingfield
Newton
Wandlebury
Cherry Hinton
Great Wilbraham
Little Wilbraham
Stow-cum-Quy
Horningsea
Fen Ditton
Dullingham
Stetchworth
Cheveley
Ashley
Moulton
Gazeley
Dalham
Kirtling
Lidgate
Cowlinge
Great Bradley
Great Thurlow
Little Thurlow
Kedington
Withersfield
West Wickham
Weston Colville
West Wratting
Hildersham
Great Abington
Little Abington
Bartlow
Ashdon
Hadstock
Wimbish
Debden
Radwinter
Hempstead
Clavering
Arkesden
Elmdon
Heydon
Chrishall
Great Chishill
Reed
Barkway
Sandon
Kelshall
Wallington
Ashwell
Steeple Morden
Guilden Morden
Abington Pigotts
Litlington
Tadlow
Wrestlingworth
Hatley St George
East Hatley
Eyeworth
Wendy
Shingay
Whaddon
Town plan: Cambridge p.116

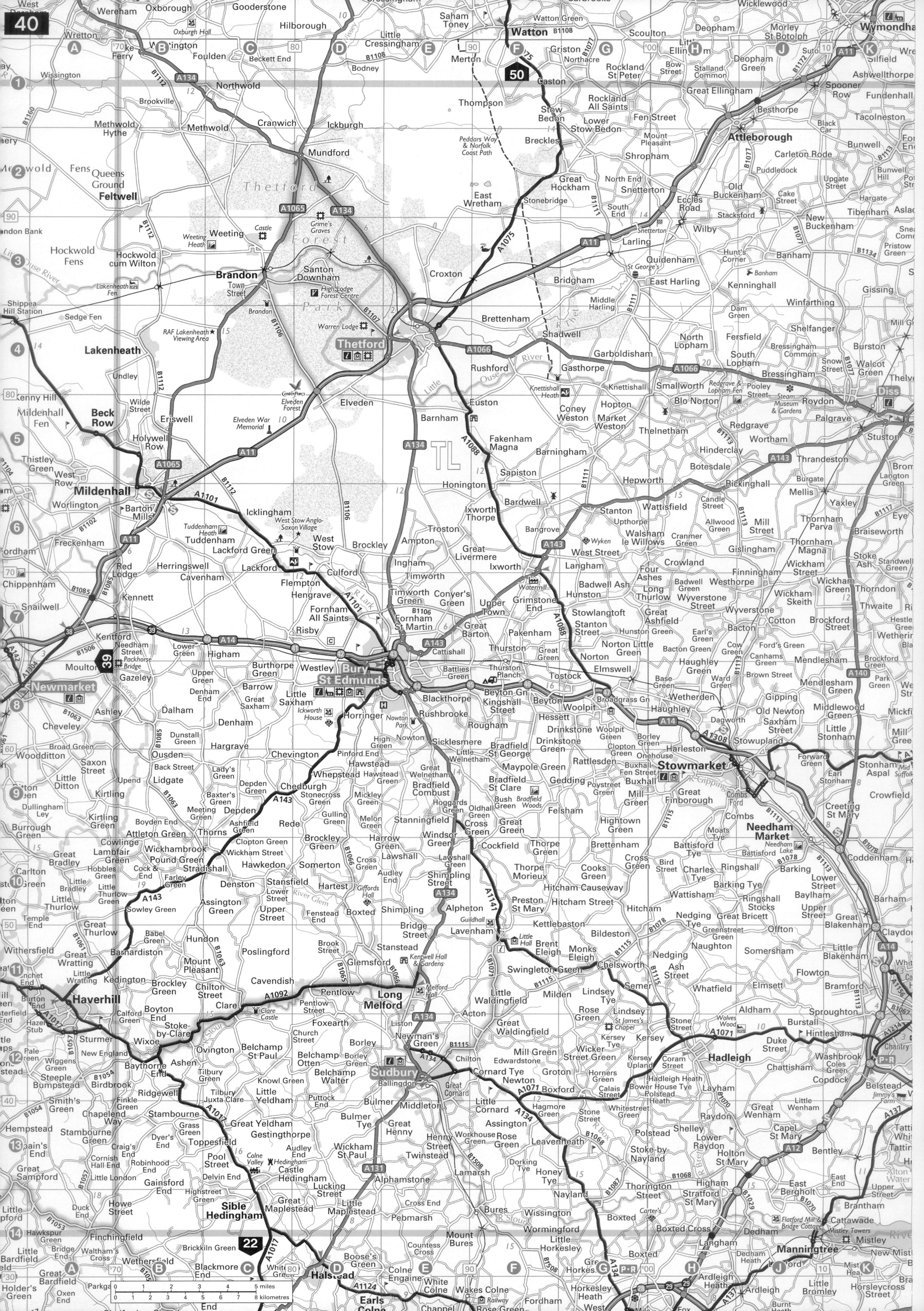
West Dereham
Wereham
Oxborough
Oxburgh Hall
Gooderstone
Hilborough
Little Cressingham
Saham Toney
Watton
Watton Green
Wicklewood
Morley St Botolph
Wymondham
Wretton
Stoke Ferry
Whittington
Foulden
Beckett End
Bodney
Merton
Griston
Northacre
Scoulton
Rockland St Peter
Deopham
Deopham Green
Little Ellingham
Bow Street
Stalland Common
Suton
Silfield
Ashwellthorpe
Wissington
Northwold
Caston
Great Ellingham
Spooner Row
Fundenhall
Brookville
Thompson
Rockland All Saints
Besthorpe
Tacolneston
Methwold Hythe
Methwold
Cranwich
Ickburgh
Stow Bedon
Lower Stow Bedon
Fen Street
Black Car
Peddars Way & Norfolk Coast Path
Breckles
Mount Pleasant
Attleborough
Mundford
Shropham
Carleton Rode
Bunwell
Fens
Queens Ground
Feltwell
Thetford Forest Park
Great Hockham
North End
Snetterton
Puddledock
Bunwell Hill
East Wretham
Stonebridge
Old Buckenham
Cake Street
Upgate Street
Hargate
South End
Eccles Road
Stacksford
New Buckenham
Tibenham
Aslacton
Weeting Heath
Weeting
Castle
Grime's Graves
Snetterton
Wilby
Landon Bank
Larling
Pristow Green
Hockwold Fens
Hockwold cum Wilton
Quidenham
Hunt's Corner
Banham
Little Ouse River
Brandon
Town Street
Santon Downham
Croxton
Bridgham
St George's
East Harling
Kenninghall
Lakenheath Fen
High Lodge Forest Centre
Middle Harling
Gissing
Shippea Hill Station
Brandon
Dam Green
Winfarthing
Sedge Fen
Warren Lodge
Brettenham
Shelfanger
RAF Lakenheath Viewing Area
Thetford
Shadwell
North Lopham
Fersfield
Bressingham Common
Burston
Lakenheath
Garboldisham
South Lopham
Snow Street
Walcot Green
Rushford
River Ouse
Gasthorpe
Bressingham
Undley
Knettishall Heath
Knettishall
Smallworth
Redgrave & Lopham Fen
Pooley Street
Steam Museum & Gardens
Diss
Roydon
Kenny Hill
CenterParcs Elveden Forest
Elveden
Euston
Hopton
Blo Norton
Palgrave
Mildenhall Fen
Beck Row
Wilde Street
Eriswell
Elveden War Memorial
Barnham
Coney Weston
Market Weston
Thelnetham
Redgrave
Wortham
Stuston
Holywell Row
Fakenham Magna
Barningham
Hinderclay
Thistley Green
Thrandeston
West Row
Sapiston
Botesdale
Mildenhall
Honington
Hepworth
Rickinghall
Burgate
Langton Green
Mellis
Worlington
Barton Mills
Bardwell
Candle Street
Yaxley
Icklingham
West Stow Anglo-Saxon Village
Ixworth Thorpe
Stanton
Wattisfield
Upthorpe
Allwood Green
Mill Street
Thornham Parva
Eye
Freckenham
Tuddenham
Troston
Bangrove
Walsham le Willows
Cranmer Green
Braiseworth
Lackford Green
West Stow
Brockley
Ampton
Great Livermere
West Street
Wyken
Gislingham
Thornham Magna
Stoke Ash
Fordham
Red Lodge
Herringswell
Cavenham
Lackford
Ingham
Timworth
Ixworth
Langham
Four Ashes
Crowland
Finningham
Wickham Street
Standwell Green
Chippenham
Flempton
Culford
Hengrave
Timworth Green
Conyer's Green
Watermill
Badwell Ash
Long Thurlow
Badwell Green
Westhorpe
Wickham Green
Thorndon
Kennett
Snailwell
Fornham All Saints
Upper Town
Grimstone End
Hunston
Wyverstone Street
Wickham Skeith
Thwaite
Fornham St Martin
Stowlangtoft
Great Ashfield
Wyverstone
Cotton
Brockford Street
Risby
Great Barton
Pakenham
Stanton Street
Hunston Green
Bacton
Kentford
Needham Street
Packhorse Bridge
Lower Green
Higham
Cattishall
Thurston
Great Green
Norton Little Green
Norton
Earl's Green
Cow Green
Bacton Green
Ford's Green
Canhams Green
Mendlesham
Brockford Green
Moulton
Burthorpe Green
Westley
Bury St Edmunds
Battlies Green
Thurston Planch
Tostock
Elmswell
Haughley Green
Ward Green
Brown Street
Newmarket
Gazeley
Upper Green
Barrow
Denham End
Little Saxham
Great Saxham
Blackthorpe
Beyton Green
Beyton
Kingshall Street
Broadgrass Green
Base Green
Wetherden
Mendlesham Green
Park Green
Ashley
Dalham
Ickworth House
Horringer
Rushbrooke
Rougham
Woolpit
Hessett
Haughley
Dagworth
Gipping
Old Newton
Middlewood Green
Cheveley
Denham
Dunstall Green
Nowton Park
Nowton
High Green
Sicklesmere
Little Welnetham
Drinkstone
Drinkstone Green
Bradfield St George
Woolpit Green
Borley Green
Clopton Green
Onehouse
Harleston
Saxham Street
Stowupland
Little Stonham
Broad Green
Woodditton
Ousden
Hargrave
Chevington
Pinford End
Hawstead
Great Welnetham
Maypole Green
Rattlesden
Buxhall Fen Street
Stowmarket
Forward Green
Stonham Aspal
Saxon Street
Little Ditton
Back Street
Lady's Green
Lidgate
Upend
Depden Green
Chedburgh
Whepstead
Hawstead Green
Bradfield Combust
Bradfield St Clare
Gedding
Buxhall
Poystreet Green
Earl Stonham
Kirtling
Baxter's Green
Stonecross Green
Mickley Green
Hoggards Green
Oldhall Green
Bush Green
Bradfield Woods
Mill Green
Great Finborough
Combs Ford
Creeting St Mary
Crowfield
Dullingham Ley
Kirtling Green
Meeting Green
Depden
Gulling Green
Melon Green
Stanningfield
Cross Green
Felsham
Combs
Needham Market
Burrough Green
Boyden End
Attleton Green
Thorns
Ashfield Green
Rede
Brockley Green
Windsor Green
Great Green
Hightown Green
Moats Tye
Needham Lake
Cowlinge
Lambfair Green
Wickhambrook
Clopton Green
Wickham Street
Harrow Green
Cockfield
Thorpe Green
Brettenham
Battisford Tye
Battisford
Barking
Coddenham
Great Bradley
Hobbles Green
Pound Green
Hawkedon
Somerton
Cross Green
Lawshall
Lawshall Green
Cross Green
Bird Street
Charles Tye
Ringshall
Carlton Green
Little Bradley
Cock & End
Stradishall
Farley Green
Denston
Stansfield
Hartest
Audley End
Shimpling Street
Thorpe Morieux
Cooks Green
Barking Tye
Lower Street
Little Thurlow Green
Little Thurlow
Sowley Green
Assington Green
Lower Street
River Glem
Giffords Hall
Shimpling
Alpheton
Preston St Mary
Hitcham Causeway
Hitcham Street
Hitcham
Wattisham
Ringshall Stocks
Baylham
Barham
Temple End
Great Thurlow
Upper Street
Fenstead End
Boxted
Bridge Street
Guildhall
Kettlebaston
Nedging Tye
Great Bricett
Upper Street
Great Blakenham
Babel Green
Hundon
Lavenham
Little Hall
Brent Eleigh
Bildeston
Greenstreet Green
Offton
Claydon
Withersfield
Great Wratting
Barnardiston
Poslingford
Brook Street
Stanstead
Kentwell Hall & Gardens
Monks Eleigh
Naughton
Somersham
Little Blakenham
Little Wratting
Kedington
Mount Pleasant
Glemsford
Swingleton Green
Chelsworth
Nedging
Ash Street
Flowton
Burton End
Brockley Green
Chilton Street
Cavendish
Pentlow
Long Melford
Melford Hall
Little Waldingfield
Milden
Lindsey Tye
Semer
Whatfield
Elmsett
Bramford
Haverhill
Clare
Pentlow Street
Lindsey
Aldham
Sproughton
Hazel Stub
Calford Green
Boyton End
Clare Castle
Foxearth
Liston
Acton
Great Waldingfield
Rose Green
St James's Chapel
Kersey Tye
Stone Street
Wolves Wood
Burstall
Hintlesham
Sturmer
Stoke-by-Clare
Wixoe
Church Street
Belchamp St Paul
Borley
Newman's Green
Chilton
Mill Green
Wicker Street Green
Kersey
Kersey Upland
Coram Street
Hadleigh
Duke Street
Washbrook
Chantry
Pale Green
New England
Ovington
Belchamp Otten
Borley Green
Edwardstone
Groton
Horners Green
Chattisham
Wiggens Green
Steeple Bumpstead
Baythorne End
Ashen
Tilbury Green
Knowl Green
Belchamp Walter
Sudbury
Ballingdon
Great Cornard
Cornard Tye
Newton
Boxford
Calais Street
Bower House Tye
Hadleigh Heath
Polstead Heath
Layham
Copdock
Belstead
Birdbrook
Ridgewell
Tilbury Juxta Clare
Little Yeldham
Puttock End
Bulmer
Middleton
Little Cornard
Hagmore Green
Stone Street
Whitestreet Green
Raydon
Great Wenham
Little Wenham
Jimmy's Farm
Smith's Green
Finkle Green
Chapelend Way
Stambourne
Great Yeldham
Gestingthorpe
Bulmer Tye
Great Henny
Assington
Polstead
Shelley
Lower Raydon
Capel St Mary
Tattingstone
Hempstead
Stambourne Green
Grass Green
Toppesfield
Audley End
Wickham St Paul
Henny Street
Workhouse Green
Rose Green
Leavenheath
Stoke-by-Nayland
Holton St Mary
Bentley
Cornish Hall End
Craig's End
Dyer's End
Robinhood End
Pool Street
Colne Valley
Hedingham Castle
Twinstead
Dorking Tye
Honey Tye
Raydon
Great Sampford
Little London
Gainsford End
Delvin End
Castle Hedingham
Lucking Street
Alphamstone
Lamarsh
Nayland
Thorington Street
Higham
Stratford St Mary
East Bergholt
East End
Alton Water
Upper Street
Little Sampford
Howe Street
Duck End
Highstreet Green
Sibble Hedingham
Great Maplestead
Little Maplestead
Cross End
Pebmarsh
Bures
Wissington
Boxted
Carter's
Flatford Mill & Bridge Cottage
Brantham
Cattawade
Hawkspur Green
Finchingfield
Brickkiln Green
Mount Bures
Wormingford
Boxted Cross
Dedham
Mistley Towers
Mistley
Little Bardfield
Bridge End
Waltham's Cross
Countess Cross
Little Horkesley
Langham
Dedham Heath
Manningtree
New Mistley
Great Bardfield
Wethersfield
Blackmore End
White Green
Halstead
Boose's Green
Colne Engaine
White Colne
Wakes Colne
Great Horkesley
Boxted
Ardleigh Heath
Lawford
Mistley Heath
Bradfield
Holder's Green
Oxen End
Parkgate
Earls Colne
Chappel
Rose Green
Fordham
Horkesley Heath
West Bergholt
Ardleigh
Little Bromley
Horsleycross Street
TL
A11
A134
A1065
A1066
A1075
A1088
A1101
A143
A14
A1308
A140
A1141
A131
A1017
A1092
A1071
A12
A137
A1214
B1108
B1112
B1106
B1107
B1111
B1113
B1077
B1134
B1085
B1506
B1063
B1066
B1065
B1061
B1054
B1057
B1053
B1115
B1078
B1070
B1068
B1087
B1508
B1029
B1113
B1124
50
39
22
0 1 2 3 4 5 miles
0 1 2 3 4 5 6 7 8 kilometres

Suffolk
41
Hopton on Sea
Corton
Blundeston
Somerleyton
Herringfleet
St Olaves
Fritton
Haddiscoe
Thurlton
Norton Subcourse
Hales
Loddon
Mundham
Brooke
Shotesham
Bergh Apton
Thurton
Hardley Street
Reedham
Browston Green
Hobland Hall
51
Seething
Kirstead Green
Raveningham
Thwaite St Mary
Stockton
Kirby Cane
Maypole Green
Toft Monks
Wheatacre
Burgh St Peter
Aldeby
Bull's Green
Gillingham
Ellingham
Geldeston
Broome
Shipmeadow
Ditchingham
Bungay
Hedenham
Woodton
Topcroft
Topcroft Street
Hempnall
Hempnall Green
Saxlingham Thorpe
Saxlingham Nethergate
Saxlingham Green
Tasburgh
Upper Tasburgh
Flordon
Hapton
Tharston
Stratton St Michael
Forncett St Mary
Forncett St Peter
Fritton
Morningthorpe
Shelton
Shelton Green
Long Stratton
Hardwick
Great Moulton
High Green
Colegate End
Bush Green
Pulham Market
Pulham St Mary
Tivetshall St Mary
Starston
Harleston
Needham
Dickleburgh
Rushall
Garlic Street
Shimpling
Scole
Billingford
Hoxne
Syleham
Weybread
Brockdish
Thorpe Abbotts
Upper Weybread
Wingfield
Wingfield Green
Cross Green
Brome Street
Heckfield Green
Denham
Stradbroke
Horham
Wilby
Athelington
Redlingfield
Redlingfield Green
Occold
Southolt
Bedingfield
Tannington
Worlingworth
Bedfield
Saxtead
Saxtead Green
Saxtead Little Green
Dennington
Badingham
Kenton
Monk Soham
Earl Soham
Debenham
Framlingham
Winston
Ashfield cum Thorpe
Cretingham
Brandeston
Kettleburgh
Pettaugh
Framsden
Monewden
Helmingham
Otley
Gosbeck
Clopton
Ashbocking
Swilland
Grundisburgh
Witnesham
Burgh
Hasketon
Culpho
Tuddenham
Playford
Great Bealings
Little Bealings
Westerfield
Rushmere St Andrew
Kesgrave
IPSWICH
Martlesham Heath
Martlesham
Woodbridge
Melton
Ufford
Bromeswell
Eyke
Rendlesham
Sutton Hoo
Sutton
Waldringfield
Brightwell
Bucklesham
Newbourne
Hemley
Shottisham
Nacton
Levington
Kirton
Falkenham
Trimley St Martin
Trimley St Mary
Felixstowe
Old Felixstowe
Walton
Felixstowe Ferry
Landguard Fort
Landguard Point
Harwich
Dovercourt
Parkeston
Parkeston Quay
Shotley
Shotley Gate
Shotley Street
Erwarton
Chelmondiston
Pin Mill
Woolverstone
Freston
Holbrook Bay
Harkstead
Stutton
Wrabness
Hook of Holland
International Ferry Terminal
23
Harwich Harbour
River Orwell
River Deben
River Stour
Alderton
Ramsholt
Bawdsey
Hollesley
Hollesley Bay
Shingle Street
Boyton
Capel St Andrew
Butley
Chillesford
Orford
Orford Ness
Sudbourne
Tunstall
Iken
Snape
Snape Maltings
Snape Street
Aldeburgh
Aldeburgh Bay
River Alde
River Ore
Thorpeness
Thorpe Ness
Knodishall
Knodishall Common
Friston
Leiston
Aldringham
Sizewell
Leiston Abbey
Theberton
Eastbridge
Westleton
Dunwich
Dunwich Heath
Dunwich Forest
Minsmere
Middleton
Yoxford
Darsham
Kelsale
Saxmundham
Carlton
Benhall Green
Sternfield
Farnham
Friday Street
Stratford St Andrew
Great Glemham
Little Glemham
Marlesford
Hacheston
Parham
Easton
Wickham Market
Campsea Ash
Pettistree
Blaxhall
Sweffling
Rendham
Bruisyard
Cransford
Peasenhall
Sibton
Heveningham
Ubbeston Green
Laxfield
Huntingfield
Walpole
Cookley
Halesworth
Holton
Blyford
Wenhaston
Blythburgh
Walberswick
Southwold
Reydon
Wangford
Uggeshall
Westhall
Brampton
Stoven
Wrentham
Covehithe
South Cove
Benacre
Benacre Ness
Henstead
Kessingland
Kessingland Beach
Rushmere
Gisleham
Carlton Colville
Mutford
Barnby
North Cove
Worlingham
Beccles
Ringsfield
Barsham
Mettingham
Ilketshall St Andrew
Ilketshall St Margaret
Ilketshall St John
Homersfield
Flixton
Earsham
St Margaret South Elmham
St Cross South Elmham
All Saints South Elmham
St James South Elmham
St Michael South Elmham
Rumburgh
Spexhall
Wissett
Chediston
Mendham
Metfield
Fressingfield
Linstead Parva
Cratfield
Redisham
Sotterley
Shadingfield
Ellough
Weston
Oulton
Oulton Broad
LOWESTOFT
Lowestoft Ness
Pakefield
Kirkley
Sole Bay
Suffolk Heritage Coast
TM
A12
A14
A140
A143
A144
A145
A146
A1095
A1094
A1120
A1152

CAERNARFON BAY
CARDIGAN BAY
LLEYN PENINSULA
Newborough
Caernarfon
Dinas Dinlle
Llandwrog
Penygroes
Clynnog-fawr
Trefor
Llanaelhaearn
Nefyn
Morfa Nefyn
Pistyll
Edern
Tudweiliog
Aberdaron
Abersoch
Pwllheli
Llanbedrog
Criccieth
Bardsey Sound
BARDSEY ISLAND
St Tudwal's Island East
St Tudwal's Island West
Tremadog Bay
Lleyn Heritage Coast

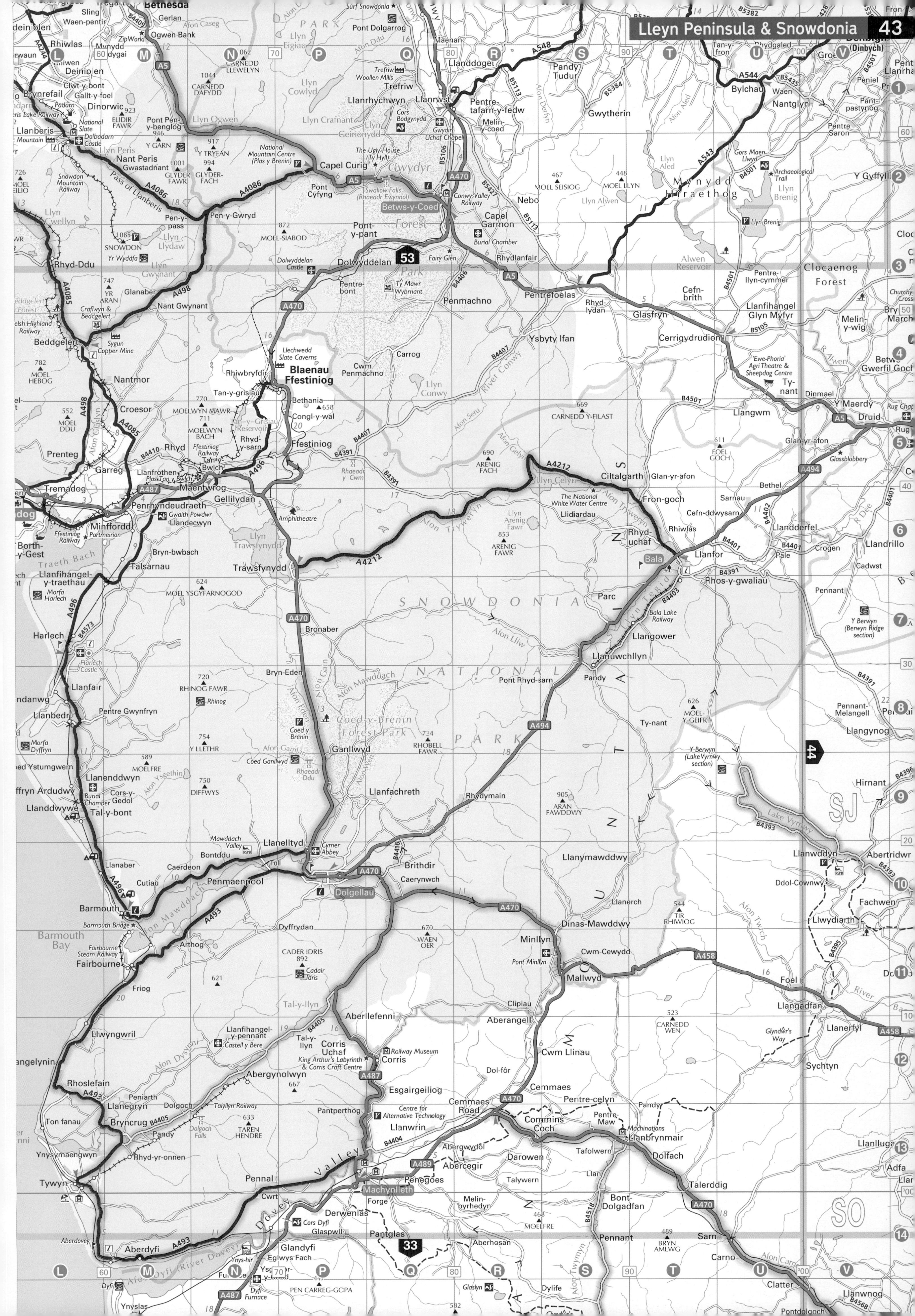
Bethesda
Gerlan
Ogwen Bank
Rhiwlas
Deiniolen
Brynrefail
Dinorwic
Llanberis
Nant Peris
Pen-y-pass
Pen-y-Gwryd
Capel Curig
Pont Dolgarrog
Maenan
Llanddoget
Trefriw
Llanrhychwyn
Llanrwst
Pentre-tafarn-y-fedw
Melin-y-coed
Betws-y-Coed
Capel Garmon
Nebo
Pandy Tudur
Gwytherin
Bylchau
Nantglyn
Y Gyffylliog
Clocaenog Forest
Rhyd-Ddu
Beddgelert
Nantmor
Croesor
Prenteg
Garreg
Tremadog
Penrhyndeudraeth
Minffordd
Maentwrog
Gellilydan
Trawsfynydd
Talsarnau
Llanfihangel-y-traethau
Harlech
Llanfair
Llanbedr
Pentre Gwynfryn
Llanenddwyn
Tal-y-bont
Llanaber
Barmouth
Barmouth Bay
Fairbourne
Arthog
Friog
Llwyngwril
Rhoslefain
Llanegryn
Bryncrug
Tywyn
Aberdyfi
Dolwyddelan
Pont-y-pant
Penmachno
Blaenau Ffestiniog
Ffestiniog
Cwm Penmachno
Pentrefoelas
Rhydlanfair
Ysbyty Ifan
Glasfryn
Cerrigydrudion
Llangwm
Y Maerdy
Druid
Frongoch
Llanfor
Bala
Rhos-y-gwaliau
Llandderfel
Llandrillo
Parc
Llangower
Llanuwchllyn
Pandy
Bronaber
Bryn-Eden
Ganllwyd
Llanfachreth
Rhydymain
Llanelltyd
Dolgellau
Penmaenpool
Bontddu
Brithdir
Caerynwch
Dinas-Mawddwy
Minllyn
Mallwyd
Cwm-Cewydd
Llanymawddwy
Llangadfan
Foel
Llanerfyl
Aberllefenni
Corris
Corris Uchaf
Abergynolwyn
Esgairgeiliog
Cemmaes Road
Cemmaes
Commins Coch
Llanbrynmair
Darowen
Machynlleth
Penegoes
Pennal
Derwenlas
Glandyfi
Talerddig
Carno
Sarn
Llanwddyn
Lake Vyrnwy
SNOWDONIA NATIONAL PARK
SJ
SO

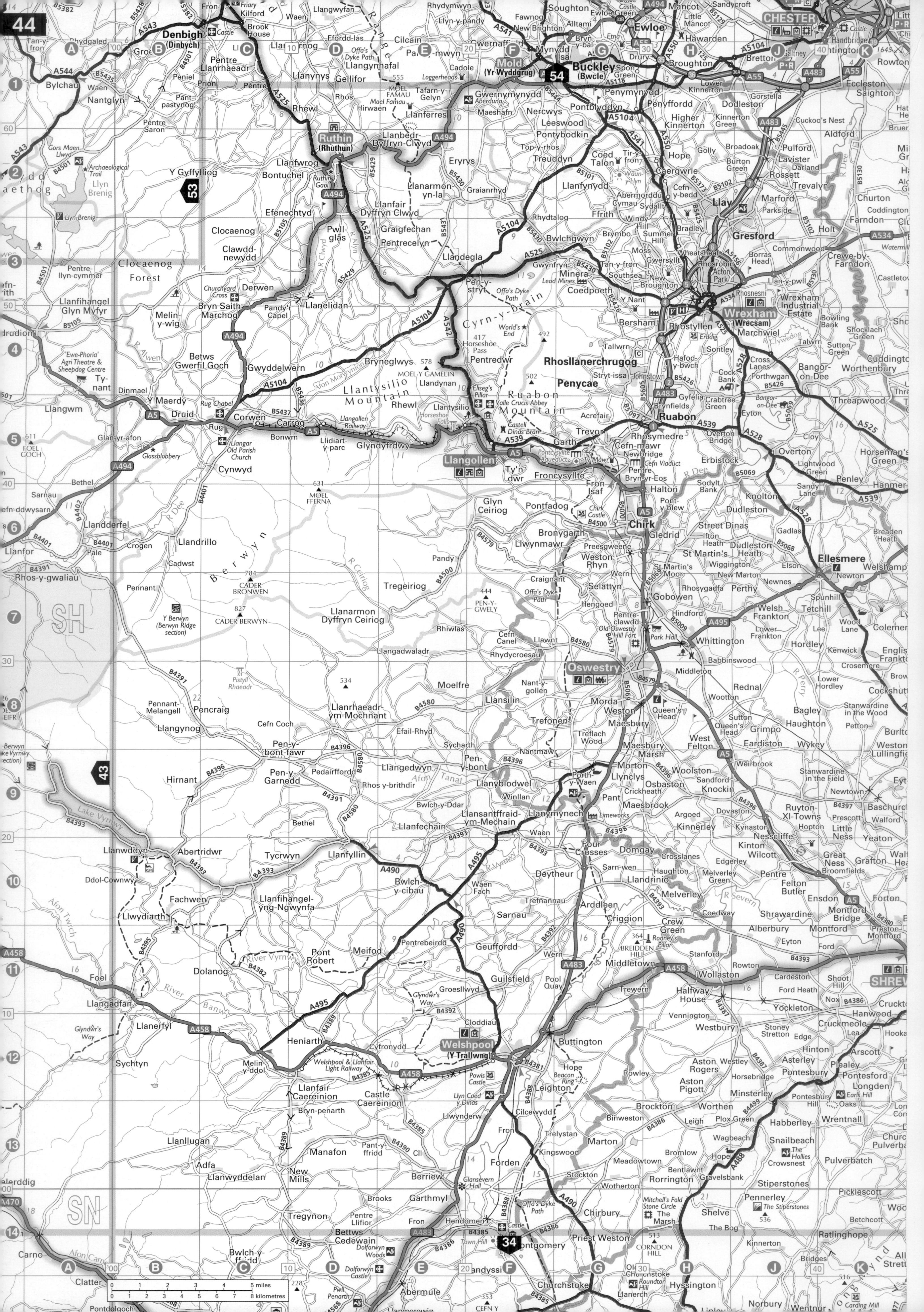

44
Friary
Kilford
Brook House
Fron
Denbigh
(Dinbych)
Castle
Tan-y-fron
Rhydgaled
Groes
Llandyrnog
Waen
Llangwyfan
Ffordd-las
Offa's Dyke Path
Llangynhafal
Cilcain
Pant-y-mwyn
Rhydymwyn
Llyn-y-pandy
Gwernaffield
Fawnog
New Brighton
Soughton
Alltami
Mynydd Isa
Bryn-y-baal
Ewloe Green
Ewloe
Mancot
Little Mancot
Sandycroft
Hawarden
CHESTER
Castle
Handbridge
Huntington
Rowton
Mold
(Yr Wyddgrug)
54
Buckley
(Bwcle)
Drury
Spon Green
Broughton
Bretton
Saltney
Pentre Llanrhaeadr
Llanynys
Gellifor
Peniel
Prion
Pentre
Bylchau
Waen
Nantglyn
Pant-pastynog
Pentre Saron
Moel Famau
Loggerheads
Cadole
Tafarn-y-Gelyn
Hirwaen
Rhewl
Rhos
Llanferres
Gwernymynydd
Aberduna
Maeshafn
Nercwys
Penymynydd
Pontblyddyn
Penyffordd
Higher Kinnerton
Lower Kinnerton
Kinnerton Green
Dodleston
Gorstella
Eccleston
Saighton
Cuckoo's Nest
Aldford
Ruthin
(Rhuthun)
Llanbedr-Dyffryn-Clwyd
Leeswood
Pontybodkin
Top-y-rhos
Treuddyn
Coed Talon
Tir-y-fron
Waun-y-Llyn
Hope
Golly
Broadoak
Pulford
Lavister
Darland
Rossett
Trevalyn
Churton
Gors Maen Llwyd
Archaeological Trail
Llyn Brenig
Y Gyffylliog
53
Llanfwrog
Bontuchel
Ruthin Gaol
Eryrys
Llanarmon-yn-Ial
Graianrhyd
Llanfynydd
Caergwrle
Burton Green
Cefn-y-bedd
Abermorddu
Cymau
Sydallt
Llay
Marford
Parkside
Coddington
Farndon
Efenechtyd
Llanfair Dyffryn Clwyd
Pwll-glâs
Graigfechan
Pentrecelyn
Rhydtalog
Ffrith
Windy Hill
Summerhill
Brymbo
Bradley
Gresford
Holt
Clocaenog
Clawdd-newydd
Clocaenog Forest
Llandegla
Bwlchgwyn
Moss
Gwersyllt
Wheatsheaf
Commonwood
Borras Head
Crewe-by-Farndon
Castletown
Pentre-llyn-cymmer
Churchyard Cross
Derwen
Bryn Saith Marchog
Pen-y-stryt
Offa's Dyke Path
Gwynfryn
Minera
Lead Mines
Tan-y-fron
Southsea
New Broughton
Rhosrobin
Acton Park
Llan-y-pwll
Coedpoeth
Llanfihangel Glyn Myfyr
Melin-y-wig
Pandy'r Capel
Llanelidan
Cyrn-y-brain
Y Nant
Bersham
Rhostyllen
Wrexham
(Wrecsam)
Rhosnesni
Wrexham Industrial Estate
Erddig
Marchwiel
Bowling Bank
Shocklach Green
World's End
Horseshoe Pass
Pentredwr
Bryneglwys
Moel y Gamelin
Llandynan
Rhosllanerchrugog
Tallwrn
Sontley
Hafod-y-bwch
Stryt-issa
Johnstown
Cock Bank
Cross Lanes
Porthwgan
Bangor-on-Dee
Worthenbury
Cuddington
Sutton Green
Betws Gwerfil Goch
Gwyddelwern
'Ewe-Phoria' Agri Theatre & Sheepdog Centre
Ty-nant
Dinmael
Afon Morwynion
Llantysilio Mountain
Eliseg's Pillar
Valle Crucis Abbey
Ruabon Mountain
Penycae
Gyfelia
Crabtree Green
Bryn-fields
Ruabon
Eyton
Threapwood
Llangwm
Y Maerdy
Druid
Rug Chapel
Rug
Corwen
Carrog
Rhewl
Llantysilio
Horseshoe Falls
Llangollen Railway
Castell Dinas Bran
Acrefair
Trevor
Rhosymedre
Cefn-mawr
Newbridge
Overton Bridge
Overton
Glan-yr-afon
Foel Goch
Glassblobbery
Llangar Old Parish Church
Bonwm
Lliadiart-y-parc
Glyndyfrdwy
Llangollen
Pontcysyllte Aqueduct
Garth
Ty Mawr
Cefn Viaduct
Pentre
Bryn-yr-Eos
Erbistock
Lightwood Green
Horseman's Green
Cynwyd
Bethel
Sarnau
Moel Fferna
Ty'n-dwr
Froncysyllte
Fron Isaf
Halton
Sodylt Bank
Penley
Hanmer
Llandderfel
Llandrillo
Glyn Ceiriog
Pontfadog
Chirk Castle
Chirk
Pont-y-blew
Dudleston
Knolton
Sandy Lane
Llanfor
Pale
Crogen
Bronygarth
Llwynmawr
Gledrid
Street Dinas
Ifton Heath
Dudleston Heath
Gadlas
Breaden Heath
Rhos-y-gwaliau
Cadwst
Berwyn
Pandy
Preesgweene
Weston Rhyn
St Martin's
Wiggington
Ellesmere
Welshampton
Pennant
Cader Bronwen
Tregeiriog
Craignant
Wern
St Martin's Moor
New Marton
Elson
Newton
SH
Y Berwyn (Berwyn Ridge section)
Cader Berwyn
Llanarmon Dyffryn Ceiriog
Pen-y-Gwely
Offa's Dyke Path
Selattyn
Hengoed
Gobowen
Rhosygadfa
Perthy
Newnes
Spunhill
Tetchill
Welsh Frankton
Lower Frankton
Pentre-clawdd
Old Oswestry Hill Fort
Hindford
Park Hall
Whittington
Lee
Wood Lane
Colemere
Rhiwlas
Cefn Canel
Llawnt
Rhydycroesau
Llangadwaladr
Hordley
Kenwick
English Frankton
Babbinswood
Crosemere
Oswestry
Middleton
Pistyll Rhaeadr
Moelfre
Nant-y-gollen
Rednal
Lower Hordley
Stanwardine in the Wood
Cockshutt
Pennant-Melangell
Pencraig
Llanrhaeadr-ym-Mochnant
Llansilin
Morda
Weston
Queen's Head
Wootton
Bagley
Haughton
Petton
Llangynog
Cefn Coch
Efail-Rhyd
Trefonen
Treflach Wood
Maesbury
Sutton
Queen's Head
Grimpo
Maesbury Marsh
West Felton
Eardiston
Wykey
Weston Lullingfields
Berwyn Lake Vyrnwy section
43
Pen-y-bont-fawr
Sycharth
Nantmawr
Pen-y-bont
Porth-y-Waen
Morton
Llynclys
Woolston
Weirbrook
Stanwardine in the Field
Hirnant
Pen-y-Garnedd
Pedairffordd
Llangedwyn
Rhos y-brithdir
Afon Tanat
Llanyblodwel
Winllan
Crickheath
Osbaston
Sandford
Knockin
Pant
Maesbrook
Newtown
Baschurch
Lake Vyrnwy
Bwlch-y-Ddar
Lansantffraid-ym-Mechain
Llanymynech
Limeworks
Argoed
Kinnerley
Dovaston
Ruyton-XI-Towns
Prescott
Walford
Hopton
Little Ness
Bethel
Llanfechain
Kynaston
Nesscliffe
Yeaton
Llanwddyn
Abertridwr
Tycrwyn
Llanfyllin
Waen
Four Crosses
Domgay
Crosslanes
Kinton
Wilcott
Great Ness
Grafton
Ddol-Cownwy
Bwlch-y-cibau
Deytheur
Sarn-wen
Llandrinio
Haughton
Edgerley
Melverley Green
Pentre
Broomfields
Afon Twrch
Fachwen
Llanfihangel-yng-Ngwynfa
Waen Fach
Melverley
Felton Butler
Ensdon
Forton
Llwydiarth
Trefnannau
Sarnau
Arddleen
Criggion
Coedway
R Severn
Shrawardine
Montford Bridge
Crew Green
Alberbury
Montford
Preston Montford
Pentrebeirdd
Geufford
Breidden Hill
Rodney's Pillar
Wern
Eyton
Ford
River Vyrnwy
Pont Robert
Meifod
Stanford
Foel
Dolanog
Middletown
Wollaston
Rowton
Cardeston
Shoot Hill
Shrewsbury
Guilsfield
Pool Quay
Trewern
Ford Heath
Llangadfan
River Banwy
Groesllwyd
Glyndŵr's Way
Halfway House
Yockleton
Nox
Cruckton
Vennington
Llanerfyl
Heniarth
Cloddiau
Cyfronydd
Buttington
Westbury
Hanwood
Cruckmeole
Stoney Stretton
Edge
Hookagate
Sychtyn
Melin-y-ddol
Welshpool & Llanfair Light Railway
Welshpool
(Y Trallwng)
Hope
Beacon Ring
Aston Rogers
Westley
Hinton
Arscott
Asterley
Pontesbury
Plealey
Pontesford
Longden
Llanfair Caereinion
Castle Caereinion
Powis Castle
Leighton
Rowley
Aston Pigott
Horsebridge
Minsterley
Pontesbury Hill
Earl's Hill
Oaks
Llyn Coed y Dinas
Bryn-penarth
Llwynderw
Cilcewydd
Brockton
Binweston
Worthen
Leigh
Plox Green
Habberley
Wrentnall
Llanllugan
Manafon
Pant-y-ffridd
Cil
Fron
Trelystan
Kingswood
Marton
Wagbeach
Hope
Snailbeach
The Hollies
Crowsnest
Church Pulverbatch
Pulverbatch
Adfa
Llanwyddelan
New Mills
Berriew
Forden
Glansevern Hall
Stockton
Meadowtown
Bentlawnt
Rorrington
Gravelsbank
Stiperstones
Wotherton
Brooks
Garthmyl
Tregynon
Pentre Llifior
Offa's Dyke Path
Chirbury
Mitchell's Fold Stone Circle
The Marsh
Shelve
Pennerley
The Stiperstones
Picklescott
SN
Bettws Cedewain
Fron
Hendomen
Castle
Town Hill
34
Montgomery
Priest Weston
Corndon Hill
The Bog
Betchcott
Ratlinghope
Kinnerton
Dolforwyn Woods
Carno
Afon Carno
Bwlch-y-ffridd
Clatter
Dolforwyn Castle
Abermule
Sarn
Llandyssil
Churchstoke
Old Churchstoke
Roundton Hill
Hyssington
Llanerch
Norbury
Bridges
Wentnor
Carding Mill
Cefn Y
Pontdolgoch
Penarth
0 1 2 3 4 5 miles
0 1 2 3 4 5 6 7 8 kilometres

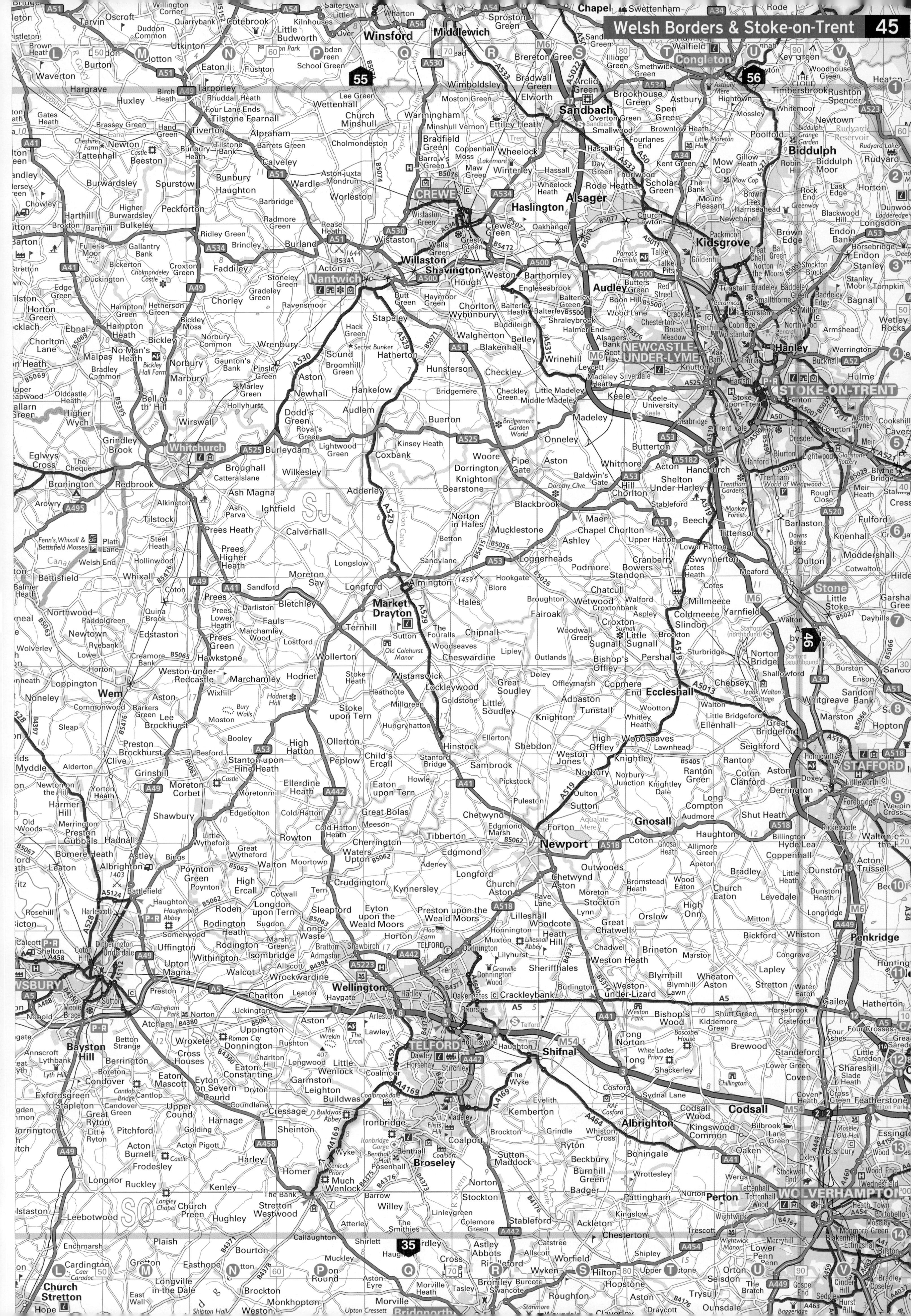
Winsford
Middlewich
Congleton
Sandbach
Biddulph
Crewe
Nantwich
Haslington
Alsager
Kidsgrove
Willaston
Shavington
Audley
Newcastle-under-Lyme
Hanley
Stoke-on-Trent
Whitchurch
Market Drayton
Eccleshall
Stone
Stafford
Newport
Gnosall
Penkridge
Wellington
Telford
Shifnal
Broseley
Much Wenlock
Albrighton
Codsall
Wolverhampton
Bayston Hill
Church Stretton
Wem
Sandbach
Kidsgrove
SJ
SO
55
56
46
35

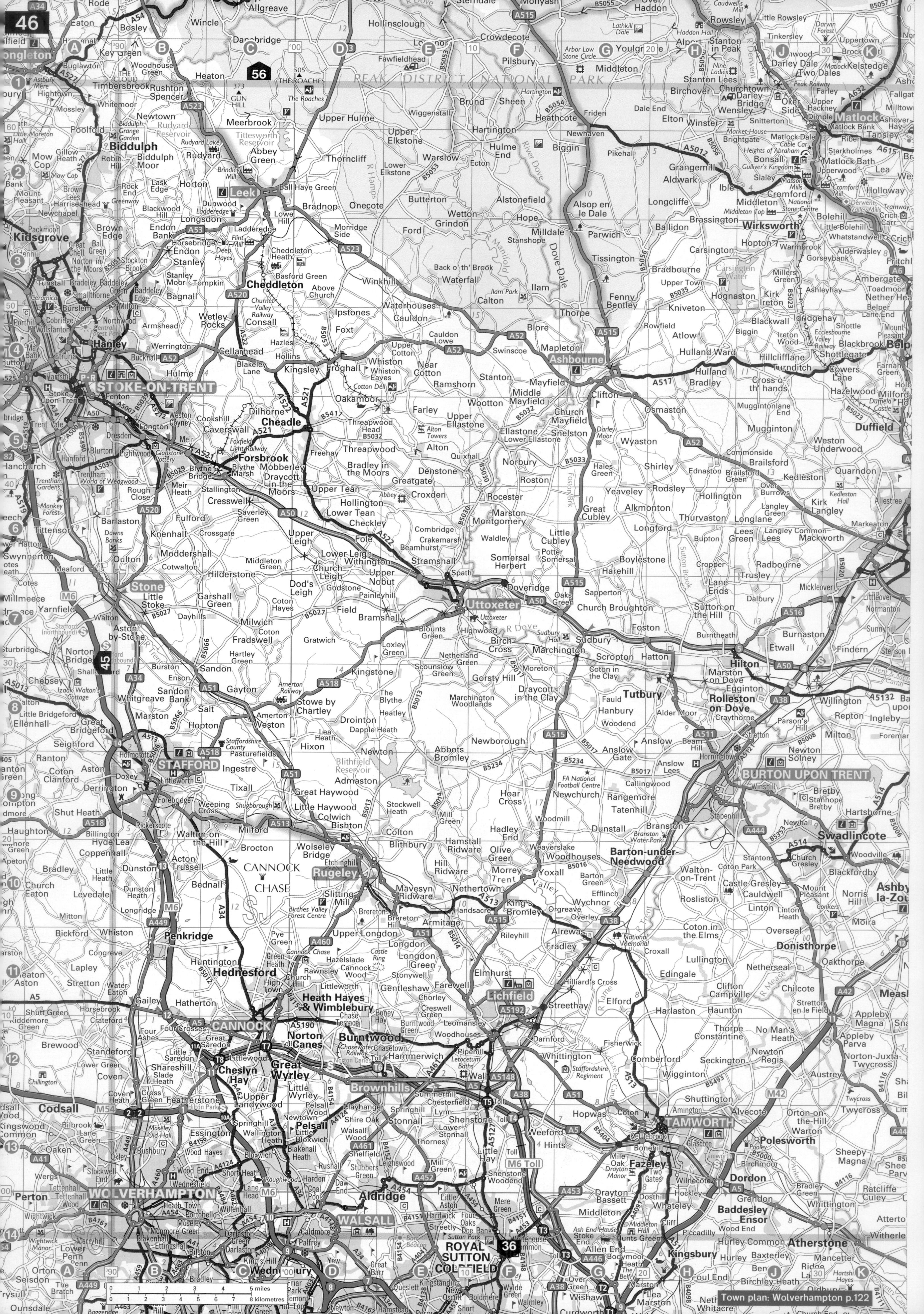

PEAK DISTRICT NATIONAL PARK
Congleton
Allgreave
Wincle
Hollinsclough
Crowdecote
Monyash
Over Haddon
Rowsley
Little Rowsley
Bosley
Danebridge
Longnor
Fawfieldhead
Pilsbury
Youlgreave
Alport
Stanton in Peak
Darley Dale
Two Dales
Rushton Spencer
Heaton
56
The Roaches
Gun Hill
Meerbrook
Upper Hulme
Brund
Sheen
Hartington
Heathcote
Middleton
Birchover
Churchtown
Darley Bridge
Wensley
Winster
Elton
Matlock
Matlock Bath
Cromford
Tansley
Biddulph
Biddulph Moor
Rudyard
Rudyard Reservoir
Tittesworth Reservoir
Abbey Green
Thorncliff
Upper Elkstone
Lower Elkstone
Warslow
Hulme End
Biggin
Newhaven
Pikehall
Grangemill
Aldwark
Ible
Bonsall
Middleton
Wirksworth
Mow Cop
Kidsgrove
Horton
Leek
Ball Haye Green
Bradnop
Onecote
Butterton
Alstonefield
Alsop en le Dale
Longcliffe
Brassington
Ballidon
Wetton
Grindon
Hope
Milldale
Parwich
Ford
Morridge Side
Longsdon
Endon
Endon Bank
Stanley
Cheddleton
Cheddleton Heath
Basford Green
Above Church
Winkhill
Waterhouses
Cauldon
Back o' th' Brook
Waterfall
Ilam
Dove Dale
Tissington
Bradbourne
Carsington
Carsington Water
Kirk Ireton
Idridgehay
Ambergate
Tunstall
Burslem
Bagnall
Wetley Rocks
Consall
Ipstones
Foxt
Calton
Thorpe
Fenny Bentley
Kniveton
Atlow
Hulland Ward
Hanley
STOKE-ON-TRENT
Cellarhead
Kingsley
Froghall
Whiston
Cauldon Lowe
Upper Cotton
Near Cotton
Swinscoe
Blore
Mapleton
Ashbourne
Hulland
Turnditch
Belper
Cross o' th' hands
Oakamoor
Ramshorn
Stanton
Mayfield
Clifton
Osmaston
Cheadle
Dilhorne
Caverswall
Forsbrook
Blythe Bridge
Meir
Longton
Farley
Upper Ellastone
Wootton
Middle Mayfield
Church Mayfield
Ellastone
Snelston
Wyaston
Muggington
Duffield
Alton
Alton Towers
Denstone
Threapwood
Bradley in the Moors
Greatgate
Croxden
Norbury
Roston
Shirley
Brailsford
Kedleston
Quarndon
Trentham
Barlaston
Stone
Upper Tean
Hollington
Lower Tean
Checkley
Rocester
Marston Montgomery
Great Cubley
Yeaveley
Rodsley
Alkmonton
Longford
Kirk Langley
Mackworth
Fulford
Knenhall
Moddershall
Oulton
Hilderstone
Upper Leigh
Fole
Beamhurst
Stramshall
Combridge
Crakemarsh
Somersal Herbert
Little Cubley
Boylestone
Sutton on the Hill
Radbourne
Mickleover
Church Leigh
Lower Leigh
Withington
Dod's Leigh
Upper Nobut
Spath
Uttoxeter
Doveridge
Sapperton
Church Broughton
Dalbury
Littleover
Eccleshall
Little Stoke
Garshall Green
Aston-by-Stone
Milwich
Fradswell
Field
Bramshall
Blounts Green
Highwood
Birch Cross
Sudbury
Marchington
Foston
Scropton
Hatton
Hilton
Etwall
Findern
Norton Bridge
Sandon
Gratwich
Kingstone
Loxley Green
Scounslow Green
Gorsty Hill
Moreton
Tutbury
Rolleston on Dove
Egginton
Willington
Repton
Chebsey
Burston
Gayton
Amerton
Stowe by Chartley
The Blythe
Heatley
Marchington Woodlands
Draycott in the Clay
Hanbury
Fauld
Anslow
Anslow Gate
Newborough
Abbots Bromley
Stafford
Ingestre
Hixon
Drointon
Newton
Blithfield Reservoir
Admaston
Rangemore
Tatenhill
Newchurch
BURTON UPON TRENT
Stapenhill
Swadlincote
Bretby
Hartshorne
Tixall
Great Haywood
Little Haywood
Colwich
Bishton
Stockwell Heath
Hoar Cross
Dunstall
Branston
Barton-under-Needwood
Milford
Walton-on-the-Hill
Brocton
Wolseley Bridge
Colton
Blithbury
Hamstall Ridware
Hill Ridware
Olive Green
Yoxall
Woodhouses
Walton-on-Trent
Rosliston
Castle Gresley
Cauldwell
Linton
Church Gresley
Woodville
Ashby-de-la-Zouch
CANNOCK CHASE
Rugeley
Penkridge
Dunston
Acton Trussell
Bednall
Slitting Mill
Brereton
Mavesyn Ridware
Armitage
Handsacre
King's Bromley
Nethertown
Wychnor
Alrewas
Fradley
Coton in the Elms
Overseal
Donisthorpe
Hednesford
Huntington
Pye Green
Upper Longdon
Longdon
Longdon Green
Gentleshaw
Farewell
Elmhurst
Lichfield
Streethay
Elford
Edingale
Lullington
Netherseal
Clifton Campville
Chilcote
Measham
Gailey
Hatherton
Heath Hayes & Wimblebury
Cannock
Norton Canes
Burntwood
Chase Terrace
Whittington
Harlaston
Haunton
Thorpe Constantine
No Man's Heath
Appleby Magna
Appleby Parva
Norton-Juxta-Twycross
Cheslyn Hay
Great Wyrley
Hammerwich
Brownhills
Little Wyrley
Wall
Shenstone
Hopwas
Tamworth
Wigginton
Seckington
Newton Regis
Austrey
Twycross
Codsall
Featherstone
Pelsall
Stonnall
Lower Stonnall
Weeford
Hints
Fazeley
Polesworth
Orton-on-the-Hill
Warton
Sheepy Magna
Perton
Essington
Wednesfield
WOLVERHAMPTON
Walsall
Aldridge
Shire Oak
Walsall Wood
Little Hay
Drayton Bassett
Mile Oak
Dordon
Grendon
Baddesley Ensor
Atherstone
Ratcliffe Culey
Bilston
Darlaston
Wednesbury
Four Oaks
ROYAL SUTTON COLDFIELD
Middleton
Kingsbury
Hurley
Whittington
Seisdon
Orton
Mancetter
Witherley
36
45

Town plan: Wolverhampton p.122

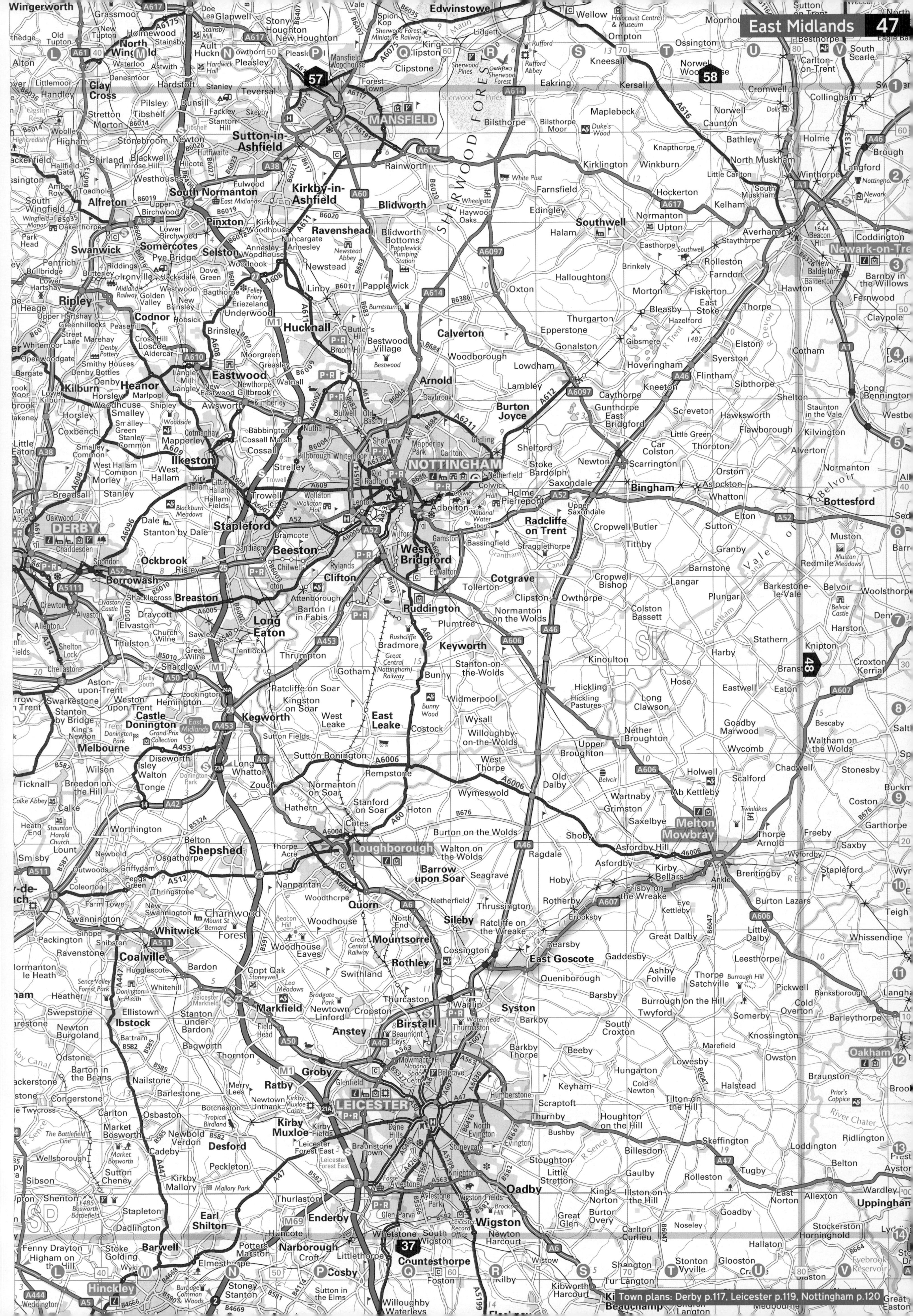

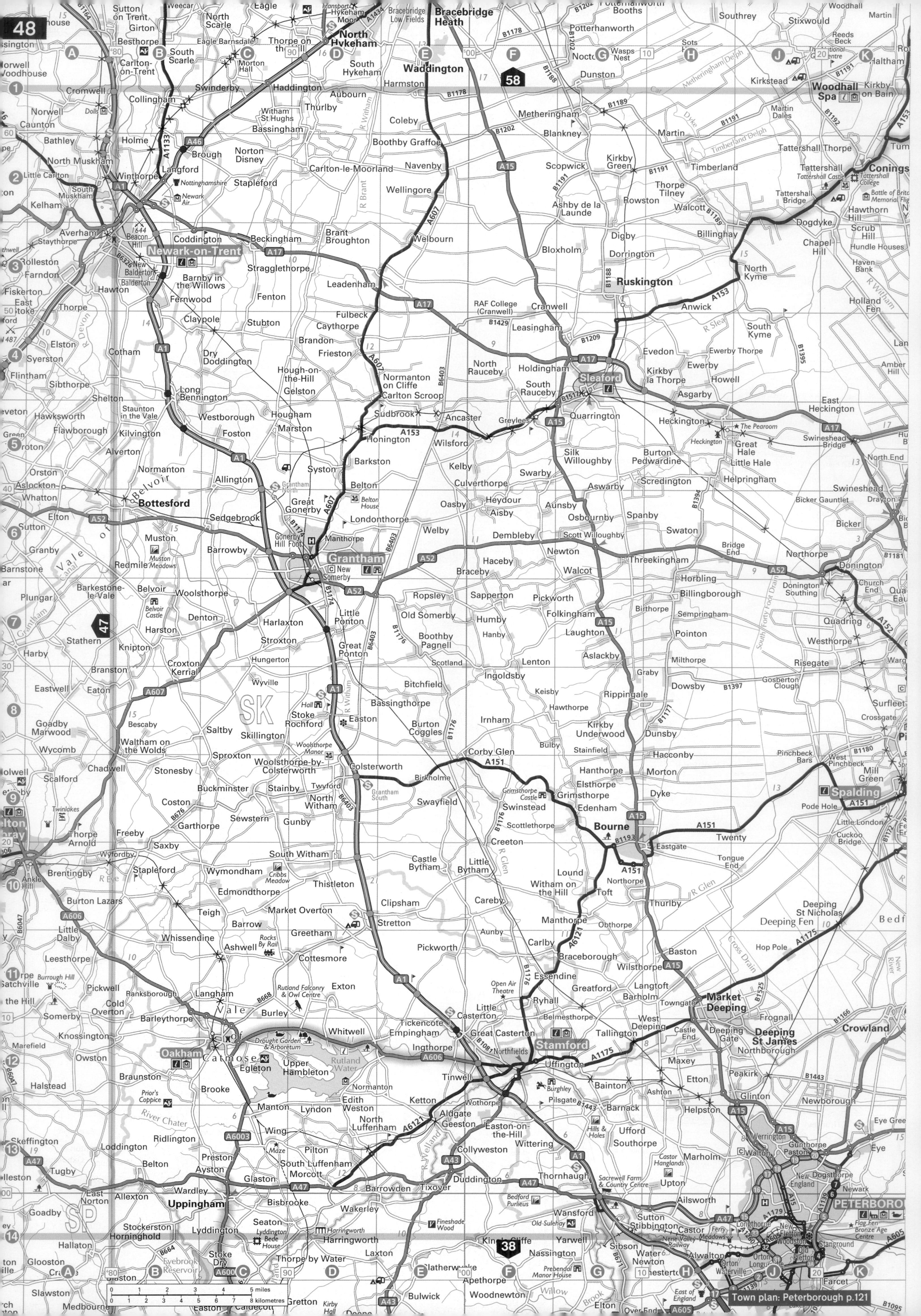

North Hykeham
Bracebridge Heath
Waddington
Woodhall Spa
Newark-on-Trent
Collingham
Swinderby
Brough
Winthorpe
Langford
Coddington
Beckingham
Balderton
Barnby in the Willows
Fernwood
Claypole
Long Bennington
Westborough
Foston
Bottesford
Sedgebrook
Muston
Barrowby
Grantham
Gonerby Hill Foot
Great Gonerby
Belton
Barkston
Syston
Honington
Ancaster
Sudbrook
Wilsford
Caythorpe
Fulbeck
Leadenham
Navenby
Wellingore
Welbourn
Brant Broughton
Stragglethorpe
Ruskington
Sleaford
Leasingham
Cranwell
RAF College (Cranwell)
Holdingham
Quarrington
North Rauceby
South Rauceby
Heckington
Great Hale
Helpringham
Swineshead
Billinghay
Tattershall
Tattershall Castle
Dogdyke
Metheringham
Martin
Timberland
Walcott
Digby
Dorrington
North Kyme
South Kyme
Anwick
Threekingham
Billingborough
Horbling
Donington
Quadring
Folkingham
Aslackby
Rippingale
Dowsby
Kirkby Underwood
Dunsby
Hacconby
Morton
Bourne
Spalding
Pinchbeck
Corby Glen
Colsterworth
Woolsthorpe-by-Colsterworth
Skillington
Stoke Rochford
Great Ponton
Little Ponton
Harlaxton
Denton
Belvoir
Knipton
Croxton Kerrial
Waltham on the Wolds
Buckminster
Coston
Wymondham
South Witham
North Witham
Castle Bytham
Little Bytham
Witham on the Hill
Thurlby
Baston
Langtoft
Market Deeping
Deeping St James
Deeping St Nicholas
Crowland
Stamford
Tallington
Uffington
Barnack
Ryhall
Essendine
Great Casterton
Empingham
Oakham
Rutland Water
Egleton
Upper Hambleton
Manton
Edith Weston
Uppingham
Wing
Morcott
South Luffenham
North Luffenham
Ketton
Collyweston
Easton-on-the-Hill
Wittering
Duddington
Wansford
Castor
Peterborough
Stanground
Farcet
Yaxley
Helpston
Glinton
Peakirk
Bainton
Ufford
Kings Cliffe
Nassington
Harringworth
Wakerley
Lyddington
Seaton
Bisbrooke
Glaston
Ayston
Preston
Ridlington
Braunston
Langham
Cottesmore
Greetham
Exton
Whitwell
Burley
Market Overton
Teigh
Whissendine
Ashwell
Barrow
Clipsham
Stretton
Pickworth
Melton Mowbray
Somerby
Knossington
Tugby
Skeffington
Hallaton
Gretton
Bulwick
Woodnewton
Apethorpe
Oundle
SK
SP
Vale of Belvoir
Vale of Catmoss
A1
A15
A17
A46
A52
A151
A153
A606
A607
A6121
A47
A43
A1175
58
47
38
Town plan: Peterborough p.121
0 1 2 3 4 5 miles
0 1 2 3 4 5 6 7 8 kilometres

THE WASH
TF
TL
Skegness
Boston
Hunstanton
Heacham
Dersingham
King's Lynn
Holbeach
Long Sutton
Terrington St Clement
Wisbech
Downham Market
March
Whittlesey
Spilsby
Burgh le Marsh
Wainfleet All Saints
Friskney
Wrangle
Old Leake
Butterwick
Freiston
Kirton
Frampton
Sutterton
Fosdyke
Gedney
Sutton Bridge
Tilney All Saints
Clenchwarton
Snettisham
Sandringham
Castle Rising
Gaywood
Wiggenhall St Germans
Outwell
Upwell
Emneth
Elm
Guyhirn
Thorney
Denver
Hilgay
Southery
Welney
Methwold
Stoke Ferry
Narborough
Middleton
Gibraltar Point
Holme next the Sea
Old Hunstanton
Ringstead
Sedgeford
Fring
Shernborne
Flitcham
Hillington
Congham
Grimston
Gayton
Ashwicken
Pentney
Marham
Shouldham
Wereham
Oxborough
Boughton
Stow Bardolph
Wimbotsham
Terrington St John
Walpole St Andrew
Walpole St Peter
Tydd St Giles
Tydd St Mary
Gedney Hill
Holbeach Drove
Whaplode Drove
Moulton
Whaplode
Weston
Cowbit
Crowland
Eastrea
Coates
Turves
Benwick
Chatteris
Doddington
Wimblington
Stonea
Coldham
Friday Bridge
Leverington
Parson Drove
Murrow
Wisbech St Mary
Walsoken
Magdalen
Watlington
Runcton Holme
Wormegay
Tottenhill
Blackborough End
Setchey
North Runcton
West Winch
Saddlebow
Wiggenhall St Mary Magdalen
Fincham
Barton Bendish
Crimplesham
Bexwell
West Dereham
Fordham
Nordelph
Three Holes
Ten Mile Bank
Hilgay Fen
Lakesend
Christchurch
Manea
Whittington
Foulden
Brookville
Methwold Hythe
Northwold
59
50
39

A 70 B C 80 D E 90 F G 00 H J 10 K

TF

North Norfolk Heritage Coast

Blakeney Point

Brancaster Bay Scolt Head Island Holkham Bay Blakeney Point Morston Marshes Cley Marshes Muckleburgh Collection

Holme Dunes Holme next the Sea Brancaster Brancaster Staithe Burnham Norton Burnham Overy Staithe Holkham Wells-next-the-Sea Morston Blakeney Cley next the Sea Sheringham

Old Hunstanton Titchwell Burnham Deepdale A149 Newgate Salthouse Weybourne Upper Sheringham

Thornham Branodunum Roman Fort B1155 Holkham Hall Stiffkey Cockthorpe Kelling

Hunstanton Ringstead Burnham Market Burnham Overy B1355 Warham Langham Glandford Sheringham Park High Kelling

Heacham Norfolk Lavender Summerfield B1153 North Creake New Holkham Creake Abbey Wells & Walsingham Light Railway Wighton Westgate Saxlingham B1156 North Norfolk Railway Holt Bodham High Kelling

Peddars Way & Norfolk Coast Path Docking B1155 Stanhoe Burnham Thorpe The Shrine of Our Lady Copy's Green Binham Priory & Market Cross Binham Field Dalling Sharrington Letheringsett Little Thornage Brinton Hempstead Baconsthorpe

Snettisham Sedgeford B1454 Fring South Creake Southgate Little Walsingham Great Walsingham Hindringham Lower Green Bale Thornage Hunworth Edgefield Green Plumstead Baconsthorpe Castle

Ingoldisthorpe Shernborne Bircham Newton Barmer West Barsham Houghton St Giles Thursford Stody Briningham Edgefield Little Barningham

Dersingham Doddshill Great Bircham Bircham Tofts Syderstone Wicken Green Village Sculthorpe Thursford Gunthorpe Swanton Novers Craymere Beck Saxthorpe Mannington Gardens

Dersingham Bog Anmer Houghton Hall Dunton Coxford Shereford Fakenham Kettlestone Fulmodeston Hindolveston Nethergate Thurning Corpusty Oulton

Sandringham West Newton New Houghton West Rudham Broomsthorpe Hempton Pensthorpe Waterfowl Park Croxton Stibbard Wood Norton Guestwick Wood Dalling Heydon

Flitcham Harpley East Rudham Helhoughton Tatterford Toftrees Little Ryburgh Great Ryburgh B1146 Guist Twyford Themelthorpe Reepham Salle Southgate

Castle Rising Hillington Little Massingham West Raynham East Raynham Colkirk Oxwick Gateley Broom Green Bintree Foxley Wood Foxley Whitwell Street Great Witchingham

Congham Grimston Great Massingham South Raynham Whissonsett Potthorpe Brisley North Elmham Billingford Bawdeswell B1145 Sparham Alderford Swan

Roydon Pott Row Weasenham St Peter Wellingham Tittleshall Stanfield North Elmham Chapel B1110 Worthing B1147 Lyng Sparhamhill Lenwade Dinosaur Attleb

King's Lynn Bawsey Gayton Weasenham All Saints Rougham East Bilney Old Beetley Beetley Bylaugh Elsing Morton on the Hill Weston Longville

Fairstead Brow-of-the-Hill Ashwicken Gayton Thorpe Mileham B1146 Swanton Morley Hoe Woodgate Primrose Green Greensgate

Fair Green East Winch West Acre Litcham Litcham East Lexham Beeston Longham Gressenhall Green Northall Green North Tuddenham Hockering Ringland T

North Runcton West Bilney West Lexham Newton Priory Castle Woodgate Gressenhall Hoe Etling Green Weston

Setchey Blackborough End Pentney Great Dunham Crane's Corner Sparrow Green Dereham A47 North Tuddenham Honingham Eastor

Middleton West Bilney Narborough Little Dunham Great Dunham Mattishall Burgh Mattishall Clint Green South Green East Tuddenham Welborne Royal Norfolk

Tottenhill Wormegay River Nar A47 Sporle Great Fransham Wendling Scarning Toftwood Dereham Westfield Yaxham Whinburgh Brandon Parva Barford Colton Marlingford

Marham A1122 Swaffham Ecotech Discovery Centre Necton Little Fransham Hulver Street West End Daffy Green Westfield Garvestone Runhall Coston Barnham Broom Great Melton

Shouldham Barton Bendish Beachamwell North Pickenham Holme Hale Ivy Todd East Bradenham West Bradenham Shipdham A1075 Brandon Parva Reymerston Thuxton Danemoor Green Wramplingham Hethersett

Crimplesham Fincham Cockley Cley A1065 South Pickenham Ashill Saham Hills Cranworth Southburgh Hardingham Hingham Hackford Crownthorpe Kimberley Kidd's Moor

Stradsett Iceni Village Great Cressingham Saham Toney Woodrising Mid Norfolk Railway Morley St Botolph Suton

West Dereham Wereham Boughton Oxborough Gooderstone Hilborough Watton Green Ovington Carbrooke Deopham Deopham Green Silfield

Wretton Oxburgh Hall Foulden Beckett End R Wissey Little Cressingham Bodney Watton B1108 Griston Scoulton Rockland St Peter Bow Street Stalland Common Deopham Green Wymondha

Stoke Ferry Whittington Northwold Merton Northacre Little Ellingham Rockland All Saints Fen Street Great Ellingham A11

Wissington B1112 A134 TL Thompson Stow Bedon Mount Pleasant Spooner Row Fundenhall

Methwold Hythe Methwold Cranwich Ickburgh Peddars Way & Norfolk Coast Path Breckles Stow Bedon Great Ellingham Besthorpe Bunwell Kineton

Mundford Brookville Breckles Attleborough Carleton Rode

0 1 2 3 4 5 miles
0 1 2 3 4 5 6 7 8 kilometres

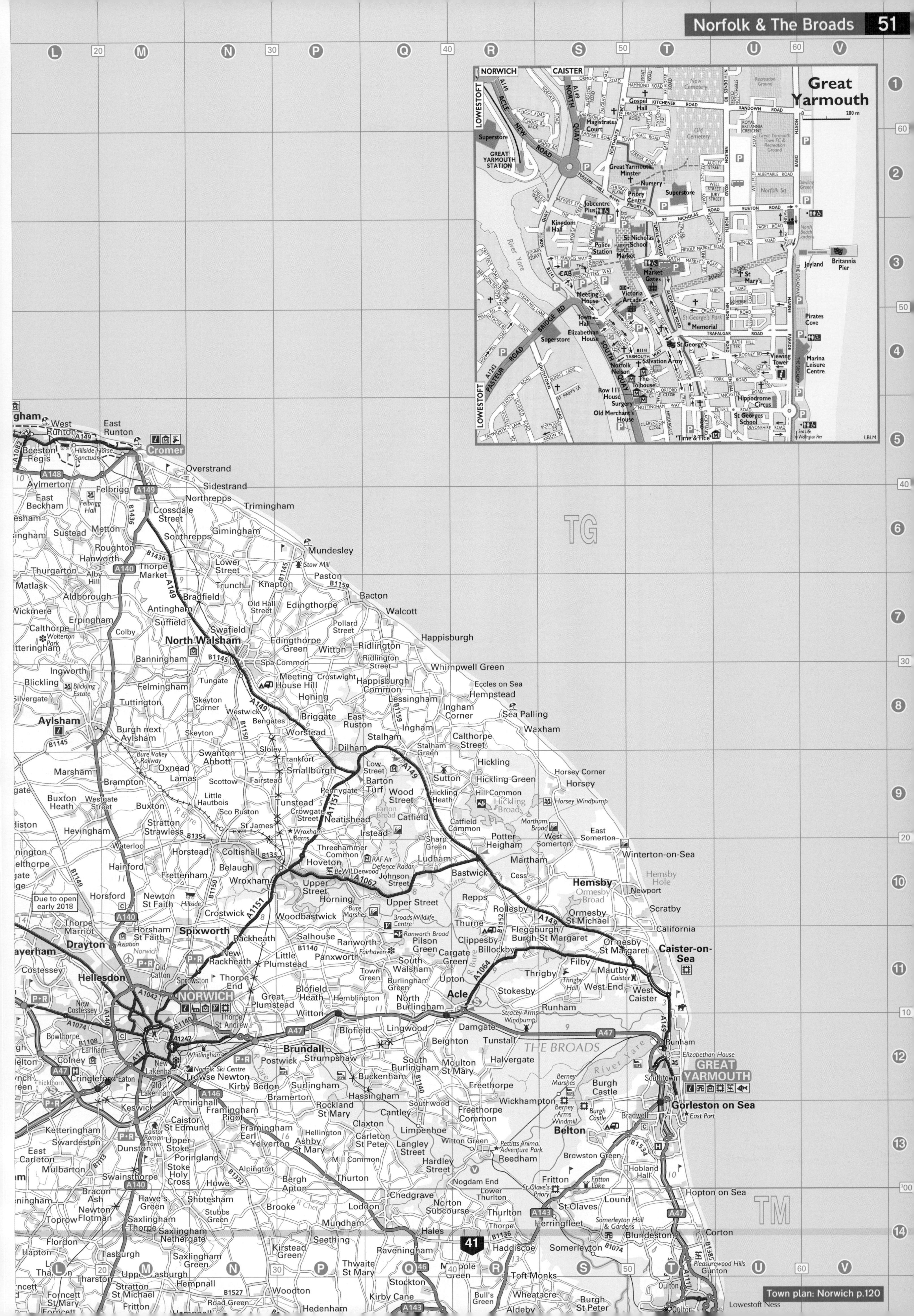

Great Yarmouth

NORWICH   CAISTER

Norwich

Great Yarmouth

Gorleston on Sea

Caister-on-Sea

North Walsham

Aylsham

Cromer

Acle

Hemsby

Belton

THE BROADS

TG

TM

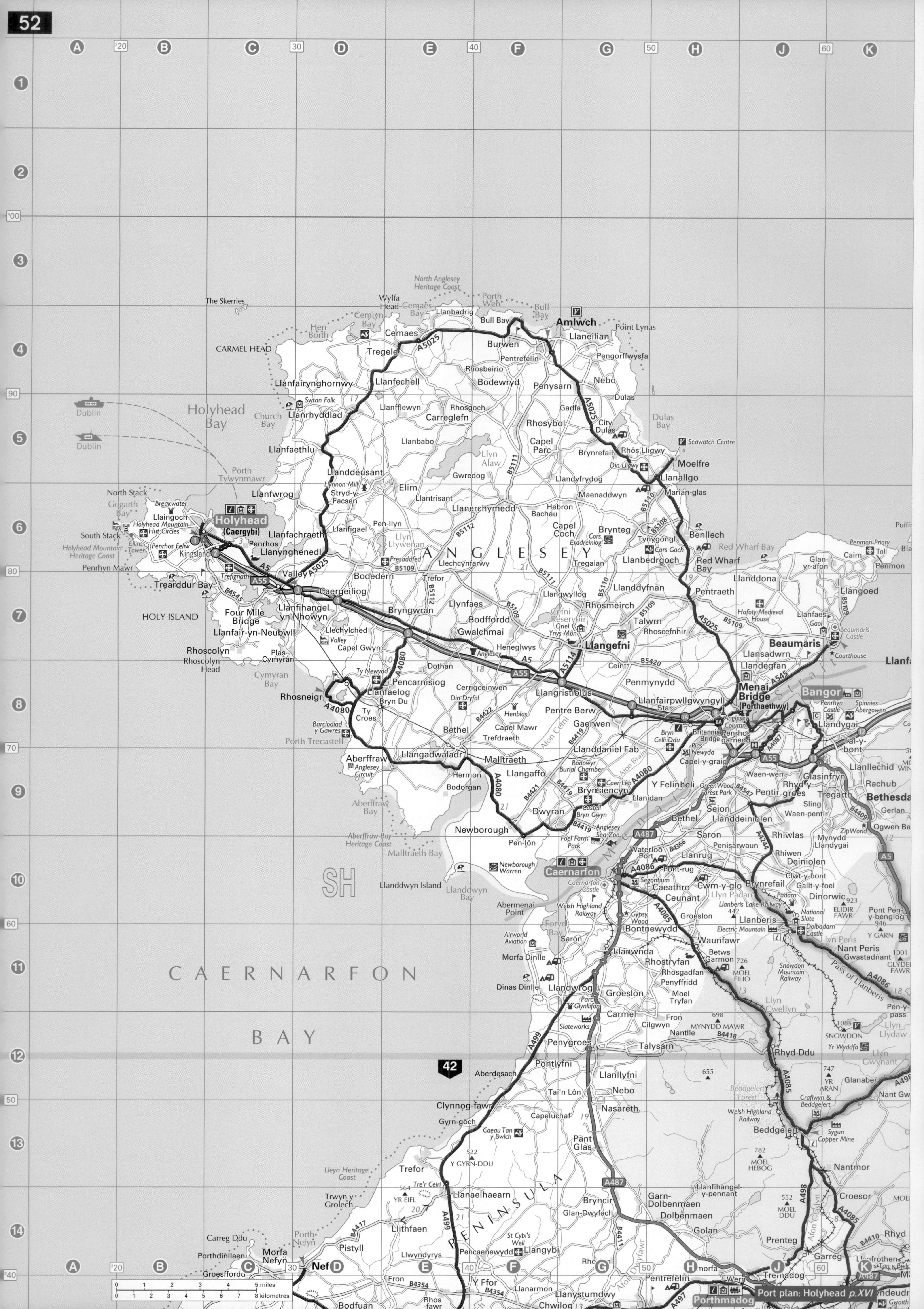

52
The Skerries
North Anglesey Heritage Coast
Wylfa Head
Cemaes Bay
Porth Wen
Bull Bay
Amlwch
Point Lynas
Cemlyn Bay
Hen Borth
Cemaes
Llanbadrig
Burwen
Llaneilian
CARMEL HEAD
Tregele
Pentrefelin
Pengorffwysfa
Rhosbeirio
Nebo
Llanfairynghornwy
Llanfechell
Bodewryd
Penysarn
Dulas
Holyhead Bay
Dublin
Church Bay
Swtan Folk
Llanrhyddlad
Llanfflewyn
Rhosgoch
Carreglefn
Gadfa
Rhosybol
City Dulas
Dulas Bay
Llanbabo
Capel Parc
Seawatch Centre
Llanfaethlu
Llyn Alaw
Brynrefail
Rhôs Lligwy
Moelfre
Porth Tywynmawr
Llanddeusant
Gwredog
Din Lligwy
Llanallgo
Llynnon Mill
Llandyfrydog
Marian-glas
North Stack
Llanfwrog
Stryd-y-Facsen
Elim
Llantrisant
Maenaddwyn
Gogarth Bay
Breakwater
Llaingoch
Holyhead Mountain Hut Circles
Holyhead (Caergybi)
Llanerchymedd
Hebron
Bachau
Benllech
Pen-llyn
Capel Coch
Brynteg
South Stack
Llanfachraeth
Llanfigael
Llyn Llywenan
Tynygongl
Cors Goch
Red Wharf Bay
Penmon Priory
Holyhead Mountain Heritage Coast
Ellins Tower
Penrhos Feliw
Penrhos
Kingsland
Llanynghenedl
ANGLESEY
Tregaian
Llanbedrgoch
Red Wharf Bay
Caim
Glan-yr-afon
Penmon
Penrhyn Mawr
Presaddfed
Llechcynfarwy
Valley
Trefignath
Trearddur Bay
Bodedern
Trefor
Llangwyllog
Llanddyfnan
Pentraeth
Llanddona
Llangoed
Caergeiliog
Rhosmeirch
HOLY ISLAND
Four Mile Bridge
Llanfihangel yn Nhowyn
Bryngwran
Llynfaes
Cefni Reservoir
Talwrn
Hafoty Medieval House
Llanfaes
Beaumaris
Beaumaris Castle
Llanfair-yn-Neubwll
Llechylched
Bodffordd
Oriel Ynys Môn
Rhoscefnhir
Valley
Gwalchmai
Rhoscolyn
Capel Gwyn
Anglesey
Heneglwys
Llangefni
Llansadwrn
Courthouse
Rhoscolyn Head
Plas Cymyran
Cymyran Bay
Dothan
Ceint
Llandegfan
Ty Newydd
Pencarnisiog
Penmynydd
Menai Bridge (Porthaethwy)
Bangor
Penrhyn Castle
Spinnies Abergwenan
Rhosneigr
Llanfaelog
Bryn Du
Cerrigceinwen
Din Dryfol
Llangristiolus
Llanfairpwllgwyngyll
Star
Llandygai
Ty Croes
Henblas
Pentre Berw
Barclodiad y Gawres
Bethel
Capel Mawr
Gaerwen
Bryn Celli Ddu
Britannia Bridge
Anglesey Column
Penrhos garnedd
Tal-y-bont
Porth Trecastell
Trefdraeth
Plas Newydd
Llanddaniel Fab
Aberffraw
Llangadwaladr
Malltraeth
Bodowyr Burial Chamber
Capel-y-graig
Llanllechid
Anglesey Circuit
Hermon
Llangaffo
Caer Lêb
Y Felinheli
Waen-wen
Glasinfryn
Rachub
Bodorgan
Brynsiencyn
Greenwood Forest Park
Pentir
Rhyd-y-groes
Tregarth
Bethesda
Aberffraw Bay
Dwyran
Llanidan
Castell Bryn Gwyn
Seion
Sling
Gerlan
Wern-pentir
Newborough
Anglesey Sea Zoo
Bethel
Llanddeiniolen
Ogwen Bank
Aberffraw Bay Heritage Coast
Pen-lôn
Foel Farm Park
Saron
Rhiwlas
Mynydd Llandygai
Malltraeth Bay
Waterloo Port
Penisarwaun
Zip World
Newborough Warren
Caernarfon
Llanrug
Rhiwen
Deiniolen
SH
Llanddwyn Island
Llanddwyn Bay
Caernarfon Castle
Pont-rug
Segontium
Caeathro
Cwm-y-glo
Brynrefail
Clwt-y-bont
Gallt-y-foel
Ceunant
Llyn Padarn
Dinorwic
Abermenai Point
Welsh Highland Railway
Llanberis Lake Railway
Gypsy Wood
Groeslon
Llanberis
National Slate
Foryd Bay
Bontnewydd
Electric Mountain
Dolbadarn Castle
ELIDIR FAWR
Pont Pen-y-benglog
Airworld Aviation
Saron
Waunfawr
Llyn Peris
Y GARN
Nant Peris
Gwastadnant
Morfa Dinlle
Llanwnda
Betws Garmon
Rhostryfan
MOEL EILIO
GLYDER FAWR
CAERNARFON
Rhosgadfan
Snowdon Mountain Railway
Pass of Llanberis
Dinas Dinlle
Llandwrog
Penyffridd
Groeslon
Moel Tryfan
Parc Glynllifon
Llyn Cwellyn
Pen-y-pass
Carmel
Fron
Cilgwyn
MYNYDD MAWR
Nantlle
SNOWDON
Llyn Llydaw
BAY
Slateworks
Penygroes
Talysarn
Yr Wyddfa
Rhyd-Ddu
Llyn Gwynant
Pontllyfni
Aberdesach
Llanllyfni
YR ARAN
Glanaber
Tai'n Lôn
Nebo
Beddgelert Forest
Nant Gwynant
Clynnog-fawr
Nasareth
Craflwyn & Beddgelert
Capeluchaf
Welsh Highland Railway
Gyrn-goch
Beddgelert
Sygun Copper Mine
Caeau Tan y Bwlch
Pant Glas
Y GYRN-DDU
MOEL HEBOG
Nantmor
Lleyn Heritage Coast
Trefor
Tre'r Ceiri
YR EIFL
Llanaelhaearn
Garn-Dolbenmaen
Llanfihangel-y-pennant
Croesor
Trwyn y Groloch
PENINSULA
Bryncir
Dolbenmaen
MOEL DDU
Glan-Dwyfach
Llithfaen
Golan
Carreg Ddu
Porth Nefyn
Pistyll
St Cybi's Well
Llangybi
Prenteg
Rhyd
Porthdinllaen
Morfa Nefyn
Llwyndyrys
Pencaenewydd
Rhos
Garreg
Llanfrothen
Groesffordd
Nefyn
Penmorfa
Tremadog
Fron
Y Ffor
Pentrefelin
Wern
Llanarmon
Llanystumdwy
Rhos-fawr
Bodfuan
Chwilog
Porthmadog
Port plan: Holyhead p.XVI
5 miles
8 kilometres

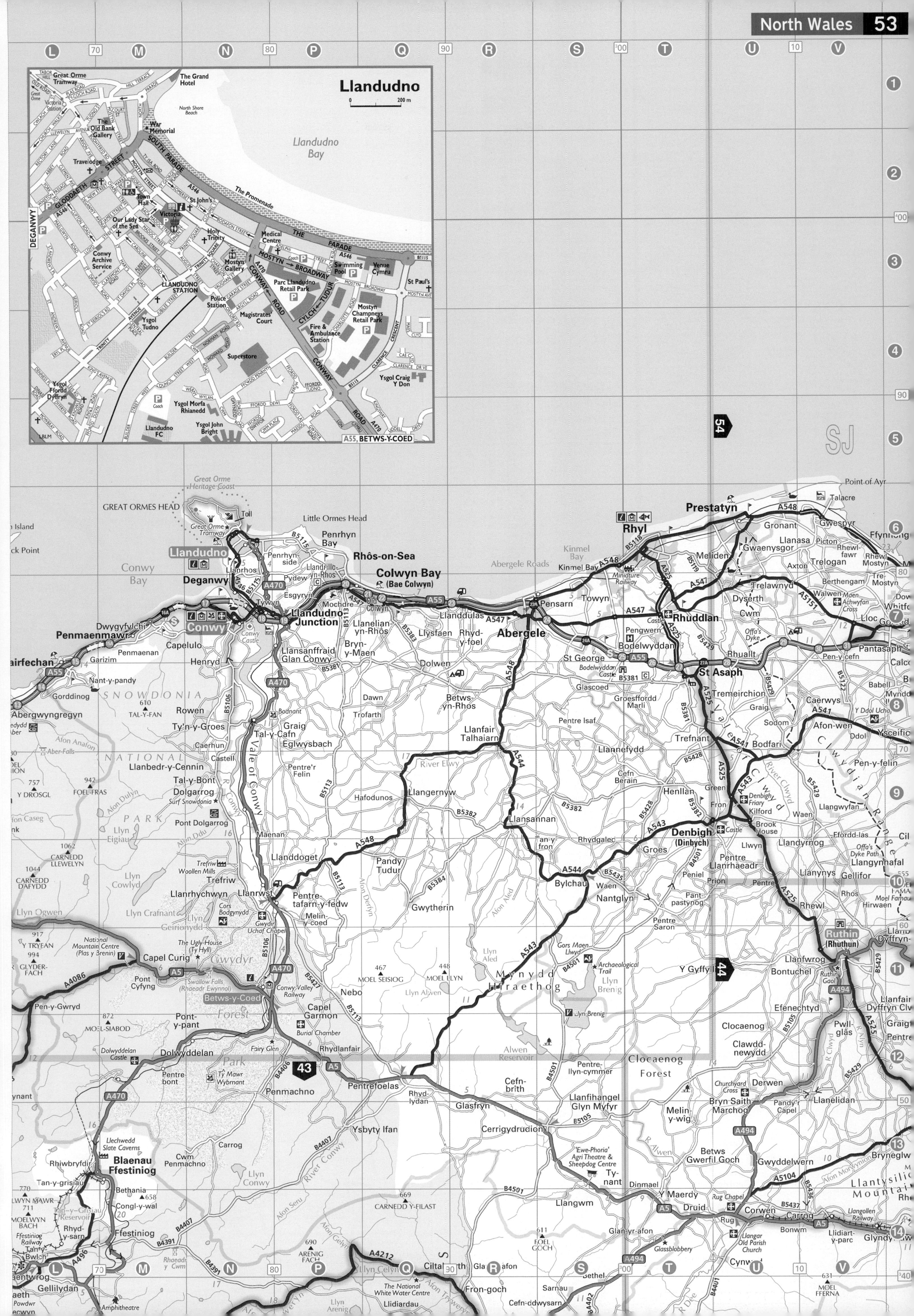

Llandudno

0   200 m

SJ

54

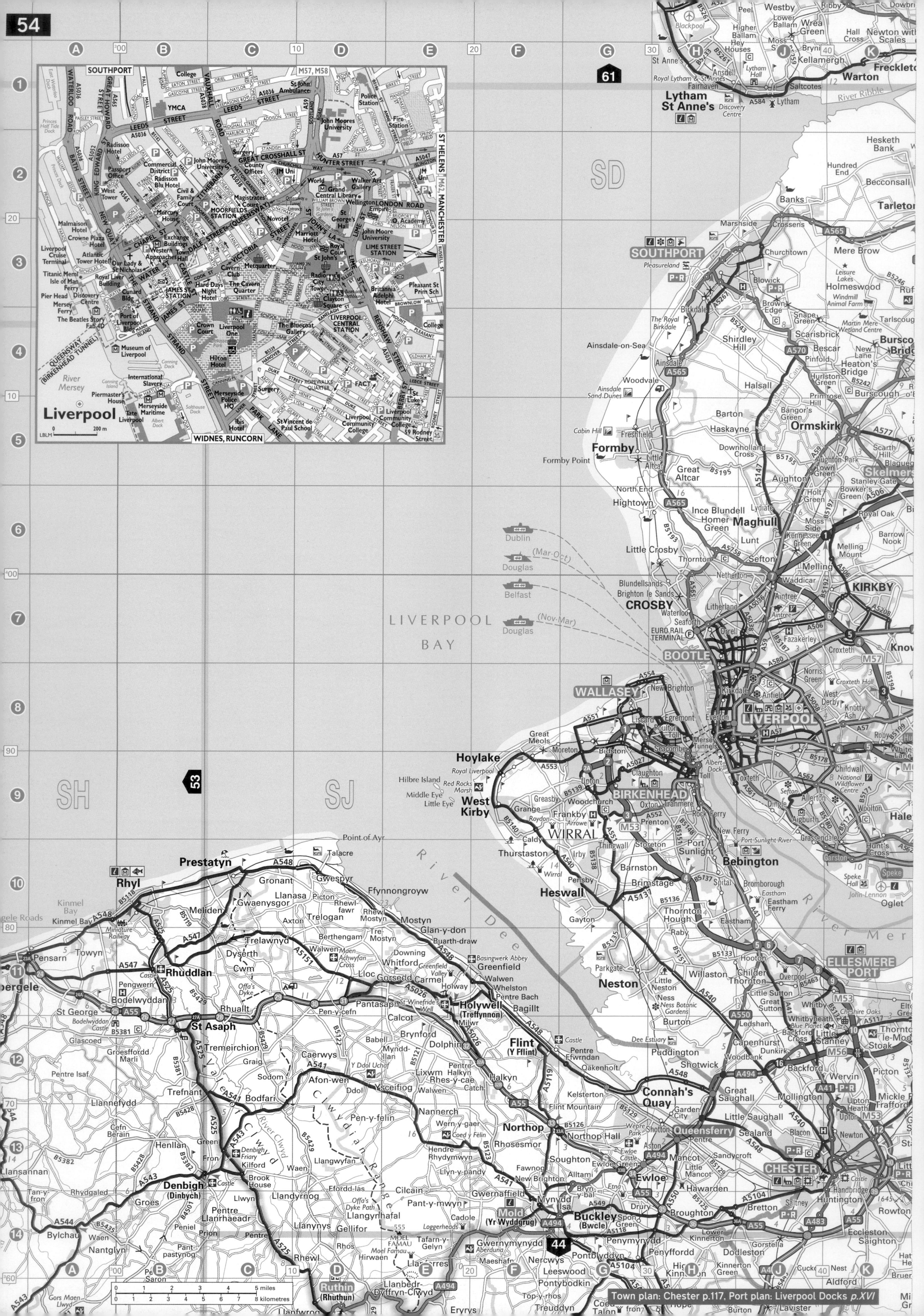

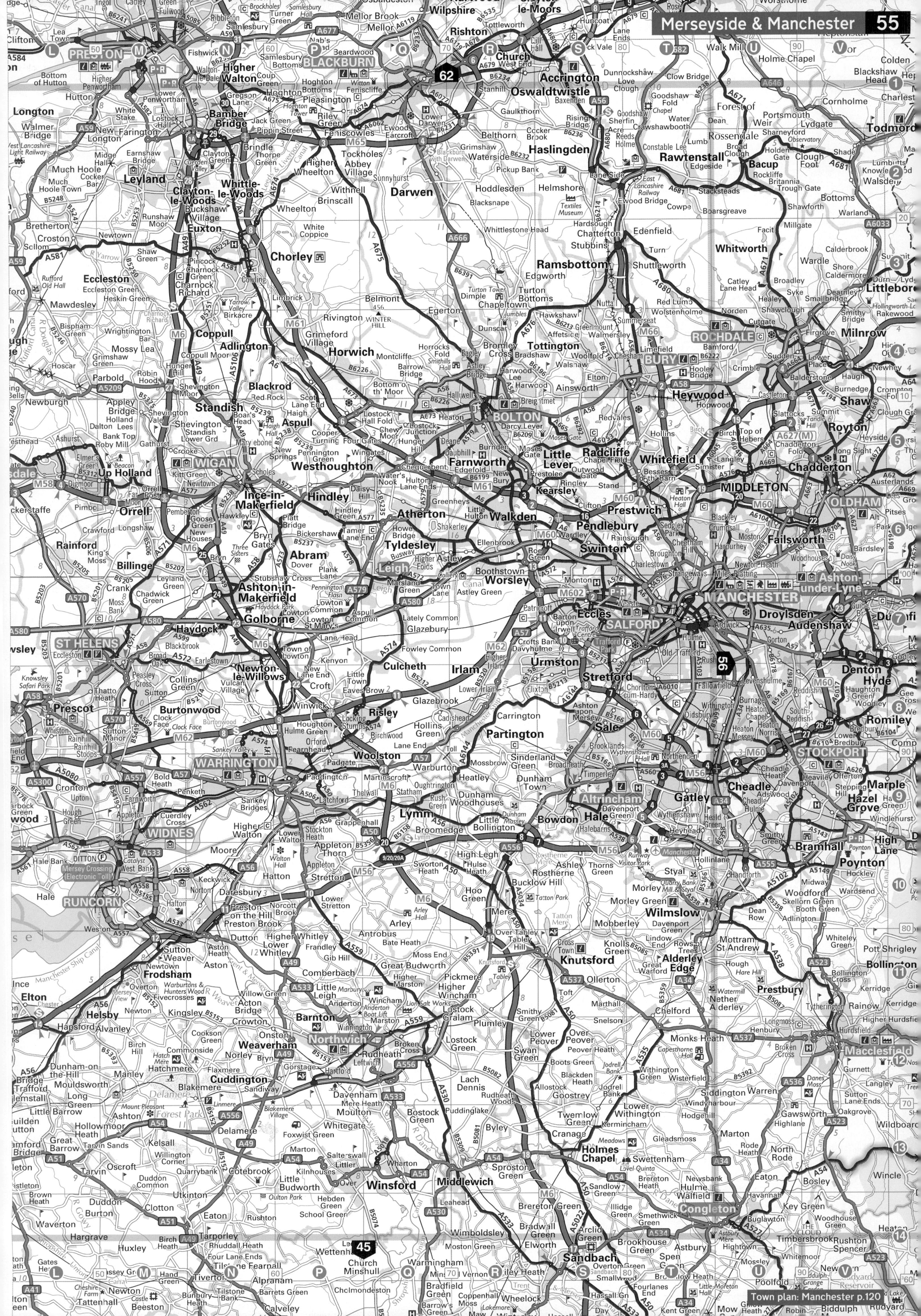
PRESTON
BLACKBURN
Accrington
Oswaldtwistle
Haslingden
Rawtenstall
Bacup
Todmorden
Leyland
Chorley
Darwen
Ramsbottom
Whitworth
Littleborough
Horwich
ROCHDALE
BURY
Heywood
Milnrow
Shaw
Royton
BOLTON
Farnworth
Radcliffe
Whitefield
MIDDLETON
Chadderton
OLDHAM
WIGAN
Up Holland
Orrell
Ince-in-Makerfield
Hindley
Westhoughton
Atherton
Walkden
Prestwich
Failsworth
Tyldesley
Swinton
Pendlebury
Leigh
Worsley
Ashton-in-Makerfield
Golborne
MANCHESTER
SALFORD
Eccles
Ashton-under-Lyne
Droylsden
Audenshaw
ST HELENS
Haydock
Newton-le-Willows
Prescot
Urmston
Stretford
Denton
Hyde
Irlam
Culcheth
Sale
Romiley
Partington
STOCKPORT
WARRINGTON
Cheadle
Gatley
Marple
Altrincham
Hale
Lymm
Bramhall
WIDNES
RUNCORN
Poynton
Wilmslow
Knutsford
Alderley Edge
Frodsham
Helsby
Prestbury
Macclesfield
Northwich
Weaverham
Cuddington
Holmes Chapel
Winsford
Middlewich
Congleton
Sandbach
Town plan: Manchester p.120

62
63
55
45
46
Accrington
Oswaldtwistle
Haslingden
Rawtenstall
Bacup
Todmorden
Hebden Bridge
HALIFAX
BRADFORD
Queensbury
Cleckheaton
Heckmondwike
Batley
Brighouse
Elland
Sowerby Bridge
Ripponden
HUDDERSFIELD
Mirfield
Ramsbottom
Whitworth
Littleborough
ROCHDALE
BURY
Heywood
Milnrow
Shaw
Royton
Radcliffe
Whitefield
MIDDLETON
Chadderton
OLDHAM
Prestwich
Pendlebury
Swinton
Failsworth
Ashton-under-Lyne
MANCHESTER
SALFORD
Eccles
Droylsden
Audenshaw
Stalybridge
Dukinfield
Mossley
Urmston
Stretford
Sale
Denton
Hyde
Romiley
STOCKPORT
Marple
Cheadle
Gatley
Altrincham
Hale
Bowdon
Hazel Grove
Bramhall
Poynton
High Lane
Disley
New Mills
Glossop
Hadfield
Whaley Bridge
Chapel-en-le-Frith
Wilmslow
Knutsford
Alderley Edge
Prestbury
Bollington
Macclesfield
Buxton
Bakewell
Congleton
Holmes Chapel
Sandbach
Biddulph
Meltham
Holmfirth
Kirkburton
Penistone
Marsden
Slaithwaite
Saddleworth Moor
Howden Moors
PEAK DISTRICT NATIONAL PARK
HIGH PEAK
ROAD CLOSED SAT/SUN/BH MON
Snake Pass
Kinder Scout
Edale
Castleton
Hope
Tideswell
Pennine Way
5 miles
8 kilometres

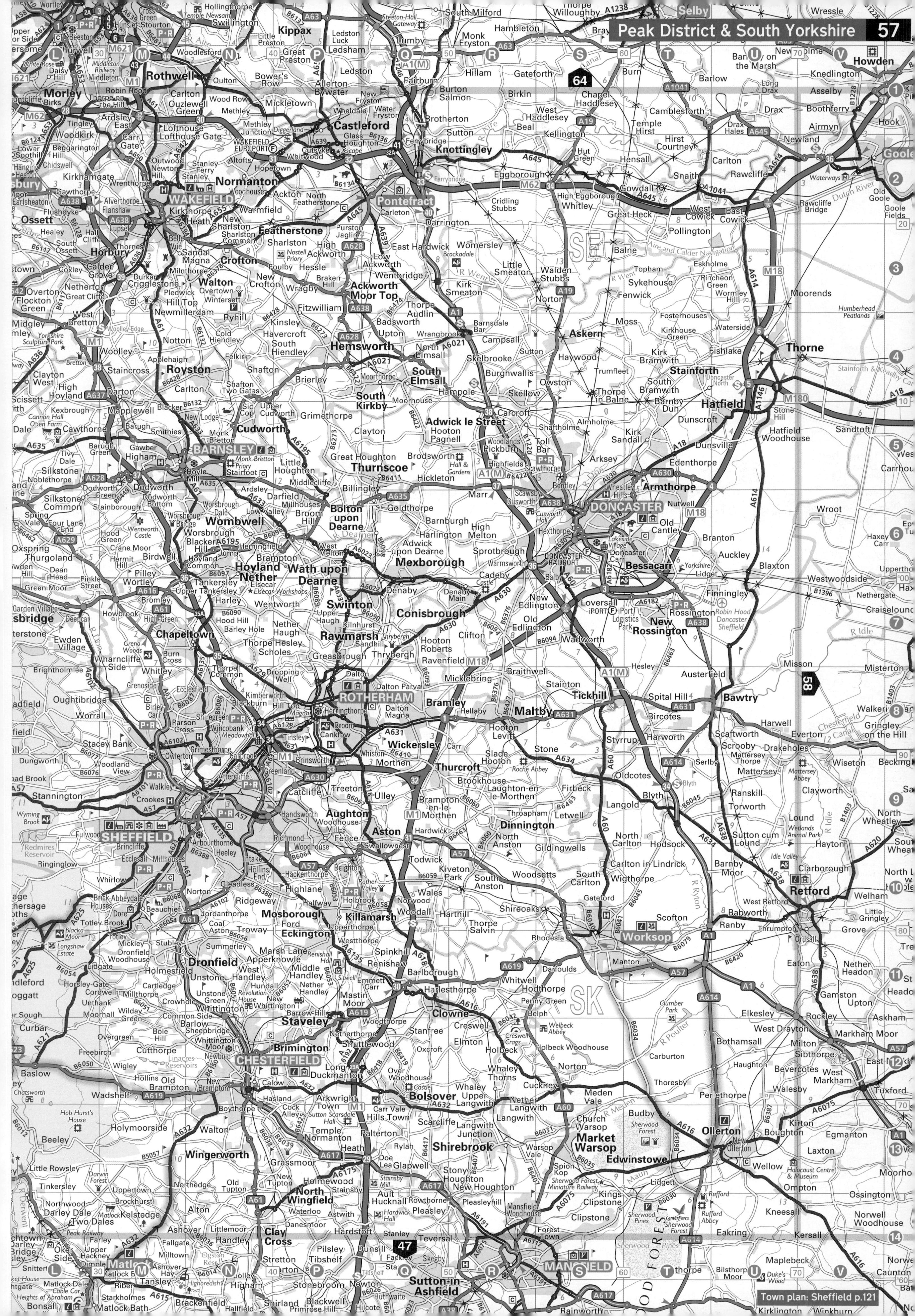
Selby
Howden
Kippax
Castleford
Knottingley
Rothwell
Morley
Normanton
WAKEFIELD
Pontefract
Ossett
Horbury
Featherstone
Crofton
Walton
Ackworth Moor Top
Hemsworth
South Elmsall
South Kirkby
Askern
Thorne
Stainforth
Hatfield
Royston
Cudworth
BARNSLEY
Adwick le Street
Thurnscoe
Wombwell
Bolton upon Dearne
Hoyland Nether
Wath upon Dearne
Mexborough
Conisbrough
Swinton
Rawmarsh
DONCASTER
Armthorpe
Bessacarr
New Rossington
Chapeltown
ROTHERHAM
Maltby
Tickhill
Bawtry
Bramley
Wickersley
Thurcroft
Dinnington
Aughton
Aston
SHEFFIELD
Mosborough
Killamarsh
Eckington
Dronfield
Staveley
Clowne
Brimington
CHESTERFIELD
Bolsover
Shirebrook
Market Warsop
Edwinstowe
Ollerton
Worksop
Retford
Wingerworth
North Wingfield
Clay Cross
Matlock
MANSFIELD
Sutton-in-Ashfield
Tuxford
64
58
47

Town plan: Sheffield p.121

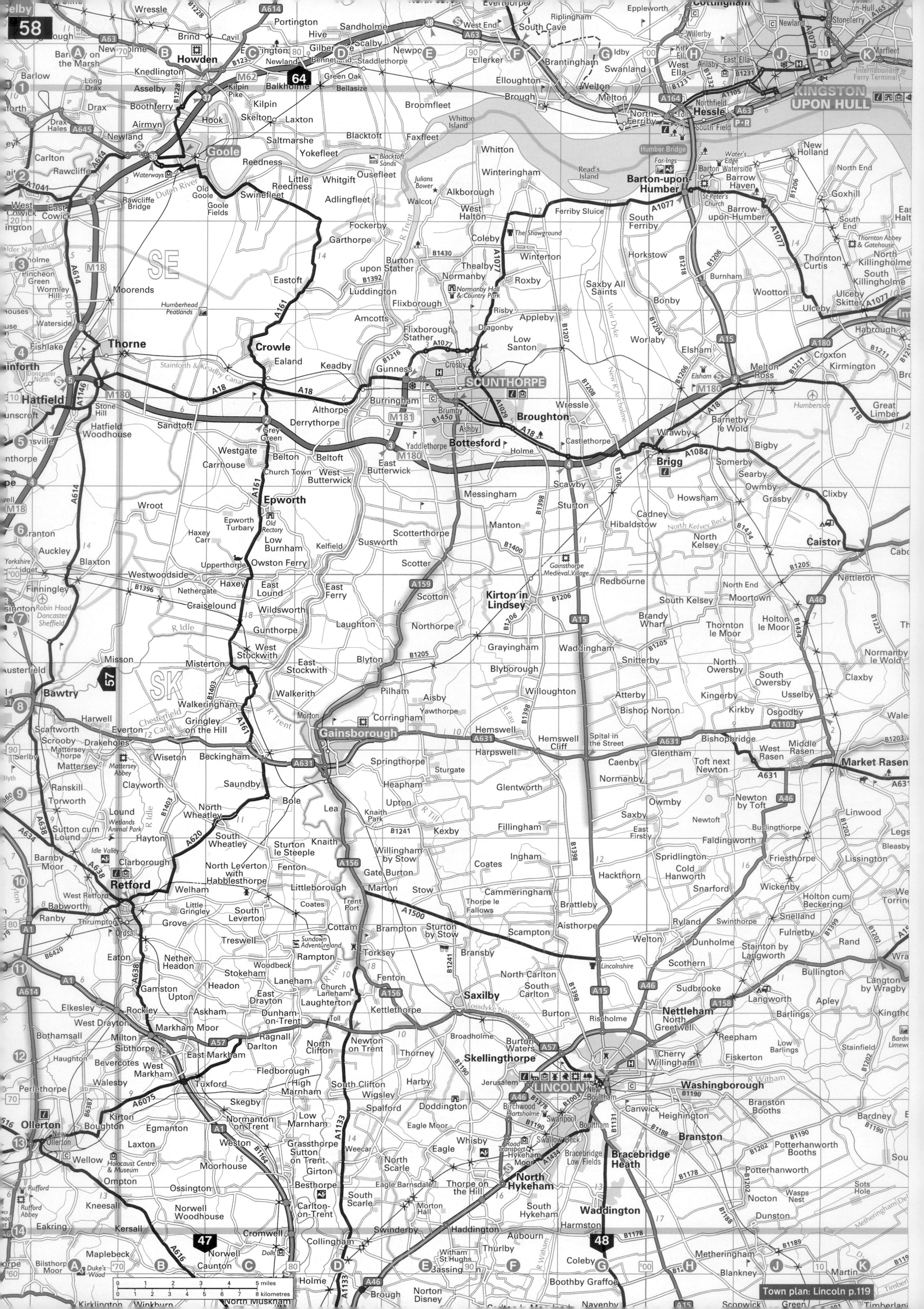
Howden
Goole
Thorne
Hatfield
Crowle
Epworth
Scunthorpe
Bottesford
Broughton
Brigg
Barton-upon-Humber
Hessle
Kingston upon Hull
Caistor
Kirton in Lindsey
Gainsborough
Market Rasen
Retford
Bawtry
Ollerton
Lincoln
North Hykeham
Waddington
Bracebridge Heath
Washingborough
Nettleham
Saxilby
Skellingthorpe
Branston
Portington
Sandholme
Wressle
Brind
Newport
Gilberdyke
Scalby
Staddlethorpe
Balkholme
Kilpin
Knedlington
Asselby
Barlow
Drax
Boothferry
Airmyn
Hook
Skelton
Laxton
Saltmarshe
Blacktoft
Faxfleet
Yokefleet
Reedness
Whitgift
Ousefleet
Adlingfleet
Swinefleet
Rawcliffe
Carlton
Old Goole
Goole Fields
Rawcliffe Bridge
Whitton
Winteringham
Alkborough
West Halton
Walcot
Fockerby
Garthorpe
Luddington
Eastoft
Moorends
Amcotts
Flixborough
Flixborough Stather
Burton upon Stather
Normanby
Thealby
Coleby
Winterton
Roxby
Risby
Appleby
Dragonby
Low Santon
Crosby
Gunness
Burringham
Keadby
Ealand
Althorpe
Derrythorpe
Grey Green
Belton
Beltoft
Westgate
Carrhouse
Church Town
West Butterwick
East Butterwick
Sandtoft
Stone Hill
Hatfield Woodhouse
Wroot
Epworth Turbary
Haxey Carr
Low Burnham
Kelfield
Susworth
Scotterthorpe
Scotter
Owston Ferry
Upperthorpe
Westwoodside
Haxey
East Lound
Nethergate
Graiselound
Wildsworth
East Ferry
Scotton
Laughton
Northorpe
Gunthorpe
West Stockwith
East Stockwith
Misterton
Misson
Blyton
Walkerith
Walkeringham
Gringley on the Hill
Pilham
Aisby
Yawthorpe
Corringham
Morton
Everton
Harwell
Scaftworth
Scrooby
Drakeholes
Mattersey
Mattersey Thorpe
Wiseton
Beckingham
Saundby
Clayworth
Ranskill
Torworth
Lound
Sutton cum Lound
Hayton
North Wheatley
South Wheatley
Bole
Lea
Knaith
Knaith Park
Sturton le Steeple
North Leverton with Habblesthorpe
Fenton
Littleborough
Coates
Clarborough
Welham
Little Gringley
South Leverton
Grove
Ordsall
Thrumpton
Babworth
Ranby
West Retford
Barnby Moor
Treswell
Cottam
Rampton
Torksey
Brampton
Sturton by Stow
Stow
Marton
Gate Burton
Willingham by Stow
Upton
Heapham
Springthorpe
Sturgate
Kexby
Glentworth
Fillingham
Ingham
Cammeringham
Thorpe le Fallows
Brattleby
Aisthorpe
Scampton
Hemswell
Hemswell Cliff
Harpswell
Spital in the Street
Caenby
Glentham
Normanby
Owmby
Saxby
East Firsby
Spridlington
Cold Hanworth
Hackthorn
Snarford
Faldingworth
Friesthorpe
Welton
Dunholme
Ryland
Scothern
Sudbrooke
Reepham
Cherry Willingham
Fiskerton
Langworth
Barlings
Apley
Stainton by Langworth
Snelland
Wickenby
Lissington
Holton cum Beckering
Linwood
Newton by Toft
Toft next Newton
West Rasen
Middle Rasen
Bishopbridge
Osgodby
Kirkby
Usselby
Kingerby
Claxby
Normanby le Wold
Owersby
North Owersby
South Owersby
Snitterby
Atterby
Bishop Norton
Waddingham
Grayingham
Blyborough
Willoughton
Redbourne
Hibaldstow
Cadney
Howsham
North Kelsey
South Kelsey
Brandy Wharf
Thornton le Moor
Holton le Moor
Moortown
North End
Nettleton
Searby
Owmby
Grasby
Clixby
Somerby
Bigby
Barnetby le Wold
Wrawby
Melton Ross
Elsham
Kirmington
Croxton
Great Limber
Worlaby
Bonby
Saxby All Saints
Horkstow
South Ferriby
Ferriby Sluice
Barrow-upon-Humber
Barrow Haven
Goxhill
New Holland
Thornton Curtis
Burnham
Wootton
Ulceby
Ulceby Skitter
North Killingholme
South Killingholme
Habrough
Scawby
Sturton
Manton
Messingham
Holme
Castlethorpe
Wressle
Brumby
Ashby
Yaddlethorpe
Eaton
Nether Headon
Headon
Upton
Gamston
Stokeham
Laneham
Church Laneham
East Drayton
Dunham-on-Trent
Ragnall
Darlton
Askham
Rockley
Elkesley
West Drayton
Milton
Markham Moor
Bothamsall
Haughton
Sibthorpe
Bevercotes
West Markham
East Markham
Tuxford
Walesby
Perlethorpe
Kirton
Boughton
Egmanton
Laxton
Wellow
Ompton
Kneesall
Eakring
Kersall
Maplebeck
Bilsthorpe Moor
Caunton
Norwell
Norwell Woodhouse
Ossington
Moorhouse
Weston
Grassthorpe
Sutton on Trent
Normanton on Trent
Skegby
Low Marnham
High Marnham
Fledborough
North Clifton
South Clifton
Newton on Trent
Kettlethorpe
Thorney
Wigsley
Harby
Spalford
Girton
Besthorpe
Carlton-on-Trent
Cromwell
Collingham
South Scarle
North Scarle
Eagle
Eagle Moor
Eagle Barnsdale
Doddington
Whisby
Thorpe on the Hill
Morton Hall
Swinderby
Haddington
Thurlby
Aubourn
Witham St Hughs
Bassingham
South Hykeham
Harmston
Coleby
Boothby Graffoe
Norton Disney
Brough
Holme
Broadholme
Burton Waters
Jerusalem
Birchwood
Hartsholme
Swanpool
Boultham
Swallow Beck
Bracebridge Low Fields
Canwick
Heighington
Branston Booths
Potterhanworth
Potterhanworth Booths
Nocton
Dunston
Metheringham
Blankney
Martin
Riseholme
Burton
North Carlton
South Carlton
Ellerker
Brantingham
Elloughton
Welton
Brough
Melton
North Ferriby
Swanland
Broomfleet
Cottingham
West Ella
Kirk Ella
Anlaby
Willerby
Bellasize
Green Oak
Newland
Fishlake
Stainforth
Barnby Dun
Auckley
Blaxton
Finningley
Austerfield
Hatfield Woodhouse
Wormley Hill
Waterside
Pincheon Green
SE
SK
57
64
47
48
Town plan: Lincoln p.119
0 1 2 3 4 5 miles
0 1 2 3 4 5 6 7 8 kilometres

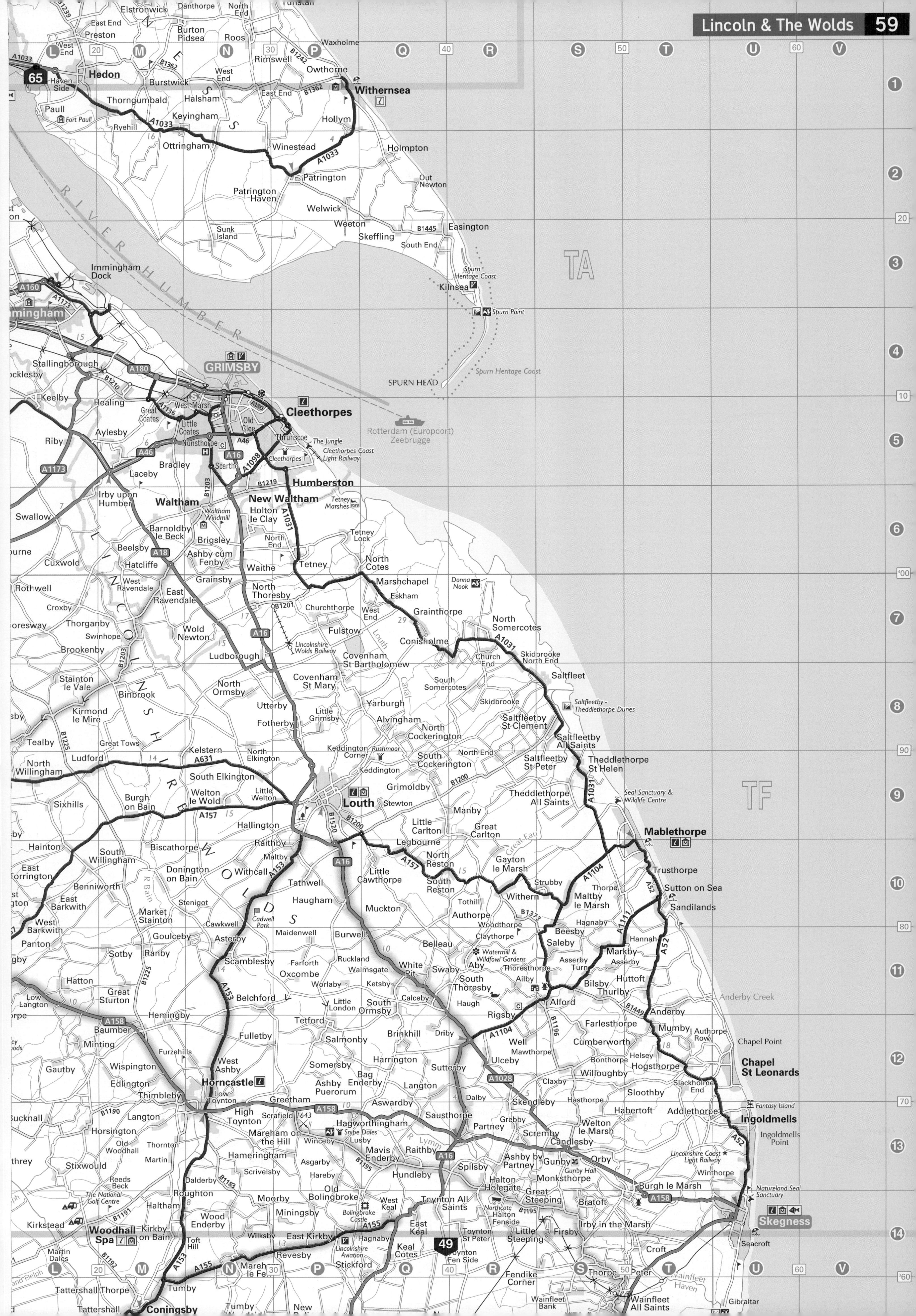
Hedon
Withernsea
Patrington
Easington
Kilnsea
Spurn Point
SPURN HEAD
RIVER HUMBER
GRIMSBY
Cleethorpes
Rotterdam (Europoort)
Zeebrugge
Humberston
New Waltham
Waltham
Tetney
North Cotes
Marshchapel
Grainthorpe
North Somercotes
Saltfleet
Saltfleetby - Theddlethorpe Dunes
Louth
Mablethorpe
Trusthorpe
Sutton on Sea
Sandilands
Alford
Anderby Creek
Chapel Point
Chapel St Leonards
Ingoldmells
Ingoldmells Point
Skegness
Seacroft
Gibraltar
Horncastle
Woodhall Spa
Coningsby
Tattershall
Spilsby
Burgh le Marsh
Wainfleet All Saints
Binbrook
Ludford
North Willingham
Market Stainton
Tetford
LINCOLNSHIRE WOLDS
TA
TF

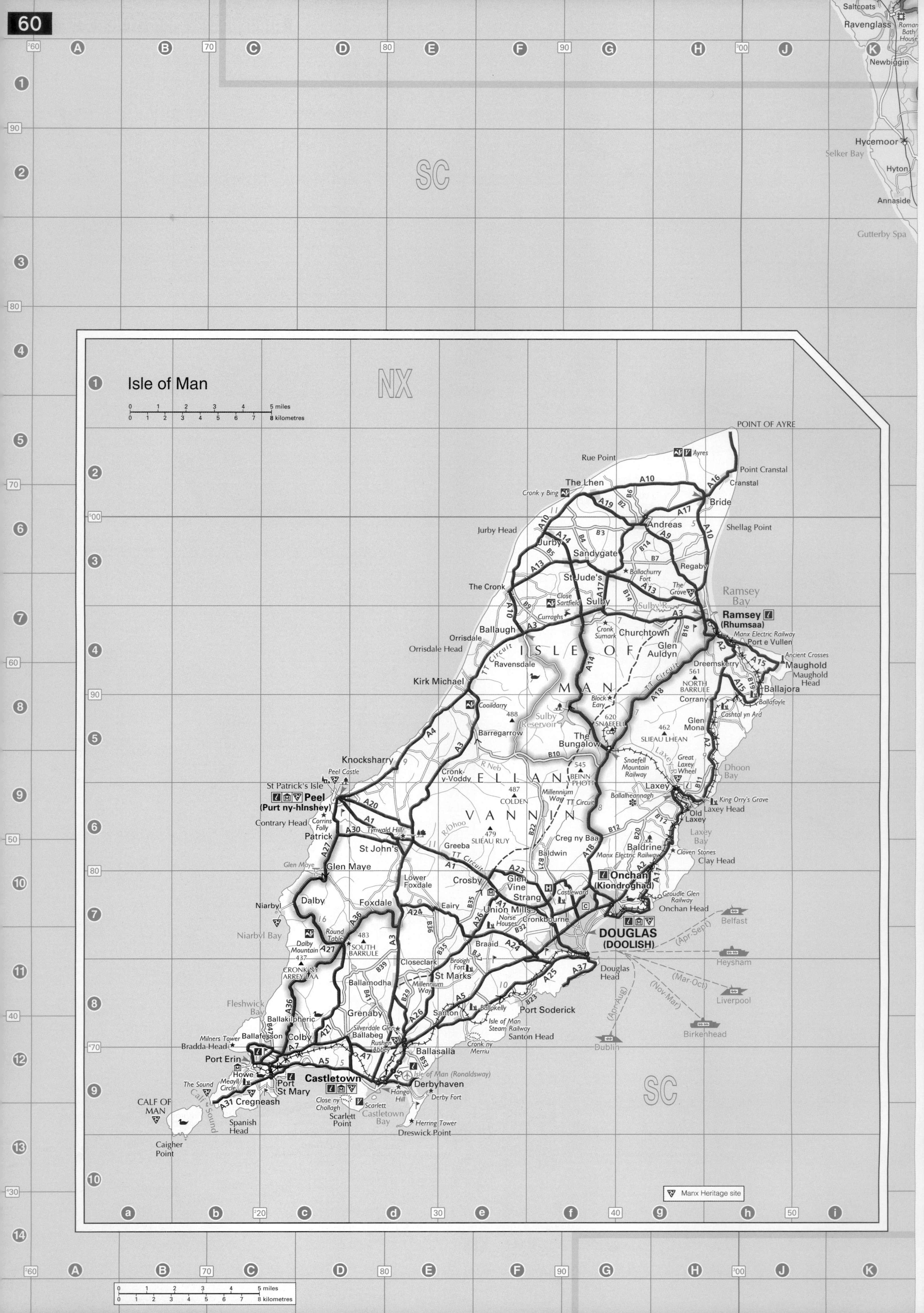

Isle of Man

NX

Saltcoats
Ravenglass
Roman Bath House
Newbiggin

Hycemoor
Selker Bay
Hyton
Annaside
Gutterby Spa

SC

POINT OF AYRE

Rue Point
Ayres
Point Cranstal
Cranstal
The Lhen
A10
Bride
Cronk y Bing
A19
B6
B2
A17
A16
Jurby Head
A10
Andreas
A9
Shellag Point
Jurby
A14
B3
B14
Sandygate
B4
St Jude's
A17
Ballachurry Fort
Regaby
B7
The Cronk
A13
A13
The Grove
Ramsey Bay
Close Sortfield
Sulby
B14
Sulby
Ballaugh
A3
Curraghs
A3
Ramsey (Rhumsaa)
Orrisdale
Cronk Sumark
Churchtown
B16
Manx Electric Railway
Orrisdale Head
ISLE OF
Glen Auldyn
Port e Vullen
Kirk Michael
Ravensdale
MAN
NORTH BARRULE 561
Dreemskerry
Maughold
Cooildarry
488
Block Eary
A18
Corrany
Ballajora
Maughold Head
Barregarrow
Sulby Reservoir
620 SNAEFELL
A15
Ballafayle
Cashtal yn Ard
The Bungalow
462 SLIEAU LHEAN
Glen Mona
Knocksharry
Peel Castle
Cronk-y-Voddy
R Neb
545
Snaefell Mountain Railway
Dhoon Bay
St Patrick's Isle
BEINN-Y-PHOTT
ELLAN
Great Laxey Wheel
Peel (Purt ny-hInshey)
A20
487
Millennium Way
King Orry's Grave
Contrary Head
Corrins Folly
A1
VANNIN
COLDEN
Laxey
Laxey Head
Patrick
A30
Tynwald Hill
Ballalheannagh
Old Laxey
A27
479 SLIEAU RUY
Creg ny Baa
B20
B12
St John's
Greeba
A18
Baldrine
Laxey Bay
Glen Maye
A1
TT Circuit
Baldwin
B10
Manx Electric Railway
Cloven Stones
Glen Maye
A23
Crosby
Glen Vine
Clay Head
Dalby
Lower Foxdale
B35
Strang
Castleward
Onchan (Kiondroghad)
Niarbyl
A1
Eairy
A26
Norse Houses
Groudle Glen Railway
Foxdale
A24
Cronkbourne
B32
Onchan Head
Niarbyl Bay
16
Round Table
Union Mills
DOUGLAS (DOOLISH)
Belfast
483
Braaid
A24
(Apr-Sept)
Dalby Mountain
SOUTH BARRULE
A3
B31
437
Closeclark
Brogh Fort
A25
A37
Heysham
CRONK NY ARREY LAA
Ballamodha
B39
St Marks
Douglas Head
Fleshwick Bay
A36
Millennium Way
A5
10
(Mar-Oct)
Grenaby
B39
B26
Santon
Liverpool
Ballakilpheric
Silverdale Glen
A5
Ballakelly
Port Soderick
Ballafesson
Ballabeg
Isle of Man Steam Railway
(Nov-Mar)
Milners Tower
Colby
Rushen Abbey
Santon Head
Bradda Head
A7
Cronk ny Merriu
Birkenhead
Port Erin
A5
Ballasalla
Isle of Man (Ronaldsway)
Dublin
Howe
A7
Castletown
Derbyhaven
The Sound
Meayll Circle
Port St Mary
Hango Hill
Derby Fort
CALF OF MAN
A31 Cregneash
Close ny Chollagh
Castletown Bay
Spanish Head
Scarlett Point
Herring Tower
Caigher Point
Dreswick Point

SC

Manx Heritage site

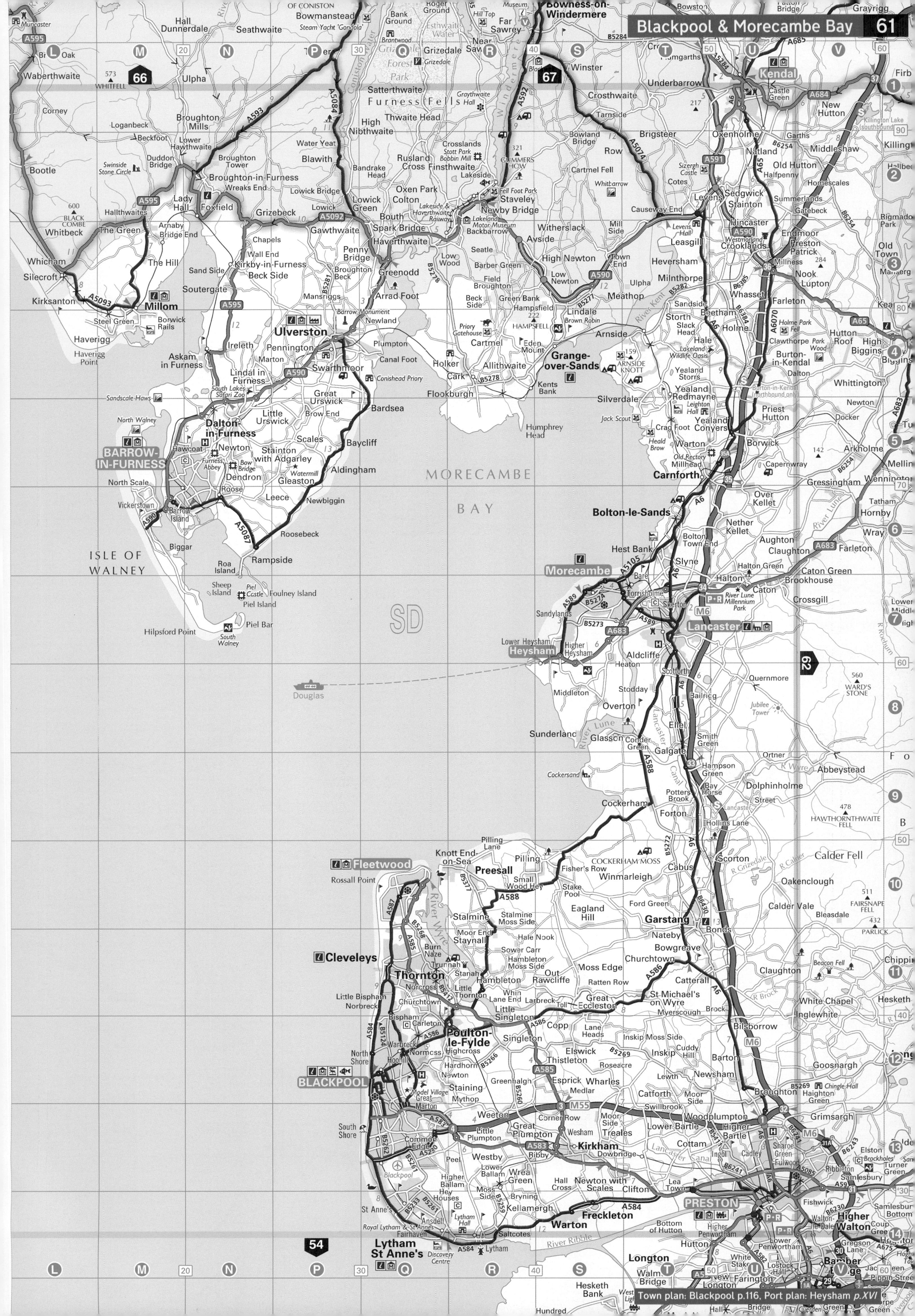
MORECAMBE
BAY
ISLE OF
WALNEY
SD
Bowness-on-Windermere
Kendal
Ulverston
Millom
BARROW-IN-FURNESS
Dalton-in-Furness
Grange-over-Sands
Carnforth
Bolton-le-Sands
Morecambe
Lancaster
Heysham
Fleetwood
Cleveleys
Thornton
Poulton-le-Fylde
BLACKPOOL
Lytham St Anne's
Kirkham
Preston
Garstang
Preesall
Knott End-on-Sea
Cockerham
Galgate
Glasson
Silverdale
Arnside
Milnthorpe
Cartmel
Flookburgh
Newby Bridge
Broughton-in-Furness
Coniston Water
Windermere
Grizedale Forest Park
Furness Fells
Askam in Furness
Rampside
Roa Island
Piel Island
Walney
Douglas
Bilsborrow
Freckleton
Warton
Longton
Calder Fell
Abbeystead
Dolphinholme
Quernmore
Halton
Caton
Arkholme
Kirkby Lonsdale
Crooklands
Levens
Sedgwick
Beetham
Holme
Burton-in-Kendal
Whittington
Hornby
Wray
M6
M55
A6
A590
A595
A5092
A5093
A587
A585
A586
A588
A583
A584
River Lune
River Wyre
River Ribble
River Kent

Town plan: Blackpool p.116, Port plan: Heysham p.XVI

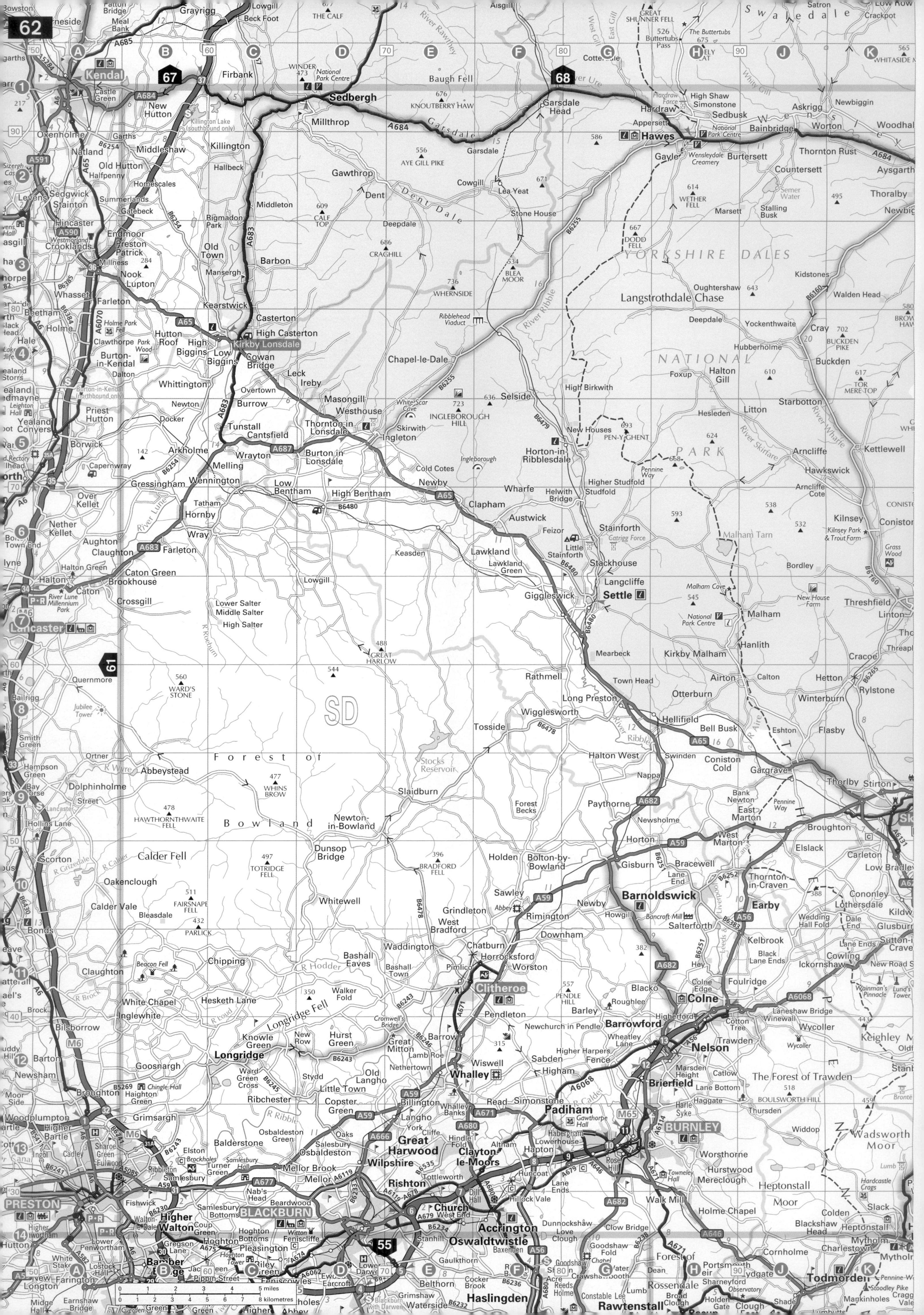

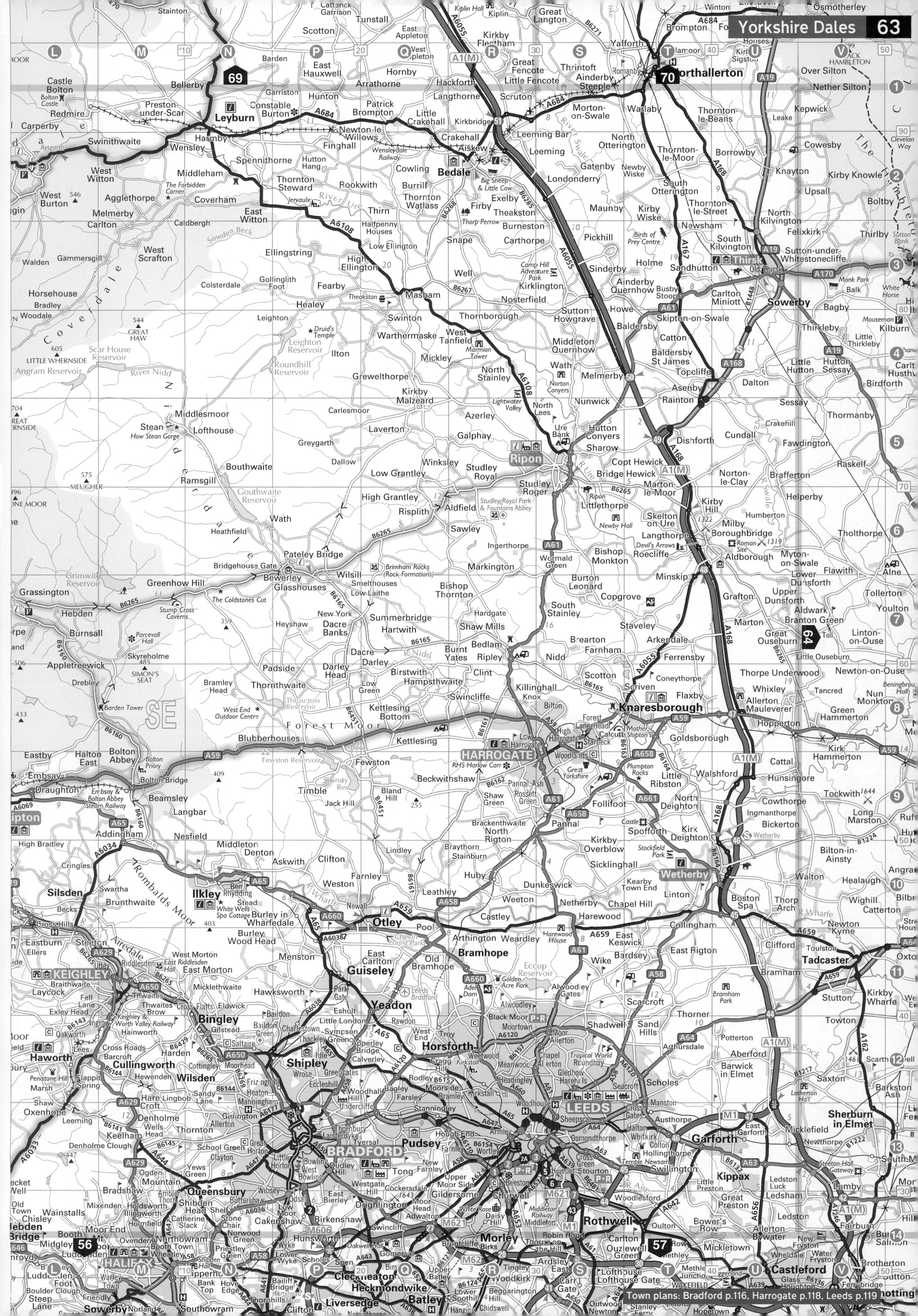

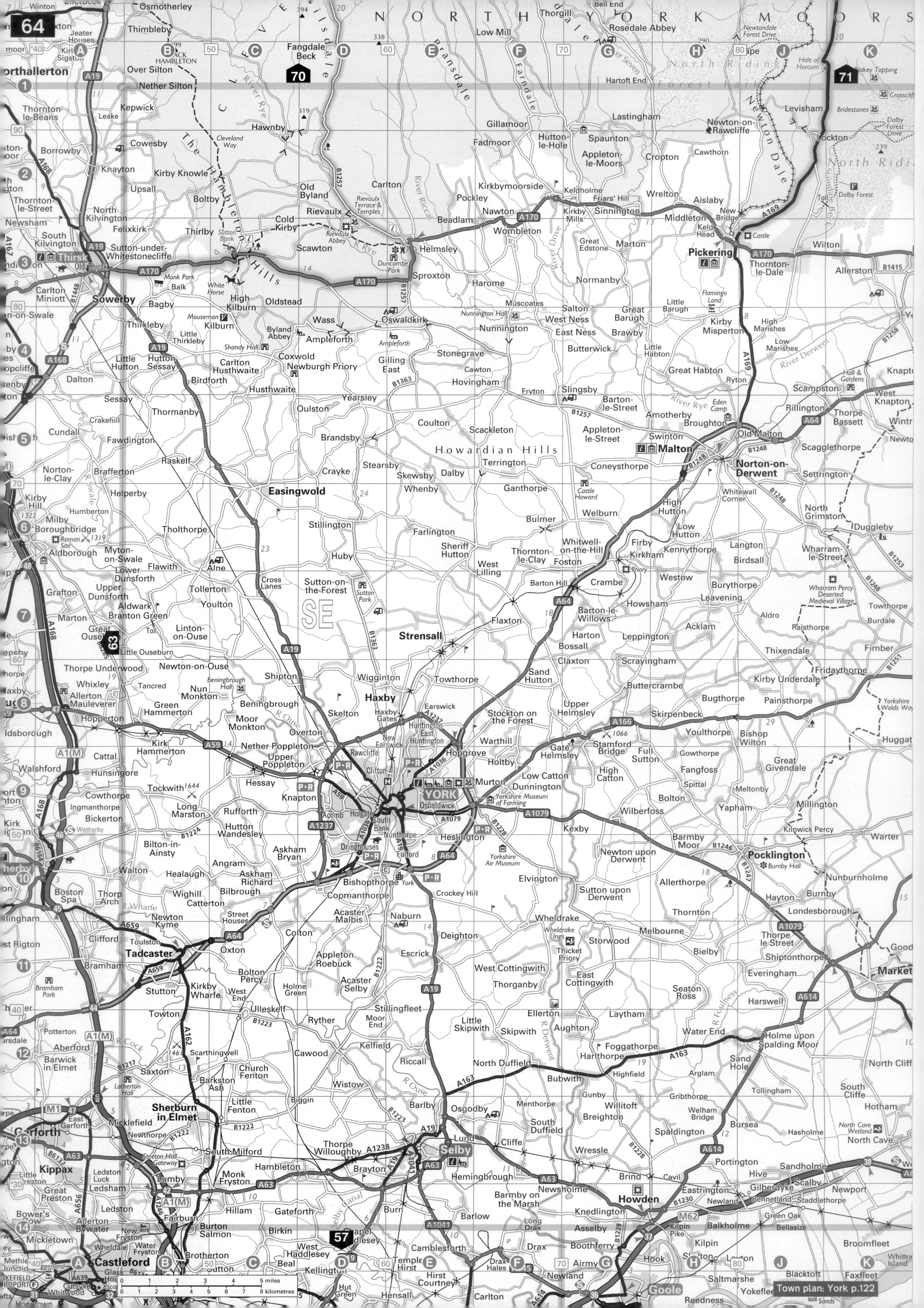
NORTH YORK MOORS
Winton
Osmotherley
Thimbleby
Jeater Houses
Kirby Sigston
Northallerton
Over Silton
Nether Silton
Black Hambleton
Cleveland Way
Bilsdale
Fangdale Beck
70
Low Mill
Bransdale
Farndale
Thorgill
Rosedale Abbey
Hartoft End
North Riding Forest Park
Newtondale Forest Drive
Hole of Horcum
Blakey Topping
71
Crosscliff
Levisham
Bridestones
Dalby Forest Drive
Newton Dale
Thornton-le-Beans
Kepwick
Leake
Hawnby
River Rye
Gillamoor
Lastingham
Newton-on-Rawcliffe
Lockton
Fadmoor
Hutton-le-Hole
Spaunton
Appleton-le-Moors
Cropton
Cawthorn
North Riding
Borrowby
Cowesby
Knayton
Kirby Knowle
The Hambleton Hills
Upsall
Old Byland
Carlton
Kirkbymoorside
Keldholme
Friars' Hill
Wrelton
Aislaby
Dalby Forest
Thornton-le-Street
Boltby
Rievaulx
Rievaulx Terrace & Temples
Pockley
Nawton
Kirkby Mills
Sinnington
Middleton
New Bridge
North Kilvington
Newsham
South Kilvington
Felixkirk
Thirlby
Cold Kirby
Rievaulx Abbey
Beadlam
Wombleton
Keld Head
Castle
Thirsk
Sutton-under-Whitestonecliffe
Sutton Bank
Scawton
Helmsley
Great Edstone
Marton
Pickering
Wilton
Carlton Miniott
Monk Park
Balk
White Horse
Duncombe Park
Sproxton
Harome
Normanby
Thornton-le-Dale
Allerston
Sowerby
Bagby
High Kilburn
Oldstead
Flamingo Land
Little Barugh
Muscoates
Salton
Great Barugh
Kirby Misperton
High Marishes
Sand Hutton
Thirkleby
Mouseman
Kilburn
Wass
Oswaldkirk
Nunnington Hall
Nunnington
West Ness
East Ness
Brawby
Little Thirkleby
Shandy Hall
Byland Abbey
Ampleforth
Butterwick
Little Habton
Low Marishes
River Derwent
Little Hutton
Hutton Sessay
Carlton Husthwaite
Coxwold
Newburgh Priory
Gilling East
Stonegrave
Cawton
Hovingham
Great Habton
Ryton
Knapton
Dalton
Birdforth
Husthwaite
Fryton
Slingsby
Barton-le-Street
Scampston
Hall & Gardens
West Knapton
Sessay
Yearsley
Oulston
Eden Camp
Amotherby
Rillington
Thorpe Bassett
Crakehill
Thormanby
Coulton
Scackleton
Appleton-le-Street
Broughton
Swinton
Old Malton
Cundall
Fawdington
Brandsby
Howardian Hills
Malton
Scagglethorpe
Raskelf
Terrington
Norton-on-Derwent
Norton-le-Clay
Brafferton
Stearsby
Crayke
Skewsby
Dalby
Coneysthorpe
Settrington
Helperby
Easingwold
Whenby
Ganthorpe
Castle Howard
Whitewall Corner
Kirby Hill
Humberton
Milby
Boroughbridge
Roman Site
Stillington
Welburn
High Hutton
North Grimston
Tholthorpe
Farlington
Bulmer
Low Hutton
Duggleby
Aldborough
Myton-on-Swale
Huby
Sheriff Hutton
Whitwell-on-the-Hill
Firby
Kirkham
Kennythorpe
Langton
Wharram-le-Street
Lower Dunsforth
Flawith
Alne
West Lilling
Thornton-le-Clay
Foston
Birdsall
Grafton
Upper Dunsforth
Tollerton
Cross Lanes
Sutton-on-the-Forest
Sutton Park
Barton Hill
Crambe
Westow
Burythorpe
Wharram Percy Deserted Medieval Village
Aldwark
Branton Green
Youlton
Leavening
Towthorpe
Marton
Linton-on-Ouse
Great Ouseburn
Toll
Flaxton
Barton-le-Willows
Howsham
Aldro
Burdale
Acklam
Raisthorpe
Strensall
Harton
Leppington
Fimber
Little Ouseburn
Bossall
Thixendale
Thorpe Underwood
Newton-on-Ouse
Claxton
Scrayingham
Fridaythorpe
Whixley
Tancred
Beningbrough Hall
Shipton
Wigginton
Towthorpe
Sand Hutton
Kirby Underdale
Allerton Mauleverer
Nun Monkton
Green Hammerton
Beningbrough
Haxby
Buttercrambe
Bugthorpe
Painsthorpe
Yorkshire Wolds Way
Earswick
Hopperton
Moor Monkton
Skelton
Haxby Gates
Huntington
Stockton on the Forest
Upper Helmsley
Skirpenbeck
Kirk Hammerton
Overton
East Huntington
Youlthorpe
Bishop Wilton
Huggate
Idsborough
Cattal
Nether Poppleton
Upper Poppleton
New Earswick
Warthill
Gate Helmsley
Stamford Bridge
Full Sutton
Walshford
Hunsingore
Rawcliffe
Hopgrove
Holtby
Gowthorpe
Great Givendale
Clifton
High Catton
Fangfoss
Tockwith
Hessay
Murton
Low Catton
Dunnington
Spittal
Meltonby
Cowthorpe
Knapton
YORK
Osbaldwick
Yorkshire Museum of Farming
Bolton
Millington
Ingmanthorpe
Long Marston
Rufforth
Acomb
Holgate
Wilberfoss
Yapham
Bickerton
Wetherby
South Bank
Heslington
Kexby
Kilnwick Percy
Hutton Wandesley
Nunthorpe
Barmby Moor
Warter
Bilton-in-Ainsty
Askham Bryan
Dringhouses
Fulford
Yorkshire Air Museum
Newton upon Derwent
Pocklington
Burnby Hall
Angram
Askham Richard
Walton
Healaugh
Bishopthorpe
York
Elvington
Allerthorpe
Nunburnholme
Boston Spa
Thorp Arch
Wighill
Bilbrough
Catterton
Copmanthorpe
Crockey Hill
Sutton upon Derwent
Hayton
Burnby
Acaster Malbis
Naburn
Thornton
Londesborough
Street Houses
Newton Kyme
Wheldrake
Wheldrake Ings
Melbourne
Clifford
Toulston
Colton
Deighton
Storwood
Thicket Priory
Thorpe le Street
Shiptonthorpe
Tadcaster
Oxton
Appleton Roebuck
Escrick
Bielby
Market
Bramham
West Cottingwith
East Cottingwith
Everingham
Bramham Park
Bolton Percy
Acaster Selby
Thorganby
Seaton Ross
Stutton
Kirkby Wharfe
West End
Holme Green
Harswell
Towton
Ulleskelf
Stillingfleet
Ellerton
Laytham
Ryther
Moor End
Little Skipwith
Skipwith
Aughton
Water End
Holme upon Spalding Moor
Potterton
Aberford
Kelfield
Foggathorpe
Barwick in Elmet
Scarthingwell
Cawood
Harlthorpe
Sand Hole
North Cliffe
Saxton
Church Fenton
Riccall
North Duffield
Bubwith
Highfield
Arglam
Barkston Ash
Wistow
Lotherton Hall
Gunby
Tollingham
South Cliffe
Biggin
Little Fenton
Barlby
Osgodby
Menthorpe
Willitoft
Gribthorpe
Sherburn in Elmet
Breighton
Welham Bridge
Hotham
Garforth
East Garforth
Micklefield
Newthorpe
South Duffield
Bursea
North Cave Wetland
Spaldington
Hasholme
North Cave
Thorpe Willoughby
Lund
Cliffe
Wressle
Steeton Hall Gateway
South Milford
Selby
Portington
Sandholme
Kippax
Little Preston
Ledston Luck
Lumby
Monk Fryston
Hambleton
Brayton
Hemingbrough
Brind
Cavil
Hive
Scalby
Ledsham
Great Preston
Newsholme
Barmby on the Marsh
Eastrington
Gilberdyke
Newport
Howden
Bennetland
Newland
Staddlethorpe
Hillam
Gateforth
Burn
Knedlington
Ledston
Fairburn
Barlow
Asselby
Green Oak
Bellasize
Allerton Bywater
Burton Salmon
Birkin
Long Drax
Balkholme
Bower's Row
New Fryston
Water Fryston
Chapel Haddlesey
Kilpin Pike
Kilpin
Broomfleet
Mickletown
Brotherton
West Haddlesey
Camblesforth
Drax
Boothferry
Methley Junction
Castleford
Glass
Sutton
Beal
Kellington
Temple Hirst
Drax Hales
Newland
Airmyn
Hook
Skelton
Laxton
Whitton Island
Whitwood
Cutsyke
Hut Green
Hirst Courtney
Blacktoft
Faxfleet
Saltmarshe
Yokefleet
Hensall
Carlton
Goole
Reedness
Sands
Town plan: York p.122
63
57
SE
0 1 2 3 4 5 miles
0 1 2 3 4 5 6 7 8 kilometres

Scarborough
Filey
Filey Bay
Hunmanby
Bridlington
BRIDLINGTON BAY
FLAMBOROUGH HEAD
Flamborough
Driffield
Hornsea
Beverley
Cottingham
KINGSTON UPON HULL
Hedon
Withernsea
Hessle
Weighton
TA
58
59
Town plan: Kingston upon Hull p.119

66
Dalbeattie
Little Knox
Carlingwark Loch
Rhonehouse
Gelston
Craigley
Barlochan
Palnackie
Airieland
Barnbarroch
Kippford / Scaur
Mote of Mark
Orchardton Tower
343 SCREEL HILL
390 BENGAIRN
East Stewartry Coast
Drumburn
Rockcliffe
Colvend
Portling
Sandyhills
Fairgirth
Caulkerbush
Mainsriddle
Loaningfoot
74
569 CRIFFELL
Carse Bay
Kirkbean
Carsethorn
Borron Point
Arbigland
Gill Foot Bay
Southerness
Southerness Point
Castlehill Point
Sypland
Auchencairn
Culnaightrie
Auchencairn Bay
Heston Island
Balcary
Balcary Point
Rascarrel
Orroland
Dundrennan Abbey
73
Abbey Head
SOLWAY FIRTH
NX
Solway
Campfield Marsh
Glasson Moss
Bowness Common
Drum
Longcroft
Cardurnock
Grune Point
Anthorn
Whitrigg
Angerton
Moricambe Bay
Kirkbride
Skinburness
Powhill
Newton Arlosh
Silloth
East Cote
Calvo
Causewayhead
Border
Salt Coates
Seaville
Blackdyke
Brownrigg
South Solway Mosses
Bigland
Blitterlees
Moss Side
Raby
Abbey Town
Holm Cultram
Kingside Hill
Wolsty
Kelsick
Oulton
Lessonhall
Beckfoot
Dundraw
Moor Row
Aikhead
Pelutho
Highlaws
Newtown
Aldoth
Wheyrigg
Blencogo
Waverbridge
Waverton
Holme St Cuthbert
Tarns
Bromfield
Parkgate
Mawbray
Salta
Mealrigg
High Scales
Waterside
Dubmill Point
Edderside
New Cowper
Langrigg
Westnewton
Yearngill
Low Row
Bolton Low Houses
Crookdale
Allonby
Allonby Bay
Watchill
Fletchertown
Hayton
Aspatria
Harriston
Baggrow
Blennerhasset
Mealsgate
Prospect
Oughterside
Arkleby
Kirkland Guards
Torpenhow
Allerby
Threapland
Crosscanonby
Crosby
Crosby Villa
Bullgill
Parsonby
Plumbland
Bothel
Whitrigg
Ireby
Fort
River Ellen
Gilcrux
Greengill
High Ireby
Uldale
Maryport
Dearham
Ruthwaite
Ellenborough
Townhead
447 BINSEY
Risehow
Tallentire
Sunderland
Bewaldeth
Fothergill
Woodside
Broughton Moor
Blindcrake
Bridekirk
Redmain
Lake District Wildlife Park
High Bewaldeth
Flimby
Standingstone
Dovenby
R Derwent
Kilnhill
Bassenthwaite
St Helens
Great Broughton
Little Broughton
Papcastle
Jennings
North Row
Chapel
Siddick
High Seaton
Camerton
Embleton
High Side
Seaton
Great Clifton
Cockermouth
Scarness
Brigham
Wythop Mill
North Side
Bridgefoot
Greysouthen
Bassenthwaite Lake
Workington
Stainburn
Little Clifton
Eaglesfield
Mirehouse
Little Crosthwaite
Mossbay
Armaside
Moss Bay
Westfield
Salterbeck
High Harrington
Winscales
Deanscales
552 LORDS SEAT
Harrington
Branthwaite
Dean
Low Lorton
Mosser Mains
High Lorton
Thornthwaite
Grayson Green
Ullock
Pardshaw
Whinlatter
Distington
Thackthwaite
318 Whinlatter Pass
Braithwaite
Common End
Mockerkin
Waterend
790 GRISEDALE PIKE
Gilgarran
Pica
Kidburngill
770 HOBCARTON PIKE
Swinside
Lowca
Howgate
Low Moresby
Stair
Parton
Loweswater
Lamplugh
Loweswater
Brownrigg
851 GRASMOOR
572
Little Town
Moresby Parks
Arlecdon
Asby
Kirkland
Crummock Water
Whitehaven
Rowrah
High Leys
Winder
Grange
Kells
Hensingham
Frizington
Scale Force
Saltom Bay
Buttermere
Hassness
Mirehouse
Cleator Moor
615
636
Ennerdale Bridge
Ennerdale Water
Buttermere
806 HIGH STILE
Gatesgarth
754 DALE HEAD
Sandwith
Sandwith Newtown
Moor Row
356 Honister Pass
Honister Slate Mine
River Liza
Rottington
Bigrigg
St Bees Head
St Bees Head Heritage Coast
Cleator
River Calder
533 LANK RIGG
892 PILLAR
St Bees
Egremont
LAKE DISTRICT
798 HAYCOCK
802 KIRK FELL
899 GREAT GABLE
Wilton
Worm Gill
Coulderton
Thornhill
Carleton
Wasdale Head
NATIONAL PARK
Middletown
Haile
691 SEATALLAN
River Bleng
910 GREAT END
Nethertown
Blackbeck
978 SCAFELL PIKE
964 SCAFELL
902 BOW FELL
Beckermet
Calder Bridge
Wast Water
Braystones
Ponsonby
R Ehen
Cross
Wellington
Nether Wasdale
Burnmoor Tarn
Sellafield Station
Calder
R Irt
Gosforth
R Mite
Santon
Santon Bridge
Boot
Hardknott Fort
393 Hardknott Pass
Seascale
Eskdale Green
Beckfoot
Hallsenna Moor
Eskdale
652 HARTER FELL
Drigg
Holmrook
Muncaster Mill
Ravenglass & Eskdale Railway
River Esk
Devoke Water
River Duddon
Saltcoats
Muncaster
Ravenglass
Roman Bath House
Hall Dunnerdale
Seathwaite
Broad Oak
SD
Newbiggin
Waberthwaite
573 WHITFELL
Ulpha
Corney
Logan
Broughton Mills
Beckfoot
Lower Hawthwaite
Hycemoor
Selker Bay
Swinside
Duddon Bridge
Broughton Tower
A75
A710
A711
B793
B736
A596
B5299
B5300
B5301
B5302
B5307
A591
A594
A595
A66
B5291
B5292
A597
B5306
A5086
B5295
B5294
B5345
B5343
B5289
A593
0 1 2 3 4 5 miles
0 1 2 3 4 5 6 7 8 kilometres

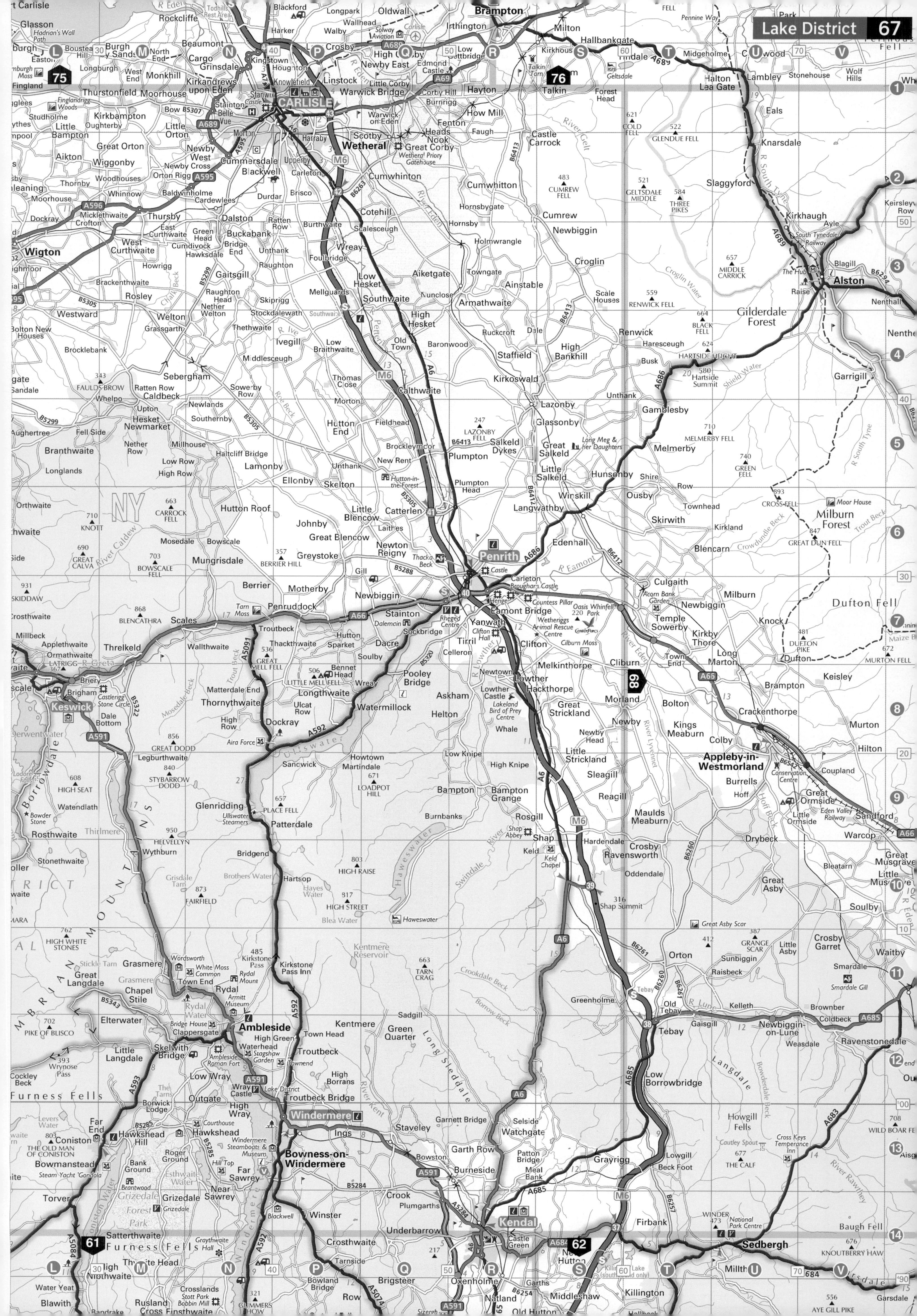

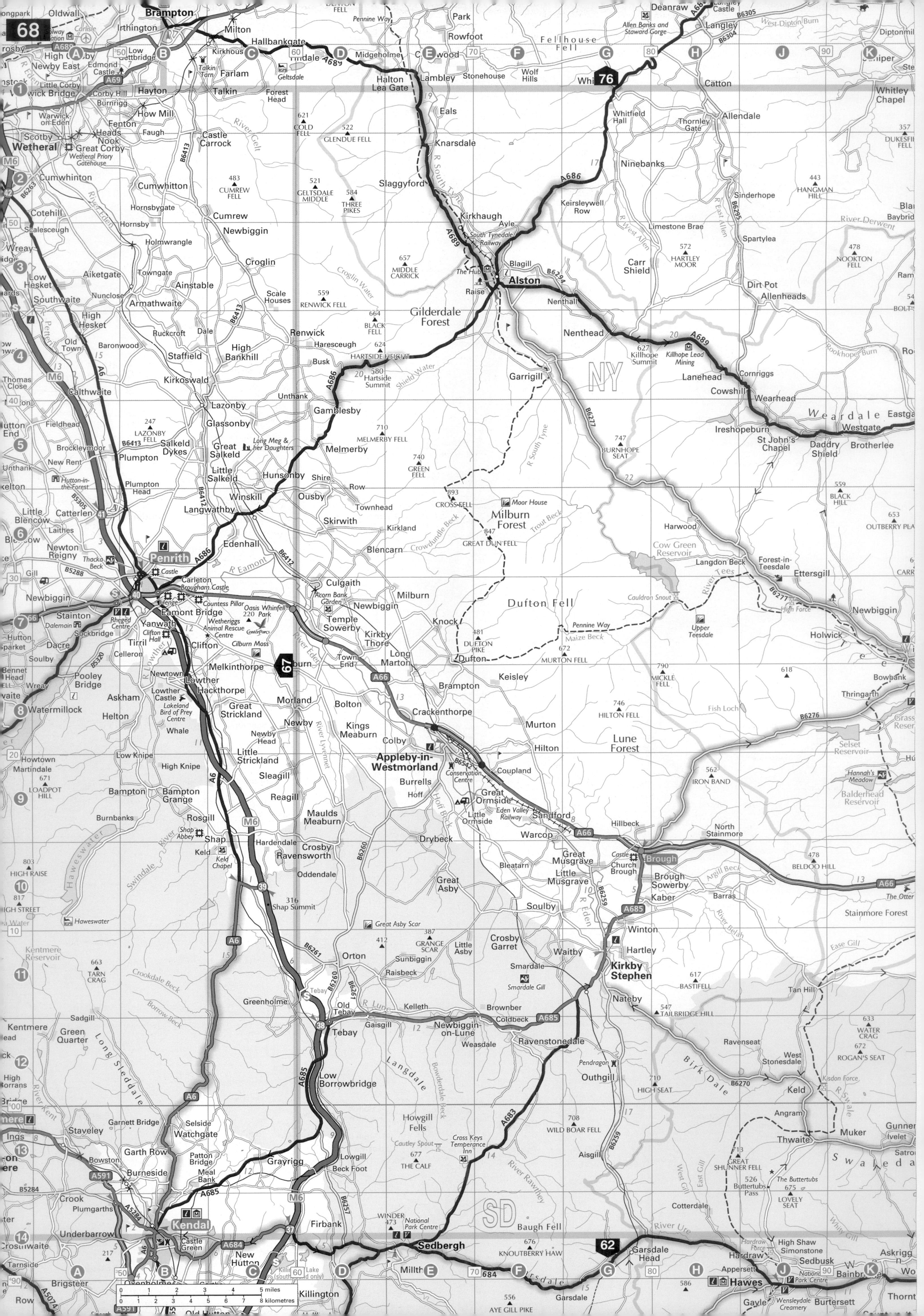
Oldwall
Brampton
Irthington
Milton
Hallbankgate
Kirkhouse
Tindale
Midgeholme
Coanwood
Park
Rowfoot
Fellhouse Fell
Allen Banks and Staward Gorge
Deanraw
Langley Castle
Langley
B6305
B6304
West Dipton Burn
Diptonmill
A689
A69
Low Row
Newby East
High Crosby
Low Gelt Bridge
Edmond Castle
Talkin Tarn
Farlam
Geltsdale
Halton Lea Gate
Lambley
Stonehouse
Wolf Hills
Whitfield
Catton
Little Corby
Warwick Bridge
Corby Hill
Hayton
Talkin
Forest Head
Whitley Chapel
Burnrigg
How Mill
Eals
Whitfield Hall
Allendale
Warwick-on-Eden
Fenton
Heads Nook
Faugh
Castle Carrock
River Gelt
621 COLD FELL
522 GLENDUE FELL
Knarsdale
Thornley Gate
357 DUKESFIELD FELL
Scotby
Wetheral
Great Corby
Wetheral Priory Gatehouse
B6413
M6
Cumwhinton
Cumwhitton
483 CUMREW FELL
521 GELTSDALE MIDDLE
584 THREE PIKES
Slaggyford
R South Tyne
A686
Ninebanks
443 HANGMAN HILL
B6263
Cotehill
Hornsbygate
Hornsby
Cumrew
Newbiggin
Kirkhaugh
Ayle
Keirsleywell Row
Sinderhope
Baybridge
River Derwent
Scaleseugh
Holmwrangle
South Tynedale Railway
Limestone Brae
Spartylea
R West Allen
R East Allen
B6295
Wreay
Croglin
Carr Shield
572 HARTLEY MOOR
478 NOOKTON FELL
Low Hesket
Aiketgate
Towngate
Ainstable
Croglin Water
657 MIDDLE CARRICK
The Hub
Blagill
Alston
B6294
Southwaite
Nunclose
Armathwaite
Scale Houses
559 RENWICK FELL
Raise
Nenthall
Dirt Pot
Allenheads
High Hesket
Ruckcroft
Dale
Renwick
664 BLACK FELL
Gilderdale Forest
Nenthead
Old Town
Baronwood
Staffield
High Bankhill
Haresceugh
624 HARTSIDE HEIGHT
627 Killhope Summit
Killhope Lead Mining
Rookhope Burn
Busk
580 Hartside Summit
Shield Water
Garrigill
NY
Lanehead
Cornriggs
Cowshill
Thomas Close
Kirkoswald
Calthwaite
Unthank
Gamblesby
Wearhead
Lazonby
Glassonby
Weardale
Westgate
Eastgate
Ireshopeburn
St John's Chapel
Daddry Shield
Brotherlee
Fieldhead
247 LAZONBY FELL
710 MELMERBY FELL
B6277
747 BURNHOPE SEAT
Brockleymoor
B6413
Salkeld Dykes
Great Salkeld
Long Meg & her Daughters
Melmerby
740 GREEN FELL
R South Tyne
Plumpton
New Rent
Little Salkeld
Hunsonby
Shire
Hutton-in-the-Forest
Plumpton Head
Row
893 CROSS FELL
Moor House
Milburn Forest
559 BLACK HILL
B5305
Winskill
Ousby
Townhead
Trout Beck
Langwathby
Skirwith
Kirkland
Crowdundle Beck
847 GREAT DUN FELL
Harwood
653 OUTBERRY PLAIN
Little Blencow
Catterlen
Laithes
Edenhall
Blencarn
Cow Green Reservoir
Langdon Beck
Forest-in-Teesdale
Ettersgill
Newton Reigny
Thacka Beck
Penrith
A686
B6412
River Tees
Gill
B5288
Castle
R Eamont
Culgaith
Carleton
Brougham Castle
Acorn Bank Garden
Milburn
Dufton Fell
Cauldron Snout
B6277
High Force
Newbiggin
Countess Pillar
Henge
Oasis Whinfell 220 Park
Newbiggin
Temple Sowerby
Knock
Pennine Way
Stainton
Eamont Bridge
Rheged Centre
Yanwath
Dalemain
Sockbridge
Wetheriggs Animal Rescue Centre
Center Parcs
Kirkby Thore
481 DUFTON PIKE
Maize Beck
Upper Teesdale
Holwick
Tirril
Clifton Hall
Clifton
Cilburn Moss
Hutton
Dacre
Celleron
River Eden
Long Marton
Town End
672 MURTON FELL
Dufton
790 MICKLE FELL
618
Soulby
B5320
Newtown
Melkinthorpe
67
Kirkby Thore
A66
Keisley
Bowbank
Pooley Bridge
Lowther
Hackthorpe
Brampton
Bennet Head
Askham
Lowther Castle
Lakeland Bird of Prey Centre
Great Strickland
Morland
Bolton
Crackenthorpe
746 HILTON FELL
Fish Loch
Thringarth
Watermillock
Helton
Whale
Newby
Kings Meaburn
Murton
B6276
Newby Head
Colby
Lune Forest
Selset Reservoir
Howtown
Martindale
Low Knipe
Little Strickland
River Lyvennet
Hilton
671 LOADPOT HILL
High Knipe
Appleby-in-Westmorland
B6542
Coupland
562 IRON BAND
Hannah's Meadow
Sleagill
Conservation Centre
Burrells
Balderhead Reservoir
Bampton
Bampton Grange
A6
Reagill
Hoff
Great Ormside
Hoff Beck
Little Ormside
Eden Valley Railway
Sandford
Burnbanks
Rosgill
Maulds Meaburn
Hillbeck
North Stainmore
Shap Abbey
Shap
M6
Hardendale
Crosby Ravensworth
Drybeck
Warcop
A66
Keld
Keld Chapel
B6260
Great Musgrave
Castle
Brough
803 HIGH RAISE
Haweswater
Swindale
Oddendale
Bleatarn
Church Brough
Little Musgrave
Brough Sowerby
Argill Beck
478 BELDOO HILL
817 HIGH STREET
39
316 Shap Summit
Great Asby
R Eden
B6259
Kaber
Barras
A66
The Otter
Stainmore Forest
Soulby
A685
Haweswater
Great Asby Scar
Winton
River Belah
387 GRANGE SCAR
Little Asby
Crosby Garret
Hartley
Ease Gill
Kentmere Reservoir
A6
412
B6261
Orton
Sunbiggin
Waitby
Kirkby Stephen
663 TARN CRAG
Crookdale Beck
Raisbeck
Smardale
Smardale Gill
617 BASTIFELL
Tan Hill
Tebay
B6260
B6261
Borrow Beck
Greenholme
Old Tebay
R Lune
Kelleth
Brownber
Nateby
547 TAILBRIDGE HILL
Sadgill
38
Gaisgill
Newbiggin-on-Lune
Coldbeck
A685
Green Quarter
Long Sleddale
Tebay
Weasdale
Ravenstonedale
633 WATER CRAG
Kentmere
Ravenseat
672 ROGAN'S SEAT
Langdale
Bowderdale Beck
Pendragon
West Stonesdale
High Borrans
A685
Low Borrowbridge
Outhgill
Birk Dale
710 HIGH SEAT
B6270
Kisdon Force
Keld
River Kent
A6
R Swale
Garnett Bridge
Howgill Fells
A683
708 WILD BOAR FELL
Angram
Staveley
Selside
Watchgate
Cross Keys Temperance Inn
Muker
Gunnerside
Ivelet
Thwaite
Caultey Spout
677 THE CALF
Lowgill
Beck Foot
Aisgill
B6259
Garth Row
Patton Bridge
Grayrigg
River Rawthey
713 GREAT SHUNNER FELL
526 Buttertubs Pass
The Buttertubs
675 LOVELY SEAT
Swaledale
Bowston
Burneside
Meal Bank
West Gill
East Gill
Satron
A591
A685
B5284
Crook
M6
B6257
SD
Cotterdale
Plumgarths
A5284
Kendal
Firbank
WINDER 473
National Park Centre
Baugh Fell
River Ure
Whitfield Gill
Underbarrow
Castle Green
A684
37
Sedbergh
676 KNOUTBERRY HAW
62
Garsdale Head
Hardraw Force
Hardraw
High Shaw Simonstone
Sedbusk
Askrigg
Crosthwaite
217
A6
New Hutton
Killington Lake (southbound only)
Millthrop
684
Garsdale
Appersett
National Park Centre
Bainbridge
Tarnside
Brigsteer
Oxenholme
A590
Killington
556 AYE GILL PIKE
Garsdale
586
Hawes
Gayle
Wensleydale Creamery
Burtersett
Thornton Rust
Old Hutton
A590
A5074
Row
0 1 2 3 4 5 miles
0 1 2 3 4 5 6 7 8 kilometres

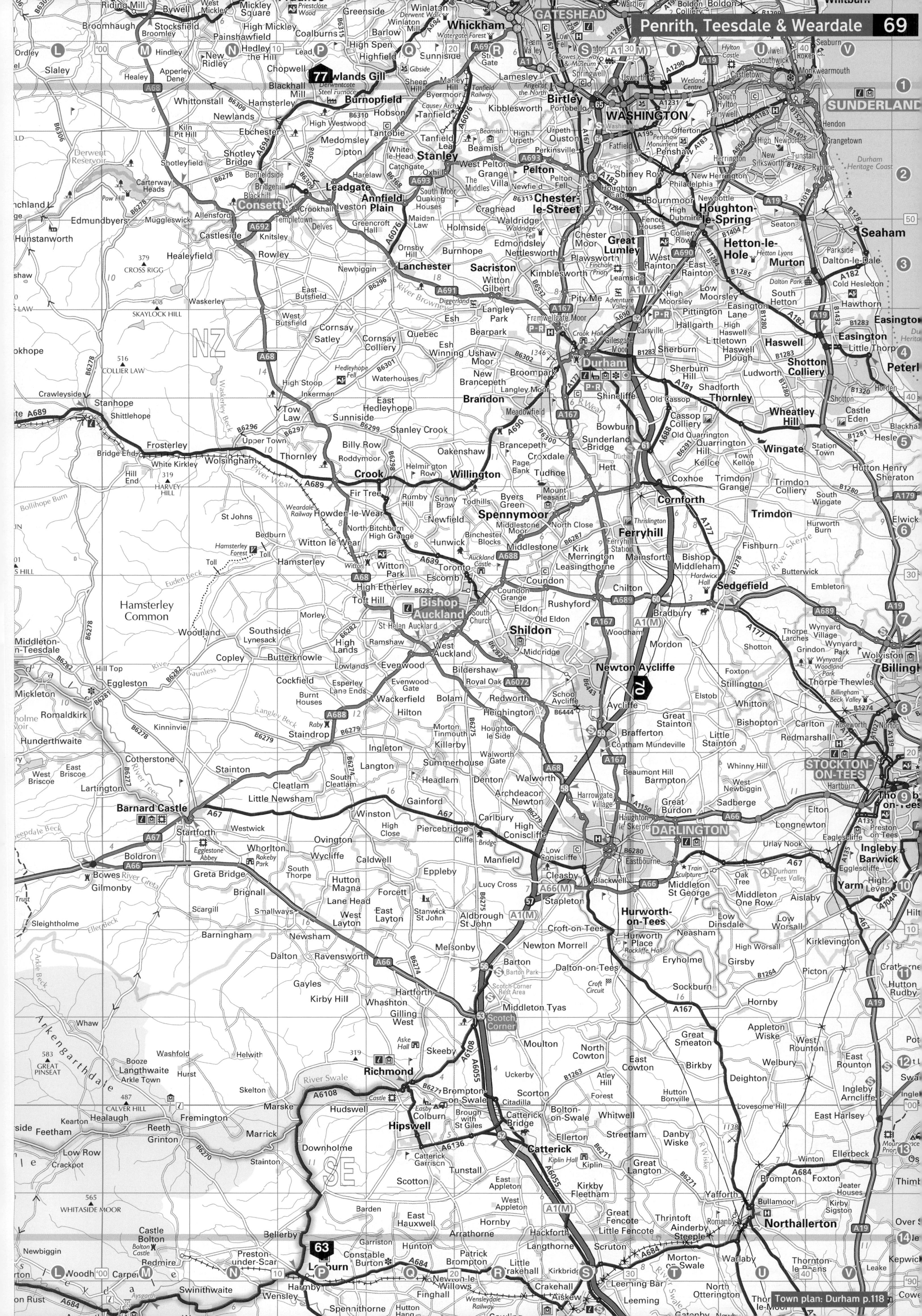

70
77
69
63
GATESHEAD
Whickham
Whitburn
Whitburn Bay
Boldon
East Boldon
SUNDERLAND
Birtley
WASHINGTON
Stanley
Pelton
Chester-le-Street
Houghton-le-Spring
Hetton-le-Hole
Murton
Seaham
Lanchester
Sacriston
Great Lumley
Easington Colliery
Easington
Haswell
Shotton Colliery
Peterlee
Durham
Brandon
Blackhall Colliery
Wheatley Hill
Thornley
Wingate
Willington
Crook
Spennymoor
Cornforth
Ferryhill
Trimdon
HARTLEPOOL
Hartlepool Bay
Bishop Auckland
Shildon
Sedgefield
Newton Aycliffe
Billingham
Tees Bay
Redcar
Marske-by-the-Sea
New Marske
STOCKTON-ON-TEES
MIDDLESBROUGH
Thornaby-on-Tees
Eston
Guisborough
DARLINGTON
Yarm
Ingleby Barwick
Great Ayton
Stokesley
Hurworth-on-Tees
Scotch Corner
Richmond
Hipswell
Catterick
Catterick Bridge
Northallerton
NZ
SE
CLEVELAND HILLS
NORTH YORK MOORS
Durham Heritage Coast
River Tees
River Wear
0 1 2 3 4 5 miles
0 1 2 3 4 5 6 7 8 kilometres

Sunderland

Middlesbrough

Saltburn-by-the-Sea
New Brotton
Brotton
Skelton
New Skelton
North Skelton
Kilton
Kilton Thorpe
Lingdale
Liverton Mines
Stanghow
Woodhill
Liverton
Moorsholm
Gerrick
Scaling
Scaling Dam
Danby
Castleton
Ainthorpe
Westerdale
Danby Bottom
Street
Glaisdale
The Green
Lealholm
Lealholm Side
Stonegate
Mickleby
West Barnby
East Barnby
Dunsley
Newholm
Hutton Mulgrave
Ugthorpe
Egton
Egton Bridge
Grosmont
Key Green
Beck Hole
Goathland
Church Houses
Low Mill
Thorgill
Rosedale Abbey
Low Bell End
Hartoft End
Stape
Carlin How
Skinningrove
Upton
Boulby
Loftus
Dalehouse
Easington
Staithes
Port Mulgrave
Hinderwell
Newton Mulgrave
Roxby
Handale
Borrowby
Runswick
Kettleness
Goldsborough
Ellerby
Lythe
Raithwaite
Sandsend
Whitby
Abbey
Saltwick Bay
Ruswarp
Stainsacre
Aislaby
Briggswath
Sleights
Sneaton
Ugglebarnby
Low Hawsker
High Hawsker
Iburndale
Sneatonthorpe
Raw
Robin Hood's Bay
Littlebeck
Fylingthorpe
Old Peak or South Cheek
Ravenscar
Staintondale
Harwood Dale
Cloughton Newlands
Hayburn Wyke
Cloughton
Cloughton Wyke
Cromer Point
Burniston
Scalby
Scarborough

Hummersea Scar
Runswick Bay
Overdale Wyke
Sandsend Wyke
Ness Point or North Cheek
Robin Hood's Bay

North Yorkshire and Cleveland Heritage Coast
Captain Cook & Staithes Heritage Centre
The Moors National Park Centre
North York Moors Railway
North Yorkshire Moors Railway
Wheeldale Roman Road
Newtondale Forest Drive
Blakey Topping
Hole of Horcum

NORTH YORK MOORS NATIONAL PARK
THE YORK MOORS
NORTH RIDING FOREST PARK

River Esk
Esk Dale
Rosedale
Farndale

Pike Hill 326
369
301
290
292
239

A171
A174
A169
B1266
B1366
B1410
B1447
B1416
A165

64
65

Gillamoor
Fadmoor
Hutton-le-Hole
Spaunton
Appleton-le-Moors
Cropton
Cawthorn
Lastingham
Spaunton
Newton-on-Rawcliffe
Levisham
Lockton
Stape
Bickley
Broxa
Silpho
Suffield
Hackness
Wrench Green
Everley
Scalby
Falsgrave
Dolby Forest Drive
Bridestones
Crosscliff
Cleveland Way
North Bay Railway
Castle
Shire Horse Centre

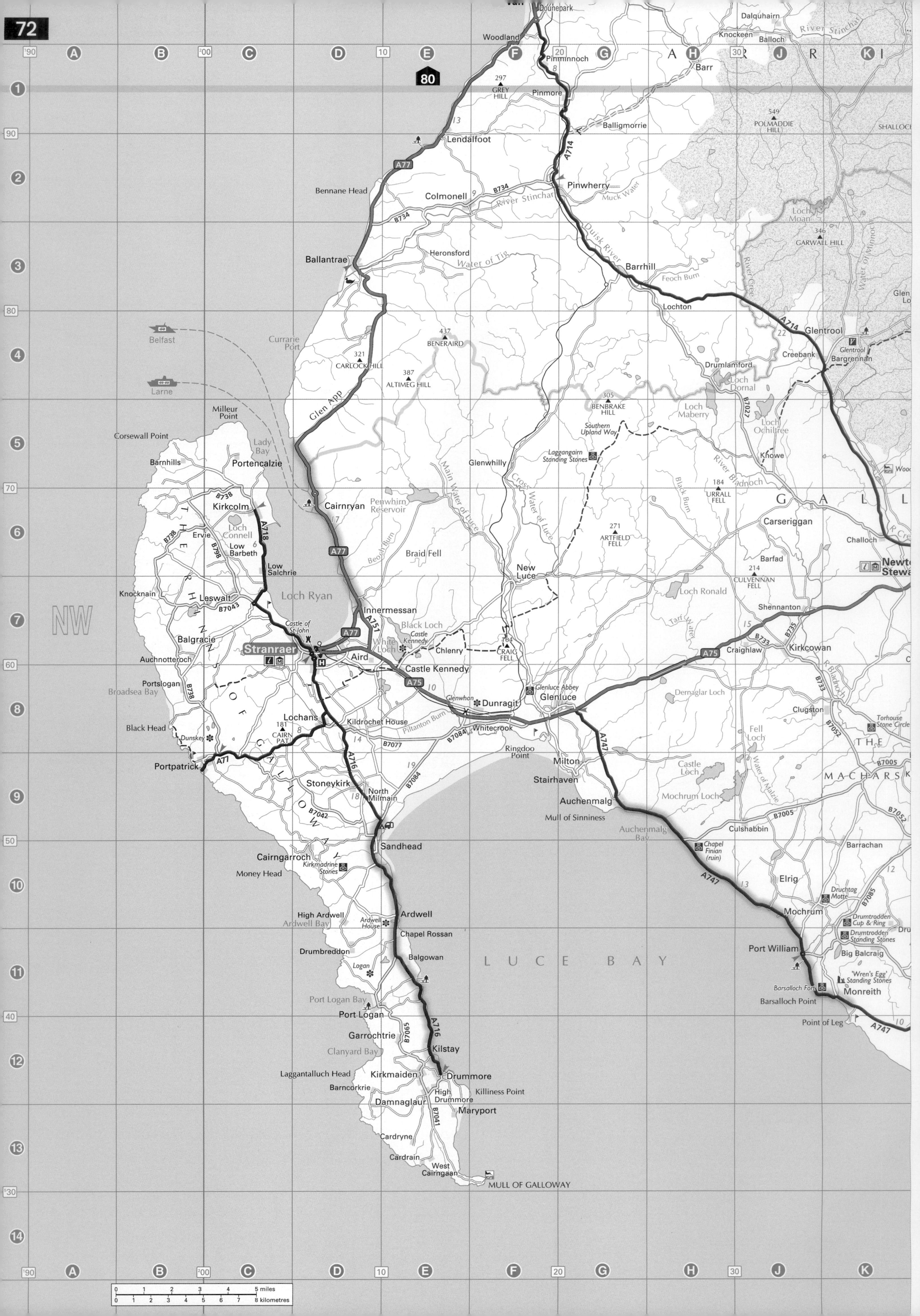
80
NW
Dalquhairn
Knockeen
Balloch
River Stinchar
Dounepark
Woodland
Pinmmnoch
Barr
297 GREY HILL
Pinmore
Balligmorrie
549 POLMADDIE HILL
SHALLOCH
Lendalfoot
A77
A714
Pinwherry
Muck Water
Bennane Head
Colmonell
B734
River Stinchar
B734
Loch Moan
346 GARWALL HILL
Duisk River
Heronsford
Water of Tig
Ballantrae
Barrhill
Feoch Burn
River Cree
Water of Minnoch
Lochton
Glen
Belfast
Currarie Port
437 BENERAIRD
A714
Glentrool
Glentrool
Bargrennan
Creebank
321 CARLOCK HILL
387 ALTIMEG HILL
Drumlamford
Loch Dornal
Larne
Milleur Point
Glen App
305 BENBRAKE HILL
Loch Maberry
B7027
Loch Ochiltree
Southern Upland Way
Corsewall Point
Lady Bay
Laggangairn Standing Stones
Knowe
Barnhills
Portencalzie
Glenwhilly
Main Water of Luce
River Bladnoch
B738
Cross Water of Luce
Black Burn
184 URRALL FELL
Kirkcolm
Cairnryan
Penwhirn Reservoir
G A L L
THE RHINNS OF GALLOWAY
Loch Connell
A718
Carseriggan
B738
Ervie
B798
Low Barbeth
271 ARTFIELD FELL
Challoch
A77
Braid Fell
Beoch Burn
Barfad
Low Salchrie
New Luce
214 CULVENNAN FELL
Newton Stewart
Knocknain
Leswalt
B7043
Loch Ryan
Loch Ronald
Innermessan
A751
Shennanton
Black Loch
Castle of St John
Tarf Water
B733
B735
A77
White Loch
Castle Kennedy
Chlenry
164 CRAIG FELL
A75
Craighlaw
Kirkcowan
Balgracie
Stranraer
Aird
Auchnotteroch
Castle Kennedy
R Bladnoch
A75
B733
Portslogan
Broadsea Bay
B738
Glenwhan
Dunragit
Glenluce Abbey
Glenluce
Dernaglar Loch
Lochans
Kildrochet House
Clugston
Torhouse Stone Circle
Black Head
Dunskey
181 CAIRN PAT
Piltanton Burn
B7084
Whitecrook
A747
Fell Loch
B7052
THE
B7077
Ringdoo Point
Portpatrick
A77
A716
B7084
Milton
Castle Loch
Water of Malzie
B7005
Stairhaven
MACHARS
Stoneykirk
North Milmain
Auchenmalg
Mochrum Loch
B7042
Mull of Sinniness
B7005
B7052
Auchenmalg Bay
Culshabbin
Sandhead
Chapel Finian (ruin)
Barrachan
Cairngarroch
Kirkmadrine Stones
Money Head
A747
Elrig
Druchtag Motte
B7085
High Ardwell
Ardwell
Ardwell Bay
Ardwell House
Mochrum
Drumtrodden Cup & Ring
Chapel Rossan
Drumtrodden Standing Stones
Drumbreddon
Balgowan
LUCE BAY
Port William
Big Balcraig
Logan
'Wren's Egg' Standing Stones
Barsalloch Fort
Monreith
Port Logan Bay
Barsalloch Point
Port Logan
B7065
A716
Point of Leg
A747
Garrochtrie
Clanyard Bay
Kilstay
Laggantalluch Head
Kirkmaiden
Drummore
Barncorkrie
Killiness Point
High Drummore
Damnaglaur
B7041
Maryport
Cardryne
Cardrain
West Cairngaan
MULL OF GALLOWAY
5 miles
8 kilometres

Carsphairn
Knowehead
Moniaive
Kirkland
Tynron
Keir Mill
Closeburn
Kirkpatrick
Dunscore
Glenhoul
Blawquhairn
St John's Town of Dalry
Bogue
Balmaclellan
New Galloway
Corsock
Clatteringshaws Loch
Minnigaff
Creebridge
Palnure
Creetown
Kirkmabreck
Wigtown
Bladnoch
Kirkinner
Sorbie
Garlieston
Whithorn
Isle of Whithorn
BURROW HEAD
Wigtown Bay
Gatehouse of Fleet
Anwoth
Laurieston
Loch Ken
Crossmichael
Castle Douglas
Dalbeattie
Kirkcudbright
Tongland
Twynholm
Borgue
Dundrennan
Auchencairn
Kippford / Scaur
Rockcliffe
Palnackie
Mossdale
Airds of Kells
Ringford
Bridge of Dee
Rhonehouse
Gelston
Haugh of Urr
Springholm
Kirkpatrick Durham
Crocketford
Lochfoot
Abbey Head
Little Ross
Ross
Borness
NX
81
74
69

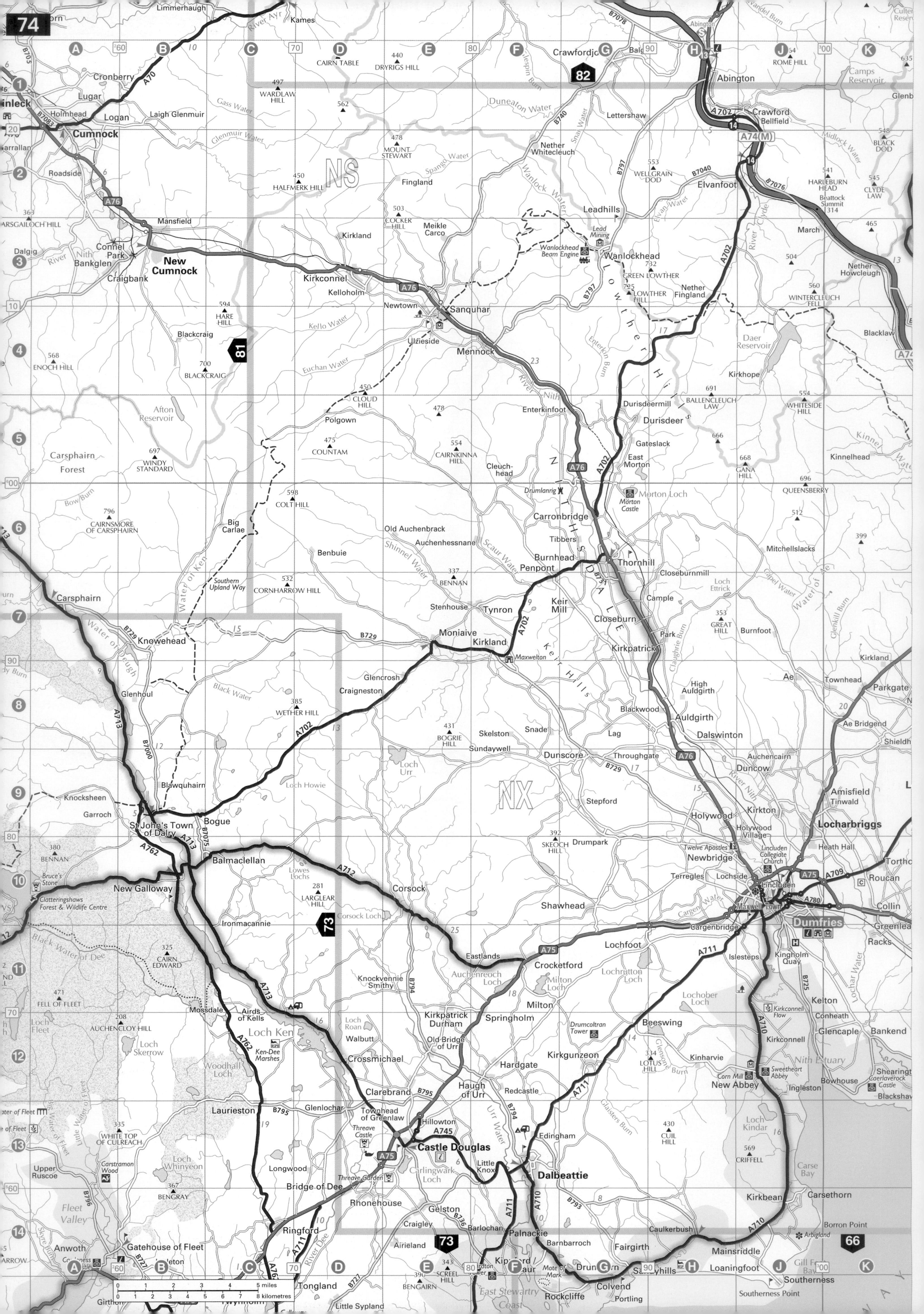

Limmerhaugh
Kames
Cronberry
Lugar
Logan
Laigh Glenmuir
Cumnock
Holmhead
Roadside
Mansfield
Connel Park
Bankglen
Craigbank
New Cumnock
Dalgig
Kirkconnel
Kelloholm
Newtown
Sanquhar
Ulzieside
Mennock
Blackcraig
HARE HILL
ENOCH HILL
BLACKCRAIG
Afton Reservoir
Carsphairn Forest
WINDY STANDARD
CAIRNSMORE OF CARSPHAIRN
Big Carlae
Southern Upland Way
Carsphairn
Knowehead
Glenhoul
Blawquhairn
Knocksheen
Garroch
St John's Town of Dalry
Bogue
Balmaclellan
New Galloway
Clatteringshaws Forest & Wildlife Centre
Bruce's Stone
Ironmacannie
CAIRN EDWARD
FELL OF FLEET
AUCHENCLOY HILL
Mossdale
Airds of Kells
Loch Ken
Ken-Dee Marshes
Woodhall Loch
Loch Skerrow
Laurieston
WHITE TOP OF CULREACH
Loch Whinyeon
Carstramon Wood
Upper Ruscoe
BENGRAY
Fleet Valley
Anwoth
Gatehouse of Fleet
Ringford
Tongland
Little Sypland
Bridge of Dee
Longwood
Glenlochar
Rhonehouse
Threave Garden
Threave Castle
Castle Douglas
Carlingwark Loch
Gelston
Craigley
Airieland
SCREEL HILL
BENGAIRN
Barlochan
Palnackie
Barnbarroch
Kippford
Mote of Mark
Rockcliffe
Colvend
Portling
Sandyhills
Fairgirth
Caulkerbush
Mainsriddle
Loaningfoot
Southerness
Southerness Point
Arbigland
Borron Point
Kirkbean
Carsethorn
Carse Bay
CRIFFELL
Loch Kindar
New Abbey
Sweetheart Abbey
Ingleston
Kinharvie
LOTUS HILL
CUIL HILL
Beeswing
Lochober Loch
Kirkgunzeon
Drumcoltran Tower
Hardgate
Redcastle
Edingham
Dalbeattie
Little Knox
Haugh of Urr
Hillowton
Townhead of Greenlaw
Clarebrand
Crossmichael
Walbutt
Loch Roan
Old Bridge of Urr
Kirkpatrick Durham
Springholm
Milton
Milton Loch
Crocketford
Auchenreoch Loch
Lochrutton Loch
Knockvennie Smithy
Eastlands
Lochfoot
Cargenbridge
Corsock
Corsock Loch
LARGLEAR HILL
Lowes Lochs
Loch Howie
WETHER HILL
Craigneston
Glencrosh
Moniaive
Kirkland
Maxwelton
Tynron
Stenhouse
Keir Mill
Penpont
Burnhead
Tibbers
Carronbridge
Drumlanrig
Thornhill
Closeburnmill
Closeburn
Cample
Park
Kirkpatrick
Loch Ettrick
GREAT HILL
Burnfoot
Blackwood
High Auldgirth
Auldgirth
Dalswinton
Lag
Snade
Skelston
Sundaywell
BOGRIE HILL
Loch Urr
Dunscore
Throughgate
Stepford
SKEOCH HILL
Drumpark
Shawhead
Twelve Apostles
Newbridge
Terregles
Lochside
Lincluden
Lincluden Collegiate Church
Maxwell Town
Dumfries
Holywood
Holywood Village
Kirkton
Duncow
Auchencairn
Locharbriggs
Amisfield
Tinwald
Heath Hall
Roucan
Collin
Greenlea
Racks
Kingholm Quay
Islesteps
Kelton
Conheath
Kirkconnell
Kirkconnell Flow
Glencaple
Bankend
Nith Estuary
Bowhouse
Shearington
Caerlaverock Castle
Blackshaw
Ae
Ae Bridgend
Townhead
Parkgate
Kirkland
Shieldhill
Mitchellslacks
Kinnelhead
QUEENSBERRY
GANA HILL
WHITESIDE HILL
BALLENCLEUCH LAW
Durisdeermill
Durisdeer
Gateslack
East Morton
Morton Loch
Morton Castle
Enterkinfoot
Cleuchhead
CAIRNKINNA HILL
BENNAN
Old Auchenbrack
Auchenhessnane
Benbuie
CORNHARROW HILL
COLT HILL
COUNTAM
Polgown
CLOUD HILL
Kirkland
Meikle Carco
COCKER HILL
Fingland
HALFMERK HILL
MOUNT STEWART
WARDLAW HILL
CAIRN TABLE
DRYRIGS HILL
Crawfordjohn
Lettershaw
Nether Whitecleuch
WELLGRAIN DOD
Leadhills
Lead Mining
Wanlockhead
Wanlockhead Beam Engine
GREEN LOWTHER
LOWTHER HILL
Nether Fingland
Lowther Hills
Nithsdale
Keir Hills
Elvanfoot
Abington
Crawford
Bellfield
Camps Reservoir
ROME HILL
BLACK DOD
HARLEBURN HEAD
CLYDE LAW
Beattock Summit
March
Nether Howcleuch
WINTERCLEUCH FELL
Daer Reservoir
Kirkhope
Blacklaw
River Nith
River Clyde
River Ayr
River Dee
Water of Ken
Black Water of Dee
Urr Water
Cargen Water
Scaur Water
Shinnel Water
Euchan Water
Kello Water
Duneaton Water
Gass Water
Glenmuir Water
Spango Water
Wanlock Water
Snar Water
Elvan Water
Enterkin Burn
Water of Ae
Kinnel Water
Lochar Water
Water of Deugh
Black Water
Bow Burn
NS
NX
0 1 2 3 4 5 miles
0 1 2 3 4 5 6 7 8 kilometres

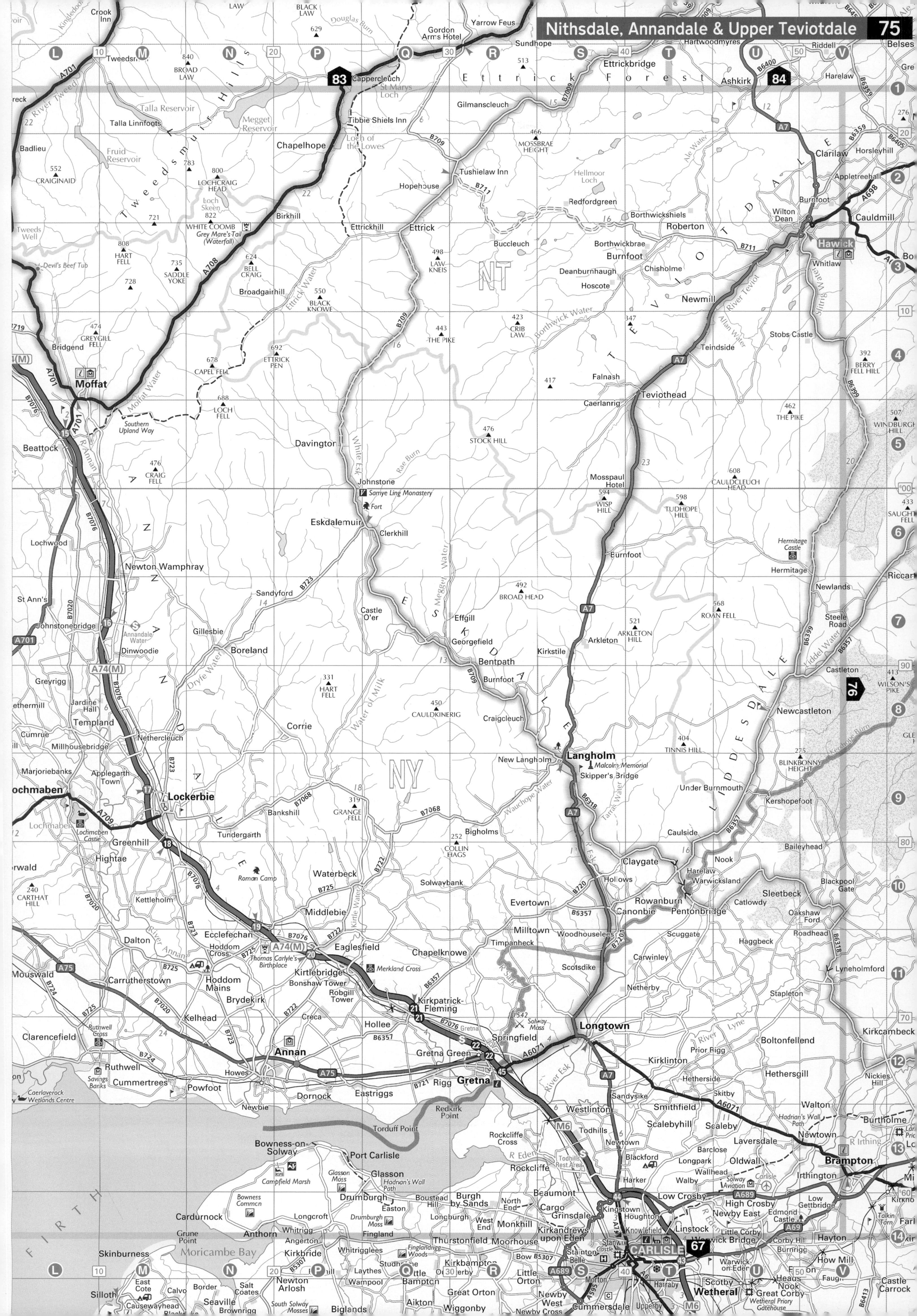

L · M · N · P · Q · R · S · T · U · V

83 · **84**

Crook Inn
Tweedsmuir
A701
River Tweed
BROAD LAW 840
Talla Reservoir
Talla Linnfoots
Chapelhope
Megget Reservoir
Cappercleuch
St Marys Loch
Tibbie Shiels Inn
Loch of the Lowes
Black Law
Douglas Burn
Gordon Arms Hotel
Yarrow Feus
Sundhope
Gilmanscleuch
Ettrickbridge
Ashkirk
Hartwoodmyres
Riddell
Belses
B6400
Harelaw
B6359

ETTRICK FOREST

Fruid Reservoir
CRAIGINAID 552
Tweeds Well
721
Loch Skeen 822
WHITE COOMB
Grey Mare's Tail (Waterfall)
Birkhill
Ettrickhill
Ettrick
Hopehouse
Tushielaw Inn
Hellmoor Loch
MOSSBRAE HEIGHT 466
Redfordgreen
Borthwickshiels
Roberton
Clarilaw
Horsleyhill
Appletreehall
Burnfoot
Wilton Dean
Hawick
Cauldmill
A698
A7

Tweedsmuir Hills

BADLIEU
783
800
LOCHCRAIG HEAD
Loch Skeen
HART FELL 808
Devil's Beef Tub
A708
SADDLE YOKE 735
728
GREYGILL FELL 474
Bridgend
Moffat
A701
Beattock
Southern Upland Way
CRAIG FELL 476
Lochwood
Newton Wamphray
A701
Johnstonebridge
Annandale Water
Dinwoodie
Greyrigg
Jardine Hall
Templand
Netherscleuch
Applegarth Town
B723
Lochmaben
Lochmaben Castle
A709
Greenhill
Hightae
CARTHAT HILL 240
Hoddom Mains
Brydekirk
Kelhead
Kirtlebridge
Bonshaw Tower
Robgill Tower
Kirkpatrick-Fleming

BELL CRAIG 624
Broadgairhill
BLACK KNOWE 550
CAPEL FELL 678
ETTRICK PEN 692
LOCH FELL 688
Davington
White Esk
Rae Burn
Johnstone
Samye Ling Monastery
Fort
Eskdalemuir
Clerkhill
Sandyford
Castle O'er
Gillesbie
Boreland
Effgill
Georgefield
Bentpath
Burnfoot
B709
HART FELL 331
Corrie
CAULDKINERIG 450
Craigcleuch
Bankshill
GRANGE FELL 319
Tundergarth
Bigholms
COLLIN HAGS
Waterbeck
Solwaybank
Middlebie
Ecclefechan
A74(M)
Hoddom Cross
Thomas Carlyle's Birthplace
Eaglesfield
Merkland Cross
Chapelknowe

THE PIKE 443
CRIB LAW 423
LAW KNEIS 498
Buccleuch
Burnfoot
Deanburnhaugh
Hoscote
Chisholme
Newmill
347
Teindside
Falnash
Caerlanrig
Teviothead
A7
STOCK HILL 476
Mosspaul Hotel
WISP HILL 594
BROAD HEAD 492
Kirkstile
BERRY FELL HILL 392
THE PIKE 462
WINDBURGH HILL 507
Stobs Castle
SAUGH FELL 433
CAULDCLEUCH HEAD 608
TUDHOPE HILL 598
Burnfoot
Hermitage Castle
Hermitage
Newlands
Riccar
ROAN FELL 568
ARKLETON HILL 521
Arkleton
New Langholm
Langholm
Malcolm Memorial
Skipper's Bridge
TINNIS HILL 404
Under Burnmouth
Castleton
WILSON'S PIKE 413
Newcastleton
BLINKBONNY HEIGHT 225
Kershopefoot
Claygate
Harelaw
Warwicksland
Nook
Baileyhead
Blackpool Gate
Catlowdy
Oakshaw Ford
Roadhead
Haggbeck
Lyneholmford
Stapleton
Netherby
Carwinley
Scotsdike
Longtown
A7
Kirklinton
Hetherside
Smithfield
Scaleby
Walton
Burtholme

A74(M)
Lockerbie
NY
B7068
Tundergarth
Roman Camp
Kettleholm
Dalton
Carrutherstown
Mouswald
A75
Ruthwell Cross
Clarencefield
Ruthwell Savings Banks
Cummertrees
Powfoot
Howes
Dornock
Eastriggs
Newbie
Annan
B722
Creca
Hollee
B6357
Springfield
Gretna Green
Gretna
Rigg
Solway Moss
Timpanheck
Milltown
Woodhouselees
Scuggate
Carwinley
Scotsdike
Longtown
Kirkandrews upon Eden

Canonbie
Rowanburn
Pentonbridge
Caulside
Hollows
B6318
Wauchope Water
B6357
Tarras Water
Esk
Sleetbeck
B6318
Nickies Hill
Kirkcambeck
Boltonfellend
Prior Rigg
Hethersgill

Moricambe Bay
Skinburness
Silloth
East Cote
Calvo
Causewayhead
Border
Abbeytown
Newton Arlosh
Kirkbride
Angerton
Whitrigg
Anthorn
Cardurnock
Longcroft
Bowness-on-Solway
Port Carlisle
Glasson
Drumburgh
Easton
Boustead Hill
Burgh by Sands
Monkhill
Kirkbampton
Little Orton
Great Orton
Wiggonby
Aikton
Gamblesby
Biglands
Fingland
Thurstonfield
Moorhouse
West End
Longburgh

Caerlaverock Wetlands Centre
Bowness Common
Campfield Marsh
Glasson Moss
Drumburgh Moss
Hadrian's Wall Path
Grune Point
FIRTH
South Solway Mosses

M6
Rockcliffe Cross
Todhills
Westlinton
Blackford
Harker
Rockcliffe
Cargo
Grinsdale
Kingstown
Houghton
Stanwix
CARLISLE
67
A689
Low Crosby
High Crosby
Edmond Castle
Newby East
Little Corby
Warwick Bridge
Corby Hill
Hayton
How Mill
Talkin
Farlam
Brampton
A69
Irthington
Newtown
Laversdale
Crosby-on-Eden
Wall Head
Scaleby
Hadrian's Wall Path
Lanercost
Newton
A6071
River Eden
Longpark
Wallhead
Oldwall
Walby
Scaleby Hill
Skitby
Smithfield
Sandysike
Westlinton
Linstock
Harraby
Botcherby
Wetheral
Great Corby
Wetheral Priory Gatehouse
Scotby
Cummersdale
Upperby
Newby West
Newby Cross
Durdar

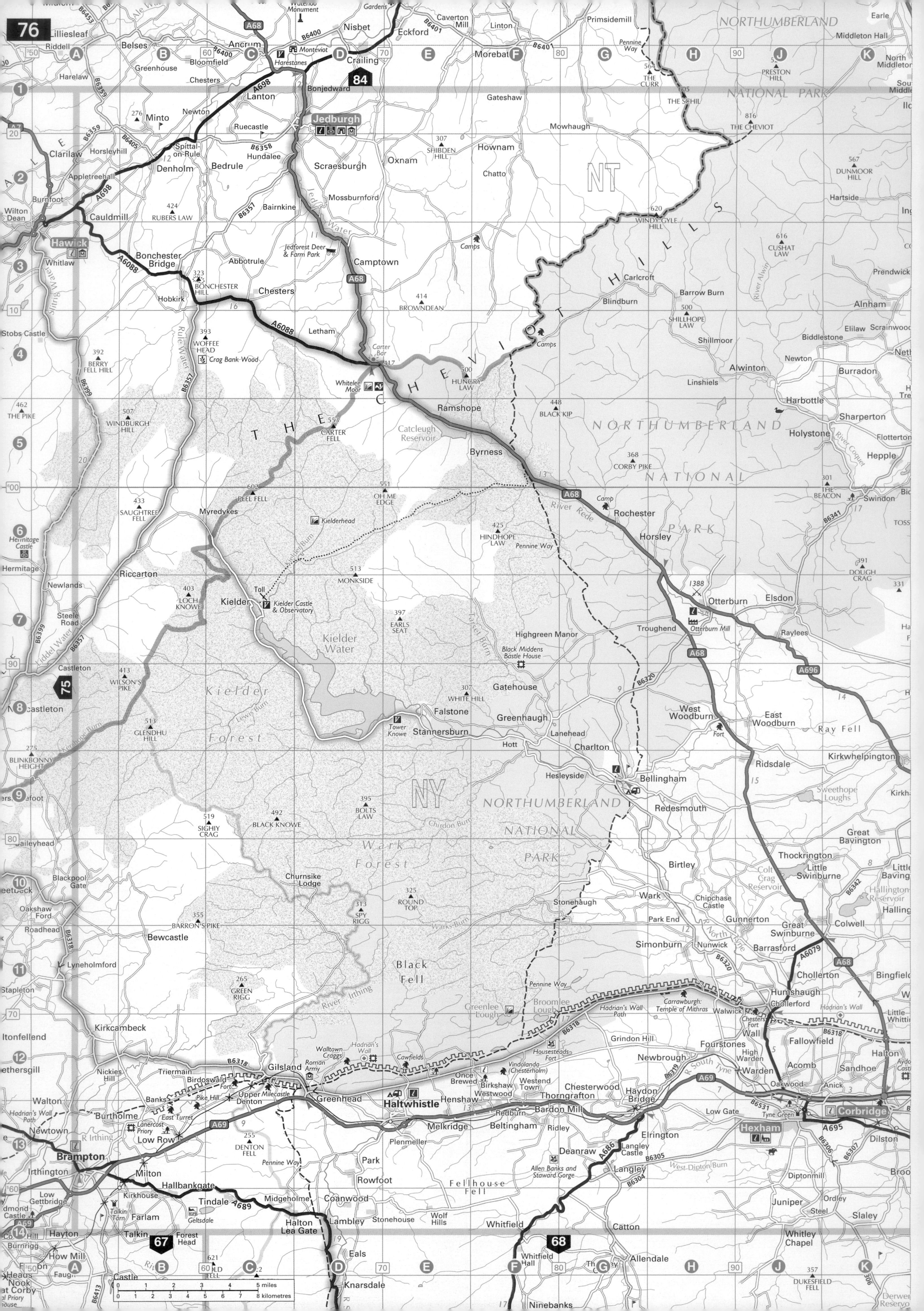
Lilliesleaf
Riddell
Ancrum
Nisbet
Eckford
Caverton Mill
Linton
Primsidemill
NORTHUMBERLAND
Earle
Middleton Hall
Belses
Bloomfield
Greenhouse
Chesters
Harestanes
Monteviot
Crailing
Morebattle
Pennine Way
Preston Hill
North Middleton
Harelaw
Bonjedward
The Curr
The Schil
NATIONAL PARK
Lanton
Gateshaw
Minto
Newton
Ruecastle
Jedburgh
Mowhaugh
The Cheviot
Clarilaw
Horsleyhill
Spittal-on-Rule
Hundalee
Shibden Hill
Hownam
Denholm
Bedrule
Scraesburgh
Oxnam
Chatto
Dunmoor Hill
Appletreehall
NT
Burnfoot
Mossburnford
Hartside
Wilton Dean
Cauldmill
Rubers Law
Bairnkine
Windy Gyle Hill
Hawick
Jedforest Deer & Farm Park
Camps
Cushat Law
Whitlaw
Bonchester Bridge
Abbotrule
Camptown
Prendwick
Carlcroft
Bonchester Hill
Hobkirk
Chesters
Blindburn
Barrow Burn
Browndean
Alnham
Shillhope Law
Stobs Castle
Letham
Woffee Head
Crag Bank Wood
Berry Fell Hill
Carter Bar
Hungry Law
Shillmoor
Elilaw
Scrainwood
Biddlestone
Newton
Alwinton
Burradon
Linshiels
Whitelee Moor
The Pike
Windburgh Hill
Ramshope
Black Kip
Harbottle
Sharperton
THE CHEVIOT HILLS
Carter Fell
Catcleugh Reservoir
NORTHUMBERLAND
Holystone
Flotterton
Byrness
Corby Pike
NATIONAL
Hepple
Peel Fell
Oh Me Edge
Camp
Rochester
The Beacon
Swindon
Saughtree Fell
Myredykes
Kielderhead
River Rede
Hermitage Castle
Hindhope Law
Pennine Way
Horsley
PARK
Dough Crag
Hermitage
Riccarton
Monkside
Newlands
Loch Knowe
Kielder
Toll
Kielder Castle & Observatory
Otterburn
Elsdon
Steele Road
Earls Seat
Troughend
Otterburn Mill
Raylees
Kielder Water
Highgreen Manor
Black Middens Bastle House
Castleton
Wilson's Pike
Kielder Forest
Gatehouse
White Hill
West Woodburn
East Woodburn
Ray Fell
Newcastleton
Glendhu Hill
Falstone
Greenhaugh
Tower Knowe
Stannersburn
Lanehead
Hott
Charlton
Fort
Blinkbonny Height
Hesleyside
Bellingham
Ridsdale
Kirkwhelpington
NY
Bolts Law
Sweethope Loughs
Black Knowe
Redesmouth
Sighty Crag
Chirdon Burn
NATIONAL
Great Bavington
Baileyhead
Wark Forest
PARK
Thockrington
Birtley
Little Swinburne
Blackpool Gate
Churnsike Lodge
Colt Crag Reservoir
Little Bavington
Hallington Reservoir
Wark
Oakshaw Ford
Round Top
Chipchase Castle
Spy Rigg
Stonehaugh
Park End
Gunnerton
Colwell
Roadhead
Barron's Pike
Great Swinburne
Bewcastle
Simonburn
Nunwick
River North Tyne
Barrasford
Lyneholmford
Black Fell
Chollerton
Bingfield
Green Rigg
Pennine Way
Humshaugh
Stapleton
River Irthing
Greenlee Lough
Broomlee Lough
Carrawburgh: Temple of Mithras
Chollerford
Hadrian's Wall Path
Walwick
Chesters Fort
Little Whittington
Kirkcambeck
Hadrian's Wall
Itonfellend
Grindon Hill
Wall
Fallowfield
Walltown Crags
Roman Army Museum
Cawfields
Housesteads Fort
Vindolanda (Chesterholm)
Fourstones
High Warden
Halton
Nickies Hill
Triermain
Gilsland
Newbrough
Birdoswald Fort
Once Brewed
Birkshaw
Westwood
Westend Town
Acomb
Sandhoe
Warden
Walton
Banks
Pike Hill
Upper Denton
Milecastle
Greenhead
Haltwhistle
Henshaw
Thorngrafton
Chesterwood
Haydon Bridge
River South Tyne
Oakwood
Anick
Hadrian's Wall Path
Burtholme
East Turret
Redburn
Bardon Mill
Low Gate
Tyne Green
Corbridge
Lanercost Priory
Melkridge
Beltingham
Ridley
Hexham
Newtown
Low Row
Denton Fell
Plenmeller
Elrington
Dilston
River Irthing
Pennine Way
Park
Deanraw
Langley Castle
Allen Banks and Staward Gorge
Brampton
Langley
West Dipton Burn
Irthington
Milton
Rowfoot
Fellhouse Fell
Diptonmill
Hallbankgate
Midgeholme
Coanwood
Low Gettbridge
Kirkhouse
Tindale
Ordley
Juniper
Talkin Tarn
Farlam
Geltsdale
Wolf Hills
Steel
Slaley
Lambley
Stonehouse
Whitfield
Hayton
Talkin
Forest Head
Halton Lea Gate
Catton
Whitley Chapel
Burnrigg
How Mill
Eals
Allendale
Whitfield Hall
Dukesfield Fell
Faugh
Castle
Knarsdale
Ninebanks
Derwent Reservoir
A68
A698
A6088
A696
A69
A689
A686
A695
A6079
B6400
B6401
B6405
B6358
B6357
B6359
B6399
B6453
B6318
B6320
B6341
B6342
B6319
B6531
B6305
B6304
B6306
B6307
B6413
75
84
67
68
A
B
C
D
E
F
G
H
J
K
1
2
3
4
5
6
7
8
9
10
11
12
13
14
0 1 2 3 4 5 miles
0 1 2 3 4 5 6 7 8 kilometres

Port of Tyne
TYNEMOUTH
MEADOW WELL
PERCY MAIN
NEWCASTLE THE NORTH
Wet'n'Wild Water Park
Royal Quays Outlet
Premier Inn
Royal Quays Marina
East Howdon
HOWDON ROAD
TYNE VIEW
TYNE TUNNEL
INTERNATIONAL PASSENGER TERMINAL
River Tyne
Jarrow
PRIORY
SUNDERLAND
500 m
Haugh Head
Chillingham
Wild Cattle Park
Ros Castle
Newtown
Lilburn Tower
Hepburn
85
267 CATERAN HILL
Newstead
Ellingham
Tughall
Preston
Preston Tower
Brunton
Christon Bank
Newton-by-the-Sea
Embleton & Newton Links
Embleton
Embleton Bay
Brownieside
Doxford
North Charlton
Falloden
Dunstan Steads
Dunstanburgh Castle
Old Bewick
West Ditchburn
South Charlton
Dunstan
Craster
Roddam
Wooperton
New Bewick
Harehope
Eglingham
Rock
Rennington
Stamford
Howick Hall
Howick
Cullernose Point
Brandon
Beanley
Branton
Powburn
Broxfield
Littlehoughton
Longhoughton
Fawdon
Glanton
East Bolton
Boulmer
Denwick
River Aln
Abberwick
Alnwick
Glanton Pike
Shawdon Hill
Bolton
Great Ryle
Broome Park
Hawkhill
Seaton Point
Lesbury
334 COCHRANE PIKE
Little Ryle
Whittingham
Aln Valley Railway
Hipsburn
Bilton
Thrunton
Alnmouth
Alnmouth Bay
Castle
Yetlington
Edlingham
Bilton Banks
High Buston
Low Buston
Shilbottle
NU
319 LONG CRAG
Lorbottle
260 GLANTLEES HILL
Newton-on-the-Moor
Birling
Warkworth Castle & Hermitage
Warkworth
Amble
Coquet Island
Cartington
Gloster Hill
Warton
Snitter
Cragside
Swarland
Guyzance
North Togston
High Hauxley
Rothbury
Old Swarland
Acklington
Togston
Radcliffe
Thropton
North End
Felton
Whitton
Longframlington
East Thirston
Broomhill
Great Tosson
Newtown
Pauperhaugh
South Broomhill
Lordenshaws
Brinkburn Priory
Weldon Bridge
West Thirston
Red Row
Druridge Bay
Eshott
Druridge Bay
Forestburn Gate
West Chevington
Druridge
Helm
Todburn
Causey Park
Stobswood
Widdrington
North Northumberland Heritage Coast
Wingates
Causey Park Bridge
Widdrington Station
Cresswell
Longhorsley
Earsdon
Fontburn Reservoir
Tritlington
Ulgham
Ellington
Fenrother
Linton
Lynemouth
Rothley Lakes
Netherwitton
Stanton
Hebron
Longhirst
Woodhorn
Beacon Point
Longwitton
River Font
Pegswood
Ashington
Woodhorn Demesne
Herterton House
Rothley
Pigdon
Hirst
North Seaton
Newbiggin-by-the-Sea
Scot's Gap
Hart Burn
Newton Underwood
Bothal
Wansbeck Riverside
Hartburn
Meldon Park
Throphill
Mitford
Sheepwash
Cambo
Wallington House & Gardens
Morpeth
Stakeford
North Seaton Colliery
High Angerton
Guide Post
West Sleekburn
Middleton
Molesden
Hepscott
Scotland Gate
Bomarsund
Wansbeck
Low Angerton
Meldon
Choppington
Cambois
North Blyth
Tranwell
Clifton
Shaftoe Crags
Bolam Lake
Bolam
Edington
Nedderton
Bedlington
East Sleekburn
Whalton
Blyth
Cowpen
Capheaton
Harnham
Saltwick
Stannington Station
Bebside
Newsham
Plessey Woods
East Hartford
New Delaval
Bradford
Belsay
Belsay Hall, Castle & Gardens
Ogle
Stannington
Shotton
Shankhouse
New Hartley
Seaton Sluice
NZ
Kirkheaton
Black Heddon
Northumberland
Cramlington
East Cramlington
Seaton
Hartley
Higham Dykes
Seaton Delaval
St Mary's
Kearsley
Milbourne
Berwick Hill
Brenkley
Big Waters
Seghill
Ryal
Ingoe
Seaton Burn
Annitsford
Holywell
Heugh
Mason
Dudley
Ponteland
Dinnington
Brunswick Village
Wide Open
Burradon
Earsdon
Whitley Bay
Fenwick
Stamfordham
Dalton
Darras Hall
Prestwick
Camperdown
Backworth
Monkseaton
Great Whittington
Matfen
Hawkwell
Newcastle
Hazlerigg
Killingworth
Cullercoats
River Pont
Woolsington
Shiremoor
Murton
Tynemouth
Clarewood
Eachwick
High Callerton
Great Park
Forest Hall
New York
Tynemouth Priory & Castle
Wall Houses
Black Callerton
Kenton Bankfoot
Amsterdam (IJmuiden)
Harlow Hill
Hadrian's Wall Path
Fawdon
Rising Sun
North Shields
Halton Shields
Rudchester
North Walbottle
Gosforth
South Gosforth
Longbenton
SOUTH SHIELDS
Houghton
Throckley
Westerhope
Kenton
Willington
Aydon
Horsley
Heddon-on-the-Wall
Walbottle
Jesmond
Wallsend
Int. Ferry Terminal
Tyne Riverside
Heaton
Jarrow
Tyne Tunnel
Westoe
Marsden Bay
George Stephenson's Birthplace
Newburn
Harton
Newton
Wylam
NEWCASTLE UPON TYNE
Walker
Ovington
Ovingham
Claravale
Ryton
Stella
Byker
Hebburn
Marsden
Souter Lighthouse & The Leas
West Wylam
Crawcrook
Scotswood
Elswick
Felling
Monkton
Souter Point
Cleadon
Eltringham
Prudhoe
Ryton Woodside
Blaydon
Metro Centre
Dunston
Whitburn
Riding Mill
Bywell
West Mickley
Mickley Square
Priestclose Wood
Greenside
Winlaton
Derwent Walk
GATESHEAD
Wardley
Bolden Colliery
West Boldon
Stocksfield
High Mickley
Winlaton Mill
Whickham
Whitburn Bay
East Boldon
Broomley
Painshawfield
Coalburns
Barlow
Watergate Forest
Low Fell
Seaburn
Hindley
New Ridley
Hedley on the Hill
Leadgate
High Spen
Highfield
Sunniside
Street Gate
Team Valley
Wrekenton
Hylton Castle
Fulwell
Southwick
Roker
Apperley Dene
Chopwell
Gibside
Bowes Railway & Museum
Springwell
Healey
Blackhall Mill
Rowlands Gill
Lamesley
Wetland Centre
Castletown
Monkwearmouth
Whittonstall
Hamsterley
Derwentcote Steel Furnace
Burnopfield
Sheep Hill
Marley Hill
Byermoor
Tanfield Railway
Angel of the North
Birtley
Usworth
SUNDERLAND
70
69
Newlands
Hobson
Causey Arch
Tanfield
Kibblesworth
Portobello
WASHINGTON
Pennywell
Hendon
Ebchester
Westwood
Tantobie
Tanfield Lea
Beamish
High Urpeth
Urpeth
Ouston
Offerton
Kiln Pit Hill
Medomsley
Shotley Bridge
Dipton
White-le-Head
Stanley
West Pelton
Perkinsville
Fatfield
Penshaw Monument
Penshaw
Herrington
High Newport
New Silksworth
Durham
Shotleyfield
Catchgate
Rothbury Forest
River Coquet
River Blyth
River Wansbeck
River Breamish
Town plan: Newcastle upon Tyne p.120

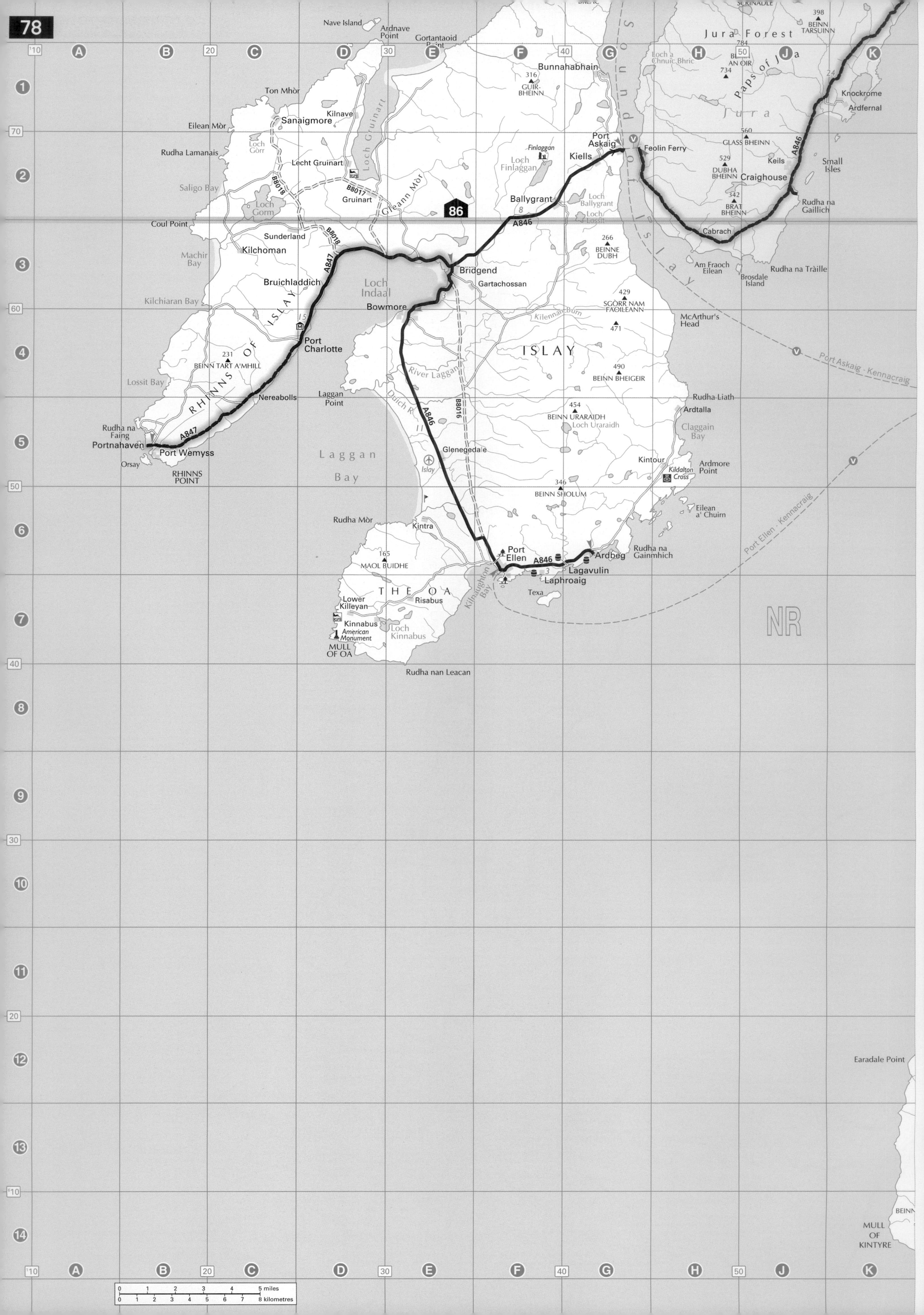
Nave Island
Ardnave Point
Gortantaoid Point
Jura Forest
398 BEINN TARSUINN
784 BEINN AN OIR
734
Paps of Jura
Loch a Chnuic Bhric
Bunnahabhain
316 GUIR-BHEINN
Knockrome
Ardfernal
Ton Mhòr
Kilnave
Sanaigmore
Eilean Mòr
Loch Gruinart
Jura
Loch Gòrr
Rudha Lamanais
Lecht Gruinart
Finlaggan
Loch Finlaggan
Port Askaig
Kiells
Feolin Ferry
560 GLASS BHEINN
529 DUBHA BHEINN
Keils
Craighouse
Small Isles
A846
Saligo Bay
B8018
B8017
Gruinart
Gleann Mòr
Loch Gorm
86
Ballygrant
Loch Ballygrant
Loch Lossit
342 BRAT BHEINN
Rudha na Gaillich
Coul Point
Sunderland
Kilchoman
Machir Bay
266 BEINNE DUBH
Cabrach
Sound of Islay
A847
Bridgend
Gartachossan
Bruichladdich
Loch Indaal
Am Fraoch Eilean
Brosdale Island
Rudha na Tràille
Kilchiaran Bay
Bowmore
429 SGÒRR NAM FAOILEANN
Kilennan Burn
471
McArthur's Head
RHINNS OF ISLAY
Port Charlotte
231 BEINN TART A'MHILL
ISLAY
Port Askaig - Kennacraig
Lossit Bay
River Laggan
490 BEINN BHEIGEIR
Nereabolls
Laggan Point
Duich R.
B8016
Rudha Liath
Ardtalla
454 BEINN URARAIDH
Loch Uraraidh
Claggain Bay
Rudha na Faing
Portnahaven
Port Wemyss
Orsay
RHINNS POINT
Laggan Bay
Glenegedale
Islay
Kintour
Ardmore Point
Kildalton Cross
346 BEINN SHOLUM
Eilean a' Chuirn
Port Ellen - Kennacraig
Rudha Mòr
Kintra
Port Ellen
Ardbeg
Rudha na Gainmhich
165 MAOL BUIDHE
Lagavulin
Laphroaig
Kilnaughton Bay
Texa
THE OA
Lower Killeyan
Risabus
Kinnabus
American Monument
Loch Kinnabus
MULL OF OA
NR
Rudha nan Leacan
Earadale Point
MULL OF KINTYRE
0 1 2 3 4 5 miles
0 1 2 3 4 5 6 7 8 kilometres

Kintyre
Arran
Bute
Gigha
Campbeltown
Tarbert
Lochranza
Brodick
Lamlash
Rothesay
Tighnabruaich
Kilberry
Skipness
Carradale
Saddell
Southend
Machrihanish
Sound of Bute
Kilbrannan Sound
West Loch Tarbert
Sound of Gigha
Loch Caolisport
Blackwaterfoot
Whiting Bay
Kildonan
Sannox
Corrie
Pirnmill
Tayinloan
Glenbarr
Muasdale
Bellochantuy
Kennacraig
Clachan
Claonaig
Portavadie
Kames
Colintraive
Port Bannatyne
Kilchattan
Garroch Head
Holy Island
Pladda
Sanda Island
Island Davaar
Mull of Kintyre
Goatfell
North Arran
Campbeltown - Ardrossan (May-Sept)

Sound of Bute
KILBRANNAN SOUND
FIRTH OF CLYDE
ARRAN
North Arran
NR
NS
NW
87
88
79
72
Skipness
Skipness Point
Claonaig
Claonaig Bay
Crossaig
Cour Bay
Cour
Grogport
Barmollack
Carradale
Carradale House
Waterfoot
Carradale Point
Carradale Bay
Saddell Bay
Cock of Arran
Lochranza
Catacol
Isle of Arran
Glen Catacol
Glen Chalmadale
A841
Sannox
Corrie
Pirnmill
Penrioch
Loch Tanna
834 CAISTEAL ABHAIL
715 BEINN BHARRAIN
Glen Iorsa
874 GOATFELL
Whitefarland
Imachar
Balliekine
792 BEINN NUIS
Glen Rosa
Merkland Point
Brodick Castle, Garden & Country Park
Brodick Bay
Iorsa Water
Brodick
Strathwhillan
Corriegills
Auchagallon Stone Circle
Machrie Bay
Machrie
Machrie Moor Stone Circles
Tormore
Moss Farm Road Stone Circle
B880
Balmichael
512 A'CHRUACH
503 BEINN BHREAC
Clauchlands Point
Margnaheglish
Lamlash
Lamlash Bay
Holy Island
Cordon
Torbeg
Shiskine
Drumadoon Point
Blackwaterfoot
Drumadoon Bay
Kilpatrick
Kilpatrick Dun
Brown Head
Glen Scorrodale
Carn Ban
Auchencairn
Kingscross
Knockenkelly
Whiting Bay
Glen Ashdale
Largymore
Largybeg
Dippen Head
Dippen
Corriecravie
Torr a' Chaisteal Fort
Sliddery
Kilmory Water
Kilmory
Lagg
Torrylin Cairn
Bennan
Kildonan
Bennan Head
Pladda
340 Ailsa Craig
Campbeltown - Brodick (May-Sept, Sat only)
Campbeltown - Ardrossan (May-Sept)
(Apr-Oct)
Ballanlay
Meikle Kilmory
Loch Fad
Loch Ascog
Kerrycroy
Mount Stuart
Bruchag
Inchmarnock
Ardscalpsie Bay
Kingarth
Stravanan Bay
Kilchattan
Kilchattan Bay
St Blane's Church
Garrochty
Garroch Head
GREAT CUMBRAE ISLAND
Millport
Little Cumbrae Island
Fairlie Roads
Quarter
Routenburn
Skelmorlie Aisle
Largs
483 IRISH LAW
Kelburn Castle & Country Centre
Fairlie
Camphill Reservoir
371 COCK LAW
Hunterston Power Station
Drakemyre
Portencross
Farland Head
Munnoch
West Kilbride
Seamill
Dalgarven
Kilwinning
Ardrossan
Horse Isle
Saltcoats
Ardeer
Irvine Bay
Lady Isle
Heads of Ayr
Fisherton
Dunure
Drumshang
Croy Brae (Electric Brae)
Knoweside
Culzean Bay
Culzean Castle & Country Park
Pennyglen
Whitefaulds
Maidenhead Bay
Maidens
Crossraguel Abbey
Kirkoswald
Souter Johnnie's Cottage
Turnberry
Turnberry Bay
Roan of Craigoch
Wallacetown
Dipple
Kilgrammie
Water of Girvan
Dailly
Old Dailly
Penkill
Girvan
Dounepark
Woodland
Pinminnoch
Barr
297 GREY HILL
Pinmore
Lendalfoot
Illigmorrie
A719
A77
B741
B7035
B734
A714
A760
A78
A738
B780
B781
B7047
B7048
B896
B899
B881
B8001
B842
B879
0 1 2 3 4 5 miles
0 1 2 3 4 5 6 7 8 kilometres

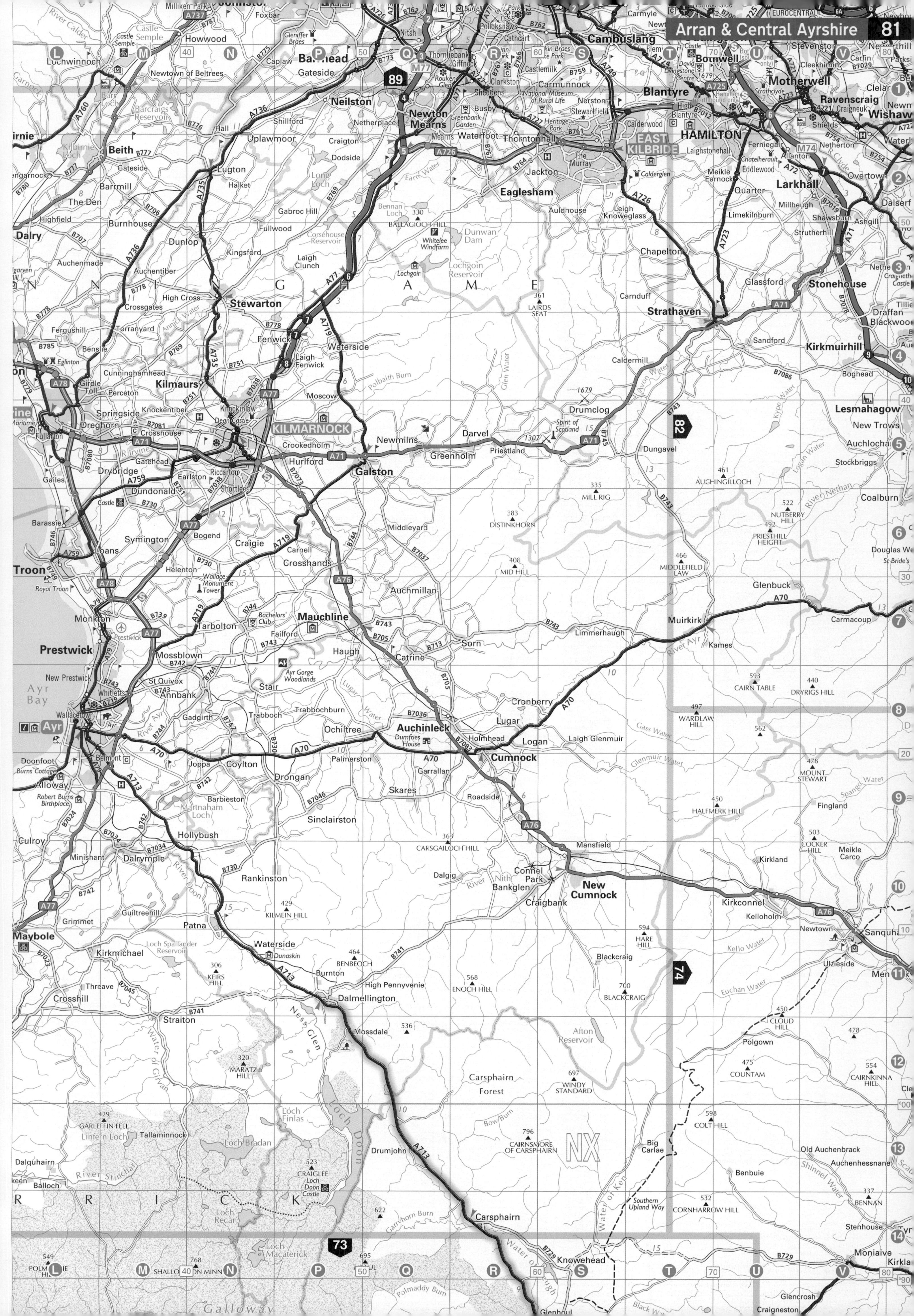

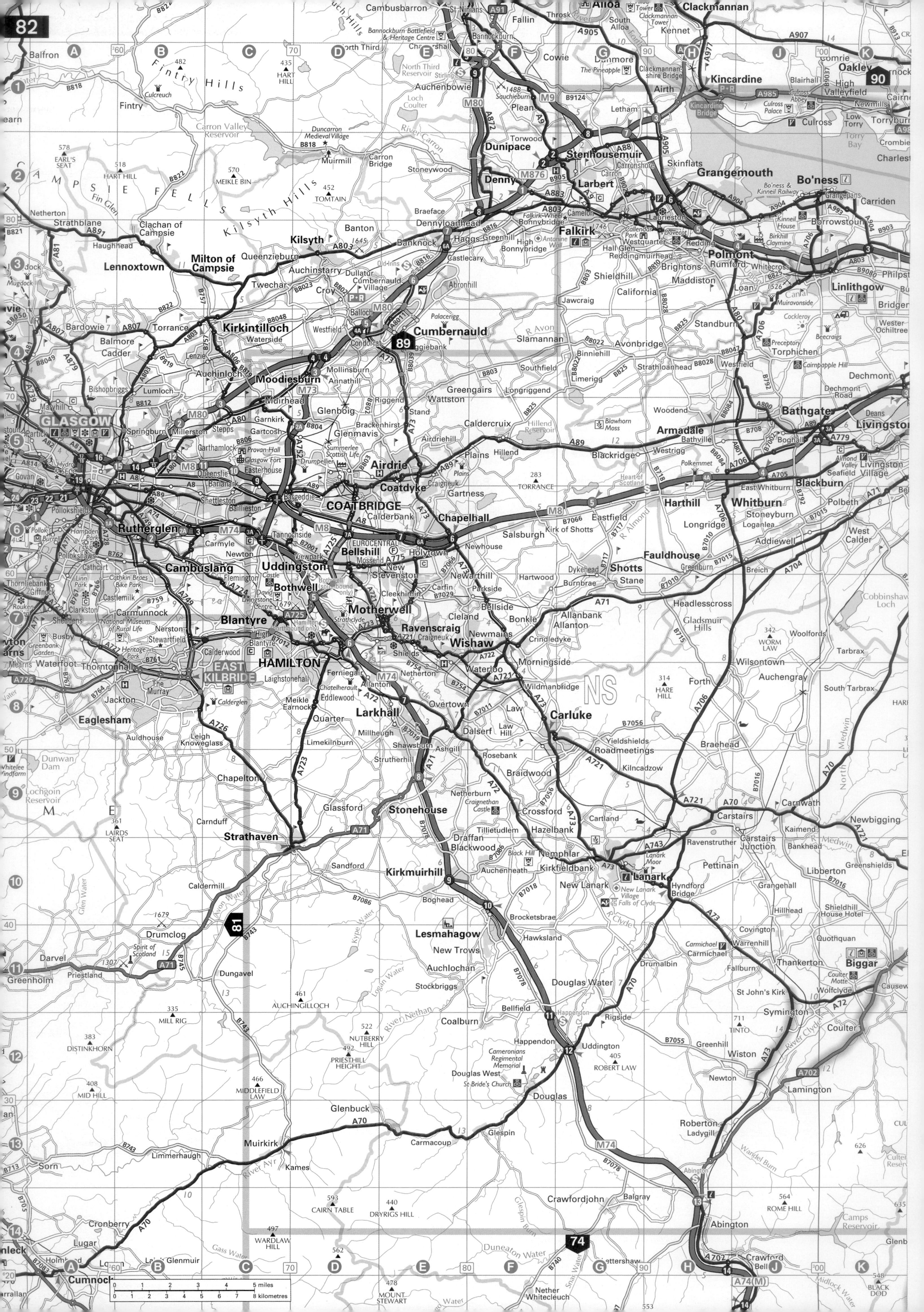

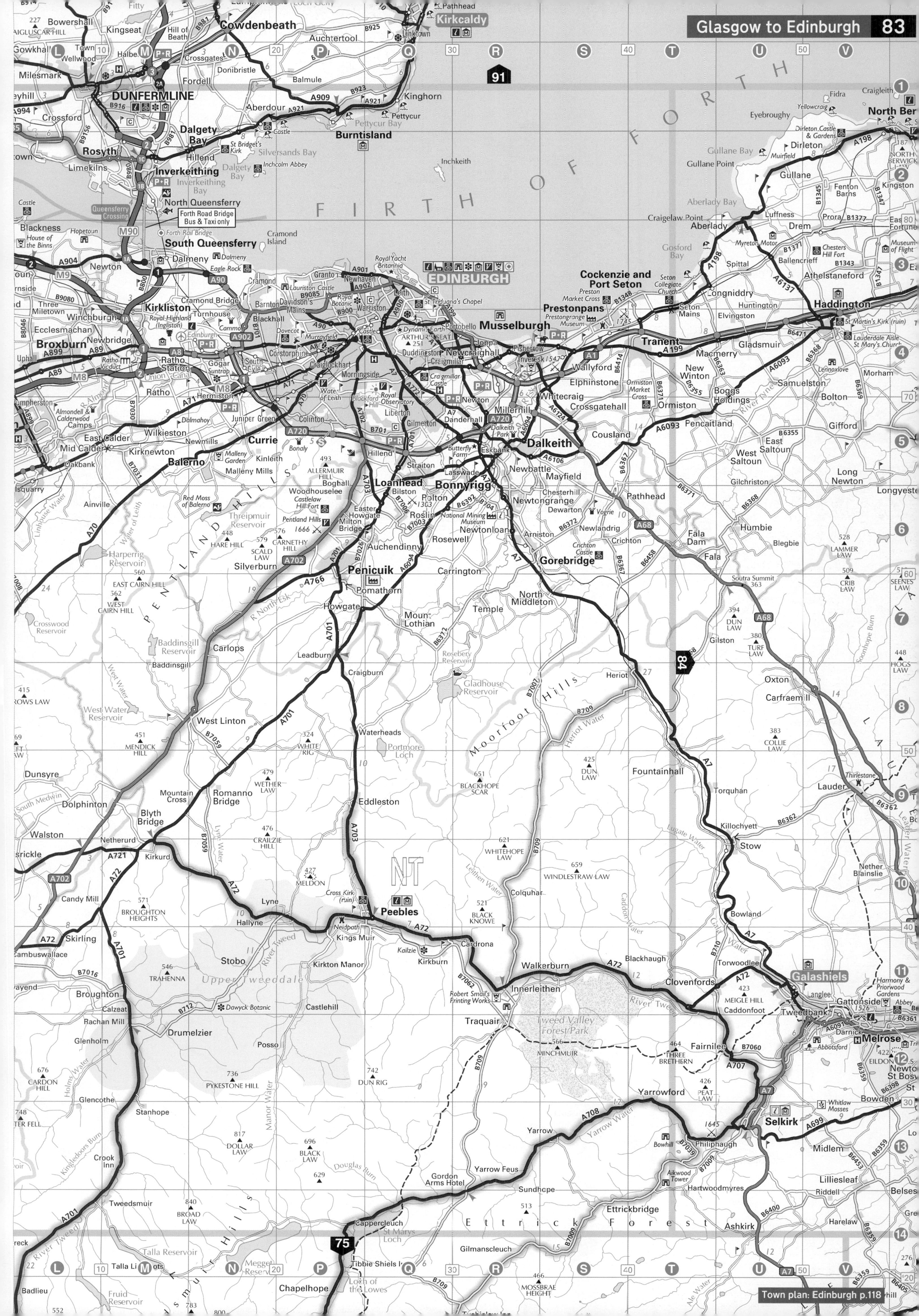
FIRTH OF FORTH
EDINBURGH
DUNFERMLINE
Kirkcaldy
Musselburgh
Dalkeith
Penicuik
Peebles
Galashiels
Selkirk
Melrose
Haddington
Pentland Hills
Moorfoot Hills
Ettrick Forest
Town plan: Edinburgh p.118

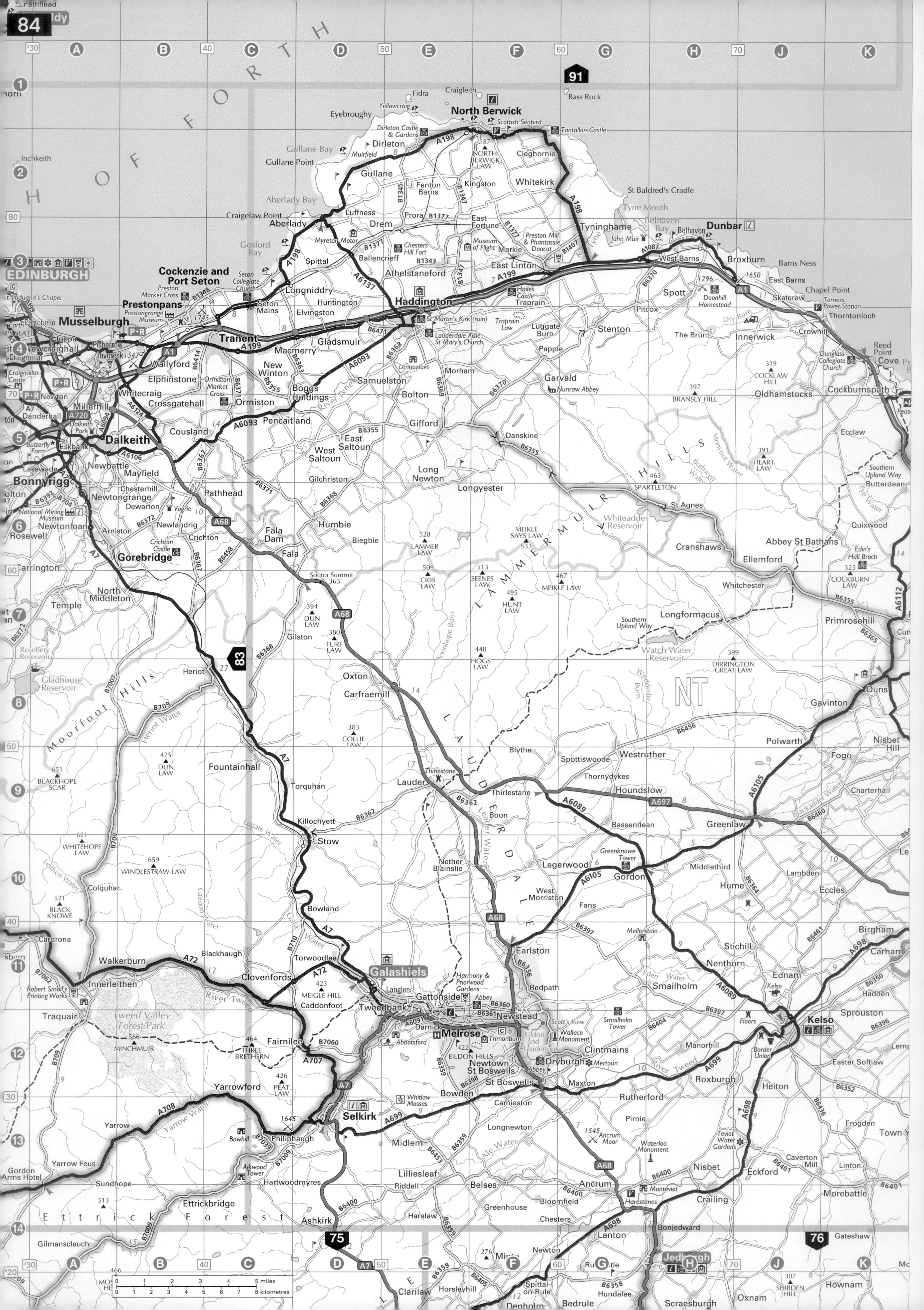

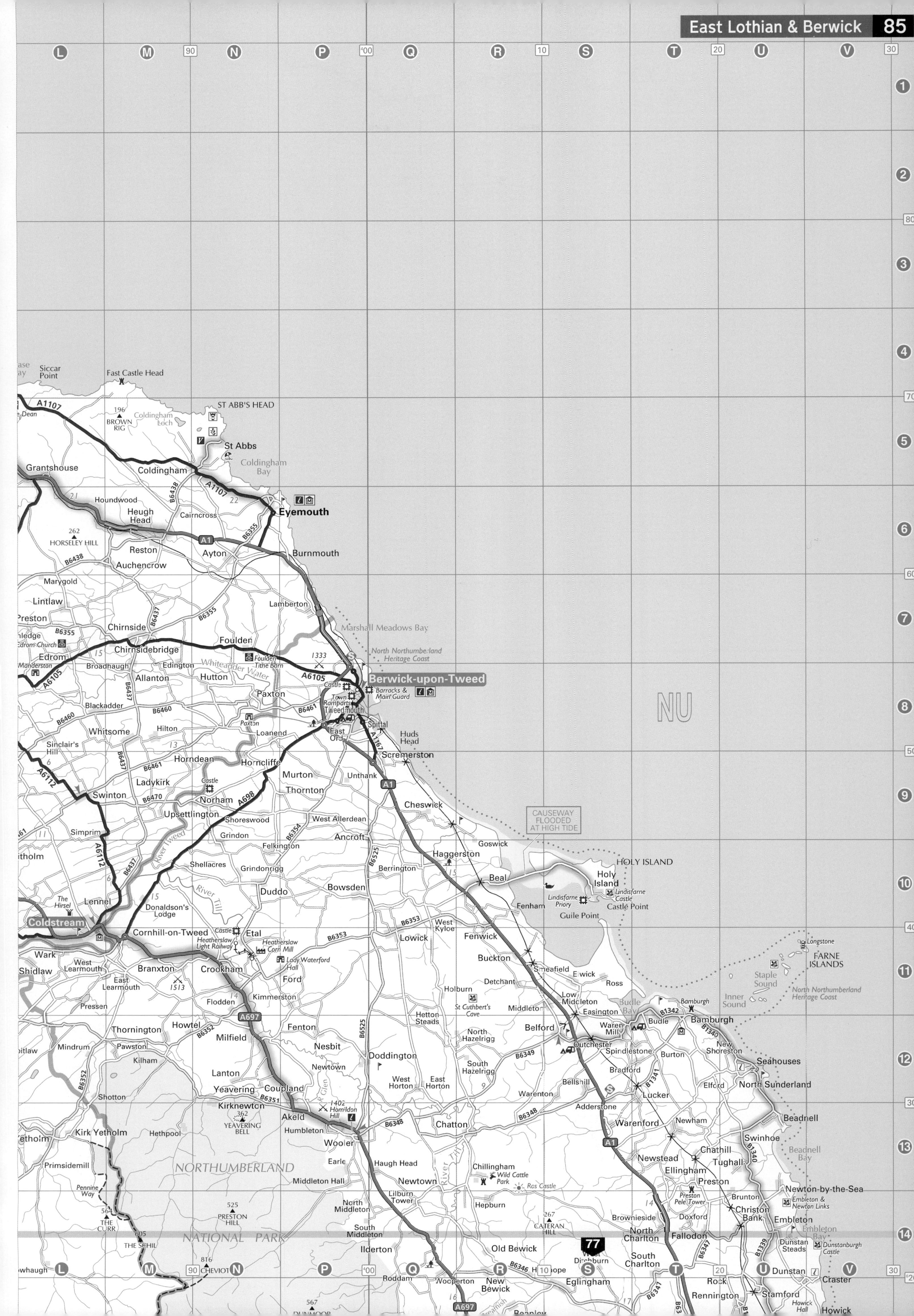

L M 90 N P '00 Q R 10 S T 20 U V 30

NU

Berwick-upon-Tweed

Coldstream

Eyemouth

ST ABB'S HEAD

St Abbs

Coldingham
Coldingham Bay

Fast Castle Head

Siccar Point

A1107

BROWN RIG

Grantshouse

Houndwood

Heugh Head
Cairncross

Reston

Ayton

Burnmouth

Auchencrow

Marygold

Lintlaw

Preston

Chirnside

Lamberton

Foulden

HORSELEY HILL

B6438

B6437

Chirnsidebridge

Edrom
Edrom Church

Broadhaugh

Edington

Allanton

Hutton

Manderston

Whiteadder Water

Foulden Tithe Barn

Marshall Meadows Bay

North Northumberland Heritage Coast

A6105

Castle

Town Ramparts
Tweedmouth

Barracks & Main Guard

Spittal

Huds Head

Blackadder

Hilton

Paxton

Loanend

East Ord

Scremerston

Whitsome

Sinclair's Hill

Horndean

Horncliffe

Murton

Unthank

A167

A1

Cheswick

CAUSEWAY FLOODED AT HIGH TIDE

Ladykirk

Norham

Thornton

West Allerdean

Ancroft

Goswick

HOLY ISLAND

Swinton

Upsettlington

Shoreswood

Grindon

Felkington

Berrington

Haggerston

Holy Island

Lindisfarne Castle Point

Simprim

Shellacres

Grindonrigg

Duddo

Bowsden

Beal

Lindisfarne Priory

Guile Point

The Hirsel

Lennel

Donaldson's Lodge

West Kyloe

Fenham

Longstone

FARNE ISLANDS

Coldstream

Cornhill-on-Tweed

Etal

Heatherslaw Light Railway

Heatherslaw Corn Mill

Lady Waterford Hall

B6353

Lowick

Fenwick

Buckton

Staple Sound

Inner Sound

North Northumberland Heritage Coast

Wark

West Learmouth

Shidlaw

Branxton

East Learmouth

Crookham

Ford

Kimmerston

Holburn

St Cuthbert's Cave

Middleton

Sneafield

E wick

Ross

Low Midleton

Bamburgh

Budle Bay

Waren Mill

Budle

New Shoreston

Pressen

Flodden

Hetton Steads

North Hazelrigg

Belford

Easington

Spindlestone

Burton

Bamburgh

Thornington

Howtel

Milfield

Fenton

Nesbit

Doddington

South Hazelrigg

Outchester

B6349

Bradford

Bellshill

Lucker

Elford

Seahouses

North Sunderland

Mindrum

Pawston

Kilham

Lanton

Newtown

West Horton

East Horton

Warenton

Adderstone

Warenford

Newham

Beadnell

Shotton

Yeavering

Coupland

HOMILDON HILL

Kirknewton

YEAVERING BELL

Akeld

Humbleton

Wooler

Earle

Haugh Head

Chatton

Chillingham
Wild Cattle Park

Ros Castle

Newstead

Chathill

Tughall

Ellingham

Preston

Swinhoe

Beadnell Bay

Kirk Yetholm

Hethpool

NORTHUMBERLAND

Middleton Hall

Newtown

Lilburn Tower

Hepburn

Brunton

Brownieside

Doxford

Christon Bank

Newton-by-the-Sea

Embleton & Newton Links

Embleton

Primsidemill

Pennine Way

THE CURR

PRESTON HILL

North Middleton

South Middleton

Ilderton

CATERAN HILL

North Charlton

South Charlton

Falloden

Dunstan Steads

Dunstanburgh Castle

NATIONAL PARK

THE SCHIL

CHEVIOT

West Ditchburn

Old Bewick

77

New Bewick

Eglingham

Rock

Dunstan

Craster

Roddam

Wooperton

Howick Hall

L M 90 N P '00 Q R B6346 10 S T 20 U V 30

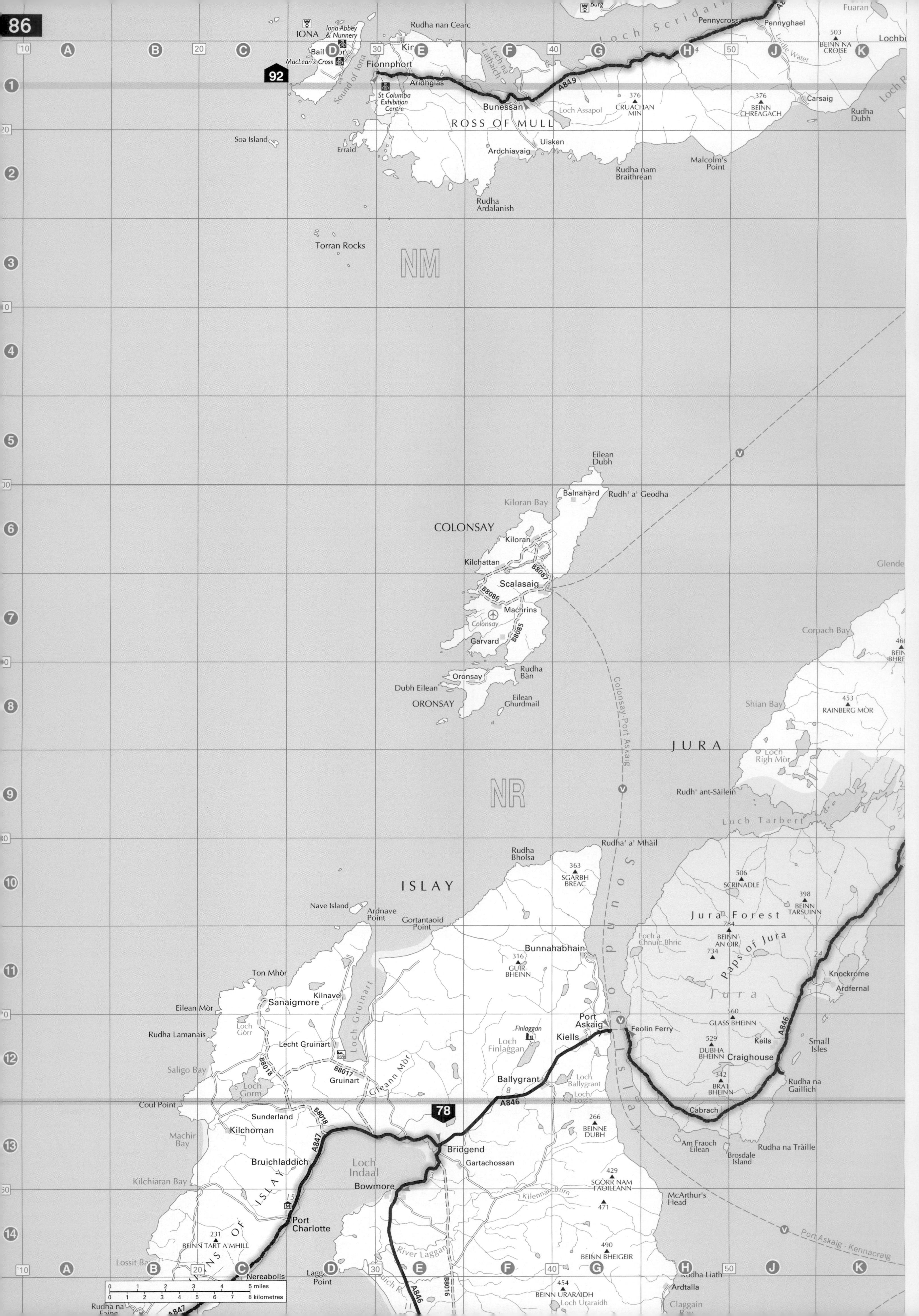

IONA

Iona Abbey & Nunnery

Rudha nan Cearc

Bail Mòr

MacLean's Cross

92

Fionnphort

Aridhglas

St Columba Exhibition Centre

Bunessan

ROSS OF MULL

Soa Island

Erraid

Ardchiavaig

Uisken

Rudha Ardalanish

Rudha nam Braithrean

Malcolm's Point

Torran Rocks

NM

Eilean Dubh

Balnahard

Rudh' a' Geodha

Kiloran Bay

COLONSAY

Kiloran

Kilchattan

B8087

Scalasaig

B8086

Machrins

Colonsay

B8085

Garvard

Oronsay

Rudha Bàn

Dubh Eilean

Eilean Ghurdmail

ORONSAY

NR

Colonsay–Port Askaig

JURA

Corpach Bay

BEINN BHRE

Shian Bay

453 ▲ RAINBERG MÒR

Rudh' ant-Sàilein

Loch Righ Mòr

Glende

Rudha' a' Mhàil

Sound of Islay

Loch Tarbert

Rudha Bholsa

363 ▲ SGARBH BREAC

506 ▲ SCRINADLE

398 ▲ BEINN TARSUINN

Jura Forest

784 ▲ BEINN AN ÒIR

ISLAY

Nave Island

Ardnave Point

Gortantaoid Point

Bunnahabhain

316 ▲ GUIR-BHEINN

Loch a Chnuic Bhric

734 ▲

J u r a

Knockrome

Ardfernal

Ton Mhòr

Kilnave

Sanaigmore

Eilean Mòr

Rudha Lamanais

Loch Gòrr

Lecht Gruinart

B8018

Gruinart

B8017

Loch Gruinart

Gleann Mòr

Finlaggan

Loch Finlaggan

Port Askaig

Kiells

Feolin Ferry

GLASS BHEINN

560 ▲

Keils

Small Isles

Paps of Jura

529 ▲ DUBHA BHEINN

342 ▲ BRAT BHEINN

Craighouse

Rudha na Gaillich

Saligo Bay

Loch Gorm

Coul Point

Sunderland

Kilchoman

Ballygrant

A846

Loch Ballygrant

Loch Lossit

Bridgend

Gartachossan

266 ▲ BEINNE DUBH

Cabrach

Am Fraoch Eilean

Brosdale Island

Rudha na Tràille

Machir Bay

Bruichladdich

Loch Indaal

Bowmore

78

A847

Kilchiaran Bay

Port Charlotte

231 ▲ BEINN TART A'MHILL

RINNS OF ISLAY

Lossit Ba

Nereabolls

Rudha na Faing

Lagg Point

River Laggan

B8016

A846

429 ▲ SGÒRR NAM FAOILEANN

471 ▲

McArthur's Head

490 ▲ BEINN BHEIGEIR

Port Askaig – Kennacraig

454 ▲ BEINN URARAIDH

Loch Uraraidh

Rudha Liath

Ardtalla

Claggain

Pennycross

Pennyghael

A849

Loch Scridain

A849

503 ▲ BEINN NA CROISE

Lochb

376 ▲ CRUACHAN MIN

Loch Assapol

376 ▲ BEINN CHREAGACH

Carsaig

Rudha Dubh

Kir

Rudha na Lathaich

Leille Water

burg

Fuaran

Loch

0 1 2 3 4 5 miles

0 1 2 3 4 5 6 7 8 kilometres

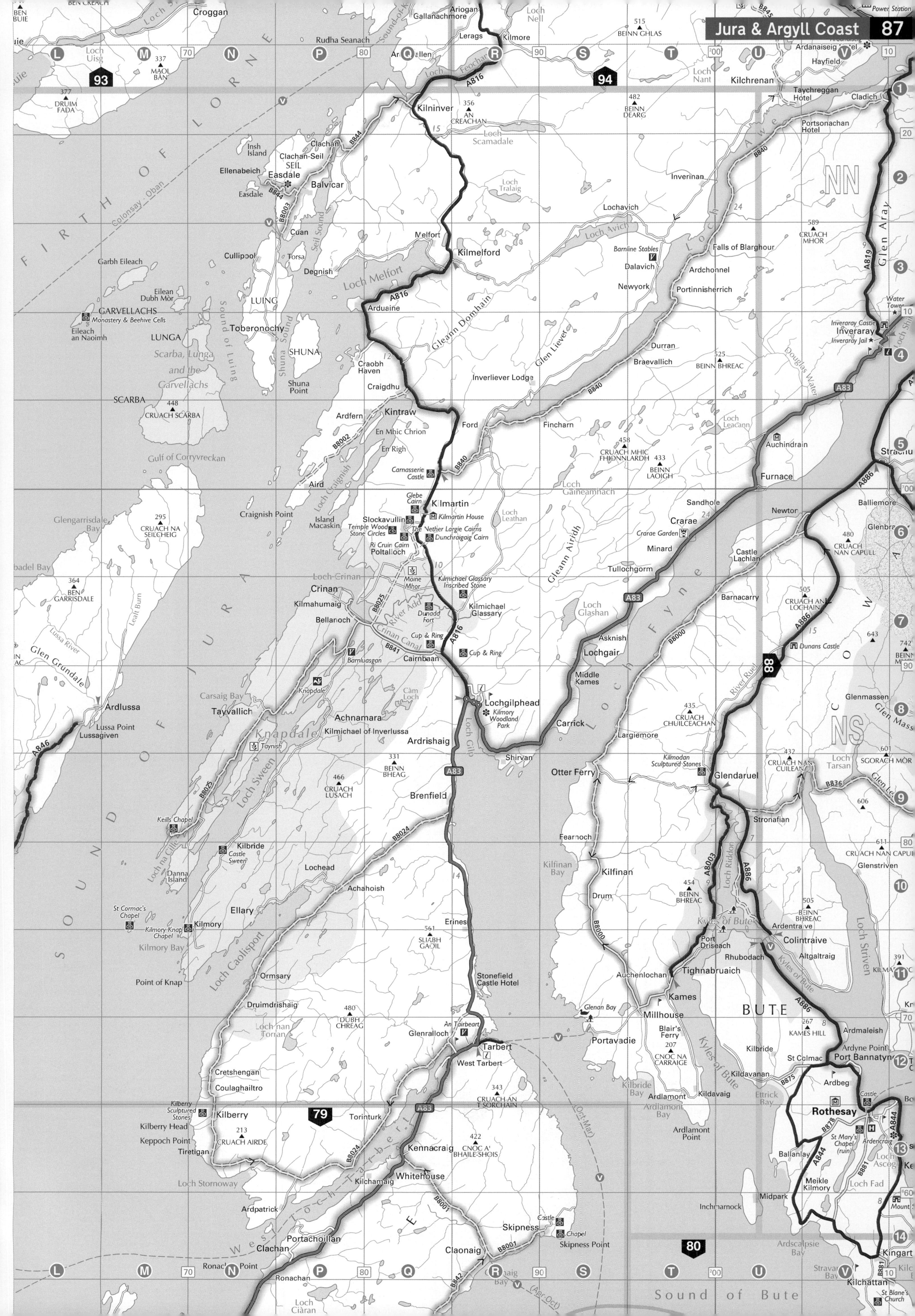

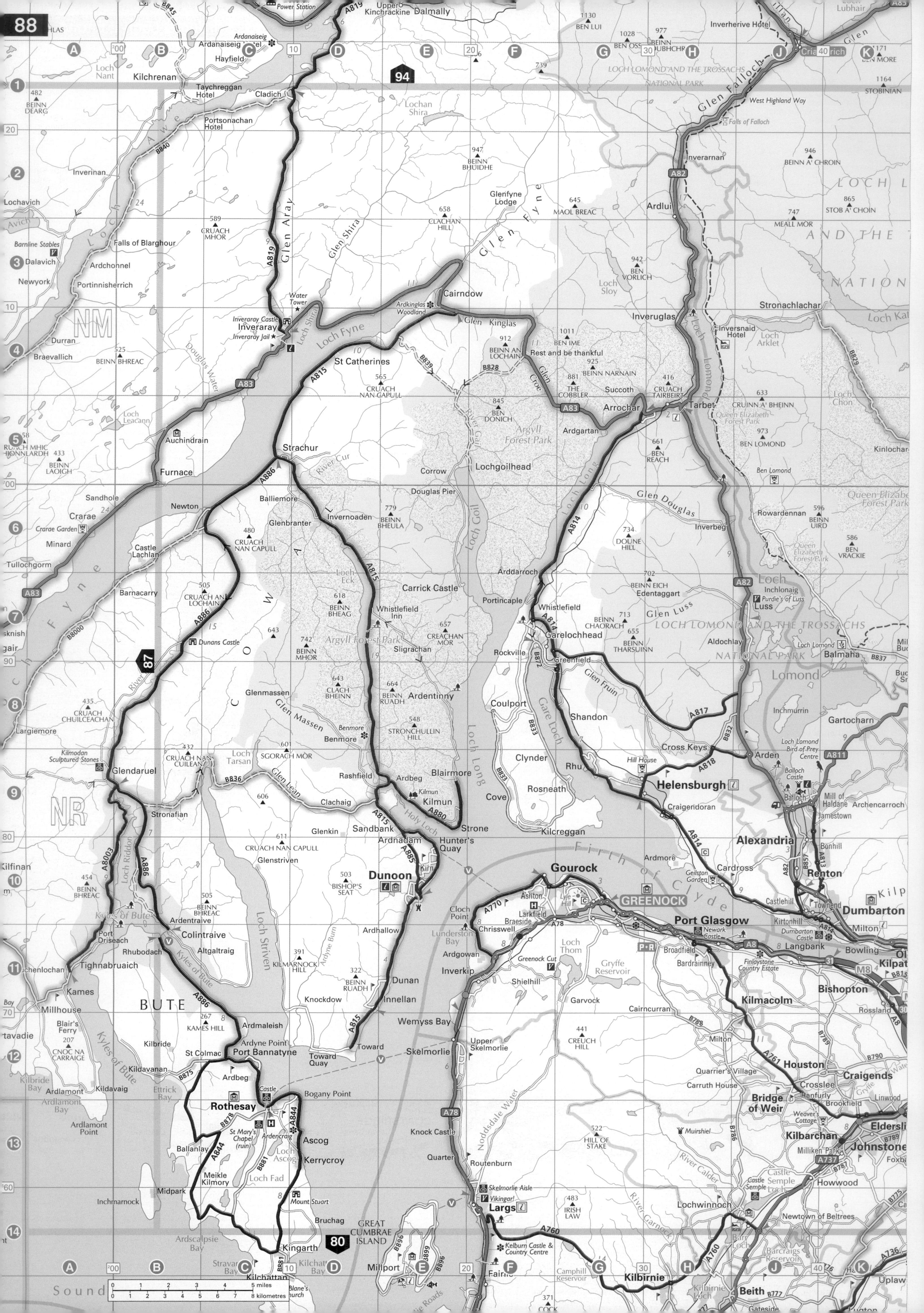

Inveraray
Loch Fyne
Strachur
Lochgoilhead
Arrochar
Tarbet
Ardlui
Luss
Helensburgh
Alexandria
Dumbarton
Gourock
Greenock
Port Glasgow
Dunoon
Rothesay
Bute
Largs
Kilbirnie
Kilmacolm
Bridge of Weir
Johnstone
Kilchrenan
Cairndow
Tighnabruaich
Colintraive
Glendaruel
Furnace
Loch Long
Gare Loch
Firth of Clyde
Loch Lomond and The Trossachs National Park
Argyll Forest Park
Cowal
Great Cumbrae Island
Millport

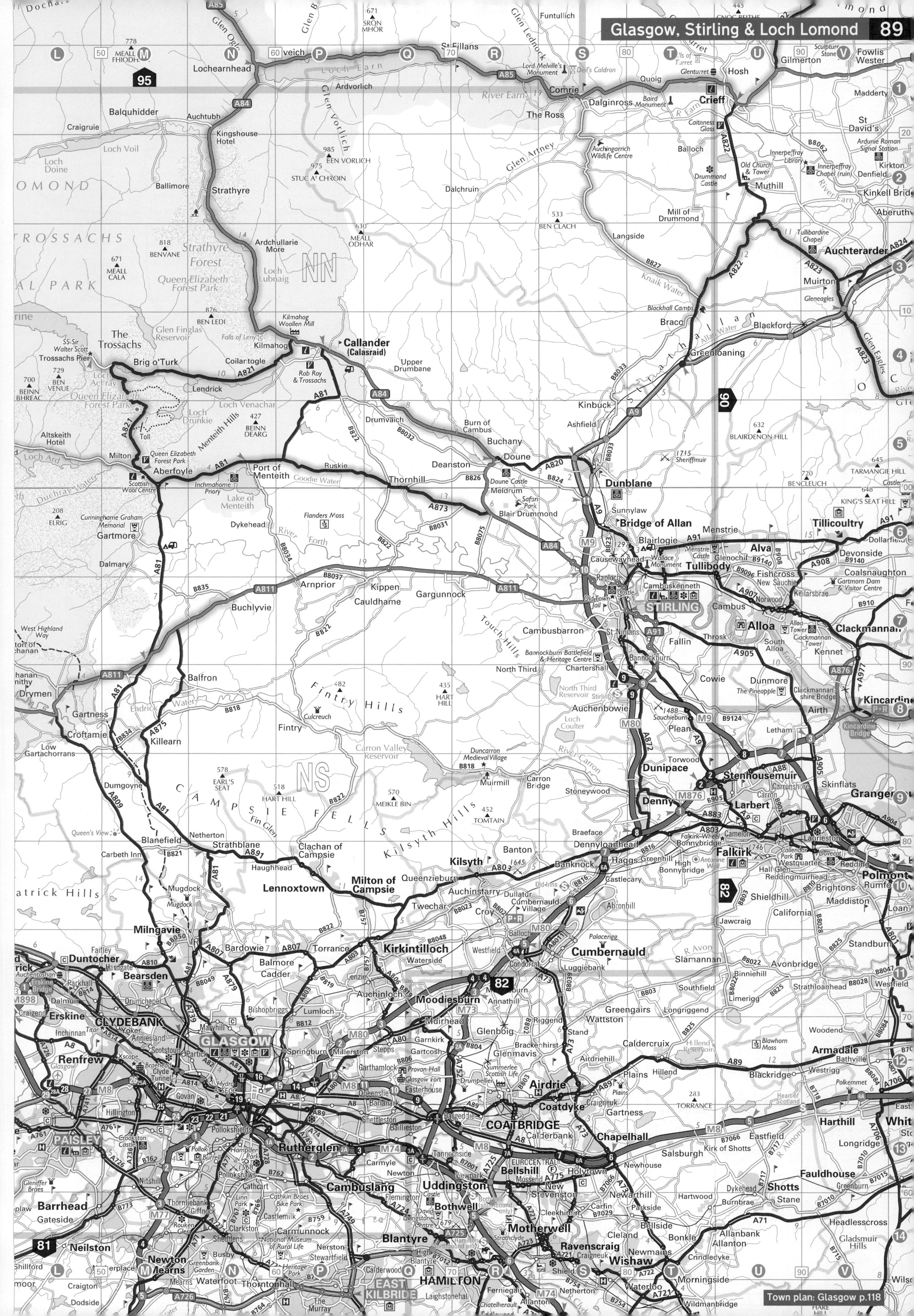

Lochearnhead
St Fillans
Comrie
Crieff
Balquhidder
Kingshouse Hotel
Strathyre
Callander (Calasraid)
The Trossachs
Brig o'Turk
Aberfoyle
Port of Menteith
Thornhill
Doune
Dunblane
Bridge of Allan
Braco
Blackford
Auchterarder
Gleneagles
Greenloaning
Kinbuck
Muthill
Tillicoultry
Alva
Tullibody
Menstrie
STIRLING
Alloa
Clackmannan
Kincardine
Bannockburn
Cambusbarron
Kippen
Gargunnock
Arnprior
Buchlyvie
Balfron
Killearn
Drymen
Gartness
Croftamie
Fintry
Campsie Fells
Fintry Hills
Kilsyth Hills
Kilsyth
Denny
Dunipace
Larbert
Stenhousemuir
Falkirk
Grangemouth
Polmont
Cumbernauld
Kirkintilloch
Milngavie
Bearsden
Lennoxtown
Milton of Campsie
Strathblane
Blanefield
CLYDEBANK
GLASGOW
Erskine
Renfrew
PAISLEY
Barrhead
Newton Mearns
Rutherglen
Cambuslang
Uddingston
Bothwell
COATBRIDGE
Airdrie
Bellshill
Motherwell
Wishaw
HAMILTON
EAST KILBRIDE
Blantyre
Shotts
Harthill
Armadale
Whitburn
Fauldhouse
Chapelhall
Moodiesburn
Stepps
Clarkston
Neilston

Town plan: Glasgow p.118

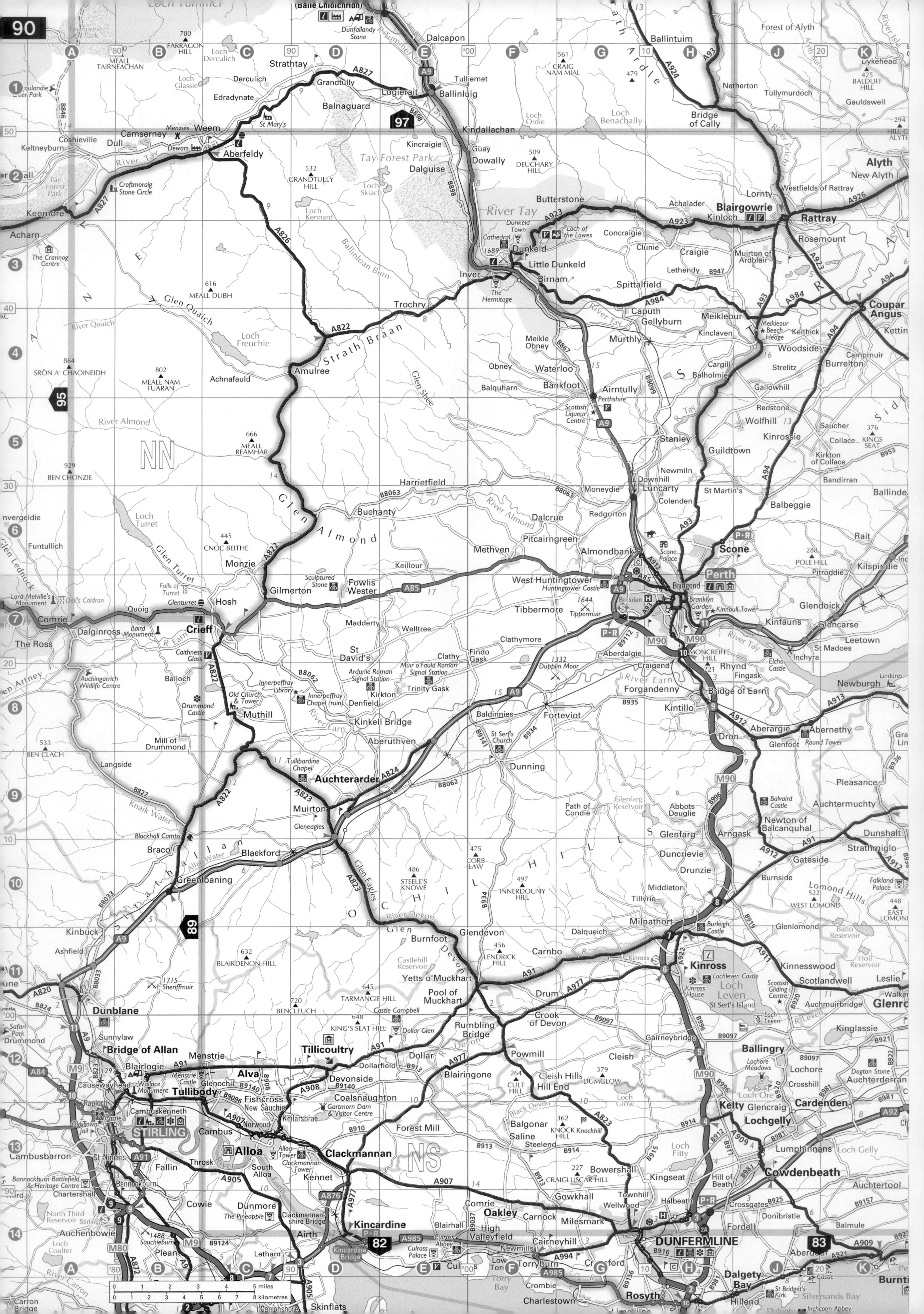

Dalcapon
Ballintuim
Forest of Alyth
Strathtay
Tulliemet
Derculich
Grandtully
Logierait
Ballinluig
Edradynate
Balnaguard
Netherton
Tullymurdoch
Bridge of Cally
Kindallachan
Keltneyburn
Coshieville
Dull
Camserney
Weem
Aberfeldy
Kincraigie
Tay Forest Park
Guay
Dowally
Dalguise
Kenmore
Croftmoraig Stone Circle
Butterstone
River Tay
Dunkeld
Little Dunkeld
Birnam
Inver
Concraigie
Clunie
Craigie
Blairgowrie
Kinloch
Achalader
Rattray
Rosemount
Alyth
New Alyth
Lornty
Acharn
The Crannog Centre
Spittalfield
Caputh
Gellyburn
Meikleour
Kinclaven
Coupar Angus
Keithick
Woodside
Burrelton
Trochry
Strath Braan
Amulree
Glen Quaich
Loch Freuchie
Meikle Obney
Obney
Waterloo
Bankfoot
Murthly
Airntully
Cargill
Balholmie
Strelitz
Balquharn
Scottish Liqueur Centre
Achnafauld
Stanley
Wolfhill
Guildtown
Kinrossie
Saucher
Collace
Kinrick of Collace
River Almond
Harrietfield
Moneydie
Luncarty
Newmiln
Colenden
St Martin's
Balbeggie
Bandirran
Buchanty
Glen Almond
Dalcrue
Redgorton
Pitcairngreen
Methven
Almondbank
Scone
Scone Palace
Rait
Kilspindie
Monzie
Glen Turret
Loch Turret
Keillour
Fowlis Wester
Gilmerton
Hosh
West Huntingtower
Huntingtower Castle
Perth
Bridgend
Tibbermore
Glendoick
Kinfauns
Glencarse
Comrie
Quoig
Crieff
Dalginross
The Ross
Madderty
Welltree
Clathymore
St David's
Clathy
Findo Gask
Aberdalgie
Dupplin Moor
Craigend
Moncreiffe Hill
Rhynd
Fingask
Elcho Castle
Leetown
St Madoes
Inchyra
Balloch
Innerpeffray Library
Trinity Gask
Forgandenny
River Earn
Bridge of Earn
Newburgh
Drummond Castle
Muthill
Denfield
Kirkton
Kinkell Bridge
Baldinnies
Forteviot
Kintillo
Aberargie
Abernethy
Dron
Glenfoot
Mill of Drummond
Aberuthven
Dunning
Langside
Auchterarder
Tullibardine Chapel
Muirton
Gleneagles
Path of Condie
Abbots Deuglie
Glenfarg
Arngask
Pleasance
Auchtermuchty
Newton of Balcanquhal
Braco
Blackford
Greenloaning
Strathallan
Glen Eagles
Duncrievie
Drunzie
Gateside
Dunshalt
Strathmiglo
Middleton
Tillyrie
Milnathort
Burleigh Castle
Falkland Palace
Lomond Hills
West Lomond
Ochil Hills
Glendevon
Burnfoot
Dalqueich
Carnbo
Glenlomond
Kinbuck
Ashfield
Blairdenon Hill
Yetts o'Muckhart
Pool of Muckhart
Kinross
Lochleven Castle
Loch Leven
St Serf's Island
Kinnesswood
Scotlandwell
Leslie
Dunblane
Sheriffmuir
Tarmangie Hill
Bencleuch
Castle Campbell
Drum
Crook of Devon
Gairneybridge
Kinglassie
Sunnylaw
Bridge of Allan
Menstrie
Tillicoultry
Dollar
Rumbling Bridge
Powmill
Cleish
Ballingry
Lochore
Blairlogie
Alva
Dollarfield
Blairingone
Cleish Hills
Hill End
Crosshill
Auchterderran
Causewayhead
Wallace Monument
Tullibody
Glenochil
Fishcross
Devonside
Coalsnaughton
Kelty
Glencraig
Lochgelly
Cardenden
Raploch
Cambuskenneth
Stirling
Cambus
New Sauchie
Kellarsbrae
Gartmorn Dam
Balgonar
Saline
Steelend
Knockhill
Forest Mill
Cambusbarron
St Ninians
Alloa
Fallin
Throsk
South Alloa
Clackmannan
Lumphinnans
Cowdenbeath
Bannockburn
Chartershall
Kennet
Bowershall
Kingseat
Hill of Beath
Auchtertool
Cowie
Dunmore
The Pineapple
Comrie
Oakley
Carnock
Milesmark
Townhill
Wellwood
Halbeath
Crossgates
Donibristle
North Third Reservoir
Auchenbowie
Airth
Kincardine
Blairhall
High Valleyfield
Cairneyhill
Dunfermline
Fordell
Balmule
Aberdour
Plean
Letham
Culross
Culross Palace
Newmills
Torryburn
Crossford
Dalgety Bay
Rosyth
Charlestown
Crombie
Torry Bay
Hillend
Burntisland
Skinflats
Carron Bridge
Carronshore
M90
M9
M80
A9
A91
A977
A823
A822
A826
A827
A923
A984
A93
A94
A85
A824
A912
A913
A907
A908
A876
A985
A92
A909
A921
A905
A872
A84
A820
A994
0 1 2 3 4 5 miles
0 1 2 3 4 5 6 7 8 kilometres

Loch of Coul
Braes of Coul
Bridge of Craigisla
Loch of Lintrathen
L
Bridge of Lintrathen
M
Braes of Coul
Kingoldrum
Northmuir
Finavon
Oathlaw
Crosston
Aberlemno
Sculptured Stones
Kemp's Castle
B957
B9134
Mains of Melgunds
Barnhead
Scurdie Ness
Farnell
Westerton of Rossie
Usan
V
Bridge of Craigisla
B951
B954
Kirriemuir
Kirkton of Airlie
Airlie
Craigton of Airlie
Roundyhill
Ballinshoe
Padanaram
A926
Drumgley
Lunanhead
Restenneth Priory
Reswallie
Bolshan
Glasterlaw
WUDDY LAW
Braehead
Boddin Point
Lunan
Westmuir
Southmuir
98
Forfar Loch
Forfar
Guthrie
Kinnell
Lunan Bay
River Isla
Ruthven
Kirkton of Airlie
Littleton
A926
A928
St Orland's Stone
Glamis
A94
Douglastown
B9127
Kingsmuir
Dunnichen
Letham
Friockheim
Leysmill
Chapelton
Cauldcots
Inverkeilor
99
Red Head
Glamis
Charleston
Thornton
Leys of Cossans
Eassie Sculptured Stone
Bowriefauld
Craichie
Whigstreet
Redford
Greystone
Colliston
Letham Grange
St Vigeans
Marywell
Auchmithie
Carlingheugh Bay
Meigle
Newbigging
Ardler
Newtyle
Eassie and Nevay
Kirkinch
Sculptured Stone Museum
KINPURNEY HILL
379 GALLOW HILL
Gateside
Hatton
Kirkbuddo
Hayhillock
Carmyllie
B961
B9127
Bonnington
Arbirlot
Condor
Arbroath
The Deil's Head
Newtyle
Glenduckie
Nether Handwick
CRAIGOWL HILL
Petterden
Todhills
CARROT HILL
Monikie
Kirkton of Monikie
Craigton
Elliot Water
Arbroath
Bonnyton
Auchterhouse
Tealing Earth-House
Newbigging
Monikie
Muirdrum
East Haven
Lundie
Kirkton of Auchterhouse
Kirkton of Tealing Tealing Dovecot
Wellbank
Carlungie Earth-House
Upper Victoria
Panbride
West Haven
Dronley
Kirkton of Strathmartine
Kellas
Murroes
Ardestie Earth-House
Barry Mill
Barry
Carnoustie
Muirhead
Birkhill
Mains of Fintry
Newbigging
Carnoustie
Fowlis
Clatto
Whitfield
Baldovie
B962
Liff
Gourdie
Camperdown
Douglas and Angus
Baldovie
A92
Claypotts Castle
Barnhill
Monifieth
BUDDON NESS
Benvie
Denhead of Gray
Downfield
Broughty Ferry
NO
Abernyte
Lochee
Mills Observatory
Ancrum Outdoor Centre
North Carr lightship
Broughty Castle
Baledgarno
Invergowrie
Kingoodie
DUNDEE
Discovery Point
HM Frigate 'Unicorn'
Tayport
Tentsmuir Point
Longforgan
Dundee
A92 Tay Bridge
Newport-on-Tay
Inchture
A90
Firth of Tay
Balmerino Abbey
Wormit
Kirkton
A914
B946
A945
Tentsmuir Point
Grange
Balmerino
Bottomcraig
Scottish National Golf Centre
Errol
Coultra
Gauldry
Hazelton Walls
Kilmany
Lucklawhill
Leuchars
ST ANDREWS BAY
NORMANS LAW
Creich
Brunton
Rathillet
Logie
A919
Balmullo
Den of Lindores
Dunbog
Lindores
Luthrie
Moonzie
Denbrae
A914
Dairsie
Guardbridge
River Eden
Kincaple
St Andrews Castle
St Andrews
Brownhills
Boarhills
Fernie
Cupar
Strathkinness
Botanic
Monimail
Letham
Bow of Fife
Kemback
Blebocraigs
Denhead
Craigtoun
B939
Collessie
Cupar Muir
Hill of Tarvit Mansion
Pitscottie
Cameron Reservoir
Dunino
Kingsbarns
Cambo
Kingsbarns
Lochieheads
Giffordtown
Charlottetown
Deer Centre
Scotstarvit Tower
Bridgend
Ceres
Baldinnie
B940
Peat Inn
Radernie
Kingsmuir
Scotland's Secret Bunker
Balcomie Links
FIFE NESS
Ladybank
Craigrothie
Struthers
New Gilston
Woodside
Largoward
Lathones
Carnbee
Crail
Kingskettle
Balmalcolm
Pitlessie
CLATTO HILL
Langdyke
Praytis
Upper Largo
Colinsburgh
Arncroach
Kellie Castle
Wester Pitkierie
Easter Pitkierie
Kilrenny
Cellardyke
Falkland
Freuchie
Muirhead
Star
Baintown
Bonnybank
Lundin Mill
Drumeldrie
Newton of Balcormo
Fisheries
Anstruther
Kennoway
Scoonie
Lundin Links
Lower Largo
Largo Bay
Kilconquhar
Pittenweem
St Monans
Cadham
Markinch
Windygates
A915
Leven
Innerleven
Earlsferry
Elie
Isle of May
Thornton
Milton of Balgonie
Methilhill
Methil
Buckhaven
East Wemyss
Coaltown of Balgonie
Coaltown of Wemyss
West Wemyss
River Ore
NT
Gallatown
Ravenscraig Castle
Pathhead
Kirkcaldy
Dysart
Craigleith
Yellowcraig
Fidra
Bass Rock
84
North Berwick
Dirleton Castle & Gardens
A198
Tantallon Castle
Kinghorn
Pettycur Bay
Gullane Bay
Gullane Point
Muirfield
Dirleton
Cleghornie
Inchkeith
FIRTH OF FORTH

Town plan: Dundee p.117

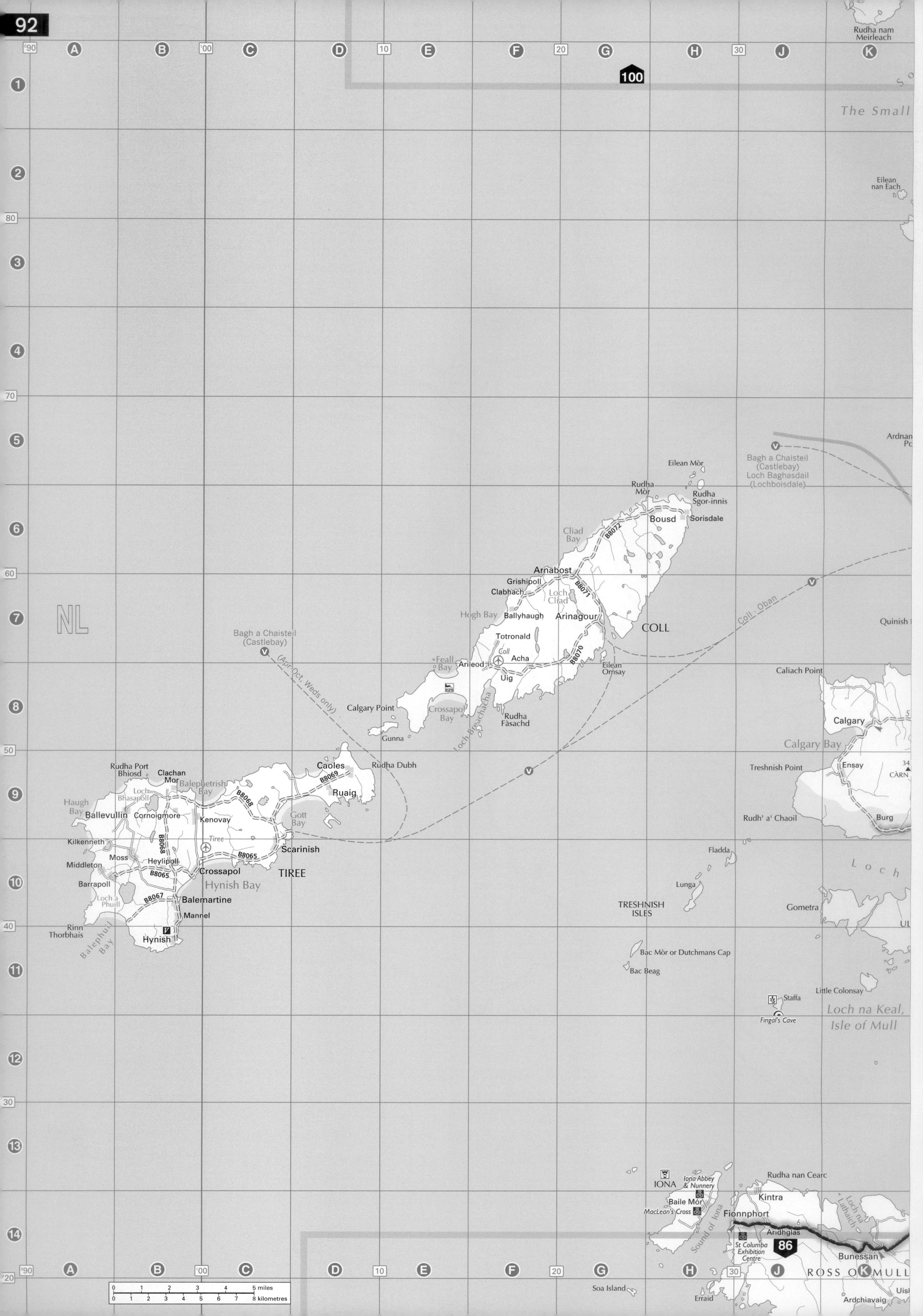

100

The Small

Rudha nam
Meirleach

Eilean
nan Each

NL

Ardnan
Po

Bagh a Chaisteil
(Castlebay)
Loch Baghasdail
(Lochboisdale)

Eilean Mòr

Rudha
Mòr

Rudha
Sgor-innis

Bousd

Sorisdale

Cliad
Bay

B8072

Arnabost

Grishipoll

Clabhach

Loch
Cliad

B8071

Coll - Oban

COLL

Quinish

Caliach Point

Hogh Bay

Ballyhaugh

Arinagour

Totronald

B8070

Coll

Acha

Feall
Bay

Arileod

Uig

Eilean
Ornsay

Calgary

Calgary Point

Crossapol
Bay

Rudha
Fàsachd

Calgary Bay

Gunna

Bagh a Chaisteil
(Castlebay)

(Apr-Oct. Weds only)

Loch Breachacha

Treshnish Point

Ensay

CÀRN

Caoles

Rùdha Dubh

Rudh' a' Chaoil

Burg

Rudha Port
Bhiosd

Clachan
Mòr

Balephetrish
Bay

B8069

Ruaig

B8068

Loch

Haugh
Bay

Loch
Bhasapoll

Ballevullin

Cornoigmore

Kenovay

Gott
Bay

Fladda

Kilkenneth

B8068

Tiree

Scarinish

Lunga

Moss

Heylipoll

B8065

Middleton

Crossapol

TIREE

TRESHNISH
ISLES

Gometra

Barrapoll

B8065

Hynish Bay

UL

Loch a
Phuill

B8067

Balemartine

Rinn
Thorbhais

Mannel

Bac Mòr or Dutchmans Cap

Hynish

Bac Beag

Little Colonsay

Balephuil Bay

Staffa

Loch na Keal,
Isle of Mull

Fingal's Cave

IONA

Iona Abbey
& Nunnery

Rudha nan Cearc

Baile Mòr

Kintra

MacLean's Cross

Fionnphort

Sound of Iona

Aridhglas

86

St Columba
Exhibition
Centre

Bunessan

Soa Island

ROSS OK MULL

Uisl

Erraid

Ardchiavaig

Swordland
Glenancross
Loch Morar
Lettermorar
Bunacaimb
503 CÀRN A' MHADAIDH-RUAIDH
Cleadale
Bay of Laig
299 AN CRUACHAN
Rudha an Fhasaidh
Laig
EIGG
Kildonnan
393 AN SGURR
Sandavore
Isles
Sound of Eigg
Eilean Chathastail
MUCK
Port Mor
100
Eilean Ighe
Back of Keppoch
Arisaig
Luinga Mhòr
Loch nan Ceall
Rudh' Arisaig
103 CRUACH DOIRE
Druimindarroch
Arisaig House
600 SIDHEAN MÒR
Prince Charlie's Cairn
Kinlochnanuagh
Loch nan Uamh
Meoble
River Meoble
710 MEITH BHEINN
101
716 AN STAC
Loch Beoriad
796 SGURR AN UTHA
Polnish
Lochailort
Inverailort
Loch Eilt
A830
Glenfinnan
Ardnish
Sound of Arisaig
Rudha Chοalais
Loch Ailort
A861
877 ROIS-BHEINN
882 BEINN ODHAR BHEAG
NM
Smearisary
Glenuig
712
664 BEINN GAIRE
Eilean Shona
Rudha Aird Druimnich
Ockle Point
Morar, Moidart and Ardnamurchan
Loch Moidart
Tioram
Seven Men of Moidart
Kinlochmoidart
Ardmolich
Brunery
Glen Forsian
Glen Moidart
Scamodale
758 MEALL MÒR
Loch Shiel
754 SGOR AN TARMACHAIN
239 BEINN BHREAC
MOIDART
Sanna Point
Sanna Bay
Kilmory
Ockle
Ardtoe
Shielfoot
Dalnabreck
Portuairk
Achnaha
Branault
356 BEINN BHREAC
Kentra
B8044
Blain
Mingarrypark
Dalelia
Glen Hurich
436 MEALL NAN CON
ARDNAMURCHAN
Arevegaig
Polloch
Loch Doilet
888 SGURR DHOMHNUILL
Achosnich
B8007
Loch Mudle
437
Acharacle
Claish Moss
846 BEINN RESIPOL
SUNART
342 BEINN NA SEILG
Kilchoan
Ormsaigmore
Mingary
527 BEN HIANT
Salen
Resipole
Ariundle Oakwood
Glenbeg
512 BEN LAGA
Loch Sunart
Anaheilt
Strontian
Ardslignish
Glenborrodale
Laga
339 GEARR CHREAG
Glencripesdale
Camasine
Woodend
Ardnastang
Camasachoirce
Achnalea
Glen Tarbert
Ardmore Point
Sorne Point
Oronsay
Carna
Auliston Point
Liddesdale
A884
Glengorm Castle
620 GLAS BHEINN
853 CREACH BHEINN
Tobermory
571 BEINN LADAIN
522 MEALL A' CHOISE
Lochuisge
Calve Island
Loch Teacuis
292 'S AIRDE BEINN
Drimnin
Glen Dubh
94
BEINN NA CILLE
B8043
Dervaig
B8073
Achnadrish House
437 BEINN BHUIDHE
550 SÌTHEAN NA RAPLAICH
B849
Loch Arienas
Acharn
Loch a' Choire
738 BEINN MHEADHOIN
A848
444 SPEINNE MÒR
Loch Frisa
Gleann Geal
Claggan
568 SGÙRR A' BHUIC
Larachbeg
339 MEALL DAMH
Sound of Mull
Rannoch River
Achranich
Loch Tèarnait
Port Ramsay
Glen Aros
Funiary
Loch Aline
390 CNOC AN DA CHINN
Fanmore
Aros
Lochaline
Glenaros House
Tirefour Castle (ruin)
464 GLAIS BHEINN
514 AN SLEAGHOCH
Clachan
Eriska
Ballygown
Loch Tuath
Eas Fors
333 BEINN NAN CÀRN
Killiechronan
B8035
Salen
A849
Fishnish Point
Fishnish Pier
Eilean Dubh
LISMORE
B8045
Lynn of Lorne
Achnacroish
Oskamull
B8073
Gruline
Macquarie Mausoleum
408 BEINN NAN LUS
Glen Forsa
Rudha an Ridire
Scallastle Bay
Kilcheran
Bernera Island
Eorsa
Loch na Keal
ISLE
Loch Bà
636 BEINN MHEADHON
Altcreich
591 BEINN A' GHRÀIG
Craignure
Lynn of Lorne
Ardmucknish Bay
Inch Kenneth
Inchkenneth Chapel (ruin)
B8035
766 DÙN DA GHAOITHE
OF
Duart Bay
Duart Point
Torosay
Duart
Dunstaffnage Castle & Chapel
Balnahard
North Connel
966 BEN MORE
704 CRUACHAN DEARG
MULL
Lochdonhead
Lochdon
Dunbeg
Gorten
Dunollie Castle
Ganavan Bay
A849
Loch Don
Grass Point
McCaig's Tower
519 BEIN-NA SREINE
Strathcoil
A85
491 CREACH BHEINN
Tiroran
Aird of Kinloch
Glen More
247 CÀRN BÀN
Oban (An t-Oban)
KERRERA
Fossil Tree
Burg
A849
Loch Fuaran
717 BEN BUIE
698 BEN CREACH
Loch Spelve
Croggan
Gallanachbeg
Ariogan
Gallanachmore
Loch Nell
Loch Scridain
Pennycross
Pennyghael
Sound of Kerrera
Leidle Water
503 BEINN NA CROISE
Lochbuie
Loch Uisg
Rudha Seanach
Lerags
Kilmore
Ardentallen
337 MAOL BÀN
Loch Feochan
A816
Loch Buie
376 CRUACHAN MIN
376 BEINN CHREAGACH
Carsaig
377 DRUIM FADA
87
Kilninver
356 AN CREACHAN
Loch Assapol
Rudha
THE FIRTH OF LORNE
Loch Scamadale
Insh Island
Clachan
Clachan-Seil
SEIL
B844
Malcolm's
LOCH LINNHE

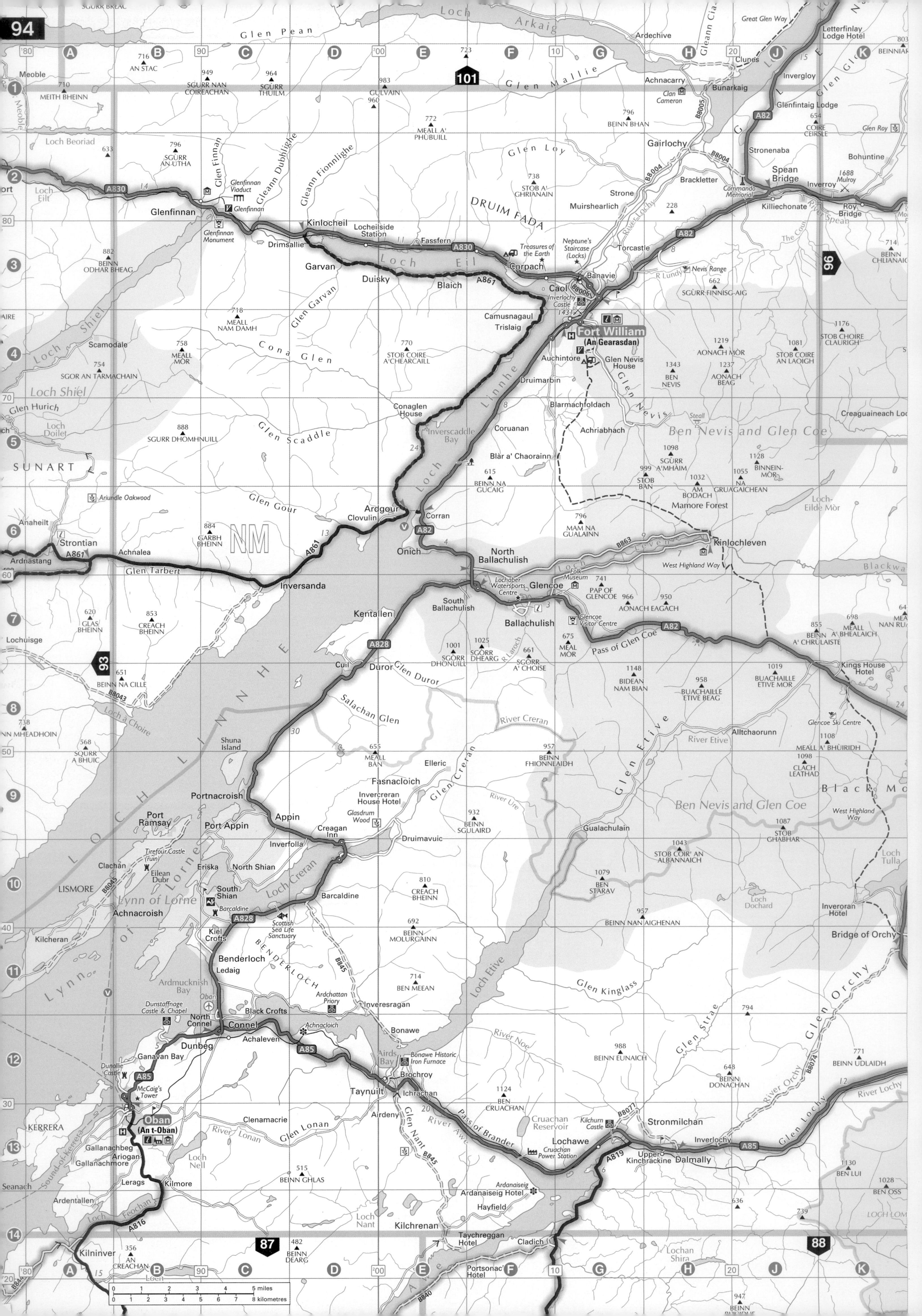
Loch Arkaig
Glen Pean
Glen Mallie
101
Ardechive
Achnacarry
Clan Cameron
Gleann Cia-aig
Great Glen Way
Letterfinlay Lodge Hotel
Clunes
Bunarkaig
Invergloy
Glenfintaig Lodge
Meoble
MEITH BHEINN
AN STAC
SGURR NAN COIREACHAN
SGURR THUILM
GULVAIN
Loch Beoriad
SGURR AN UTHA
Glen Finnan
Gleann Dubh-lighe
Gleann Fionnlighe
MEALL A' PHUBUILL
Glen Loy
BEINN BHAN
Gairlochy
Stronenaba
Spean Bridge
Bohuntine
Glen Roy
COIRE CEIRSLE
Inverroy
Mulroy
Roy Bridge
Killiechonate
Commando Memorial
Brackletter
Strone
STOB A' GHRIANAIN
DRUIM FADA
Muirshearlich
Glenfinnan Viaduct
Glenfinnan
Glenfinnan Monument
Loch Eilt
A830
Kinlocheil
Locheilside Station
Drimsallie
Fassfern
Garvan
Duisky
Blaich
Loch Eil
Corpach
Treasures of the Earth
Neptune's Staircase (Locks)
Torcastle
Banavie
Caol
Inverlochy Castle
Nevis Range
SGÙRR FINNISG-AIG
BEINN ODHAR BHEAG
MEALL NAM DAMH
Glen Garvan
Camusnagaul
Trislaig
Fort William
(An Gearasdan)
Loch Shiel
Scamodale
MEALL MOR
SGOR AN TARMACHAIN
Cona Glen
STOB COIRE A'CHEARCAILL
Auchintore
Glen Nevis House
Druimarbin
BEN NEVIS
AONACH MÒR
AONACH BEAG
STOB COIRE AN LAOIGH
STOB CHOIRE CLAURIGH
Glen Hurich
Loch Doilet
SGURR DHOMHNUILL
Glen Scaddle
Conaglen House
Inverscaddle Bay
Loch Linnhe
Blarmachfoldach
Achriabhach
Coruanan
Glen Nevis
Steall
Ben Nevis and Glen Coe
Creaguaineach Lodge
SUNART
Blàr a' Chaorainn
BEINN NA GUCAIG
SGÙRR A' MHÀIM
STOB BAN
AM BODACH
NA GRUAGAICHEAN
BINNEIN MÒR
Mamore Forest
Loch Eilde Mòr
Ariundle Oakwood
Glen Gour
Ardgour
Clovulin
Corran
Anaheilt
Strontian
GARBH BHEINN
NM
MAM NA GUALAINN
Onich
North Ballachulish
Kinlochleven
Loch Leven
West Highland Way
Ardnastang
A861
Achnalea
Glen Tarbert
Inversanda
Lochaber Watersports Centre
Glencoe
Folk Museum
PAP OF GLENCOE
AONACH EAGACH
Blackwater
South Ballachulish
Ballachulish
Glencoe Visitor Centre
GLAS BHEINN
CREACH BHEINN
Kentallen
Lochuisge
A828
SGORR DHONUILL
SGORR DHEARG
SGORR A' CHOISE
MEALL MOR
Pass of Glen Coe
A82
BEINN A' CHRULAISTE
MEALL A' BHEALAICH
MEALL NAN RUADHAG
Cuil
Duror
Glen Duror
BEINN NA CILLE
B8043
BIDEAN NAM BIAN
BUACHAILLE ETIVE BEAG
BUACHAILLE ETIVE MOR
Kings House Hotel
SGURR MHEADHOIN
Loch a' Choire
Salachan Glen
River Creran
Glencoe Ski Centre
SGURR A BHUIC
Shuna Island
MEALL BAN
Elleric
BEINN FHIONNLAIDH
Glen Etive
River Etive
Alltchaorunn
MEALL A' BHÙIRIDH
CLACH LEATHAD
Fasnacloich
Invercreran House Hotel
Glen Creran
River Ure
Black Mount
Portnacroish
Port Ramsay
Port Appin
Appin
Glasdrum Wood
Creagan Inn
BEINN SGULAIRD
Druimavuic
Gualachulain
STOB GHABHAR
West Highland Way
Inverfolla
STOB COIR' AN ALBANNAICH
Loch Tulla
LOCH LINNHE
Tirefour Castle (ruin)
Clachan
Eriska
North Shian
Eilean Dubh
Loch Creran
LISMORE
South Shian
Barcaldine
CREACH BHEINN
BEN STARAV
Loch Dochard
Inveroran Hotel
Lynn of Lorne
Achnacroish
Barcaldine
Scottish Sea Life Sanctuary
BEINN NAN AIGHENAN
Kilcheran
Kiel Crofts
BENDERLOCH
BEINN MOLURGAINN
Bridge of Orchy
Benderloch
Ledaig
B845
Loch Etive
Glen Kinglass
Glen Orchy
Ardmucknish Bay
BEN MEEAN
Dunstaffnage Castle & Chapel
Ardchattan Priory
Inveresragan
Black Crofts
North Connel
Connel
Achnacloich
Bonawe
Glen Strae
Achaleven
Dunbeg
A85
River Noe
BEINN EUNAICH
BEINN UDLAIDH
Ganavan Bay
Airds Bay
Bonawe Historic Iron Furnace
Dunollie Castle
McCaig's Tower
Brochroy
Taynuilt
Ichrachan
BEN CRUACHAN
BEINN DONACHAN
River Orchy
B8074
River Lochy
Oban
(An t-Oban)
Clenamacrie
Glen Lonan
River Lonan
Airdeny
Glen Nant
River Awe
Pass of Brander
Cruachan Reservoir
Kilchurn Castle
B8077
Stronmilchan
Glen Lochy
KERRERA
Lochawe
Inverlochy
Gallanachbeg
Ariogan
Gallanachmore
Loch Nell
Cruachan Power Station
Upper Kinchrackine
Dalmally
A819
Sound of Kerrera
BEINN GHLAS
Ardanaiseig
Ardanaiseig Hotel
BEN LUI
BEN OSS
Seanach
Lerags
Kilmore
Ardentallen
Hayfield
Loch Feochan
Loch Nant
Kilchrenan
LOCH LOMOND
A816
87
BEINN DEARG
Taychreggan Hotel
Cladich
88
Kilninver
AN CREACHAN
Loch Awe
Portsonachan Hotel
Lochan Shira
B844
B840
BEINN BHUIDHE
5 miles
8 kilometres

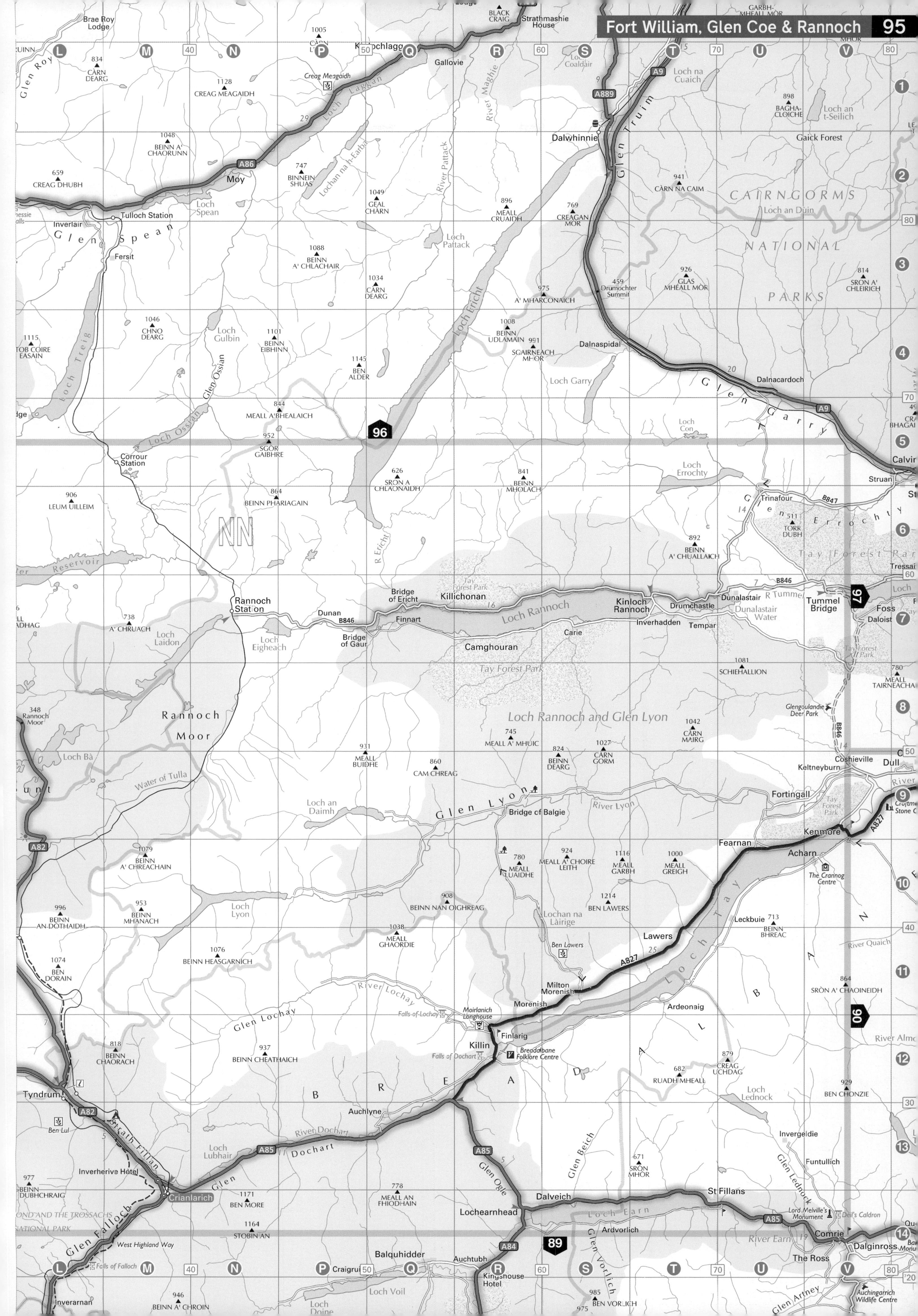
Brae Roy Lodge
Glen Roy
834 CARN DEARG
1128 CREAG MEAGAIDH
Creag Meagaidh
1005
Kinlochlaggan
Loch Laggan
Gallovie
BLACK CRAIG
Strathmashie House
River Mashie
Loch Coaldair
A9
A889
Loch na Cuaich
Dalwhinnie
Glen Truim
898 BAGHA-CLOICHE
Loch an t-Seilich
Gaick Forest
1048 BEINN A' CHAORUNN
659 CREAG DHUBH
A86
Moy
747 BINNEIN SHUAS
Lochan na h-Earba
River Pattack
1049 GEAL CHARN
896 MEALL CRUAIDH
769 CREAGAN MOR
941 CÀRN NA CAIM
CAIRNGORMS NATIONAL PARKS
Loch an Dùin
Loch Spean
Inverlair
Tulloch Station
Glen Spean
Fersit
1088 BEINN A' CHLACHAIR
Loch Pattack
1034 CARN DEARG
975 A' MHARCONAICH
459 Drumochter Summit
926 GLAS MHEALL MÒR
814 SRON A' CHLEIRICH
Loch Treig
1115 STOB COIRE EASAIN
1046 CHNO DEARG
Loch Gulbin
1101 BEINN EIBHINN
Glen Ossian
1145 BEN ALDER
Loch Ericht
1008 BEINN UDLAMAIN
991 SGAIRNEACH MHOR
Dalnaspidal
Loch Garry
Glen Garry
Dalnacardoch
844 MEALL A' BHEALAICH
Loch Ossian
96
952 SGOR GAIBHRE
Loch Con
Corrour Station
626 SRON A CHLAONAIDH
841 BEINN MHOLACH
Loch Errochty
Struan
Calvine
906 LEUM UILLEIM
864 BEINN PHARIAGAIN
Trinafour
B847
Glen Errochty
511 TORR DUBH
NN
R Ericht
892 BEINN A' CHUALLAICH
Tay Forest Park
Reservoir
Tressait
Rannoch Station
Bridge of Ericht
Killichonan
Kinloch Rannoch
Drumchastle
Dunalastair
B846
R Tummel
Tummel Bridge
97
Foss
Daloist
Dunan
Finnart
Loch Rannoch
Inverhadden
Tempar
Dunalastair Water
738 A' CHRUACH
Loch Laidon
Loch Eigheach
Bridge of Gaur
Camghouran
Carie
1081 SCHIEHALLION
780 MEALL TAIRNEACHAN
348 Rannoch Moor
Rannoch Moor
Loch Rannoch and Glen Lyon
Glengoulandie Deer Park
1042 CARN MAIRG
745 MEALL A' MHUIC
824 BEINN DEARG
1027 CARN GORM
Loch Bà
931 MEALL BUIDHE
860 CAM CHREAG
Coshieville
Keltneyburn
Dull
Water of Tulla
Loch an Daimh
Glen Lyon
Bridge of Balgie
River Lyon
Fortingall
Kenmore
A827
A82
1079 BEINN A' CHREACHAIN
780 MEALL LUAIDHE
924 MEALL A' CHOIRE LEITH
1116 MEALL GARBH
1000 MEALL GREIGH
Fearnan
Acharn
The Crannog Centre
996 BEINN AN DOTHAIDH
953 BEINN MHANACH
Loch Lyon
908 BEINN NAN OIGHREAG
1214 BEN LAWERS
Lochan na Làirige
Leckbuie
713 BEINN BHREAC
1038 MEALL GHAORDIE
Ben Lawers
Lawers
Loch Tay
River Quaich
1074 BEN DORAIN
1076 BEINN HEASGARNICH
Milton Morenish
864 SRÒN A' CHAOINEIDH
River Lochay
Glen Lochay
Falls-of-Lochay
Moirlanich Longhouse
Morenish
Ardeonaig
BREADALBANE
90
818 BEINN CHAORACH
937 BEINN CHEATHAICH
Finlarig
Killin
Falls of Dochart
Breadalbane Folklore Centre
879 CREAG UCHDAG
682 RUADH MHEALL
River Almond
929 BEN CHONZIE
Tyndrum
A82
Ben Lui
Auchlyne
Loch Lednock
Strath Fillan
River Dochart
Glen Dochart
Loch Lubhair
A85
Glen Ogle
Glen Beich
671 SRÒN MHOR
Invergeldie
Glen Lednock
Funtullich
977 BEINN DUBHCHRAIG
Inverherive Hotel
Crianlarich
1171 BEN MORE
778 MEALL AN FHIODHAIN
Dalveich
St Fillans
Lochearnhead
Loch Earn
Lord Melville's Monument
Deil's Caldron
Comrie
LOCH LOMOND AND THE TROSSACHS NATIONAL PARK
1164 STOBINIAN
Ardvorlich
Glen Vorlich
River Earn
Dalginross
Glen Falloch
West Highland Way
A84
89
Balquhidder
Auchtubh
Falls of Falloch
Craigruie
Kingshouse Hotel
The Ross
Inverarnan
946 BEINN A' CHROIN
Loch Voil
Loch Doine
985 BEN VORLICH
975
Glen Artney
Auchingarrich Wildlife Centre

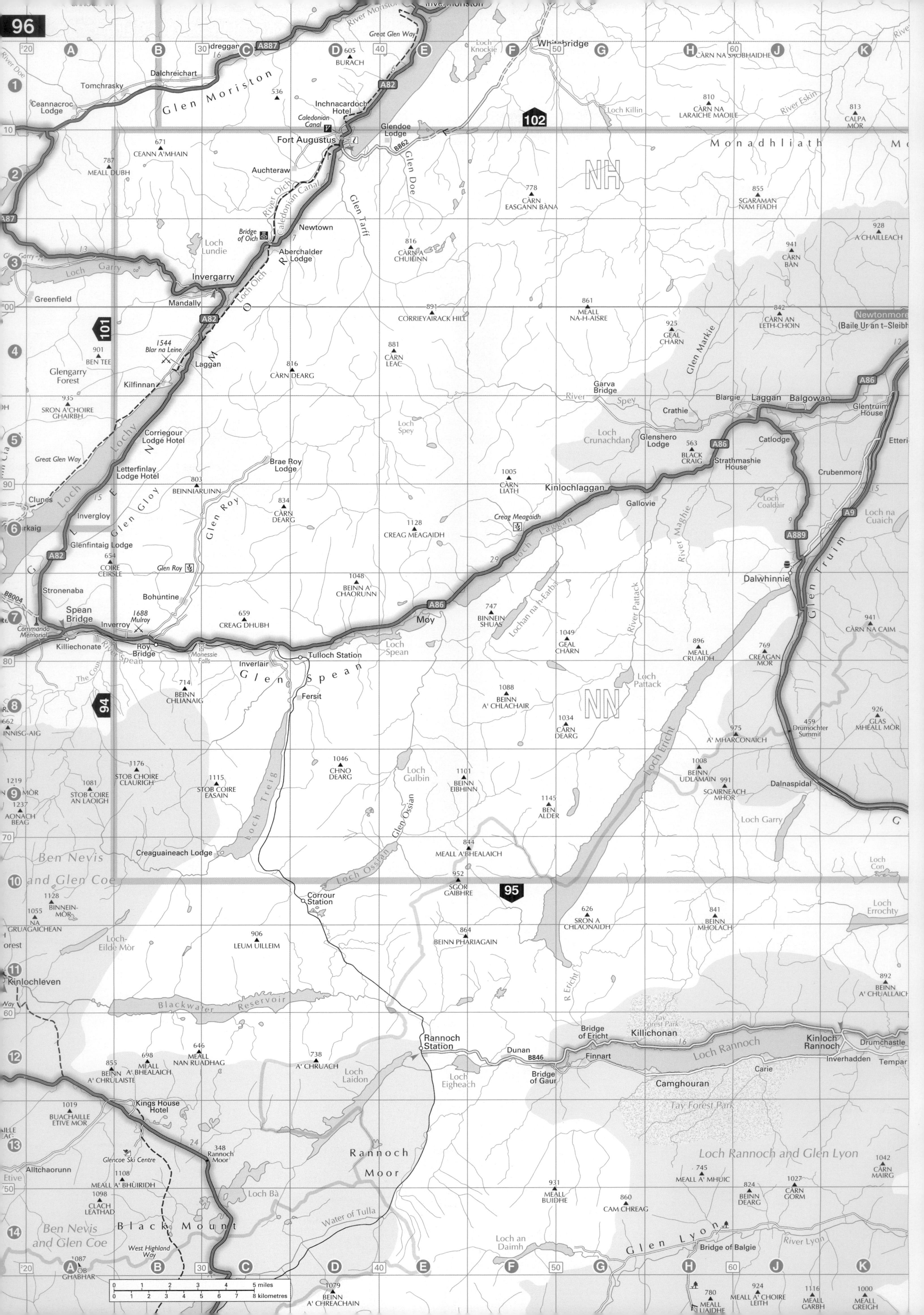

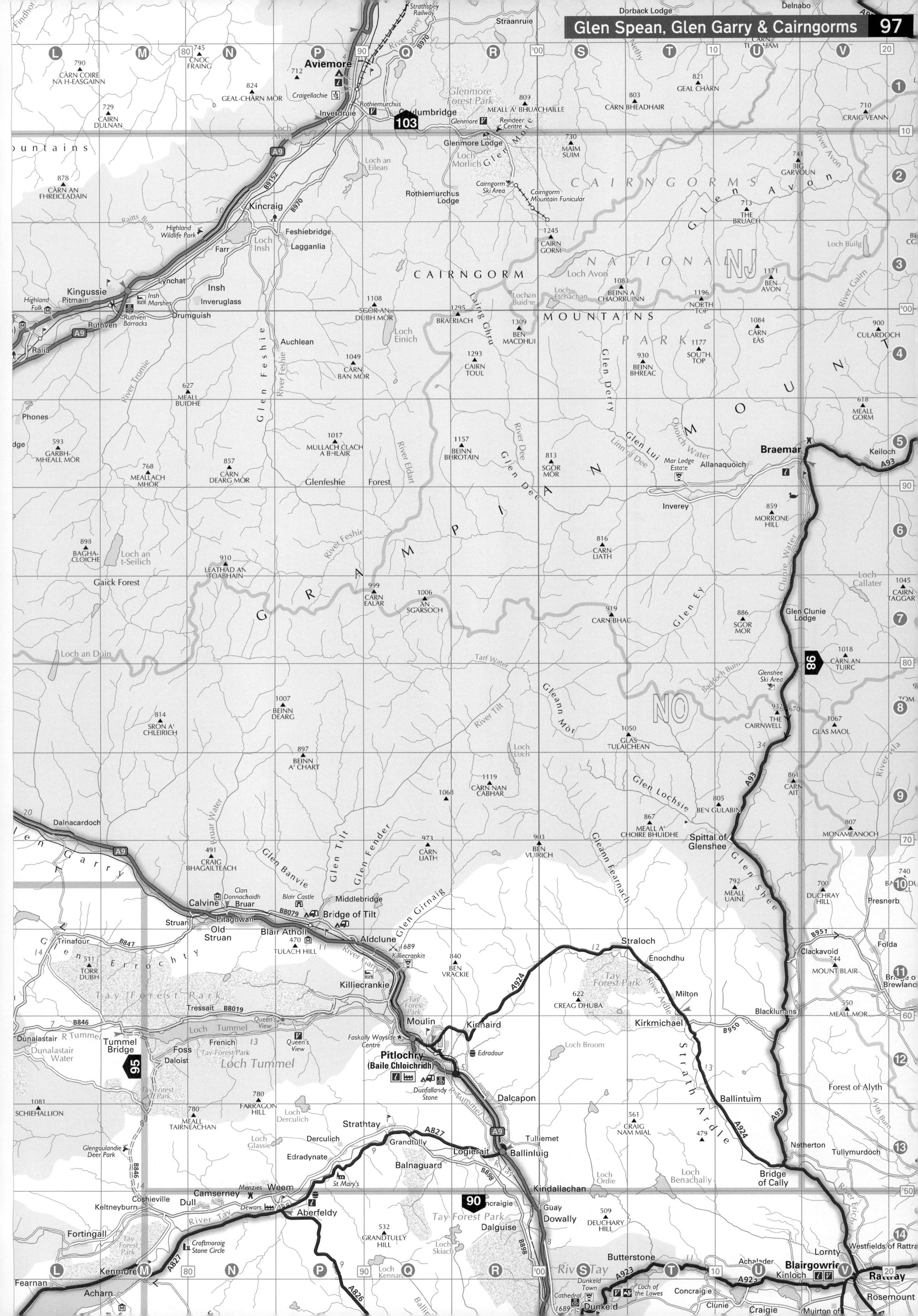
Aviemore
Coylumbridge
Inverdruie
Rothiemurchus
Craigellachie
Glenmore Forest Park
Glenmore
Reindeer Centre
Glenmore Lodge
Loch Morlich
Glen More
Loch an Eilean
Rothiemurchus Lodge
Cairngorm Ski Area
Cairngorm Mountain Funicular
MEALL A' BHUACHAILLE
GEAL-CHÀRN MÓR
CNOC FRAING
CÀRN COIRE NA H-EASGAINN
CAIRN DULNAN
CÀRN AN FHREICEADAIN
Kincraig
Highland Wildlife Park
Loch Insh
Feshiebridge
Lagganlia
Farr
Lynchat
Kingussie
Pitmain
Highland Folk
Insh Marshes
Insh
Inveruglass
Ruthven Barracks
Ruthven
Drumguish
Ralia
Auchlean
Glen Feshie
River Feshie
River Tromie
Phones
MEALL BUIDHE
GARBH-MHEALL MÓR
MEALLACH MHÓR
CÀRN DEARG MÓR
MULLACH CLACH A' BHLAIR
Glenfeshie Forest
River Eidart
SGÒR AN DUBH MÓR
Loch Einich
CÀRN BAN MÓR
BRAERIACH
CAIRN TOUL
Lairig Ghru
BEN MACDHUI
CAIRN GORM
CAIRNGORM MOUNTAINS
CAIRNGORMS NATIONAL PARK
Loch Avon
Loch Etchachan
Lochan Buidhe
BEINN A' CHAORRUINN
MAIM SUIM
BIG GARVOUN
THE BRUACH
Glen Avon
River Avon
Loch Builg
BEN AVON
NORTH TOP
SOUTH TOP
CÀRN EAS
BEINN BHREAC
Glen Derry
CULARDOCH
River Gairn
MEALL GORM
Glen Lui
Linn of Dee
Quoich Water
Mar Lodge Estate
Allanaquoich
Braemar
Keiloch
Inverey
MORRONE HILL
BEINN BHROTAIN
River Dee
Glen Dee
SGOR MOR
GRAMPIAN MOUNTAINS
BAGHA-CHLOICHE
Loch an t-Seilich
LEATHAD AN TOABHAIN
Gaick Forest
CÀRN EALAR
AN SGARSOCH
CÀRN LIATH
CÀRN BHAC
Glen Ey
SGOR MOR
Glen Clunie Lodge
Clunie Water
Loch Callater
CAIRN TAGGAR
CÀRN AN TUIRC
Loch an Dùin
Tarf Water
Glenshee Ski Area
Baddoch Burn
THE CAIRNWELL
GLAS MAOL
BEINN DEARG
SRON A' CHLEIRICH
River Tilt
Gleann Mòr
GLAS TULAICHEAN
Loch Loch
BEINN A' CHAIT
CÀRN NAN CABHAR
Glen Lochsie
BEN GULABIN
CÀRN AIT
River Isla
MEALL A' CHOIRE BHUIDHE
Spittal of Glenshee
Glen Shee
MONAMEANOCH
Dalnacardoch
Glen Garry
Bruar Water
CRAIG BHAGAILTEACH
Glen Banvie
Glen Tilt
Glen Fender
CÀRN LIATH
BEN VUIRICH
Gleann Fearnach
MEALL UAINE
DUCHRAY HILL
Presnerb
Calvine
Clan Donnachaidh
Bruar
Blair Castle
Middlebridge
Bridge of Tilt
Glen Girnaig
Struan
Pitagowan
Old Struan
Blair Atholl
TULACH HILL
Aldclune
Killiecrankie
BEN VRACKIE
Straloch
Enochdhu
Trinafour
TORR DUBH
Glen Errochty
Tay Forest Park
Tressait
Loch Tummel
Queen's View
Moulin
Kinnaird
CREAG DHUBA
River Ardle
Milton
Kirkmichael
Blacklunans
Folda
Clackavoid
MOUNT BLAIR
Brewlands
MEALL MOR
Dunalastair
Dunalastair Water
Tummel Bridge
Foss
Frenich
Daloist
Faskally Wayside Centre
Pitlochry (Baile Chloichridh)
Edradour
Loch Broom
Strath Ardle
Dunfallandy Stone
Dalcapon
Ballintuim
Forest of Alyth
SCHIEHALLION
FARRAGON HILL
MEALL TAIRNEACHAN
Loch Derculich
Strathtay
Derculich
CRAIG NAM MIAL
Loch Glassie
Edradynate
Grandtully
Logierait
Tulliemet
Ballinluig
Netherton
Tullymurdoch
Glengoulandie Deer Park
Balnaguard
St Mary's
Loch Ordie
Loch Benachally
Bridge of Cally
Camserney
Menzies
Weem
Coshieville
Dull
Keltneyburn
Dewars
Aberfeldy
Kindallachan
Guay
Dowally
DEUCHARY HILL
Dalguise
Fortingall
River Tay
Croftmoraig Stone Circle
GRANDTULLY HILL
Loch Skiach
Loch Kennard
Butterstone
Lornty
Westfields of Rattray
Kenmore
Fearnan
Acharn
Dunkeld
Cathedral
Loch of the Lowes
Concraigie
Clunie
Craigie
Achalader
Blairgowrie
Kinloch
Rattray
Rosemount
Delnabo
Dorback Lodge
Straanruie
Strathspey Railway
River Spey
Nethy
GEAL CHÀRN
CÀRN BHEADHAIR
CRAIG VEANN
A9
A93
A924
A827
A826
A923
B970
B9152
B8079
B847
B8019
B846
B898
B950
B951
NJ
NO
103
86
95
90

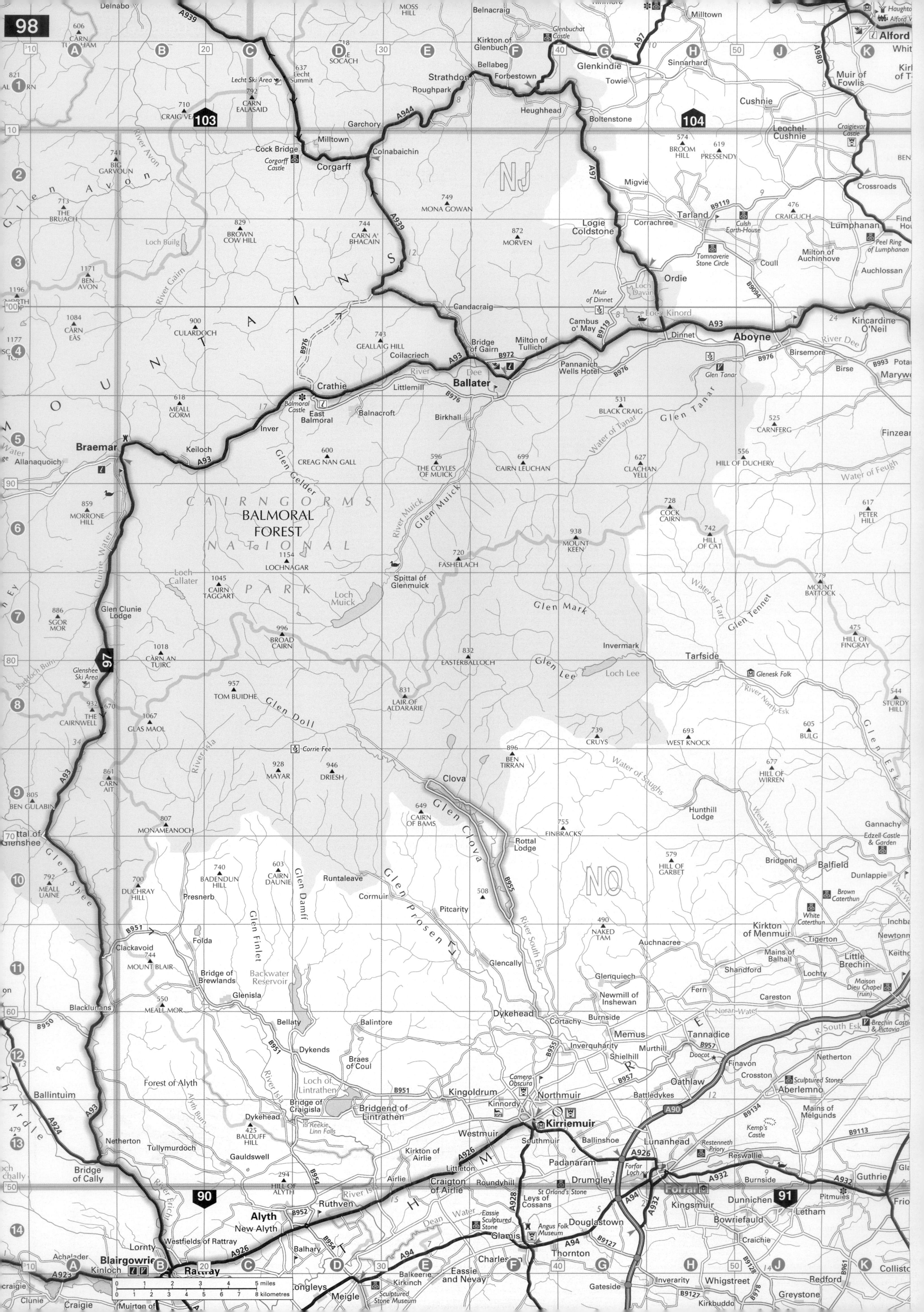

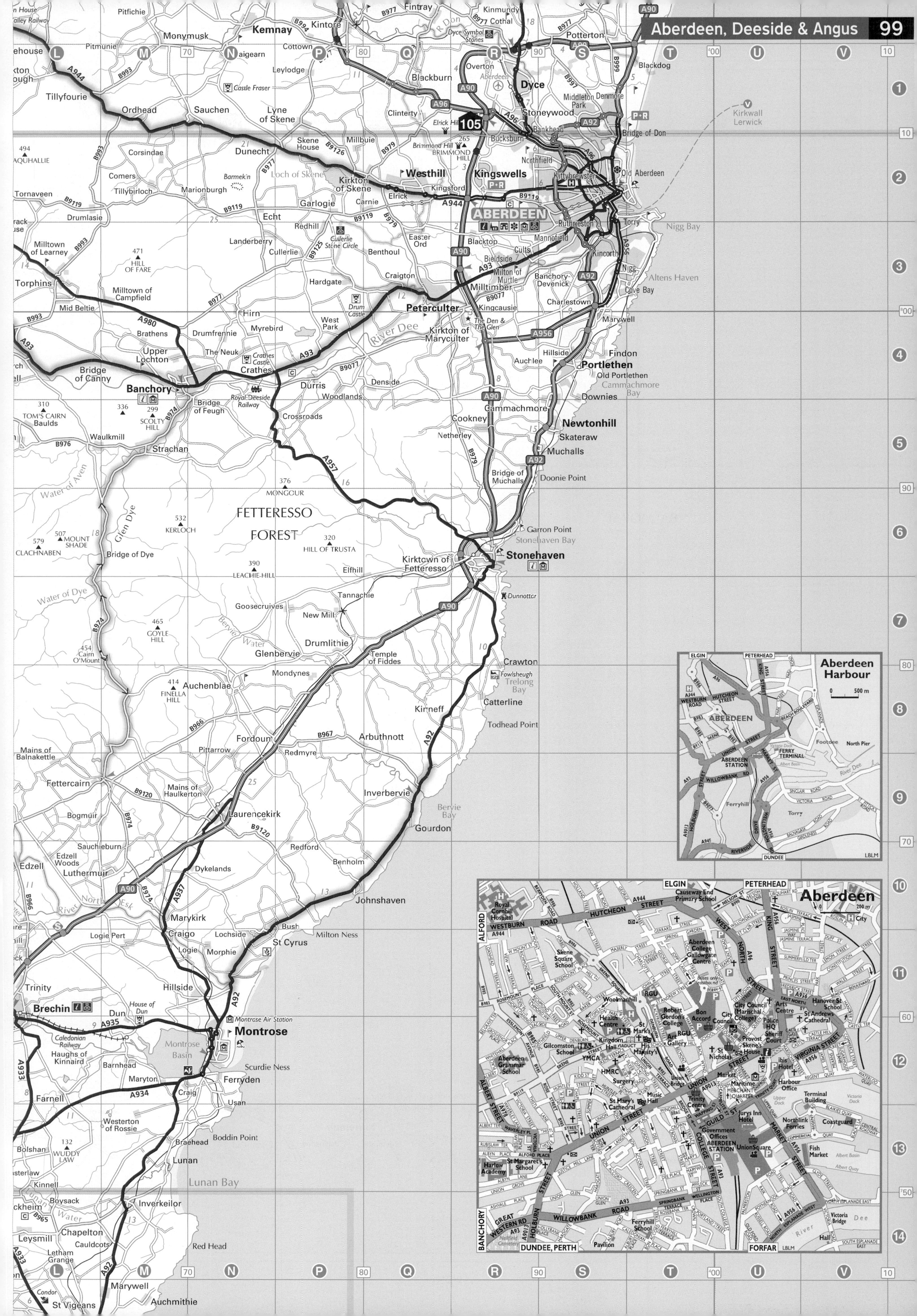

L M 70 N P 80 Q R 90 S T '00 U V 10

① 10 ② ③ '00 ④ ⑤ 90 ⑥ ⑦ 80 ⑧ ⑨ 70 ⑩ ⑪ 60 ⑫ ⑬ '50 ⑭

Pitfichie
Pitmunie
Kemnay
Kintore
B977 Fintray
Kinmundy
B977 Cothal
A90
Monymusk
B994
Cottown
Leylodge
Blackburn
R Don
Dyce Symbol
Stones
Potterton
Blackdog

House
ley Railway
L M 70 N
aigearn
P 80 Q
Overton
Aberdeen
R
Dyce
S
Middleton Denmore
Park
T U V 10

Ordhead
Sauchen
Lyne of Skene
Castle Fraser
Clinterty
Stoneywood
A90
A92
Bridge of Don
Kirkwall
Lerwick

Tillyfourie
A944
B993
Ordhead

494
AQUHALLIE
Corsindae
Dunecht
Skene House
B9126
Millbuie
B979
Elrick Hill
105
Brimmond Hill 265
BRIMMOND HILL
Bucksburn
Bankhead
A96
P·R

Tornaveen
Comers
Tillybirloch
Marionburgh
Barmekin
Loch of Skene
Kirkton of Skene
Westhill
Kingswells
Kittybrewster
Old Aberdeen

Drumlasie
B9119
B9119
Garlogie
Carnie
Kingsford
Elrick
A944
P·R
H
B9119

Milltown of Learney
Torphins
B993
Redhill
Landerberry
Cullerlie
Cullerlie Stone Circle
Echt
Benthoul
Easter Ord
ABERDEEN
Ruthrieston
Torry
Nigg Bay

471
HILL OF FARE
Hardgate
Craigton
Blacktop
A90
Mannofield
Cults
Kincorth
Altens Haven

Mid Beltie
A980
Hirn
Drum Castle
Peterculter
A93
Bieldside
Milton of Murtle
Banchory-Devenick
Nigg
Cove Bay

Brathens
Drumfrennie
Myrebird
West Park
B9077
Kingcausie
Charlestown

Upper Lochton
The Neuk
Crathes Castle
Kirkton of Maryculter
The Den & The Glen
A956
Marywell

Bridge of Canny
Crathes
C
B9077
Denside
Auchlee
Hillside
Findon
Portlethen
Old Portlethen
Cammachmore Bay

336
299
SCOLTY HILL
Durris
Woodlands
A90
Downies

310
TOM'S CAIRN
Baulds
Banchory
Bridge of Feugh
Royal Deeside Railway
Crossroads
Cammachmore
Newtonhill
Skateraw

B976
Waulkmill
Strachan
Cookney
Netherley
Muchalls
A92

579
CLACHNABEN
507
532
KERLOCH
Bridge of Dye
FETTERESSO FOREST
A957
376
MONGOUR
Bridge of Muchalls
Doonie Point

Water of Aven
Glen Dye
320
HILL OF TRUSTA
Garron Point
Stonehaven Bay

Water of Dye
B974
465
GOYLE HILL
390
LEACHIE-HILL
Elfhill
Kirktown of Fetteresso
Stonehaven
i

454
Cairn O'Mount
Goosecruives
New Mill
Tannachie
A90
Dunnottar

414
FINELLA HILL
Auchenblae
Mondynes
Drumlithie
Glenbervie
Temple of Fiddes
Crawton
Fowlsheugh
Trelong Bay

Mains of Balnakettle
Fettercairn
Pittarrow
Fordoun
Redmyre
B967
Arbuthnott
A92
Catterline
Todhead Point

Bogmuir
B9120
Mains of Haulkerton
Laurencekirk
Inverbervie
Bervie Bay

Sauchieburn
B974
B9120
Redford
Gourdon

Edzell Woods
Luthermuir
Dykelands
Benholm

Edzell
A90
B974
A937
Marykirk
Craigo
Logie
Bush
Milton Ness
Johnshaven

Brechin
i
Dun
House of Dun
Logie Pert
Lochside
Morphie
St Cyrus

Caledonian Railway
A935
Craigo
Hillside

Haughs of Kinnaird
Barnhead
Maryton
Montrose Air Station
Montrose
A92
Scurdie Ness

Farnell
A934
Craig
Ferryden
Boddin Point

132
WUDDY LAW
Bolshan
Braehead
Lunan

Kinnell
B965
Westerton of Rossie
Usan
Lunan Bay

Leysmill
Boysack
Chapelton
Red Head

L M 70 N P 80 Q R 90 S T '00 U V 10

Aberdeen Harbour

ELGIN
PETERHEAD
Aberdeen Harbour
0   500 m
WESTBURN ROAD
HUTCHEON STREET
ABERDEEN
A944
A96
BEACH BOULEVARD
KING STREET
FERRY TERMINAL
ABERDEEN STATION
Footdee
North Pier
UNION STREET
WILLOWBANK RD
River Dee
Albert Basin
Ferryhill
Torry
HOLBURN STREET
RIVERSIDE
VICTORIA ROAD
A956
A945
A9013
DUNDEE
LBLM

Aberdeen

ELGIN
PETERHEAD
Aberdeen
0   200 m
City
ALFORD
WESTBURN ROAD
A944
HUTCHEON STREET
Causeway End Primary School
Nelson St
King St
A96
Royal Cornhill Hospital
Aberdeen College Gallowgate Centre
Jasmine Terrace
Constitution St
ALBERT STREET
Skene Square School
Woolmanhill
RGU
City Council Marischal
Arts Centre
Hanover St School
St Andrews Cathedral
Health Centre
Robert Gordon College
City Council
Police HQ
Sheriff Court
Provost Skene's House
St Nicholas
Aberdeen Grammar School
Gilcomston School
YMCA
His Majesty's
Art Gallery
Kingdom Hall
VIADUCT
St Mark's
Bon Accord
Ibis Hotel
Maritime Museum
Merchant Quarter
Terminal Building
ALBERT STREET
Surgery
HMRC
Union Bridge
Music Hall
Trinity Centre
VIRGINIA STREET
St Mary's Cathedral
UNION STREET
Provost Ross's House
Northlink Ferries
Coastguard
Government Offices
ABERDEEN STATION
UnionSquare
Jurys Inn Hotel
Quay
Fish Market
BANCHORY
GREAT WESTERN RD
Harlaw Academy
St Margaret's School
ALFORD PLACE
Maberly
COLLEGE STREET
MARKET STREET
Albert Basin
Albert Quay
GREAT WESTERN ROAD
HOLBURN STREET
Ferryhill School
WILLOWBANK ROAD
WELLINGTON PLACE
Victoria Bridge
River Dee
Hall
DUNDEE, PERTH
Pavilion
FORFAR
NORTH ESPLANADE EAST
SOUTH ESPLANADE EAST
LBLM

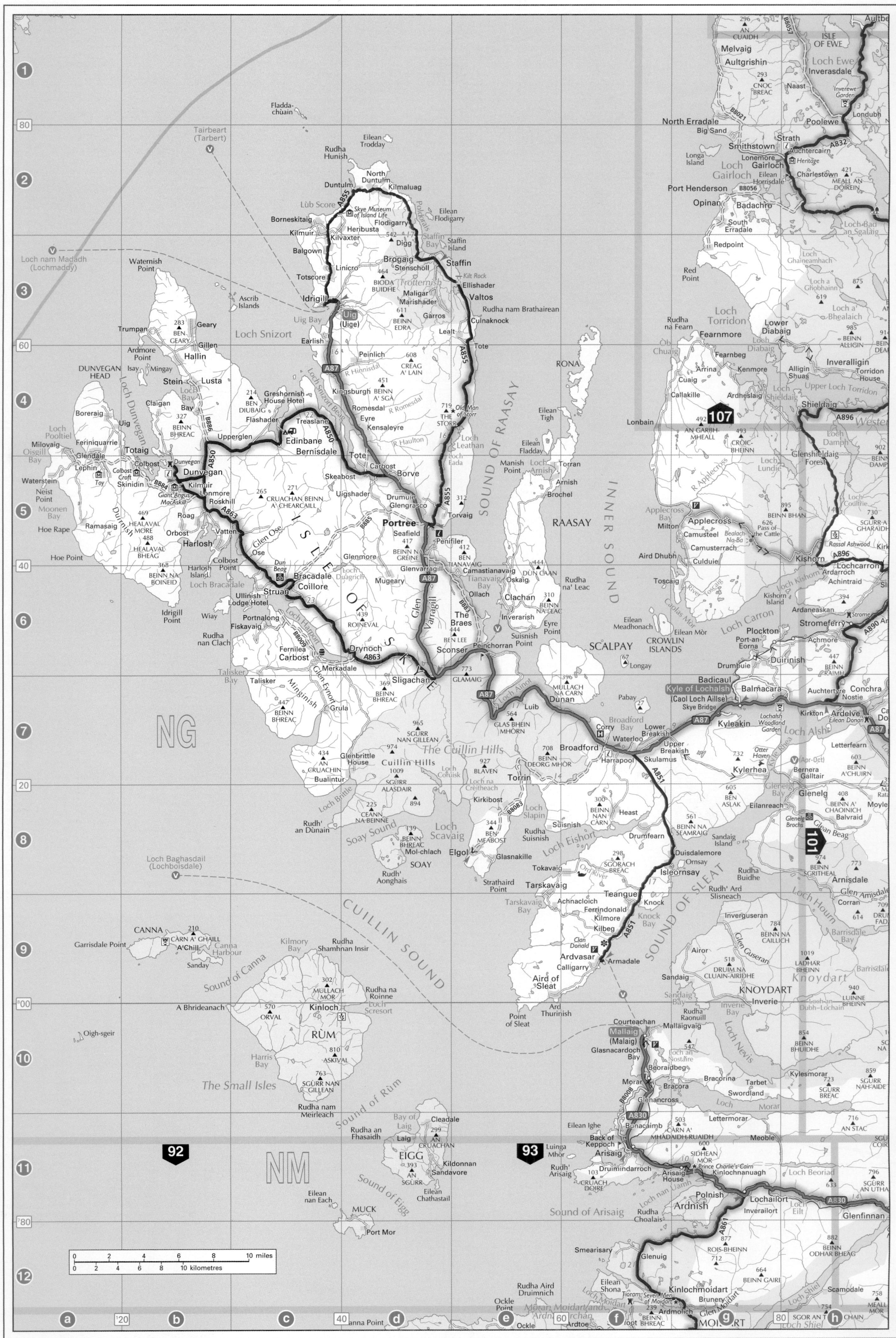
ISLE OF SKYE
RAASAY
SOUND OF RAASAY
INNER SOUND
SOUND OF SLEAT
CUILLIN SOUND
The Small Isles
CANNA
RÙM
EIGG
MUCK
SOAY
SCALPAY
RONA
Portree
Dunvegan
Uig
Broadford
Kyleakin
Kyle of Lochalsh
Mallaig
Armadale
Sligachan
The Cuillin Hills
KNOYDART
NG
NM
107
101
92
93
0 2 4 6 8 10 miles
0 2 4 6 8 10 kilometres

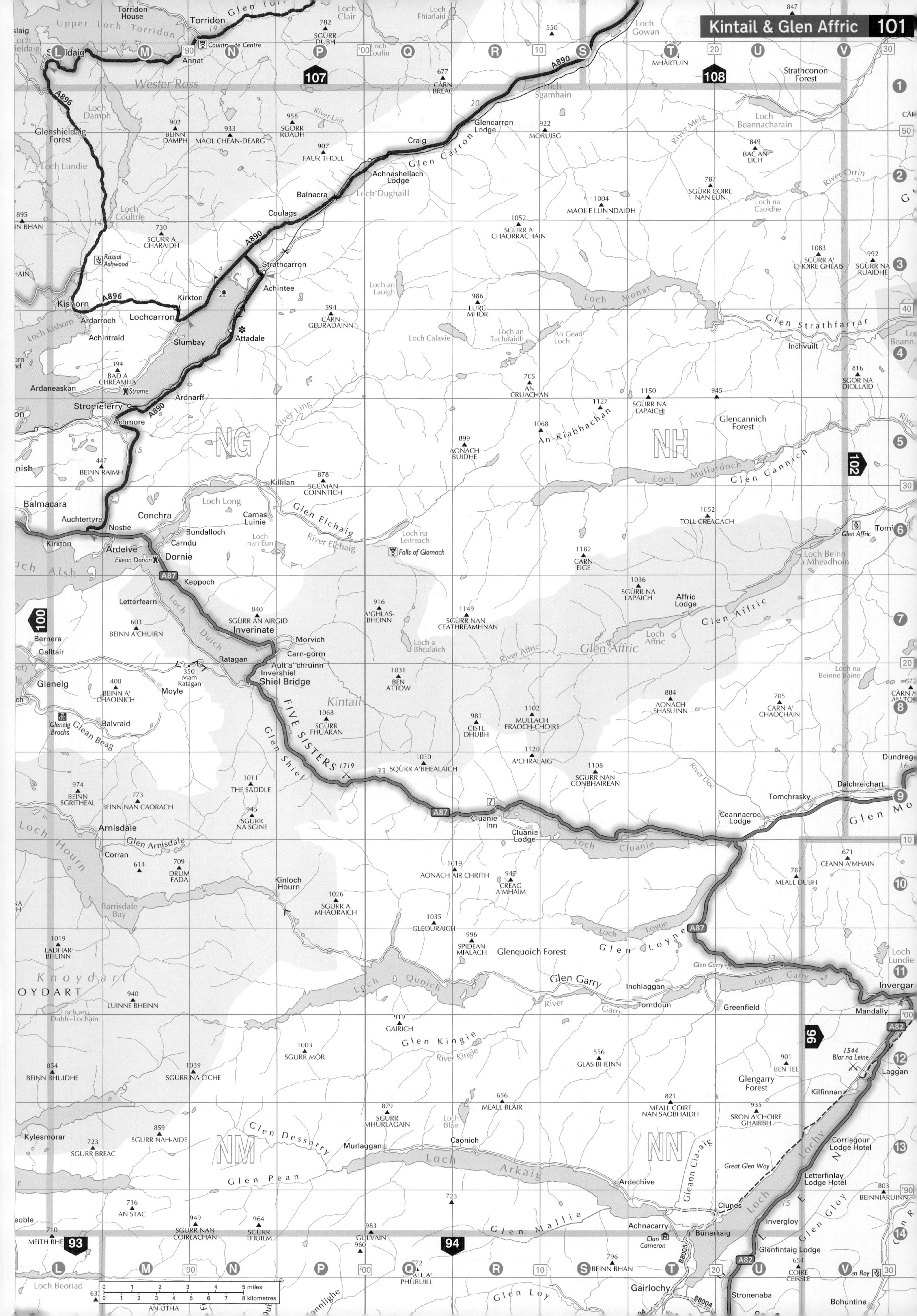
Torridon
Upper Loch Torridon
Shieldaig
Wester Ross
A896
Loch Damph
Glenshieldaig Forest
Loch Lundie
Loch Coultrie
Rassal Ashwood
Kishorn
Ardarroch
Lochcarron
Loch Kishorn
Achintraid
Slumbay
Attadale
Strathcarron
Achintee
Coulags
Balnacra
Achnashellach Lodge
Loch Dughaill
Glen Carron
Craig
Glencarron Lodge
A890
Loch Sgamhain
Ardaneaskan
Strome
Stromeferry
Achmore
Ardnarff
BEINN RAIMH
Balmacara
Auchtertyre
Kirkton
Nostie
Conchra
Ardelve
Eilean Donan
Dornie
Carndu
Bundalloch
Loch Long
Camas Luinie
Killilan
Glen Elchaig
River Elchaig
Loch na Leitreach
Falls of Glomach
Loch Alsh
A87
Keppoch
Letterfearn
Loch Duich
Invernate
Morvich
Carn-gorm
Ratagan
Shiel Bridge
Inverinate
Bernera
Galltair
Glenelg
Moyle
Balvraid
Glenelg Brochs
Glean Beag
Kintail
FIVE SISTERS
Glen Shiel
THE SADDLE
Arnisdale
Glen Arnisdale
Loch Hourn
Corran
Kinloch Hourn
Barrisdale Bay
Knoydart
Cluanie Inn
Cluanie Lodge
Loch Cluanie
Ceannacroc Lodge
Tomchrasky
Dalchreichart
Dundreggan
Glen Moriston
Glen Affric
Loch Affric
Affric Lodge
River Affric
Loch Beinn a Mheadhoin
Loch Mullardoch
Glen Cannich
Glencannich Forest
Loch Monar
Glen Strathfarrar
Inchvuilt
Loch Calavie
Loch an Laoigh
An-Riabhachan
Glenquoich Forest
Glen Loyne
Loch Loyne
Glen Garry
Loch Quoich
Inchlaggan
Tomdoun
Greenfield
Invergarry
Mandally
Glen Kingie
River Kingie
Glengarry Forest
Laggan
Kilfinnan
Loch Lochy
Great Glen Way
Corriegour Lodge Hotel
Letterfinlay Lodge Hotel
Loch Arkaig
Glen Dessarry
Murlaggan
Caonich
Glen Pean
Glen Mallie
Achnacarry
Clan Cameron
Bunarkaig
Clunes
Gleann Cia-aig
Ardechive
Invergloy
Glenfintaig Lodge
Glen Gloy
Gairlochy
Glen Loy
Stronenaba
Bohuntine
Kylesmorar
Strathconon Forest
Loch Beannacharain
River Meig
River Orrin
NG
NH
NM
NN
5 miles
8 kilometres

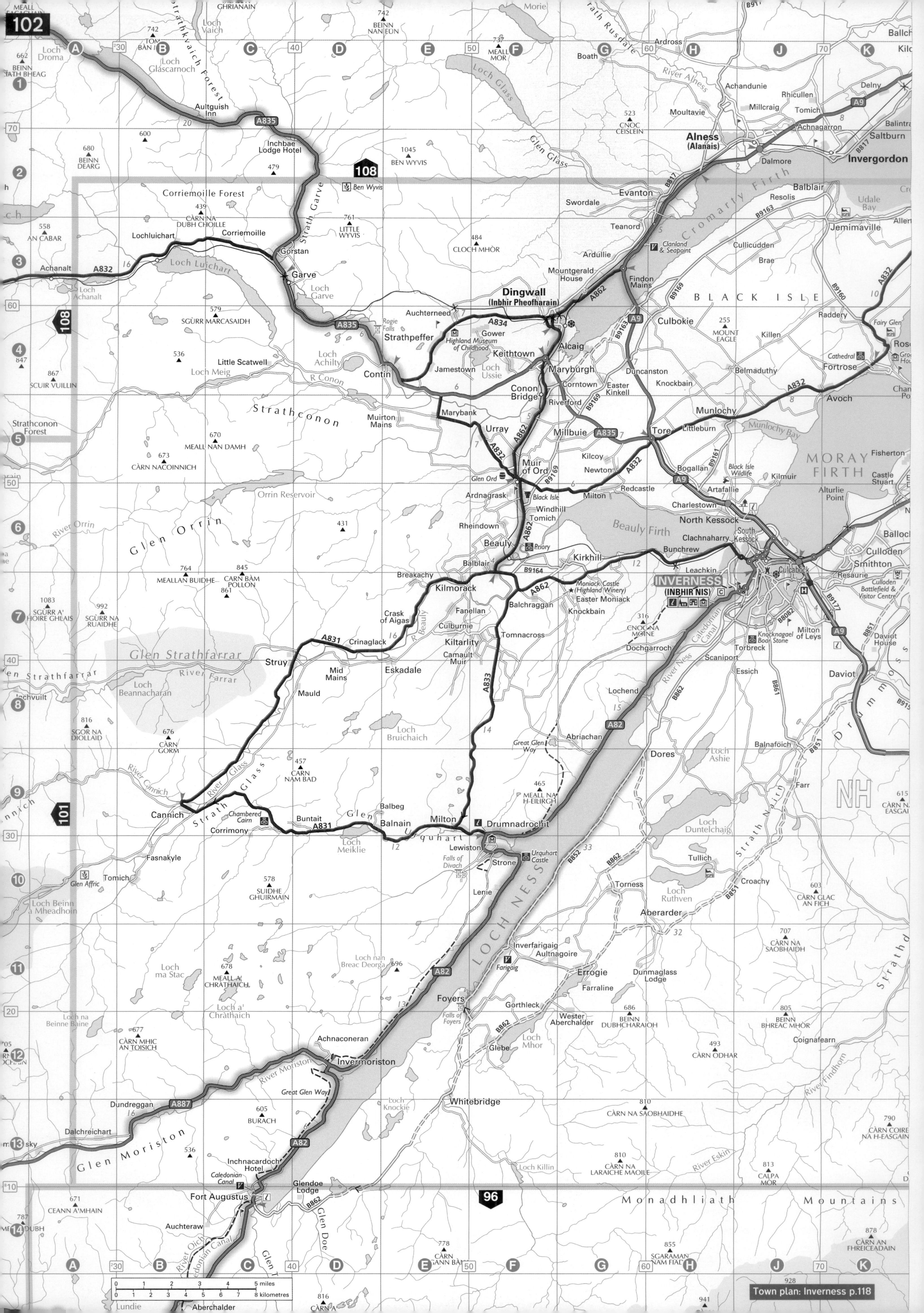
A
B
C
D
E
F
G
H
J
K
1
2
3
4
5
6
7
8
9
10
11
12
13
14
30
40
50
60
70
108
101
96
Loch Droma
Loch Vaich
Loch Glascarnoch
Strathvaich Forest
Aultguish Inn
A835
Inchbae Lodge Hotel
742 BEINN NAN EUN
737 MEALL MÒR
Loch Glass
Boath
Ardross
Strath Rusdale
River Alness
Achandunie
Rhicullen
Delny
Millcraig
Tomich
Moultavie
523 CNOC CEISLEIN
Alness (Alanais)
Achnagarron
Saltburn
Invergordon
Dalmore
Balintraid
Glen Glass
1045 BEN WYVIS
680 BEINN DEARG
600
479
Ben Wyvis
Corriemoille Forest
439 CÀRN NA DUBH CHOILLE
Corriemoille
Lochluichart
558 AN CABAR
Strath Garve
761 LITTLE WYVIS
484 CLOCH MHÒR
Evanton
Swordale
Teanord
Cromarty Firth
Balblair
Resolis
Udale Bay
Jemimaville
Clanland & Seaport
Cullicudden
Brae
Ardullie
Mountgerald House
Findon Mains
Gorstan
Garve
Loch Garve
Achanalt
Loch Achanalt
A832
Loch Luichart
Dingwall (Inbhir Pheofharain)
A862
B9169
B9160
BLACK ISLE
Auchterneed
A834
Rogie Falls
Strathpeffer
Highland Museum of Childhood
Gower
Keithtown
Alcaig
579 SGÙRR MARCASAIDH
Culbokie
255 MOUNT EAGLE
Raddery
Fairy Glen
Killen
Rosemarkie
Cathedral
Fortrose
536
Little Scatwell
Loch Meig
Loch Achilty
Contin
Jamestown
Loch Ussie
Maryburgh
Duncanston
Belmaduthy
847
867 SCUIR VUILLIN
R Conon
Strathconon
Conon Bridge
Corntown
Easter Kinkell
Knockbain
Avoch
Chanonry Point
Strathconon Forest
Muirton Mains
Marybank
Riverford
Urray
Millbuie
A835
Tore
Munlochy
Littleburn
Munlochy Bay
670 MEALL NAN DAMH
673 CÀRN NACOINNICH
A832
Muir of Ord
Kilcoy
Newton
Bogallan
B9161
Black Isle Wildlife
Kilmuir
MORAY FIRTH
Fisherton
Castle Stuart
Alturlie Point
Glen Ord
Ardnagrask
Black Isle
Milton
Redcastle
Charlestown
Orrin Reservoir
Windhill
Tomich
River Orrin
Glen Orrin
431
Rheindown
Beauly Firth
North Kessock
Clachnaharry
South Kessock
Balloch
Beauly
Priory
Bunchrew
Culloden
Smithton
Kirkhill
Balblair
B9164
Leachkin
Culcabock
Resaurie
Culloden Battlefield & Visitor Centre
764 MEALLAN BUIDHE
845 CÀRN BÀN POLLON
861
Breakachy
Kilmorack
Moniack Castle (Highland Winery)
Easter Moniack
INVERNESS (INBHIR NIS)
1083 SGÙRR A' CHOIRE GHLAIS
992 SGÙRR NA RUAIDHE
Crask of Aigas
Fanellan
Balchraggan
Knockbain
316 CNOC NA MÒINE
Caledonian Canal
B8082
Milton of Leys
B9177
B851
Daviot House
Culburnie
Kiltarlity
Tomnacross
Knocknagael Boar Stone
Dochgarroch
Torbreck
A9
Glen Strathfarrar
A831
Crinaglack
R Beauly
Camault Muir
Scaniport
River Ness
Strathfarrar
Struy
River Farrar
Mid Mains
Eskadale
Essich
B861
Daviot
Loch Beannacharan
Mauld
Lochend
A833
B862
816 SGÒR NA DIOLLAID
676 CÀRN GORM
Loch Bruichaich
Great Glen Way
Abriachan
A82
Balnafoich
Drummossie
Dores
Loch Ashie
River Cannich
River Glass
Strath Glass
457 CÀRN NAM BAD
465 MEALL NA H-EILIRGH
Farr
NH
615 CÀRN NA H-EASGAIN
Cannich
Chambered Cairn
Corrimony
Buntait
Glen Urquhart
Balbeg
Balnain
Milton
Drumnadrochit
Loch Meiklie
Lewiston
Urquhart Castle
Strone
Falls of Divach
B852
Loch Duntelchaig
Strath Nairn
Fasnakyle
Glen Affric
Tomich
Tullich
578 SUIDHE GHUIRMAIN
Lenie
LOCH NESS
Torness
Loch Ruthven
Croachy
603 CÀRN GLAC AN FHÌCH
Loch Beinn a Mheadhoin
Aberarder
707 CÀRN NA SAOBHAIDHE
Inverfarigaig
Aultnagoire
Farigaig
Loch nan Breac Dearga
696
Loch ma Stac
678 MEALL A' CHRATHAICH
Errogie
Dunmaglass Lodge
Farraline
Strathdearn
Foyers
Falls of Foyers
Gorthleck
Loch a' Chrathaich
Wester Aberchalder
686 BEINN DUBHCHARAIDH
805 BEINN BHREAC MHÒR
Loch na Beinne Baine
677 CÀRN MHIC AN TOISICH
Loch Mhor
Glebe
Coignafearn
493 CÀRN ODHAR
Achnaconeran
Invermoriston
River Moriston
River Findhorn
Great Glen Way
Loch Knockie
Whitebridge
810 CÀRN NA SAOBHAIDHE
790 CÀRN COIRE NA H-EASGAIN
Dundreggan
A887
605 BURACH
Dalchreichart
Glen Moriston
536
Inchnacardoch Hotel
Loch Killin
810 CÀRN NA LARAICHE MAOILE
River Eskin
813 CALPA MÒR
Caledonian Canal
Fort Augustus
Glendoe Lodge
B862
Monadhliath Mountains
671 CEANN A'MHAIN
787
Auchteraw
River Oich
Glen Doe
778 CÀRN GANN BÀN
855 SGARAMAN NAM FIADH
878 CÀRN AN FHREICEADAIN
928
941
816 CÀRN A'
Lundie
Aberchalder
5 miles
8 kilometres
Town plan: Inverness p.118

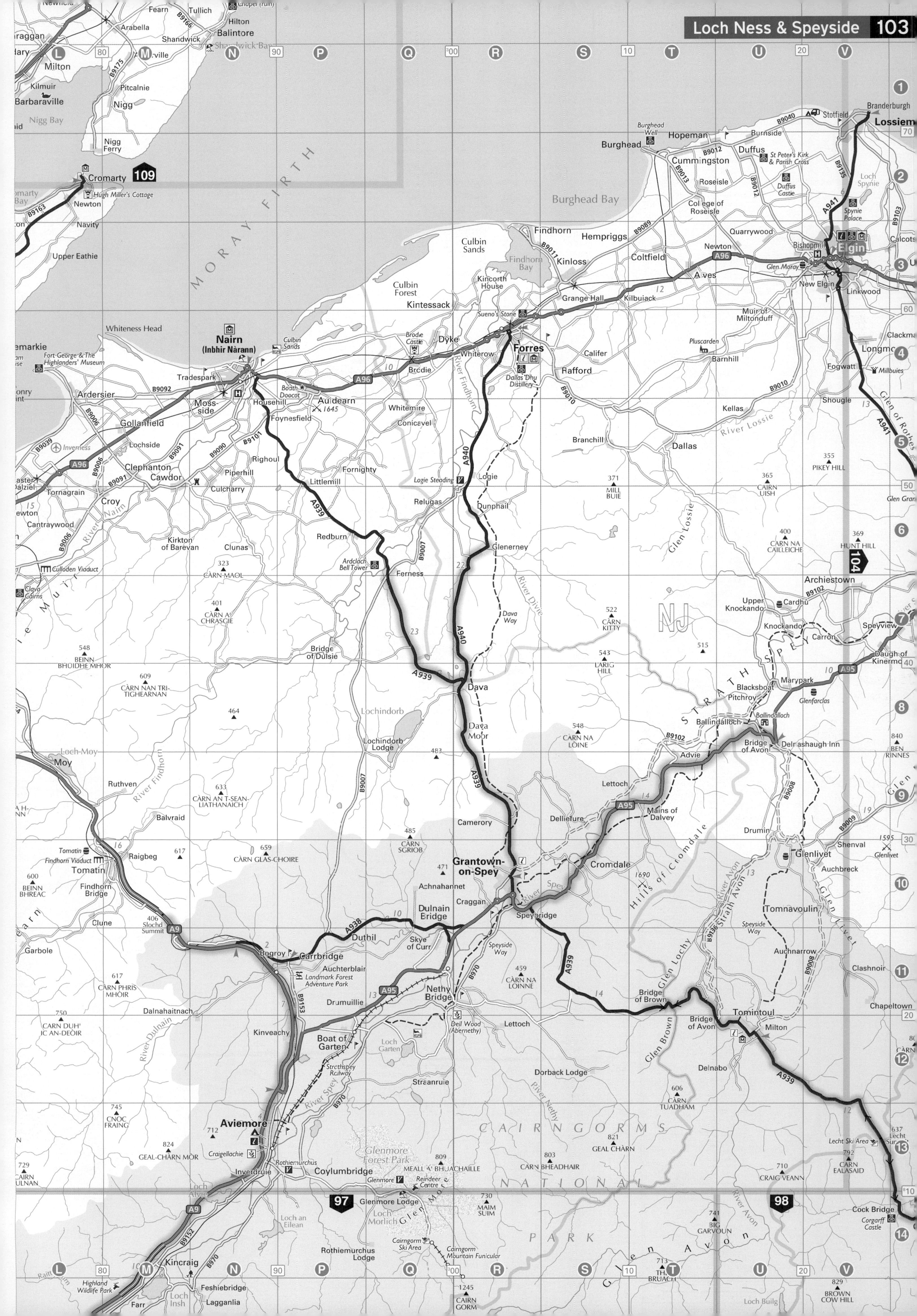
Moray Firth
Burghead Bay
Nigg Bay
Cromarty
109
Nairn (Inbhir Nàrann)
Forres
Elgin
Lossiemouth
Burghead
Hopeman
Duffus
Findhorn
Kinloss
Culbin Forest
Kintessack
Brodie
Dyke
Auldearn
Cawdor
Croy
Ardersier
Dallas
Archiestown
Knockando
Cardhu
Strath Spey
Ballindalloch
Bridge of Avon
Dava
Dava Moor
Lochindorb
Grantown-on-Spey
Cromdale
Hills of Cromdale
Dulnain Bridge
Carrbridge
Nethy Bridge
Boat of Garten
Aviemore
Coylumbridge
Glenmore Lodge
Glenmore Forest Park
Kincraig
Feshiebridge
Tomatin
Moy
Glenlivet
Tomnavoulin
Tomintoul
Cock Bridge
Cairngorms National Park
Glen Avon
Lecht Ski Area
104
97
98
NJ

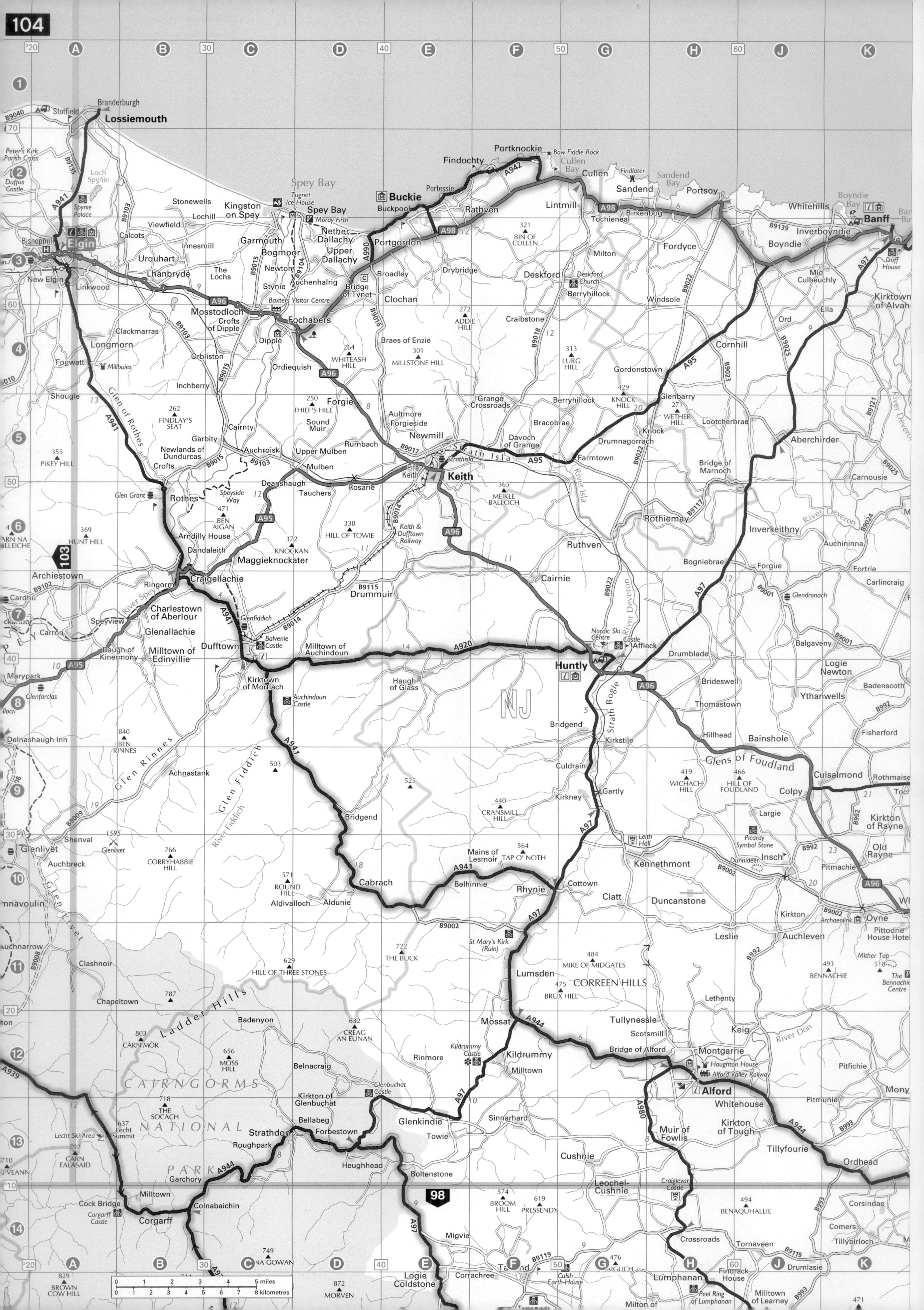

Branderburgh
Stotfield
Lossiemouth
Peter's Kirk Parish Cross
Duffus Castle
Loch Spynie
Spynie Palace
Bishopmill
Elgin
New Elgin
Linkwood
Stonewells
Lochill
Kingston on Spey
Tugnet Ice House
Spey Bay
Moray Firth
Viewfield
Calcots
Innesmill
Garmouth
Nether Dallachy
Upper Dallachy
Urquhart
Lhanbryde
The Lochs
Bogmoor
Newton
Stynie
Auchenhalrig
Bridge of Tynet
Baxters Visitor Centre
Mosstodloch
Crofts of Dipple
Fochabers
Dipple
Clackmarras
Longmorn
Fogwatt
Millbuies
Orbliston
Ordiequish
Inchberry
Shougle
Glen of Rothes
Findlay's Seat
Cairnty
Garbity
Newlands of Dundurcas
Crofts
Auchroisk
Pikey Hill
Glen Grant
Rothes
Speyside Way
Ben Aigan
Arndilly House
Dandaleith
Maggieknockater
Craigellachie
Hunt Hill
Archiestown
Ringorm
River Spey
Charlestown of Aberlour
Glenallachie
Speyview
Carron
Daugh of Kinermony
Milltown of Edinvillie
Dufftown
Glenfiddich
Balvenie Castle
Marypark
Glenfarclas
Kirktown of Mortlach
Auchindoun Castle
Delnashaugh Inn
Ben Rinnes
Glen Rinnes
Achnastank
Glen Fiddich
River Fiddich
Glenlivet
Shenval
Auchbreck
Corryhabbie Hill
Glen Livet
Clashnoir
Chapeltown
Ladder Hills
Carn Mor
Badenyon
Moss Hill
Cairngorms National Park
The Socach
Lecht Summit
Lecht Ski Area
Carn Ealasaid
Strathdon
Roughpark
Garchory
Milltown
Cock Bridge
Corgarff Castle
Corgarff
Colnabaichin
Na Gowan
Brown Cow Hill
Buckie
Buckpool
Portessie
Portgordon
Findochty
Portknockie
Bow Fiddle Rock
Cullen Bay
Cullen
Rathven
Broadley
Drybridge
Clochan
Bin of Cullen
Adie Hill
Braes of Enzie
Whiteash Hill
Millstone Hill
Thief's Hill
Forgie
Sound Muir
Aultmore
Forgieside
Rumbach
Newmill
Upper Mulben
Mulben
Deanshaugh
Tauchers
Rosarie
Keith
Strathisla
Strath Isla
Hill of Towie
Knockan
Keith & Dufftown Railway
Drummuir
Milltown of Auchindoun
Haugh of Glass
Bridgend
Cabrach
Round Hill
Aldivalloch
Aldunie
The Buck
Hill of Three Stones
Creag an Eunan
Belnacraig
Kirkton of Glenbuchat
Glenbuchat Castle
Bellabeg
Forbestown
Heughhead
Glenkindie
Towie
Boltenstone
Findlater
Sandend
Sandend Bay
Portsoy
Lintmill
Tochieneal
Birkenbog
Milton
Fordyce
Deskford
Deskford Church
Berryhillock
Craibstone
Windsole
Lurg Hill
Gordonstown
Knock Hill
Grange Crossroads
Bracobrae
Davoch of Grange
Drumnagorrach
Knock
Farmtown
River Isla
Meikle Balloch
Rothiemay
Ruthven
Cairnie
River Deveron
Nordic Ski Centre
Huntly Castle
Huntly
Strath Bogie
Bridgend
Kirkstile
Culdrain
Gartly
Kirkney
Cransmill Hill
Mains of Lesmoir
Tap o' Noth
Belhinnie
Rhynie
Cottown
Clatt
Leith Hall
Kennethmont
St Mary's Kirk (Ruin)
Mire of Midgates
Lumsden
Correen Hills
Brux Hill
Mossat
Kildrummy Castle
Kildrummy
Rinmore
Milltown
Sinnarhard
Cushnie
Leochel-Cushnie
Broom Hill
Pressendy
Migvie
Tarland
Cush Earth-House
Aiguch
Logie Coldstone
Corrachree
Morven
Whitehills
Boyndie Bay
Banff
Inverboyndie
Boyndie
Duff House
Mid Culbeuchly
Kirktown of Alvah
Ord
Ella
Cornhill
Glenbarry
Wether Hill
Lootcherbrae
Aberchirder
River Deveron
Bridge of Marnoch
Carnousie
Inverkeithny
Auchininna
Bogniebrae
Forgue
Fortrie
Carlincraig
Glendronach
Balgaveny
Drumblade
Logie Newton
Brideswell
Badenscoth
Thomastown
Ythanwells
Fisherford
Hillhead
Bainshole
Glens of Foudland
Wichach Hill
Hill of Foudland
Culsalmond
Colpy
Rothmaise
Largie
Kirkton of Rayne
Picardy Symbol Stone
Dunnideer
Insch
Old Rayne
Pitmachie
Duncanstone
Kirkton
Archaeolink
Oyne
Leslie
Auchleven
Pittodrie House Hotel
Mither Tap
Bennachie
The Bennachie Centre
Lethenty
Tullynessle
Scotsmill
Keig
River Don
Bridge of Alford
Montgarrie
Haughton House
Alford Valley Railway
Alford
Whitehouse
Pitfichie
Pitmunie
Muir of Fowlis
Kirkton of Tough
Tillyfourie
Ordhead
Craigievar Castle
Benaquhallie
Corsindae
Comers
Tillybirloch
Crossroads
Tornaveen
Lumphanan
Findrack House
Drumlasie
Peel Ring of Lumphanan
Milltown of Learney
NJ

Macduff
Gardenstown
Crovie
Pennan
Rosehearty
Pittulie
Sandhaven
Kinnaird Head
Fraserburgh
Peathill
Craigiefold
Cairnbulg
Inverallochy
St Combs
Memsie
Rathen
Crofts of Savoch
Lonmay
Rattray Head
Loch of Strathbeg
Crimond
Blackhill
Newburgh
Strichen
New Pitsligo
New Aberdour
Turriff
Cuminestown
New Byth
Garmond
Fetterangus
St Fergus
Rora
Longside
Mintlaw
Old Deer
Maud
New Deer
Stuartfield
Peterhead
Burnhaven
Boddam
Auchnagatt
Methlick
Fyvie
Hatton
Cruden Bay
Ellon
Oldmeldrum
Pitmedden
Udny Green
Newburgh
Inverurie
Kintore
Kemnay
Balmedie
Dyce
Potterton
Blackdog
Westhill
Kingswells
Bucksburn
Bridge of Don
Old Aberdeen
Aberdeen
Nigg Bay
NK
Kirkwall
Lerwick
99

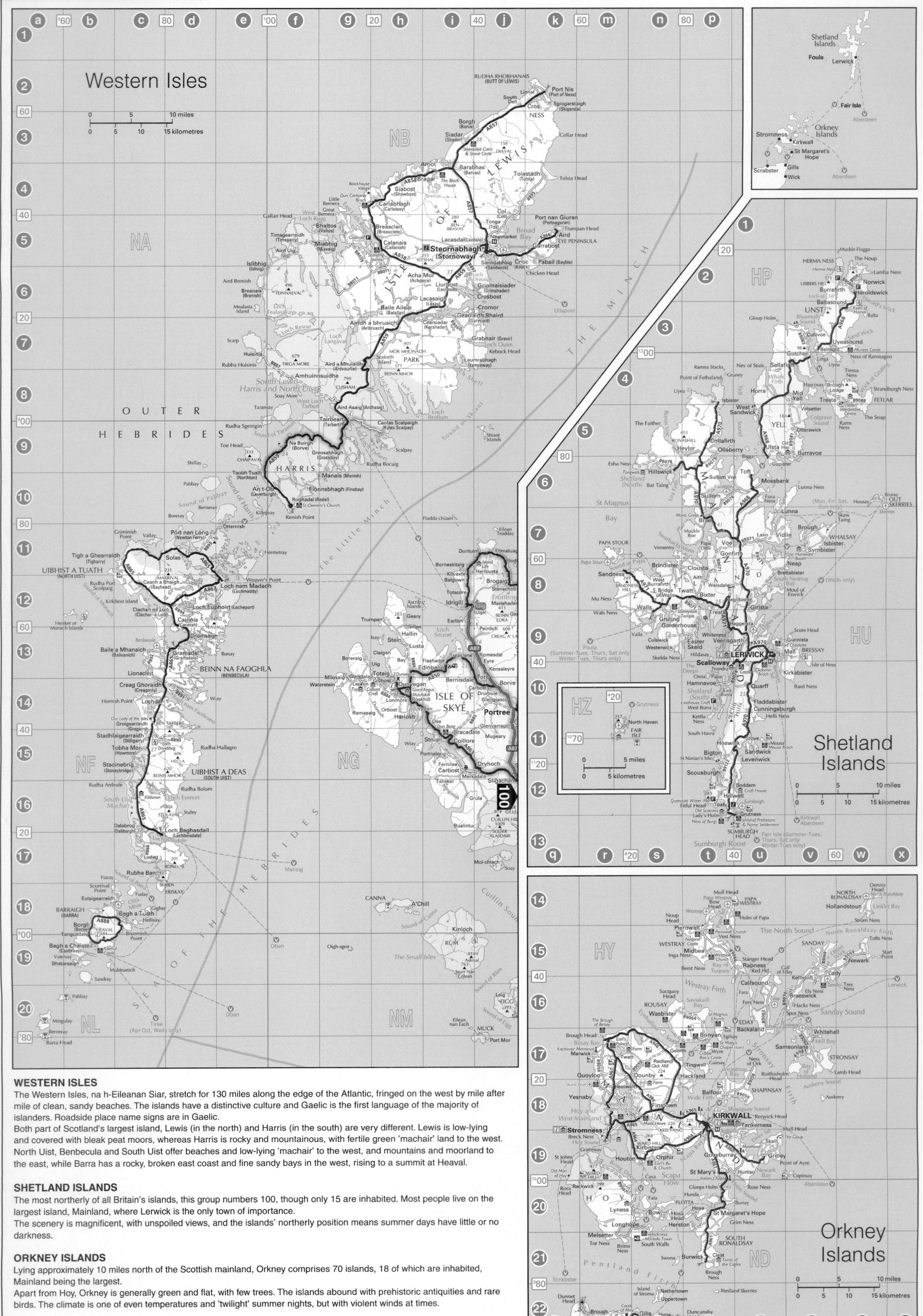

WESTERN ISLES

The Western Isles, na h-Eileanan Siar, stretch for 130 miles along the edge of the Atlantic, fringed on the west by mile after mile of clean, sandy beaches. The islands have a distinctive culture and Gaelic is the first language of the majority of islanders. Roadside place name signs are in Gaelic.

Both part of Scotland's largest island, Lewis (in the north) and Harris (in the south) are very different. Lewis is low-lying and covered with bleak peat moors, whereas Harris is rocky and mountainous, with fertile green 'machair' land to the west. North Uist, Benbecula and South Uist offer beaches and low-lying 'machair' to the west, and mountains and moorland to the east, while Barra has a rocky, broken east coast and fine sandy bays in the west, rising to a summit at Heaval.

SHETLAND ISLANDS

The most northerly of all Britain's islands, this group numbers 100, though only 15 are inhabited. Most people live on the largest island, Mainland, where Lerwick is the only town of importance.

The scenery is magnificent, with unspoiled views, and the islands' northerly position means summer days have little or no darkness.

ORKNEY ISLANDS

Lying approximately 10 miles north of the Scottish mainland, Orkney comprises 70 islands, 18 of which are inhabited, Mainland being the largest.

Apart from Hoy, Orkney is generally green and flat, with few trees. The islands abound with prehistoric antiquities and rare birds. The climate is one of even temperatures and 'twilight' summer nights, but with violent winds at times.

For information on ferry services see page XVI.

110

108

L 70 M N 80 P Q 90 R S 00 T U 10 V

SUILVEN 732

Loch Inver

Soyea Island

Inverkirkaig

River Kirkaig

Fionn Loch

Eilear Mòr

Enard Bay

Loch Sionascaig

CUL M

Rhu Coigach

Achnahaird

612

STAC POLLAIDH

Rubha Mòr

Reiff

769

CUL BEAG

Isle Ristol

Polbain

Badentarbet

Loch Lurgainn

Glas-leac Mòr

SUMMER ISLES

Achiltibuie

Polglass

Ben Mor Coigach

COIGACH

Tanera Beg

Badentarbat Bay

652

BEN MORE COIGACH

Steornabhagh (Stornoway)

Tanera Mòr

Culnacraig

Strathcanaird

Glas-leac Beag

Horse Island

Horse Sound

Strath Canaird

NC

Eilean Dubh

Achduart

Priest Island

Leac Dhonn

Isle Martin

A835

Greenstone Point

Cailleach Head

Annat Bay

Ardmair

Rudha Beag

Scoraig

Morefield

Ullapool (Ulapul)

Mellon Udrigle

Stattic Point

Rhireavach

635

BEINN GHOBHLACH

A83

Rudha Reidh

Foura

Cove

Laide

Gruinard Bay

Badluarach

Little Loch Broom

EIL

Melvaig

Mellon Charles

Ormiscaig

GRUINARD ISLAND

A832

Badcaul

Badrallach

Ardessie

Camusnagaul

296

AN CUAIDH

Aultbea

Gruinard

764

SÀIL MHÒR

32

Dundonnell

Ardindrean

Let

Aultgrishin

ISLE OF EWE

Loch Ewe

Loch Fada

Little Gruinard River

Gruinard River

Lochan Gaineamhach

Strathnasheallag Forest

Dundonnell Forest

Inverasdale

347

CREAG-MHEAL BEAG

1062

AN TEALLACH

507

CARN BHIORAIN

Crofte

293

CNOC BREAC

Naast

Inverewe Garden

13

250

MEALL NA MEINE

681

BEINN A' CHAISGEIN BEAG

Fisherfield Forest

Loch na Sealga

Dundonnell Forest

80

North Erradale

Poolewe

Londubh

Fionn Loch

Wester Ross

906

BEINN DEARG MHÒR

Big Sand

Strath

A832

Dubh Loch

MEALL AN T-SITHE

601

Smithstown

Auchtercairn

Lonemore

Heritage

421

MEALL AN DOIREIN

791

BEINN AIRIDH CHARR

974

SGÙRRBÀN

Loch-a' Bhraoin

Longa Island

Loch Gairloch

Gairloch

Charlestown

1019

MULLACH COIRE MHIC F-HEARCHAIR

Eilean Horrisdale

Loch

859

BEINN LÀIR

Lochan Fada

999

A' CHAILLEACH

Port Henderson

B8056

Letterewe Forest

70

Badachro

Opinan

Loch Bad an Sgalaig

Letterewe

Loch Garbhaig

South Erradale

Loch Maree Hotel

Maree

Redpoint

19

Talladale

A832

981

SLIOCH

NH

Red Point

Loch Ghaineamhach

NG

Loch na A-Oidhche

Loch Maree

680

BEINN A' MHÙINIDH

711

BEINN NAN RAMH

875

BAOSBHEINN

855

BEINN AN EOIN

724

Kinlochewe Forest

619

BEINN BHREAC

Loch a' Bhealaich

Kinlochewe Forest

933

FIONN BHEINN

12

Rudha na Fearn

Fearnmore

Lower Diabaig

Falls River

985

BEINN ALLIGIN

914

BEINN DEARG

1009

RUADH-STAC MÒR

972

Incheril

Beinn Eighe

Kinlochewe

Glen Docherty

A832

10

60

Fearnbeg

Loch Diabaig

Inveralligin

1024

1053

LIATHACH

BEINN EIGHE

A896

Ob Chuaig

Cuaig

Arrina

Kenmore

Allligin Shuas

Torridon House

Glen Torridon

550

Loch a' Chroisg

13

Callakille

Upper Loch Torridon

Torridon

782

SGÙRR DUBH

Loch Clair

Loch Fhiarlaid

Loch Gowa

Ardheslaig

Countryside Centre

Loch Coulin

677

CARN BREAC

A890

Lonbain

492

AN GARBH-MHEALL

Shieldaig

Annat

West Ross

14

493

CROIC-BHEINN

A896

Loch Damph

902

BEINN DAMPH

958

SGÒRR RUADH

River Lair

20

A890

Loch Sgamhain

Glensheldaig Forest

907

FUAR THOLL

Craig

Glen Carron Lodge

MORUISG

Glen Carron

L 70 M N 80 P Q 90 R S 00 T U 10 V

0 1 2 3 4 5 miles
0 1 2 3 4 5 6 7 8 kilometres

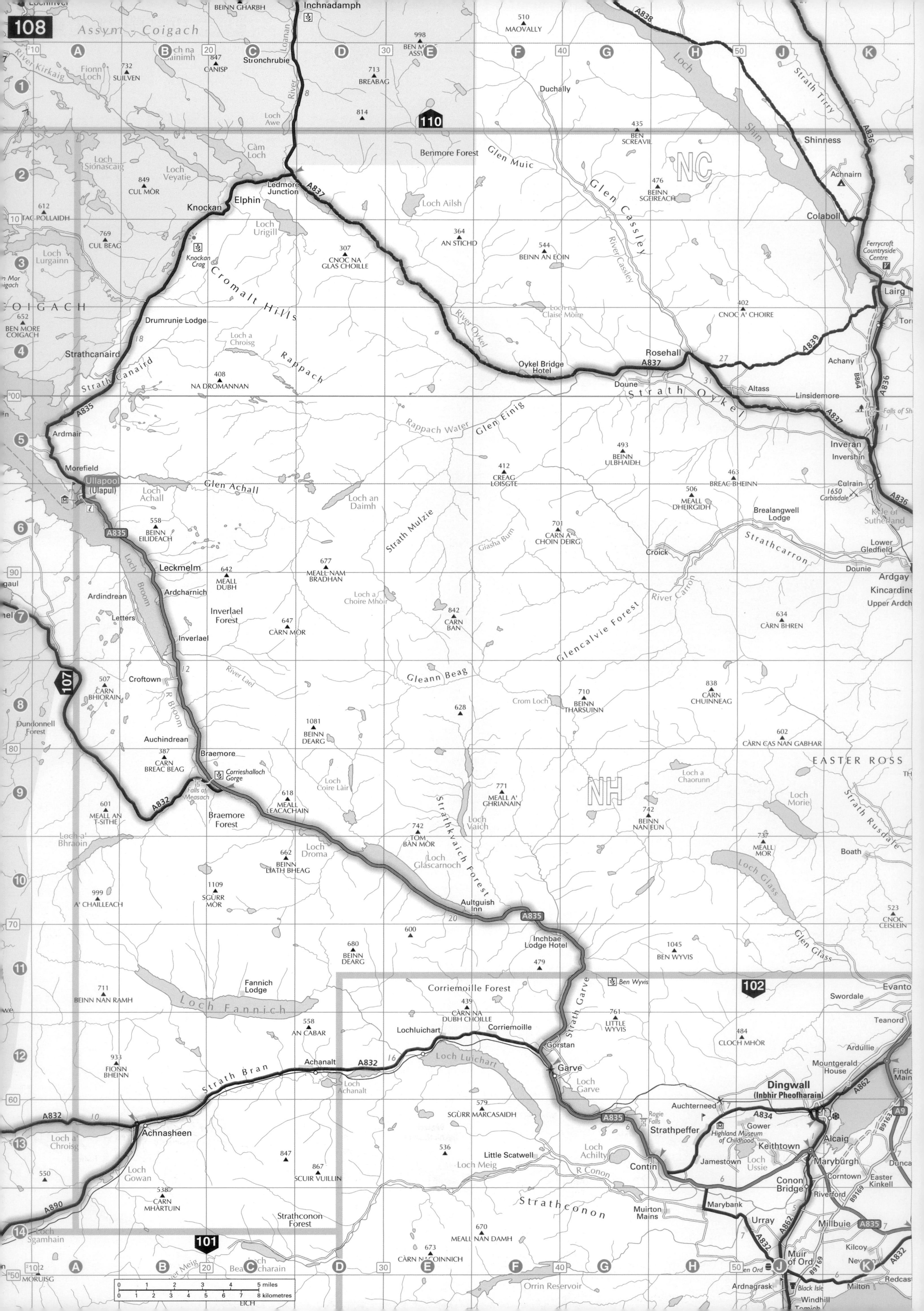
Assynt - Coigach
BEINN GHARBH
Inchnadamph
510
MAOVALLY
A838
Loch na Gainimh
847
CANISP
Stronchrubie
Loanan
998
BEN MORE ASSYNT
River Kirkaig
Fionn Loch
732
SUILVEN
713
BREABAG
Duchally
Loch Shin
Strath Tirry
River
814
Loch Awe
110
435
BEN SCREAVIL
Shinness
A836
Loch Sionascaig
Càm Loch
Benmore Forest
Glen Muic
NC
849
CUL MOR
Loch Veyatie
Ledmore Junction
A837
Glen Cassley
476
BEINN SGEIREACH
Achnairn
612
STAC POLLAIDH
Knockan
Elphin
Loch Urigill
Loch Ailsh
Colaboll
769
CUL BEAG
364
AN STICHD
544
BEINN AN EOIN
Loch Lurgainn
Knockan Crag
307
CNOC NA GLAS CHOILLE
River Cassley
Ferrycroft Countryside Centre
Cromalt Hills
Lairg
COIGACH
652
BEN MORE COIGACH
Drumrunie Lodge
River Oykel
Loch na Claise Mòire
402
CNOC A' CHOIRE
Loch a' Chroisg
Strathcanaird
Rappach
A839
Rosehall
Oykel Bridge Hotel
Achany
408
NA DROMANNAN
Strath Canaird
Doune
Strath Oykel
B864
Altass
Linsidemore
A835
Rappach Water
Glen Einig
Falls of Shin
Ardmair
Inveran
Invershin
493
BEINN ULBHAIDH
Morefield
412
CREAG LOISGTE
463
BREAC-BHEINN
Culrain
Ullapool (Ulapul)
Loch Achall
Glen Achall
Loch an Daimh
506
MEALL DHEIRGIDH
1650 Carbisdale
Kyle of Sutherland
558
BEINN EILIDEACH
Strath Mulzie
701
CARN A' CHOIN DEIRG
Brealangwell Lodge
Giasha Burn
Strathcarron
Lower Gledfield
Loch Broom
Leckmelm
677
MEALL NAM BRADHAN
642
MEALL DUBH
Croick
Dounie
Ardgay
Kincardine
Ardindrean
Ardcharnich
Loch a' Choire Mhòir
River Carron
Upper Ardch
Letters
Inverlael Forest
842
CARN BAN
634
CÀRN BHREN
647
CÀRN MÒR
Glencalvie Forest
Inverlael
107
River Lael
Gleann Beag
507
CARN BHIORAIN
Croftown
838
CARN CHUINNEAG
710
BEINN THARSUINN
Crom Loch
R Broom
628
Dundonnell Forest
1081
BEINN DEARG
602
CÀRN CAS NAN GABHAR
Auchindrean
387
CARN BREAC BEAG
Braemore
EASTER ROSS
Corrieshalloch Gorge
Loch a' Chaorunn
Falls of Measach
Loch Coire Làir
NH
771
MEALL A' GHRIANAIN
Loch Morie
A832
618
MEALL LEACACHAIN
Strathkvaich Forest
Strath Rusdale
601
MEALL AN T-SITHE
Braemore Forest
742
TOM BÀN MÒR
Loch Vaich
742
BEINN NAN EUN
Loch a' Bhraoin
737
MEALL MOR
Loch Droma
662
BEINN LIATH BHEAG
Loch Glascarnoch
Boath
Loch Glass
1109
SGÙRR MÒR
999
A' CHAILLEACH
Aultguish Inn
20
523
CNOC CEISLEIN
600
680
BEINN DEARG
Inchbae Lodge Hotel
1045
BEN WYVIS
Glen Glass
479
711
BEINN NAN RAMH
Fannich Lodge
Corriemoille Forest
Ben Wyvis
102
Evanton
Loch Fannich
439
CÀRN NA DUBH CHOILLE
Strath Garve
761
LITTLE WYVIS
Swordale
558
AN CABAR
Lochluichart
Corriemoille
Teanord
484
CLOCH MHÒR
933
FIONN BHEINN
Loch Luichart
Gorstan
Ardullie
Achanalt
A832
Garve
Mountgerald House
Strath Bran
Loch Achanalt
Loch Garve
Dingwall (Inbhir Pheofharain)
A862
Auchterneed
579
SGÙRR MARCASAIDH
Rogie Falls
A834
A9
A832
Strathpeffer
Highland Museum of Childhood
Gower
Alcaig
Achnasheen
Loch a' Chroisg
536
Keithtown
Little Scatwell
Loch Achilty
Jamestown
Loch Ussie
Maryburgh
550
Loch Gowan
847
867
SCUIR VUILLIN
Loch Meig
R Conon
Contin
Conon Bridge
Corntown
Easter Kinkell
538
CARN MHARTUIN
Strathconon
Riverford
A890
Marybank
Muirton Mains
Urray
Strathconon Forest
670
MEALL NAN DAMH
Millbuie
Loch Sgamhain
101
673
CÀRN NAN CONNICH
Muir of Ord
Kilcoy
MORUISG
Orrin Reservoir
Ardnagrask
Black Isle
Milton
Windhill
0 1 2 3 4 5 miles
0 1 2 3 4 5 6 7 8 kilometres

Ben Armine Forest

L   M   N   P   Q   R   S   T   U   V

Glas-loch Mòr

462 ▲ MEALLAN LIATH MÒR

Kildonan 416
BEINN DUBHAIN
River Helmsdale
Strath of Kildonan
A897
Torrish
CREAG THORARAIDH 404
Badbea Historic Villa

Ord of Caithness

111

CNOC NA H-INNSE MOIRE
3
Q
CNOC NAN CRÙBAG MCR

421
624 ▲ BEINN DHORAIN
591 ▲ BEINN NA MÈILICH
West Helmsdale
Timespan
Navidale House Hotel
East Helmsdale
Gartymore
Portgower
Helmsdale 112

ND

293 ▲ CNOC LEAMHNACHD
Balnacoil Lodge
539 ▲ COL-BHEINN
Lothmore
Lothbeg
21

317 SITHEAN ACHADH NAN EUN
Loch Beannach
Strath Brora
River Brora
Dalreavoch Lodge
Loch Brora
Lothbeg

323 ▲ BEN DOULA
Loch Craggie
Black Water
River Brora
520 ▲ BEN HORN
Loch Horn
Dalchalm

Tomich
A839
14
Rogart
378 ▲ CAGAR FEOSAIG
Brora
Doll
A9

313 CREAGAN GLAS
446 ▲ BEN LUNDIE
383 BEN BHRAGGIE
Rhives
Backies
Corn Liath

333 MEALL EACHAINN
Loch Buidhe
Torboll
Golspie-Burn
Dunrobin Castle
Golspie

349 ▲ BEINN DONUILL
Sleasdairidh
River Evelix
Cambusavie Platform
Loch Fleet
Skelbo
Skelbo Street
Fourpenny
Embo

Badninish
Achvaich
Rearquhar
Astle
Birichin
B9168
Embo Street
Pitgrudy
Royal Dornoch

Bonar Bridge
Loch Migdale
Spinningdale
A949
10
Clashmore
Evelix
A949
A9
3
Camore
Dornoch
Historylinks

ronie
A836
Whiteface
Ferrytown
Cuthill
Camore
Dornoch Firth
Tarbat Ness

Dornoch Firth
Struie Hill
Ardmore
Cambuscurrie Bay
Ferry Point
Dornoch Point
Innis Mhor
Brucefield
Wilkhaven

Edderton
A836
BEINN CLACH AN FHEADAIN 477
19
Dornoch Firth Bridge
Glenmorangie
Morangie
Portmahomack
Inver
Rockfield

Aultnamain Inn
284 ▲
Tain (Baile Dhubhthaich)
Arboll
B9165
Rockfield

MORANGIE FOREST
692 ▲ BEINN ARSUINN
379 ▲ CNOC AN T-SABHAIL
B9176
Newfield
B9165
Toulvaddie
Loch Eye
Hill of Fearn
Rhynie
Lochslin
Balmuchy
Hilton of Cadboll Chapel (ruin)
Hilton

Ardross
Ballchraggan
Kildary
Milton
Arabella
Fearn
B9166
Tullich
Shandwick
Balintore
Shandwick Bay

Achandunie
Rhicullen
Delny
Kilmuir
Barbaraville
B9175
Ankerville
Nigg

Moultavie
Millcraig
Tomich
A9
8
Balintraid
Pitcalnie
Nigg Bay

Alness (Alanais)
Dalmore
Achnagarron
Saltburn
Nigg Ferry

B817
Invergordon
Cromarty

NJ

Balblair
Resolis
Udale Bay
Hugh Miller's Cottage
Newton
Navity
103

Clanland & Seapoint
B9163
Jemimaville
Allerton
Upper Eathie
Burghead
Burghead Bay

BLACK ISLE
B9160
Cullicudden
Brae
B9169

Culbokie
255 ▲ MOUNT EAGLE
Killen
Raddery
Fairy Glen
Rosemarkie
Whiteness Head
Culbin Sands
Findhorn
Hempriggs
Kinloss
B9011

Culbokie
Belmaduthy
Cathedral
Fortrose
Groam House
Fort George & The Highlanders' Museum
Nairn (Inbhir Narann)
Culbin Forest
Kincorth House
Kintessack
Brodie Castle
Dyke
Sueno's Stone
Forres
Califer
Rafford
B9010

Knockbain
A832
Munlochy
Avoch
Chanonry Point
Ardersier
B9092
Tradespark
Moss-side
Housenill
Auldearn 1645
Whitemire
Conicavel
Branchill

MORAY FIRTH
Littleburn
Munlochy Bay
Fisherton
B9039
B9006
Gollanfield
Lochside
Boath Doocot
Foynesfield
Righoul
A940

L   N   P   Q   S   T   U   V

MORAY FIRTH

70   80   90

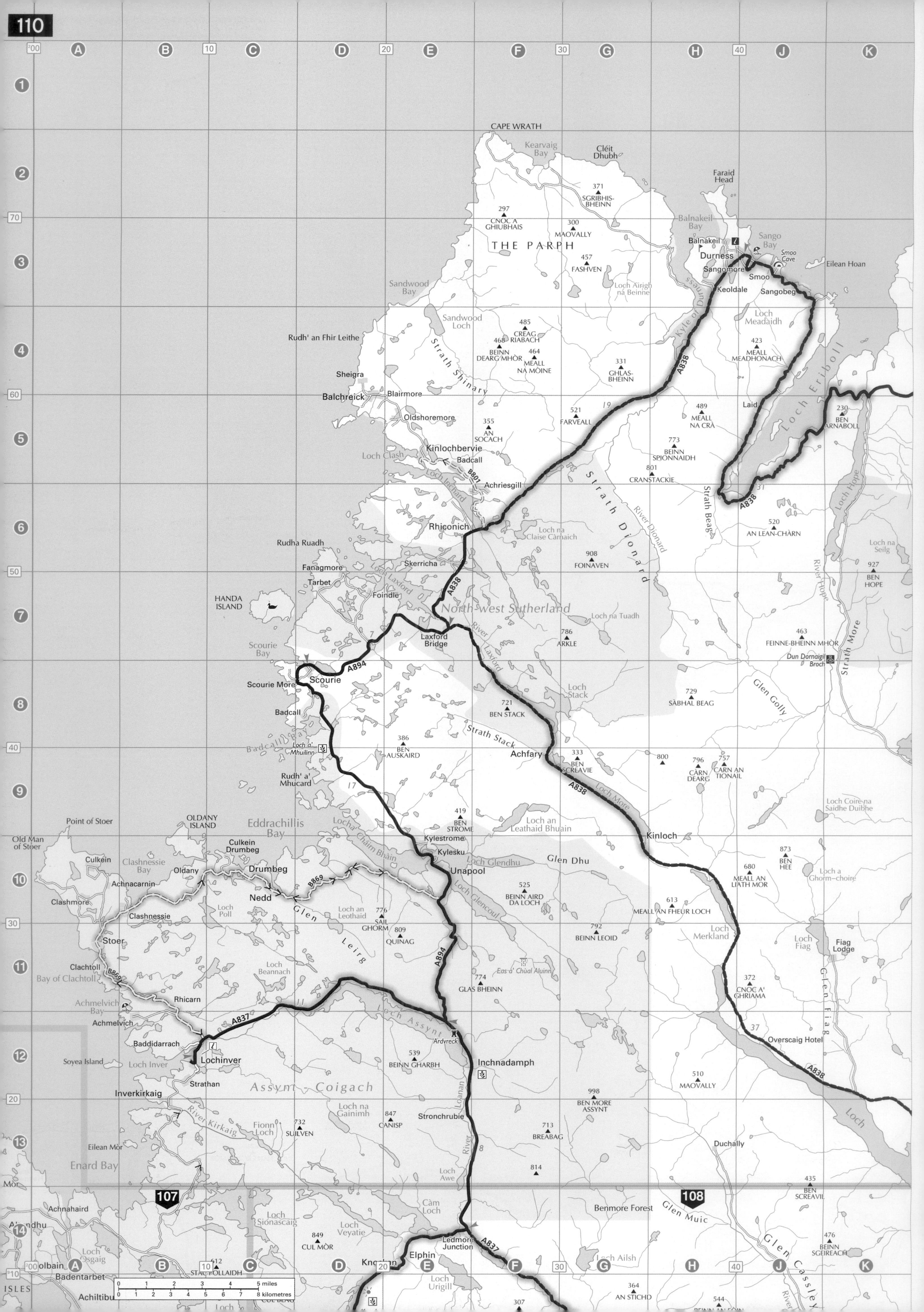
CAPE WRATH
Kearvaig Bay
Cléit Dhubh
Faraid Head
371 SGRIBHIS-BHEINN
297 CNOC A' GHIUBHAIS
300 MAOVALLY
THE PARPH
Balnakeil Bay
Balnakeil
Durness
Sango Bay
Smoo Cave
Eilean Hoan
Sangomore
Smoo
457 FASHVEN
Loch Airigh na Beinne
Keoldale
Sangobeg
Sandwood Bay
Sandwood Loch
485 CREAG RIABACH
468 BEINN DEARG MHÒR
464 MEALL NA MÒINE
Loch Meadaidh
423 MEALL MEADHONACH
Rudh' an Fhir Leithe
Strath Shinary
331 GHLAS-BHEINN
Kyle of Durness
A838
Loch Eriboll
Sheigra
Balchreick
Blairmore
Oldshoremore
Laid
230 BEN ARNABOLL
521 FARVEALL
489 MEALL NA CRA
355 AN SOCACH
773 BEINN SPIONNAIDH
Kinlochbervie
Loch Clash
Badcall
801 CRANSTACKIE
B801
Achriesgill
Strath Dionard
River Dionard
Strath Beag
Loch Hope
Rhiconich
Loch na Claise Carnaich
520 AN LEAN-CHÀRN
Rudha Ruadh
Loch na Seilg
908 FOINAVEN
927 BEN HOPE
Fanagmore
Skerricha
Tarbet
Loch Laxford
Foindle
River Hope
HANDA ISLAND
North-west Sutherland
Loch na Tuadh
Laxford Bridge
River Laxford
786 ARKLE
463 FEINNE-BHEINN MHÒR
Strath More
Scourie Bay
Dun Dornaigil Broch
A894
Scourie
Scourie More
Loch Stack
729 SÀBHAL BEAG
Glen Golly
721 BEN STACK
Badcall
Strath Stack
Badcall Bay
Loch a' Mhuilinn
386 BEN AUSKAIRD
Achfary
333 BEN SCREAVIE
800
796 CARN DEARG
757 CARN AN TIONAIL
Rudh' a' Mhucard
Loch More
Loch Coire na Saidhe Duibhe
Point of Stoer
OLDANY ISLAND
Eddrachillis Bay
419 BEN STROME
Loch an Leathaid Bhuain
Kinloch
Old Man of Stoer
Culkein Drumbeg
Kylestrome
Loch a' Chairn Bhàin
Culkein
Clashnessie Bay
Kylesku
Loch Glendhu
Glen Dhu
873 BEN HEE
Oldany
Drumbeg
Unapool
Loch a Ghorm-choire
Achnacarnin
B869
680 MEALL AN LIATH MOR
Clashmore
Nedd
Loch Poll
Glen Leirg
Loch an Leothaid
776 SAIL GHORM
525 BEINN AIRD DA LOCH
Loch Glencoul
613 MEALL AN FHEUR LOCH
Clashnessie
809 QUINAG
792 BEINN LEOID
Loch Merkland
Stoer
Loch Fiag
Fiag Lodge
Clachtoll
Bay of Clachtoll
Loch Beannach
Eas a' Chùal Aluinn
774 GLAS BHEINN
372 CNOC A' GHRIAMA
Glen Fiag
Achmelvich Bay
Rhicarn
A837
Loch Assynt
Achmelvich
Ardvreck
37
Overscaig Hotel
Baddidarrach
539 BEINN GHARBH
Inchnadamph
Soyea Island
Loch Inver
Lochinver
Strathan
Assynt – Coigach
510 MAOVALLY
Inverkirkaig
998 BEN MORE ASSYNT
Loch na Gainimh
847 CANISP
Stronchrubie
River Loanan
River Kirkaig
Fionn Loch
732 SUILVEN
713 BREABAG
Eilean Mor
Duchally
Enard Bay
814
Loch Awe
435 BEN SCREAVIE
107
108
Achnahaird
Càm Loch
Benmore Forest
Glen Muic
Loch Sionascaig
Loch Veyatie
476 BEINN SGEIREACH
Altandhu
849 CUL MÒR
Ledmore Junction
Glen Cassley
Loch Osgaig
Elphin
Polbain
612 STAC POLLAIDH
Knockan
Loch Ailsh
Badentarbet
Loch Urigill
ISLES
Achiltibuie
364 AN STICHD
307
544
5 miles
8 kilometres

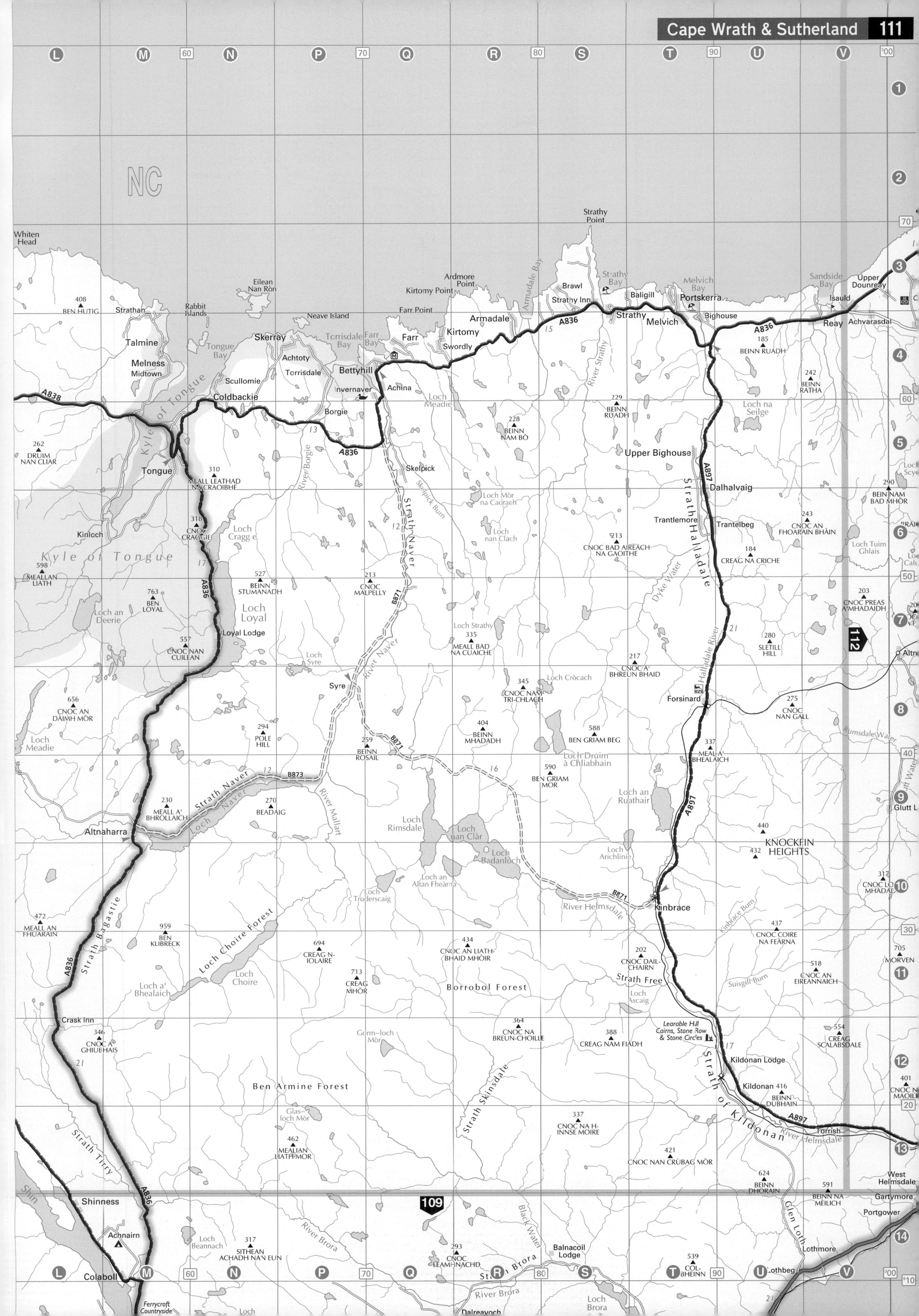

NC

Whiten
Head

408
BEN HUTIG

Strathan
Talmine

Melness
Midtown

262
DRUIM
NAN CLIAR

Tongue

A838

Kyle of Tongue

598
MEALLAN
LIATH

Kinloch

Eilean
Nan Ròn

Rabbit
Islands

Skerray

Achtoty

Scullomie

Coldbackie

Borgie

310
MEALL LEATHAD
NA CRAOIBHE

318
CNOC
CRAGGIE

A836

763
BEN
LOYAL

Loch an
Deerie

557
CNOC NAN
CUILEAN

Neave Island

Torrisdale
Bay

Farr
Bay

Torrisdale

Bettyhill
Invernaver

Achina

River Borgie

Loch
Cragge

527
BEINN
STUMANADH

Loch
Loyal

Loyal Lodge

Loch
Syre

Syre

294
POLE
HILL

Ardmore
Point

Kirtomy Point

Farr Point

Farr

Swordly

Kirtomy

Loch
Meadie

Skelpick

213
CNOC
MALPELLY

Strath Naver

Skelpick Burn

River Naver

B871

259
BEINN
ROSAIL

Brawl

Strathy Inn

Armadale

A836

15

River Strathy

Loch Mòr
na Caoraeh

Loch
nan Clach

Loch Strathy

335
MEALL BAD
NA CUAICHE

345
CNOC NAM
TRI-CHLACH

404
BEINN
MHADADH

Strathy
Bay

Baligill

Strathy

Strathy
Point

Melvich

Melvich
Bay

Bighouse

Upper Bighouse

Dalhalvaig

Trantlemore

Trantlebeg

229
BEINN
RUADH

228
BEINN
NAM BÒ

213
CNOC BAD AIREACH
NA GAOITHE

217
CNOC A'
BHREUN BHAID

Portskerra

Sandside
Bay

A836

185
BEINN RUADH

242
BEINN
RATHA

Loch na
Seilge

A897

Strath Halladale

243
CNOC AN
FHOARAIN BHÀIN

184
CREAG NA CRICHE

Halladale River

21

Upper
Dounreay

Isauld

Reay

Achvarasdal

BEIN NAM
BAD MHOR

290

BRÀI

Loch Tuim
Ghlais

203
CNOC PREAS
A'MHADAIDH

280
SLETILL
HILL

112

Loc
Scye

Calt

Loc

275
CNOC
NAN GALL

Forsinard

588
BEN GRIAM BEG

590
BEN GRIAM
MOR

Loch Druim
à Chliabhain

Loch an
Ruathair

337
MEALL A'
BHEALAICH

Rumsdale Water

40

Glutt L

9

Loch
Meadie

656
CNOC AN
DÀIMH MOR

230
MEALL A'
BHROLLAICH

Altnaharra

Strath Naver

12

B873

270
BEADAIG

River Mallart

Loch Naver

16

Loch
Rimsdale

Loch
nan Clàr

Loch
Badanloch

Loch an
Altan Fheàrna

Loch
Truderscaig

Loch
Arichlinie

River Helmsdale

B871

Kinbrace

440

KNOCKFIN
HEIGHTS

432

A897

Kinbrace Burn

317
CNOC LO
MHADAI

10

30

472
MEALL AN
FHUARAIN

A836

Strath Bagastie

959
BEN
KLIBRECK

Loch a'
Bhealaich

Loch Choire Forest

Loch
Choire

694
CREAG N-
IOLAIRE

713
CREAG
MHÒR

Borrobol Forest

434
CNOC AN LIATH-
BHAID MHÒR

202
CNOC DAIL-
CHAIRN

Strath Free

Loch
Ascaig

437
CNOC COIRE
NA FEÀRNA

518
CNOC AN
EIREANNAICH

705
MORVEN

11

Crask Inn

346
CNOC A'
GHIUBHAIS

21

Ben Armine Forest

462
MEALIAN
LIATH MÒR

Strath Skinsdale

Gorm-loch
Mòr

364
CNOC NA
BREUN-CHOILLE

388
CREAG NAM FIADH

Learable Hill
Cairns, Stone Row
& Stone Circ'es

17

Kildonan Lodge

Kildonan

416
BEINN
DUBHAIN

A897

Strath of Kildonan

554
CREAG
SCALABSDALE

401
CNOC
MAOIL

12

20

Strath Tirry

Shinness

Achnairn

A836

Colaboll

Loch
Beannach

317
SITHEAN
ACHADH NAN EUN

River Brora

337
CNOC NA H-
INNSE MOIRE

421
CNOC NAN CRÙBAG MÒR

293
CNOC NA
LEAMH-NACHD

Balnacoil
Lodge

River Helmsdale

Strath of Kildonan

Torrish

624
BEINN
DHORAIN

591
BEINN NA
MEILICH

West
Helmsdale

Gartymore

Portgower

13

539
COL-
BHEINN

Lothmore

Lothbeg

14

Shin

Ferrycroft
Countryside

Loch

Dalreavoch

River Brora

Black Water

St R Brora

Loch
Brora

Glen Loth

21

109

L M 60 N 70 P Q 80 R S 90 T U V 00

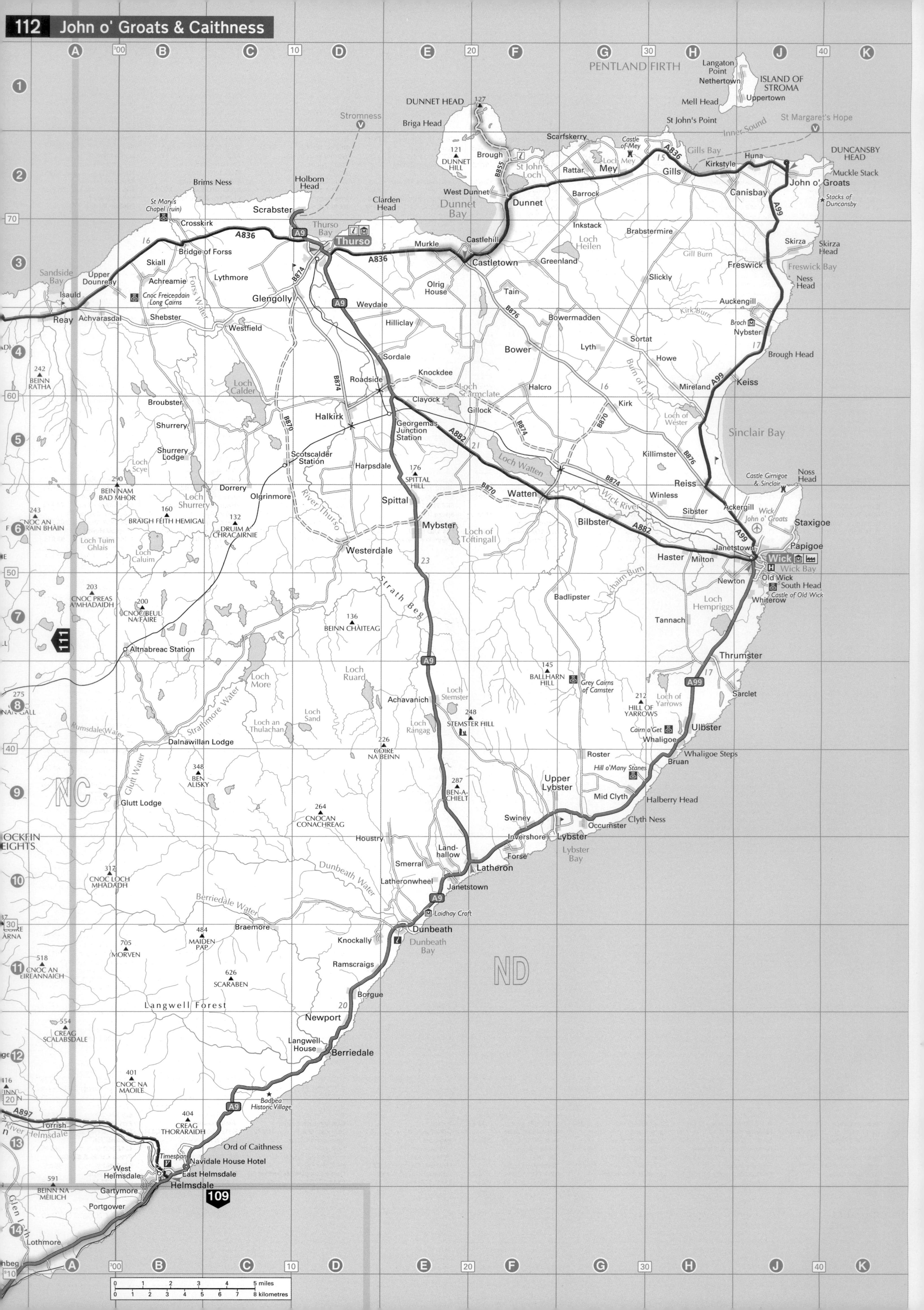
PENTLAND FIRTH
ISLAND OF STROMA
DUNNET HEAD
DUNCANSBY HEAD
John o' Groats
Thurso
Scrabster
Castletown
Dunnet
Mey
Gills
Canisbay
Halkirk
Georgemas Junction Station
Watten
Spittal
Wick
Keiss
Sinclair Bay
Reiss
Thrumster
Ulbster
Lybster
Latheron
Dunbeath
Berriedale
Helmsdale
Reay
Loch Watten
Loch Calder
Langwell Forest
NC
ND
111
109
5 miles
8 kilometres

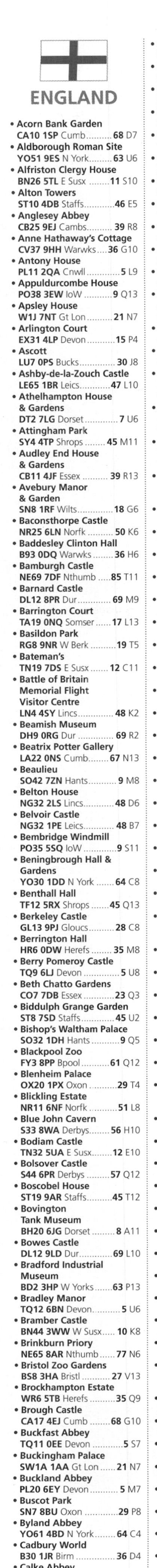

ENGLAND

- Acorn Bank Garden CA10 1SP Cumb 68 D7
- Aldborough Roman Site YO51 9ES N York 63 U6
- Alfriston Clergy House BN26 5TL E Susx 11 S10
- Alton Towers ST10 4DB Staffs 46 E5
- Anglesey Abbey CB25 9EJ Cambs 39 R8
- Anne Hathaway's Cottage CV37 9HH Warwks 36 G10
- Antony House PL11 2QA Cnwll 5 L9
- Appuldurcombe House PO38 3EW IoW 9 Q13
- Apsley House W1J 7NT Gt Lon 21 N7
- Arlington Court EX31 4LP Devon 15 P4
- Ascott LU7 0PS Bucks 30 J8
- Ashby-de-la-Zouch Castle LE65 1BR Leics 47 L10
- Athelhampton House & Gardens DT2 7LG Dorset 7 U6
- Attingham Park SY4 4TP Shrops 45 M11
- Audley End House & Gardens CB11 4JF Essex 39 R13
- Avebury Manor & Garden SN8 1RF Wilts 18 G6
- Baconsthorpe Castle NR25 6LN Norfk 50 K6
- Baddesley Clinton Hall B93 0DQ Warwks 36 H6
- Bamburgh Castle NE69 7DF Nthumb 85 T11
- Barnard Castle DL12 8PR Dur 69 M9
- Barrington Court TA19 0NQ Somset 17 L13
- Basildon Park RG8 9NR W Berk 19 T5
- Bateman's TN19 7DS E Susx 12 C11
- Battle of Britain Memorial Flight Visitor Centre LN4 4SY Lincs 48 K2
- Beamish Museum DH9 0RG Dur 69 R2
- Beatrix Potter Gallery LA22 0NS Cumb 67 N13
- Beaulieu SO42 7ZN Hants 9 M8
- Belton House NG32 2LS Lincs 48 D6
- Belvoir Castle NG32 1PE Leics 48 B7
- Bembridge Windmill PO35 5SQ IoW 9 S11
- Beningbrough Hall & Gardens YO30 1DD N York 64 C8
- Benthall Hall TF12 5RX Shrops 45 Q13
- Berkeley Castle GL13 9PJ Gloucs 28 C8
- Berrington Hall HR6 0DW Herefs 35 M8
- Berry Pomeroy Castle TQ9 6LJ Devon 5 U8
- Beth Chatto Gardens CO7 7DB Essex 23 Q3
- Biddulph Grange Garden ST8 7SD Staffs 45 U2
- Bishop's Waltham Palace SO32 1DH Hants 9 Q5
- Blackpool Zoo FY3 8PP Bpool 61 Q12
- Blenheim Palace OX20 1PX Oxon 29 T4
- Blickling Estate NR11 6NF Norfk 51 L8
- Blue John Cavern S33 8WA Derbys 56 H10
- Bodiam Castle TN32 5UA E Susx 12 E10
- Bolsover Castle S44 6PR Derbys 57 Q12
- Boscobel House ST19 9AR Staffs 45 T12
- Bovington Tank Museum BH20 6JG Dorset 8 A11
- Bowes Castle DL12 9LD Dur 69 L10
- Bradford Industrial Museum BD2 3HP W Yorks 63 P13
- Bradley Manor TQ12 6BN Devon 5 U6
- Bramber Castle BN44 3WW W Susx 10 K8
- Brinkburn Priory NE65 8AR Nthumb 77 N6
- Bristol Zoo Gardens BS8 3HA Bristl 27 V13
- Brockhampton Estate WR6 5TB Herefs 35 Q9
- Brough Castle CA17 4EJ Cumb 68 G10
- Buckfast Abbey TQ11 0EE Devon 5 S7
- Buckingham Palace SW1A 1AA Gt Lon 21 N7
- Buckland Abbey PL20 6EY Devon 5 M7
- Buscot Park SN7 8BU Oxon 29 P8
- Byland Abbey YO61 4BD N York 64 C4
- Cadbury World B30 1JR Birm 36 D4
- Calke Abbey DE73 7LE Derbys 47 L9
- Canons Ashby House NN11 3SD Nhants 37 Q10
- Canterbury Cathedral CT1 2EH Kent 13 N4
- Carisbrooke Castle PO30 1XY IoW 9 P11
- Carlyle's House SW3 5HL Gt Lon 21 N7
- Castle Drogo EX6 6PB Devon 5 S2
- Castle Howard YO60 7DA N York 64 G5
- Castle Rising Castle PE31 6AH Norfk 49 U9
- Charlecote Park CV35 9ER Warwks 36 J9
- Chartwell TN16 1PS Kent 21 S12
- Chastleton House GL56 0SU Oxon 29 P2
- Chatsworth DE45 1PP Derbys 57 L12
- Chedworth Roman Villa GL54 3LJ Gloucs 29 L5
- Chessington World of Adventures KT9 2NE Gt Lon 21 L10
- Chester Cathedral CH1 2HU Ches W 54 K13
- Chester Zoo CH2 1EU Ches W 54 K12
- Chesters Roman Fort & Museum NE46 4EU Nthumb 76 J11
- Chiswick House & Gardens W4 2RP Gt Lon 21 M7
- Chysauster Ancient Village TR20 8XA Cnwll 2 D10
- Claremont Landscape Garden KT10 9JG Surrey 20 K10
- Claydon House MK18 2EY Bucks 30 F7
- Cleeve Abbey TA23 0PS Somset 16 D8
- Clevedon Court BS21 6QU N Som 17 M2
- Cliveden SL6 0JA Bucks 20 F5
- Clouds Hill BH20 7NQ Dorset 7 V6
- Clumber Park S80 3AZ Notts 57 T12
- Colchester Zoo CO3 0SL Essex 23 N3
- Coleridge Cottage TA5 1NQ Somset 16 G9
- Coleton Fishacre TQ6 0EQ Devon 6 B14
- Compton Castle TQ3 1TA Devon 5 V8
- Conisbrough Castle DN12 3BU Donc 57 R7
- Corbridge Roman Town NE45 5NT Nthumb 76 K13
- Corfe Castle BH20 5EZ Dorset 8 D12
- Corsham Court SN13 0BZ Wilts 18 C6
- Cotehele PL12 6TA Cnwll 5 L7
- Coughton Court B49 5JA Warwks 36 E8
- Courts Garden BA14 6RR Wilts 18 C8
- Cragside NE65 7PX Nthumb 77 M5
- Crealy Great Adventure Park EX5 1DR Devon 6 D6
- Crich Tramway Village DE4 5DP Derbys 46 K2
- Croft Castle HR6 9PW Herefs 34 K7
- Croome Park WR8 9JS Worcs 35 U12
- Deddington Castle OX15 0TE Oxon 29 U1
- Didcot Railway Centre OX11 7NJ Oxon 19 R2
- Dover Castle CT16 1HU Kent 13 R7
- Drayton Manor Theme Park B78 3SA Staffs 46 G13
- Dudmaston Estate WV15 6QN Shrops 35 R3
- Dunham Massey WA14 4SJ Traffd 55 R9
- Dunstanburgh Castle NE66 3TT Nthumb 77 R1
- Dunster Castle TA24 6SL Somset 16 C8
- Durham Cathedral DH1 3EH Dur 69 S4
- Dyrham Park SN14 8HY S Glos 28 D12
- East Riddlesden Hall BD20 5EL Brad 63 M11
- Eden Project PL24 2SG Cnwll 3 R6
- Eltham Palace & Gardens SE9 5QE Gt Lon 21 R8
- Emmetts Garden TN14 6BA Kent 21 S12
- Exmoor Zoo EX31 4SG Devon 15 Q4
- Farleigh Hungerford Castle BA2 7RS Somset 18 B9
- Farnborough Hall OX17 1DU Warwks 37 M11
- Felbrigg Hall NR11 8PR Norfk 51 L6
- Fenton House & Garden NW3 6SP Gt Lon 21 N5
- Finch Foundry EX20 2NW Devon 5 Q2
- Finchale Priory DH1 5SH Dur 69 S3
- Fishbourne Roman Palace PO19 3QR W Susx 10 C10
- Flamingo Land YO17 6UX N York 64 H4
- Forde Abbey TA20 4LU Somset 7 L3
- Fountains Abbey & Studley Royal HG4 3DY N York 63 R6
- Gawthorpe Hall BB12 8UA Lancs 62 G13
- Gisborough Priory TS14 6HG R & Cl 70 K9
- Glendurgan Garden TR11 5JZ Cnwll 2 K11
- Goodrich Castle HR9 6HY Herefs 28 A4
- Great Chalfield Manor & Garden SN12 8NH Wilts 18 C8
- Great Coxwell Barn SN7 7LZ Oxon 29 Q9
- Greenway TQ5 0ES Devon 5 V10
- Haddon Hall DE45 1LA Derbys 56 K13
- Hailes Abbey GL54 5PB Gloucs 29 L1
- Ham House & Garden TW10 7RS Gt Lon 21 L8
- Hampton Court Palace KT8 9AU Gt Lon 21 L9
- Hanbury Hall WR9 7EA Worcs 36 B8
- Hardwick Hall S44 5QJ Derbys 57 Q14
- Hardy's Cottage DT2 8QJ Dorset 7 T6
- Hare Hill SK10 4PY Ches E 56 C11
- Hatchlands Park GU4 7RT Surrey 20 J12
- Heale Gardens SP4 6NU Wilts 18 H13
- Helmsley Castle YO62 5AB N York 64 E3
- Hereford Cathedral HR1 2NG Herefs 35 M13
- Hergest Croft Gardens HR5 3EG Herefs 34 G9
- Hever Castle & Gardens TN8 7NG Kent 21 S13
- Hidcote Manor Garden GL55 6LR Gloucs 36 G12
- Hill Top LA22 0LF Cumb 67 N13
- Hinton Ampner SO24 0LA Hants 9 R3
- Holkham Hall NR23 1AB Norfk 50 E5
- Housesteads Roman Fort NE47 6NN Nthumb 76 F12
- Howletts Wild Animal Park CT4 5EL Kent 13 N4
- Hughenden Manor HP14 4LA Bucks 20 E3
- Hurst Castle SO41 0TP Hants 9 L11
- Hylands House & Park CM2 8WQ Essex 22 G7
- Ickworth IP29 5QE Suffk 40 D8
- Ightham Mote TN15 0NT Kent 21 U12
- Ironbridge Gorge Museums TF8 7DQ Wrekin 45 Q13
- Kedleston Hall DE22 5JH Derbys 46 K5
- Kenilworth Castle & Elizabethan Garden CV8 1NE Warwks 36 J6
- Kenwood House NW3 7JR Gt Lon 21 N5
- Killerton EX5 3LE Devon 6 C4
- King John's Hunting Lodge BS26 2AP Somset 17 M6
- Kingston Lacy BH21 4EA Dorset 8 D8
- Kirby Hall NN17 3EN Nhants 38 D2
- Knightshayes Court EX16 7RQ Devon 16 C13
- Knole House TN13 1HU Kent 21 T12
- Knowsley Safari Park L34 4AN Knows 55 L8
- Lacock Abbey SN15 2LG Wilts 18 D7
- Lamb House TN31 7ES E Susx 12 H11
- Lanhydrock House PL30 5AD Cnwll 3 R4
- Launceston Castle PL15 7DR Cnwll 4 J4
- Leeds Castle ME17 1PB Kent 12 F5
- Legoland SL4 4AY W&M 20 F8
- Lindisfarne Castle TD15 2SH Nthumb 85 S10
- Lindisfarne Priory TD15 2RX Nthumb 85 S10
- Little Moreton Hall CW12 4SD Ches E 45 T2
- Liverpool Cathedral L1 7AZ Lpool 54 J9
- London Zoo ZSL NW1 4RY Gt Lon 21 N6
- Longleat BA12 7NW Wilts 18 B12
- Loseley Park GU3 1HS Surrey 20 G13
- Ludgershall Castle SP11 9QR Wilts 19 L10
- Lydford Castle EX20 4BH Devon 5 N4
- Lyme Park, House & Garden SK12 2NX Ches E 56 E10
- Lytes Cary Manor TA11 7HU Somset 17 P11
- Lyveden New Bield PE8 5AT Nhant 38 E3
- Maiden Castle DT2 9PP Dorset 7 S7
- Mapledurham Estate RG4 7TR Oxon 19 U5
- Marble Hill House TW1 2NL Gt Lon 21 L8
- Marwell Zoo SO21 1JH Hants 9 Q4
- Melford Hall CO10 9AA Suffk 40 E11
- Merseyside Maritime Museum L3 4AQ Lpool 54 H9
- Minster Lovell Hall OX29 0RR Oxon 29 R5
- Mompesson House SP1 2EL Wilts 8 G3
- Monk Bretton Priory S71 5QD Barns 57 N5
- Montacute House TA15 6XP Somset 17 N13
- Morwellham Quay PL19 8JL Devon 5 L7
- Moseley Old Hall WV10 7HY Staffs 46 B13
- Mottisfont SO51 0LP Hants 9 L3
- Mottistone Manor Garden PO30 4ED IoW 9 N12
- Mount Grace Priory DL6 3JG N York 70 F13
- National Maritime Museum SE10 9NF Gt Lon 21 Q7
- National Motorcycle Museum B92 0ED Solhll 36 H4
- National Portrait Gallery WC2H 0HE Gt Lon 21 N6
- National Railway Museum YO26 4XJ York 64 D9
- National Space Centre LE4 5NS C Leic 47 Q12
- Natural History Museum SW7 5BD Gt Lon 21 N7
- Needles Old Battery PO39 0JH IoW 9 L12
- Nene Valley Railway PE8 6LR Cambs 38 H1
- Netley Abbey SO31 5FB Hants 9 P7
- Newark Air Museum NG24 2NY Notts 48 B2
- Newtown Old Town Hall PO30 4PA IoW 9 N10
- North Leigh Roman Villa OX29 6QB Oxon 29 S4
- Norwich Cathedral NR1 4DH Norfk 51 M12
- Nostell Priory WF4 1QE Wakefd 57 P3
- Nunnington Hall YO62 5UY N York 64 F4
- Nymans RH17 6EB W Susx 11 M5
- Old Royal Naval College SE10 9NN Gt Lon 21 Q7
- Old Sarum SP1 3SD Wilts 8 G2
- Old Wardour Castle SP3 6RR Wilts 8 C3
- Oliver Cromwell's House CB7 4HF Cambs 39 R4
- Orford Castle IP12 2ND Suffk 41 R10
- Ormesby Hall TS3 0SR R & Cl 70 H9
- Osborne House PO32 6JX IoW 9 Q9
- Osterley Park & House TW7 4RB Gt Lon 20 K7
- Overbeck's TQ8 8LW Devon 5 S13
- Oxburgh Hall PE33 9PS Norfk 50 B13
- Packwood House B94 6AT Warwks 36 G6
- Paignton Zoo TQ4 7EU Torbay 6 A13
- Paycocke's House & Garden CO6 1NS Essex 22 K3
- Peckover House & Garden PE13 1JR Cambs 49 Q12
- Pendennis Castle TR11 4LP Cnwll 3 L10
- Petworth House & Park GU28 0AE W Susx 10 F6
- Pevensey Castle BN24 5LE E Susx 11 U10
- Peveril Castle S33 8WQ Derbys 56 J10
- Polesden Lacey RH5 6BD Surrey 20 K12
- Portland Castle DT5 1AZ Dorset 7 S10
- Portsmouth Historic Dockyard PO1 3LJ C Port 9 S8
- Powderham Castle EX6 8JQ Devon 6 C8
- Prior Park Landscape Garden BA2 5AH BaNES 17 U4
- Prudhoe Castle NE42 6NA Nthumb 77 M13
- Quarry Bank Mill & Styal SK9 4LA Ches E 55 T10
- Quebec House TN16 1TD Kent 21 R12
- Ramsey Abbey Gatehouse PE17 1DH Cambs 39 L3
- Reculver Towers & Roman Fort CT6 6SU Kent 13 P2
- Red House DA6 8JF Gt Lon 21 S7
- Restormel Castle PL22 0EE Cnwll 4 E8
- Richborough Roman Fort CT13 9JW Kent 13 R3
- Richmond Castle DL10 4QW N York 69 Q12
- Roche Abbey S66 8NW Rothm 57 R9
- Rochester Castle ME1 1SW Medway 12 D2
- Rockbourne Roman Villa SP6 3PG Hants 8 G5
- Roman Baths & Pump Room BA1 1LZ BaNES 17 U4
- Royal Botanic Gardens, Kew TW9 3AB Gt Lon 21 L7
- Royal Observatory Greenwich SE10 8XJ Gt Lon 21 Q7
- Rufford Old Hall L40 1SG Lancs 55 L3
- Runnymede SL4 2JJ W & M 20 G8
- Rushton Triangular Lodge NN14 1RP Nhants 38 B4
- Rycote Chapel OX9 2PA Oxon 30 E12
- St Leonard's Tower ME19 6PE Kent 12 C4
- St Michael's Mount TR17 0HT Cnwll 2 E11
- St Paul's Cathedral EC4M 8AD Gt Lon 21 P6
- Salisbury Cathedral SP1 2EJ Wilts 8 G3
- Saltram PL7 1UH C Plym 5 N9
- Sandham Memorial Chapel RG20 9JT Hants 19 Q8
- Sandringham House & Grounds PE35 6EN Norfk 49 U8
- Saxtead Green Post Mill IP13 9QQ Suffk 41 N8
- Scarborough Castle YO11 1HY N York 65 P2
- Science Museum SW7 2DD Gt Lon 21 N7
- Scotney Castle TN3 8JN Kent 12 C8
- Shaw's Corner AL6 9BX Herts 31 Q9
- Sheffield Park & Garden TN22 3QX E Susx 11 Q6
- Sherborne Old Castle DT9 3SA Dorset 17 R13
- Sissinghurst Castle Garden TN17 2AB Kent 12 F8
- Sizergh Castle & Garden LA8 8AE Cumb 61 T2
- Smallhythe Place TN30 7NG Kent 12 G10
- Snowshill Manor & Garden WR12 7JU Gloucs 36 E14
- Souter Lighthouse SR6 7NH S Tyne 77 U13
- Speke Hall, Garden & Estate L24 1XD Lpool 54 K10
- Spinnaker Tower, Emirates PO1 3TT C Port 9 S9
- Stokesay Castle SY7 9AH Shrops 34 K4
- Stonehenge SP4 7DE Wilts 18 H12
- Stourhead BA12 6QD Wilts 17 U10
- Stowe Landscape Gardens MK18 5EQ Bucks 30 E5
- Sudbury Hall DE6 5HT Derbys 46 G7
- Sulgrave Manor OX17 2SD Nhants 37 Q11
- Sunnycroft TF1 2DR Wrekin 45 Q11
- Sutton Hoo IP12 3DJ Suffk 41 N11
- Sutton House E9 6JQ Gt Lon 21 Q5
- Tate Britain SW1P 4RG Gt Lon 21 N7
- Tate Liverpool L3 4BB Lpool 54 H9
- Tate Modern SE1 9TG Gt Lon 21 P6
- Tattershall Castle LN4 4LR Lincs 48 K2
- Tatton Park WA16 6QN Ches E 55 R10
- The British Library NW1 2DB Gt Lon 21 N6
- The British Museum WC1B 3DG Gt Lon 21 N6
- The Lost Gardens of Heligan PL26 6EN Cnwll 3 P7
- The Lowry M50 3AZ Salfd 55 T7
- The National Gallery WC2N 5DN Gt Lon 21 N6
- The Vyne RG24 9HL Hants 19 T9
- The Weir Garden HR4 7QF Herefs 34 K12
- Thornton Abbey & Gatehouse DN39 6TU N Linc 58 K3
- Thorpe Park KT16 8PN Surrey 20 H9
- Tilbury Fort RM18 7NR Thurr 22 G12
- Tintagel Castle PL34 0HE Cnwll 4 C3
- Tintinhull Garden BA22 8PZ Somset 17 P13
- Totnes Castle TQ9 5NU Devon 5 U8
- Tower of London EC3N 4AB Gt Lon 21 P6
- Townend LA23 1LB Cumb 67 P12
- Treasurer's House YO1 7JL York 64 E9
- Trelissick Garden TR3 6QL Cnwll 3 L9
- Trengwainton Garden TR20 8RZ Cnwll 2 C10
- Trerice TR8 4PG Cnwll 3 L5
- Twycross Zoo CV9 3PX Leics 46 K12
- Upnor Castle ME2 4XG Medway 22 J13
- Uppark House & Garden GU31 5QR W Susx 10 B7
- Upton House & Garden OX15 6HT Warwks 37 L11
- Victoria & Albert Museum SW7 2RL Gt Lon 21 N7
- Waddesdon Manor HP18 0JH Bucks 30 F9
- Wakehurst Place RH17 6TN W Susx 11 N4
- Wall Roman Site WS14 0AW Staffs 46 E12
- Wallington NE61 4AR Nthumb 77 L9
- Walmer Castle & Gardens CT14 7LJ Kent 13 S6
- Warkworth Castle & Hermitage NE65 0UJ Nthumb 77 Q4
- Warner Bros Studio Tour London WD25 7LS Herts 31 N12
- Warwick Castle CV34 4QU Warwks 36 J8
- Washington Old Hall NE38 7LE Sundld 70 D1
- Waterperry Gardens OX33 1LG Oxon 30 D11
- Weeting Castle IP27 0RQ Norfk 40 C3
- Wenlock Priory TF13 6HS Shrops 45 P13
- West Midland Safari & Leisure Park DY12 1LF Worcs 35 T5
- West Wycombe Park HP14 3AJ Bucks 20 D4
- Westbury Court Garden GL14 1PD Gloucs 28 D5
- Westminster Abbey SW1P 3PA Gt Lon 21 N7
- Westonbirt Arboretum GL8 8QS Gloucs 28 G9
- Westwood Manor BA15 2AF Wilts 18 B9
- Whipsnade Zoo ZSL LU6 2LF Becs C 31 M9
- Whitby Abbey YO22 4JT N York 71 R10
- Wightwick Manor & Gardens WV6 8EE Wolves 45 U14
- Wimpole Estate SG8 0BW Cambs 39 M10
- Winchester Cathedral SO23 9LS Hants 9 P3
- Winchester City Mill SO23 0EJ Hants 9 P3
- Windsor Castle SL4 1NJ W & M 20 G7
- Winkworth Arboretum GU8 4AD Surrey 10 F2
- Wisley RHS Garden GU23 6QB Surrey 20 J11
- Woburn Safari Park MK17 9QN Beds C 31 L6
- Wookey Hole Caves BA5 1BA Somset 17 P7
- Woolsthorpe Manor NG33 5PD Lincs 48 D9
- Wordsworth House CA13 9RX Cumb 66 H6
- Wrest Park MK45 4HR Beds C 31 N5
- Wroxeter Roman City SY5 6PR Shrops 45 N12
- WWT Arundel Wetland Centre BN18 9PB W Susx 10 G9
- WWT Slimbridge Wetland Centre GL2 7BT Gloucs 28 D6
- Yarmouth Castle PO41 0PB IoW 9 M11
- York Minster YO1 7HH York 64 E9

SCOTLAND

- Aberdour Castle KY3 0SL Fife 83 N1
- Alloa Tower FK10 1PP Clacks 90 C13
- Angus Folk Museum DD8 1RT Angus 91 N2
- Arbroath Abbey DD11 1EG Angus 91 T3
- Arduaine Garden PA34 4XQ Ag & B 87 P3
- Bachelors' Club KA5 5RB S Ayrs 81 N7
- Balmoral Castle Grounds AB35 5TB Abers 98 D5
- Balvenie Castle AB55 4DH Moray 104 C7
- Bannockburn Battlefield & Heritage Centre FK7 0LJ Stirlg 89 S7
- Blackness Castle EH49 7NH Falk 83 L2
- Blair Castle PH18 5TL P & K 97 P10
- Bothwell Castle G71 8BL S Lans 82 C7
- Branklyn Garden PH2 7BB P & K 90 H7
- Brodick Castle, Garden & Country Park KA27 8HY N Ayrs 80 E5
- Brodie Castle IV36 2TE Moray 103 Q4
- Broughton House & Garden DG6 4JX D & G 73 R9
- Burleigh Castle KY13 9GG P & K 90 H11
- Caerlaverock Castle DG1 4RU D & G 74 K12
- Cardoness Castle DG7 2EH D & G 73 P8
- Carnasserie Castle PA31 8RQ Ag & B 87 Q5
- Castle Campbell & Garden FK14 7PP Clacks 90 E12
- Castle Fraser, Garden & Estate AB51 7LD Abers 105 L13
- Castle Kennedy & Gardens DG9 8BX D & G 72 E7
- Castle Menzies PH15 2JD P & K 90 B2
- Corgarff Castle AB36 8YP Abers 98 D2
- Craigievar Castle AB33 8JF Abers 98 K2
- Craigmillar Castle EH16 4SY C Edin 83 Q4
- Crarae Garden PA32 8YA Ag & B 87 T6
- Crathes Castle & Garden AB31 5QJ Abers 99 N4
- Crichton Castle EH37 5XA Mdloth 83 S6
- Crossraguel Abbey KA19 8HQ S Ayrs 80 K11
- Culloden Battlefield IV2 5EU Highld 102 K6
- Culross Palace KY12 8JH Fife 82 J1
- Culzean Castle & Country Park KA19 8LE S Ayrs 80 J10
- Dallas Dhu Distillery IV36 2RR Moray 103 R4
- David Livingstone Centre G72 9BY S Lans 82 C7
- Dirleton Castle & Garden EH39 5ER E Loth 84 E2
- Doune Castle FK16 6EA Stirlg 89 R5
- Drum Castle, Garden & Estate AB31 5EY Abers 99 P3
- Dryburgh Abbey TD6 0RQ Border 84 F12
- Duff House AB45 3SX Abers 104 K3
- Dumbarton Castle G82 1JJ W Duns 88 J11
- Dundrennan Abbey DG6 4QH D & G 73 S10
- Dunnottar Castle AB39 2TL Abers 99 R7
- Dunstaffnage Castle PA37 1PZ Ag & B 94 B12
- Edinburgh Castle EH1 2NG C Edin 83 Q4
- Edinburgh Zoo RZSS EH12 6TS C Edin 83 P4
- Edzell Castle & Garden DD9 7UE Angus 98 K10
- Eilean Donan Castle IV40 8DX Highld 101 M6
- Elgin Cathedral IV30 1HU Moray 103 V3
- Falkland Palace & Garden KY15 7BU Fife 91 L10
- Fort George IV2 7TE Highld 103 L4
- Fyvie Castle AB53 8JS Abers 105 M8
- Georgian House EH2 4DR C Edin 83 P4
- Gladstone's Land EH1 2NT C Edin 83 Q4
- Glamis Castle DD8 1RJ Angus 91 N2
- Glasgow Botanic Gardens G12 0UE C Glas 89 N12
- Glasgow Cathedral G4 0QZ C Glas 89 P12
- Glasgow Science Centre G51 1EA C Glas 89 N12
- Glen Grant Distillery AB38 7BS Moray 104 B6
- Glenluce Abbey DG8 0AF D & G 72 F8
- Greenbank Garden G76 8RB E Rens 81 R1
- Haddo House AB41 7EQ Abers 105 P9
- Harmony Garden TD6 9LJ Border 84 E12
- Hermitage Castle TD9 0LU Border 75 U6
- Highland Wildlife Park RZSS PH21 1NL Highld 97 N3
- Hill House G84 9AJ Ag & B 88 G9
- Hill of Tarvit Mansion & Garden KY15 5PB Fife 91 N9
- Holmwood G44 3YG C Glas 89 N14
- House of Dun DD10 9LQ Angus 99 M12
- House of the Binns EH49 7NA W Loth 83 L3
- Huntingtower Castle PH1 3JL P & K 90 G7
- Huntly Castle AB54 4SH Abers 104 G7
- Hutchesons' Hall G1 1EJ C Glas 89 N12
- Inchmahome Priory FK8 3RA Stirlg 89 N5
- Inveresk Lodge Garden EH21 7TE E Loth 83 R4
- Inverewe Garden & Estate IV22 2LG Highld 107 Q8
- Inverlochy Castle PH33 6SN Highld 94 G3
- Kellie Castle & Garden KY10 2RF Fife 91 R10
- Kildrummy Castle AB33 8RA Abers 104 F12
- Killiecrankie Visitor Centre PH16 5LG P & K 97 Q11
- Leith Hall Garden & Estate AB54 4NQ Abers 104 G10
- Linlithgow Palace EH49 7AL W Loth 82 K3
- Lochleven Castle KY13 8UF P & K 90 H11
- Logan Botanic Garden DG9 9ND D & G 72 D11
- Malleny Garden EH14 7AF C Edin 83 N5
- Melrose Abbey TD6 9LG Border 84 E12
- National Museum of Scotland EH1 1JF C Edin 83 Q4
- Newark Castle PA14 5NH Inver 88 H11
- Palace of Holyroodhouse EH8 8DX C Edin 83 Q4
- Pitmedden Garden AB41 7PD Abers 105 P10
- Preston Mill & Phantassie Doocot EH40 3DS E Loth 84 F3
- Priorwood Garden TD6 9PX Border 84 E12
- Robert Smail's Printing Works EH44 6HA Border 83 R11
- Rothesay Castle PA20 0DA Ag & B 88 C13
- Royal Botanic Garden Edinburgh EH3 5LR C Edin 83 P3
- Royal Yacht Britannia EH6 6JJ C Edin 83 Q3
- St Andrews Aquarium KY16 9AS Fife 91 R8
- Scone Palace PH2 6BD P & K 90 H6
- Smailholm Tower TD5 7PG Border 84 G12
- Souter Johnnie's Cottage KA19 8HY S Ayrs 80 J11
- Stirling Castle FK8 1EJ Stirlg 89 S7
- Sweetheart Abbey DG2 8BU D & G 74 J12
- Tantallon Castle EH39 5PN E Loth 84 F1
- Tenement House G3 6QN C Glas 89 N12
- The Burrell Collection G43 1AT C Glas 89 N13
- The Falkirk Wheel FK1 4RS Falk 82 G2
- The Hunterian Museum G12 8QQ C Glas 89 N12
- Threave Castle DG7 1TJ D & G 74 D13
- Threave Garden DG7 1RX D & G 74 E13
- Tolquhon Castle AB41 7LP Abers 105 P10
- Traquair House EH44 6PW Border 83 R11
- Urquhart Castle IV63 6XJ Highld 102 F10
- Weaver's Cottage PA10 2JG Rens 88 K13
- Whithorn Priory & Museum DG8 8PY D & G 73 L11

WALES

- Aberconwy House LL32 8AY Conwy 53 N7
- Aberdulais Tin Works & Waterfall SA10 8EU Neath 26 D8
- Beaumaris Castle LL58 8AP IoA 52 K7
- Big Pit: National Coal Museum NP4 9XP Torfn 27 N6
- Bodnant Garden LL28 5RE Conwy 53 P8
- Caerleon Roman Fortress & Baths NP18 1AE Newpt 27 Q9
- Caernarfon Castle LL55 2AY Gwynd 52 G10
- Caldicot Castle & Country Park NP26 4HU Mons 27 T10
- Cardiff Castle CF10 3RB Cardif 27 M12
- Castell Coch CF15 7JS Cardif 27 L11
- Chirk Castle LL14 5AF Wrexhm 44 G6
- Colby Woodland Garden SA67 8PP Pembks 25 L9
- Conwy Castle LL32 8AY Conwy 53 N7
- Criccieth Castle LL52 0DP Gwynd 42 K6
- Dinefwr Park & Castle SA19 6RT Carmth 25 V6
- Dolaucothi Gold Mines SA19 8US Carmth 33 N12
- Erddig LL13 0YT Wrexhm 44 H4
- Ffestiniog Railway LL49 9NF Gwynd 43 N5
- Harlech Castle LL46 2YH Gwynd 43 L7
- Llanerchaeron SA48 8DG Cerdgn 32 J8
- National Showcaves Centre for Wales SA9 1GJ Powys 26 E4
- Penrhyn Castle LL57 4HT Gwynd 52 K8
- Plas Newydd LL61 6DQ IoA 52 H9
- Plas yn Rhiw LL53 8AB Gwynd 42 D8
- Portmeirion LL48 6ER Gwynd 43 L6
- Powis Castle & Garden SY21 8RF Powys 44 F12
- Raglan Castle NP15 2BT Mons 27 S6
- Sygun Copper Mine LL55 4NE Gwynd 43 M4
- Tintern Abbey NP16 6SE Mons 27 U7
- Tudor Merchant's House SA70 7BX Pembks 24 K10
- Tŷ Mawr Wybrnant LL25 0HJ Conwy 43 Q3
- Valle Crucis Abbey LL20 8DD Denbgs 44 F5

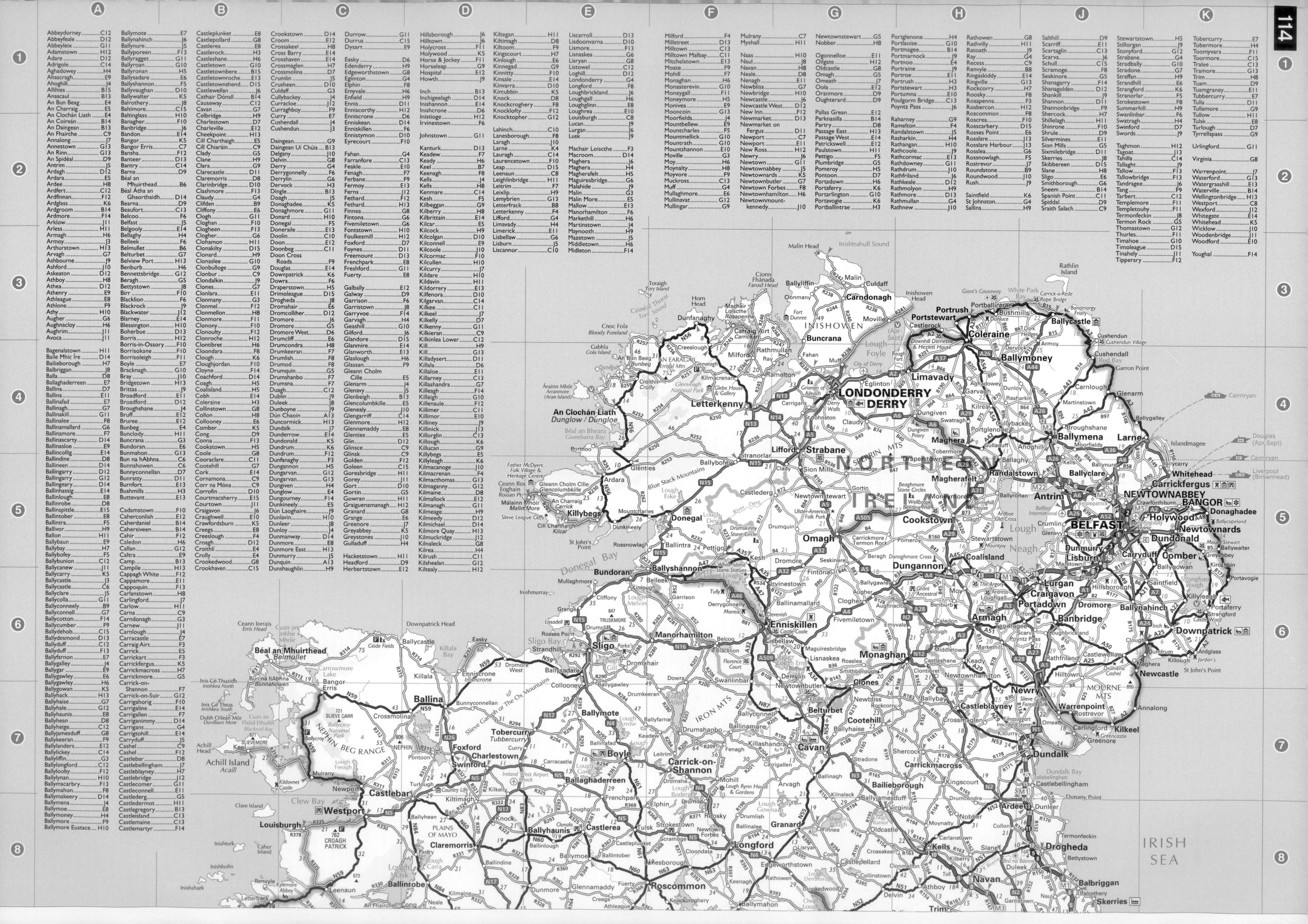

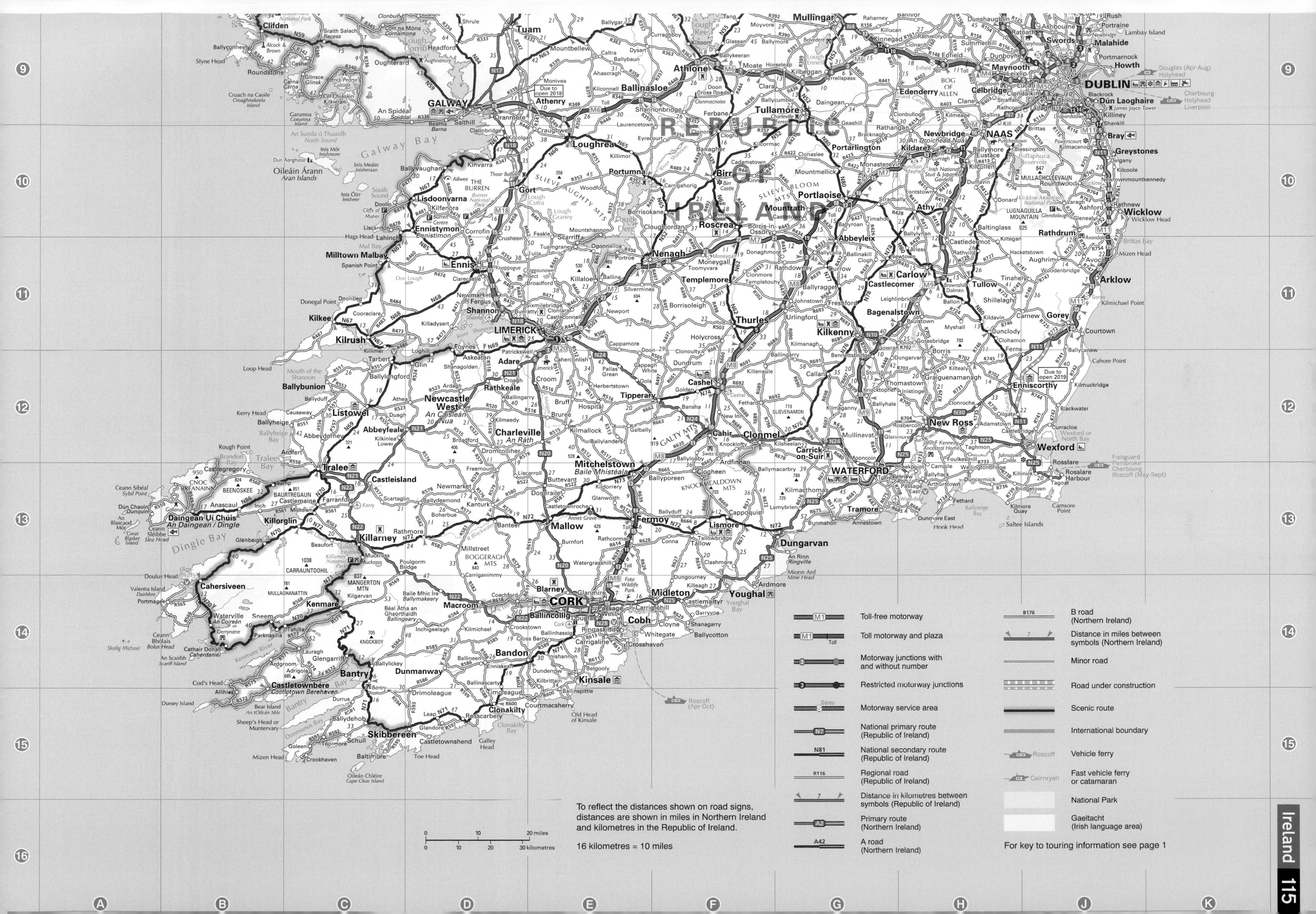
REPUBLIC OF IRELAND
DUBLIN
Dún Laoghaire
Howth
Swords
Malahide
Maynooth
Celbridge
NAAS
Bray
Greystones
Wicklow
Arklow
Rathdrum
Gorey
Enniscorthy
Wexford
Rosslare Harbour
New Ross
WATERFORD
Tramore
Dungarvan
Youghal
Midleton
Cobh
CORK
Kinsale
Bandon
Clonakilty
Skibbereen
Bantry
Kenmare
Killarney
Tralee
Listowel
Dingle Bay
Cahersiveen
Castletownbere
Mallow
Fermoy
Mitchelstown
Lismore
Clonmel
Carrick-on-Suir
Cahir
Cashel
Tipperary
Thurles
Kilkenny
Carlow
Athy
Kildare
Newbridge
Portlaoise
Portarlington
Tullamore
Birr
Roscrea
Nenagh
LIMERICK
Shannon
Ennis
Kilrush
Kilkee
GALWAY
Athenry
Loughrea
Gort
Ballinasloe
Athlone
Mullingar
Tuam
Clifden
Oughterard
Oileáin Árann
Aran Islands
Galway Bay
Killorglin
Castleisland
Charleville
Newcastle West
Abbeyfeale
Macroom
To reflect the distances shown on road signs, distances are shown in miles in Northern Ireland and kilometres in the Republic of Ireland.
16 kilometres = 10 miles
Toll-free motorway
Toll motorway and plaza
Motorway junctions with and without number
Restricted motorway junctions
Motorway service area
National primary route (Republic of Ireland)
National secondary route (Republic of Ireland)
Regional road (Republic of Ireland)
Distance in kilometres between symbols (Republic of Ireland)
Primary route (Northern Ireland)
A road (Northern Ireland)
B road (Northern Ireland)
Distance in miles between symbols (Northern Ireland)
Minor road
Road under construction
Scenic route
International boundary
Vehicle ferry
Fast vehicle ferry or catamaran
National Park
Gaeltacht (Irish language area)
For key to touring information see page 1

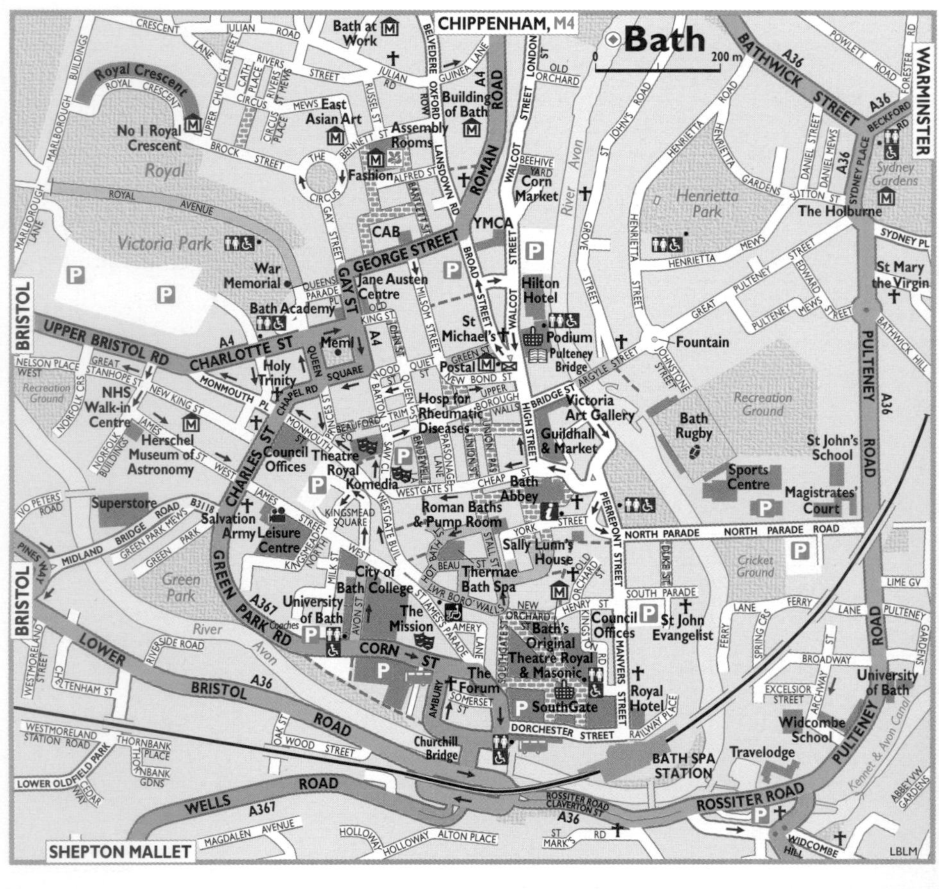
Bath
0
200 m
CHIPPENHAM, M4
WARMINSTER
BRISTOL
SHEPTON MALLET
Royal Crescent
No 1 Royal Crescent
Royal Victoria Park
Victoria Park
Bath at Work
Building of Bath
East Asian Art
Assembly Rooms
Fashion
CAB
YMCA
Corn Market
Henrietta Park
The Holburne
Sydney Gardens
St Mary the Virgin
War Memorial
Jane Austen Centre
Bath Academy
St Michael's
Hilton Hotel
Podium
Pulteney Bridge
Fountain
Holy Trinity
Memi
Postal
NHS Walk-in Centre
Hosp for Rheumatic Diseases
Victoria Art Gallery
Guildhall & Market
Bath Rugby
Recreation Ground
St John's School
Herschel Museum of Astronomy
Council Offices
Theatre Royal
Komedia
Bath Abbey
Sports Centre
Magistrates' Court
Superstore
Salvation Army
Roman Baths & Pump Room
Leisure Centre
Sally Lunn's House
NORTH PARADE
Cricket Ground
Green Park
City of Bath College
Thermae Bath Spa
University of Bath
The Mission
Bath's Original Theatre Royal & Masonic
Council Offices
St John Evangelist
CORN ST
The Forum
SouthGate
Royal Hotel
University of Bath
Churchill Bridge
Widcombe School
Travelodge
BATH SPA STATION
ROSSITER ROAD
WELLS ROAD
A367
A36
A4
LOWER BRISTOL ROAD
UPPER BRISTOL RD
CHARLOTTE ST
GEORGE STREET
PULTENEY ROAD
ROMAN ROAD
GREEN PARK RD
CHARLES ST
BATHWICK STREET
Kennet & Avon Canal
River Avon
LBLM

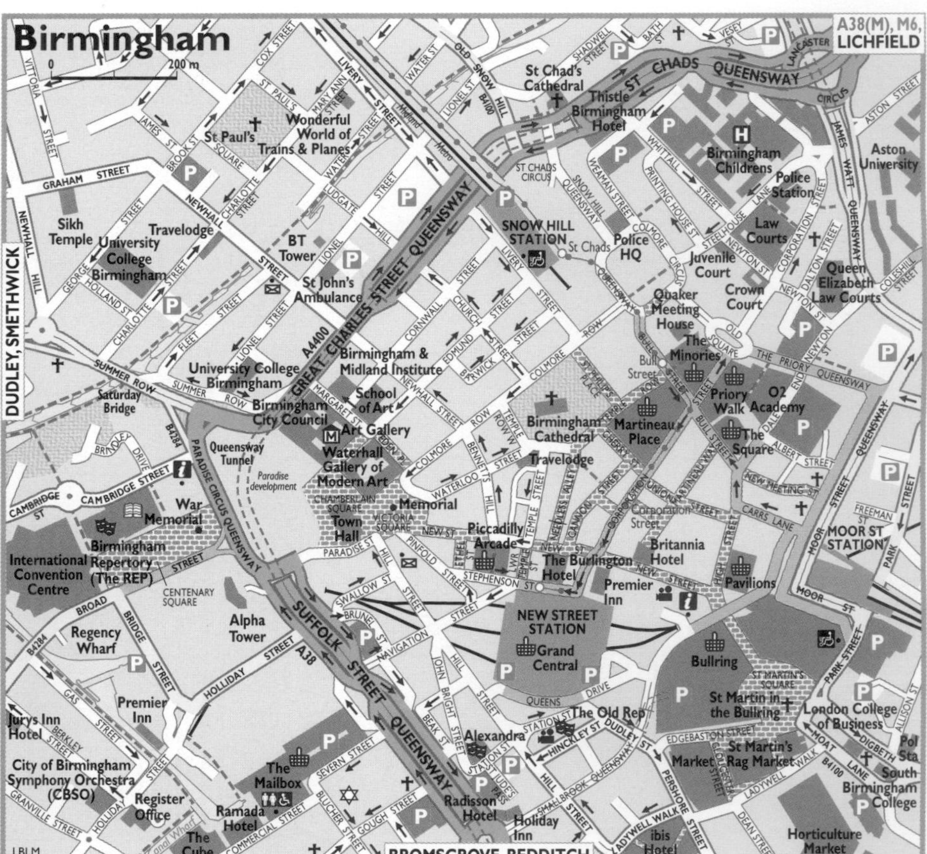
Birmingham
0
200 m
A38(M), M6, LICHFIELD
DUDLEY, SMETHWICK
BROMSGROVE, REDDITCH
St Chad's Cathedral
Thistle Birmingham Hotel
ST CHADS QUEENSWAY
St Paul's
Wonderful World of Trains & Planes
Birmingham Children's
Police Station
Aston University
Sikh Temple
Travelodge
University College Birmingham
BT Tower
St John's Ambulance
SNOW HILL STATION
St Chad's
Police HQ
Law Courts
Juvenile Court
Crown Court
Queen Elizabeth Law Courts
Quaker Meeting House
The Minories
University College Birmingham
Birmingham & Midland Institute
School of Art
Birmingham City Council
Art Gallery
Birmingham Cathedral
Martineau Place
Priory Walk
O2 Academy
The Square
Travelodge
Queensway Tunnel
Waterhall Gallery of Modern Art
Saturday Bridge
War Memorial
Birmingham Repertory (The REP)
International Convention Centre
Town Hall
Memorial
Piccadilly Arcade
The Burlington Hotel
Corporation Street
Britannia Hotel
MOOR ST STATION
Pavilions
NEW STREET STATION
Grand Central
Premier Inn
Bullring
Regency Wharf
Alpha Tower
CENTENARY SQUARE
St Martin in the Bullring
London College of Business
Premier Inn
The Old Rep
Alexandra
Market
St Martin's Rag Market
South Birmingham College
Jurys Inn Hotel
City of Birmingham Symphony Orchestra (CBSO)
The Mailbox
Register Office
Ramada Hotel
The Cube
Radisson Hotel
Holiday Inn
Ibis Hotel
Horticulture Market
GREAT CHARLES STREET QUEENSWAY
SUFFOLK STREET QUEENSWAY
GRAHAM STREET
A38
A4400
LBLM

Blackpool
0
200 m
FLEETWOOD
BLACKPOOL NORTH STATION
LANCASTER
PRESTON, (M55)
LYTHAM ST ANNES
PRESTON, (M55)
Medical Centre
Sports Barn
Metropole Hotel
Grundy Art Gallery
Superstore
Superstore
Council Office
Jobcentre Plus
Sacred Heart
North Pier
Travelodge
St John the Evangelist
TALBOT ROAD
GEORGE STREET
COOKSON ST
GROSVENOR ST
CHURCH STREET
Salvation Army
St John's School
Winter Gardens
Grand
Medical Centre
Meeting House
Tower Festival Headland
The Blackpool Tower
Houndshill
Council Offices
Register Office
St John Ambulance
Spiritualist
Kingdom Hall
Blackpool & Fylde College
Coral Island
ALBERT ROAD
CORONATION STREET
Lifeboat Station
Market
Sea Life
Police Station
County Court
Blackpool & Fylde College
Madame Tussauds Blackpool
Magistrates' Court
Central Pier
CENTRAL DRIVE
PROMENADE
LBLM

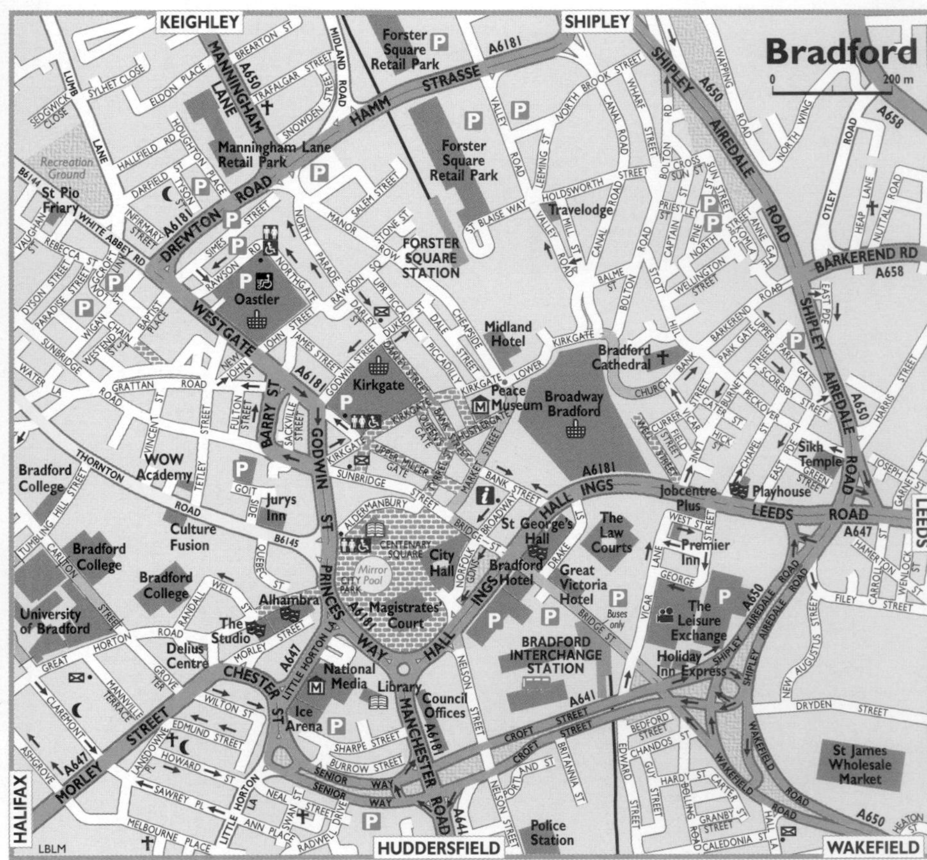
Bradford
0
200 m
KEIGHLEY
SHIPLEY
HALIFAX
HUDDERSFIELD
WAKEFIELD
LEEDS
Forster Square Retail Park
Forster Square Retail Park
Manningham Lane Retail Park
St Pio Friary
Recreation Ground
FORSTER SQUARE STATION
Travelodge
Oastler
Midland Hotel
Bradford Cathedral
Kirkgate
Peace Museum
Broadway Bradford
Bradford College
WOW Academy
Jurys Inn
Culture Fusion
Bradford College
Bradford College
University of Bradford
City Hall
St George's Hall
Bradford Hotel
Great Victoria Hotel
Law Courts
Jobcentre Plus
Sikh Temple
Playhouse
Premier Inn
The Leisure Exchange
Holiday Inn Express
BRADFORD INTERCHANGE STATION
Magistrates' Court
Alhambra
The Studio
Delius Centre
National Media
Library
Council Offices
Ice Arena
Police Station
St James Wholesale Market
MANNINGHAM LANE
DREWTON ROAD
WESTGATE
GODWIN ST
PRINCES WAY
MANCHESTER ROAD
HALL INGS
MORLEY STREET
BARKEREND RD
LEEDS ROAD
A650
A658
A6181
A641
LBLM

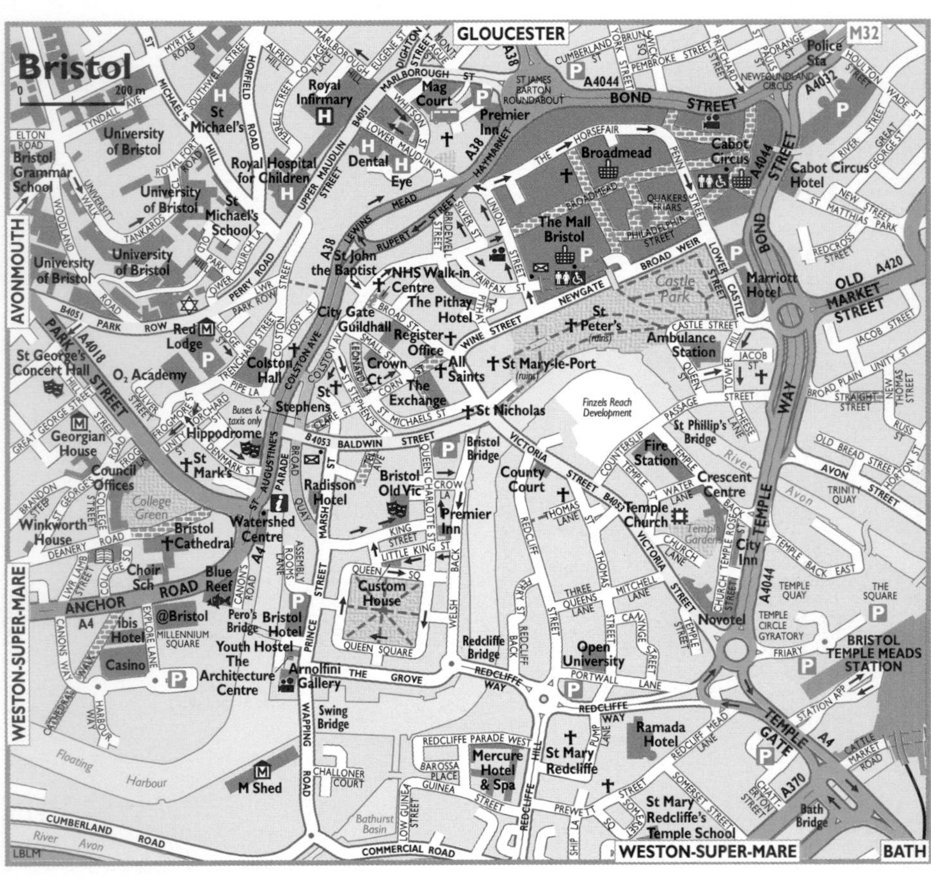
Bristol
0
200 m
GLOUCESTER
M32
AVONMOUTH
WESTON-SUPER-MARE
WESTON-SUPER-MARE
BATH
St Michael's
University of Bristol
Royal Infirmary
Mag Court
Premier Inn
Police Sta
Bristol Grammar School
Royal Hospital for Children
Dental
Eye
Broadmead
Cabot Circus
Cabot Circus Hotel
University of Bristol
St Michael's School
University of Bristol
University of Bristol
St John the Baptist
NHS Walk-in Centre
The Mall Bristol
The Pithay Hotel
Marriott Hotel
Castle Park
City Gate
Guildhall
Register Office
St Peter's
Ambulance Station
Red Lodge
St George's Concert Hall
O2 Academy
Colston Hall
Crown Ct
All Saints
St Mary-le-Port
The Exchange
St Stephens
St Nicholas
Finzels Reach Development
St Philip's Bridge
Hippodrome
Georgian House
St Mark's
Council Offices
College Green
Radisson Hotel
Bristol Old Vic
Bristol Bridge
County Court
Fire Station
Crescent Centre
Premier Inn
Temple Church
Winkworth House
Bristol Cathedral
Watershed Centre
Choir Sch
Blue Reef
Custom House
Novotel
@Bristol
Ibis Hotel
Millennium Square
Pero's Bridge
Bristol Hotel
Youth Hostel
Casino
The Architecture Centre
Arnolfini Gallery
Redcliffe Bridge
Open University
BRISTOL TEMPLE MEADS STATION
Swing Bridge
Floating Harbour
M Shed
Mercure Hotel & Spa
St Mary Redcliffe
Ramada Hotel
St Mary Redcliffe's Temple School
Bathurst Basin
Bath Bridge
TEMPLE GATE
TEMPLE WAY
BOND STREET
OLD MARKET STREET
PARK STREET
ANCHOR ROAD
CUMBERLAND ROAD
COMMERCIAL ROAD
A4044
A420
A38
A4
LBLM

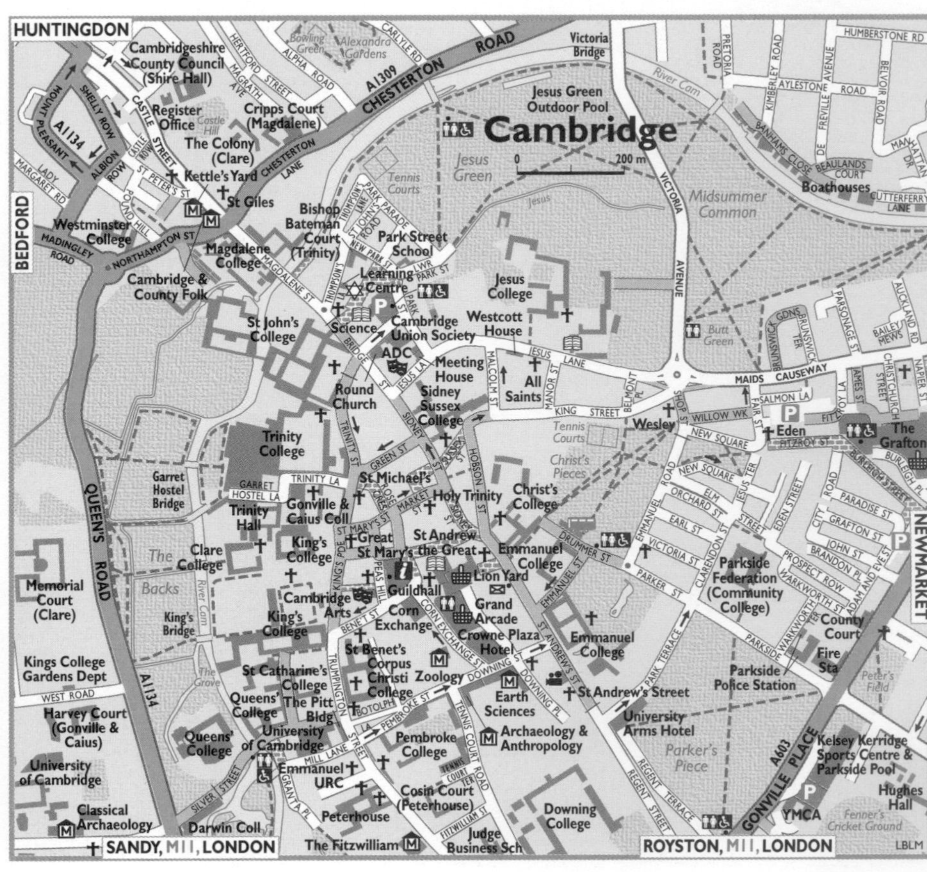
Cambridge
0
200 m
HUNTINGDON
BEDFORD
NEWMARKET
SANDY, M11, LONDON
ROYSTON, M11, LONDON
Cambridgeshire County Council (Shire Hall)
Victoria Bridge
Jesus Green Outdoor Pool
Register Office
Castle Hill
Cripps Court (Magdalene)
The Colony (Clare)
Kettle's Yard
St Giles
Jesus Green
Midsummer Common
Boathouses
Westminster College
Bishop Bateman Court (Trinity)
Park Street School
Magdalene College
Jesus College
Cambridge & County Folk
Learning Centre
St John's College
Science
Cambridge Union Society
Westcott House
ADC
Meeting House
All Saints
Round Church
Sidney Sussex College
Wesley
Eden
The Grafton
Trinity College
Garret Hostel Bridge
St Michael's
Holy Trinity
Christ's College
Christ's Pieces
Trinity Hall
Gonville & Caius Coll
Clare College
King's College
Great St Mary's
St Andrew the Great
Emmanuel College
Parkside Federation (Community College)
Memorial Court (Clare)
The Backs
King's Bridge
Cambridge Arts
Guildhall
Lion Yard
Grand Arcade
Corn Exchange
Crowne Plaza Hotel
Emmanuel College
County Court
Fire Sta
Kings College Gardens Dept
St Catharine's College
Queens' College
The Pitt Bldg
St Benet's
Corpus Christi College
Zoology
Earth Sciences
St Andrew's Street
Parkside Police Station
Harvey Court (Gonville & Caius)
University of Cambridge
Queens' College
University of Cambridge
Archaeology & Anthropology
University Arms Hotel
Parker's Piece
University of Cambridge
Emmanuel URC
Pembroke College
Cosin Court (Peterhouse)
Downing College
Kelsey Kerridge Sports Centre & Parkside Pool
Hughes Hall
Classical Archaeology
Darwin Coll
Peterhouse
YMCA
The Fitzwilliam
Judge Business Sch
Fenner's Cricket Ground
CHESTERTON ROAD
QUEEN'S ROAD
MAIDS CAUSEWAY
GONVILLE PLACE
A1134
A1303
A603
LBLM

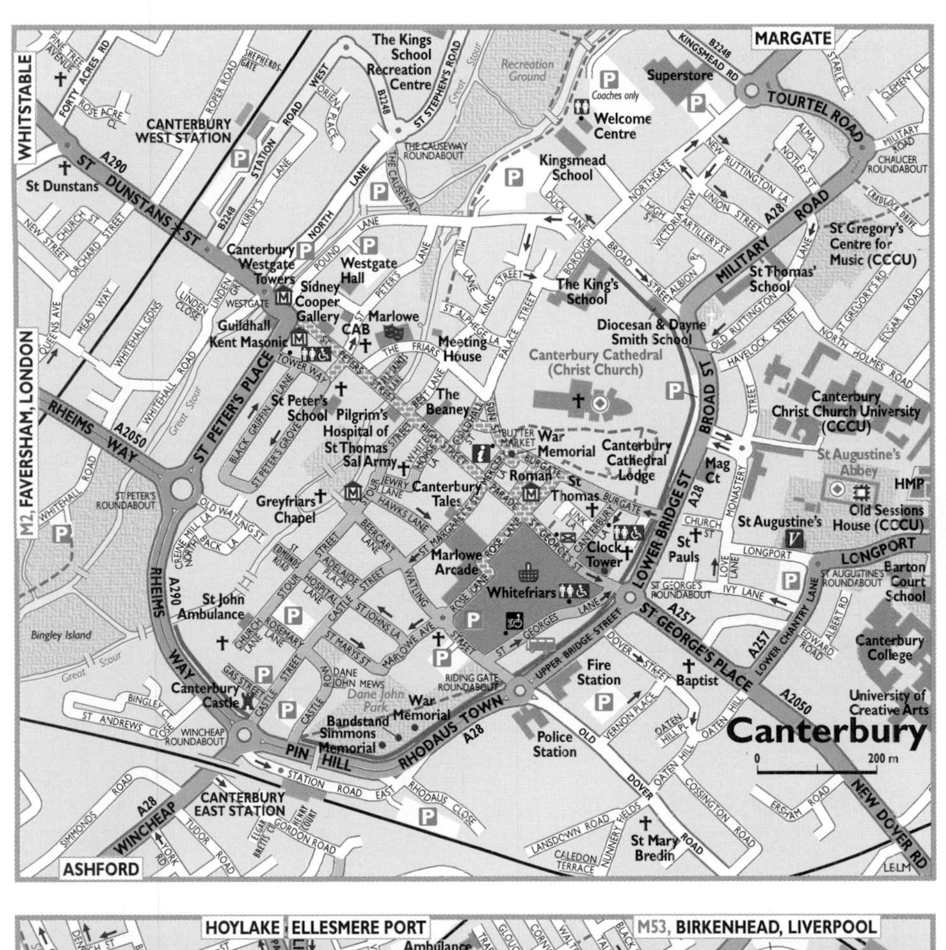
Canterbury
MARGATE
WHITSTABLE
M2, FAVERSHAM, LONDON
ASHFORD
NEW DOVER RD
CANTERBURY WEST STATION
CANTERBURY EAST STATION
St Dunstans
ST DUNSTANS ST
The Kings School Recreation Centre
Superstore
Welcome Centre
Kingsmead School
TOURTEL ROAD
MILITARY ROAD
St Gregory's Centre for Music (CCCU)
St Thomas' School
The King's School
Canterbury Westgate Towers
Westgate Hall
Sidney Cooper Gallery
Marlowe
Guildhall
Kent Masonic
CAB
Meeting House
Diocesan & Dayne Smith School
Canterbury Cathedral (Christ Church)
Canterbury Christ Church University (CCCU)
St Peter's School
Pilgrim's Hospital of St Thomas
The Beaney
ST PETER'S PLACE
RHEIMS WAY
War Memorial
Canterbury Cathedral Lodge
St Augustine's Abbey
HMP
Old Sessions House (CCCU)
Greyfriars Chapel
Sal Army
Canterbury Tales
Roman
St Thomas
Mag Ct
St Augustine's
St Pauls
Clock Tower
Marlowe Arcade
Whitefriars
LONGPORT
Barton Court School
St John Ambulance
Canterbury College
Fire Station
Baptist
ST GEORGE'S PLACE
LOWER BRIDGE ST
Canterbury Castle
War Memorial
Bandstand
Simmons Memorial
University of Creative Arts
Police Station
RHODAUS TOWN
PIN HILL
WINCHEAP
St Mary Bredin
200 m
LBLM

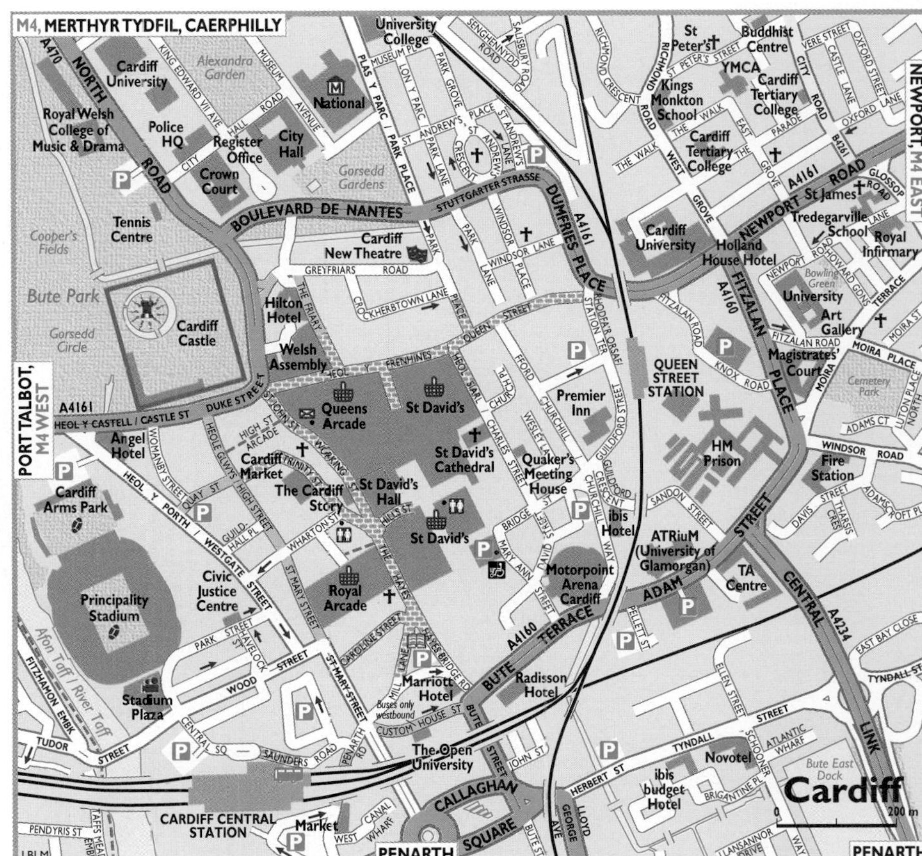
Cardiff
M4, MERTHYR TYDFIL, CAERPHILLY
NEWPORT, M4 EAST
PORT TALBOT, M4 WEST
PENARTH
University College
Cardiff University
National
Royal Welsh College of Music & Drama
Police HQ
Register Office
City Hall
Crown Court
Gorsedd Gardens
Tennis Centre
BOULEVARD DE NANTES
Cardiff New Theatre
St Peter's
Buddhist Centre
YMCA
Kings Monkton School
Cardiff Tertiary College
Cardiff University
Holland House Hotel
Tredegarville School
Royal Infirmary
University Art Gallery
Magistrates' Court
Bute Park
Cardiff Castle
Hilton Hotel
Welsh Assembly
Queens Arcade
St David's
St David's Cathedral
Premier Inn
Quaker's Meeting House
QUEEN STREET STATION
HM Prison
Fire Station
Angel Hotel
Cardiff Arms Park
Cardiff Market
The Cardiff Story
St David's Hall
ibis Hotel
ATRiuM (University of Glamorgan)
TA Centre
Principality Stadium
Civic Justice Centre
Royal Arcade
Motorpoint Arena Cardiff
Stadium Plaza
Marriott Hotel
Radisson Hotel
BUTE TERRACE
CENTRAL LINK
The Open University
CARDIFF CENTRAL STATION
Market
CALLAGHAN SQUARE
ibis budget Hotel
Novotel
200 m
LBLM

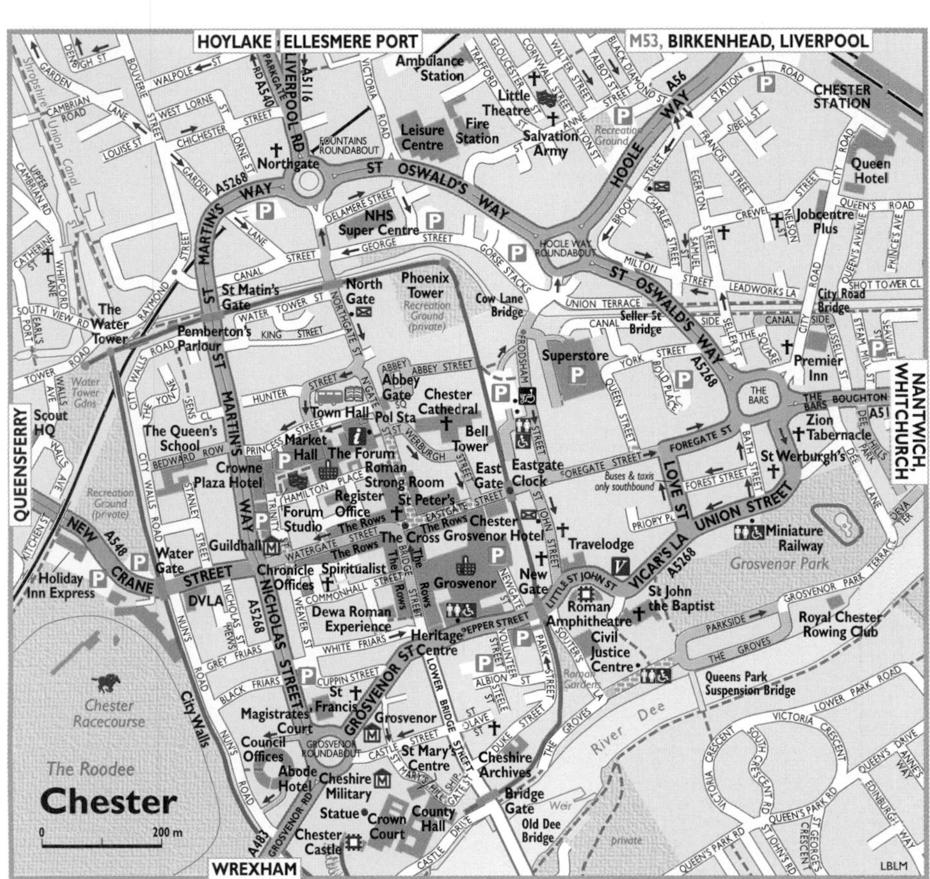
Chester
HOYLAKE
ELLESMERE PORT
M53, BIRKENHEAD, LIVERPOOL
QUEENSFERRY
NANTWICH, WHITCHURCH
WREXHAM
Ambulance Station
Little Theatre
Fire Station
Salvation Army
Leisure Centre
CHESTER STATION
Queen Hotel
Northgate
ST OSWALD'S WAY
NHS Super Centre
Jobcentre Plus
St Matin's Gate
North Gate
Phoenix Tower
Cow Lane Bridge
City Road Bridge
The Water Tower
Pemberton's Parlour
Superstore
Premier Inn
Abbey Gate
Chester Cathedral
Town Hall
Pol Sta
Bell Tower
Zion Tabernacle
St Werburgh's
The Queen's School
Market Hall
The Forum
Roman Strong Room
Eastgate Clock
Crowne Plaza Hotel
Forum Studio
Register Office
St Peter's
The Cross
Grosvenor Hotel
Guildhall
Chronicle Offices
Spiritualist
Travelodge
Miniature Railway
Grosvenor Park
Water Gate
DVLA
Grosvenor
New Gate
Roman Amphitheatre
St John the Baptist
Holiday Inn Express
Dewa Roman Experience
Heritage Centre
Civil Justice Centre
Royal Chester Rowing Club
Queens Park Suspension Bridge
Chester Racecourse
The Roodee
St Francis
Magistrates' Court
Grosvenor
St Mary Centre
Council Offices
Abode Hotel
Cheshire Archives
Cheshire Military Statue
Crown Court
County Hall
Chester Castle
Bridge Gate
Old Dee Bridge
River Dee
City Walls
200 m
LBLM

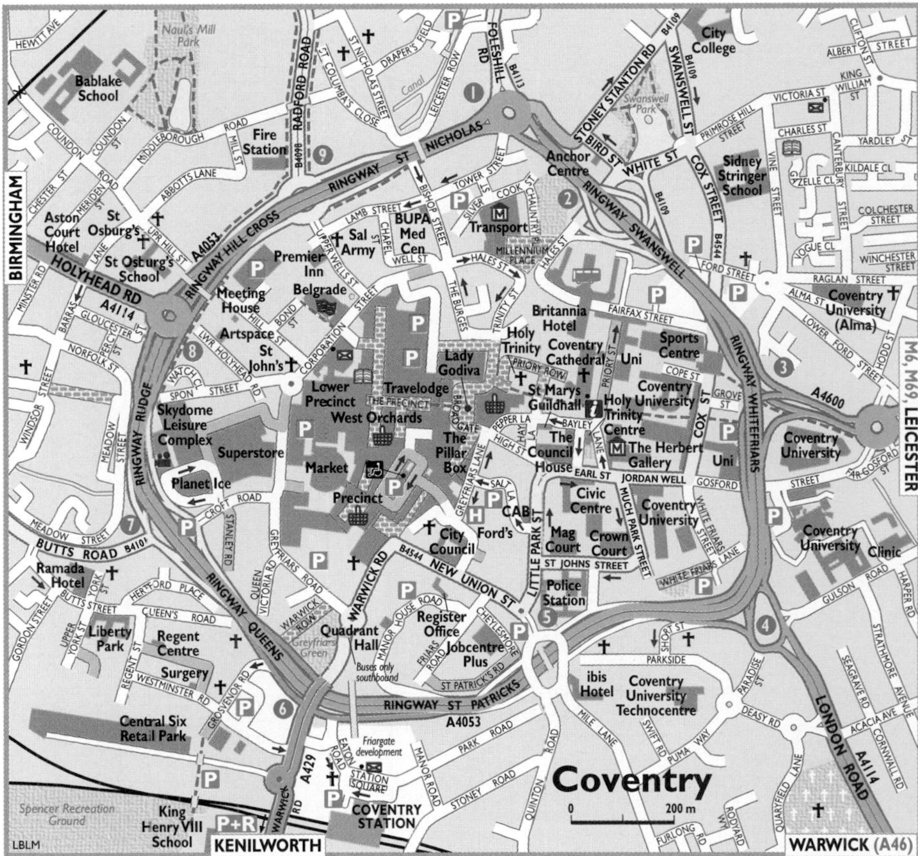
Coventry
BIRMINGHAM
M6, M69, LEICESTER
KENILWORTH
WARWICK (A46)
Bablake School
City College
Fire Station
Sidney Stringer School
Anchor Centre
RINGWAY ST NICHOLAS
Aston Court Hotel
St Osburg's
St Osburg's School
Sal Army
BUPA Med Cen
Transport
Premier Inn
Belgrade
Meeting House
Artspace
St John's
Britannia Hotel
Sports Centre
Coventry University (Alma)
Holy Trinity
Coventry Cathedral
Uni
Lady Godiva
Travelodge
Lower Precinct
West Orchards
Skydome Leisure Complex
Superstore
St Mary's Guildhall
Holy Trinity Centre
The Herbert Gallery
Coventry University
Planet Ice
Market
The Pillory Box
The Council House
Precinct
Civic Centre
Coventry University
CAB
City Council
Ford's
Mag Court
Crown Court
Ramada Hotel
Police Station
Liberty Park
Regent Centre
Surgery
Register Office
Quadrant Hall
Jobcentre Plus
ibis Hotel
Coventry University Technocentre
Central Six Retail Park
RINGWAY ST PATRICKS
RINGWAY QUEENS
King Henry VIII School
COVENTRY STATION
LONDON ROAD
200 m
LBLM

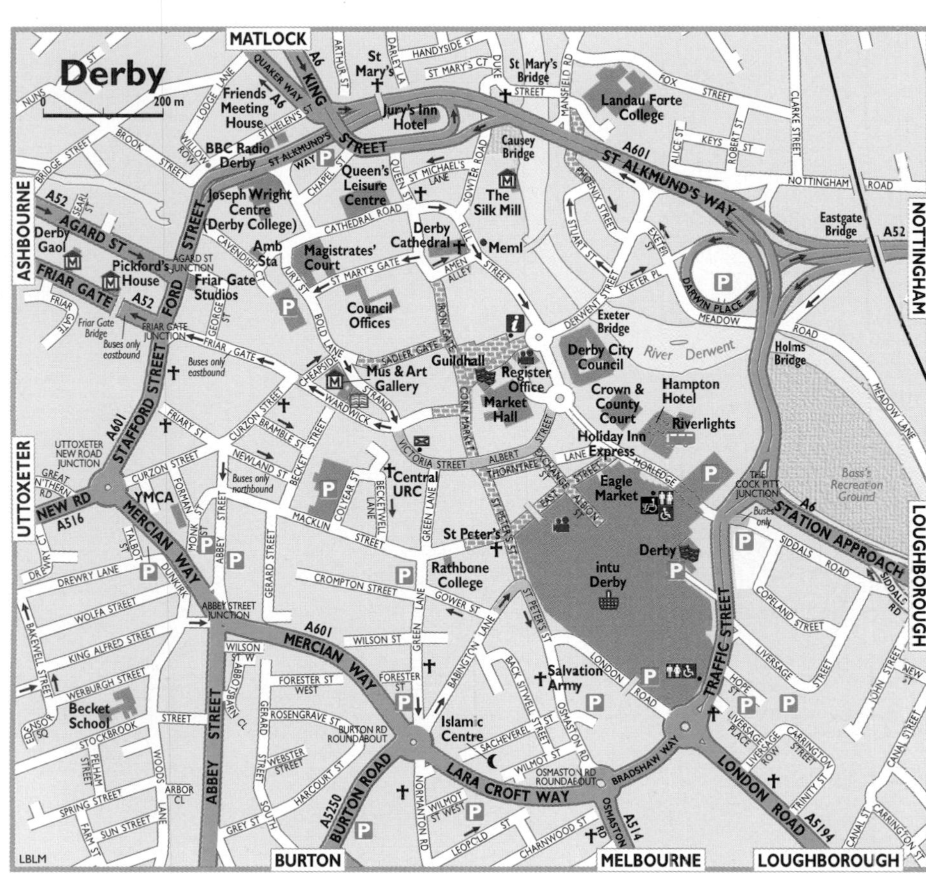
Derby
MATLOCK
ASHBOURNE
UTTOXETER
NOTTINGHAM
LOUGHBOROUGH
BURTON
MELBOURNE
St Mary's
St Mary's Bridge
Friends Meeting House
Jury's Inn Hotel
Landau Forte College
BBC Radio Derby
ST ALKMUND'S WAY
Queen's Leisure Centre
Causey Bridge
Joseph Wright Centre (Derby College)
The Silk Mill
Eastgate Bridge
Derby Gaol
Pickford's House
Derby Cathedral
Magistrates' Court
Friar Gate Studios
Meml
Council Offices
Exeter Bridge
Derby City Council
Holms Bridge
Guildhall
Mus & Art Gallery
Register Office
Market Hall
Crown & County Court
Hampton Hotel
Riverlights
Holiday Inn Express
River Derwent
YMCA
Central URC
Eagle Market
STATION APPROACH
St Peter's
Rathbone College
intu Derby
Derby
Salvation Army
Islamic Centre
MERCIAN WAY
LARA CROFT WAY
ABBEY STREET
BURTON ROAD
LONDON ROAD
TRAFFIC STREET
Becket School
200 m
LBLM

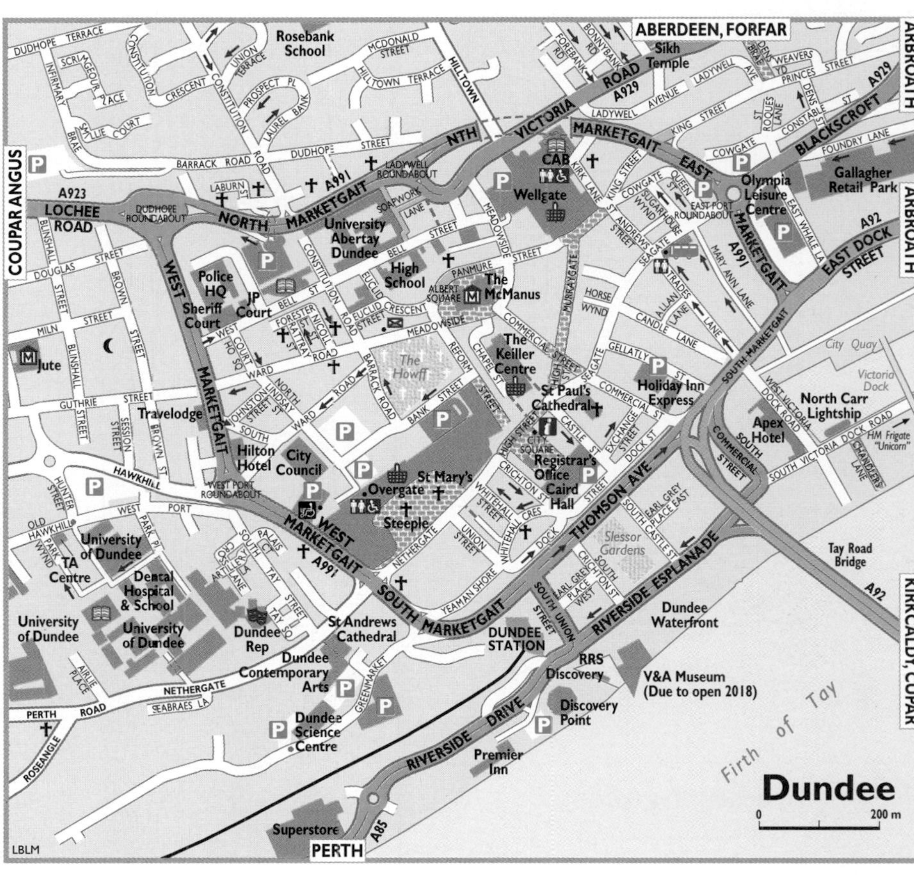
ABERDEEN, FORFAR
ARBROATH
COUPAR ANGUS
KIRKCALDY, CUPAR
PERTH
Rosebank School
Sikh Temple
VICTORIA ROAD
BLACKSCROFT
CAB
Wellgate
Gallagher Retail Park
Olympia Leisure Centre
NORTH MARKETGAIT
University Abertay Dundee
High School
Police HQ
Sheriff Court
JP Court
The McManus
EAST DOCK STREET
Jute
The Howff
The Keiller Centre
St Paul's Cathedral
Holiday Inn Express
North Carr Lightship
Apex Hotel
Travelodge
Hilton Hotel
City Council
Overgate
St Mary's
Steeple
Registrar's Office
Caird Hall
WEST MARKETGAIT
University of Dundee
TA Centre
Dental Hospital & School
University of Dundee
Dundee Rep
St Andrews Cathedral
SOUTH MARKETGAIT
DUNDEE STATION
Dundee Waterfront
Tay Road Bridge
RRS Discovery
V&A Museum (Due to open 2018)
Discovery Point
Dundee Contemporary Arts
Dundee Science Centre
RIVERSIDE DRIVE
RIVERSIDE ESPLANADE
Premier Inn
Superstore
Firth of Tay
Dundee
200 m
LBLM

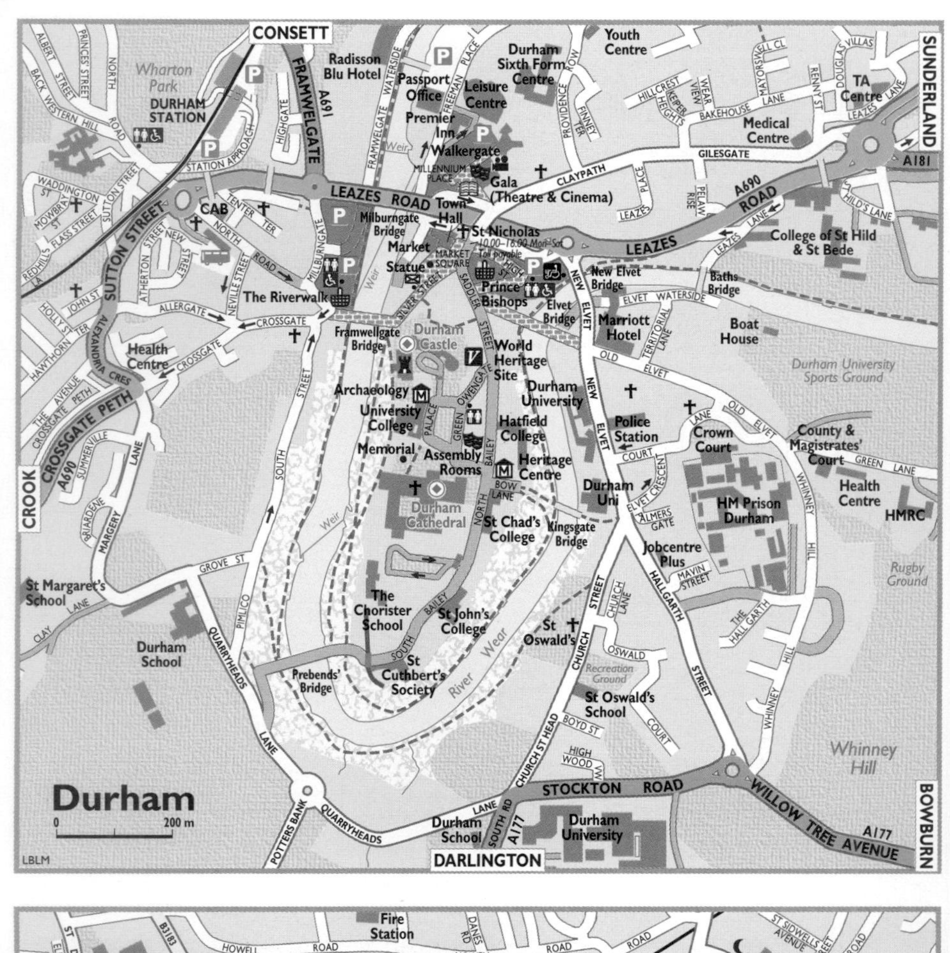

Durham
CONSETT
SUNDERLAND
DARLINGTON
BOWBURN
DURHAM STATION
Durham Cathedral
Durham Castle
World Heritage Site
Durham University
HM Prison Durham
County & Magistrates' Court
College of St Hild & St Bede
Gala (Theatre & Cinema)
LEAZES ROAD
STOCKTON ROAD
WILLOW TREE AVENUE

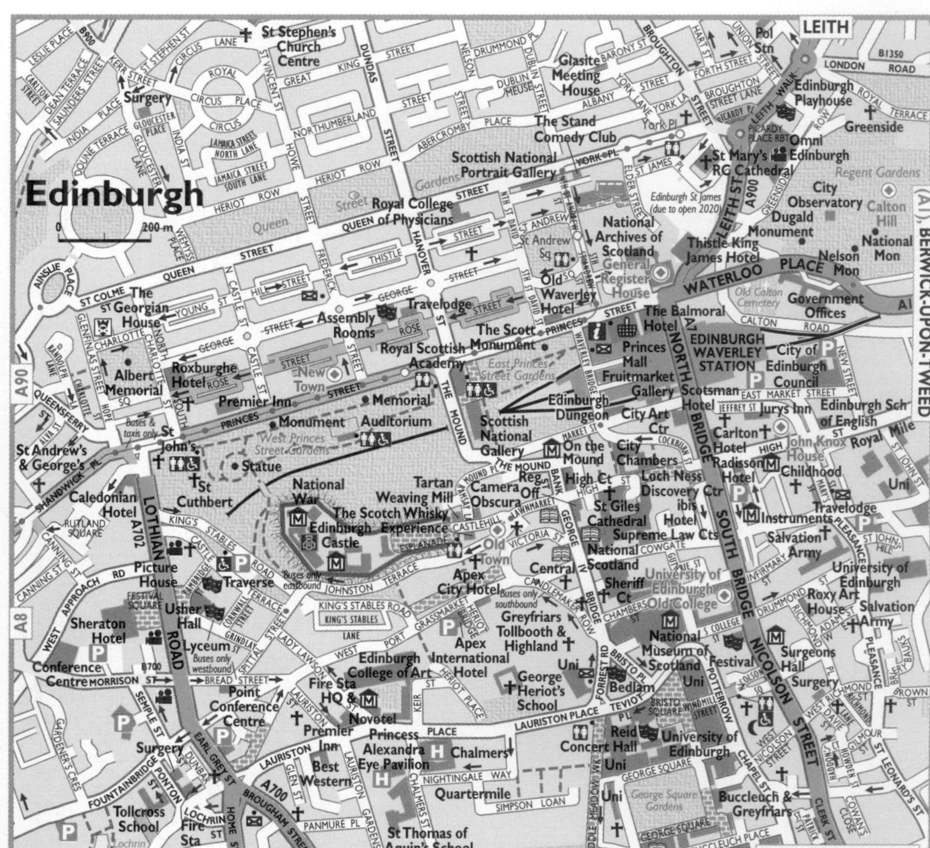

Edinburgh
LEITH
BERWICK-UPON-TWEED
PEEBLES, JEDBURGH
EDINBURGH WAVERLEY STATION
Edinburgh Castle
Scottish National Portrait Gallery
Scottish National Gallery
National Museum of Scotland
The Scotch Whisky Experience
Camera Obscura
St Giles Cathedral
PRINCES STREET
GEORGE STREET
QUEEN STREET
LOTHIAN ROAD

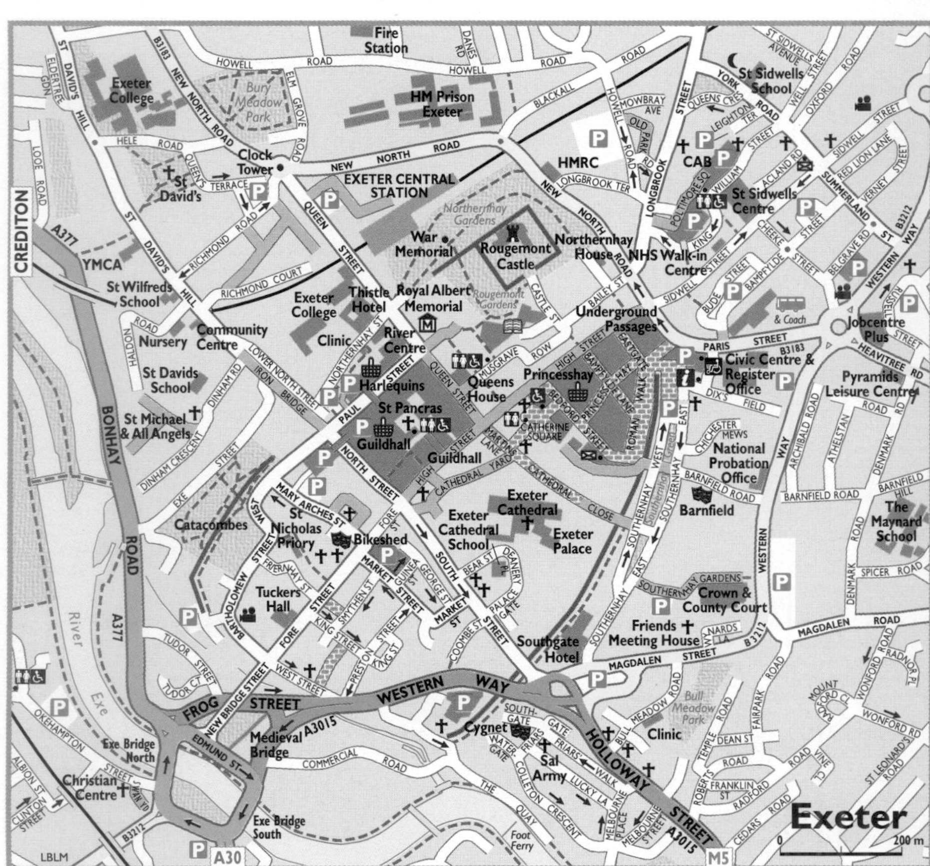

Exeter
CREDITON
EXETER CENTRAL STATION
HM Prison Exeter
Rougemont Castle
Exeter Cathedral
Underground Passages
Princesshay
Guildhall
Civic Centre & Register Office
Crown & County Court
WESTERN WAY
FROG STREET
A30
M5

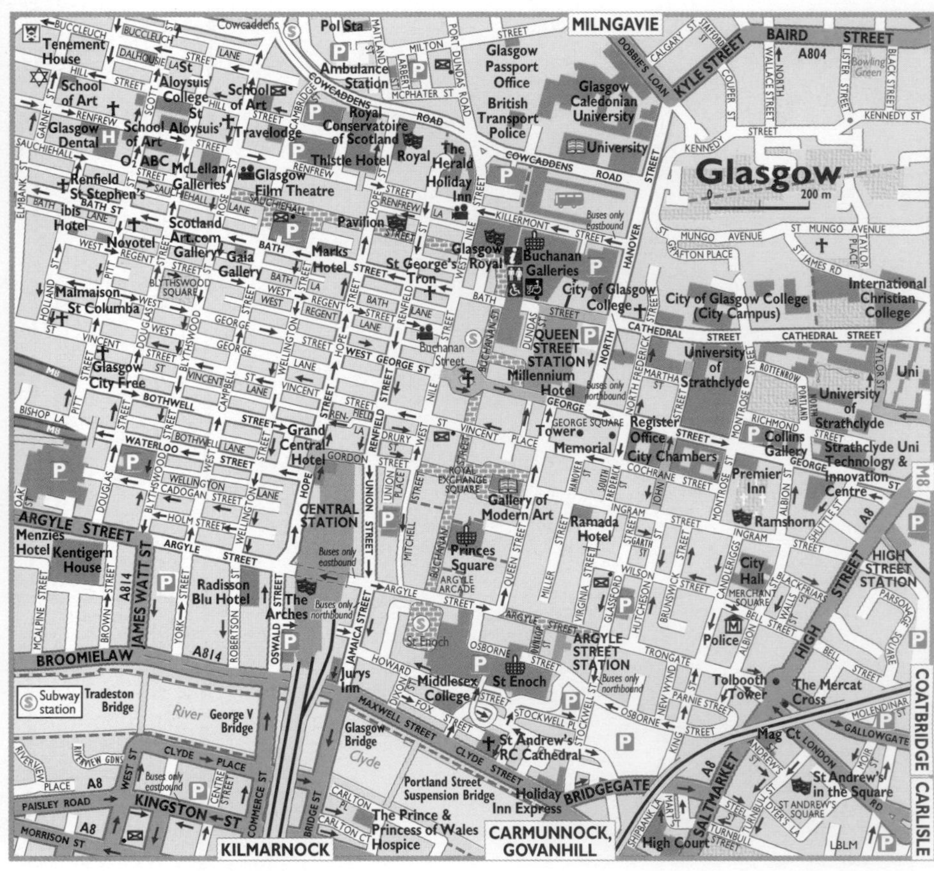

Glasgow
MILNGAVIE
KILMARNOCK
CARMUNNOCK, GOVANHILL
COATBRIDGE
CARLISLE
CENTRAL STATION
QUEEN STREET STATION
HIGH STREET STATION
Glasgow Caledonian University
University of Strathclyde
City Chambers
Gallery of Modern Art
Glasgow School of Art
ARGYLE STREET
BROOMIELAW
KINGSTON ST

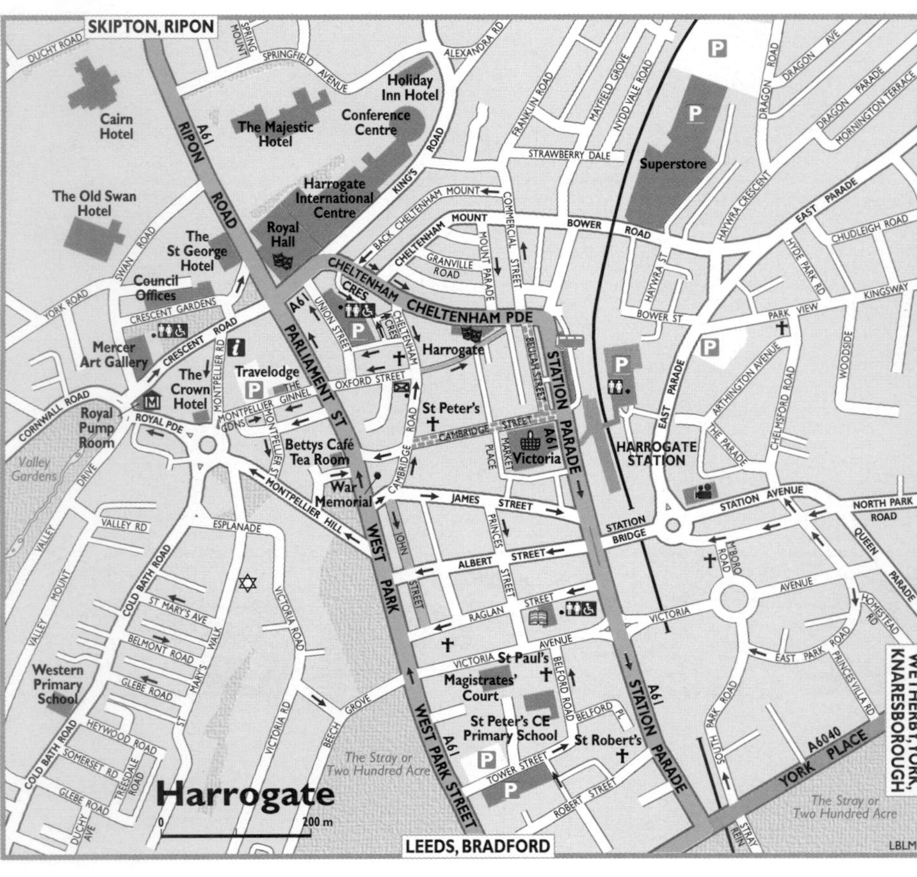

Harrogate
SKIPTON, RIPON
LEEDS, BRADFORD
WETHERBY, YORK, KNARESBOROUGH
HARROGATE STATION
Harrogate International Centre
Royal Hall
Royal Pump Room
Mercer Art Gallery
Bettys Café Tea Room
The Majestic Hotel
The Old Swan Hotel
RIPON ROAD
PARLIAMENT ST
STATION PARADE
YORK PLACE

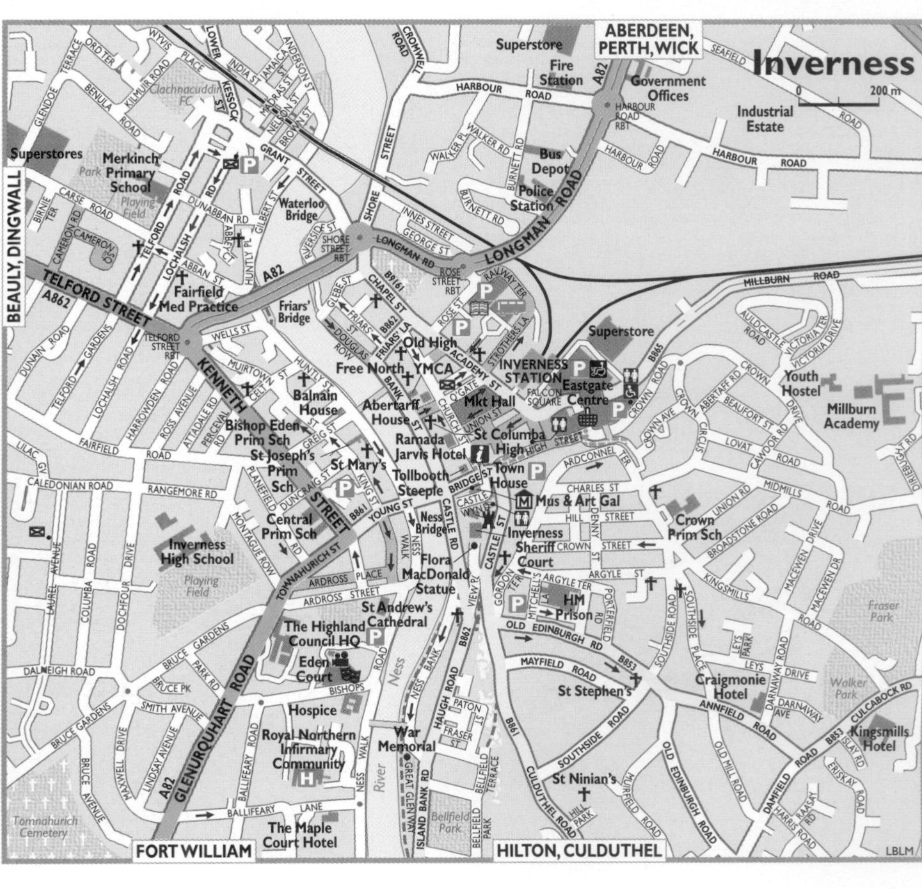

Inverness
ABERDEEN, PERTH, WICK
BEAULY, DINGWALL
FORT WILLIAM
HILTON, CULDUTHEL
INVERNESS STATION
Inverness Castle
St Andrew's Cathedral
Eden Court
Mus & Art Gal
Town House
LONGMAN ROAD
TELFORD STREET
KENNETH STREET
GLENURQUHART ROAD

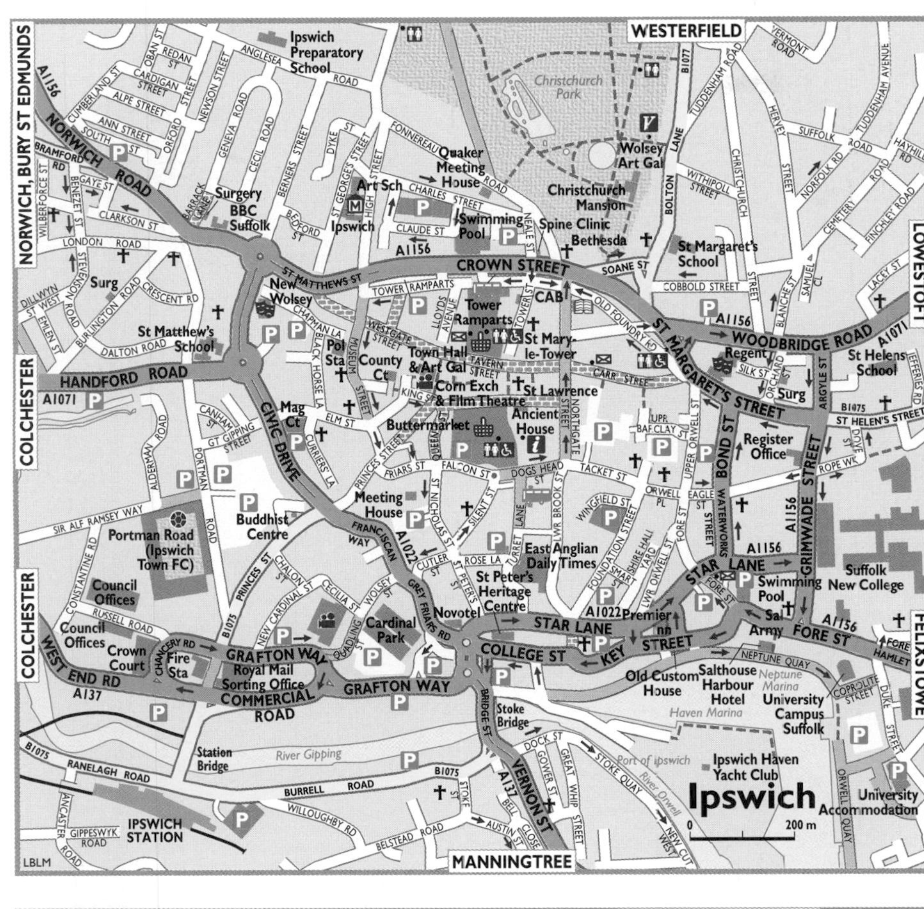
Ipswich
WESTERFIELD
LOWESTOFT
FELIXSTOWE
MANNINGTREE
COLCHESTER
NORWICH, BURY ST EDMUNDS
0 200 m

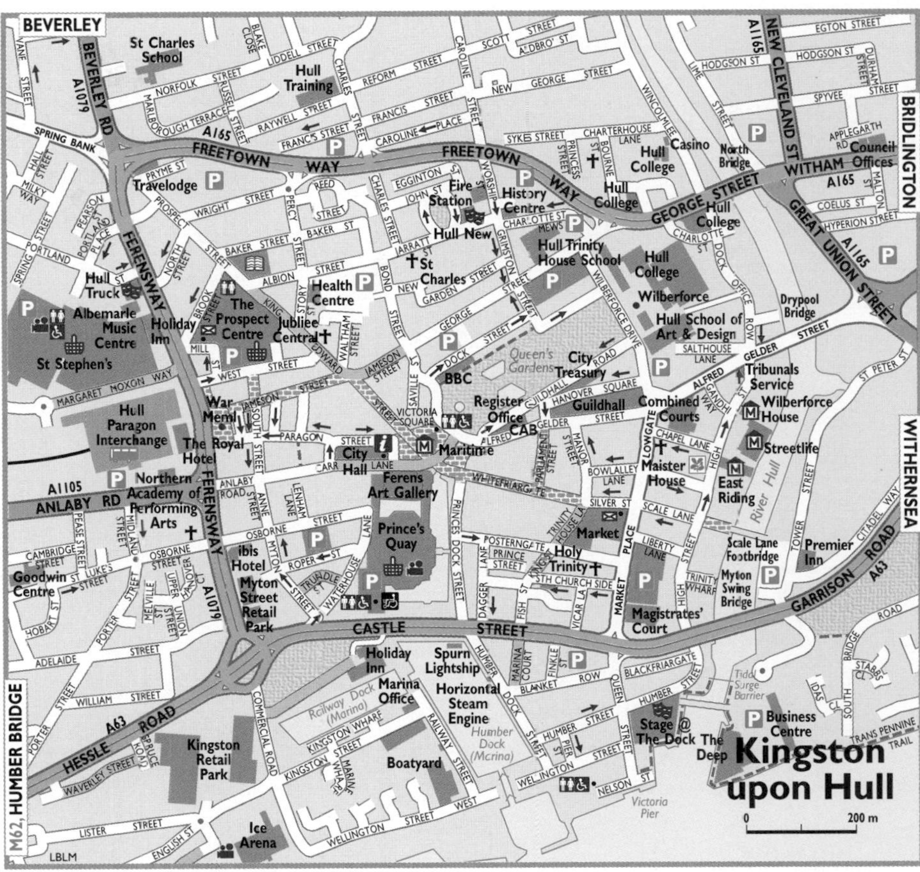
Kingston upon Hull
BEVERLEY
BRIDLINGTON
WITHERNSEA
M62, HUMBER BRIDGE
0 200 m

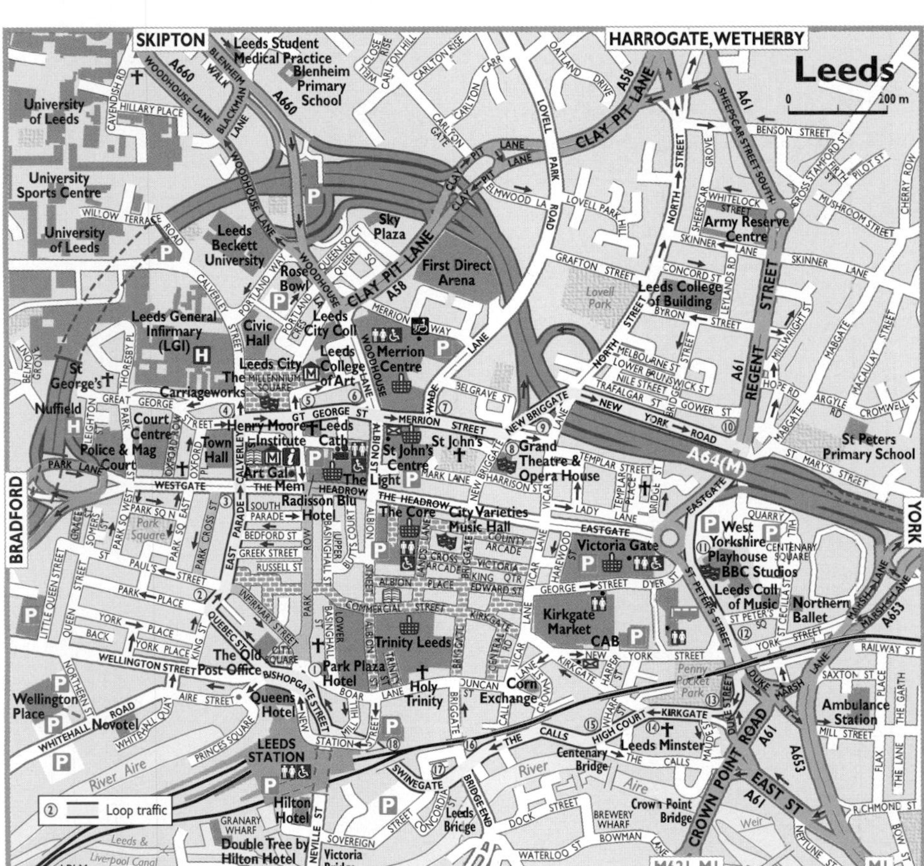
Leeds
SKIPTON
HARROGATE, WETHERBY
YORK
BRADFORD
M621, M1
M1
0 200 m

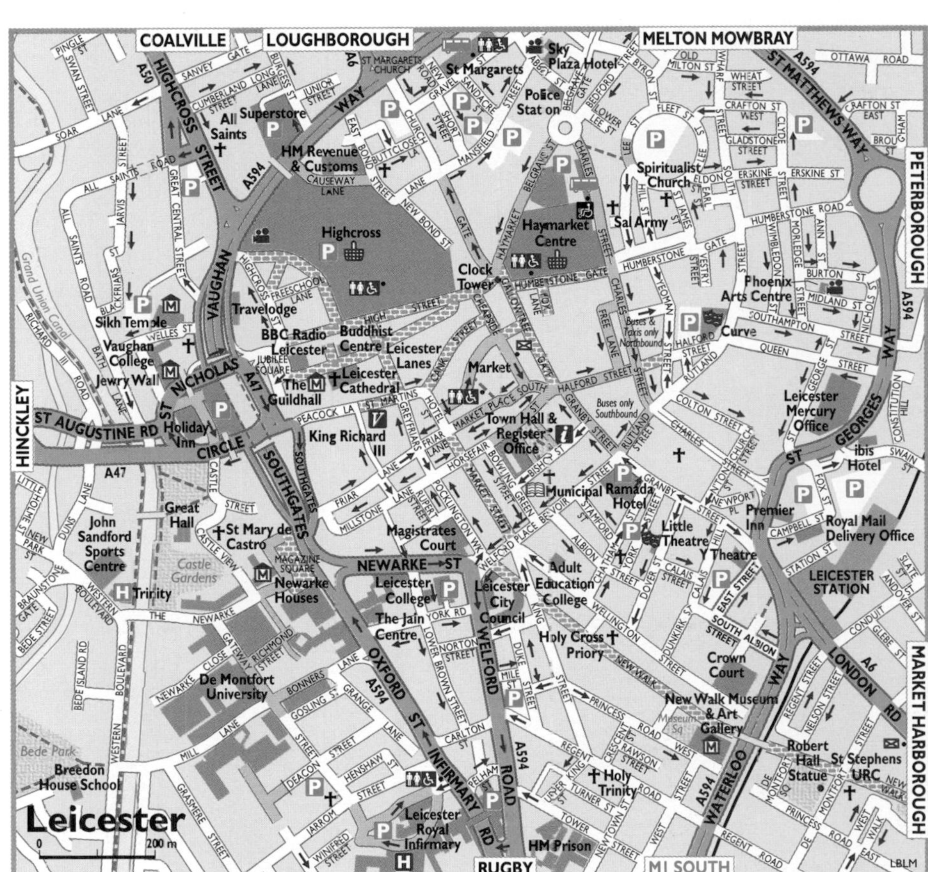
Leicester
COALVILLE
LOUGHBOROUGH
MELTON MOWBRAY
PETERBOROUGH
MARKET HARBOROUGH
HINCKLEY
RUGBY
M1 SOUTH
0 200 m

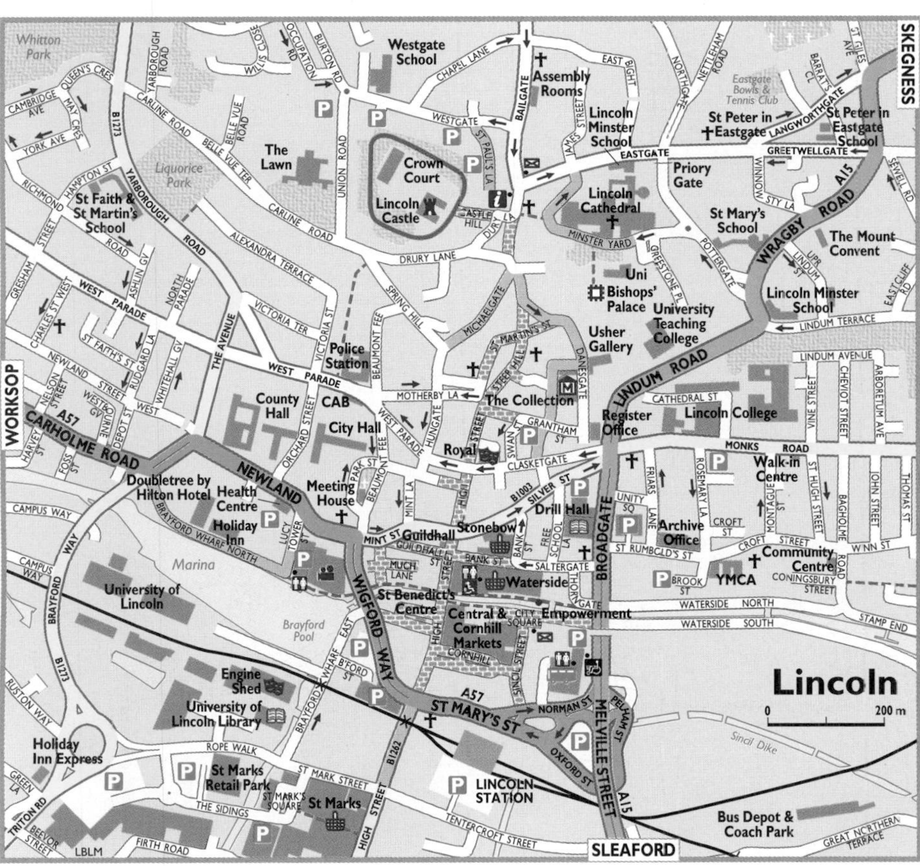
Lincoln
SKEGNESS
WORKSOP
SLEAFORD
0 200 m

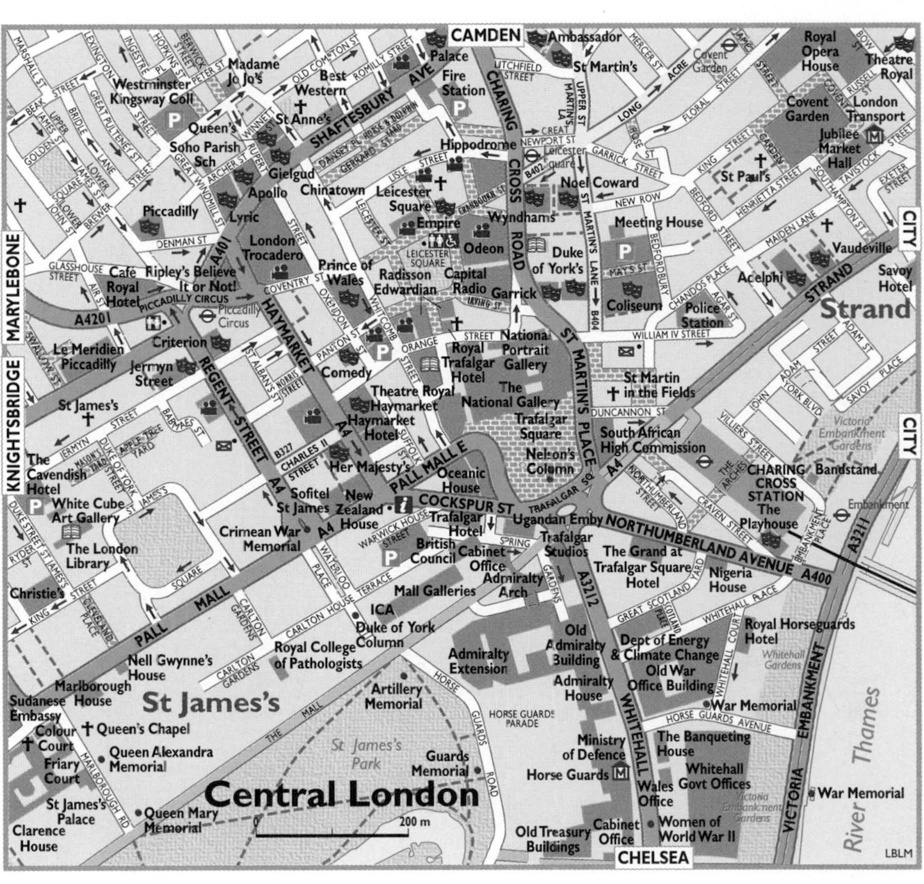
Central London
CAMDEN
CITY
MARYLEBONE
KNIGHTSBRIDGE
CHELSEA
St James's
Strand
0 200 m

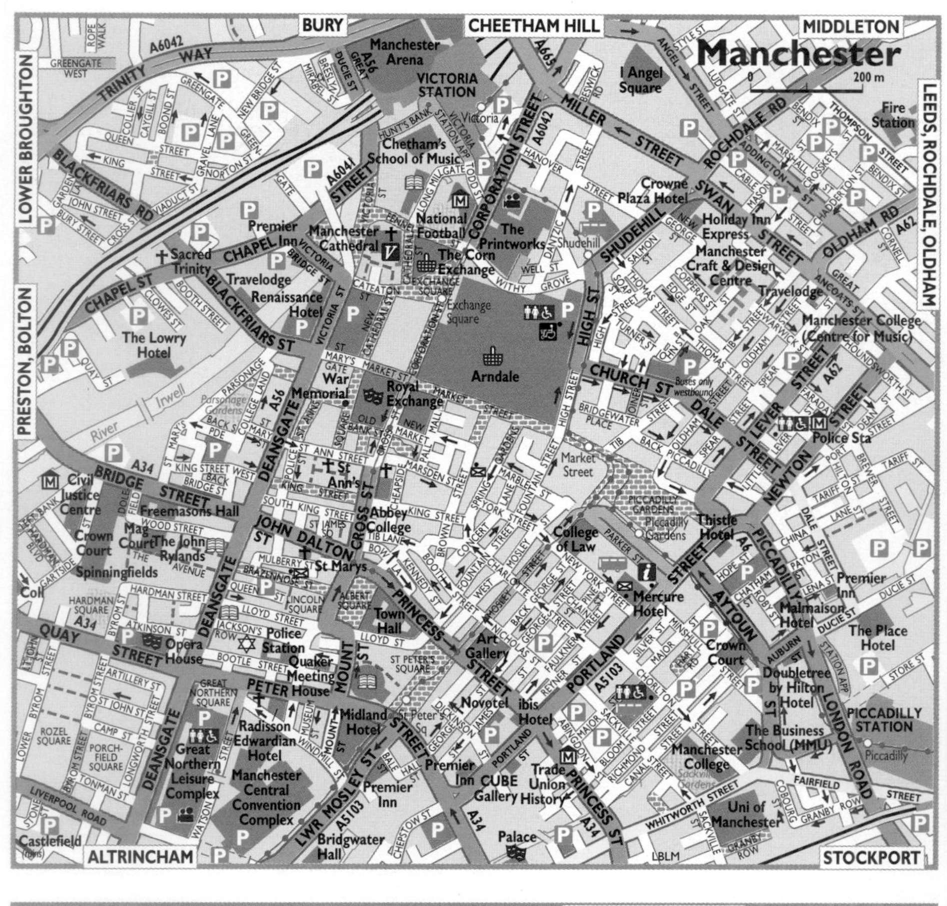
Manchester
0 200 m
BURY
CHEETHAM HILL
MIDDLETON
LEEDS, ROCHDALE, OLDHAM
LOWER BROUGHTON
PRESTON, BOLTON
ALTRINCHAM
STOCKPORT
LBLM

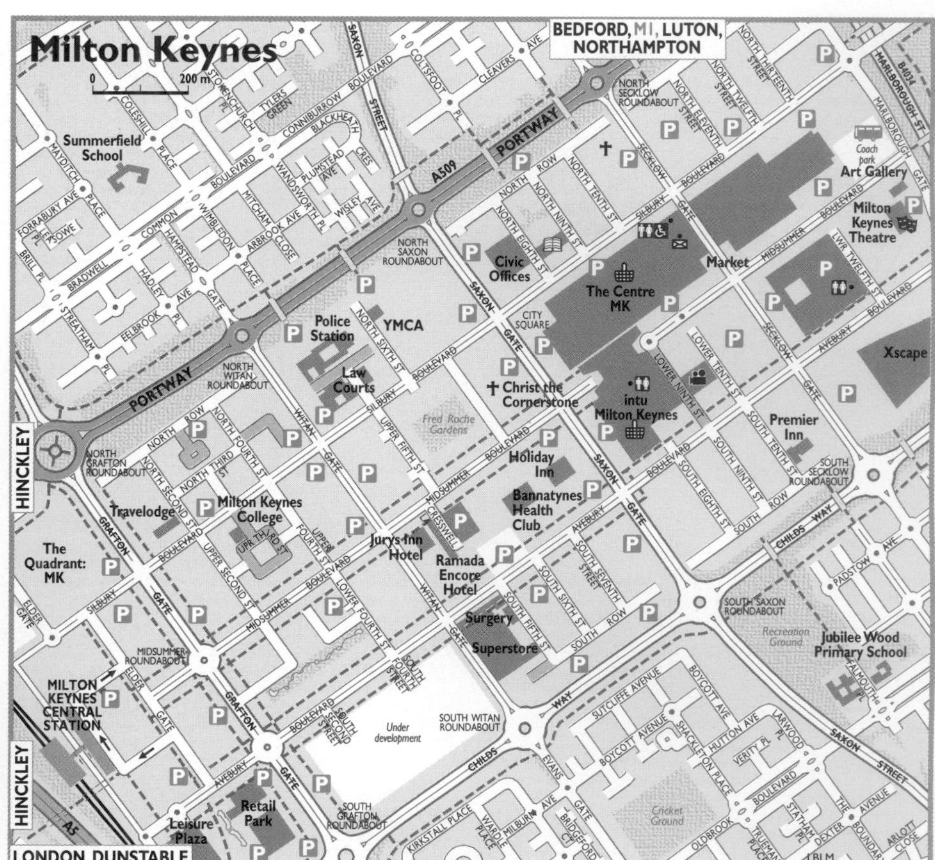
Milton Keynes
0 200 m
BEDFORD, M1, LUTON, NORTHAMPTON
HINCKLEY
LONDON, DUNSTABLE
LBLM

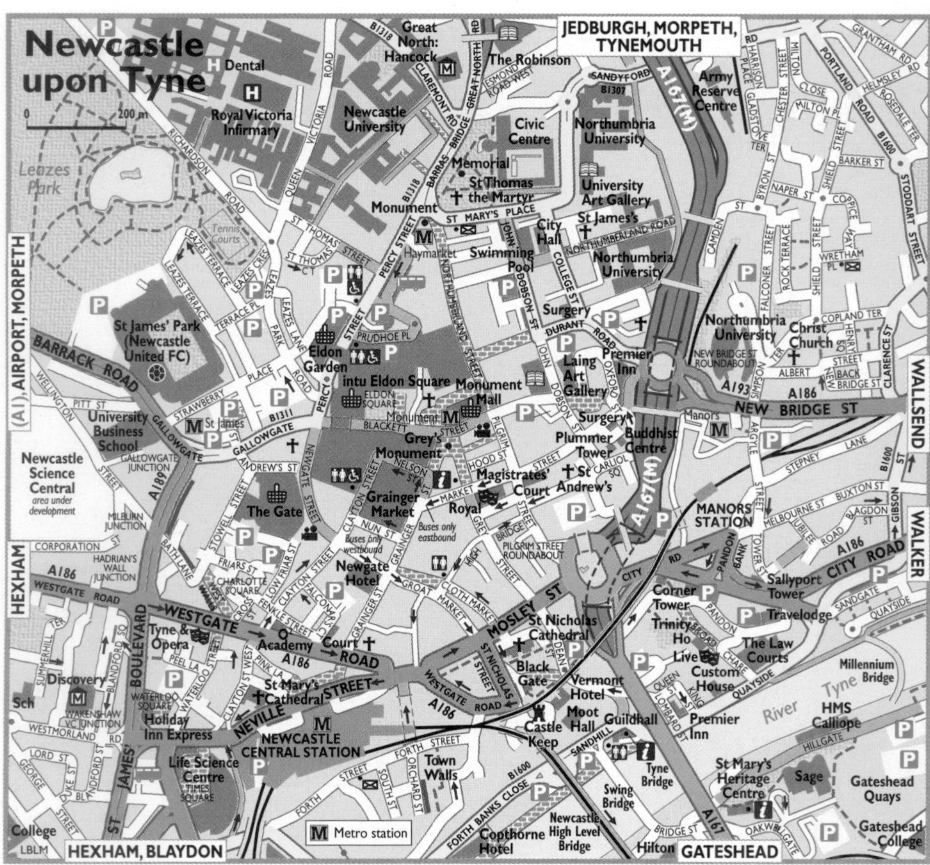
Newcastle upon Tyne
0 200 m
JEDBURGH, MORPETH, TYNEMOUTH
(A1), AIRPORT, MORPETH
WALLSEND
WALKER
HEXHAM
HEXHAM, BLAYDON
GATESHEAD
Metro station
LBLM

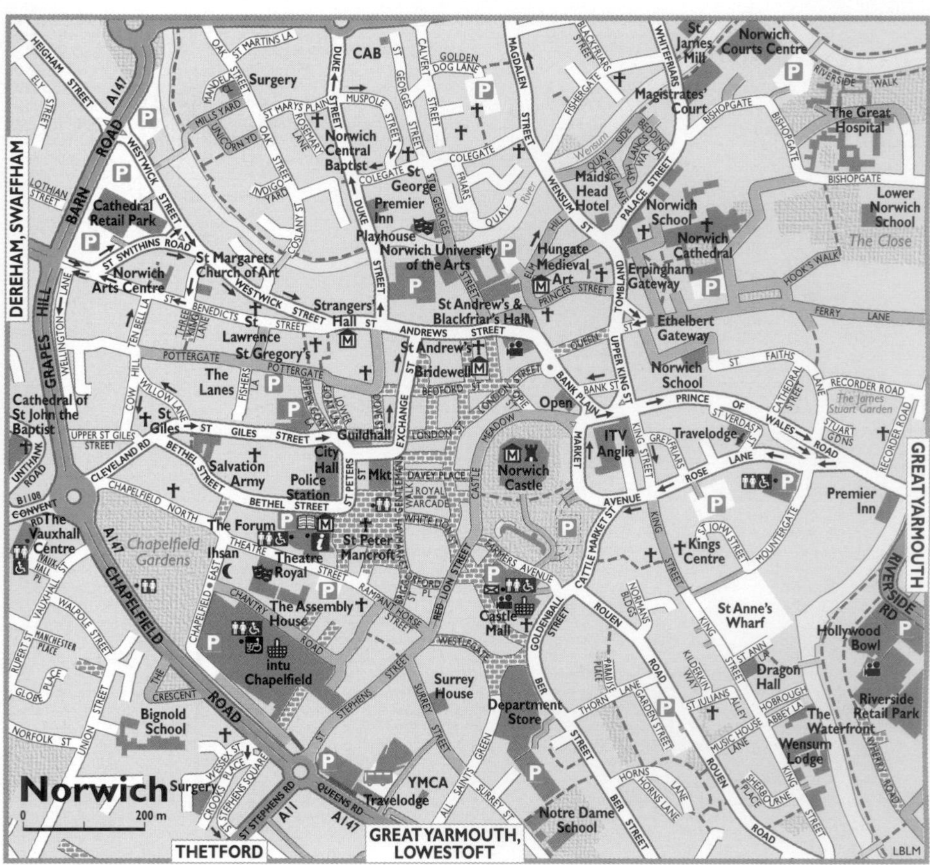
Norwich
0 200 m
DEREHAM, SWAFFHAM
GREAT YARMOUTH
THETFORD
GREAT YARMOUTH, LOWESTOFT
LBLM

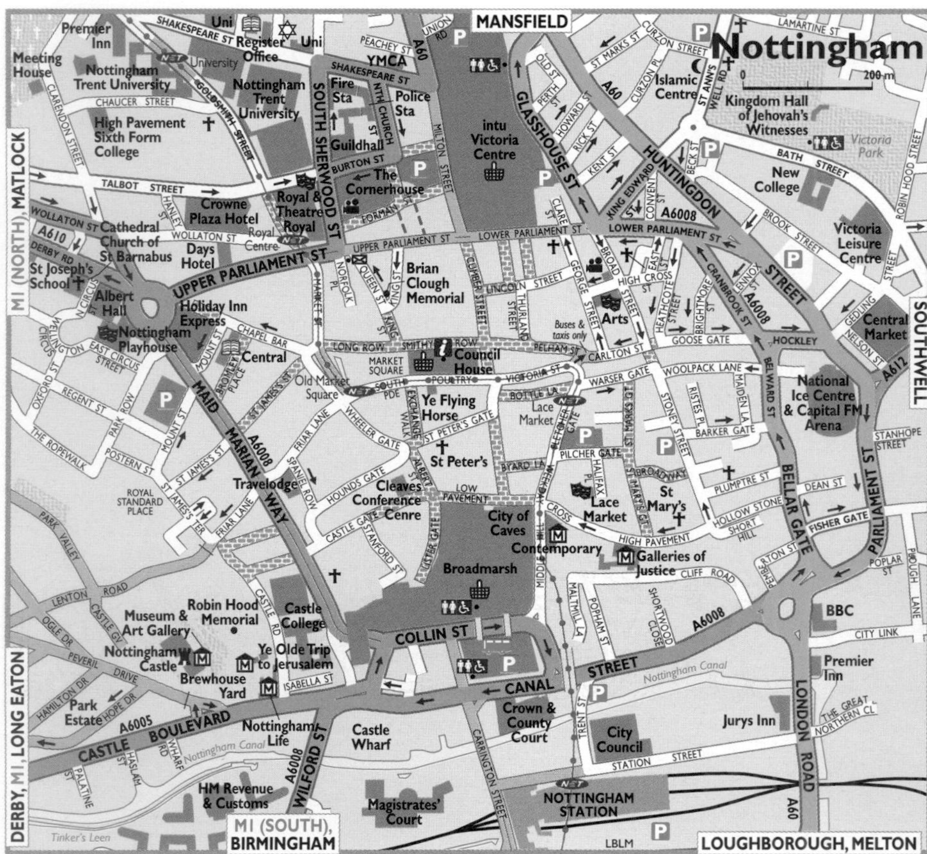
Nottingham
0 200 m
MANSFIELD
M1 (NORTH), MATLOCK
SOUTHWELL
DERBY, M1, LONG EATON
M1 (SOUTH), BIRMINGHAM
LOUGHBOROUGH, MELTON
LBLM

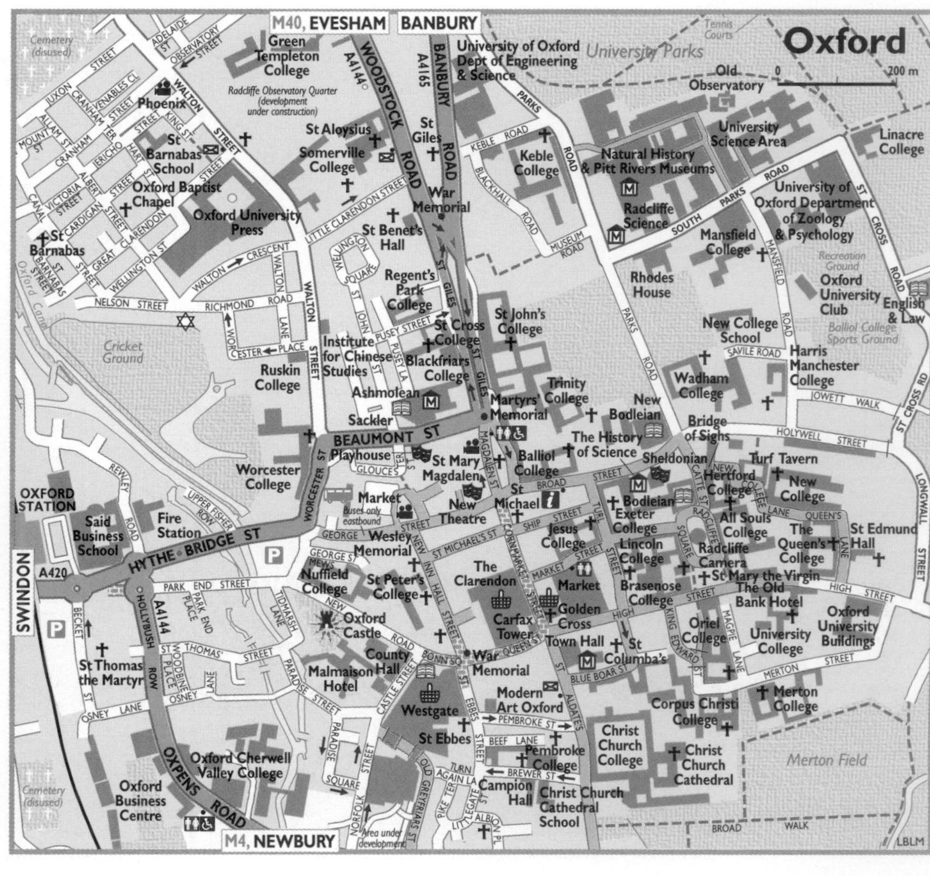
Oxford
0 200 m
M40, EVESHAM
BANBURY
SWINDON
M4, NEWBURY
LBLM

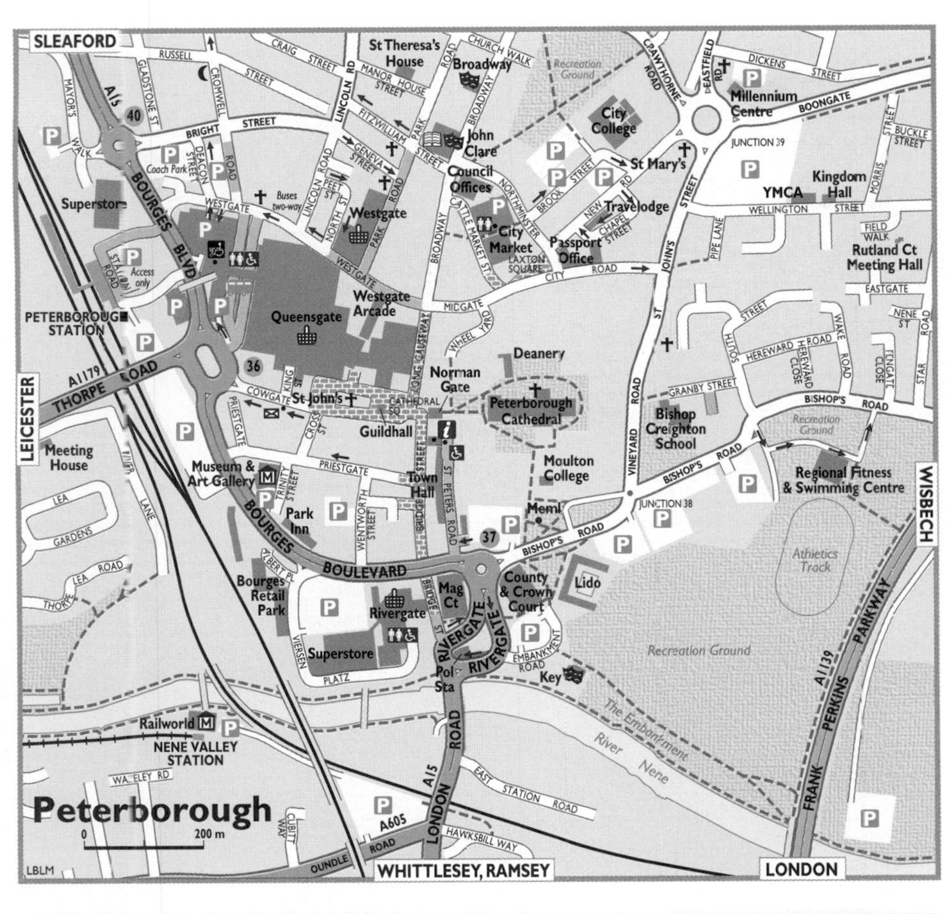
Peterborough
SLEAFORD
LEICESTER
WISBECH
WHITTLESEY, RAMSEY
LONDON
Queensgate
Westgate Arcade
Peterborough Cathedral
Deanery
Guildhall
Town Hall
Museum & Art Gallery
Bishop Creighton School
Moulton College
Regional Fitness & Swimming Centre
Athletics Track
Recreation Ground
Rivergate
County & Crown Court
Lido
Key
Railworld
NENE VALLEY STATION
PETERBOROUGH STATION
Meeting House
Bourges Retail Park
Superstore
Travelodge
YMCA
Kingdom Hall
Rutland Ct Meeting Hall
Millennium Centre
City College
St Theresa's House
Broadway
John Clare
Council Offices
City Market
Passport Office
River Nene
The Embankment
200 m
LBLM

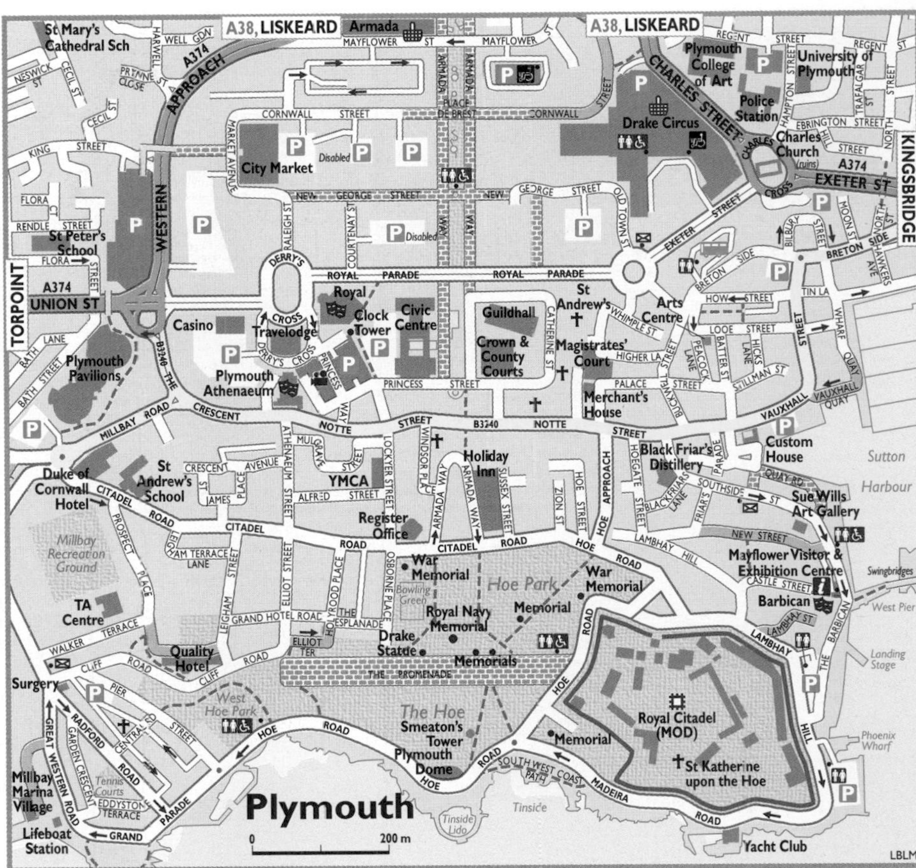
Plymouth
A38, LISKEARD
TORPOINT
KINGSBRIDGE
St Mary's Cathedral Sch
Armada
Plymouth College of Art
University of Plymouth
Drake Circus
Police Station
Charles Church
City Market
Western Approach
Royal Parade
Casino
Travelodge
Clock Tower
Civic Centre
Guildhall
Crown & County Courts
Magistrates' Court
St Andrew's
Arts Centre
Merchant's House
Plymouth Pavilions
Plymouth Athenaeum
Holiday Inn
Black Friar's Distillery
Custom House
Sutton Harbour
Sue Wills Art Gallery
Mayflower Visitor & Exhibition Centre
Barbican
Duke of Cornwall Hotel
St Andrew's School
YMCA
Register Office
Millbay Recreation Ground
TA Centre
Quality Hotel
Hoe Park
War Memorial
Royal Navy Memorial
Drake Statue
Memorials
The Promenade
Royal Citadel (MOD)
St Katherine upon the Hoe
Memorial
The Hoe
Smeaton's Tower
Plymouth Dome
West Hoe Park
Millbay Marina Village
Lifeboat Station
Yacht Club
Tinside Lido
Tinside
200 m
LBLM

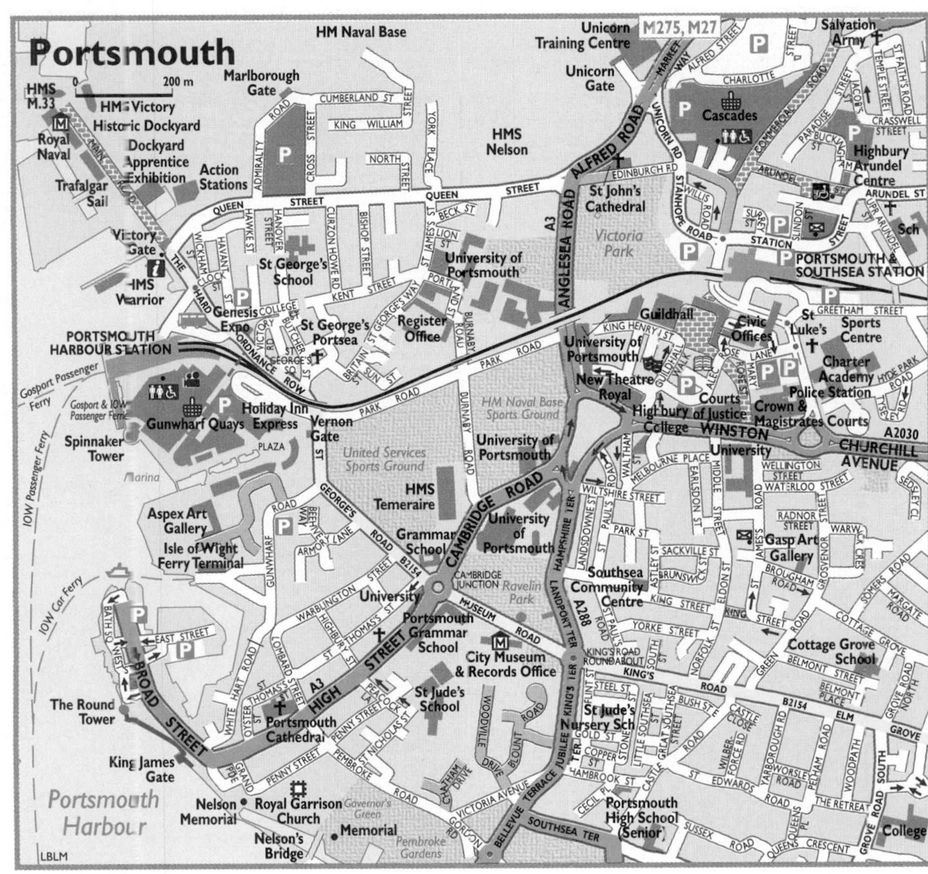
Portsmouth
HM Naval Base
HMS M.33
HMS Victory
Historic Dockyard
Dockyard Apprentice Exhibition
Royal Naval
Trafalgar Sail
Marlborough Gate
Action Stations
HMS Nelson
Unicorn Training Centre
Unicorn Gate
Cascades
Highbury Arundel Centre
St John's Cathedral
Victoria Park
PORTSMOUTH & SOUTHSEA STATION
University of Portsmouth
Guildhall
Civic Offices
Sports Centre
Charter Academy
Police Station
Crown & Magistrates Courts
New Theatre Royal
Highbury College
St George's School
Register Office
PORTSMOUTH HARBOUR STATION
Gunwharf Quays
Holiday Inn Express
Spinnaker Tower
Vernon Gate
United Services Sports Ground
HMS Temeraire
Grammar School
Aspex Art Gallery
Isle of Wight Ferry Terminal
Southsea Community Centre
Gasp Arc Gallery
Cottage Grove School
City Museum & Records Office
Portsmouth Grammar School
St Jude's School
Portsmouth Cathedral
The Round Tower
King James Gate
Nelson Memorial
Royal Garrison Church
Memorial
Nelson's Bridge
Portsmouth High School (Senior)
Portsmouth Harbour
Pembroke Gardens
WINSTON CHURCHILL AVENUE
HIGH STREET
200 m
LBLM

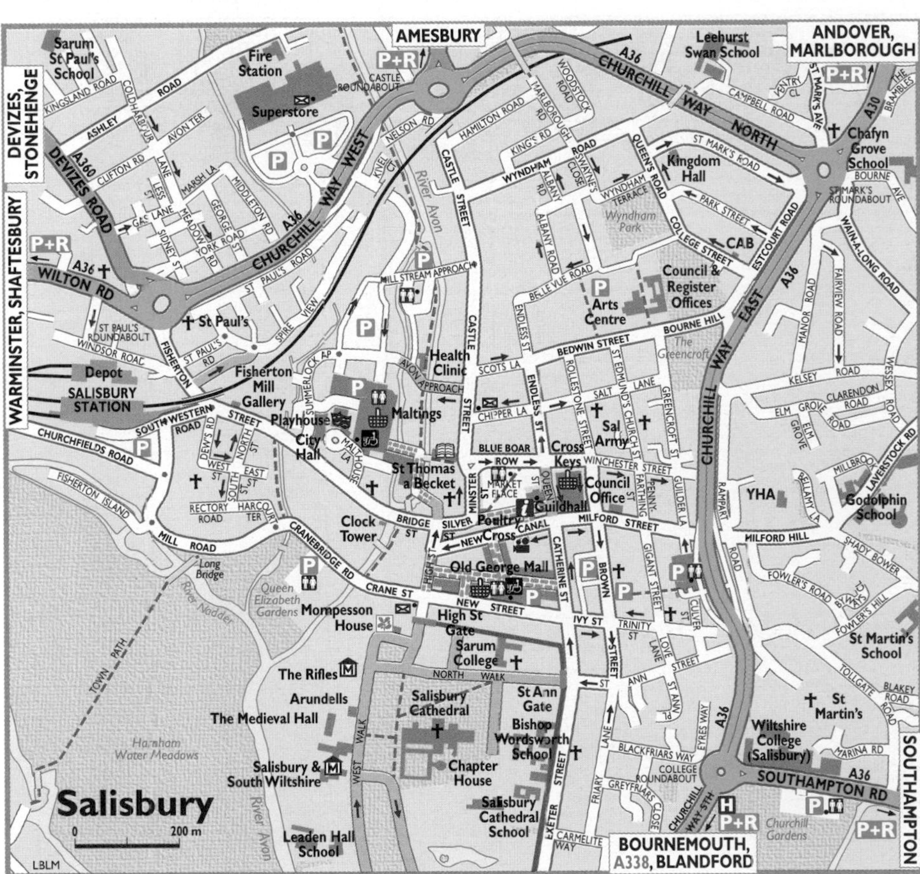
Salisbury
AMESBURY
ANDOVER, MARLBOROUGH
DEVIZES, STONEHENGE
WARMINSTER, SHAFTESBURY
SOUTHAMPTON
BOURNEMOUTH, A338, BLANDFORD
Sarum St Paul's School
Fire Station
Superstore
Leehurst Swan School
Chafyn Grove School
Kingdom Hall
CAB
Council & Register Offices
Arts Centre
St Paul's
Depot
SALISBURY STATION
Fisherton Mill Gallery
Playhouse
City Hall
Maltings
Health Clinic
St Thomas a Becket
Guildhall
Council Office
Sal Army
Poultry Cross
Old George Mall
Clock Tower
YHA
Godolphin School
Queen Elizabeth Gardens
Mompesson House
High St Gate
Sarum College
The Rifles
Arundells
The Medieval Hall
Salisbury Cathedral
St Ann Gate
Bishop Wordsworth School
Chapter House
Wiltshire College (Salisbury)
St Martin's School
St Martin's
Salisbury & South Wiltshire
Salisbury Cathedral School
Leaden Hall School
Harnham Water Meadows
River Avon
CHURCHILL WAY
200 m
LBLM

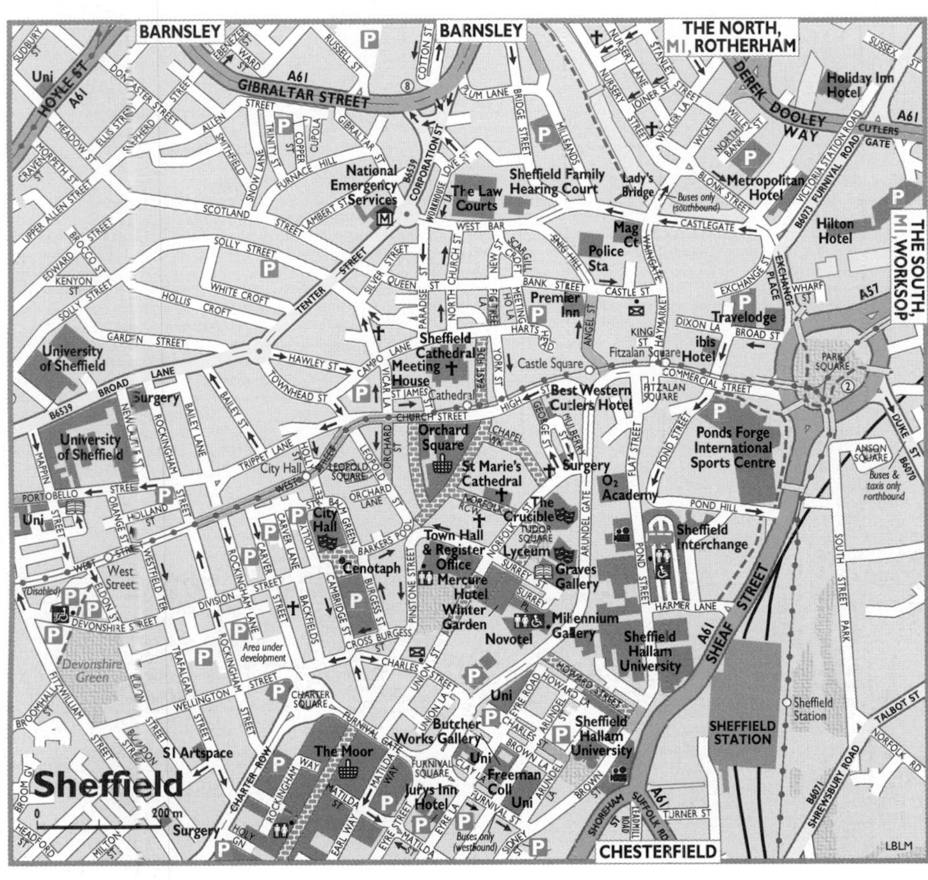
Sheffield
BARNSLEY
THE NORTH, M1, ROTHERHAM
THE SOUTH, M1, WORKSOP
CHESTERFIELD
Uni
Holiday Inn Hotel
National Emergency Services
The Law Courts
Sheffield Family Hearing Court
Metropolitan Hotel
Hilton Hotel
Police Sta
Mag Ct
Premier Inn
Travelodge
University of Sheffield
Sheffield Cathedral
Meeting House
Castle Square
Best Western Cutlers Hotel
Ponds Forge International Sports Centre
Orchard Square
St Marie's Cathedral
City Hall
Town Hall & Register Office
Lyceum
Crucible
Graves Gallery
Sheffield Interchange
Cenotaph
Mercure Hotel
Winter Garden
Millennium Gallery
Novotel
Sheffield Hallam University
SHEFFIELD STATION
Devonshire Green
Butcher Works Gallery
The Moor
St Artspace
Freeman Coll
Jurys Inn Hotel
GIBRALTAR STREET
DEREK DOOLEY WAY
SHEAF STREET
200 m
LBLM

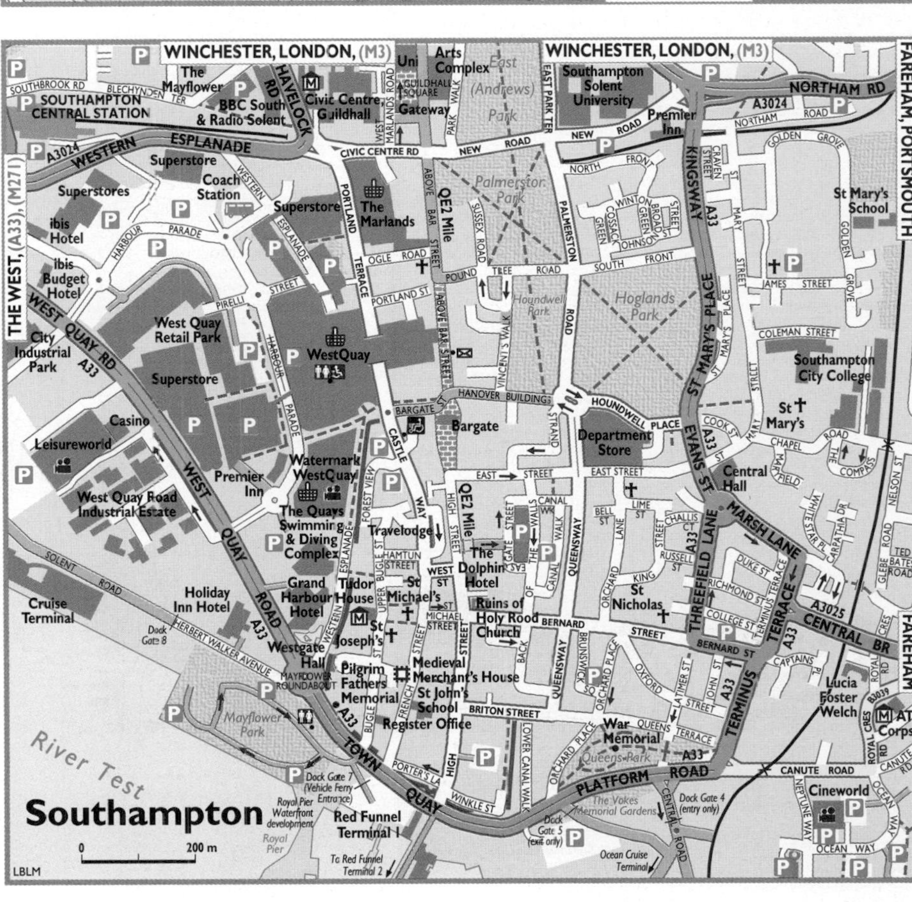
Southampton
WINCHESTER, LONDON, (M3)
FAREHAM, PORTSMOUTH
THE WEST, (A33), (M271)
FAREHAM
The Mayflower
BBC South & Radio Solent
Civic Centre, Guildhall
Arts Complex
Gateway
East (Andrews) Park
Southampton Solent University
Premier Inn
SOUTHAMPTON CENTRAL STATION
Superstore
Coach Station
Superstores
Ibis Hotel
Ibis Budget Hotel
The Marlands
Palmerston Park
Hoglands Park
St Mary's School
West Quay Retail Park
City Industrial Park
WestQuay
Bargate
Department Store
Southampton City College
St Mary's
Casino
Leisureworld
West Quay Road Industrial Estate
Premier Inn
Watermark WestQuay
The Quays Swimming & Diving Complex
Travelodge
The Dolphin Hotel
Central Hall
Cruise Terminal
Holiday Inn Hotel
Grand Harbour Hotel
Tudor House
St Michael's
Ruins of Holy Rood Church
St Nicholas
Westgate Hall
St Joseph's
Pilgrim Fathers Memorial
Medieval Merchant's House
St John's School
Register Office
War Memorial
Queens Park
Lucia Foster Welch
AT Corps
Mayflower Park
River Test
Red Funnel Terminal 1
Cineworld
TOWN QUAY
PLATFORM ROAD
200 m
LBLM

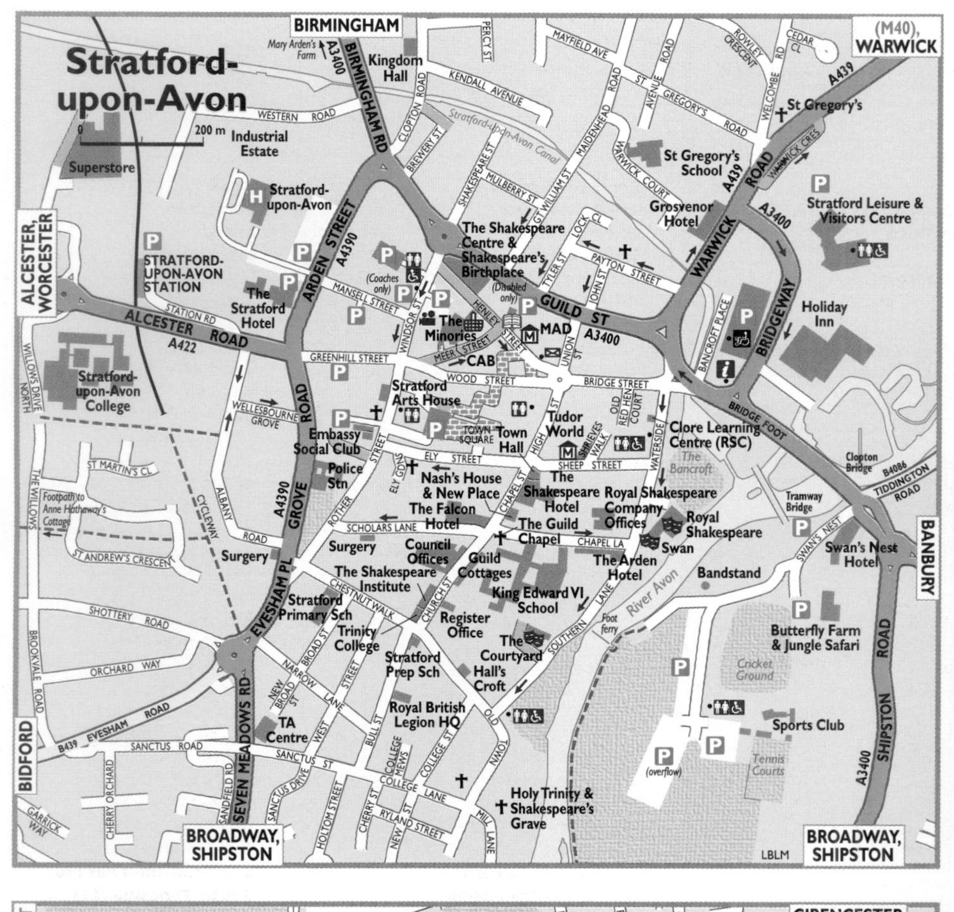

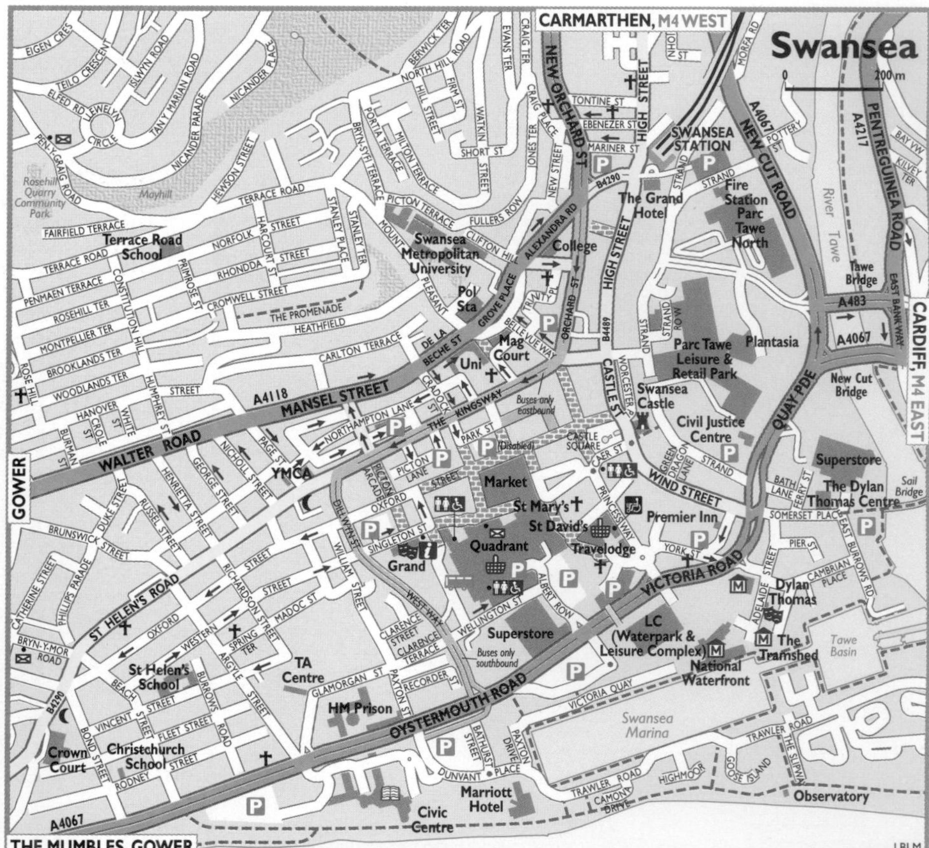

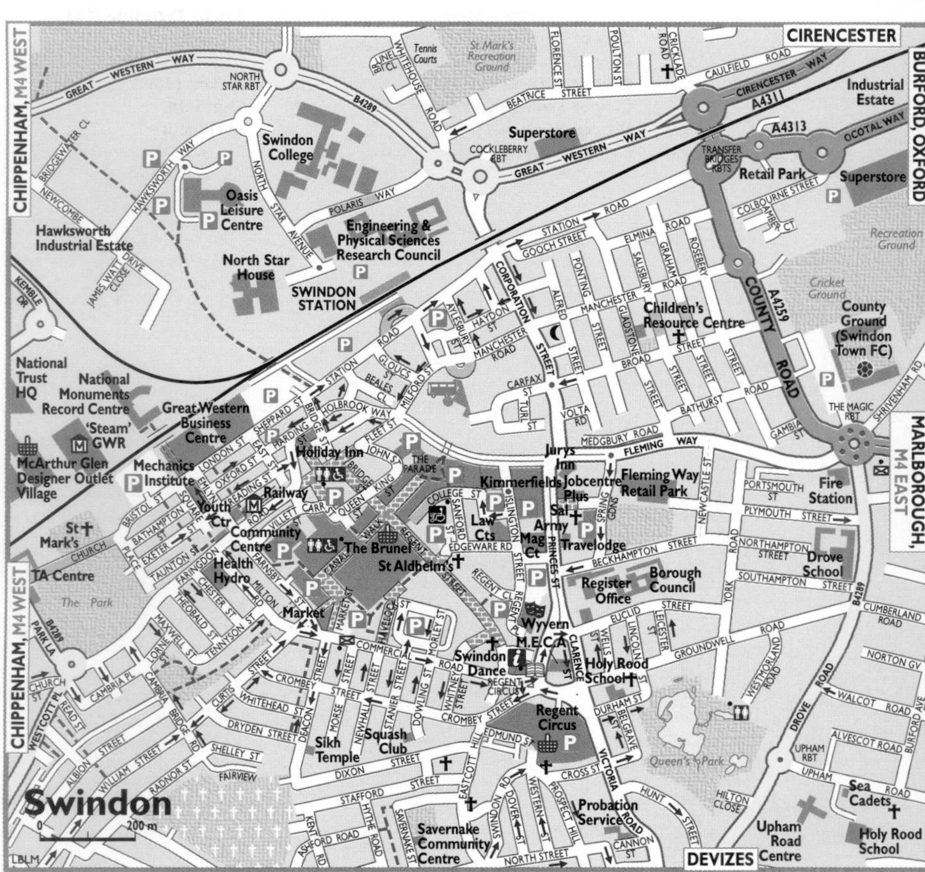

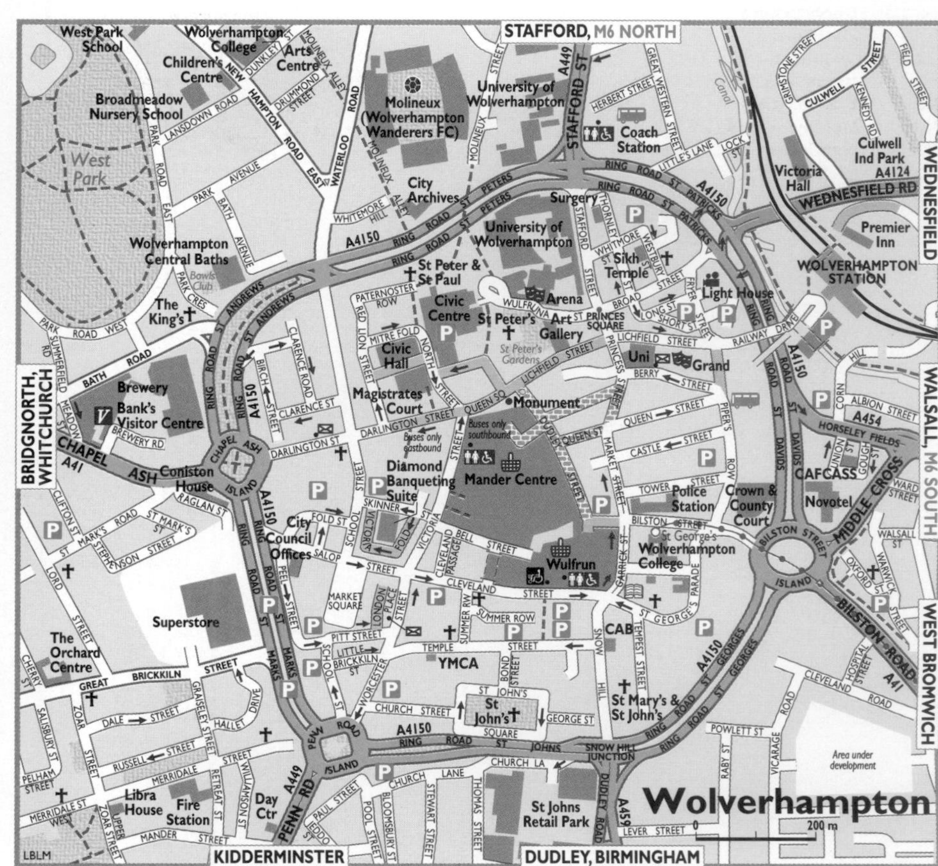

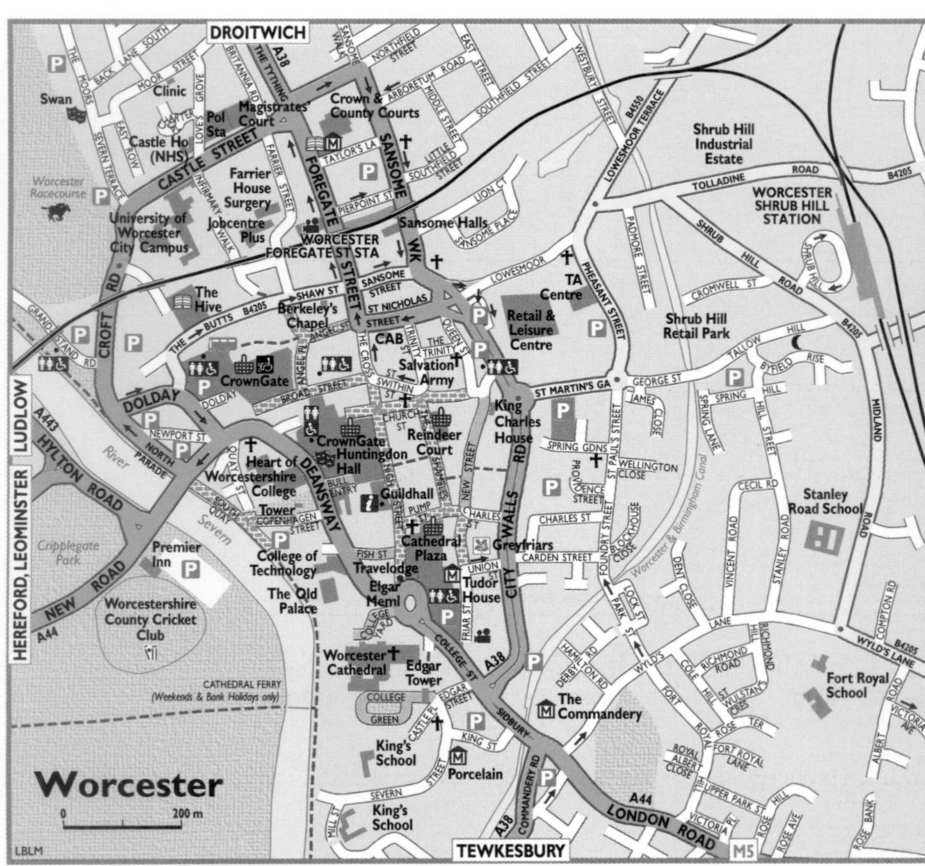

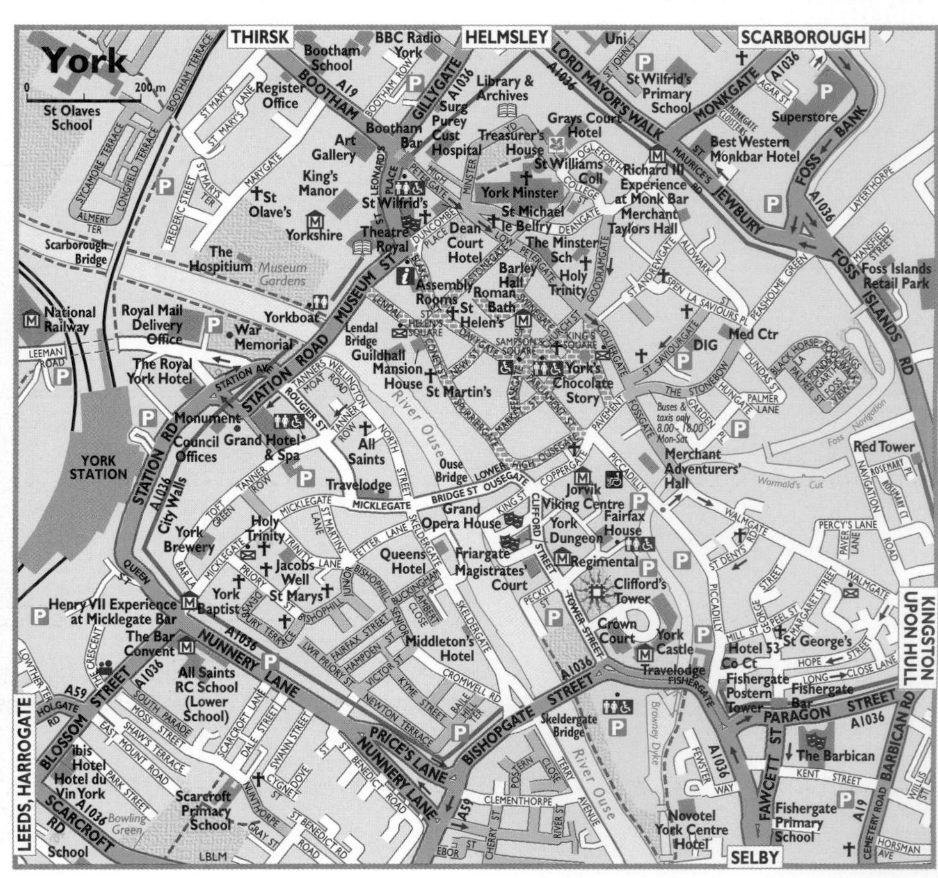

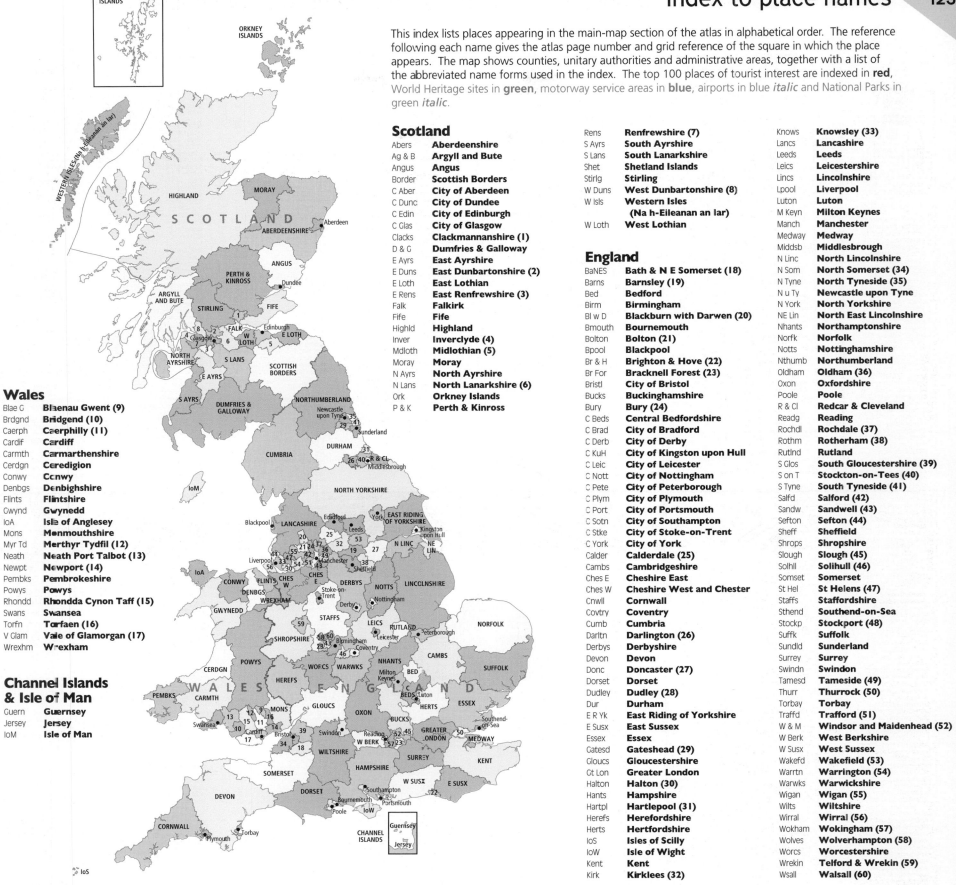

This index lists places appearing in the main-map section of the atlas in alphabetical order. The reference following each name gives the atlas page number and grid reference of the square in which the place appears. The map shows counties, unitary authorities and administrative areas, together with a list of the abbreviated name forms used in the index. The top 100 places of tourist interest are indexed in **red**, World Heritage sites in **green**, motorway service areas in **blue**, airports in **blue italic** and National Parks in **green italic**.

Scotland

Abers	**Aberdeenshire**
Ag & B	**Argyll and Bute**
Angus	**Angus**
Border	**Scottish Borders**
C Aber	**City of Aberdeen**
C Dunc	**City of Dundee**
C Edin	**City of Edinburgh**
C Glas	**City of Glasgow**
Clacks	**Clackmannanshire (1)**
D & G	**Dumfries & Galloway**
E Ayrs	**East Ayrshire**
E Duns	**East Dunbartonshire (2)**
E Loth	**East Lothian**
E Rens	**East Renfrewshire (3)**
Falk	**Falkirk**
Fife	**Fife**
Highld	**Highland**
Inver	**Inverclyde (4)**
Mdloth	**Midlothian (5)**
Moray	**Moray**
N Ayrs	**North Ayrshire**
N Lans	**North Lanarkshire (6)**
Ork	**Orkney Islands**
P & K	**Perth & Kinross**
Rens	**Renfrewshire (7)**
S Ayrs	**South Ayrshire**
S Lans	**South Lanarkshire**
Shet	**Shetland Islands**
Stirlg	**Stirling**
W Duns	**West Dunbartonshire (8)**
W Isls	**Western Isles (Na h-Eileanan an Iar)**
W Loth	**West Lothian**

England

BaNES	**Bath & N E Somerset (18)**
Barns	**Barnsley (19)**
Bed	**Bedford**
Birm	**Birmingham**
Bl w D	**Blackburn with Darwen (20)**
Bolton	**Bolton (21)**
Bmouth	**Bournemouth**
Bpool	**Blackpool**
Br & H	**Brighton & Hove (22)**
Br For	**Bracknell Forest (23)**
Bristl	**City of Bristol**
Bucks	**Buckinghamshire**
Bury	**Bury (24)**
C Beds	**Central Bedfordshire**
C Brad	**City of Bradford**
C Derb	**City of Derby**
C KuH	**City of Kingston upon Hull**
C Leic	**City of Leicester**
C Nott	**City of Nottingham**
C Pete	**City of Peterborough**
C Plym	**City of Plymouth**
C Port	**City of Portsmouth**
C Sotn	**City of Southampton**
C Stke	**City of Stoke-on-Trent**
C York	**City of York**
Calder	**Calderdale (25)**
Cambs	**Cambridgeshire**
Ches E	**Cheshire East**
Ches W	**Cheshire West and Chester**
Cnwll	**Cornwall**
Covtry	**Coventry**
Cumb	**Cumbria**
Darltn	**Darlington (26)**
Derbys	**Derbyshire**
Devon	**Devon**
Donc	**Doncaster (27)**
Dorset	**Dorset**
Dudley	**Dudley (28)**
Dur	**Durham**
E R Yk	**East Riding of Yorkshire**
E Susx	**East Sussex**
Essex	**Essex**
Gatesd	**Gateshead (29)**
Gloucs	**Gloucestershire**
Gt Lon	**Greater London**
Halton	**Halton (30)**
Hants	**Hampshire**
Hartpl	**Hartlepool (31)**
Herefs	**Herefordshire**
Herts	**Hertfordshire**
IoS	**Isles of Scilly**
IoW	**Isle of Wight**
Kent	**Kent**
Kirk	**Kirklees (32)**
Knows	**Knowsley (33)**
Lancs	**Lancashire**
Leeds	**Leeds**
Leics	**Leicestershire**
Lincs	**Lincolnshire**
Lpool	**Liverpool**
Luton	**Luton**
M Keyn	**Milton Keynes**
Manch	**Manchester**
Medway	**Medway**
Middsb	**Middlesbrough**
N Linc	**North Lincolnshire**
N Som	**North Somerset (34)**
N Tyne	**North Tyneside (35)**
N u Ty	**Newcastle upon Tyne**
N York	**North Yorkshire**
NE Lin	**North East Lincolnshire**
Nhants	**Northamptonshire**
Norfk	**Norfolk**
Notts	**Nottinghamshire**
Nthumb	**Northumberland**
Oldham	**Oldham (36)**
Oxon	**Oxfordshire**
Poole	**Poole**
R & Cl	**Redcar & Cleveland**
Readg	**Reading**
Rochdl	**Rochdale (37)**
Rothm	**Rotherham (38)**
Rutlnd	**Rutland**
S Glos	**South Gloucestershire (39)**
S on T	**Stockton-on-Tees (40)**
S Tyne	**South Tyneside (41)**
Salfd	**Salford (42)**
Sandw	**Sandwell (43)**
Sefton	**Sefton (44)**
Sheff	**Sheffield**
Shrops	**Shropshire**
Slough	**Slough (45)**
Solhll	**Solihull (46)**
Somset	**Somerset**
St Hel	**St Helens (47)**
Staffs	**Staffordshire**
Sthend	**Southend-on-Sea**
Stockp	**Stockport (48)**
Suffk	**Suffolk**
Sundld	**Sunderland**
Surrey	**Surrey**
Swindn	**Swindon**
Tamesd	**Tameside (49)**
Thurr	**Thurrock (50)**
Torbay	**Torbay**
Traffd	**Trafford (51)**
W & M	**Windsor and Maidenhead (52)**
W Berk	**West Berkshire**
W Susx	**West Sussex**
Wakefd	**Wakefield (53)**
Warrtn	**Warrington (54)**
Warwks	**Warwickshire**
Wigan	**Wigan (55)**
Wilts	**Wiltshire**
Wirral	**Wirral (56)**
Wokham	**Wokingham (57)**
Wolves	**Wolverhampton (58)**
Worcs	**Worcestershire**
Wrekin	**Telford & Wrekin (59)**
Wsall	**Walsall (60)**

Wales

Blae G	**Blaenau Gwent (9)**
Brdgnd	**Bridgend (10)**
Caerph	**Caerphilly (11)**
Cardif	**Cardiff**
Carmth	**Carmarthenshire**
Cerdgn	**Ceredigion**
Conwy	**Conwy**
Denbgs	**Denbighshire**
Flints	**Flintshire**
Gwynd	**Gwynedd**
IoA	**Isle of Anglesey**
Mons	**Monmouthshire**
Myr Td	**Merthyr Tydfil (12)**
Neath	**Neath Port Talbot (13)**
Newpt	**Newport (14)**
Pembks	**Pembrokeshire**
Powys	**Powys**
Rhondd	**Rhondda Cynon Taff (15)**
Swans	**Swansea**
Torfn	**Torfaen (16)**
V Glam	**Vale of Glamorgan (17)**
Wrexhm	**Wrexham**

Channel Islands & Isle of Man

Guern	**Guernsey**
Jersey	**Jersey**
IoM	**Isle of Man**

Using the National Grid

With an Ordnance Survey National Grid reference you can pinpoint anywhere in the country in this atlas. The blue grid lines which divide the main-map pages into 5km squares for ease of indexing also match the National Grid. A National Grid reference gives two letters and some figures. An example is how to find the summit of mount Snowdon using its 4-figure grid reference of **SH6154**.

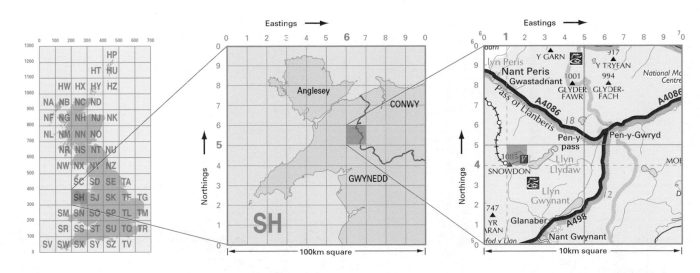

The letters **SH** indicate the 100km square of the National Grid in which Snowdon is located.

In a 4-figure grid reference the first two figures (eastings) are read along the map from left to right, the second two (northings) up the map. The figures **6** and **5**, the first and third figures of the Snowdon reference, indicate the 10km square within the **SH** square, lying above (north) and right (east) of the intersection of the vertical (easting) line **6** and horizontal (northing) line **5**.

The summit is finally pinpointed by figures **1** and **4** which locate a 1km square within the 10km square. At road atlas scales these grid lines are normally estimated by eye.

Bonehill Staffs 46 G13
Bo'ness Falk 82 K2
Boney Hay Staffs 46 D11
Bonhill W Duns 88 J10
Boningale Shrops 45 T13
Bonjedward Border 84 H14
Bonkle N Lans 82 F7
Bonnington Angus 91 S4
Bonnington Kent 13 L8
Bonnybank Fife 91 N11
Bonnybridge Falk 89 T10
Bonnykelly Abers 105 P5
Bonnyrigg Mdloth 83 R5
Bonnyton Angus 91 M4
Bonsall Derbys 46 J2
Bonshaw Tower D & G 75 P11
Bont Mons 27 R4
Bontddu Gwynd 43 N10
Bont-Dolgadfan Powys 43 S13
Bont-goch Cerdgn 33 N3
Bonthorpe Lincs 59 S12
Bontnewydd Cerdgn 33 M7
Bontnewydd Gwynd 52 G11
Bontuchel Denbgs 44 C2
Bonvilston V Glam 26 K13
Bonwm Denbgs 44 D5
Bon-y-maen Swans 26 B8
Boode Devon 15 M5
Booker Bucks 20 D4
Booley Shrops 45 N8
Boon Border 84 F9
Boon Hill Staffs 45 T3
Boorley Green Hants 9 Q6
Boosbeck R & Cl 71 L9
Boose's Green Essex 22 K1
Boot Cumb 66 J12
Booth Calder 56 F1
Boothby Graffoe Lincs 48 E2
Boothby Pagnell Lincs 48 E7
Boothferry E R Yk 58 B1
Booth Green Ches E 56 D10
Boothstown Salfd 55 R6
Booth Town Calder 56 G1
Boothville Nhants 37 U8
Bootle Cumb 61 L2
Bootle Sefton 54 H7
Boots Green Ches W 55 S12
Boot Street Suffk 41 M11
Booze N York 69 M12
Boraston Shrops 35 P7
Bordeaux Guern 6 e2
Borden Kent 12 G3
Borden W Susx 10 C6
Border Cumb 66 J2
Borders Crematorium Border 84 F12
Bordley N York 62 J6
Boreham Essex 22 J6
Boreham Wilts 18 C12
Boreham Street E Susx 11 V8
Borehamwood Herts 21 L3
Boreland D & G 75 N7
Boreraig Highld 100 a4
Boreton Shrops 45 M12
Borgh W Isls 106 b18
Borgh W Isls 106 j3
Borgie Highld 111 P5
Borgue D & G 73 Q10
Borgue Highld 112 D11
Borley Essex 40 D12
Borley Green Essex 40 D12
Borley Green Suffk 40 G8
Borneskitaig Highld 100 c2
Borness D & G 73 Q10
Boroughbridge N York 63 T6
Borough Green Kent 12 B4
Borras Head Wrexhm 44 J3
Borrowash Derbys 47 M7
Borrowby N York 63 U2
Borrowby N York 71 N9
Borrowstoun Falk 82 J2
Borstal Medway 12 D2
Borth Cerdgn 33 M2
Borthwickbrae Border 75 T3
Borthwickshiels Border 75 T2
Borth-y-Gest Gwynd 43 L6
Borve Highld 100 d5
Borve W Isls 106 b18
Borve W Isls 106 f9
Borve W Isls 106 j3
Borwick Lancs 61 U5
Borwick Lodge Cumb 67 M13
Borwick Rails Cumb 61 M4
Bosavern Cnwll 2 B10
Bosbury Herefs 35 Q12
Boscarne Cnwll 3 Q3
Boscastle Cnwll 4 D2
Boscombe Bmouth 8 G10
Boscombe Wilts 18 K13
Boscoppa Cnwll 3 Q6
Bosham W Susx 10 C10
Bosham Hoe W Susx 10 C10
Bosherston Pembks 24 G12
Boskednan Cnwll 2 C10
Boskenna Cnwll 2 C12
Bosley Ches E 56 D13
Bosoughan Cnwll 3 M4
Bossall N York 64 G7
Bossiney Cnwll 4 D3
Bossingham Kent 13 N6
Bossington Somset 15 U3
Bostock Green Ches W 55 Q13
Boston Lincs 49 M5
Boston Crematorium Lincs 49 M4
Boston Spa Leeds 63 U10
Boswarthan Cnwll 2 C10
Boswinger Cnwll 3 P8
Botallack Cnwll 2 B10
Botany Bay Gt Lon 21 N3
Botcheston Leics 47 N13
Botesdale Suffk 40 H5
Bothal Nthumb 77 Q8
Bothampstead W Berk 19 R5
Bothamsall Notts 57 U12
Bothel Cumb 66 J5
Bothenhampton Dorset 7 N6
Bothwell S Lans 82 D7
Bothwell Services S Lans 82 D7
Botley Bucks 31 L12
Botley Hants 9 Q6
Botley Oxon 29 U6
Botolph Claydon Bucks 30 F8
Botolphs W Susx 10 K9
Botolph's Bridge Kent 13 M9
Bottesford Leics 48 B6
Bottesford N Linc 58 E5
Bottisham Cambs 39 R8
Bottomcraig Fife 91 N7
Bottom of Hutton Lancs 55 L1
Bottom o' th' Moor Bolton 55 Q4
Bottoms Calder 56 D2
Bottoms Cnwll 2 B12
Botts Green Warwks 36 H2
Botusfleming Cnwll 5 L8
Botwnnog Gwynd 42 E7
Bough Beech Kent 21 S13
Boughrood Powys 34 D13
Boughspring Gloucs 27 V8
Boughton Nhants 37 U7
Boughton Norfk 49 V13
Boughton Notts 57 U13
Boughton Aluph Kent 12 K6
Boughton End C Beds 31 L5
Boughton Green Kent 12 E5
Boughton Malherbe Kent 12 G6
Boughton Monchelsea Kent 12 E5
Boughton Street Kent 13 L4
Boulby R & Cl 71 N9
Boulder Clough Calder 56 F2
Bouldnor IoW 9 M11
Bouldon Shrops 35 M3
Boulmer Nthumb 77 R3
Boulston Pembks 24 G8
Boultham Lincs 58 G13
Bourn Cambs 39 M9
Bourne Lincs 48 G9
Bournebridge Essex 22 D9
Bournebrook Birm 36 D4
Bourne End Bed 38 F8
Bourne End Bucks 20 E5
Bourne End C Beds 31 L4
Bourne End Herts 31 M11
Bournemouth Bmouth 8 F10
Bournemouth Airport Dorset 8 G9
Bournemouth Crematorium Bmouth 8 G10
Bournes Green Gloucs 28 H7
Bournes Green Sthend 23 M10
Bournheath Worcs 36 C6
Bournmoor Dur 70 D2
Bournstream Gloucs 28 D9
Bournville Birm 36 D4
Bourton Dorset 17 U10
Bourton N Som 17 L4
Bourton Oxon 29 P10
Bourton Shrops 35 N1
Bourton Wilts 18 F8
Bourton on Dunsmore Warwks 37 M6
Bourton-on-the-Hill Gloucs 29 N1
Bourton-on-the-Water Gloucs 29 N3
Bousd Ag & B 92 H6
Boustead Hill Cumb 75 Q14
Bouth Cumb 61 Q2
Bouthwaite N York 63 N5
Bouts Worcs 36 D9
Boveney Bucks 20 F7
Boveridge Dorset 8 F6
Bovey Tracey Devon 5 U5
Bovingdon Herts 31 M12
Bovingdon Green Bucks 20 D5
Bovinger Essex 22 D6
Bovington Dorset 8 A11
Bovington Camp Dorset 8 A11
Bow Cumb 67 M1
Bow Devon 5 U9
Bow Devon 15 R12
Bow Gt Lon 21 Q6
Bow Ork 106 s20
Bowbank Dur 68 K8
Bow Brickhill M Keyn 30 K6
Bowbridge Gloucs 28 G6
Bowburn Dur 70 D5
Bowcombe IoW 9 P11
Bowd Devon 6 F6
Bowden Border 84 F12
Bowden Devon 5 U11
Bowden Hill Wilts 18 D7
Bowdon Traffd 55 S9
Bower Highld 112 F4
Bower Ashton Bristl 17 Q2
Bowerchalke Wilts 8 E4
Bowerhill Wilts 18 D8
Bower Hinton Somset 17 N13
Bower House Tye Suffk 40 G12
Bowermadden Highld 112 F4
Bowers Staffs 45 T6
Bowers Gifford Essex 22 J10
Bowershall Fife 90 G13
Bower's Row Leeds 63 U14
Bowes Dur 69 L10
Bowgreave Lancs 61 T11
Bowhouse D & G 74 K12
Bowithick Cnwll 4 F4
Bowker's Green Lancs 54 K6
Bowland Border 84 D10
Bowland Bridge Cumb 61 S2
Bowley Herefs 35 M10
Bowley Town Herefs 35 M10
Bowlhead Green Surrey 10 E3
Bowling C Brad 63 P13
Bowling W Duns 88 K11
Bowling Bank Wrexhm 44 J4
Bowling Green Worcs 35 T10
Bowmanstead Cumb 67 M13
Bowmore Ag & B 78 E4
Bowness-on-Solway Cumb 75 P13
Bowness-on-Windermere Cumb 67 P13
Bow of Fife Fife 91 M9
Bowriefauld Angus 91 R2
Bowscale Cumb 67 N6
Bowsden Nthumb 85 P10
Bowston Cumb 67 Q13
Bow Street Cerdgn 33 M3
Bow Street Norfk 50 H14
Bowthorpe Norfk 51 L12
Box Gloucs 28 G7
Box Wilts 18 B7
Boxbush Gloucs 28 C3
Boxbush Gloucs 28 D5
Box End Bed 38 F11
Boxford Suffk 40 G12
Boxford W Berk 19 P6
Boxgrove W Susx 10 E9
Box Hill Surrey 21 L12
Boxley Kent 12 E4
Boxmoor Herts 31 M11
Box's Shop Cnwll 14 F12
Boxted Essex 23 P1
Boxted Essex 40 G14
Boxted Suffk 40 D10
Boxted Cross Essex 23 P1
Boxwell Gloucs 28 F9
Boxworth Cambs 39 M8
Boyden End Suffk 40 B9
Boyden Gate Kent 13 P2
Boylestone Derbys 46 G6
Boyndie Abers 104 J3
Boyndlie Abers 105 Q3
Boynton E R Yk 65 Q6
Boysack Angus 91 T2
Boys Hill Dorset 7 S2
Boythorpe Derbys 57 N13
Boyton Cnwll 4 J2
Boyton Suffk 41 Q11
Boyton Wilts 18 E13
Boyton Cross Essex 22 F6
Boyton End Suffk 40 B12
Bozeat Nhants 38 D9
Braaid IoM 60 e7
Brabling Green Suffk 41 N8
Brabourne Kent 13 M7
Brabourne Lees Kent 13 L7
Brabstermire Highld 112 H3
Bracadale Highld 100 c6
Braceborough Lincs 48 G11
Bracebridge Heath Lincs 58 G13
Bracebridge Low Fields Lincs 58 G13
Braceby Lincs 48 F6
Bracewell Lancs 62 H10
Brackenfield Derbys 47 L2
Brackenhirst N Lans 82 D5
Brackenthwaite Cumb 67 L3
Brackenthwaite N York 63 R9
Bracklesham W Susx 10 C11
Brackletter Highld 94 H2
Brackley Nhants 30 C5
Brackley Hatch Nhants 30 D4
Bracknell Br For 20 E9
Braco P & K 89 T4
Bracobrae Moray 104 G5
Bracon Ash Norfk 51 L14
Bracora Highld 100 g10
Bracorina Highld 100 g10
Bradaford Devon 4 K2
Bradbourne Derbys 46 H3
Bradbury Dur 70 D7
Bradden Nhants 37 R11
Braddock Cnwll 4 F8
Bradeley C Stke 45 U3
Bradenham Bucks 20 D3
Bradenstoke Wilts 18 F5
Bradfield Devon 6 E3
Bradfield Essex 23 R1
Bradfield Norfk 51 N7
Bradfield Sheff 57 L8
Bradfield W Berk 19 T6
Bradfield Combust Suffk 40 E9
Bradfield Green Ches E 45 Q2
Bradfield Heath Essex 23 R1
Bradfield St Clare Suffk 40 F9
Bradfield St George Suffk 40 F9
Bradford C Brad 63 P13
Bradford Cnwll 4 E5
Bradford Devon 14 K11
Bradford Nthumb 77 M10
Bradford Nthumb 85 T12
Bradford Abbas Dorset 7 Q2
Bradford Leigh Wilts 18 B8
Bradford-on-Avon Wilts 18 B8
Bradford-on-Tone Somset 16 G12
Bradford Peverell Dorset 7 S6
Bradiford Devon 15 N6
Brading IoW 9 S11
Bradley Derbys 46 H4
Bradley Hants 19 T12
Bradley Kirk 56 J2
Bradley N York 63 L3
Bradley NE Lin 59 M5
Bradley Staffs 45 U10
Bradley Wolves 36 C1
Bradley Worcs 36 C8
Bradley Wrexhm 44 H3
Bradley Common Ches W 45 M4
Bradley Green Somset 16 J9
Bradley Green Warwks 46 J13
Bradley Green Worcs 36 C8
Bradley in the Moors Staffs 46 E5
Bradley Stoke S Glos 28 B11
Bradmore Notts 47 Q7
Bradney Somset 16 K9
Bradninch Devon 6 C4
Bradninch Devon 15 P6
Bradnop Staffs 46 D2
Bradnor Green Herefs 34 G9
Bradpole Dorset 7 N6
Bradshaw Bolton 55 R4
Bradshaw Calder 63 M14
Bradshaw Kirk 56 G4
Bradstone Devon 4 K4
Bradwall Green Ches E 55 S14
Bradwell Derbys 56 J10
Bradwell Devon 15 M4
Bradwell Essex 22 K3
Bradwell M Keyn 30 H4
Bradwell Norfk 51 T13
Bradwell Crematorium Staffs 45 U4
Bradwell-on-Sea Essex 23 P6
Bradwell Waterside Essex 23 N6
Bradworthy Devon 14 H10
Brae Highld 102 J3
Brae Shet 106 t7
Braeface Falk 89 S9
Braehead Angus 99 M13
Braehead D & G 73 L9
Braehead S Lans 82 J8
Braemar Abers 98 B5
Braemore Highld 108 B9
Braemore Highld 112 C11
Brae Roy Lodge Highld 96 C5
Braeside Inver 88 F11
Braes of Coul Angus 98 D12
Braes of Enzie Moray 104 D4
Braeswick Ork 106 v16
Braevallich Ag & B 87 T4
Brafferton Darltn 69 S8
Brafferton N York 63 U5
Brafield-on-the-Green Nhants 38 B9
Bragar W Isls 106 h4
Bragbury End Herts 31 S8
Braidwood S Lans 82 F9
Brailsford Derbys 46 J5
Brailsford Green Derbys 46 J5
Brain's Green Gloucs 28 C6
Braintree Essex 22 J3
Braiseworth Suffk 40 K6
Braishfield Hants 9 M3
Braithwaite C Brad 63 L11
Braithwaite Cumb 66 K8
Braithwell Donc 57 R8
Braken Hill Wakefd 57 P3
Bramber W Susx 10 K8
Brambridge Hants 9 P4
Bramcote Notts 47 P6
Bramcote Warwks 37 M3
Bramcote Crematorium Notts 47 P6
Bramdean Hants 9 S3
Bramerton Norfk 51 N13
Bramfield Herts 31 S9
Bramfield Suffk 41 Q6
Bramford Suffk 40 K11
Bramhall Stockp 56 C10
Bramham Leeds 63 U11
Bramhope Leeds 63 R11
Bramley Hants 19 U9
Bramley Leeds 63 Q12
Bramley Rothm 57 Q8
Bramley Surrey 10 G2
Bramley Corner Hants 19 T9
Bramley Green Hants 19 U9
Bramley Head N York 63 N8
Bramling Kent 13 P4
Brampford Speke Devon 6 B5
Brampton Cambs 38 K6
Brampton Cumb 68 E8
Brampton Cumb 76 A13
Brampton Lincs 58 D11
Brampton Norfk 51 M9
Brampton Rothm 57 P6
Brampton Suffk 41 R4
Brampton Abbotts Herefs 28 B2
Brampton Ash Nhants 37 U3
Brampton Bryan Herefs 34 J6
Brampton-en-le-Morthen Rothm 57 Q9
Bramshall Staffs 46 E7
Bramshaw Hants 8 K5
Bramshill Hants 20 B10
Bramshott Hants 10 C4
Bramwell Somset 17 M11
Branault Highld 93 N5
Brancaster Norfk 50 C5
Brancaster Staithe Norfk 50 C5
Brancepeth Dur 69 R5
Branchill Moray 103 S5
Brand End Lincs 49 N4
Branderburgh Moray 104 A1
Brandesburton E R Yk 65 Q10
Brandeston Suffk 41 M8
Brand Green Gloucs 28 D2
Brandis Corner Devon 14 K12
Brandiston Norfk 50 K9
Brandon Dur 69 R4
Brandon Lincs 48 D4
Brandon Nthumb 77 L2
Brandon Suffk 40 C3
Brandon Warwks 37 M5
Brandon Bank Norfk 39 T3
Brandon Creek Norfk 39 T2
Brandon Parva Norfk 50 J12
Brandsby N York 64 D5
Brandy Wharf Lincs 58 H7
Brane Cnwll 2 C11
Bran End Essex 22 G2
Branksome Poole 8 E10
Branksome Park Poole 8 F10
Bransbury Hants 19 P12
Bransby Lincs 58 E11
Branscombe Devon 6 G7
Bransford Worcs 35 S10
Bransgore Hants 8 H9
Bransholme C KuH 65 Q13
Bransley Shrops 35 Q5
Branson's Cross Worcs 36 E6
Branston Leics 48 B8
Branston Lincs 58 H13
Branston Staffs 46 H9
Branston Booths Lincs 58 J13
Branstone IoW 9 R12
Brant Broughton Lincs 48 D3
Brantham Suffk 40 K14
Branthwaite Cumb 66 G8
Branthwaite Cumb 67 L5
Brantingham E R Yk 65 L14
Branton Donc 57 T6
Branton Nthumb 77 L2
Branton Green N York 63 U7
Branxton Nthumb 85 M11
Brassey Green Ches W 45 M1
Brassington Derbys 46 H3
Brasted Kent 21 S11
Brasted Chart Kent 21 S12
Brathens Abers 99 M4
Bratoft Lincs 59 S14
Brattleby Lincs 58 F10
Bratton Somset 16 B7
Bratton Wilts 18 D10
Bratton Wrekin 45 P11
Bratton Clovelly Devon 5 M2
Bratton Fleming Devon 15 P5
Bratton Seymour Somset 17 S11
Braughing Herts 31 U7
Braughing Friars Herts 22 B3
Braunston Nhants 37 P7
Braunston Rutlnd 48 B12
Braunstone Town Leics 47 Q13
Braunton Devon 15 L5
Brawby N York 64 G4
Brawl Highld 111 S3
Braworth N York 70 H11
Bray W & M 20 F7
Braybrooke Nhants 37 U4
Braydon Wilts 28 K10
Braydon Brook Wilts 28 J9
Braydon Side Wilts 28 K10
Brayford Devon 15 Q6
Bray's Hill E Susx 12 C13
Bray Shop Cnwll 4 J6
Braystones Cumb 66 F11
Braythorn N York 63 Q10
Brayton N York 64 E13
Braywick W & M 20 E7
Braywoodside W & M 20 E7
Brazacott Cnwll 4 H2
Breach Kent 12 F2
Breach Kent 13 N6
Breachwood Green Herts 31 Q8
Breaden Heath Shrops 44 K6
Breadsall Derbys 47 L6
Breadstone Gloucs 28 D7
Breadward Herefs 34 G10
Breage Cnwll 2 G11
Breakachy Highld 102 E7
Breakspear Crematorium Gt Lon 20 J5
Brealangwell Lodge Highld 108 J6
Bream Gloucs 28 B6
Breamore Hants 8 H5
Brean Somset 16 J5
Breanais W Isls 106 e6
Brearley Calder 56 F1
Brearton N York 63 S7
Breascleit W Isls 106 h5
Breasclete W Isls 106 h5
Breaston Derbys 47 N7
Brechfa Carmth 25 T4
Brechin Angus 99 L11
Breckles Norfk 40 G2
Brecon Powys 26 J2
Brecon Beacons National Park 26 J3
Bredbury Stockp 56 D8
Brede E Susx 12 F12
Bredenbury Herefs 35 P9
Bredfield Suffk 41 N10
Bredgar Kent 12 G3
Bredhurst Kent 12 E3
Bredon Worcs 36 B13
Bredon's Hardwick Worcs 36 B13
Bredon's Norton Worcs 36 B13
Bredwardine Herefs 34 H12
Breedon on the Hill Leics 47 M9
Breich W Loth 82 J6
Breightmet Bolton 55 R5
Breighton E R Yk 64 G13
Breinton Herefs 35 L13
Bremhill Wilts 18 E6
Bremridge Devon 15 Q7
Brenchley Kent 12 C7
Brendon Devon 14 J11
Brendon Devon 15 S3
Brendon Hill Somset 16 D10
Brenfield Ag & B 87 Q9
Brenish W Isls 106 e6
Brenkley N u Ty 77 Q10
Brent Cross Gt Lon 21 M5
Brent Eleigh Suffk 40 F11
Brentford Gt Lon 21 L7
Brentingby Leics 47 U10
Brent Knoll Somset 16 K6
Brent Mill Devon 5 R9
Brent Pelham Herts 22 B1
Brentwood Essex 22 E9
Brenzett Kent 12 K10
Brenzett Green Kent 12 K10
Brereton Staffs 46 E10
Brereton Green Ches E 55 S14
Brereton Heath Ches E 55 T13
Brereton Hill Staffs 46 E10
Bressay Shet 106 v9
Bressingham Norfk 40 J4
Bressingham Common Norfk 40 J4
Bretby Derbys 46 J9
Bretby Crematorium Derbys 46 J9
Bretford Warwks 37 M5
Bretforton Worcs 36 E12
Bretherton Lancs 55 L2
Brettabister Shet 106 u8
Brettenham Norfk 40 F4
Brettenham Suffk 40 G10
Bretton Derbys 56 K11
Bretton Flints 54 J14
Brewers End Essex 22 E3
Brewer Street Surrey 21 P12
Brewood Staffs 45 U12
Briantspuddle Dorset 7 V6
Brick End Essex 22 E2
Brickendon Herts 31 T11
Bricket Wood Herts 31 P12
Brick Houses Sheff 57 M10
Brickkiln Green Essex 22 H1
Bricklehampton Worcs 36 C12
Bride IoM 60 g2
Bridekirk Cumb 66 H6
Bridell Pembks 32 C12
Bridestowe Devon 5 N3
Brideswell Abers 104 H8
Bridford Devon 5 U3
Bridge Kent 13 N5
Bridge End Cumb 61 M3
Bridge End Cumb 67 N3
Bridge End Devon 5 R11
Bridge End Dur 69 M5
Bridge End Essex 22 G1
Bridge End Lincs 48 H6
Bridgefoot Cumb 66 G7
Bridge Green Essex 39 Q13
Bridgehampton Somset 17 Q12
Bridge Hewick N York 63 S5
Bridgehill Dur 69 N2
Bridgehouse Gate N York 63 P6
Bridgemary Hants 9 R8
Bridgemere Ches E 45 R4
Bridgend Abers 104 G8
Bridgend Ag & B 78 E3
Bridgend Ag & B 79 P8
Bridgend Angus 98 J10
Bridgend Brdgnd 26 G12
Bridgend Cerdgn 32 C11
Bridgend Cumb 67 P10
Bridgend D & G 75 L4
Bridgend Devon 5 P11
Bridgend Fife 91 N9
Bridgend Moray 104 D9
Bridgend P & K 90 H7
Bridgend W Loth 82 K3
Bridgend of Lintrathen Angus 98 D13
Bridge of Alford Abers 104 H12
Bridge of Allan Stirlg 89 S6
Bridge of Avon Moray 103 U11
Bridge of Avon Moray 103 U8
Bridge of Balgie P & K 95 R9
Bridge of Brewlands Angus 98 B11
Bridge of Brown Highld 103 T11
Bridge of Cally P & K 97 U13
Bridge of Canny Abers 99 M4
Bridge of Craigisla Angus 98 D13
Bridge of Dee D & G 74 D14
Bridge of Don C Aber 99 S2
Bridge of Dulsie Highld 103 P7
Bridge of Dye Abers 99 M6
Bridge of Earn P & K 90 H8
Bridge of Ericht P & K 95 Q7
Bridge of Feugh Abers 99 N5
Bridge of Forss Highld 112 B3
Bridge of Gairn Abers 98 F4
Bridge of Gaur P & K 95 Q7
Bridge of Marnoch Abers 104 H5
Bridge of Muchalls Abers 99 R5
Bridge of Orchy Ag & B 94 K11
Bridge of Tilt P & K 97 P10
Bridge of Tynet Moray 104 D3
Bridge of Walls Shet 106 s8
Bridge of Weir Rens 88 J12
Bridge Reeve Devon 15 Q10
Bridgerule Devon 14 G12
Bridges Shrops 34 J1
Bridge Sollers Herefs 34 K12
Bridge Street Suffk 40 E11
Bridgetown Cnwll 4 J3
Bridgetown Somset 16 B10
Bridge Trafford Ches W 55 L12
Bridge Yate S Glos 28 C13
Bridgham Norfk 40 G3
Bridgnorth Shrops 35 R2
Bridgwater Somset 16 J9
Bridgwater Services Somset 16 K10
Bridlington E R Yk 65 R6
Bridport Dorset 7 N6
Bridstow Herefs 28 A3
Brierfield Lancs 62 G12
Brierley Barns 57 P4
Brierley Gloucs 28 B4
Brierley Herefs 35 L9
Brierley Hill Dudley 36 B3
Brierlow Bar Derbys 56 G13
Brierton Hartpl 70 G6
Briery Cumb 67 L8
Brigg N Linc 58 H5
Briggate Norfk 51 P8
Briggswath N York 71 Q11
Brigham Cumb 66 G6
Brigham Cumb 67 L8
Brigham E R Yk 65 P9
Brighouse Calder 56 H2
Brighstone IoW 9 N12
Brightgate Derbys 46 J2
Brighthampton Oxon 29 S7
Brightholmlee Sheff 57 L7
Brightley Devon 15 P13
Brightling E Susx 12 C11
Brightlingsea Essex 23 Q4
Brighton Br & H 11 N10
Brighton Cnwll 3 N6
Brighton le Sands Sefton 54 H7
Brightons Falk 82 H3
Brightwalton W Berk 19 P5
Brightwalton Green W Berk 19 P5
Brightwalton Holt W Berk 19 P5
Brightwell Suffk 41 N12
Brightwell Baldwin Oxon 30 E13
Brightwell-cum-Sotwell Oxon 19 S2
Brightwell Upperton Oxon 19 U2
Brignall Dur 69 N10
Brig o'Turk Stirlg 89 M4
Brigsley NE Lin 59 N6
Brigsteer Cumb 61 T2
Brigstock Nhants 38 D3
Brill Bucks 30 E10
Brill Cnwll 2 J11
Brilley Herefs 34 G11
Brimfield Herefs 35 M7
Brimfield Cross Herefs 35 M7
Brimington Derbys 57 P12
Brimley Devon 5 U5
Brimpsfield Gloucs 28 H5
Brimpton W Berk 19 S8
Brimpton Common W Berk 19 S8
Brimscombe Gloucs 28 G7
Brimstage Wirral 54 H10
Brincliffe Sheff 57 M10
Brind E R Yk 64 G13
Brindham Somset 17 P9
Brindister Shet 106 s8
Brindle Lancs 55 N2
Brindley Ches E 45 N3
Brineton Staffs 45 T11
Bringhurst Leics 38 B2
Bringsty Common Herefs 35 R9
Brington Cambs 38 G5
Brinian Ork 106 t17
Briningham Norfk 50 H7
Brinkely Notts 47 T3
Brinkhill Lincs 59 Q12
Brinkley Cambs 39 T10
Brinklow Warwks 37 M5
Brinkworth Wilts 28 K11
Brinscall Lancs 55 P2
Brinscombe Somset 17 M6
Brinsea N Som 17 M4
Brinsley Notts 47 N4
Brinsop Herefs 34 K12
Brinsworth Rothm 57 P9
Brinton Norfk 50 H6
Brinyan Ork 106 t17
Brisco Cumb 67 P2
Brisley Norfk 50 F9
Brislington Bristl 17 R2
Brissenden Green Kent 12 H8
Bristol Bristl 28 A13
Bristol Airport N Som 17 P3
Bristol Zoo Gardens Bristl 27 V13
Briston Norfk 50 J7
Brisworthy Devon 5 P7
Britannia Lancs 56 C2
Britford Wilts 8 H3
Brithdir Caerph 27 L7
Brithdir Gwynd 43 Q10
British Legion Village Kent 12 D4
Briton Ferry Neath 26 C9
Britwell Salome Oxon 19 U2
Brixham Torbay 6 B13
Brixton Devon 5 P10
Brixton Gt Lon 21 P7
Brixton Deverill Wilts 18 C13
Brixworth Nhants 37 T6
Brize Norton Oxon 29 Q6
Brize Norton Airport Oxon 29 Q6
Broad Alley Worcs 35 U7
Broad Blunsdon Swindn 29 M9
Broadbottom Tamesd 56 E8
Broadbridge W Susx 10 C9
Broadbridge Heath W Susx 10 J4
Broad Campden Gloucs 36 G13
Broad Carr Calder 56 G3
Broad Chalke Wilts 8 E3
Broad Clough Lancs 56 C2
Broadclyst Devon 6 C5
Broadfield Inver 88 H11
Broadfield Pembks 24 K10
Broadford Highld 100 f7
Broad Ford Kent 12 D8
Broadford Bridge W Susx 10 H6
Broadgairhill Border 75 P3
Broadgrass Green Suffk 40 G8
Broad Green Cambs 39 U8
Broad Green Essex 23 L3
Broad Green Worcs 35 S9
Broad Green Worcs 36 C6
Broadhaugh Border 85 M7
Broad Haven Pembks 24 E8
Broadheath Traffd 55 S9
Broadheath Worcs 35 Q7
Broadhembury Devon 6 F4
Broadhempston Devon 5 U7
Broad Hill Cambs 39 S5
Broad Hinton Wilts 18 H5
Broadholme Lincs 58 E12
Broadland Row E Susx 12 F12
Broadlay Carmth 25 Q9
Broad Layings Hants 19 P8
Broadley Essex 22 B6
Broadley Lancs 56 C3
Broadley Moray 104 D3
Broadley Common Essex 22 B6
Broad Marston Worcs 36 F11
Broadmayne Dorset 7 T7
Broad Meadow Staffs 45 T4
Broadmere Hants 19 T11
Broadmoor Gloucs 28 B4
Broadmoor Pembks 24 J9
Broadnymett Devon 15 R12
Broad Oak Carmth 25 U6
Broad Oak Cumb 66 H14
Broadoak Dorset 7 M5
Broad Oak E Susx 11 U6
Broad Oak E Susx 12 F12
Broadoak Gloucs 28 C5
Broad Oak Hants 20 C12
Broad Oak Herefs 27 T3
Broad Oak Kent 13 N3
Broad Oak St Hel 55 M7
Broadoak Wrexhm 44 J2
Broad Road Suffk 41 N5
Broad's Green Essex 22 G5
Broadstairs Kent 13 S2
Broadstone Mons 27 U7
Broadstone Poole 8 E9
Broadstone Shrops 35 M3
Broad Street E Susx 12 G12
Broad Street Essex 22 E4
Broad Street Kent 12 F4
Broad Street Kent 13 M7
Broad Street Medway 22 J13
Broad Street Wilts 18 H9
Broad Street Green Essex 23 L6
Broad Town Wilts 18 G5
Broadwas Worcs 35 S9
Broadwater Herts 31 R8
Broadwater W Susx 10 J10
Broadwaters Worcs 35 T5
Broadway Carmth 25 N8
Broadway Carmth 25 Q9
Broadway Pembks 24 E8
Broadway Somset 16 K13
Broadway Suffk 41 Q5
Broadway Worcs 36 E13
Broadwell Gloucs 28 A5
Broadwell Gloucs 29 P2
Broadwell Oxon 29 Q7
Broadwell Warwks 37 N7
Broadwey Dorset 7 S8
Broadwindsor Dorset 7 M4
Broadwood Kelly Devon 15 P11
Broadwoodwidger Devon 5 L3
Brobury Herefs 34 H12
Brochel Highld 100 e5
Brochroy Ag & B 94 E12
Brock Lancs 61 U11
Brockamin Worcs 35 S10
Brockbridge Hants 9 S5
Brockdish Norfk 41 M5
Brockencote Worcs 35 U6
Brockenhurst Hants 9 L8
Brocketsbrae S Lans 82 F11
Brockford Green Suffk 40 K7
Brockford Street Suffk 40 K7
Brockhall Nhants 37 R8
Brockham Surrey 21 L13
Brockhampton Gloucs 28 H2
Brockhampton Gloucs 28 K3
Brockhampton Hants 9 U7
Brockhampton Herefs 28 A1
Brockhampton Green Dorset 7 T3
Brockholes Kirk 56 J4
Brockhurst Derbys 57 M14
Brockhurst Warwks 37 N4
Brocklebank Cumb 67 M4
Brocklesby Lincs 58 K4
Brockley N Som 17 N3
Brockley Suffk 40 D6
Brockley Green Suffk 40 B11
Brockley Green Suffk 40 D10
Brockleymoor Cumb 67 Q5
Brockmoor Dudley 36 B3
Brockscombe Devon 15 L13
Brock's Green Hants 19 R8
Brockton Shrops 34 H3
Brockton Shrops 35 N2
Brockton Shrops 44 H13
Brockton Shrops 45 R13
Brockton Staffs 45 T7
Brockweir Gloucs 27 U7
Brockwood Park Hants 9 S3
Brockworth Gloucs 28 G4
Brocton Cnwll 3 Q3
Brocton Staffs 46 C10
Brodick N Ayrs 80 E5
Brodie Moray 103 Q4
Brodsworth Donc 57 R5
Brogaig Highld 100 d3
Brogborough C Beds 31 L5
Brokenborough Wilts 28 H10
Broken Cross Ches E 56 C12
Broken Cross Ches W 55 Q12
Brokerswood Wilts 18 B10
Bromborough Wirral 54 J10
Brome Suffk 40 K5
Brome Street Suffk 41 L5
Bromeswell Suffk 41 P10
Bromfield Cumb 66 J3
Bromfield Shrops 35 L5
Bromham Bed 38 F10
Bromham Wilts 18 E7
Bromley Barns 57 M7
Bromley Dudley 36 B3
Bromley Gt Lon 21 R9
Bromley Shrops 35 R1
Bromley Common Gt Lon 21 R9
Bromley Cross Bolton 55 R4
Bromley Cross Essex 23 Q2
Bromley Green Kent 12 J8
Bromlow Shrops 44 H13
Brompton Medway 12 E2
Brompton N York 70 E13
Brompton-by-Sawdon N York 65 L3
Brompton-on-Swale N York 69 R13
Brompton Ralph Somset 16 E10
Brompton Regis Somset 16 C10
Bromsash Herefs 28 C3
Bromsberrow Gloucs 35 R14
Bromsberrow Heath Gloucs 35 R14
Bromsgrove Worcs 36 C6
Bromstead Heath Staffs 45 S10
Bromyard Herefs 35 Q10
Bromyard Downs Herefs 35 Q9
Bronaber Gwynd 43 P7
Bronant Cerdgn 33 M7
Broncroft Shrops 35 M3
Brongest Cerdgn 32 F11
Bronington Wrexhm 45 L6
Bronllys Powys 34 D14
Bronwydd Carmth 25 R6
Bronydd Powys 34 F11
Bronygarth Shrops 44 G6
Brook Carmth 25 N9
Brook Hants 8 K6
Brook Hants 9 L3
Brook IoW 9 M12
Brook Kent 13 L7
Brook Surrey 10 E3
Brook Surrey 20 J13
Brooke Norfk 51 N14
Brooke Rutlnd 48 B12
Brookenby Lincs 59 M7
Brook End Bed 38 G8
Brook End C Beds 38 J11
Brook End Cambs 38 G6
Brook End M Keyn 30 K4
Brookfield Rens 88 K13
Brookhampton Oxon 30 D13
Brookhampton Somset 17 R11
Brook Hill Hants 8 K6
Brook House Denbgs 54 C13
Brookhouse Lancs 61 U7
Brookhouse Rothm 57 R9
Brookhouse Green Ches E 45 T1
Brookhouses Derbys 56 F9
Brookland Kent 12 J10
Brooklands Traffd 55 S8
Brookmans Park Herts 31 R12
Brooks Powys 44 D14
Brooksby Leics 47 S10
Brooks End Kent 13 Q2
Brooks Green W Susx 10 J6
Brook Street Essex 22 E9
Brook Street Kent 12 H9
Brook Street Suffk 40 D11
Brook Street W Susx 11 N5
Brookthorpe Gloucs 28 F5
Brookville Norfk 40 B1
Brookwood Surrey 20 G11
Broom C Beds 31 Q4
Broom Rothm 57 P8
Broom Warwks 36 E10
Broome Norfk 41 Q2
Broome Shrops 34 K4
Broome Worcs 36 B5
Broomedge Warrtn 55 R9
Broome Park Nthumb 77 N3
Broomer's Corner W Susx 10 J6
Broomershill W Susx 10 H7
Broomfield Essex 22 H5
Broomfield Kent 12 F5
Broomfield Kent 13 N2
Broomfield Somset 16 H10
Broomfields Shrops 44 K10
Broomfleet E R Yk 58 E1
Broom Green Norfk 50 G9
Broomhall W & M 20 G9
Broomhaugh Nthumb 77 L13
Broom Hill Barns 57 P6
Broom Hill Dorset 8 E8
Broom Hill Notts 47 P4
Broomhill Nthumb 77 Q5
Broom Hill Worcs 36 B5
Broomhill Green Ches E 45 P4
Broomley Nthumb 77 L13
Broompark Dur 69 R4
Broom's Green Gloucs 35 R14
Broomsthorpe Norfk 50 D8
Broom Street Kent 12 K3
Brora Highld 109 S4
Broseley Shrops 45 Q13
Brotherhouse Bar Lincs 49 L11
Brotherlee Dur 68 K5
Brothertoft Lincs 49 L4
Brotherton N York 57 Q1
Brotton R & Cl 71 L9
Broubster Highld 112 B5
Brough Cumb 68 G10
Brough Derbys 56 J10
Brough E R Yk 58 F1
Brough Highld 112 F2
Brough Notts 48 B2
Brough Shet 106 v7
Broughall Shrops 45 N5
Brough Lodge Shet 106 v4
Brough Sowerby Cumb 68 G10
Broughton Border 83 M11
Broughton Bucks 30 H10
Broughton Cambs 39 L5
Broughton Flints 54 H14
Broughton Hants 9 L2
Broughton Lancs 61 U13
Broughton M Keyn 30 J5
Broughton N Linc 58 G5
Broughton N York 62 J9
Broughton N York 64 H5
Broughton Nhants 38 B5
Broughton Oxon 37 M13
Broughton Salfd 55 T6
Broughton Staffs 45 S7
Broughton V Glam 16 B2
Broughton Astley Leics 37 P2
Broughton Beck Cumb 61 P3
Broughton Gifford Wilts 18 C8
Broughton Green Worcs 36 C8
Broughton Hackett Worcs 36 B10
Broughton-in-Furness Cumb 61 N2
Broughton Mains D & G 73 M10
Broughton Mills Cumb 61 N1
Broughton Moor Cumb 66 G6
Broughton Poggs Oxon 29 P7
Broughton Tower Cumb 61 N2
Broughty Ferry C Dund 91 Q5
Brough with St Giles N York 69 R13
Brow End Cumb 61 P5
Brownber Cumb 68 F11
Brown Candover Hants 19 S13
Brown Edge Lancs 54 J4
Brown Edge Staffs 46 B3
Brown Heath Ches W 55 L14
Brownheath Shrops 45 L8
Brownhill Abers 105 P7
Brownhills Fife 91 R8
Brownhills Wsall 46 D12
Brownieside Nthumb 85 T14
Browninghill Green Hants 19 S9
Brown Lees Staffs 45 U2
Brownlow Heath Ches E 45 T1
Brownrigg Cumb 66 F8
Brownrigg Cumb 66 J2
Brownsea Island Dorset 8 E11
Brown's Green Birm 36 E2
Brownsham Devon 14 G7
Browns Hill Gloucs 28 G7
Brownsover Warwks 37 P5
Brownston Devon 5 R10
Brown Street Suffk 40 J8
Brow-of-the-Hill Norfk 49 U10
Browston Green Norfk 51 S13
Broxa N York 65 L1
Broxbourne Herts 31 U11
Broxburn E Loth 84 H3
Broxburn W Loth 83 L4
Broxfield Nthumb 77 Q2
Broxted Essex 22 E2
Broxton Ches W 45 L3
Broyle Side E Susx 11 R8
Bruan Highld 112 H9
Bruar P & K 97 N10
Brucefield Highld 109 S7
Bruchag Ag & B 88 D14
Bruera Ches W 44 K1
Bruern Abbey Oxon 29 Q3
Bruichladdich Ag & B 78 D3
Bruisyard Suffk 41 P7
Bruisyard Street Suffk 41 P7
Brumby N Linc 58 E5
Brund Staffs 46 F1
Brundall Norfk 51 P12
Brundish Suffk 41 N7
Brundish Street Suffk 41 N6
Brunery Highld 93 S4
Brunnion Cnwll 2 E9
Brunslow Shrops 34 J4
Brunswick Village N u Ty 77 Q11
Bruntcliffe Leeds 57 L1
Brunthwaite C Brad 63 M10
Bruntingthorpe Leics 37 R3
Brunton Fife 91 M7
Brunton Nthumb 85 U14
Brunton Wilts 18 K9
Brushford Devon 15 Q11
Brushford Somset 16 B11
Bruton Somset 17 S9
Bryan's Green Worcs 35 U7
Bryanston Dorset 8 B7
Bryant's Bottom Bucks 20 E3
Brydekirk D & G 75 N11
Bryher IoS 2 b2
Brymbo Wrexhm 44 G3
Brympton Somset 17 P13
Bryn Carmth 25 T10
Bryn Ches W 55 P12
Bryn Neath 26 E9
Bryn Shrops 34 G3
Bryn Wigan 55 N6
Brynamman Carmth 26 C5
Brynberian Pembks 24 K3
Brynbryddan Neath 26 D9
Bryn-bwbach Gwynd 43 M6
Bryncae Rhondd 26 H11
Bryncethin Brdgnd 26 G11
Bryncir Gwynd 42 J5
Bryn-côch Neath 26 C8
Bryncroes Gwynd 42 D7
Bryncrug Gwynd 43 M13
Bryn Du IoA 52 D8
Bryn-Eden Gwynd 43 P8
Bryneglwys Denbgs 44 D4
Brynfields Wrexhm 44 H5
Brynford Flints 54 E12
Bryn Gates Wigan 55 N6
Bryn Golau Rhondd 26 J10
Bryngwran IoA 52 E7
Bryngwyn Mons 27 R6
Bryngwyn Powys 34 E11
Bryn-Henllan Pembks 24 H3
Brynhoffnant Cerdgn 32 F10
Bryning Lancs 61 S14
Brynithel Blae G 27 N7
Brynmawr Blae G 27 M5
Bryn-mawr Gwynd 42 D7
Brynmenyn Brdgnd 26 G11
Brynmill Swans 26 A9
Brynna Rhondd 26 H11
Bryn-penarth Powys 44 D13
Brynrefail Gwynd 52 J10
Brynrefail IoA 52 G5
Brynsadler Rhondd 26 J11
Bryn Saith Marchog Denbgs 44 C3
Brynsiencyn IoA 52 G9
Brynteg IoA 52 G6
Bryn-y-bal Flints 54 G14
Bryn-y-Maen Conwy 53 P7
Bryn-yr-Eos Wrexhm 44 G5
Bualintur Highld 100 d7
Buarth-draw Flints 54 E11
Bubbenhall Warwks 37 L6
Bubwith E R Yk 64 G12
Buccleuch Border 75 R3
Buchanan Smithy Stirlg 89 L8
Buchanhaven Abers 105 U6
Buchanty P & K 90 D6
Buchany Stirlg 89 R5
Buchlyvie Stirlg 89 N7
Buckabank Cumb 67 N3
Buckden Cambs 38 J7
Buckden N York 62 J4
Buckenham Norfk 51 Q12
Buckerell Devon 6 F4
Buckfast Devon 5 S7
Buckfastleigh Devon 5 S7
Buckhaven Fife 91 N12
Buckholt Mons 27 U4
Buckhorn Devon 14 J13
Buckhorn Weston Dorset 17 U12
Buckhurst Hill Essex 21 R4
Buckie Moray 104 E2
Buckingham Bucks 30 E6
Buckland Bucks 30 J10
Buckland Devon 5 R12
Buckland Gloucs 36 E13
Buckland Hants 9 L9
Buckland Herts 31 U6
Buckland Kent 13 R7
Buckland Oxon 29 R8
Buckland Surrey 21 M12
Buckland Brewer Devon 14 K8
Buckland Common Bucks 30 K11
Buckland Dinham Somset 17 U6
Buckland Filleigh Devon 15 L11
Buckland in the Moor Devon 5 S6
Buckland Monachorum Devon 5 M7
Buckland Newton Dorset 7 S3
Buckland Ripers Dorset 7 S8
Buckland St Mary Somset 6 J2
Buckland-Tout-Saints Devon 5 T11
Bucklebury W Berk 19 S6
Bucklers Hard Hants 9 N8
Bucklesham Suffk 41 M12
Buckley Flints 54 G14
Buckley Green Warwks 36 G7
Bucklow Hill Ches E 55 R10
Buckminster Leics 48 C9
Bucknall C Stke 46 B4
Bucknall Lincs 59 L13
Bucknell Oxon 30 C7
Bucknell Shrops 34 J6
Buckpool Moray 104 E2
Bucksburn C Aber 99 R2
Buck's Cross Devon 14 J8
Bucks Green W Susx 10 H4
Buckshaw Village Lancs 55 N2
Bucks Hill Herts 31 N12
Bucks Horn Oak Hants 10 C2
Buck's Mills Devon 14 J8
Buckton E R Yk 65 R5
Buckton Herefs 34 J6
Buckton Nthumb 85 R11
Buckworth Cambs 38 H5
Budby Notts 57 T13
Buddileigh Staffs 45 R4
Bude Cnwll 14 F11
Budge's Shop Cnwll 4 J9
Budlake Devon 6 C4
Budle Nthumb 85 T11
Budleigh Salterton Devon 6 E8
Budlett's Common E Susx 11 R6
Budock Water Cnwll 2 K10
Buerton Ches E 45 Q5
Bugbrooke Nhants 37 S9
Bugford Devon 5 U10
Buglawton Ches E 56 C14
Bugle Cnwll 3 Q5
Bugley Dorset 17 U12
Bugthorpe E R Yk 64 H8
Buildwas Shrops 45 P13
Builth Road Powys 34 B10
Builth Wells Powys 34 B10
Bulbourne Herts 30 K10
Bulbridge Wilts 8 F2
Bulby Lincs 48 G8
Bulford Wilts 18 J12
Bulford Camp Wilts 18 J12
Bulkeley Ches E 45 M3
Bulkington Warwks 37 L3
Bulkington Wilts 18 D9
Bulkworthy Devon 14 J10
Bullamoor N York 70 E14
Bull Bay IoA 52 F4
Bullbridge Derbys 47 L3
Bullbrook Br For 20 E9
Bullen's Green Herts 31 R11
Bulley Gloucs 28 E4
Bullgill Cumb 66 G5
Bullinghope Herefs 35 M13
Bullington Hants 19 Q12
Bullington Lincs 58 J11
Bullockstone Kent 13 N2
Bull's Green Herts 31 S9
Bull's Green Norfk 41 R2
Bulmer Essex 40 D12
Bulmer N York 64 F6
Bulmer Tye Essex 40 D13
Bulphan Thurr 22 F10
Bulstone Devon 6 G7
Bulstrode Herts 31 M12
Bulverhythe E Susx 12 E14
Bulwark Abers 105 Q6
Bulwell C Nott 47 P5
Bulwick Nhants 38 E2
Bumble's Green Essex 22 B6
Bunacaimb Highld 100 f11
Bunarkaig Highld 101 T14
Bunbury Ches E 45 N2
Bunbury Heath Ches E 45 N2
Bunchrew Highld 102 H6
Buncton W Susx 10 J8
Bundalloch Highld 101 M6
Bunessan Ag & B 86 F1
Bungay Suffk 41 P3
Bunker's Hill Lincs 49 L3
Bunnahabhain Ag & B 86 G11
Bunny Notts 47 Q8
Buntait Highld 102 D9
Buntingford Herts 31 U7
Bunwell Norfk 40 K2
Bunwell Hill Norfk 40 K2
Bupton Derbys 46 H6
Burbage Derbys 56 F12
Burbage Leics 37 M2
Burbage Wilts 18 K8
Burcher Herefs 34 H8
Burchett's Green E Susx 12 C9
Burchett's Green W & M 20 D6
Burcombe Wilts 8 F2
Burcot Oxon 30 C13
Burcot Worcs 36 C6
Burcote Shrops 35 R1
Burcott Bucks 30 H9
Burcott Bucks 30 J8
Burdale N York 64 K7
Bures Essex 40 F14
Burford Oxon 29 Q5
Burford Shrops 35 N7
Burg Ag & B 92 K9
Burgate Suffk 40 J5
Burgates Hants 10 B5
Burge End Herts 31 P6
Burgess Hill W Susx 11 N7
Burgh Suffk 41 M10
Burgh by Sands Cumb 75 R14
Burgh Castle Norfk 51 S12
Burghclere Hants 19 Q8
Burghead Moray 103 T2
Burghfield W Berk 19 U7
Burghfield Common W Berk 19 U7
Burgh Heath Surrey 21 M11
Burgh Hill E Susx 12 D10
Burghill Herefs 35 L12
Burgh Island Devon 5 Q12
Burgh le Marsh Lincs 59 T13
Burgh next Aylsham Norfk 51 M8
Burgh on Bain Lincs 59 M9
Burgh St Margaret Norfk 51 R11
Burgh St Peter Norfk 41 S2
Burghwallis Donc 57 R4
Burham Kent 12 D3
Buriton Hants 9 U5
Burland Ches E 45 P3
Burlawn Cnwll 3 P2
Burleigh Gloucs 28 G7
Burlescombe Devon 16 E13
Burleston Dorset 7 U6
Burlestone Devon 5 U11
Burley Hants 8 J8
Burley Rutlnd 48 C11
Burley Shrops 35 L4
Burleydam Ches E 45 P5
Burley Gate Herefs 35 N11
Burley in Wharfedale C Brad 63 P10
Burley Lawn Hants 8 J8
Burley Street Hants 8 J8
Burley Wood Head C Brad 63 P11
Burlingham Green Norfk 51 Q11
Burlingjobb Powys 34 G9
Burlington Shrops 45 S11
Burlton Shrops 45 L8
Burmarsh Kent 13 M9
Burmington Warwks 36 J13
Burn N York 64 D14
Burnage Manch 56 C8
Burnaston Derbys 46 J7
Burnbanks Cumb 67 R9
Burnbrae N Lans 82 G7
Burnby E R Yk 64 J10
Burn Cross Sheff 57 M7
Burndell W Susx 10 F10
Burnden Bolton 55 R5
Burnedge Rochdl 56 D4
Burneside Cumb 67 R13
Burneston N York 63 S3
Burnett BaNES 17 S3
Burnfoot Border 75 T3
Burnfoot Border 75 V2
Burnfoot D & G 74 J7
Burnfoot D & G 75 R8
Burnfoot D & G 75 S6
Burnfoot P & K 90 E11
Burnham Bucks 20 F6
Burnham N Linc 58 J3
Burnham Deepdale Norfk 50 D5
Burnham Green Herts 31 S9
Burnham Market Norfk 50 D5
Burnham Norton Norfk 50 D5
Burnham-on-Crouch Essex 23 M8
Burnham-on-Sea Somset 16 K7
Burnham Overy Norfk 50 D5
Burnham Overy Staithe Norfk 50 D5
Burnham Thorpe Norfk 50 E5
Burnhaven Abers 105 U7
Burnhead D & G 74 G6
Burnhervie Abers 105 L12
Burnhill Green Staffs 45 S13
Burnhope Dur 69 Q3
Burnhouse N Ayrs 81 M2
Burniston N York 71 T14
Burnley Lancs 62 G13
Burnley Crematorium Lancs 62 G13
Burnmouth Border 85 P6
Burn Naze Lancs 61 Q11
Burn of Cambus Stirlg 89 R5
Burnopfield Dur 69 Q1
Burnrigg Cumb 67 Q1
Burnsall N York 63 L7
Burnside Angus 98 G12
Burnside Angus 98 J13
Burnside Fife 90 J10
Burnside Moray 103 U2
Burnside W Loth 83 L3
Burnside of Duntrune Angus 91 P5
Burntcommon Surrey 20 H12
Burntheath Derbys 46 H7
Burnt Heath Essex 23 Q2
Burnt Hill W Berk 19 S6
Burnthouse Cnwll 2 K9
Burnt Houses Dur 69 P8
Burntisland Fife 83 P1
Burnt Oak E Susx 11 S5
Burnton E Ayrs 81 P11
Burntwood Staffs 46 E12
Burntwood Green Staffs 46 E12
Burnt Yates N York 63 R7
Burnworthy Somset 16 G13
Burpham Surrey 20 H12
Burpham W Susx 10 G9
Burradon N Tyne 77 R11
Burradon Nthumb 76 K4
Burrafirth Shet 106 w2
Burras Cnwll 2 H10
Burraton Cnwll 5 L7
Burravoe Shet 106 v5
Burrells Cumb 68 E9
Burrelton P & K 90 K4
Burridge Devon 6 K3
Burridge Devon 15 N5
Burridge Hants 9 Q6
Burrill N York 63 Q2
Burringham N Linc 58 D5
Burrington Devon 15 P9
Burrington Herefs 34 K6
Burrington N Som 17 N5
Burrough End Cambs 39 T9
Burrough Green Cambs 39 T9
Burrough on the Hill Leics 47 U11
Burrow Lancs 62 C5
Burrow Somset 16 B8
Burrow Bridge Somset 17 L10
Burrowhill Surrey 20 G10
Burrows Cross Surrey 20 J13
Burry Swans 25 S12
Burry Green Swans 25 S12
Burry Port Carmth 25 R10
Burscough Lancs 54 K4
Burscough Bridge Lancs 54 K4
Bursea E R Yk 64 J13
Burshill E R Yk 65 P10
Bursledon Hants 9 P7
Burslem C Stke 45 U4
Burstall Suffk 40 J12
Burstock Dorset 7 M4
Burston Norfk 40 K4
Burston Staffs 46 B7
Burstow Surrey 11 N2
Burstwick E R Yk 65 S14
Burtersett N York 62 H2
Burtholme Cumb 76 A13
Burthorpe Green Suffk 40 C8
Burthwaite Cumb 67 P3
Burthy Cnwll 3 N5
Burtle Hill Somset 17 L8
Burtoft Lincs 49 L6
Burton Ches W 54 H12
Burton Ches W 55 M14
Burton Dorset 7 S6
Burton Dorset 8 H10
Burton Lincs 58 G12
Burton Nthumb 85 T12
Burton Pembks 24 G9
Burton Somset 7 P2
Burton Somset 16 G8
Burton Wilts 17 V10
Burton Wilts 18 B5
Burton Agnes E R Yk 65 Q7
Burton Bradstock Dorset 7 N7
Burton Coggles Lincs 48 E8
Burton Dassett Warwks 37 L10
Burton End Essex 22 D3
Burton End Suffk 39 U11
Burton Fleming E R Yk 65 P5
Burton Green Warwks 36 J5
Burton Green Wrexhm 44 H2
Burton Hastings Warwks 37 M3
Burton-in-Kendal Cumb 61 U4
Burton-in-Kendal Services Cumb 61 U4
Burton in Lonsdale N York 62 D5
Burton Joyce Notts 47 R5
Burton Latimer Nhants 38 D6
Burton Lazars Leics 47 U10

Burton Leonard – Clackmannanshire Bridge
127

Burton Leonard N York 63 S7
Burton on the Wolds Leics 47 Q9
Burton Overy Leics 47 S14
Burton Pedwardine Lincs 48 H5
Burton Pidsea E R Yk 65 S13
Burton Salmon N York 57 Q1
Burton's Green Essex 22 K2
Burton upon Stather N Linc 58 E3
Burton upon Trent Staffs 46 H9
Burton Waters Lincs 58 F12
Burtonwood Warrtn 55 N8
Burtonwood Services Warrtn 55 N8
Burwardsley Ches W 45 M2
Burwarton Shrops 35 P3
Burwash E Susx 12 C11
Burwash Common E Susx 11 U6
Burwash Weald E Susx 11 V6
Burwell Cambs 39 S7
Burwell Lincs 59 Q11
Burwen IoA 52 F4
Burwick Ork 106 t21
Bury Bury 55 T4
Bury Cambs 39 L4
Bury Somset 16 B11
Bury W Susx 10 G8
Bury End C Beds 31 P5
Bury Green Herts 22 C3
Bury St Edmunds Suffk 40 E8
Burythorpe N York 64 H7
Busby E Rens 81 R1
Busby Stoop N York 63 T3
Buscot Oxon 29 P8
Bush Abers 99 P10
Bush Cnwll 14 F11
Bush Bank Herefs 35 L10
Bushbury Wolves 46 B13
Bushbury Crematorium Wolves 46 B13
Bushby Leics 47 S13
Bushey Herts 20 K3
Bushey Heath Herts 20 K4
Bush Green Norfk 41 M3
Bush Green Suffk 40 F9
Bush Hill Park Gt Lon 21 P3
Bushley Worcs 35 U14
Bushley Green Worcs 35 U14
Bushmead Bed 38 H8
Bushmoor Shrops 34 K3
Bushton Wilts 18 G5
Busk Cumb 68 D4
Buslingthorpe Lincs 58 J9
Bussage Gloucs 28 G7
Bussex Somset 17 L10
Butcher's Cross E Susx 11 T5
Butcombe N Som 17 P4
Bute Ag & B 88 B12
Butleigh Somset 17 P10
Butleigh Wootton Somset 17 P9
Butler's Cross Bucks 30 H11
Butler's Hill Notts 47 P4
Butlers Marston Warwks 36 K10
Butley Suffk 41 Q10
Butley High Corner Suffk 41 Q11
Buttercrambe N York 64 G8
Butterdean Border 84 K6
Butterknowle Dur 69 P7
Butterleigh Devon 6 C3
Butterley Derbys 47 M3
Buttermere Cumb 66 J9
Buttermere Wilts 19 M8
Butters Green Staffs 45 T3
Buttershaw C Brad 63 N14
Butterstone P & K 90 G2
Butterton Staffs 45 T5
Butterton Staffs 46 E2
Butterwick Dur 70 E6
Butterwick Lincs 49 N4
Butterwick N York 64 G4
Butterwick N York 65 M5
Butt Green Ches E 45 Q3
Buttington Powys 44 F12
Buttonbridge Shrops 35 R5
Buttonoak Shrops 35 S5
Buttsash Hants 9 N7
Buttsbear Cross Cnwll 14 G12
Butt's Green Essex 22 J7
Buxhall Suffk 40 H9
Buxhall Fen Street Suffk 40 H9
Buxted E Susx 11 R6
Buxton Derbys 56 G12
Buxton Norfk 51 M9
Buxton Heath Norfk 51 L9
Bwlch Powys 27 M3
Bwlchgwyn Wrexhm 44 G3
Bwlchllan Cerdgn 33 L9
Bwlchnewydd Carmth 25 Q6
Bwlchtocyn Gwynd 42 F8
Bwlch-y-cibau Powys 44 E10
Bwlch-y-Ddar Powys 44 E9
Bwlchyfadfa Cerdgn 32 H11
Bwlch-y-ffridd Powys 34 C1
Bwlch-y-groes Pembks 25 M3
Bwlchymyrdd Swans 25 U11
Bwlch-y-sarnau Powys 34 B6
Byermoor Gatesd 69 Q1
Byers Green Dur 69 R6
Byfield Nhants 37 P10
Byfleet Surrey 20 J10
Byford Herefs 34 J12
Bygrave Herts 31 S5
Byker N u Ty 77 R13
Byland Abbey N York 64 D4
Bylaugh Norfk 50 H10
Bylchau Conwy 53 S10
Byley Ches W 55 R13
Bynea Carmth 25 T11
Byrness Nthumb 76 F5
Bystock Devon 6 D8
Bythorn Cambs 38 G5
Byton Herefs 34 J8
Bywell Nthumb 77 L13
Byworth W Susx 10 F6

C

Cabbacott Devon 14 K8
Cabourne Lincs 58 K6
Cabrach Ag & B 78 H3
Cabrach Moray 104 D10
Cabus Lancs 61 T10
Cackle Street E Susx 11 R5
Cackle Street E Susx 12 C12
Cackle Street E Susx 12 F12
Cadbury Devon 6 B3
Cadbury Barton Devon 15 Q9
Cadbury World Birm 36 D4
Cadder E Duns 89 P11
Caddington C Beds 31 N9
Caddonfoot Border 84 D11
Cadeby Donc 57 R6
Cadeby Leics 47 M13
Cadeleigh Devon 6 B3
Cade Street E Susx 11 U6
Cadgwith Cnwll 2 J14
Cadham Fife 91 L11
Cadishead Salfd 55 R8
Cadle Swans 25 V11
Cadley Lancs 61 U13
Cadley Wilts 18 K10
Cadley Wilts 18 K7
Cadmore End Bucks 20 C4
Cadnam Hants 9 L6
Cadney N Linc 58 H6
Cadole Flints 54 F14
Cadoxton V Glam 16 F3
Cadoxton Juxta-Neath Neath 26 D8
Cadwst Denbgs 44 B6
Caeathro Gwynd 52 H10
Caehopkin Powys 26 E5
Caenby Lincs 58 G9
Caeo Carmth 33 N12
Caerau Brdgnd 26 F9
Caerau Cardif 27 L12
Cae'r-bont Powys 26 E5
Cae'r bryn Carmth 25 U8
Caerdeon Gwynd 43 N10
Caer Farchell Pembks 24 C5
Caergeiliog IoA 52 D7
Caergwrle Flints 44 H2
Caerhun Conwy 53 N8
Caerlanrig Border 75 S5
Caerleon Newpt 27 Q9
Caernarfon Gwynd 52 G10
Caernarfon Castle Gwynd 52 G10
Caerphilly Caerph 27 M10
Caersws Powys 34 B2
Caerwedros Cerdgn 32 G9
Caerwent Mons 27 T9
Caerwys Flints 54 D12
Caerynwch Gwynd 43 Q10
Caggle Street Mons 27 R4
Caim IoA 52 K6
Cairinis W Isls 106 d12
Cairnbaan Ag & B 87 Q7
Cairnbulg Abers 105 S2
Cairncross Border 85 M6
Cairncurran Inver 88 H11
Cairndow Ag & B 88 E3
Cairneyhill Fife 82 K1
Cairngarroch D & G 72 D10
Cairngorms National Park 97 T3
Cairnie Abers 104 F7
Cairnorrie Abers 105 P7
Cairnryan D & G 72 D6
Cairnty Moray 104 C5
Caister-on-Sea Norfk 51 T11
Caistor Lincs 58 K6
Caistor St Edmund Norfk 51 M13
Cakebole Worcs 35 U6
Cake Street Norfk 40 J2
Calais Street Suffk 40 G13
Calanais W Isls 106 h5
Calbourne IoW 9 N11
Calceby Lincs 59 Q11
Calcot Flints 54 E12
Calcot Gloucs 29 L5
Calcot W Berk 19 U6
Calcot Row W Berk 19 U6
Calcots Moray 104 B3
Calcott Kent 13 N3
Calcott Shrops 44 K11
Calcutt N York 63 S8
Calcutt Wilts 29 M9
Caldbeck Cumb 67 M4
Caldbergh N York 63 M2
Caldecote Cambs 38 H3
Caldecote Cambs 39 M9
Caldecote Herts 31 R5
Caldecote Nhants 37 S10
Caldecote Highfields Cambs 39 N9
Caldecott Nhants 38 E7
Caldecott Oxon 29 U8
Caldecott RutInd 38 C2
Caldecotte M Keyn 30 J5
Calder Cumb 66 F12
Calderbank N Lans 82 E6
Calder Bridge Cumb 66 F11
Calderbrook Rochdl 56 D3
Caldercruix N Lans 82 F5
Calder Grove Wakefd 57 M3
Caldermill S Lans 81 T4
Caldermore Rochdl 56 D3
Calder Vale Lancs 61 U10
Calderwood S Lans 81 T1
Caldey Island Pembks 24 K11
Caldicot Mons 27 T10
Caldmore Wsall 46 D14
Caldwell N York 69 Q10
Caldy Wirral 54 F9
Caledfwlch Carmth 26 B2
Calenick Cnwll 3 L8
Calf of Man IoM 60 b9
Calford Green Suffk 40 B11
Calfsound Ork 106 u16
Calgary Ag & B 93 K8
Califer Moray 103 S4
California Falk 82 H3
California Norfk 51 T10
California Cross Devon 5 S10
Calke Derbys 47 L9
Calke Abbey Derbys 47 L9
Callakille Highld 107 L13
Callander Stirlg 89 P4
Callanish W Isls 106 h5
Callaughton Shrops 45 P14
Callestick Cnwll 2 K6
Calligarry Highld 100 f9
Callington Cnwll 4 K7
Callingwood Staffs 46 G9
Callow Herefs 35 L14
Callow End Worcs 35 T11
Callow Hill Wilts 28 K11
Callow Hill Worcs 36 D8
Callow Hill Worcs 35 R6
Callows Grave Worcs 35 N7
Calmore Hants 9 L6
Calmsden Gloucs 28 K6
Calne Wilts 18 E6
Calow Derbys 57 P12
Calshot Hants 9 P8
Calstock Cnwll 5 L7
Calstone Wellington Wilts 18 F7
Calthorpe Norfk 51 L7
Calthorpe Street Norfk 51 R8
Calthwaite Cumb 67 Q4
Calton N York 62 J8
Calton Staffs 46 F4
Calveley Ches E 45 N2
Calver Derbys 56 K12
Calverhall Shrops 45 P6
Calver Hill Herefs 34 J11
Calverleigh Devon 6 B2
Calverley Leeds 63 Q12
Calver Sough Derbys 56 K11
Calvert Bucks 30 E8
Calverton M Keyn 30 G5
Calverton Notts 47 R4
Calvine P & K 97 N10
Calvo Cumb 66 J2
Calzeat Border 83 M11
Cam Gloucs 28 E8
Camasachoirce Highld 93 U6
Camasine Highld 93 T6
Camas Luinie Highld 101 N6
Camastianavaig Highld 100 e6
Camault Muir Highld 102 F7
Camber E Susx 12 J12
Camberley Surrey 20 E10
Camberwell Gt Lon 21 P7
Camblesforth N York 57 T1
Cambo Nthumb 77 L9
Cambois Nthumb 77 S9
Camborne Cnwll 2 G8
Camborne & Redruth Mining District Cnwll 2 G8
Cambourne Cambs 39 M9
Cambridge Cambs 39 Q9
Cambridge Gloucs 28 D7
Cambridge Airport Cambs 39 Q9
Cambridge City Crematorium Cambs 39 N8
Cambrose Cnwll 2 H7
Cambus Clacks 90 C13
Cambusavie Platform Highld 109 P5
Cambusbarron Stirlg 89 S7
Cambuskenneth Stirlg 89 T7
Cambuslang S Lans 89 P13
Cambus o' May Abers 98 G4
Cambuswallace S Lans 82 K11
Camden Town Gt Lon 21 N6
Cameley BaNES 17 R5
Camelford Cnwll 4 E4
Camelon Falk 82 G2
Camerory Highld 103 R9
Camer's Green Worcs 35 S13
Camerton BaNES 17 S5
Camerton Cumb 66 F6
Camghouran P & K 95 R7
Camieston Border 84 F12
Cammachmore Abers 99 S4
Cammeringham Lincs 58 F10
Camore Highld 109 P7
Campbeltown Ag & B 79 N11
Campbeltown Airport Ag & B 79 M11
Camperdown N Tyne 77 R11
Cample D & G 74 G7
Campmuir P & K 90 K4
Camps W Loth 83 L5
Campsall Donc 57 R4
Campsea Ash Suffk 41 P9
Camps End Cambs 39 T12
Campton C Beds 31 P5
Camptown Border 76 D3
Camrose Pembks 24 F6
Camserney P & K 90 B2
Camusnagaul Highld 94 F4
Camusnagaul Highld 107 U7
Camusteel Highld 100 g5
Camusterrach Highld 100 g5
Canada Hants 8 K5
Canal Foot Cumb 61 Q4
Canaston Bridge Pembks 24 J7
Candacraig Abers 98 E4
Candlesby Lincs 59 S13
Candle Street Suffk 40 H6
Candover Green Shrops 45 M12
Candy Mill Border 83 L10
Cane End Oxon 19 U5
Canewdon Essex 23 L9
Canford Bottom Dorset 8 E8
Canford Cliffs Poole 8 F11
Canford Crematorium Bristl 27 V12
Canford Heath Poole 8 E10
Canford Magna Poole 8 E9
Canhams Green Suffk 40 J7
Canisbay Highld 112 H2
Canklow Rothm 57 P8
Canley Covtry 36 K5
Canley Crematorium Covtry 36 K5
Cann Dorset 8 B4
Canna Highld 100 b9
Cann Common Dorset 8 B4
Cannich Highld 102 B9
Cannington Somset 16 J9
Canning Town Gt Lon 21 R6
Cannock Staffs 46 C11
Cannock Chase Staffs 46 C10
Cannock Wood Staffs 46 D11
Cannon Bridge Herefs 34 K12
Canonbie D & G 75 S11
Canon Frome Herefs 35 P12
Canon Pyon Herefs 35 L11
Canons Ashby Nhants 37 Q10
Canonstown Cnwll 2 E9
Canterbury Kent 13 M4
Canterbury Cathedral Kent 13 N4
Cantley Norfk 51 Q13
Cantlop Shrops 45 M12
Canton Cardif 27 M12
Cantraywood Highld 103 L6
Cantsfield Lancs 62 C5
Canvey Island Essex 22 J11
Canwick Lincs 58 G13
Canworthy Water Cnwll 4 G2
Caol Highld 94 G3
Caolas Scalpaigh W Isls 106 h9
Caoles Ag & B 92 D9
Caonich Highld 101 R13
Capel Kent 12 B7
Capel Surrey 10 K2
Capel Bangor Cerdgn 33 N4
Capel Betws Lleucu Cerdgn 33 M9
Capel Coch IoA 52 G6
Capel Curig Conwy 53 M11
Capel Cynon Cerdgn 32 G11
Capel Dewi Carmth 25 S6
Capel Dewi Cerdgn 32 J12
Capel-Dewi Cerdgn 33 M4
Capel Garmon Conwy 53 P11
Capel Green Suffk 41 Q11
Capel Gwyn Carmth 25 S6
Capel Gwyn IoA 52 D7
Capel Gwynfe Carmth 26 C3
Capel Hendre Carmth 25 U8
Capel Isaac Carmth 25 U5
Capel Iwan Carmth 25 N3
Capel le Ferne Kent 13 Q8
Capelles Guern 6 d2
Capel Llanilltern Cardif 26 K12
Capel Mawr IoA 52 F8
Capel Parc IoA 52 G5
Capel St Andrew Suffk 41 Q11
Capel St Mary Suffk 40 J13
Capel Seion Cerdgn 33 M5
Capel Trisant Cerdgn 33 P5
Capeluchaf Gwynd 42 H4
Capelulo Conwy 53 M7
Capel-y-ffin Powys 27 P1
Capel-y-graig Gwynd 52 H9
Capenhurst Ches W 54 J12
Capernwray Lancs 61 U5
Cape Wrath Highld 110 F1
Capheaton Nthumb 77 L9
Caplaw E Rens 88 K14
Capon's Green Suffk 41 N7
Cappercleuch Border 83 P14
Capstone Medway 12 E2
Capton Devon 5 U10
Capton Somset 16 E9
Caputh P & K 90 G3
Caradon Mining District Cnwll 4 H6
Caradon Town Cnwll 4 H6
Carbeth Inn Stirlg 89 M10
Carbis Cnwll 3 Q5
Carbis Bay Cnwll 2 E9
Carbost Highld 100 c6
Carbost Highld 100 d5
Carbrook Sheff 57 N9
Carbrooke Norfk 50 F13
Carburton Notts 57 T12
Carclaze Cnwll 3 Q6
Car Colston Notts 47 T5
Carcroft Donc 57 R5
Cardenden Fife 90 K12
Cardeston Shrops 44 J11
Cardewlees Cumb 67 N2
Cardhu Moray 103 U7
Cardiff Cardif 27 M12
Cardiff Airport V Glam 16 E3
Cardiff & Glamorgan Crematorium Cardif 27 M11
Cardiff Gate Services Cardif 27 N11
Cardiff West Services Cardif 26 K12
Cardigan Cerdgn 32 C11
Cardinal's Green Cambs 39 T11
Cardington Bed 38 G11
Cardington Shrops 35 M1
Cardinham Cnwll 4 E7
Cardrain D & G 72 E13
Cardrona Border 83 R11
Cardross Ag & B 88 H10
Cardross Crematorium Ag & B 88 H10
Cardryne D & G 72 E13
Cardurnock Cumb 75 N14
Careby Lincs 48 F10
Careston Angus 98 J11
Carew Pembks 24 H10
Carew Cheriton Pembks 24 H10
Carew Newton Pembks 24 H10
Carey Herefs 27 V1
Carfin N Lans 82 E7
Carfraemill Border 84 E8
Cargate Green Norfk 51 Q11
Cargenbridge D & G 74 J11
Cargill P & K 90 J4
Cargo Cumb 75 S14
Cargreen Cnwll 5 L8
Cargurrel Cnwll 3 M9
Carham Nthumb 84 K11
Carhampton Somset 16 D8
Carharrack Cnwll 2 J8
Carie P & K 95 S7
Carinish W Isls 106 d12
Carisbrooke IoW 9 P11
Cark Cumb 61 R4
Carkeel Cnwll 5 L8
Carlabhagh W Isls 106 h4
Carland Cross Cnwll 3 M6
Carlbury Darltn 69 R9
Carlby Lincs 48 F11
Carlcroft Nthumb 76 G3
Carlecotes Barns 56 J6
Carleen Cnwll 2 G10
Carlesmoor N York 63 Q5
Carleton Cumb 66 F11
Carleton Cumb 67 P2
Carleton Cumb 67 R7
Carleton Lancs 61 Q12
Carleton N York 62 K10
Carleton Wakefd 57 Q2
Carleton Crematorium Bpool 61 Q12
Carleton Forehoe Norfk 50 J12
Carleton Rode Norfk 40 K2
Carleton St Peter Norfk 51 P13
Carlidnack Cnwll 2 K11
Carlincraig Abers 104 K7
Carlingcott BaNES 17 S5
Carlin How R & Cl 71 M9
Carlisle Cumb 67 N1
Carlisle Airport Cumb 75 U13
Carlisle Crematorium Cumb 67 N2
Carloggas Cnwll 3 M3
Carlops Border 83 N7
Carloway W Isls 106 h4
Carlton Barns 57 N4
Carlton Bed 38 E9
Carlton Cambs 39 T10
Carlton Leeds 57 M1
Carlton Leics 47 L13
Carlton N York 57 T2
Carlton N York 63 M3
Carlton N York 64 E2
Carlton Notts 47 R5
Carlton S on T 70 E8
Carlton Suffk 41 Q8
Carlton Colville Suffk 41 T3
Carlton Curlieu Leics 37 S1
Carlton Green Cambs 39 T10
Carlton Husthwaite N York 64 B4
Carlton-in-Cleveland N York 70 H12
Carlton in Lindrick Notts 57 S10
Carlton-le-Moorland Lincs 48 D2
Carlton Miniott N York 63 T3
Carlton-on-Trent Notts 58 C14
Carlton Scroop Lincs 48 D5
Carluke S Lans 82 F8
Carlyon Bay Cnwll 3 R6
Carmacoup S Lans 82 E13
Carmarthen Carmth 25 R6
Carmel Carmth 25 U7
Carmel Flints 54 E11
Carmel Gwynd 52 G12
Carmichael S Lans 82 H11
Carmountside Crematorium C Stke 46 B4
Carmunnock C Glas 89 N14
Carmyle C Glas 89 P13
Carmyllie Angus 91 R3
Carnaby E R Yk 65 Q6
Carnbee Fife 91 R10
Carnbo P & K 90 G11
Carn Brea Cnwll 2 H8
Carnbrogie Abers 105 P10
Carndu Highld 101 M6
Carnduff S Lans 81 T3
Carne Cnwll 2 K12
Carne Cnwll 3 N9
Carne Cnwll 3 P5
Carnell E Ayrs 81 P6
Carnewas Cnwll 3 M3
Carnforth Lancs 61 T5
Carn-gorm Highld 101 P7
Carnhedryn Pembks 24 D5
Carnhell Green Cnwll 2 G9
Carnie Abers 99 Q2
Carnkie Cnwll 2 H8
Carnkie Cnwll 2 J10
Carnkiet Cnwll 2 K6
Carno Powys 33 U1
Carnock Fife 90 F14
Carnon Downs Cnwll 2 K8
Carnousie Abers 104 K5
Carnoustie Angus 91 S5
Carnsmerry Cnwll 3 Q5
Carnwath S Lans 82 J9
Carnyorth Cnwll 2 B10
Carol Green Solhll 36 J5
Carpalla Cnwll 3 P6
Carperby N York 63 L2
Carr Rothm 57 R8
Carradale Ag & B 79 Q8
Carrbridge Highld 103 P11
Carrbrook Tamesd 56 E6
Carrefour Jersey 7 b2
Carreglefn IoA 52 E5
Carr Gate Wakefd 57 M2
Carrhouse N Linc 58 C5
Carrick Ag & B 87 S8
Carrick Castle Ag & B 88 E7
Carriden Falk 82 K2
Carrington Lincs 49 M2
Carrington Mdloth 83 R6
Carrington Traffd 55 R8
Carrog Conwy 43 Q4
Carrog Denbgs 44 D5
Carron Falk 82 G2
Carron Moray 103 V7
Carronbridge D & G 74 G6
Carron Bridge Stirlg 89 R9
Carronshore Falk 82 G2
Carrow Hill Mons 27 S9
Carr Shield Nthumb 68 H3
Carrutherstown D & G 75 M11
Carruth House Inver 88 J12
Carr Vale Derbys 57 Q13
Carrville Dur 70 D4
Carsaig Ag & B 86 J1
Carseriggan D & G 72 J6
Carsethorn D & G 74 J14
Carshalton Gt Lon 21 N10
Carsington Derbys 46 J3
Carskey Ag & B 79 M14
Carsluith D & G 73 M9
Carsphairn D & G 81 R14
Carstairs S Lans 82 H9
Carstairs Junction S Lans 82 J9
Carswell Marsh Oxon 29 R8
Carter's Clay Hants 9 L4
Carters Green Essex 22 D5
Carterton Oxon 29 Q6
Carterway Heads Nthumb 69 M2
Carthew Cnwll 3 Q5
Carthorpe N York 63 S3
Cartington Nthumb 77 L5
Cartland S Lans 82 G9
Cartledge Derbys 57 M11
Cartmel Cumb 61 R4
Cartmel Fell Cumb 61 S2
Carway Carmth 25 S9
Carwinley Cumb 75 T11
Cashe's Green Gloucs 28 F6
Cashmoor Dorset 8 D6
Cassington Oxon 29 U5
Cassop Colliery Dur 70 D5
Castallack Cnwll 2 D11
Castel Guern 6 d3
Castell Conwy 53 N9
Castell-y-bwch Torfn 27 P9
Casterton Cumb 62 C4
Castle Cnwll 3 R5
Castle Acre Norfk 50 D10
Castle Ashby Nhants 38 C9
Castlebay W Isls 106 b19
Castle Bolton N York 63 L1
Castle Bromwich Solhll 36 F3
Castle Bytham Lincs 48 E10
Castlebythe Pembks 24 H5
Castle Caereinion Powys 44 E12
Castle Camps Cambs 39 T12
Castle Carrock Cumb 67 R1
Castlecary Falk 89 S10
Castle Cary Somset 17 R10
Castle Combe Wilts 18 B5
Castlecraig Highld 109 Q11
Castle Donington Leics 47 M8
Castle Douglas D & G 74 E13
Castle Eaton Swindn 29 M8
Castle Eden Dur 70 F5
Castle End C Pete 48 H12
Castleford Wakefd 57 P1
Castle Frome Herefs 35 Q11
Castle Gate Cnwll 2 D10
Castle Green Cumb 61 U1
Castle Green Surrey 20 G10
Castle Gresley Derbys 46 J10
Castle Hedingham Essex 40 C13
Castlehill Border 83 P11
Castlehill Highld 112 E3
Castle Hill Kent 12 C7
Castle Hill Suffk 40 K11
Castlehill W Duns 88 J10
Castle Howard N York 64 G5
Castle Kennedy D & G 72 E8
Castle Lachlan Ag & B 87 U6
Castlemartin Pembks 24 F11
Castlemilk C Glas 89 N14
Castle Morris Pembks 24 F4
Castlemorton Worcs 35 S13
Castlemorton Common Worcs 35 S13
Castle O'er D & G 75 P7
Castle Rising Norfk 49 U9
Castleside Dur 69 N3
Castle Stuart Highld 102 K6
Castlethorpe M Keyn 30 H4
Castlethorpe N Linc 58 G5
Castleton Border 75 V8
Castleton Derbys 56 J10
Castleton N York 71 L11
Castleton Newpt 27 P11
Castleton Rochdl 56 C4
Castletown Ches W 44 K3
Castletown Dorset 7 S10
Castletown Highld 112 E3
Castletown IoM 60 d9
Castletown Sundld 77 T14
Castley N York 63 R10
Caston Norfk 50 G14
Castor C Pete 48 H14
Caswell Bay Swans 25 U13
Catacol N Ayrs 79 S7
Cat and Fiddle Derbys 56 F12
Catbrain S Glos 27 V11
Catbrook Mons 27 U7
Catch Flints 54 F12
Catchall Cnwll 2 C11
Catchem's Corner Solhll 36 J5
Catchgate Dur 69 Q2
Catcliffe Rothm 57 P9
Catcomb Wilts 18 F5
Catcott Somset 17 L9
Catcott Burtle Somset 17 M8
Caterham Surrey 21 P11
Catfield Norfk 51 Q9
Catfield Common Norfk 51 R9
Catford Gt Lon 21 Q8
Catforth Lancs 61 T12
Cathcart C Glas 89 N13
Cathedine Powys 27 L2
Catherine-de-Barnes Solhll 36 G4
Catherine Slack C Brad 63 M14
Catherington Hants 9 T6
Catherston Leweston Dorset 7 L6
Catherton Shrops 35 Q5
Catisfield Hants 9 R7
Catley Herefs 35 Q12
Catley Lane Head Rochdl 56 C3
Catlodge Highld 96 J5
Catlow Lancs 62 H12
Catlowdy Cumb 75 U11
Catmere End Essex 39 Q13
Catmore W Berk 19 Q4
Caton Devon 5 T6
Caton Lancs 62 B7
Caton Green Lancs 62 B6
Cator Court Devon 5 R5
Catrine E Ayrs 81 R7
Cat's Ash Newpt 27 R9
Catsfield E Susx 12 D13
Catsfield Stream E Susx 12 D13
Catsgore Somset 17 P11
Catsham Somset 17 Q10
Catshill Worcs 36 C6
Catstree Shrops 35 R1
Cattadale Ag & B 79 M13
Cattal N York 63 U9
Cattawade Suffk 40 K14
Catterall Lancs 61 T11
Catteralslane Shrops 45 N5
Catterick N York 69 R13
Catterick Bridge N York 69 R13
Catterick Garrison N York 69 Q13
Catterlen Cumb 67 Q6
Catterline Abers 99 R8
Catterton N York 64 C10
Catteshall Surrey 10 F2
Catthorpe Leics 37 Q5
Cattishall Suffk 40 E7
Cattistock Dorset 7 Q5
Catton N York 63 T4
Catton Nthumb 76 G14
Catwick E R Yk 65 Q10
Catworth Cambs 38 G6
Caudle Green Gloucs 28 H5
Caulcott C Beds 31 M4
Caulcott Oxon 30 B8
Cauldcots Angus 91 U2
Cauldhame Stirlg 89 P7
Cauldmill Border 76 A2
Cauldon Staffs 46 E4
Cauldon Lowe Staffs 46 E4
Cauldwell Derbys 46 J10
Caulkerbush D & G 66 D1
Caulside D & G 75 T9
Caundle Marsh Dorset 7 S2
Caunsall Worcs 35 U4
Caunton Notts 47 T1
Causeway Hants 9 U4
Causeway End Cumb 61 T2
Causeway End D & G 73 L8
Causeway End Essex 22 G4
Causewayend S Lans 82 K11
Causewayhead Cumb 66 H2
Causewayhead Stirlg 89 T6
Causeyend Abers 105 Q12
Causey Park Nthumb 77 P7
Causey Park Bridge Nthumb 77 P7
Cavendish Suffk 40 D11
Cavenham Suffk 40 C6
Caversfield Oxon 30 C7
Caversham Readg 20 B8
Caverswall Staffs 46 C5
Caverton Mill Border 84 J13
Cavil E R Yk 64 H13
Cawdor Highld 103 M5
Cawkwell Lincs 59 N11
Cawood N York 64 D12
Cawsand Cnwll 5 L10
Cawston Norfk 50 K9
Cawston Warwks 37 N6
Cawthorn N York 64 H2
Cawthorne Barns 57 L5
Cawton N York 64 E4
Caxton Cambs 39 M9
Caxton End Cambs 39 M9
Caxton Gibbet Cambs 39 L8
Caynham Shrops 35 N6
Caythorpe Lincs 48 D4
Caythorpe Notts 47 S4
Cayton N York 65 P3
Ceann a Bhaigh W Isls 106 c12
Ceannacroc Lodge Highld 101 U9
Cearsiadar W Isls 106 i6
Ceciliford Mons 27 U7
Cefn Newpt 27 P10
Cefn Berain Conwy 53 S9
Cefn-brith Conwy 43 T3
Cefn-bryn-brain Carmth 26 C5
Cefn Byrle Powys 26 E5
Cefn Canel Powys 44 F7
Cefn Coch Powys 44 D8
Cefn-coed-y-cymmer Myr Td 26 J6
Cefn Cribwr Brdgnd 26 F11
Cefn Cross Brdgnd 26 F11
Cefn-ddwysarn Gwynd 43 U6
Cefn-Einion Shrops 34 G3
Cefneithin Carmth 25 U8
Cefngorwydd Powys 33 T11
Cefn-mawr Wrexhm 44 G5
Cefnpennar Rhondd 26 J7
Cefn-y-bedd Flints 44 H2
Cefn-y-pant Carmth 25 L5
Ceint IoA 52 G7
Cellan Cerdgn 33 M11
Cellardyke Fife 91 S11
Cellarhead Staffs 46 C4
Celleron Cumb 67 Q7
Celynen Caerph 27 N8
Cemaes IoA 52 E4
Cemmaes Powys 43 R12
Cemmaes Road Powys 43 R13
Cenarth Cerdgn 32 E12
Cerbyd Pembks 24 D5
Ceres Fife 91 P9
Cerne Abbas Dorset 7 S4
Cerney Wick Gloucs 29 L8
Cerrigceinwen IoA 52 F8
Cerrigydrudion Conwy 43 U4
Cess Norfk 51 R10
Ceunant Gwynd 52 H10
Chaceley Gloucs 28 G1
Chacewater Cnwll 2 K8
Chackmore Bucks 30 E5
Chacombe Nhants 37 N12
Chadbury Worcs 36 D11
Chadderton Oldham 56 D5
Chadderton Fold Oldham 56 D5
Chaddesden C Derb 47 L6
Chaddesley Corbett Worcs 35 U6
Chaddlehanger Devon 5 M5
Chaddleworth W Berk 19 P5
Chadlington Oxon 29 R3
Chadshunt Warwks 36 K10
Chadwell Leics 47 U9
Chadwell Shrops 45 S11
Chadwell End Bed 38 G7
Chadwell Heath Gt Lon 21 S5
Chadwell St Mary Thurr 22 F12
Chadwick Worcs 35 T7
Chadwick End Solhll 36 H6
Chadwick Green St Hel 55 M7
Chaffcombe Somset 7 L2
Chafford Hundred Thurr 22 F12
Chagford Devon 5 S3
Chailey E Susx 11 P7
Chainbridge Cambs 49 P13
Chainhurst Kent 12 D6
Chalbury Dorset 8 E7
Chalbury Common Dorset 8 E7
Chaldon Surrey 21 P11
Chaldon Herring Dorset 7 U8
Chale IoW 9 P13
Chale Green IoW 9 P13
Chalfont Common Bucks 20 H4
Chalfont St Giles Bucks 20 G4
Chalfont St Peter Bucks 20 H4
Chalford Gloucs 28 G7
Chalford Oxon 30 F12
Chalford Wilts 18 C10
Chalgrave C Beds 31 M7
Chalgrove Oxon 30 D13
Chalk Kent 22 G13
Chalk End Essex 22 F5
Chalkhouse Green Oxon 20 B7
Chalkway Somset 7 L3
Chalkwell Kent 12 G3
Challaborough Devon 5 R12
Challacombe Devon 15 Q4
Challoch D & G 72 K6
Challock Kent 12 K5
Chalmington Dorset 7 Q4
Chalton C Beds 31 M7
Chalton C Beds 38 H10
Chalton Hants 9 U5
Chalvey Slough 20 G7
Chalvington E Susx 11 S9
Chambers Green Kent 12 H7
Chandler's Cross Herts 20 J3
Chandlers Cross Worcs 35 S13
Chandler's Ford Hants 9 N4
Channel's End Bed 38 H9
Channel Tunnel Terminal Kent 13 N8
Chanterlands Crematorium C KuH 65 P13
Chantry Somset 17 T7
Chantry Suffk 40 K12
Chapel Cumb 66 K6
Chapel Fife 91 L13
Chapel Allerton Leeds 63 S12
Chapel Allerton Somset 17 M6
Chapel Amble Cnwll 3 P1
Chapel Brampton Nhants 37 T7
Chapelbridge Cambs 38 K2
Chapel Chorlton Staffs 45 T6
Chapel Cross E Susx 11 U6
Chapel End Bed 38 H9
Chapel End C Beds 31 N4
Chapel End Cambs 38 H4
Chapel End Warwks 36 K2
Chapelend Way Essex 40 B13
Chapel-en-le-Frith Derbys 56 G10
Chapel Field Bury 55 S5
Chapelgate Lincs 49 P9
Chapel Green Warwks 36 J3
Chapel Green Warwks 37 N8
Chapel Haddlesey N York 57 S1
Chapelhall N Lans 82 E5
Chapel Hill Abers 105 T8
Chapel Hill Lincs 48 K3
Chapel Hill Mons 27 U8
Chapelhope Border 75 Q1
Chapelknowe D & G 75 R11
Chapel Lawn Shrops 34 H5
Chapel-le-Dale N York 62 E4
Chapel Leigh Somset 16 F11
Chapel Milton Derbys 56 G10
Chapel of Garioch Abers 105 L11
Chapel Rossan D & G 72 E11
Chapel Row E Susx 11 U8
Chapel Row Essex 22 J7
Chapel Row W Berk 19 S7
Chapels Cumb 61 N3
Chapel St Leonards Lincs 59 U12
Chapel Stile Cumb 67 M11
Chapelton Angus 91 T2
Chapelton Devon 15 N7
Chapelton S Lans 82 C9
Chapeltown Bl w D 55 R3
Chapel Town Cnwll 3 M5
Chapeltown Moray 104 A11
Chapeltown Sheff 57 N7
Chapmanslade Wilts 18 B11
Chapmans Well Devon 4 K2
Chapmore End Herts 31 T9
Chappel Essex 23 L2
Charaton Cnwll 4 J7
Chard Somset 6 K3
Chard Junction Somset 6 K4
Chardleigh Green Somset 6 K2
Chardstock Devon 6 K4
Charfield S Glos 28 D9
Chargrove Gloucs 28 H4
Charing Kent 12 J6
Charing Crematorium Kent 12 J6
Charing Heath Kent 12 H6
Charing Hill Kent 12 J5
Charingworth Gloucs 36 G13
Charlbury Oxon 29 S4
Charlcombe BaNES 17 T3
Charlcutt Wilts 18 E5
Charlecote Warwks 36 J9
Charlemont Sandw 36 D2
Charles Devon 15 Q6
Charleshill Surrey 10 D2
Charleston Angus 91 N2
Charlestown C Aber 99 S3
Charlestown C Brad 63 P12
Charlestown Calder 56 E1
Charlestown Cnwll 3 Q6
Charlestown Cnwll 3 Q6
Charlestown Derbys 56 F8
Charlestown Dorset 7 S9
Charlestown Fife 83 L2
Charlestown Highld 102 H6
Charlestown Highld 107 P10
Charlestown Salfd 55 T6
Charlestown of Aberlour Moray 104 B7
Charles Tye Suffk 40 H10
Charlesworth Derbys 56 F8
Charlinch Somset 16 H9
Charlottetown Fife 91 L9
Charlton Gt Lon 21 R7
Charlton Hants 19 N11
Charlton Herts 31 Q7
Charlton Nhants 30 B5
Charlton Nthumb 76 G9
Charlton Oxon 29 T10
Charlton Somset 16 J11
Charlton Somset 17 R8
Charlton Somset 17 S6
Charlton Surrey 20 J9
Charlton W Susx 10 D8
Charlton Wilts 8 C4
Charlton Wilts 28 J10
Charlton Worcs 35 T6
Charlton Worcs 36 D11
Charlton Wrekin 45 N11
Charlton Abbots Gloucs 28 K3
Charlton Adam Somset 17 P11
Charlton All Saints Wilts 8 H4
Charlton Down Dorset 7 S5
Charlton Hill Shrops 45 N12
Charlton Horethorne Somset 17 S12
Charlton Kings Gloucs 28 J3
Charlton Mackrell Somset 17 P11
Charlton Marshall Dorset 8 C8
Charlton Musgrove Somset 17 T11
Charlton-on-Otmoor Oxon 30 C9
Charlton on the Hill Dorset 8 B8
Charlton St Peter Wilts 18 H9
Charlwood Hants 9 T2
Charlwood Surrey 11 L2
Charminster Dorset 7 S6
Charmouth Dorset 7 L6
Charndon Bucks 30 E8
Charney Bassett Oxon 29 S9
Charnock Green Lancs 55 N3
Charnock Richard Lancs 55 N3
Charnock Richard Crematorium Lancs 55 N3
Charnock Richard Services Lancs 55 M3
Charsfield Suffk 41 N9
Chart Corner Kent 12 E5
Charter Alley Hants 19 S9
Charterhall Border 84 K9
Charterhouse Somset 17 N5
Chartershall Stirlg 89 S7
Charterville Allotments Oxon 29 R5
Chartham Kent 13 M5
Chartham Hatch Kent 13 M4
Chart Hill Kent 12 E6
Chartridge Bucks 30 K12
Chart Sutton Kent 12 F6
Chartway Street Kent 12 F5
Charvil Wokham 20 C7
Charwelton Nhants 37 P9
Chase Terrace Staffs 46 D12
Chasetown Staffs 46 D12
Chastleton Oxon 29 P2
Chasty Devon 14 H12
Chatburn Lancs 62 F11
Chatcull Staffs 45 S7
Chatham Caerph 27 N10
Chatham Medway 12 E2
Chatham Green Essex 22 H4
Chathill Nthumb 85 T13
Chatley Worcs 35 U8
Chatsworth House Derbys 57 L12
Chattenden Medway 22 J13
Chatter End Essex 22 C2
Chatteris Cambs 39 N3
Chatterton Lancs 55 S3
Chattisham Suffk 40 J12
Chatto Border 76 F2
Chatton Nthumb 85 R13
Chaul End C Beds 31 N8
Chawleigh Devon 15 R10
Chawley Oxon 29 U7
Chawston Bed 38 J9
Chawton Hants 19 V13
Chaxhill Gloucs 28 D5
Chazey Heath Oxon 19 U5
Cheadle Staffs 46 D5
Cheadle Stockp 56 C9
Cheadle Heath Stockp 56 C9
Cheadle Hulme Stockp 56 C9
Cheam Gt Lon 21 M10
Cheapside W & M 20 F9
Chearsley Bucks 30 F10
Chebsey Staffs 45 U8
Checkendon Oxon 19 U4
Checkley Ches E 45 R4
Checkley Herefs 35 N13
Checkley Staffs 46 D6
Checkley Green Ches E 45 R4
Chedburgh Suffk 40 C9
Cheddar Somset 17 N6
Cheddington Bucks 30 K9
Cheddleton Staffs 46 C3
Cheddleton Heath Staffs 46 C3
Cheddon Fitzpaine Somset 16 H11
Chedglow Wilts 28 H9
Chedgrave Norfk 51 Q14
Chedington Dorset 7 N3
Chediston Suffk 41 Q5
Chediston Green Suffk 41 Q5
Chedworth Gloucs 29 L5
Chedzoy Somset 16 K9
Cheeseman's Green Kent 12 K8
Cheetham Hill Manch 55 T6
Cheldon Devon 15 R10
Chelford Ches E 55 T12
Chellaston C Derb 47 L7
Chellington Bed 38 E9
Chelmarsh Shrops 35 R3
Chelmick Shrops 35 L2
Chelmondiston Suffk 41 M13
Chelmorton Derbys 56 H13
Chelmsford Essex 22 H6
Chelmsford Crematorium Essex 22 G6
Chelmsley Wood Solhll 36 G3
Chelsea Gt Lon 21 N7
Chelsfield Gt Lon 21 S10
Chelsham Surrey 21 Q11
Chelston Somset 16 G12
Chelsworth Suffk 40 G11
Cheltenham Gloucs 28 H3
Cheltenham Crematorium Gloucs 28 J3
Chelveston Nhants 38 E7
Chelvey N Som 17 N3
Chelwood BaNES 17 R4
Chelwood Common E Susx 11 Q5
Chelwood Gate E Susx 11 Q5
Chelworth Wilts 28 J9
Chelworth Lower Green Wilts 29 L9
Chelworth Upper Green Wilts 29 L9
Cheney Longville Shrops 34 K4
Chenies Bucks 20 H3
Chepstow Mons 27 V9
Chequerbent Bolton 55 Q5
Chequers Corner Norfk 49 Q12
Cherhill Wilts 18 F6
Cherington Gloucs 28 H8
Cherington Warwks 36 J13
Cheriton Devon 15 R3
Cheriton Hants 9 R3
Cheriton Kent 13 P8
Cheriton Pembks 24 G11
Cheriton Swans 25 S12
Cheriton Bishop Devon 5 T2
Cheriton Fitzpaine Devon 15 U11
Cherrington Wrekin 45 Q10
Cherry Burton E R Yk 65 M11
Cherry Hinton Cambs 39 Q9
Cherry Orchard Worcs 35 U10
Cherry Willingham Lincs 58 H12
Chertsey Surrey 20 H9
Cherwell Valley Services Oxon 30 B7
Cheselbourne Dorset 7 U5
Chesham Bucks 31 L12
Chesham Bury 55 T4
Chesham Bois Bucks 20 G3
Cheshunt Herts 31 U12
Chesil Beach Dorset 7 R9
Chesley Kent 12 G3
Cheslyn Hay Staffs 46 C12
Chessetts Wood Warwks 36 G6
Chessington Gt Lon 21 L10
Chessington World of Adventures Gt Lon 21 L10
Chester Ches W 54 K13
Chesterblade Somset 17 S8
Chester Crematorium Ches W 54 J13
Chesterfield Derbys 57 N12
Chesterfield Staffs 46 E12
Chesterfield Crematorium Derbys 57 N12
Chesterhill Mdloth 83 S6
Chester-le-Street Dur 69 S2
Chester Moor Dur 69 S3
Chesters Border 76 C3
Chesters Border 84 G14
Chester Services Ches W 55 L12
Chesterton Cambs 38 H1
Chesterton Cambs 39 Q8
Chesterton Gloucs 28 K7
Chesterton Oxon 30 C8
Chesterton Shrops 35 S1
Chesterton Staffs 45 T4
Chesterton Green Warwks 37 L9
Chesterwood Nthumb 76 G12
Chester Zoo Ches W 54 K12
Chestfield Kent 13 M2
Chestnut Street Kent 12 G3
Cheston Devon 5 R9
Cheswardine Shrops 45 R7
Cheswick Nthumb 85 Q9
Cheswick Green Solhll 36 F5
Chetnole Dorset 7 R3
Chettiscombe Devon 6 C2
Chettisham Cambs 39 R4
Chettle Dorset 8 D6
Chetton Shrops 35 Q2
Chetwode Bucks 30 D7
Chetwynd Wrekin 45 R9
Chetwynd Aston Wrekin 45 S10
Cheveley Cambs 39 U8
Chevening Kent 21 S11
Cheverton IoW 9 P12
Chevington Suffk 40 C9
Cheviot Hills 76 F4
Chevithorne Devon 16 C13
Chew Magna BaNES 17 Q4
Chew Moor Bolton 55 Q5
Chew Stoke BaNES 17 Q4
Chewton Keynsham BaNES 17 S3
Chewton Mendip Somset 17 Q6
Chichacott Devon 15 P13
Chicheley M Keyn 38 D11
Chichester W Susx 10 D10
Chichester Crematorium W Susx 10 D9
Chickerell Dorset 7 R8
Chickering Suffk 41 M5
Chicklade Wilts 8 C2
Chicksands C Beds 31 P5
Chickward Herefs 34 G10
Chidden Hants 9 T5
Chiddingfold Surrey 10 F3
Chiddingly E Susx 11 S8
Chiddingstone Kent 11 S2
Chiddingstone Causeway Kent 21 T13
Chiddingstone Hoath Kent 11 R2
Chideock Dorset 7 M6
Chidham W Susx 10 B10
Chidswell Kirk 57 L2
Chieveley W Berk 19 Q6
Chieveley Services W Berk 19 Q6
Chignall St James Essex 22 G5
Chignall Smealy Essex 22 G5
Chigwell Essex 21 R4
Chigwell Row Essex 21 S4
Chilbolton Hants 19 N12
Chilcomb Hants 9 Q3
Chilcombe Dorset 7 P6
Chilcompton Somset 17 R6
Chilcote Leics 46 J11
Childer Thornton Ches W 54 J11
Child Okeford Dorset 8 A6
Childrey Oxon 29 S10
Child's Ercall Shrops 45 Q9
Childswickham Worcs 36 E13
Childwall Lpool 54 K9
Childwick Bury Herts 31 P10
Childwick Green Herts 31 P10
Chilfrome Dorset 7 Q5
Chilgrove W Susx 10 C8
Chilham Kent 13 L5
Chilla Devon 14 K12
Chillaton Devon 5 L4
Chillenden Kent 13 Q5
Chillerton IoW 9 P12
Chillesford Suffk 41 Q10
Chillingham Nthumb 85 R13
Chillington Devon 5 T12
Chillington Somset 7 L2
Chilmark Wilts 8 D2
Chilmington Green Kent 12 J7
Chilson Oxon 29 R4
Chilsworthy Cnwll 5 L6
Chilsworthy Devon 14 H11
Chiltern Green C Beds 31 P9
Chiltern Hills 20 C3
Chilterns Crematorium Bucks 20 F3
Chilthorne Domer Somset 17 P13
Chilton Bucks 30 E10
Chilton Devon 15 U12
Chilton Dur 69 S7
Chilton Kent 13 R2
Chilton Oxon 29 U10
Chilton Suffk 40 E12
Chilton Candover Hants 19 S12
Chilton Cantelo Somset 17 Q12
Chilton Foliat Wilts 19 M6
Chilton Polden Somset 17 L9
Chilton Street Suffk 40 C11
Chilton Trinity Somset 16 J9
Chilwell Notts 47 P6
Chilworth Hants 9 N5
Chilworth Surrey 20 H13
Chimney Oxon 29 S7
Chineham Hants 19 U9
Chingford Gt Lon 21 Q4
Chinley Derbys 56 G10
Chinnor Oxon 30 G12
Chipchase Castle Nthumb 76 H10
Chipnall Shrops 45 R7
Chippenham Cambs 39 U7
Chippenham Wilts 18 D6
Chipperfield Herts 31 M12
Chipping Herts 31 U6
Chipping Lancs 62 C11
Chipping Campden Gloucs 36 G13
Chipping Hill Essex 22 K4
Chipping Norton Oxon 29 R2
Chipping Ongar Essex 22 E7
Chipping Sodbury S Glos 28 D11
Chipping Warden Nhants 37 N11
Chipshop Devon 5 L5
Chipstable Somset 16 D11
Chipstead Kent 21 T11
Chipstead Surrey 21 N11
Chirbury Shrops 44 G14
Chirk Wrexhm 44 G6
Chirnside Border 85 M7
Chirnsidebridge Border 85 M7
Chirton Wilts 18 G9
Chisbury Wilts 19 L7
Chiselborough Somset 7 N2
Chiseldon Swindn 18 J4
Chiselhampton Oxon 30 C13
Chisholme Border 75 T3
Chislehurst Gt Lon 21 R8
Chislet Kent 13 P3
Chisley Calder 63 L14
Chiswell Green Herts 31 P12
Chiswick Gt Lon 21 M7
Chiswick End Cambs 39 N11
Chisworth Derbys 56 E8
Chitcombe E Susx 12 F11
Chithurst W Susx 10 C6
Chittering Cambs 39 Q7
Chitterne Wilts 18 E12
Chittlehamholt Devon 15 Q8
Chittlehampton Devon 15 P7
Chittoe Wilts 18 E7
Chivelstone Devon 5 T13
Chivenor Devon 15 M6
Chiverton Cross Cnwll 2 J7
Chlenry D & G 72 E7
Chobham Surrey 20 G10
Cholderton Wilts 18 K12
Cholesbury Bucks 30 K11
Chollerford Nthumb 76 J11
Chollerton Nthumb 76 J11
Cholmondeston Ches E 45 P2
Cholsey Oxon 19 S3
Cholstrey Herefs 35 L9
Chop Gate N York 70 J13
Choppington Nthumb 77 R9
Chopwell Gatesd 77 N14
Chorley Ches E 45 N3
Chorley Lancs 55 N3
Chorley Shrops 35 Q4
Chorley Staffs 46 E11
Chorleywood Herts 20 H3
Chorleywood West Herts 20 H3
Chorlton Ches E 45 R3
Chorlton-cum-Hardy Manch 55 T8
Chorlton Lane Ches W 45 L4
Choulton Shrops 34 J3
Chowley Ches W 45 L2
Chrishall Essex 39 P13
Chrisswell Inver 88 F11
Christchurch Cambs 39 Q1
Christchurch Dorset 8 H10
Christchurch Gloucs 27 V5
Christchurch Newpt 27 Q10
Christian Malford Wilts 18 E5
Christleton Ches W 54 K13
Christmas Common Oxon 20 B4
Christmas Pie Surrey 20 F13
Christon N Som 17 L5
Christon Bank Nthumb 85 U14
Christow Devon 5 U3
Christ's Hospital W Susx 10 J5
Chuck Hatch E Susx 11 R4
Chudleigh Devon 5 V5
Chudleigh Knighton Devon 5 U5
Chulmleigh Devon 15 Q10
Chunal Derbys 56 F8
Church Lancs 62 F14
Churcham Gloucs 28 E4
Church Aston Wrekin 45 R10
Church Brampton Nhants 37 T7
Church Brough Cumb 68 G10
Church Broughton Derbys 46 H7
Church Cove Cnwll 2 J14
Church Crookham Hants 20 D12
Churchdown Gloucs 28 G4
Church Eaton Staffs 45 T10
Church End Bed 38 G9
Church End Bed 38 H9
Church End Bucks 30 F11
Church End C Beds 31 L6
Church End C Beds 31 M6
Church End C Beds 31 M8
Church End C Beds 31 M9
Church End C Beds 31 Q5
Church End C Beds 38 J10
Church End Cambs 38 G6
Church End Cambs 38 J4
Church End Cambs 39 M5
Church End Essex 22 F3
Church End Essex 22 H2
Church End Essex 22 H4
Churchend Essex 23 P9
Church End Gloucs 35 U13
Church End Gt Lon 21 M4
Church End Herts 20 K2
Church End Herts 31 P10
Church End Herts 31 S6
Church End Herts 31 S8
Church End Lincs 48 K7
Church End Lincs 59 R7
Church End Suffk 41 M13
Church End Warwks 36 H2
Church End Warwks 36 J2
Church Enstone Oxon 29 S2
Church Fenton N York 64 C12
Churchfield Sandw 36 D2
Churchgate Herts 31 T12
Churchgate Street Essex 22 C5
Church Green Devon 6 H5
Church Gresley Derbys 46 J10
Church Hanborough Oxon 29 T5
Church Hill Staffs 46 D11
Church Houses N York 71 L13
Churchill Devon 6 J4
Churchill Devon 15 N4
Churchill N Som 17 M5
Churchill Oxon 29 Q3
Churchill Worcs 35 U5
Churchill Worcs 36 B10
Churchinford Somset 6 H2
Church Knowle Dorset 8 C12
Church Laneham Notts 58 D11
Church Langton Leics 37 T2
Church Lawford Warwks 37 N5
Church Lawton Ches E 45 T2
Church Leigh Staffs 46 D6
Church Lench Worcs 36 D10
Church Mayfield Staffs 46 G5
Church Minshull Ches E 45 Q1
Church Norton W Susx 10 D11
Churchover Warwks 37 P4
Church Preen Shrops 35 M1
Church Pulverbatch Shrops 44 K13
Churchstanton Somset 6 G2
Churchstoke Powys 34 G2
Churchstow Devon 5 S11
Church Stowe Nhants 37 R9
Church Street Essex 40 C12
Church Street Kent 22 H13
Church Street Suffk 41 S4
Church Stretton Shrops 35 L2
Churchthorpe Lincs 59 P7
Churchtown Bpool 61 Q11
Churchtown Cnwll 4 D5
Churchtown Derbys 57 L14
Churchtown Devon 15 Q4
Churchtown IoM 60 g4
Churchtown Lancs 61 T11
Church Town N Linc 58 C5
Churchtown Sefton 54 J3
Church Village Rhondd 26 K10
Church Warsop Notts 57 S13
Church Wilne Derbys 47 M7
Churnsike Lodge Nthumb 76 D10
Churston Ferrers Torbay 6 B13
Churt Surrey 10 D3
Churton Ches W 44 K2
Churwell Leeds 63 R14
Chwilog Gwynd 42 H6
Chyandour Cnwll 2 D10
Chyanvounder Cnwll 2 H13
Chyeowling Cnwll 2 K8
Chyvarloe Cnwll 2 H12
Cil Powys 44 E13
Cilcain Flints 54 E13
Cilcennin Cerdgn 32 K8
Cilcewydd Powys 44 F13
Cilfrew Neath 26 D7
Cilfynydd Rhondd 26 K9
Cilgerran Pembks 32 C12
Cilgwyn Carmth 26 C2
Cilgwyn Gwynd 52 G12
Ciliau-Aeron Cerdgn 32 K9
Cilmaengwyn Neath 26 C6
Cilmery Powys 34 B10
Cilrhedyn Pembks 25 N4
Cilsan Carmth 25 U6
Ciltalgarth Gwynd 43 S5
Cilycwm Carmth 33 Q13
Cimla Neath 26 D9
Cinderford Gloucs 28 C5
Cinder Hill Wolves 36 B2
Cippenham Slough 20 F6
Cirencester Gloucs 28 K7
Citadilla N York 69 R13
City Gt Lon 21 P6
City V Glam 26 H12
City Airport Gt Lon 21 R6
City Dulas IoA 52 G5
City of London Crematorium Gt Lon 21 R5
Clabhach Ag & B 92 F7
Clachaig Ag & B 88 D9
Clachan Ag & B 79 P3
Clachan Ag & B 87 P2
Clachan Ag & B 88 E3
Clachan Ag & B 93 U9
Clachan Highld 100 e6
Clachan-a-Luib W Isls 106 d12
Clachan Mor Ag & B 92 B9
Clachan na Luib W Isls 106 d12
Clachan of Campsie E Duns 89 P10
Clachan-Seil Ag & B 87 P2
Clachnaharry Highld 102 H6
Clachtoll Highld 110 A12
Clackavoid P & K 97 U11
Clacket Lane Services Surrey 21 R12
Clackmannan Clacks 90 D13
Clackmannanshire Bridge Fife 90 D14

Culbokie – East Lound 129

Culbokie Highld 102 H4
Culbone Somset 15 T3
Culburnie Highld 102 E7
Culcabock Highld 102 J7
Culcharry Highld 103 N5
Culcheth Warrtn 55 Q8
Culdrain Abers 104 G9
Culduie Highld 100 g5
Culford Suffk 40 D6
Culgaith Cumb 68 D7
Culham Oxon 30 B13
Culkein Highld 110 A10
Culkein Drumbeg Highld 110 C10
Culkerton Gloucs 28 H8
Cullen Moray 104 G2
Cullercoats N Tyne 77 T11
Cullerlie Abers 99 P3
Cullicudden Highld 102 H3
Cullingworth C Brad 63 M12
Cuillin Hills Highld 100 d7
Cullipool Ag & B 87 N3
Cullivoe Shet 106 v3
Culloden Highld 102 K6
Cullompton Devon 6 D3
Cullompton Services Devon 6 D3
Culm Davy Devon 16 F13
Culmington Shrops 35 L4
Culmstock Devon 6 F2
Culnacraig Highld 107 U4
Culnaightrie D & G 73 T9
Culnaknock Highld 100 e3
Culpho Suffk 41 M11
Culrain Highld 108 K6
Culross Fife 82 J1
Culroy S Ayrs 81 L10
Culsalmond Abers 104 K9
Culscadden D & G 73 M10
Culshabbin D & G 72 J9
Culswick Shet 106 s9
Cultercullen Abers 105 Q11
Cults C Aber 99 R3
Culverstone Green Kent 12 B3
Culverthorpe Lincs 48 F5
Culworth Nhants 37 P11
Culzean Castle & Country Park S Ayrs 80 J10
Cumbernauld N Lans 89 S11
Cumbernauld Village N Lans 89 S10
Cumberworth Lincs 59 T12
Cumdivock Cumb 67 M3
Cuminestown Abers 105 N5
Cumledge Border 84 K7
Cummersdale Cumb 67 N2
Cummertrees D & G 75 M12
Cummingston Moray 103 T2
Cumnock E Ayrs 81 R8
Cumnor Oxon 29 U7
Cumrew Cumb 67 S2
Cumrue D & G 75 L8
Cumwhinton Cumb 67 Q2
Cumwhitton Cumb 67 R2
Cundall N York 63 U5
Cunninghamhead N Ayrs 81 M4
Cunningsburgh Shet 106 u10
Cupar Fife 91 N9
Cupar Muir Fife 91 N9
Curbar Derbys 57 L12
Curbridge Hants 9 Q6
Curbridge Oxon 29 R6
Curdridge Hants 9 Q6
Curdworth Warwks 36 G2
Curland Somset 16 J13
Curridge W Berk 19 Q6
Currie C Edin 83 N5
Curry Mallet Somset 16 K12
Curry Rivel Somset 17 L11
Curteis Corner Kent 12 G8
Curtisden Green Kent 12 D7
Curtisknowle Devon 5 S10
Cury Cnwll 2 H12
Cushnie Abers 104 G13
Cushuish Somset 16 G10
Cusop Herefs 34 F12
Cusworth Donc 57 R6
Cutcloy D & G 73 M13
Cutcombe Somset 16 B9
Cutgate Rochdl 56 C4
Cuthill Highld 109 P7
Cutiau Gwynd 43 M10
Cutler's Green Essex 22 E1
Cutmadoc Cnwll 3 R4
Cutmere Cnwll 4 J8
Cutnall Green Worcs 35 U7
Cutsdean Gloucs 29 L1
Cutsyke Wakefd 57 P2
Cutthorpe Derbys 57 M12
Cuttivett Cnwll 4 K8
Cuxham Oxon 30 E13
Cuxton Medway 12 D2
Cuxwold Lincs 59 L6
Cwm Blae G 27 M6
Cwm Denbgs 54 C11
Cwmafan Neath 26 D9
Cwmaman Rhondd 26 J8
Cwmann Carmth 33 L11
Cwmavon Torfn 27 P6
Cwmbach Carmth 25 N5
Cwm-bach Carmth 25 S10
Cwmbâch Powys 34 E13
Cwmbach Rhondd 26 J7
Cwmbach Llechrhyd Powys 34 B10
Cwmbelan Powys 33 T4
Cwmbran Torfn 27 P9
Cwmbrwyno Cerdgn 33 P4
Cwm Capel Carmth 25 S10
Cwmcarn Caerph 27 N9
Cwmcarvan Mons 27 T6
Cwm-celyn Blae G 27 N6
Cwm-Cewydd Gwynd 43 S11
Cwm-cou Cerdgn 32 E12
Cwm Crawnon Powys 27 L4
Cwmdare Rhondd 26 H7
Cwmdu Carmth 26 A1
Cwmdu Powys 27 M3
Cwmdu Swans 26 A9
Cwmduad Carmth 25 Q4
Cwm Dulais Swans 25 V10
Cwmdwr Carmth 33 P14
Cwmfelin Brdgnd 26 F10
Cwmfelin Myr Td 26 K7
Cwmfelin Boeth Carmth 25 L7
Cwmfelinfach Caerph 27 M9
Cwmfelin Mynach Carmth 25 M6
Cwmffrwd Carmth 25 R7
Cwmgiedd Powys 26 D5
Cwmgorse Carmth 26 C5
Cwmgwili Carmth 25 U8
Cwmgwrach Neath 26 F7
Cwmhiraeth Carmth 25 P3
Cwm-Ifor Carmth 26 B2
Cwm Irfon Powys 33 S11
Cwmisfael Carmth 25 S7
Cwm Llinau Powys 43 R12
Cwmllynfell Neath 26 C5
Cwmmawr Carmth 25 T8
Cwm Morgan Carmth 25 N4
Cwmparc Rhondd 26 G8
Cwmpengraig Carmth 25 Q3
Cwm Penmachno Conwy 43 Q4
Cwmpennar Rhondd 26 J7
Cwmrhos Powys 27 M3
Cwmrhydyceirw Swans 26 B8
Cwmsychbant Cerdgn 32 J11
Cwmtillery Blae G 27 N6
Cwm-twrch Isaf Powys 26 D5
Cwm-twrch Uchaf Powys 26 D5
Cwm-y-glo Carmth 25 U8
Cwm-y-glo Gwynd 52 J10
Cwmyoy Mons 27 P3
Cwmystwyth Cerdgn 33 Q6
Cwrt Gwynd 43 N14
Cwrt-newydd Cerdgn 32 J11
Cwrt-y-gollen Powys 27 N4
Cyfarthfa Castle Museum Myr Td 26 J6
Cyfronydd Powys 44 D12
Cylibebyll Neath 26 C7
Cymau Flints 44 G2
Cymer Neath 26 F8
Cymmer Rhondd 26 J9
Cynghordy Carmth 33 R12
Cynheidre Carmth 25 S9
Cynonville Neath 26 E8
Cynwyd Denbgs 44 C5
Cynwyl Elfed Carmth 25 Q5

D

Daccombe Devon 6 B11
Dacre Cumb 67 Q7
Dacre N York 63 P7
Dacre Banks N York 63 P7
Daddry Shield Dur 68 J5
Dadford Bucks 30 E5
Dadlington Leics 47 M14
Dafen Carmth 25 T10
Daffy Green Norfk 50 G12
Dagenham Gt Lon 22 D11
Daglingworth Gloucs 28 J6
Dagnall Bucks 31 L9
Dagworth Suffk 40 H8
Dailly S Ayrs 80 K12
Dainton Devon 5 V7
Dairsie Fife 91 P8
Daisy Hill Bolton 55 Q6
Daisy Hill Leeds 63 R14
Dalabrog W Isls 106 c16
Dalavich Ag & B 87 T3
Dalbeattie D & G 74 F13
Dalbury Derbys 46 J7
Dalby IoM 60 c7
Dalby Lincs 59 R13
Dalby N York 64 E5
Dalcapon P & K 97 R13
Dalchalm Highld 109 S3
Dalchreichart Highld 102 A13
Dalchruin P & K 89 R2
Dalcrue P & K 90 F6
Dalderby Lincs 59 N13
Dalditch Devon 6 D8
Daldowie Crematorium C Glas 82 C6
Dale Cumb 67 R4
Dale Derbys 47 M6
Dale Pembks 24 D9
Dale Bottom Cumb 67 L8
Dale End Derbys 46 H1
Dale End N York 62 K10
Dale Hill E Susx 12 D9
Dalehouse N York 71 N9
Dalelia Highld 93 S5
Dalgarven N Ayrs 80 K3
Dalgety Bay Fife 83 N2
Dalgig E Ayrs 81 R10
Dalginross P & K 89 S1
Dalguise P & K 90 E2
Dalhalvaig Highld 111 T6
Dalham Suffk 40 B8
Daliburgh W Isls 106 c16
Dalkeith Mdloth 83 R5
Dallas Moray 103 T5
Dallinghoo Suffk 41 N9
Dallington E Susx 11 V7
Dallington Nhants 37 T8
Dallow N York 63 P5
Dalmally Ag & B 94 H13
Dalmary Stirlg 89 M6
Dalmellington E Ayrs 81 P11
Dalmeny C Edin 83 M3
Dalmore Highld 109 M11
Dalmuir W Duns 89 L11
Dalnabreck Highld 93 S5
Dalnacardoch P & K 97 L9
Dalnahaitnach Highld 103 N12
Dalnaspidal P & K 96 J9
Dalnawillan Lodge Highld 112 B8
Daloist P & K 97 M12
Dalqueich P & K 90 G11
Dalquhairn S Ayrs 81 L13
Dalreavoch Lodge Highld 109 P3
Dalry N Ayrs 80 K3
Dalrymple E Ayrs 81 M10
Dalserf S Lans 82 E8
Dalsmeran Ag & B 79 L13
Dalston Cumb 67 N2
Dalston Gt Lon 21 P6
Dalswinton D & G 74 H8
Dalton Cumb 61 U4
Dalton D & G 75 M11
Dalton Lancs 55 L5
Dalton N York 63 U4
Dalton N York 69 P11
Dalton Nthumb 77 N11
Dalton Rothm 57 Q8
Dalton-in-Furness Cumb 61 N5
Dalton-le-Dale Dur 70 F3
Dalton Magna Rothm 57 Q8
Dalton-on-Tees N York 69 S11
Dalton Parva Rothm 57 Q8
Dalton Piercy Hartpl 70 G6
Dalveich Stirlg 95 S14
Dalwhinnie Highld 96 J7
Dalwood Devon 6 H4
Damask Green Herts 31 S7
Damerham Hants 8 G5
Damgate Norfk 51 R12
Dam Green Norfk 40 H3
Damnaglaur D & G 72 E12
Danaway Kent 12 G3
Danbury Essex 22 J6
Danby N York 71 M11
Danby Bottom N York 71 L12
Danby Wiske N York 70 D13
Dandaleith Moray 104 B6
Danderhall Mdloth 83 R5
Danebridge Ches E 56 E13
Dane End Herts 31 T8
Danegate E Susx 11 T4
Danehill E Susx 11 Q5
Dane Hills C Leic 47 Q13
Danemoor Green Norfk 50 J12
Danesford Shrops 35 R2
Danesmoor Derbys 57 P14
Dane Street Kent 13 L5
Daniel's Water Kent 12 J7
Danshillock Abers 105 L4
Danskine E Loth 84 F5
Danthorpe E R Yk 65 T13
Danzey Green Warwks 36 F7
Dapple Heath Staffs 46 D8
Darby Green Hants 20 D10
Darcy Lever Bolton 55 R5
Dardy Powys 27 N4
Daren-felen Mons 27 N5
Darenth Kent 22 E13
Daresbury Halton 55 N10
Darfield Barns 57 P6
Darfoulds Notts 57 S11
Dargate Kent 13 L3
Darite Cnwll 4 H7
Darland Medway 12 E2
Darland Wrexhm 44 J2
Darlaston Wsall 36 C1
Darlaston Green Wsall 36 C1
Darley N York 63 Q8
Darley Abbey C Derb 47 L6
Darley Bridge Derbys 46 J1
Darley Dale Derbys 57 L14
Darley Green Solhll 36 G6
Darleyhall Herts 31 P8
Darley Head N York 63 P8
Darlingscott Warwks 36 H12
Darlington Darltn 69 S10
Darlington Crematorium Darltn 69 S10
Darliston Shrops 45 N7
Darlton Notts 58 C12
Darnford Staffs 46 F12
Darnick Border 84 E12
Darowen Powys 43 R13
Darra Abers 105 L6
Darracott Devon 14 F9
Darracott Devon 15 L5
Darras Hall Nthumb 77 P11
Darrington Wakefd 57 Q3
Darsham Suffk 41 R7
Darshill Somset 17 R8
Dartford Kent 22 D13
Dartford Crossing Kent 22 E12
Dartington Devon 5 T8
Dartmeet Devon 5 R6
Dartmoor National Park Devon 5 R5
Dartmouth Devon 5 V10
Darton Barns 57 M4
Darvel E Ayrs 81 R5
Darwell Hole E Susx 12 C12
Darwen Bl w D 55 Q2
Datchet W & M 20 G7
Datchworth Herts 31 S9
Datchworth Green Herts 31 S9
Daubhill Bolton 55 R5
Daugh of Kinermony Moray 104 A7
Dauntsey Wilts 18 E4
Dava Highld 103 R8
Davenham Ches W 55 Q12
Davenport Stockp 56 D9
Davenport Green Ches E 55 T11
Davenport Green Traffd 55 T9
Daventry Nhants 37 Q8
Davidson's Mains C Edin 83 P3
Davidstow Cnwll 4 F3
David Street Kent 12 B3
Davington D & G 75 P5
Davington Hill Kent 12 K3
Daviot Abers 105 L10
Daviot Highld 102 K8
Daviot House Highld 102 K7
Davis's Town E Susx 11 S7
Davoch of Grange Moray 104 F5
Davyhulme Traffd 55 S7
Daw End Wsall 46 D13
Dawesgreen Surrey 21 M13
Dawley Wrekin 45 Q12
Dawlish Devon 6 C9
Dawlish Warren Devon 6 C9
Dawn Conwy 53 Q8
Daws Green Somset 16 G12
Daws Heath Essex 22 K10
Daw's House Cnwll 4 J4
Dawsmere Lincs 49 P7
Daybrook Notts 47 Q4
Day Green Ches E 45 S2
Dayhills Staffs 46 C7
Dayhouse Bank Worcs 36 C5
Daylesford Gloucs 29 P2
Ddol Flints 54 D12
Ddol-Cownwy Powys 44 B10
Deal Kent 13 S5
Dean Cumb 66 G7
Dean Devon 5 S8
Dean Devon 15 P3
Dean Devon 15 R3
Dean Dorset 8 D5
Dean Hants 9 N2
Dean Hants 9 R5
Dean Lancs 56 C1
Dean Oxon 29 R3
Dean Somset 17 S8
Dean Bottom Kent 21 U9
Deanburnhaugh Border 75 S3
Deancombe Devon 5 S8
Dean Court Oxon 29 U6
Deane Bolton 55 Q5
Deane Hants 19 R10
Dean End Dorset 8 D5
Dean Head Barns 57 L6
Deanhead Kirk 56 F3
Deanland Dorset 8 D5
Deanlane End W Susx 9 U6
Dean Prior Devon 5 S8
Deanraw Nthumb 76 G13
Dean Row Ches E 56 C10
Deans W Loth 82 K5
Deanscales Cumb 66 G7
Deanshanger Nhants 30 G5
Deanshaugh Moray 104 D5
Deanston Stirlg 89 R5
Dean Street Kent 12 D5
Dearham Cumb 66 G5
Dearnley Rochdl 56 D3
Debach Suffk 41 M10
Debden Essex 21 R3
Debden Essex 39 S14
Debden Green Essex 22 E1
Debenham Suffk 41 L8
Deblin's Green Worcs 35 T11
Dechmont W Loth 82 K4
Dechmont Road W Loth 82 K5
Deddington Oxon 29 U1
Dedham Essex 40 J14
Dedham Heath Essex 23 Q1
Dedworth W & M 20 F7
Deene Nhants 38 D2
Deenethorpe Nhants 38 E2
Deepcar Sheff 57 L7
Deepcut Surrey 20 F11
Deepdale Cumb 62 E3
Deepdale N York 62 H4
Deeping Gate C Pete 48 H12
Deeping St James Lincs 48 J12
Deeping St Nicholas Lincs 48 K10
Deerhurst Gloucs 28 G1
Deerhurst Walton Gloucs 28 G2
Deerton Street Kent 12 J3
Defford Worcs 36 B12
Defynnog Powys 26 G2
Deganwy Conwy 53 N7
Degnish Ag & B 87 P3
Deighton C York 64 E11
Deighton N York 70 E12
Deiniolen Gwynd 52 J10
Delabole Cnwll 4 D4
Delamere Ches W 55 N13
Delfrigs Abers 105 R11
Delley Devon 15 M8
Delliefure Highld 103 S9
Dell Quay W Susx 10 C10
Delly End Oxon 29 S5
Delnabo Moray 103 U12
Delnashaugh Inn Moray 103 U8
Delny Highld 109 N10
Delph Oldham 56 E5
Delves Dur 69 P3
Delvin End Essex 40 C13
Dembleby Lincs 48 F6
Demelza Cnwll 3 P4
Denaby Donc 57 Q7
Denaby Main Donc 57 Q7
Denbies Surrey 20 K12
Denbigh Denbgs 54 C13
Denbighshire Crematorium Denbgs 53 T8
Denbrae Fife 91 N8
Denbury Devon 5 U7
Denby Derbys 47 L4
Denby Bottles Derbys 47 L4
Denby Dale Kirk 56 K5
Denchworth Oxon 29 S9
Dendron Cumb 61 N5
Denel End C Beds 31 M5
Denfield P & K 90 E8
Denford Nhants 38 E5
Dengie Essex 23 N7
Denham Bucks 20 H5
Denham Suffk 40 C8
Denham Suffk 41 L6
Denham End Suffk 40 C8
Denham Green Bucks 20 H5
Denham Green Suffk 41 L6
Denhead Abers 105 R5
Denhead Fife 91 Q9
Denhead of Gray C Dund 91 N5
Denholm Border 76 B2
Denholme C Brad 63 M13
Denholme Clough C Brad 63 M13
Denio Gwynd 42 G6
Denmead Hants 9 T6
Denmore C Aber 105 Q13
Denne Park W Susx 10 K5
Dennington Suffk 41 N7
Denny Falk 89 T9
Dennyloanhead Falk 89 T9
Den of Lindores Fife 91 L8
Denshaw Oldham 56 E4
Denside Abers 99 Q4
Densole Kent 13 P7
Denston Suffk 40 C10
Denstone Staffs 46 E5
Denstroude Kent 13 M3
Dent Cumb 62 E2
Denton Cambs 38 J3
Denton Darltn 69 R9
Denton E Susx 11 R10
Denton Kent 13 P6
Denton Kent 22 G13
Denton Lincs 48 C7
Denton N York 63 N10
Denton Nhants 38 B9
Denton Norfk 41 N3
Denton Oxon 30 C12
Denton Tamesd 56 D7
Denver Norfk 49 T13
Denwick Nthumb 77 Q3
Deopham Norfk 50 H13
Deopham Green Norfk 50 H14
Depden Suffk 40 C9
Depden Green Suffk 40 C9
Deptford Gt Lon 21 Q7
Deptford Wilts 18 F13
Derby C Derb 47 L6
Derby Devon 15 N6
Derbyhaven IoM 60 d9
Derculich P & K 97 P13
Dereham Norfk 50 G11
Deri Caerph 27 L7
Derril Devon 14 H12
Derringstone Kent 13 P6
Derrington Staffs 45 U9
Derriton Devon 14 H12
Derry Hill Wilts 18 E6
Derrythorpe N Linc 58 D5
Dersingham Norfk 49 U7
Dervaig Ag & B 93 L8
Derwen Denbgs 44 C3
Derwenlas Powys 43 P14
Derwent Valley Mills Derbys 46 K2
Derwentwater Cumb 67 L8
Derwydd Carmth 25 V7
Desborough Nhants 38 B4
Desford Leics 47 N13
Deskford Moray 104 G3
Detchant Nthumb 85 R11
Detling Kent 12 E4
Deuxhill Shrops 35 Q3
Devauden Mons 27 T8
Devil's Bridge Cerdgn 33 P5
Devitts Green Warwks 36 J2
Devizes Wilts 18 F8
Devonport C Plym 5 M10
Devonside Clacks 90 D12
Devoran Cnwll 2 K9
Devoran & Perran Cnwll 2 K9
Dewarton Mdloth 83 S6
Dewlish Dorset 7 U5
Dewsbury Kirk 56 K2
Dewsbury Moor Kirk 56 K2
Dewsbury Moor Crematorium Kirk 56 K2
Deytheur Powys 44 F10
Dial N Som 17 P3
Dial Green W Susx 10 E5
Dial Post W Susx 10 K7
Dibberford Dorset 7 N4
Dibden Hants 9 N7
Dibden Purlieu Hants 9 N7
Dickens Heath Solhll 36 F5
Dickleburgh Norfk 41 L4
Didbrook Gloucs 29 L1
Didcot Oxon 19 R2
Diddington Cambs 38 J7
Diddlebury Shrops 35 M3
Didley Herefs 27 T1
Didling W Susx 10 C7
Didmarton Gloucs 28 F10
Didsbury Manch 55 T8
Didworthy Devon 5 R8
Digby Lincs 48 G3
Digg Highld 100 d3
Diggle Oldham 56 F5
Digmoor Lancs 55 L5
Digswell Herts 31 R9
Digswell Water Herts 31 S10
Dihewyd Cerdgn 32 J9
Dilham Norfk 51 P8
Dilhorne Staffs 46 C5
Dill Hall Lancs 62 F14
Dillington Cambs 38 H7
Dilston Nthumb 76 K13
Dilton Wilts 18 C11
Dilton Marsh Wilts 18 B11
Dilwyn Herefs 34 K10
Dimple Bolton 55 R3
Dimple Derbys 46 J1
Dinas Carmth 25 N4
Dinas Cnwll 3 N2
Dinas Gwynd 42 E6
Dinas Pembks 24 H3
Dinas Rhondd 26 J9
Dinas Dinlle Gwynd 52 F11
Dinas-Mawddwy Gwynd 43 S10
Dinas Powys V Glam 16 G2
Dinder Somset 17 Q8
Dinedor Herefs 35 M13
Dingestow Mons 27 T5
Dingle Lpool 54 J9
Dingleden Kent 12 F9
Dingley Nhants 37 U3
Dingwall Highld 102 F4
Dinmael Conwy 44 B5
Dinnet Abers 98 H4
Dinnington N u Ty 77 Q11
Dinnington Rothm 57 R9
Dinnington Somset 7 M2
Dinorwic Gwynd 52 J10
Dinton Bucks 30 G10
Dinton Wilts 8 E2
Dinwoodie D & G 75 M7
Dinworthy Devon 14 H9
Dipford Somset 16 H12
Dipley Hants 20 B11
Dippen Ag & B 79 Q8
Dippen N Ayrs 80 E8
Dippenhall Surrey 20 D13
Dippermill Devon 14 K11
Dippertown Devon 5 L4
Dipple Moray 104 C4
Dipple S Ayrs 80 J12
Diptford Devon 5 S9
Dipton Dur 69 Q2
Diptonmill Nthumb 76 J13
Dirleton E Loth 84 E2
Dirt Pot Nthumb 68 J3
Discoed Powys 34 G8
Diseworth Leics 47 N9
Dishforth N York 63 T5
Disley Ches E 56 E10
Diss Norfk 40 K4
Disserth Powys 34 B9
Distington Cumb 66 F8
Distington Hall Crematorium Cumb 66 F8
Ditchampton Wilts 8 F2
Ditcheat Somset 17 R9
Ditchingham Norfk 41 P2
Ditchling E Susx 11 N7
Ditherington Shrops 45 M11
Ditteridge Wilts 18 B7
Dittisham Devon 5 V9
Ditton Kent 12 D4
Ditton Green Cambs 39 U9
Ditton Priors Shrops 35 P3
Dixton Gloucs 28 J1
Dixton Mons 27 U5
Dizzard Cnwll 14 E13
Dobcross Oldham 56 E5
Dobwalls Cnwll 4 G7
Doccombe Devon 5 T3
Dochgarroch Highld 102 H7
Dockenfield Surrey 10 C2
Docker Lancs 62 B5
Docking Norfk 50 C6
Docklow Herefs 35 N9
Dockray Cumb 67 L3
Dockray Cumb 67 N8
Dodbrooke Devon 5 S12
Doddinghurst Essex 22 E8
Doddington Cambs 39 P2
Doddington Kent 12 H4
Doddington Lincs 58 E12
Doddington Nthumb 85 P12
Doddington Shrops 35 P5
Doddiscombsleigh Devon 5 V3
Dodd's Green Ches E 45 P5
Doddshill Norfk 49 U7
Doddy Cross Cnwll 4 J8
Dodford Nhants 37 R8
Dodford Worcs 36 B6
Dodington S Glos 28 E11
Dodington Somset 16 G8
Dodleston Ches W 44 J1
Dodscott Devon 15 M9
Dodside E Rens 81 Q2
Dod's Leigh Staffs 46 D7
Dodworth Barns 57 M5
Dodworth Bottom Barns 57 M6
Dodworth Green Barns 57 M6
Doe Bank Birm 46 F14
Doe Lea Derbys 57 Q13
Dogdyke Lincs 48 K2
Dogley Lane Kirk 56 J4
Dogmersfield Hants 20 C12
Dogridge Wilts 29 L10
Dogsthorpe C Pete 48 J13
Dog Village Devon 6 C5
Dolanog Powys 44 C11
Dolau Powys 34 D7
Dolaucothi Carmth 33 N12
Dolbenmaen Gwynd 42 K5
Doley Staffs 45 R8
Dolfach Powys 43 T13
Dolfor Powys 34 D3
Dol-fôr Powys 43 R12
Dolgarrog Conwy 53 N9
Dolgellau Gwynd 43 P10
Dolgoch Gwynd 43 N13
Dol-gran Carmth 25 R4
Doll Highld 109 R4
Dollar Clacks 90 E12
Dollarfield Clacks 90 E12
Dolley Green Powys 34 G7
Dollwen Cerdgn 33 N4
Dolphin Flints 54 E12
Dolphinholme Lancs 61 U9
Dolphinton S Lans 83 M9
Dolton Devon 15 N10
Dolwen Conwy 53 Q8
Dolwyddelan Conwy 43 P3
Dolybont Cerdgn 33 M3
Dolyhir Powys 34 F9
Domgay Powys 44 G10
Donaldson's Lodge Nthumb 85 M10
Doncaster Donc 57 S6
Doncaster Carr Donc 57 S6
Doncaster North Services Donc 57 U4
Donhead St Andrew Wilts 8 C4
Donhead St Mary Wilts 8 C4
Donibristle Fife 90 J14
Doniford Somset 16 E8
Donington Lincs 48 K6
Donington on Bain Lincs 59 M10
Donington Park Services Leics 47 N8
Donington Southing Lincs 48 K7
Donisthorpe Leics 46 K11
Donkey Street Kent 13 M9
Donkey Town Surrey 20 F10
Donnington Gloucs 29 N2
Donnington Herefs 35 R14
Donnington Shrops 45 N12
Donnington W Berk 19 Q7
Donnington W Susx 10 D10
Donnington Wrekin 45 R11
Donnington Wood Wrekin 45 R11
Donyatt Somset 6 K2
Doomsday Green W Susx 10 K5
Doonfoot S Ayrs 81 L9
Dorback Lodge Highld 103 S12
Dorchester Dorset 7 S6
Dorchester-on-Thames Oxon 19 S2
Dordon Warwks 46 J13
Dore Sheff 57 M10
Dores Highld 102 G9
Dorking Surrey 21 L13
Dorking Tye Suffk 40 F13
Dormansland Surrey 11 Q2
Dormans Park Surrey 11 P2
Dormington Herefs 35 N12
Dormston Worcs 36 C9
Dorn Gloucs 36 H14
Dorney Bucks 20 F7
Dornie Highld 101 M6
Dornoch Highld 109 P7
Dornock D & G 75 P12
Dorrery Highld 112 C6
Dorridge Solhll 36 G6
Dorrington Lincs 48 G3
Dorrington Shrops 45 L13
Dorrington Shrops 45 R5
Dorsington Warwks 36 F11
Dorstone Herefs 34 H12
Dorton Bucks 30 E10
Dosthill Staffs 46 H14
Dothan IoA 52 E8
Dottery Dorset 7 N5
Doublebois Cnwll 4 F8
Doughton Gloucs 28 G9
Douglas IoM 60 f7
Douglas S Lans 82 F12
Douglas and Angus C Dund 91 P5
Douglas Crematorium IoM 60 f7
Douglas Pier Ag & B 88 E6
Douglastown Angus 91 P2
Douglas Water S Lans 82 G11
Douglas West S Lans 82 F12
Doulting Somset 17 R8
Dounby Ork 106 r17
Doune Highld 108 G4
Doune Stirlg 89 R5
Dounepark S Ayrs 80 H13
Dounie Highld 108 K6
Dousland Devon 5 N7
Dovaston Shrops 44 J9
Dove Dale Derbys 46 F3
Dove Green Notts 47 N3
Dove Holes Derbys 56 G11
Dovenby Cumb 66 G6
Dover Kent 13 R7
Dover Wigan 55 P6
Dover Castle Kent 13 R7
Dovercourt Essex 23 T1
Doverdale Worcs 35 U7
Doveridge Derbys 46 F7
Doversgreen Surrey 21 N13
Dowally P & K 90 F2
Dowbridge Lancs 61 S13
Dowdeswell Gloucs 28 K4
Dowlais Myr Td 26 K6
Dowland Devon 15 N10
Dowlish Ford Somset 7 L2
Dowlish Wake Somset 7 L2
Down Ampney Gloucs 29 L8
Downderry Cnwll 4 J10
Downe Gt Lon 21 R10
Downend Gloucs 28 F8
Downend IoW 9 Q11
Downend S Glos 28 C12
Downend W Berk 19 Q5
Downfield C Dund 91 N5
Downgate Cnwll 4 H6
Downgate Cnwll 4 K6
Downham Essex 22 H8
Downham Gt Lon 21 Q8
Downham Lancs 62 F11
Downham Market Norfk 49 T13
Down Hatherley Gloucs 28 G3
Downhead Somset 17 Q11
Downhead Somset 17 S7
Downhill Cnwll 3 M3
Downhill P & K 90 G6
Downholland Cross Lancs 54 J5
Downholme N York 69 P13
Downicarey Devon 4 K2
Downies Abers 99 S5
Downing Flints 54 E11
Downley Bucks 20 D3
Down St Mary Devon 15 R12
Downs Crematorium Br & H 11 N9
Downside Somset 17 R6
Downside Somset 17 R8
Downside Surrey 20 K11
Down Thomas Devon 5 N10
Downton Hants 8 K10
Downton Wilts 8 H4
Dowsby Lincs 48 H8
Dowsdale Lincs 49 L11
Doxey Staffs 45 U9
Doxford Nthumb 85 T14
Doynton S Glos 28 D13
Draethen Caerph 27 N10
Draffan S Lans 82 E9
Dragonby N Linc 58 F4
Dragons Green W Susx 10 J6
Drakeholes Notts 58 B8
Drakelow Worcs 35 T4
Drakemyre N Ayrs 80 K2
Drakes Broughton Worcs 36 B11
Drakewalls Cnwll 5 L6
Draughton N York 63 L9
Draughton Nhants 37 U5
Drax N York 57 U1
Drax Hales N York 57 U1
Draycote Warwks 37 M6
Draycot Foliat Swindn 18 J5
Draycott Derbys 47 M7
Draycott Gloucs 36 G13
Draycott Shrops 35 T2
Draycott Somset 17 N6
Draycott Somset 17 Q12
Draycott Worcs 35 U11
Draycott in the Clay Staffs 46 G8
Draycott in the Moors Staffs 46 C5
Drayford Devon 15 S10
Drayton C Port 9 T7
Drayton Leics 38 B2
Drayton Lincs 48 K6
Drayton Norfk 51 L11
Drayton Oxon 29 U9
Drayton Oxon 37 M12
Drayton Somset 17 M12
Drayton Worcs 36 B5
Drayton Bassett Staffs 46 G13
Drayton Beauchamp Bucks 30 K10
Drayton Manor Park Staffs 46 G13
Drayton Parslow Bucks 30 H7
Drayton St Leonard Oxon 30 C13
Drebley N York 63 M8
Dreemskerry IoM 60 h4
Dreen Hill Pembks 24 F8
Drefach Carmth 25 Q3
Drefach Carmth 25 T8
Drefach Cerdgn 32 J11
Drefelin Carmth 25 Q3
Dreghorn N Ayrs 81 M5
Drellingore Kent 13 P7
Drem E Loth 84 E3
Dresden C Stke 46 B5
Drewsteignton Devon 5 S2
Driby Lincs 59 Q12
Driffield E R Yk 65 N8
Driffield Gloucs 29 L8
Driffield Cross Roads Gloucs 29 L8
Drift Cnwll 2 C11
Drigg Cumb 66 G13
Drighlington Leeds 63 Q14
Drimnin Highld 93 P8
Drimpton Dorset 7 M4
Drimsallie Highld 94 D3
Dringhouses C York 64 D10
Drinkstone Suffk 40 G8
Drinkstone Green Suffk 40 G8
Drive End Dorset 7 Q3
Driver's End Herts 31 R8
Drointon Staffs 46 D8
Droitwich Spa Worcs 35 U8
Dron P & K 90 H8
Dronfield Derbys 57 N11
Dronfield Woodhouse Derbys 57 M11
Drongan E Ayrs 81 N9
Dronley Angus 91 M4
Droop Dorset 7 U3
Dropping Well Rothm 57 N8
Droxford Hants 9 S5
Droylsden Tamesd 56 D7
Druid Denbgs 44 B5
Druidston Pembks 24 E7
Druimarbin Highld 94 F4
Druimavuic Ag & B 94 E9
Druimdrishaig Ag & B 87 N11
Druimindarroch Highld 93 R2
Drum Ag & B 87 S10
Drum P & K 90 F11
Drumalbin S Lans 82 H11
Drumbeg Highld 110 C10
Drumblade Abers 104 H7
Drumbreddon D & G 72 D11
Drumbuie Highld 100 g6
Drumburgh Cumb 75 Q14
Drumburn D & G 66 C2
Drumchapel C Glas 89 M11
Drumchastle P & K 95 T7
Drumclog S Lans 81 S5
Drumeldrie Fife 91 P11
Drumelzier Border 83 M12
Drumfearn Highld 100 f8
Drumfrennie Abers 99 N4
Drumgley Angus 98 G13
Drumguish Highld 97 M3
Drumin Moray 103 U9
Drumjohn D & G 81 Q13
Drumlamford S Ayrs 72 H4
Drumlasie Abers 99 L2
Drumleaning Cumb 67 L2
Drumlemble Ag & B 79 M12
Drumlithie Abers 99 P7
Drummoddie D & G 72 K10
Drummore D & G 72 E12
Drummuir Moray 104 D7
Drumnadrochit Highld 102 F9
Drumnagorrach Moray 104 G5
Drumpark D & G 74 G10
Drumrunie Lodge Highld 108 B4
Drumshang S Ayrs 80 K10
Drumuie Highld 100 d5
Drumuillie Highld 103 P11
Drumvaich Stirlg 89 Q5
Drunzie P & K 90 H10
Druridge Nthumb 77 R6
Drury Flints 54 G14
Drybeck Cumb 68 E9
Drybridge Moray 104 E3
Drybridge N Ayrs 81 M5
Drybrook Gloucs 28 B4
Dryburgh Border 84 F12
Dry Doddington Lincs 48 C4
Dry Drayton Cambs 39 N8
Drymen Stirlg 89 L8
Drymuir Abers 105 Q6
Drynoch Highld 100 d6
Dry Sandford Oxon 29 U7
Dryslwyn Carmth 25 U6
Dry Street Essex 22 G10
Dryton Shrops 45 N12
Dubford Abers 105 M3
Dublin Suffk 41 L7
Duchally Highld 110 H13
Duck End Bed 31 N4
Duck End Cambs 38 K8
Duck End Essex 22 G2
Duck End Essex 39 U14
Duckend Green Essex 22 H3
Duckington Ches W 45 L3
Ducklington Oxon 29 S6
Duck's Cross Bed 38 H9
Duddenhoe End Essex 39 Q13
Duddingston C Edin 83 Q4
Duddington Nhants 48 E13
Duddlestone Somset 16 H12
Duddleswell E Susx 11 R5
Duddlewick Shrops 35 Q4
Duddo Nthumb 85 N10
Duddon Ches W 55 M14
Duddon Bridge Cumb 61 M2
Duddon Common Ches W 55 M13
Dudleston Shrops 44 H6
Dudleston Heath Shrops 44 J6
Dudley Dudley 36 B2
Dudley N Tyne 77 R11
Dudley Hill C Brad 63 P13
Dudley Port Sandw 36 C2
Dudnill Shrops 35 P6
Dudsbury Dorset 8 F9
Dudswell Herts 31 L11
Duffield Derbys 46 K5
Duffryn Neath 26 E8
Dufftown Moray 104 C7
Duffus Moray 103 U2
Dufton Cumb 68 E7
Duggleby N York 64 K6
Duirinish Highld 100 g6
Duisdalemore Highld 100 g8
Duisky Highld 94 E3
Dukestown Blae G 27 L5
Duke Street Suffk 40 J12
Dukinfield Tamesd 56 D7
Dukinfield Crematorium Tamesd 56 D7
Dulas IoA 52 G5
Dulcote Somset 17 Q8
Dulford Devon 6 E3
Dull P & K 90 B2
Dullatur N Lans 89 R10
Dullingham Cambs 39 T9
Dullingham Ley Cambs 39 T9
Dulnain Bridge Highld 103 Q11
Duloe Bed 38 J8
Duloe Cnwll 4 G9
Dulverton Somset 16 B11
Dulwich Gt Lon 21 P8
Dumbarton W Duns 88 J10
Dumbleton Gloucs 36 D13
Dumfries D & G 74 J10
Dumgoyne Stirlg 89 M9
Dummer Hants 19 S11
Dumpton Kent 13 S2
Dun Angus 99 M12
Dunalastair P & K 95 U7
Dunan Ag & B 88 E11
Dunan Highld 100 e7
Dunan P & K 95 P7
Dunaverty Ag & B 79 M14
Dunball Somset 16 K8
Dunbar E Loth 84 H3
Dunbeath Highld 112 E11
Dunbeg Ag & B 94 B12
Dunblane Stirlg 89 S5
Dunbog Fife 91 L8
Dunbridge Hants 9 L3
Duncanston Highld 102 G4
Duncanstone Abers 104 H10
Dunchideock Devon 6 A7
Dunchurch Warwks 37 N6
Duncote Nhants 37 S10
Duncow D & G 74 J9
Duncrievie P & K 90 H10
Duncton W Susx 10 F7
Dundee C Dund 91 P5
Dundee Airport C Dund 91 N6
Dundee Crematorium C Dund 91 N5
Dundon Somset 17 N10
Dundonald S Ayrs 81 M6
Dundonnell Highld 107 U7
Dundraw Cumb 66 K3
Dundreggan Highld 102 B13
Dundrennan D & G 73 S10
Dundry N Som 17 Q3
Dunecht Abers 99 P2
Dunfermline Fife 83 L1
Dunfermline Crematorium Fife 83 M1
Dunfield Gloucs 29 M8
Dunford Bridge Barns 56 J6
Dungate Kent 12 H4
Dungavel S Lans 81 T5
Dunge Wilts 18 C10
Dungeness Kent 13 L12
Dungworth Sheff 57 L9
Dunham Massey Traffd 55 R9
Dunham-on-the-Hill Ches W 55 L12
Dunham-on-Trent Notts 58 D12
Dunhampstead Worcs 36 B8
Dunhampton Worcs 35 T7
Dunham Town Traffd 55 R9
Dunham Woodhouses Traffd 55 R9
Dunholme Lincs 58 H11
Dunino Fife 91 R9
Dunipace Falk 89 T9
Dunkeld P & K 90 F3
Dunkerton BaNES 17 T5
Dunkeswell Devon 6 F3
Dunkeswick N York 63 S10
Dunkirk Ches W 54 J12
Dunkirk Kent 13 L4
Dunkirk S Glos 28 E10
Dunkirk Wilts 18 E8
Dunk's Green Kent 12 B5
Dunlappie Angus 98 K10
Dunley Hants 19 Q10
Dunley Worcs 35 S7
Dunlop E Ayrs 81 N3
Dunmaglass Highld 102 G11
Dunmere Cnwll 3 Q3
Dunmore Falk 90 C14
Dunnet Highld 112 F2
Dunnichen Angus 91 R2
Dunning P & K 90 F9
Dunnington C York 64 F9
Dunnington E R Yk 65 R9
Dunnington Warwks 36 E10
Dunnockshaw Lancs 62 G14
Dunn Street Kent 12 E3
Dunoon Ag & B 88 E10
Dunphail Moray 103 R6
Dunragit D & G 72 F8
Duns Border 84 K8
Dunsa Derbys 56 K12
Dunsby Lincs 48 H8
Dunscar Bolton 55 R4
Dunscore D & G 74 G9
Dunscroft Donc 57 T5
Dunsdale R & Cl 70 K9
Dunsden Green Oxon 20 B7
Dunsdon Devon 14 H11
Dunsfold Surrey 10 G3
Dunsford Devon 5 U3
Dunshalt Fife 90 K9
Dunshillock Abers 105 R6
Dunsill Notts 47 N1
Dunsley N York 71 Q10
Dunsley Staffs 35 U4
Dunsmore Bucks 30 J11
Dunsop Bridge Lancs 62 D10
Dunstable C Beds 31 M8
Dunstall Staffs 46 G9
Dunstall Common Worcs 35 U12
Dunstall Green Suffk 40 B8
Dunstan Nthumb 77 Q2
Dunstan Steads Nthumb 77 Q1
Dunster Somset 16 C8
Duns Tew Oxon 29 U2
Dunston Gatesd 77 Q13
Dunston Lincs 58 J14
Dunston Norfk 51 M13
Dunston Staffs 46 B10
Dunstone Devon 5 P10
Dunstone Devon 5 S5
Dunston Heath Staffs 46 B10
Dunsville Donc 57 T5
Dunswell E R Yk 65 P12
Dunsyre S Lans 83 L9
Dunterton Devon 4 K5
Dunthrop Oxon 29 S2
Duntisbourne Abbots Gloucs 28 J6
Duntisbourne Leer Gloucs 28 J6
Duntisbourne Rouse Gloucs 28 J6
Duntish Dorset 7 S3
Duntocher W Duns 89 L11
Dunton Bucks 30 H8
Dunton C Beds 31 R4
Dunton Norfk 50 E7
Dunton Bassett Leics 37 P2
Dunton Green Kent 21 T11
Dunton Wayletts Essex 22 G9
Duntulm Highld 100 d2
Dunure S Ayrs 80 K9
Dunvant Swans 25 U12
Dunvegan Highld 100 b5
Dunwich Suffk 41 S6
Dunwood Staffs 46 B2
Durdar Cumb 67 P2
Durgan Cnwll 2 K11
Durham Dur 69 S4
Durham Cathedral Dur 69 S4
Durham Crematorium Dur 69 S4
Durham Services Dur 70 D5
Durham Tees Valley Airport S on T 70 E10
Durisdeer D & G 74 G5
Durisdeermill D & G 74 G5
Durkar Wakefd 57 M3
Durleigh Somset 16 J9
Durley Hants 9 Q5
Durley Wilts 18 K8
Durley Street Hants 9 Q5
Durlock Kent 13 Q4
Durlock Kent 13 R3
Durlow Common Herefs 35 P13
Durn Rochdl 56 D3
Durness Highld 110 J3
Durno Abers 105 L10
Duror Highld 94 D7
Durran Ag & B 87 T4
Durrington W Susx 10 J9
Durrington Wilts 18 J12
Durris Abers 99 P4
Dursley Gloucs 28 E8
Dursley Cross Gloucs 28 C3
Durston Somset 16 J11
Durweston Dorset 8 B7
Duston Nhants 37 T8
Duthil Highld 103 P11
Dutlas Powys 34 F5
Duton Hill Essex 22 F2
Dutson Cnwll 4 J3
Dutton Ches W 55 N11
Duxford Cambs 39 Q11
Duxford Oxon 29 S8
Duxford IWM Cambs 39 Q11
Dwygyfylchi Conwy 53 M7
Dwyran IoA 52 F9
Dyce C Aber 105 P13
Dyer's End Essex 40 B13
Dyfatty Carmth 25 S10
Dyffrydan Gwynd 43 N11
Dyffryn Brdgnd 26 F9
Dyffryn Myr Td 26 K7
Dyffryn V Glam 16 E2
Dyffryn Ardudwy Gwynd 43 L9
Dyffryn Castell Cerdgn 33 Q4
Dyffryn Cellwen Neath 26 F5
Dyke Lincs 48 H9
Dyke Moray 103 Q4
Dykehead Angus 98 C13
Dykehead Angus 98 F12
Dykehead N Lans 82 G7
Dykehead Stirlg 89 N6
Dykelands Abers 99 N10
Dykends Angus 98 D12
Dykeside Abers 105 L7
Dylife Powys 33 S2
Dymchurch Kent 13 M10
Dymock Gloucs 28 D1
Dyrham S Glos 28 D12
Dysart Fife 91 M13
Dyserth Denbgs 54 C11

E

Eachway Worcs 36 C5
Eachwick Nthumb 77 N11
Eagland Hill Lancs 61 S10
Eagle Lincs 58 E13
Eagle Barnsdale Lincs 58 E13
Eagle Moor Lincs 58 E13
Eaglescliffe S on T 70 F9
Eaglesfield Cumb 66 G7
Eaglesfield D & G 75 P11
Eaglesham E Rens 81 R2
Eagley Bolton 55 R4
Eairy IoM 60 d7
Eakring Notts 47 S1
Ealand N Linc 58 C4
Ealing Gt Lon 21 L6
Eals Nthumb 68 E1
Eamont Bridge Cumb 67 R7
Earby Lancs 62 J10
Earcroft Bl w D 55 Q2
Eardington Shrops 35 R2
Eardisland Herefs 34 K9
Eardisley Herefs 34 H11
Eardiston Shrops 44 J8
Eardiston Worcs 35 Q7
Earith Cambs 39 N5
Earle Nthumb 85 P13
Earlestown St Hel 55 N7
Earley Wokham 20 B8
Earlham Norfk 51 L12
Earlham Crematorium Norfk 51 M12
Earlish Highld 100 c3
Earls Barton Nhants 38 C8
Earls Colne Essex 23 L2
Earls Common Worcs 36 C9
Earl's Croome Worcs 35 U12
Earlsditton Shrops 35 P5
Earlsdon Covtry 36 K5
Earl's Down E Susx 11 U7
Earlsferry Fife 91 Q11
Earlsfield Gt Lon 21 N8
Earlsford Abers 105 N9
Earl's Green Suffk 40 H7
Earlsheaton Kirk 57 L2
Earl Shilton Leics 47 N14
Earl Soham Suffk 41 M8
Earl Sterndale Derbys 56 G13
Earlston Border 84 F11
Earlston E Ayrs 81 N5
Earl Stonham Suffk 40 K9
Earlswood Surrey 21 N13
Earlswood Warwks 36 F6
Earlswood Common Mons 27 T9
Earnley W Susx 10 C11
Earnshaw Bridge Lancs 55 M2
Earsdon N Tyne 77 S11
Earsdon Nthumb 77 P7
Earsham Norfk 41 P3
Earswick C York 64 E8
Eartham W Susx 10 E9
Earthcott S Glos 28 C10
Easby N York 70 J11
Easdale Ag & B 87 N2
Easebourne W Susx 10 E6
Easenhall Warwks 37 N5
Eashing Surrey 10 E2
Easington Bucks 30 E10
Easington Dur 70 F4
Easington E R Yk 59 Q3
Easington Nthumb 85 S12
Easington Oxon 30 E13
Easington R & Cl 71 M9
Easington Colliery Dur 70 F4
Easington Lane Sundld 70 E3
Easingwold N York 64 C6
Easole Street Kent 13 Q5
Eassie and Nevay Angus 91 M3
East Aberthaw V Glam 16 D3
East Allington Devon 5 T11
East Anstey Devon 15 U7
East Anton Hants 19 N11
East Appleton N York 69 R13
East Ashey IoW 9 R11
East Ashling W Susx 10 C9
East Aston Hants 19 P11
East Ayton N York 65 M2
East Balsdon Cnwll 14 G13
East Bank Blae G 27 N6
East Barkwith Lincs 59 L10
East Barming Kent 12 D5
East Barnby N York 71 P10
East Barnet Gt Lon 21 N3
East Barns E Loth 84 J3
East Barsham Norfk 50 F7
East Beckham Norfk 51 L6
East Bedfont Gt Lon 20 J8
East Bergholt Suffk 40 J14
East Bierley Kirk 63 P14
East Bilney Norfk 50 G10
East Blatchington E Susx 11 R10
East Bloxworth Dorset 8 B10
East Boldon S Tyne 77 T13
East Boldre Hants 9 M8
East Bolton Nthumb 77 N2
Eastbourne Darltn 70 D10
Eastbourne E Susx 11 U11
Eastbourne Crematorium E Susx 11 U10
East Bower Somset 16 K9
East Bradenham Norfk 50 F12
East Brent Somset 16 K6
Eastbridge Suffk 41 S7
East Bridgford Notts 47 S5
East Briscoe Dur 69 L9
Eastbrook V Glam 16 G2
East Buckland Devon 15 Q6
East Budleigh Devon 6 E8
Eastburn C Brad 63 L11
Eastburn E R Yk 65 M8
East Burnham Bucks 20 G6
East Burton Dorset 8 A11
Eastbury Herts 20 K4
Eastbury W Berk 19 M5
East Butsfield Dur 69 P3
East Butterwick N Linc 58 D5
Eastby N York 63 L9
East Calder W Loth 83 L5
East Carleton Norfk 51 L13
East Carlton Leeds 63 Q11
East Carlton Nhants 38 B3
East Chaldon (Chaldon Herring) Dorset 7 U8
East Challow Oxon 29 S10
East Charleton Devon 5 T12
East Chelborough Dorset 7 Q3
East Chiltington E Susx 11 P7
East Chinnock Somset 7 N2
East Chisenbury Wilts 18 H10
East Cholderton Hants 19 L11
Eastchurch Kent 23 N13
East Clandon Surrey 20 J12
East Claydon Bucks 30 F7
East Clevedon N Som 17 M2
East Coker Somset 7 P2
Eastcombe Gloucs 28 G7
Eastcombe Somset 16 G10
East Compton Somset 17 R8
East Cornworthy Devon 5 U9
East Cote Cumb 66 H1
Eastcote Gt Lon 20 K5
Eastcote Nhants 37 S10
Eastcote Solhll 36 G5
Eastcott Cnwll 14 G9
Eastcott Wilts 18 F9
East Cottingwith E R Yk 64 G11
Eastcourt Wilts 18 K8
Eastcourt Wilts 28 J9
East Cowes IoW 9 Q9
East Cowick E R Yk 57 U2
East Cowton N York 70 D12
East Cramlington Nthumb 77 R10
East Cranmore Somset 17 S8
East Creech Dorset 8 C12
East Curthwaite Cumb 67 M3
East Dean E Susx 11 T11
East Dean Gloucs 28 C3
East Dean Hants 8 K3
East Dean W Susx 10 E8
East Devon Crematorium Devon 6 E5
Eastdown Devon 5 U11
East Down Devon 15 P4
East Drayton Notts 58 C11
East Dulwich Gt Lon 21 P7
East Dundry N Som 17 Q3
East Ella C KuH 65 P14
East End Bed 38 H9
East End C Beds 31 L4
East End E R Yk 59 N1
East End E R Yk 65 R13
East End Essex 22 B5
Eastend Essex 23 M9
East End Hants 9 M9
East End Hants 19 P8
East End Herts 22 C2
East End Kent 12 F8
East End Kent 23 N13
East End M Keyn 30 K4
East End N Som 17 N2
East End Oxon 29 S4
East End Somset 17 S7
East End Suffk 40 K13
Easter Balmoral Abers 98 D5
Easter Compton S Glos 27 V11
Easter Dalziel Highld 103 L5
Eastergate W Susx 10 E9
Easterhouse C Glas 82 C5
Easter Howgate Mdloth 83 P6
Easter Kinkell Highld 102 G4
Easter Moniack Highld 102 G7
Eastern Green Covtry 36 J5
Easter Ord Abers 99 Q3
Easter Pitkierie Fife 91 S10
Easter Skeld Shet 106 t9
Easter Softlaw Border 84 K12
Easterton Wilts 18 F10
Eastertown Somset 16 K6
East Everleigh Wilts 18 K10
East Farleigh Kent 12 D5
East Farndon Nhants 37 T4
East Ferry Lincs 58 D7
Eastfield N Lans 82 G6
Eastfield N York 65 N3
East Firsby Lincs 58 H9
East Fortune E Loth 84 E3
East Garforth Leeds 63 U13
East Garston W Berk 19 N5
Eastgate Dur 69 L5
Eastgate Lincs 48 H10
Eastgate Norfk 50 K9
East Ginge Oxon 29 T10
East Goscote Leics 47 R11
East Grafton Wilts 19 L8
East Green Suffk 41 R7
East Grimstead Wilts 8 J3
East Grinstead W Susx 11 P3
East Guldeford E Susx 12 H11
East Haddon Nhants 37 S7
East Hagbourne Oxon 19 R3
East Halton N Linc 58 K3
East Ham Gt Lon 21 R6
Eastham Wirral 54 J10
Eastham Ferry Wirral 54 J10
Easthampstead Park Crematorium Br For 20 D9
Easthampton Herefs 34 K8
East Hanney Oxon 29 T9
East Hanningfield Essex 22 J7
East Hardwick Wakefd 57 Q3
East Harling Norfk 40 G3
East Harlsey N York 70 F13
East Harnham Wilts 8 G3
East Harptree BaNES 17 Q5
East Hartford Nthumb 77 R10
East Harting W Susx 10 B7
East Hatch Wilts 8 C3
East Hatley Cambs 39 L10
East Hauxwell N York 69 Q14
East Haven Angus 91 S4
Eastheath Wokham 20 C9
East Heckington Lincs 48 J5
East Hedleyhope Dur 69 Q4
East Helmsdale Highld 112 B13
East Hendred Oxon 29 U10
East Heslerton N York 65 L4
East Hewish N Som 17 M4
East Hoathly E Susx 11 S7
East Holme Dorset 8 B11
Easthope Shrops 35 N1
Easthorpe Essex 23 M3
Easthorpe Notts 47 T3
East Horrington Somset 17 Q7
East Horsley Surrey 20 J12
East Horton Nthumb 85 Q12
East Howe Bmouth 8 F9
East Huntington C York 64 E8
East Huntspill Somset 16 K7
East Hyde C Beds 31 P9
East Ilkerton Devon 15 R3
East Ilsley W Berk 19 Q4
Eastington Devon 15 R11
Eastington Gloucs 28 E6
Eastington Gloucs 29 M5
East Keal Lincs 59 Q14
East Kennett Wilts 18 H7
East Keswick Leeds 63 T11
East Kilbride S Lans 81 S2
East Kimber Devon 15 L13
East Kirkby Lincs 49 M1
East Knighton Dorset 7 V7
East Knowstone Devon 15 T8
East Knoyle Wilts 8 B2
East Lambrook Somset 17 M13
East Lancashire Crematorium Bury 55 S5
Eastlands D & G 74 F11
East Langdon Kent 13 R6
East Langton Leics 37 T2
East Lavant W Susx 10 D9
East Lavington W Susx 10 E7
East Layton N York 69 Q11
Eastleach Martin Gloucs 29 P7
Eastleach Turville Gloucs 29 N6
East Leake Notts 47 Q8
East Learmouth Nthumb 85 M11
East Leigh Devon 5 R10
East Leigh Devon 5 T9
Eastleigh Devon 15 L7
East Leigh Devon 15 Q11
Eastleigh Hants 9 P5
East Lexham Norfk 50 E10
Eastling Kent 12 J4
East Linton E Loth 84 F3
East Liss Hants 10 B5
East Lockinge Oxon 29 T10
East London Crematorium Gt Lon 21 Q6
East Lound N Linc 58 C7

130 East Lulworth – Friar Waddon

East Lulworth Dorset 8 B12
East Lutton N York 65 L6
East Lydeard Somset 16 G11
East Lydford Somset 17 Q10
East Malling Kent 12 D4
East Malling Heath Kent 12 C4
East Marden W Susx 10 C8
East Markham Notts 58 B12
East Martin Hants 8 F5
East Marton N York 62 J9
East Meon Hants 9 T4
East Mere Devon 16 C13
East Mersea Essex 23 P5
East Midlands Airport Leics 47 N8
East Molesey Surrey 20 K9
Eastmoor Norfk 50 B13
East Morden Dorset 8 C10
East Morton C Brad 63 M11
East Morton D & G 74 G5
East Ness N York 64 F4
East Newton E R Yk 65 T12
Eastney C Port 9 T9
Eastnor Herefs 35 R13
East Norton Leics 47 U13
Eastoft N Linc 58 D3
East Ogwell Devon 5 U6
Easton Cambs 38 H6
Easton Cumb 75 Q14
Easton Devon 5 S3
Easton Dorset 7 S10
Easton Hants 9 Q2
Easton Lincs 48 D8
Easton Norfk 50 K11
Easton Somset 17 P7
Easton Suffk 41 N9
Easton W Berk 19 P6
Easton Wilts 18 C6
Easton Grey Wilts 28 G10
Easton-in-Gordano N Som 27 U12
Easton Maudit Nhants 38 C9
Easton-on-the-Hill Nhants 48 F13
Easton Royal Wilts 18 K8
East Orchard Dorset 8 A5
East Ord Nthumb 85 P8
East Panson Devon 4 K2
East Parley Dorset 8 F9
East Peckham Kent 12 C6
East Pennar Pembks 24 G10
East Pennard Somset 17 Q9
East Perry Cambs 38 J7
East Portlemouth Devon 5 T13
East Prawle Devon 5 T13
East Preston W Susx 10 H10
East Pulham Dorset 7 T3
East Putford Devon 14 J9
East Quantoxhead Somset 16 F8
East Rainham Medway 12 F2
East Rainton Sundld 70 D3
East Ravendale NE Lin 59 M7
East Raynham Norfk 50 E8
Eastrea Cambs 39 L1
East Riding Crematorium E R Yk 65 N6
Eastriggs D & G 75 P12
East Rigton Leeds 63 T11
Eastrington E R Yk 64 H14
East Rolstone N Som 17 L4
Eastrop Swindn 29 P9
East Rounton N York 70 F12
East Rudham Norfk 50 D8
East Runton Norfk 51 L5
East Ruston Norfk 51 P8
Eastry Kent 13 R5
East Saltoun E Loth 84 D5
Eastshaw W Susx 10 D6
East Sheen Gt Lon 21 M8
East Shefford W Berk 19 N6
East Sleekburn Nthumb 77 R9
East Somerton Norfk 51 S10
East Stockwith Lincs 58 C8
East Stoke Dorset 8 B11
East Stoke Notts 47 U4
East Stour Dorset 17 V12
East Stourmouth Kent 13 Q3
East Stowford Devon 15 P7
East Stratton Hants 19 R12
East Studdal Kent 13 R6
East Sutton Kent 12 F6
East Taphouse Cnwll 4 F8
East-the-Water Devon 15 L7
East Thirston Nthumb 77 P5
East Tilbury Thurr 22 G12
East Tisted Hants 9 U2
East Torrington Lincs 58 K10
East Tuddenham Norfk 50 J11
East Tytherley Hants 8 K3
East Tytherton Wilts 18 E6
East Village Devon 15 T11
Eastville Bristl 28 B13
Eastville Lincs 49 P2
East Wall Shrops 35 M2
East Walton Norfk 50 B10
East Water Somset 17 P6
East Week Devon 5 R2
Eastwell Leics 47 U8
East Wellow Hants 9 L4
East Wemyss Fife 91 M12
East Whitburn W Loth 82 J5
Eastwick Herts 22 B5
East Wickham Gt Lon 21 S7
East Williamston Pembks 24 J10
East Winch Norfk 49 U10
East Winterslow Wilts 8 J2
East Wittering W Susx 10 B11
East Witton N York 63 N2
Eastwood Notts 47 N4
Eastwood Sthend 22 K10
East Woodburn Nthumb 76 J8
Eastwood End Cambs 39 P2
East Woodhay Hants 19 P8
East Woodlands Somset 17 U8
East Worldham Hants 10 B3
East Wretham Norfk 40 F2
East Youlstone Devon 14 G9
Eathorpe Warwks 37 L7
Eaton Ches E 56 C13
Eaton Ches W 55 N14
Eaton Leics 47 U8
Eaton Norfk 51 M12
Eaton Notts 58 B11
Eaton Oxon 29 T7
Eaton Shrops 34 J3
Eaton Shrops 35 M3
Eaton Bishop Herefs 34 K13
Eaton Bray C Beds 31 L8
Eaton Constantine Shrops 45 N12
Eaton Ford Cambs 38 J9
Eaton Green C Beds 31 L8
Eaton Hastings Oxon 29 Q8
Eaton Mascott Shrops 45 M12
Eaton Socon Cambs 38 J9
Eaton upon Tern Shrops 45 Q9
Eaves Brow Warrtn 55 P8
Eaves Green Solhll 36 J4
Ebberston N York 64 K3
Ebbesborne Wake Wilts 8 D4
Ebbw Vale Blae G 27 M6
Ebchester Dur 69 P1
Ebdon N Som 17 L4
Ebford Devon 6 C7
Ebley Gloucs 28 F6
Ebnal Ches W 45 L4
Ebnall Herefs 35 L9
Ebrington Gloucs 36 G12
Ebsworthy Devon 5 N2
Ecchinswell Hants 19 Q9
Ecclaw Border 84 K5
Ecclefechan D & G 75 N11
Eccles Border 84 K10
Eccles Kent 12 D3
Eccles Salfd 55 S7
Ecclesall Sheff 57 M10
Ecclesfield Sheff 57 N8
Eccles Green Herefs 34 J11
Eccleshall Staffs 45 T8
Eccleshill C Brad 63 P12
Ecclesmachan W Loth 83 L4
Eccles on Sea Norfk 51 R8
Eccles Road Norfk 40 H3
Eccleston Ches W 44 K1
Eccleston Lancs 55 M3
Eccleston St Hel 55 L7
Eccleston Green Lancs 55 M3
Echt Abers 99 N2
Eckford Border 84 J13
Eckington Derbys 57 P11
Eckington Worcs 36 B12
Ecton Nhants 38 B8
Ecton Staffs 46 E2
Edale Derbys 56 H9
Eday Ork 106 u16
Eday Airport Ork 106 u16
Edburton W Susx 11 L8
Edderside Cumb 66 H3
Edderton Highld 109 N8
Eddington Kent 13 N2
Eddleston Border 83 P9
Eddlewood S Lans 82 D8
Edenbridge Kent 21 R13
Edenfield Lancs 55 T3
Edenhall Cumb 67 S6
Edenham Lincs 48 G9
Eden Mount Cumb 61 S4
Eden Park Gt Lon 21 Q9
Eden Project Cnwll 3 Q6
Edensor Derbys 56 K13
Edentaggart Ag & B 88 H7
Edenthorpe Donc 57 T5
Edern Gwynd 42 E6
Edgarley Somset 17 P9
Edgbaston Birm 36 E4
Edgcombe Cnwll 2 J10
Edgcott Bucks 30 E8
Edgcott Somset 15 T5
Edge Gloucs 28 F6
Edge Shrops 44 J12
Edgebolton Shrops 45 N9
Edge End Gloucs 28 A5
Edgefield Norfk 50 J7
Edgefield Green Norfk 50 J7
Edgefold Bolton 55 R5
Edge Green Ches W 45 L3
Edgehill Warwks 37 L11
Edgerley Shrops 44 J10
Edgerton Kirk 56 H3
Edgeside Lancs 55 T2
Edgeworth Gloucs 28 H6
Edgeworthy Devon 15 T10
Edginswell Torbay 6 A11
Edgiock Worcs 36 D8
Edgmond Wrekin 45 R10
Edgmond Marsh Wrekin 45 R9
Edgton Shrops 34 J3
Edgware Gt Lon 21 L4
Edgworth Bl w D 55 R3
Edinbane Highld 100 c4
Edinburgh C Edin 83 Q4
Edinburgh Airport C Edin 83 M4
Edinburgh Castle C Edin 83 Q4
Edinburgh Old & New Town C Edin 83 Q4
Edinburgh Royal Botanic Gardens C Edin 83 P3
Edinburgh Zoo RZSS C Edin 83 P4
Edingale Staffs 46 H11
Edingham D & G 74 F13
Edingley Notts 47 S2
Edingthorpe Norfk 51 P7
Edingthorpe Green Norfk 51 P7
Edington Border 85 M7
Edington Nthumb 77 P9
Edington Somset 17 L9
Edington Wilts 18 D10
Edington Burtle Somset 17 L8
Edingworth Somset 17 L6
Edistone Devon 14 G8
Edithmead Somset 16 K7
Edith Weston Rutlnd 48 D12
Edlesborough Bucks 31 L9
Edlingham Nthumb 77 N4
Edlington Lincs 59 M12
Edmond Castle Cumb 75 U14
Edmondsham Dorset 8 F6
Edmondsley Dur 69 R3
Edmondthorpe Leics 48 C10
Edmonton Cnwll 3 P2
Edmonton Gt Lon 21 P4
Edmundbyers Dur 69 M2
Ednam Border 84 J11
Ednaston Derbys 46 H5
Edney Common Essex 22 G7
Edradynate P & K 97 P13
Edrom Border 85 L7
Edstaston Shrops 45 M7
Edstone Warwks 36 G8
Edvin Loach Herefs 35 Q9
Edwalton Notts 47 Q6
Edwardstone Suffk 40 F12
Edwardsville Myr Td 26 K8
Edwinsford Carmth 33 M14
Edwinstowe Notts 57 T13
Edworth C Beds 31 R4
Edwyn Ralph Herefs 35 P9
Edzell Angus 99 L10
Edzell Woods Abers 99 L10
Efail-fach Neath 26 D8
Efail Isaf Rhondd 26 K11
Efailnewydd Gwynd 42 G6
Efail-Rhyd Powys 44 E8
Efailwen Carmth 24 K5
Efenechtyd Denbgs 44 D2
Effgill D & G 75 R7
Effingham Surrey 20 K12
Efflinch Staffs 46 G10
Efford Devon 15 U12
Efford Crematorium C Plym 5 N9
Egbury Hants 19 P10
Egdean W Susx 10 F6
Egerton Bolton 55 R4
Egerton Kent 12 H6
Egerton Forstal Kent 12 G6
Eggborough N York 57 S2
Eggbuckland C Plym 5 N9
Eggesford Devon 15 Q10
Eggington C Beds 31 L7
Egginton Derbys 46 J8
Egglescliffe S on T 70 F10
Eggleston Dur 69 L8
Egham Surrey 20 H8
Egham Wick Surrey 20 G8
Egleton Rutlnd 48 C12
Eglingham Nthumb 77 N2
Egloshayle Cnwll 3 Q2
Egloskerry Cnwll 4 H3
Eglwysbach Conwy 53 P8
Eglwys-Brewis V Glam 16 D3
Eglwys Cross Wrexhm 45 L5
Eglwys Fach Cerdgn 33 N1
Eglwyswrw Pembks 24 K3
Egmanton Notts 58 B13
Egremont Cumb 66 F10
Egremont Wirral 54 H8
Egton N York 71 P11
Egton Bridge N York 71 P12
Egypt Bucks 20 G5
Egypt Hants 19 Q12
Eigg Highld 93 M1
Eight Ash Green Essex 23 M2
Eilanreach Highld 100 h8
Eilean Donan Castle Highld 101 M6
Eisteddfa Gurig Cerdgn 33 Q4
Elan Valley Powys 33 S8
Elan Village Powys 33 T8
Elberton S Glos 28 B10
Elbridge W Susx 10 E10
Elburton C Plym 5 N10
Elcombe Swindn 18 H4
Elcot W Berk 19 N7
Eldernell Cambs 49 M14
Eldersfield Worcs 28 E1
Elderslie Rens 88 K13
Elder Street Essex 39 S14
Eldon Dur 69 R7
Eldwick C Brad 63 N11
Elerch Cerdgn 33 N3
Elfhill Abers 99 Q6
Elford Nthumb 85 T12
Elford Staffs 46 G11
Elgin Moray 103 V3
Elgol Highld 100 e8
Elham Kent 13 N7
Elie Fife 91 Q11
Elilaw Nthumb 76 K4
Elim IoA 52 E6
Eling Hants 9 M6
Elkesley Notts 57 U11
Elkstone Gloucs 28 J5
Ella Abers 104 J4
Ellacombe Torbay 6 B12
Elland Calder 56 H2
Elland Lower Edge Calder 56 H2
Ellary Ag & B 87 N10
Ellastone Staffs 46 F5
Ellel Lancs 61 T8
Ellemford Border 84 J6
Ellenabeich Ag & B 87 N2
Ellenborough Cumb 66 F5
Ellenbrook Salfd 55 R6
Ellenhall Staffs 45 T8
Ellen's Green Surrey 10 H3
Ellerbeck N York 70 F13
Ellerby N York 71 N10
Ellerdine Heath Wrekin 45 P9
Ellerhayes Devon 6 C4
Elleric Ag & B 94 E9
Ellerker E R Yk 65 L14
Ellers N York 63 L11
Ellerton E R Yk 64 G12
Ellerton N York 69 S13
Ellerton Shrops 45 R8
Ellesborough Bucks 30 H11
Ellesmere Shrops 44 J7
Ellesmere Port Ches W 54 K11
Ellingham Hants 8 G7
Ellingham Norfk 41 Q2
Ellingham Nthumb 85 T13
Ellingstring N York 63 P3
Ellington Cambs 38 J6
Ellington Nthumb 77 R7
Ellington Thorpe Cambs 38 J6
Elliots Green Somset 17 U7
Ellisfield Hants 19 T11
Ellishader Highld 100 e3
Ellistown Leics 47 M11
Ellon Abers 105 R9
Ellonby Cumb 67 P5
Ellough Suffk 41 R3
Elloughton E R Yk 65 L14
Ellwood Gloucs 28 A6
Elm Cambs 49 Q12
Elmbridge Worcs 36 B7
Elmdon Essex 39 Q13
Elmdon Solhll 36 G4
Elmdon Heath Solhll 36 G4
Elmer W Susx 10 F10
Elmers End Gt Lon 21 Q9
Elmer's Green Lancs 55 M5
Elmesthorpe Leics 37 N1
Elm Green Essex 22 J6
Elmhurst Staffs 46 F11
Elmley Castle Worcs 36 C12
Elmley Lovett Worcs 35 U7
Elmore Gloucs 28 E4
Elmore Back Gloucs 28 E4
Elm Park Gt Lon 22 D10
Elmscott Devon 14 F8
Elmsett Suffk 40 J11
Elms Green Worcs 35 R7
Elmstead Heath Essex 23 Q3
Elmstead Market Essex 23 Q3
Elmstead Row Essex 23 Q3
Elmsted Kent 13 M7
Elmstone Kent 13 Q3
Elmstone Hardwicke Gloucs 28 H2
Elmswell E R Yk 65 M8
Elmswell Suffk 40 G8
Elmton Derbys 57 R12
Elphin Highld 108 C2
Elphinstone E Loth 83 S4
Elrick Abers 99 Q2
Elrig D & G 72 J10
Elrington Nthumb 76 H13
Elsdon Nthumb 76 J7
Elsecar Barns 57 N7
Elsenham Essex 22 D2
Elsfield Oxon 30 B10
Elsham N Linc 58 H4
Elsing Norfk 50 J10
Elslack N York 62 J10
Elson Hants 9 S8
Elson Shrops 44 J6
Elsrickle S Lans 83 L10
Elstead Surrey 10 E2
Elsted W Susx 10 C7
Elsthorpe Lincs 48 G9
Elstob Dur 70 D8
Elston Lancs 62 B13
Elston Notts 47 U4
Elston Wilts 18 G12
Elstone Devon 15 Q9
Elstow Bed 38 G11
Elstree Herts 21 L3
Elstronwick E R Yk 65 S13
Elswick Lancs 61 S12
Elswick N u Ty 77 Q13
Elsworth Cambs 39 M8
Elterwater Cumb 67 M12
Eltham Gt Lon 21 R8
Eltham Crematorium Gt Lon 21 R8
Eltisley Cambs 39 L9
Elton Bury 55 S4
Elton Cambs 38 G2
Elton Ches W 55 L11
Elton Derbys 46 H1
Elton Gloucs 28 D5
Elton Herefs 35 L6
Elton Notts 47 U6
Elton S on T 70 F9
Elton Green Ches W 55 L12
Eltringham Nthumb 77 M13
Elvanfoot S Lans 74 J2
Elvaston Derbys 47 M7
Elveden Suffk 40 D4
Elvetham Heath Hants 20 D11
Elvingston E Loth 84 D4
Elvington C York 64 G10
Elvington Kent 13 Q5
Elwell Devon 15 Q6
Elwick Hartpl 70 G6
Elwick Nthumb 85 S11
Elworth Ches E 45 R1
Elworthy Somset 16 E10
Ely Cambs 39 R4
Ely Cardif 27 L12
Emberton M Keyn 38 C11
Embleton Cumb 66 J6
Embleton Dur 70 F7
Embleton Nthumb 85 U14
Embo Highld 109 Q6
Emborough Somset 17 R6
Embo Street Highld 109 Q6
Embsay N York 63 L9
Emery Down Hants 8 K7
Emley Kirk 56 K4
Emley Moor Kirk 56 K4
Emmbrook Wokham 20 D9
Emmer Green Readg 20 B7
Emmett Carr Derbys 57 Q11
Emmington Oxon 30 F12
Emneth Norfk 49 Q12
Emneth Hungate Norfk 49 R12
Empingham Rutlnd 48 D12
Empshott Hants 10 B4
Empshott Green Hants 9 U2
Emstrey Crematorium Shrops 45 M11
Emsworth Hants 9 U7
Enborne W Berk 19 P7
Enborne Row W Berk 19 P8
Enchmarsh Shrops 35 M1
Enderby Leics 47 P14
Endmoor Cumb 61 U3
Endon Staffs 46 B3
Endon Bank Staffs 46 B3
Enfield Gt Lon 21 Q3
Enfield Crematorium Gt Lon 21 P3
Enfield Lock Gt Lon 21 Q3
Enfield Wash Gt Lon 21 Q3
Enford Wilts 18 H10
Engine Common S Glos 28 C11
England's Gate Herefs 35 M10
Englefield W Berk 19 T6
Englefield Green Surrey 20 G8
Engleseabrook Ches E 45 S3
English Bicknor Gloucs 28 A4
Englishcombe BaNES 17 T4
English Frankton Shrops 45 L8
Engollan Cnwll 3 M2
Enham-Alamein Hants 19 N11
Enmore Somset 16 H9
Enmore Green Dorset 8 B4
Ennerdale Bridge Cumb 66 G9
Enniscaven Cnwll 3 P5
Enochdhu P & K 97 T11
Ensay Ag & B 92 K9
Ensbury Bmouth 8 F9
Ensdon Shrops 44 K10
Ensis Devon 15 N7
Enson Staffs 46 B8
Enstone Oxon 29 S3
Enterkinfoot D & G 74 G5
Enterpen N York 70 G11
Enville Staffs 35 T3
Eolaigearraidh W Isls 106 c18
Epney Gloucs 28 E5
Epperstone Notts 47 S4
Epping Essex 22 C7
Epping Green Essex 22 B6
Epping Green Herts 31 S11
Epping Upland Essex 22 B7
Eppleby N York 69 Q10
Eppleworth E R Yk 65 N13
Epsom Surrey 21 M10
Epwell Oxon 37 L12
Epworth N Linc 58 C6
Epworth Turbary N Linc 58 C6
Erbistock Wrexhm 44 J5
Erdington Birm 36 F2
Eridge Green E Susx 11 T3
Eridge Station E Susx 11 S4
Erines Ag & B 87 R10
Eriska Ag & B 94 C10
Eriskay W Isls 106 c18
Eriswell Suffk 40 B5
Erith Gt Lon 22 D12
Erlestoke Wilts 18 E10
Ermington Devon 5 Q10
Erpingham Norfk 51 L7
Erriottwood Kent 12 H4
Errogie Highld 102 G11
Errol P & K 90 K7
Erskine Rens 89 L11
Erskine Bridge Rens 89 L11
Ervie D & G 72 C6
Erwarton Suffk 41 M14
Erwood Powys 34 C12
Eryholme N York 70 D11
Eryrys Denbgs 44 F2
Escalls Cnwll 2 B11
Escomb Dur 69 Q6
Escott Somset 16 E9
Escrick N York 64 E11
Esgair Carmth 25 Q5
Esgair Cerdgn 33 L7
Esgairgeiliog Powys 43 Q12
Esgerdawe Carmth 33 M12
Esgyryn Conwy 53 P7
Esh Dur 69 Q4
Esher Surrey 20 K10
Esholt C Brad 63 P11
Eshott Nthumb 77 Q6
Eshton N York 62 J8
Esh Winning Dur 69 Q4
Eskadale Highld 102 E7
Eskbank Mdloth 83 R5
Eskdale Green Cumb 66 H12
Eskdalemuir D & G 75 Q6
Eske E R Yk 65 P11
Eskham Lincs 59 Q7
Eskholme Donc 57 T3
Esperley Lane Ends Dur 69 P8
Esprick Lancs 61 S12
Essendine Rutlnd 48 F11
Essendon Herts 31 S11
Essich Highld 102 H8
Essington Staffs 46 C13
Esslemont Abers 105 Q10
Eston R & Cl 70 H9
Etal Nthumb 85 N11
Etchilhampton Wilts 18 F8
Etchingham E Susx 12 D10
Etchinghill Kent 13 N8
Etchinghill Staffs 46 D10
Etchingwood E Susx 11 S6
Etling Green Norfk 50 H11
Etloe Gloucs 28 C6
Eton W & M 20 G7
Eton Wick W & M 20 F7
Etruria C Stke 45 U4
Etteridge Highld 96 K5
Ettersgill Dur 68 J7
Ettiley Heath Ches E 45 R1
Ettingshall Wolves 36 B1
Ettington Warwks 36 J11
Etton C Pete 48 H12
Etton E R Yk 65 M11
Ettrick Border 75 Q3
Ettrickbridge Border 83 S14
Ettrickhill Border 75 Q3
Etwall Derbys 46 J7
Eudon George Shrops 35 Q3
Euston Suffk 40 E5
Euximoor Drove Cambs 49 Q14
Euxton Lancs 55 N3
Evancoyd Powys 34 G8
Evanton Highld 102 H2
Evedon Lincs 48 G4
Evelith Shrops 45 R12
Evelix Highld 109 P6
Evenjobb Powys 34 G8
Evenley Nhants 30 C6
Evenlode Gloucs 29 P2
Evenwood Dur 69 Q8
Evenwood Gate Dur 69 Q8
Evercreech Somset 17 R9
Everingham E R Yk 64 J11
Everleigh Wilts 18 K10
Everley N York 65 M2
Eversholt C Beds 31 L6
Evershot Dorset 7 Q4
Eversley Hants 20 C10
Eversley Cross Hants 20 C10
Everthorpe E R Yk 65 L13
Everton C Beds 38 K10
Everton Hants 8 K10
Everton Lpool 54 H8
Everton Notts 57 U8
Evertown D & G 75 S10
Evesbatch Herefs 35 Q11
Evesham Worcs 36 D12
Evington C Leic 47 R13
Ewden Village Sheff 57 L7
Ewell Surrey 21 M10
Ewell Minnis Kent 13 Q7
Ewelme Oxon 19 T2
Ewen Gloucs 28 K8
Ewenny V Glam 26 G12
Ewerby Lincs 48 H4
Ewerby Thorpe Lincs 48 H4
Ewhurst Surrey 10 H2
Ewhurst Green E Susx 12 E11
Ewhurst Green Surrey 10 H3
Ewloe Flints 54 H13
Ewloe Green Flints 54 G13
Ewood Bl w D 55 Q1
Ewood Bridge Lancs 55 S2
Eworthy Devon 14 K13
Ewshot Hants 20 D13
Ewyas Harold Herefs 27 R2
Exbourne Devon 15 P12
Exbury Hants 9 N8
Exceat E Susx 11 S11
Exebridge Somset 16 B12
Exelby N York 63 R2
Exeter Devon 6 B6
Exeter Airport Devon 6 C6
Exeter & Devon Crematorium Devon 6 B6
Exeter Services Devon 6 C6
Exford Somset 15 U5
Exfordsgreen Shrops 45 L12
Exhall Warwks 36 F9
Exhall Warwks 37 L3
Exlade Street Oxon 19 U4
Exley Head C Brad 63 L11
Exminster Devon 6 B7
Exmoor National Park 15 U5
Exmouth Devon 6 D8
Exning Suffk 39 T7
Exted Kent 13 N7
Exton Devon 6 C7
Exton Hants 9 S4
Exton Rutlnd 48 D11
Exton Somset 16 B10
Exwick Devon 6 B6
Eyam Derbys 56 K11
Eydon Nhants 37 P11
Eye C Pete 48 K13
Eye Herefs 35 L8
Eye Suffk 40 K6
Eye Green C Pete 48 K13
Eye Kettleby Leics 47 T10
Eyemouth Border 85 N6
Eyeworth C Beds 39 L11
Eyhorne Street Kent 12 F5
Eyke Suffk 41 P10
Eynesbury Cambs 38 J9
Eynsford Kent 21 T9
Eynsham Oxon 29 T6
Eype Dorset 7 M6
Eyre Highld 100 d4
Eythorne Kent 13 Q6
Eyton Herefs 35 L8
Eyton Shrops 34 J3
Eyton Shrops 44 J11
Eyton Shrops 44 K9
Eyton Wrexhm 44 J5
Eyton on Severn Shrops 45 N12
Eyton upon the Weald Moors Wrekin 45 Q11

F

Faccombe Hants 19 N9
Faceby N York 70 G12
Fachwen Powys 44 B10
Facit Lancs 56 C3
Fackley Notts 47 N1
Faddiley Ches E 45 N3
Fadmoor N York 64 F2
Faerdre Swans 26 B7
Fagwyr Swans 26 B7
Faifley W Duns 89 L11
Failand N Som 17 P2
Failford S Ayrs 81 P7
Failsworth Oldham 56 C6
Fairbourne Gwynd 43 M11
Fairburn N York 64 B14
Fairfield Derbys 56 G12
Fairfield Kent 12 J10
Fairfield Worcs 36 B5
Fairfield Park Herts 31 R6
Fairford Gloucs 29 N7
Fairford Park Gloucs 29 N7
Fairgirth D & G 66 C1
Fair Green Norfk 49 U10
Fairhaven Lancs 61 Q14
Fair Isle Shet 106 r11
Fair Isle Airport Shet 106 r11
Fairlands Surrey 20 G12
Fairlie N Ayrs 80 J2
Fairlight E Susx 12 G13
Fairmile Devon 6 E5
Fairmile Surrey 20 K10
Fairnilee Border 84 D12
Fair Oak Hants 9 P5
Fairoak Staffs 45 S7
Fair Oak Green Hants 19 U8
Fairseat Kent 12 B3
Fairstead Essex 22 J4
Fairstead Norfk 49 T9
Fairstead Norfk 51 N9
Fairwarp E Susx 11 R5
Fairwater Cardif 27 L12
Fairy Cross Devon 14 K8
Fakenham Norfk 50 F8
Fakenham Magna Suffk 40 F5
Fala Mdloth 84 C6
Fala Dam Mdloth 84 C6
Falcut Nhants 30 C4
Faldingworth Lincs 58 J10
Faldouët Jersey 7 f2
Falfield S Glos 28 C9
Falkenham Suffk 41 N13
Falkirk Falk 82 G2
Falkirk Crematorium Falk 82 G2
Falkirk Wheel Falk 82 G2
Falkland Fife 91 L10
Fallburn S Lans 82 J11
Fallgate Derbys 47 L1
Fallin Stirlg 89 T7
Fallodon Nthumb 85 T14
Fallowfield Manch 56 C8
Fallowfield Nthumb 76 J12
Falls of Blarghour Ag & B 87 T3
Falmer E Susx 11 P9
Falmouth Cnwll 3 L10
Falnash Border 75 S4
Falsgrave N York 65 N2
Falstone Nthumb 76 E8
Fanagmore Highld 110 D7
Fancott C Beds 31 M7
Fanellan Highld 102 E7
Fangdale Beck N York 70 J14
Fangfoss E R Yk 64 H9
Fanmore Ag & B 93 L10
Fannich Lodge Highld 108 C11
Fans Border 84 G10
Far Bletchley M Keyn 30 J6
Farcet Cambs 38 K2
Far Cotton Nhants 37 U9
Farden Shrops 35 N5
Fareham Hants 9 R7
Far End Cumb 67 M13
Farewell Staffs 46 E11
Far Forest Worcs 35 R5
Farforth Lincs 59 P11
Far Green Gloucs 28 E7
Faringdon Oxon 29 Q8
Farington Lancs 55 M1
Farlam Cumb 76 B14
Farleigh N Som 17 P3
Farleigh Surrey 21 Q10
Farleigh Hungerford Somset 18 B9
Farleigh Wallop Hants 19 T11
Farlesthorpe Lincs 59 S12
Farleton Cumb 61 U3
Farleton Lancs 62 B6
Farley Derbys 46 J1
Farley Staffs 46 E5
Farley Wilts 8 J3
Farley Green Suffk 40 B10
Farley Green Surrey 20 J13
Farley Hill Wokham 20 B10
Farleys End Gloucs 28 E5
Farlington C Port 9 T7
Farlington N York 64 E6
Farlow Shrops 35 P4
Farmborough BaNES 17 S4
Farmbridge End Essex 22 F5
Farmcote Gloucs 29 L2
Farmcote Shrops 35 S2
Farmers Carmth 33 M12
Farmington Gloucs 29 M4
Farmoor Oxon 29 U6
Far Moor Wigan 55 M6
Farms Common Cnwll 2 H10
Farm Town Leics 47 L10
Farmtown Moray 104 G5
Farnah Green Derbys 46 K4
Farnborough Gt Lon 21 R10
Farnborough Hants 20 E12
Farnborough W Berk 19 P4
Farnborough Warwks 37 M11
Farnborough Park Hants 20 E11
Farncombe Surrey 10 F2
Farndish Bed 38 D8
Farndon Ches W 44 K3
Farndon Notts 47 U3
Farne Islands Nthumb 85 U11
Farnell Angus 99 L12
Farnham Dorset 8 D5
Farnham Essex 22 C3
Farnham N York 63 S7
Farnham Suffk 41 Q8
Farnham Surrey 20 D13
Farnham Common Bucks 20 G5
Farnham Green Essex 22 C2
Farnham Royal Bucks 20 G6
Farningham Kent 21 T9
Farnley Leeds 63 R13
Farnley N York 63 Q10
Farnley Tyas Kirk 56 J4
Farnsfield Notts 47 R2
Farnworth Bolton 55 R5
Farnworth Halton 55 M9
Far Oakridge Gloucs 28 H7
Farr Highld 97 N3
Farr Highld 102 J9
Farr Highld 111 Q4
Farraline Highld 102 G11
Farringdon Devon 6 D6
Farrington Gurney BaNES 17 R5
Far Sawrey Cumb 67 N13
Farsley Leeds 63 Q12
Farther Howegreen Essex 22 K7
Farthing Green Kent 12 F6
Farthinghoe Nhants 30 B5
Farthingloe Kent 13 Q7
Farthingstone Nhants 37 R10
Farthing Street Gt Lon 21 R10
Fartown Kirk 56 J3
Farway Devon 6 G5
Fasnacloich Ag & B 94 E9
Fasnakyle Highld 102 B10
Fassfern Highld 94 E3
Fatfield Sundld 69 S2
Faugh Cumb 67 R2
Fauld Staffs 46 G8
Fauldhouse W Loth 82 H6
Faulkbourne Essex 22 J4
Faulkland Somset 17 T6
Fauls Shrops 45 N7
Faversham Kent 12 K3
Fawdington N York 63 U5
Fawdon N u Ty 77 Q12
Fawdon Nthumb 77 L2
Fawfieldhead Staffs 56 G14
Fawkham Green Kent 21 U9
Fawler Oxon 29 S4
Fawley Bucks 20 C5
Fawley Hants 9 P8
Fawley W Berk 19 N4
Fawley Chapel Herefs 28 A2
Fawnog Flints 54 F13
Fawsley Nhants 37 Q9
Faxfleet E R Yk 58 E2
Faygate W Susx 11 L4
Fazakerley Lpool 54 J7
Fazeley Staffs 46 H13
Fearby N York 63 P3
Fearn Highld 109 Q9
Fearnan P & K 95 U10
Fearnbeg Highld 107 M13
Fearnhead Warrtn 55 P8
Fearnmore Highld 107 M12
Fearnoch Ag & B 87 S10
Featherstone Staffs 46 B12
Featherstone Wakefd 57 P3
Feckenham Worcs 36 D8
Feering Essex 23 L3
Feetham N York 69 L13
Feizor N York 62 F6
Felbridge Surrey 11 P3
Felbrigg Norfk 51 M6
Felcourt Surrey 11 P2
Felden Herts 31 M12
Felindre Carmth 25 Q3
Felindre Carmth 25 U6
Felindre Carmth 26 C2
Felindre Cerdgn 33 L9
Felindre Powys 27 M3
Felindre Powys 34 E4
Felindre Swans 26 A7
Felindre Farchog Pembks 24 K3
Felin Fach Cerdgn 32 K9
Felinfach Powys 34 C14
Felinfoel Carmth 25 T10
Felingwm Isaf Carmth 25 T6
Felingwm Uchaf Carmth 25 T6
Felin-newydd Powys 34 D13
Felixkirk N York 64 B3
Felixstowe Suffk 41 P14
Felixstowe Ferry Suffk 41 P13
Felkington Nthumb 85 N10
Felkirk Wakefd 57 N4
Felling Gatesd 77 R13
Fell Lane C Brad 63 L11
Fell Side Cumb 67 M5
Felmersham Bed 38 E9
Felmingham Norfk 51 N8
Felpham W Susx 10 E11
Felsham Suffk 40 F9
Felsted Essex 22 G3
Feltham Gt Lon 20 K8
Felthamhill Surrey 20 J8
Felthorpe Norfk 51 L10
Felton Herefs 35 N11
Felton N Som 17 P3
Felton Nthumb 77 P5
Felton Butler Shrops 44 J10
Feltwell Norfk 40 B2
Fenay Bridge Kirk 56 J3
Fence Lancs 62 G12
Fence Rothm 57 P9
Fence Houses Sundld 70 D3
Fencott Oxon 30 C9
Fendike Corner Lincs 49 Q1
Fen Ditton Cambs 39 Q8
Fen Drayton Cambs 39 M7
Fen End Lincs 48 K9
Fen End Solhll 36 H6
Fenham Nthumb 85 R10
Feniscliffe Bl w D 55 Q1
Feniscowles Bl w D 55 P1
Feniton Devon 6 F5
Fenland Crematorium Cambs 39 P2
Fenn Green Shrops 35 S4
Fenn Street Medway 22 J12
Fenny Bentley Derbys 46 G4
Fenny Bridges Devon 6 F5
Fenny Compton Warwks 37 M10
Fenny Drayton Leics 37 L1
Fenny Stratford M Keyn 30 J6
Fenrother Nthumb 77 P7
Fenstanton Cambs 39 M7
Fenstead End Suffk 40 D10
Fen Street Norfk 40 G1
Fen Street Suffk 41 L8
Fenton C Stke 45 U5
Fenton Cambs 39 M5
Fenton Cumb 67 R1
Fenton Lincs 48 C3
Fenton Lincs 58 D11
Fenton Notts 58 C10
Fenton Nthumb 85 P12
Fenton Barns E Loth 84 E2
Fenwick Donc 57 S3
Fenwick E Ayrs 81 P4
Fenwick Nthumb 77 M11
Fenwick Nthumb 85 R10
Feock Cnwll 3 L9
Feolin Ferry Ag & B 86 G12
Fergushill N Ayrs 81 L4
Feriniquarrie Highld 100 a4
Fermain Bay Guern 6 e3
Fern Angus 98 H11
Ferndale Rhondd 26 H8
Ferndown Dorset 8 F8
Ferness Highld 103 Q6
Fernham Oxon 29 Q9
Fernhill Heath Worcs 35 U9
Fernhurst W Susx 10 D5
Fernie Fife 91 M8
Ferniegair S Lans 82 D8
Fernilea Highld 100 c6
Fernilee Derbys 56 F11
Fernwood Notts 48 B3
Ferrensby N York 63 T7
Ferriby Sluice N Linc 58 G2
Ferrindonald Highld 100 f9
Ferring W Susx 10 H10
Ferrybridge Wakefd 57 Q2
Ferrybridge Services Wakefd 57 Q2
Ferryden Angus 99 N12
Ferryhill Dur 69 S6
Ferryhill Station Dur 69 S6
Ferry Point Highld 109 N7
Ferryside Carmth 25 Q8
Ferrytown Highld 109 N7
Fersfield Norfk 40 J4
Fersit Highld 96 D8
Feshiebridge Highld 97 P3
Fetcham Surrey 20 K11
Fetlar Shet 106 w4
Fetterangus Abers 105 R5
Fettercairn Abers 99 M9
Fewcott Oxon 30 B7
Fewston N York 63 P9
Ffairfach Carmth 26 A3
Ffair Rhos Cerdgn 33 P7
Ffald-y-Brenin Carmth 33 M12
Ffawyddog Powys 27 N4
Ffestiniog Gwynd 43 P5
Ffestiniog Railway Gwynd 43 N5
Ffordd-las Denbgs 54 D14
Fforest Carmth 25 U10
Fforest Mons 27 P3
Fforest Fach Swans 26 A8
Fforest Gôch Neath 26 C7
Ffostrasol Cerdgn 32 G11
Ffrith Flints 44 G2
Ffynnonddewi Cerdgn 32 G10
Ffynnongroyw Flints 54 D10
Ffynnon-Oer Cerdgn 32 K10
Fiag Lodge Highld 110 K11
Fickleshole Surrey 21 Q10
Fiddington Gloucs 28 H1
Fiddington Somset 16 H8
Fiddleford Dorset 7 V2
Fiddlers Green Cnwll 3 L5
Fiddlers Hamlet Essex 22 C7
Field Staffs 46 D7
Field Broughton Cumb 61 R3
Field Dalling Norfk 50 H6
Fieldhead Cumb 67 Q5
Field Head Leics 47 N12
Fifehead Magdalen Dorset 17 U12
Fifehead Neville Dorset 7 U2
Fifehead St Quintin Dorset 7 U2
Fife Keith Moray 104 E5
Fifield Oxon 29 P4
Fifield W & M 20 F7
Fifield Wilts 18 H10
Figheldean Wilts 18 J11
Filands Wilts 28 H10
Filby Norfk 51 S11
Filey N York 65 Q3
Filgrave M Keyn 38 C11
Filkins Oxon 29 P7
Filleigh Devon 15 Q7
Filleigh Devon 15 R10
Fillingham Lincs 58 F9
Fillongley Warwks 36 J3
Filmore Hill Hants 9 T3
Filton S Glos 28 B12
Fimber E R Yk 64 K7
Finavon Angus 98 H12
Fincham Norfk 49 U12
Finchampstead Wokham 20 C10
Fincharn Ag & B 87 S5
Finchdean Hants 9 U6
Finchingfield Essex 39 U14
Finchley Gt Lon 21 N4
Findern Derbys 46 K7
Findhorn Moray 103 R3
Findhorn Bridge Highld 103 M10
Findochty Moray 104 F2
Findo Gask P & K 90 F8
Findon Abers 99 S4
Findon W Susx 10 J9
Findon Mains Highld 102 H3
Findrack House Abers 99 L3
Finedon Nhants 38 D6
Fingal Street Suffk 41 M7
Fingask P & K 90 J8
Fingest Bucks 20 C4
Finghall N York 63 P2
Fingland Cumb 67 L1
Fingland D & G 74 E2
Finglesham Kent 13 R5
Fingringhoe Essex 23 P3
Finkle Green Essex 40 B12
Finkle Street Barns 57 M7
Finlarig Stirlg 95 R12
Finmere Oxon 30 D6
Finnart P & K 95 Q7
Finningham Suffk 40 J7
Finningley Donc 57 U7
Finsbay W Isls 106 f10
Finstall Worcs 36 C6
Finsthwaite Cumb 61 R2
Finstock Oxon 29 S4
Finstown Ork 106 s18
Fintry Abers 105 M5
Fintry Stirlg 89 P8
Finzean Abers 99 L5
Fionnphort Ag & B 92 J14
Fionnsbhagh W Isls 106 f10
Firbank Cumb 68 D14
Firbeck Rothm 57 S9
Firby N York 63 R2
Firby N York 64 G6
Firgrove Rochdl 56 D4
Firle E Susx 11 R9
Firsby Lincs 59 S14
Firsdown Wilts 8 J2
Fir Tree Dur 69 P6
Fishbourne IoW 9 R10
Fishbourne W Susx 10 C10
Fishbourne Roman Palace W Susx 10 C10
Fishburn Dur 70 E6
Fishcross Clacks 90 C12
Fisher W Susx 10 D10
Fisherford Abers 104 K8
Fisherrow E Loth 83 R4
Fisher's Pond Hants 9 P4
Fisher's Row Lancs 61 S10
Fisherstreet W Susx 10 E4
Fisherton Highld 102 K5
Fisherton S Ayrs 80 K9
Fisherton de la Mere Wilts 18 F13
Fisherwick Staffs 46 G12
Fishery Estate W & M 20 E6
Fishguard Pembks 24 G3
Fishlake Donc 57 U4
Fishleigh Devon 15 M11
Fishmere End Lincs 49 L6
Fishnish Pier Ag & B 93 R10
Fishpond Bottom Dorset 7 L5
Fishponds Bristl 28 B12
Fishtoft Lincs 49 N5
Fishtoft Drove Lincs 49 M4
Fishwick Lancs 62 B14
Fiskavaig Highld 100 c6
Fiskerton Lincs 58 H12
Fiskerton Notts 47 T3
Fitling E R Yk 65 T13
Fittleton Wilts 18 H11
Fittleworth W Susx 10 G7
Fitton End Cambs 49 P11
Fitz Shrops 44 K10
Fitzhead Somset 16 F11
Fitzroy Somset 16 G11
Fitzwilliam Wakefd 57 P3
Five Ash Down E Susx 11 R6
Five Ashes E Susx 11 T5
Five Bells Somset 16 E8
Five Bridges Herefs 35 P11
Fivecrosses Ches W 55 M11
Fivehead Somset 17 L12
Fivelanes Cnwll 4 G4
Five Lanes Mons 27 S9
Five Oak Green Kent 12 B6
Five Oaks Jersey 7 e3
Five Oaks W Susx 10 H5
Five Roads Carmth 25 S9
Five Wents Kent 12 F5
Flack's Green Essex 22 J5
Flackwell Heath Bucks 20 E5
Fladbury Worcs 36 C11
Fladdabister Shet 106 u10
Flagg Derbys 56 H13
Flamborough E R Yk 65 S5
Flamborough Head E R Yk 65 T5
Flamingo Land Theme Park N York 64 H4
Flamstead Herts 31 N10
Flamstead End Herts 31 T12
Flansham W Susx 10 F10
Flanshaw Wakefd 57 M2
Flappit Spring C Brad 63 M12
Flasby N York 62 J8
Flash Staffs 56 F13
Flashader Highld 100 c4
Flaunden Herts 31 M12
Flawborough Notts 47 U5
Flawith N York 64 B6
Flax Bourton N Som 17 P3
Flaxby N York 63 T8
Flaxley Gloucs 28 C4
Flaxmere Ches W 55 N12
Flaxpool Somset 16 F9
Flaxton N York 64 F7
Fleckney Leics 37 R2
Flecknoe Warwks 37 P8
Fledborough Notts 58 D12
Fleet Dorset 7 R8
Fleet Hants 9 U8
Fleet Hants 20 D12
Fleet Lincs 49 N9
Fleetend Hants 9 Q7
Fleet Hargate Lincs 49 N9
Fleet Services Hants 20 C11
Fleetwood Lancs 61 Q10
Fleggburgh Norfk 51 R11
Flemingston V Glam 16 D3
Flemington S Lans 89 Q14
Flempton Suffk 40 D7
Fletchersbridge Cnwll 4 E7
Fletcher's Green Kent 21 T13
Fletchertown Cumb 66 K4
Fletching E Susx 11 Q6
Fleur-de-lis Caerph 27 M8
Flexbury Cnwll 14 F11
Flexford Surrey 20 F12
Flimby Cumb 66 F6
Flimwell E Susx 12 D9
Flint Flints 54 F12
Flintham Notts 47 T4
Flint Mountain Flints 54 F12
Flinton E R Yk 65 S12
Flint's Green Solhll 36 J4
Flishinghurst Kent 12 E8
Flitcham Norfk 50 B8
Flitton C Beds 31 N5
Flitwick C Beds 31 M6
Flixborough N Linc 58 E4
Flixborough Stather N Linc 58 E4
Flixton N York 65 N4
Flixton Suffk 41 P3
Flixton Traffd 55 R8
Flockton Kirk 56 K4
Flockton Green Kirk 57 L3
Flodden Nthumb 85 N11
Flodigarry Highld 100 d2
Flookburgh Cumb 61 R4
Flordon Norfk 41 L1
Flore Nhants 37 R8
Flotterton Nthumb 76 K5
Flowers Green E Susx 11 U8
Flowton Suffk 40 J11
Flushdyke Wakefd 57 L2
Flushing Cnwll 3 L10
Fluxton Devon 6 E6
Flyford Flavell Worcs 36 C9
Fobbing Thurr 22 H11
Fochabers Moray 104 C4
Fochriw Caerph 27 L6
Fockerby N Linc 58 E3
Foddington Somset 17 Q11
Foel Powys 43 U11
Foelgastell Carmth 25 T8
Foel y Dyffryn Brdgnd 26 F9
Foggathorpe E R Yk 64 H12
Fogo Border 84 K9
Fogwatt Moray 104 A4
Foindle Highld 110 D7
Folda Angus 98 B11
Fole Staffs 46 D6
Foleshill Covtry 37 L4
Folke Dorset 7 S2
Folkestone Kent 13 P8
Folkingham Lincs 48 G7
Folkington E Susx 11 T10
Folksworth Cambs 38 H3
Folkton N York 65 P4
Folla Rule Abers 105 L9
Follifoot N York 63 S9
Folly Gate Devon 15 N13
Folly Hill Surrey 20 D13
Fonmon V Glam 16 D3
Fonthill Bishop Wilts 8 C2
Fonthill Gifford Wilts 8 C2
Fontmell Magna Dorset 8 B5
Fontmell Parva Dorset 8 A6
Fontwell W Susx 10 E9
Font-y-gary V Glam 16 E3
Foolow Derbys 56 J11
Foots Cray Gt Lon 21 S8
Forbestown Abers 104 D13
Forcett N York 69 Q10
Ford Ag & B 87 R5
Ford Bucks 30 G11
Ford Derbys 57 P10
Ford Devon 5 Q10
Ford Devon 5 T12
Ford Devon 14 K8
Ford Gloucs 29 L2
Ford Nthumb 85 N11
Ford Shrops 44 K11
Ford Somset 16 E11
Ford Somset 17 Q6
Ford Staffs 46 E3
Ford W Susx 10 F10
Ford Wilts 8 H2
Ford Wilts 18 B5
Forda Devon 5 N2
Fordcombe Kent 11 S2
Fordell Fife 90 J14
Forden Powys 44 F13
Ford End Essex 22 G4
Forder Green Devon 5 T7
Ford Green Lancs 61 T10
Fordham Cambs 39 T6
Fordham Essex 23 M2
Fordham Norfk 49 T14
Fordham Heath Essex 23 M2
Ford Heath Shrops 44 K11
Fordingbridge Hants 8 G6
Fordon E R Yk 65 N4
Fordoun Abers 99 N8
Ford's Green Suffk 40 J7
Fordstreet Essex 23 M2
Ford Street Somset 16 G13
Fordton Devon 15 T13
Fordwells Oxon 29 R5
Fordwich Kent 13 N4
Fordyce Abers 104 H3
Forebridge Staffs 46 B9
Foremark Derbys 46 K8
Forest Guern 6 d4
Forest N York 69 S12
Forest Becks Lancs 62 F9
Forestburn Gate Nthumb 77 M6
Forest Chapel Ches E 56 E12
Forest Gate Gt Lon 21 R5
Forest Green Surrey 10 J2
Forest Hall N Tyne 77 R12
Forest Head Cumb 76 B14
Forest Hill Gt Lon 21 Q8
Forest Hill Oxon 30 C11
Forest-in-Teesdale Dur 68 J6
Forest Lane Head N York 63 S8
Forest Mill Clacks 90 E13
Forest of Bowland Lancs 62 C9
Forest of Dean Gloucs 28 B5
Forest of Dean Crematorium Gloucs 28 B5
Forest Park Crematorium Gt Lon 21 S4
Forest Row E Susx 11 Q4
Forest Side IoW 9 P11
Forestside W Susx 10 B8
Forest Town Notts 47 Q1
Forfar Angus 98 H13
Forgandenny P & K 90 G8
Forge Powys 43 Q14
Forge Hammer Torfn 27 P8
Forge Side Torfn 27 N6
Forgie Moray 104 D5
Forgieside Moray 104 E5
Forgue Abers 104 J6
Forhill Worcs 36 E5
Formby Sefton 54 H5
Forncett End Norfk 40 K2
Forncett St Mary Norfk 41 L2
Forncett St Peter Norfk 41 L2
Fornham All Saints Suffk 40 D7
Fornham St Martin Suffk 40 E7
Fornighty Highld 103 P5
Forres Moray 103 R4
Forsbrook Staffs 46 C5
Forse Highld 112 F10
Forshaw Heath Warwks 36 E6
Forsinard Highld 111 T8
Forston Dorset 7 S5
Fort Augustus Highld 96 D2
Forteviot P & K 90 G8
Forth S Lans 82 H8
Forthampton Gloucs 28 G1
Fort Hommet Guern 6 c2
Forth Rail Bridge C Edin 83 M3
Forth Road Bridge Fife 83 M3
Fortingall P & K 95 U9
Fort le Marchant Guern 6 e1
Forton Hants 19 P12
Forton Lancs 61 T9
Forton Shrops 44 K10
Forton Somset 6 K3
Forton Staffs 45 S9
Fortrie Abers 104 K6
Fortrose Highld 102 K4
Fortuneswell Dorset 7 S10
Fort William Highld 94 G4
Forty Green Bucks 20 F4
Forty Hill Gt Lon 21 P3
Forward Green Suffk 40 K9
Fosbury Wilts 19 M9
Foscot Oxon 29 P3
Foscote Nhants 37 S11
Fosdyke Lincs 49 M7
Fosdyke Bridge Lincs 49 M7
Foss P & K 97 M12
Fossebridge Gloucs 29 L5
Foss-y-ffin Cerdgn 32 H8
Fosterhouses Donc 57 U4
Foster Street Essex 22 C6
Foston Derbys 46 G7
Foston Leics 37 R2
Foston Lincs 48 C5
Foston N York 64 F6
Foston on the Wolds E R Yk 65 Q8
Fotherby Lincs 59 P8
Fothergill Cumb 66 F6
Fotheringhay Nhants 38 G2
Foula Airport Shet 106 q10
Foulbridge Cumb 67 P3
Foulby Wakefd 57 N3
Foulden Border 85 N7
Foulden Norfk 50 C14
Foul End Warwks 36 H2
Foul Mile E Susx 11 U7
Foulness Island Essex 23 N9
Foulon Vale Crematorium Guern 6 d3
Foulridge Lancs 62 H11
Foulsham Norfk 50 H9
Fountainhall Border 84 C9
Four Ashes Solhll 36 G5
Four Ashes Staffs 35 T3
Four Ashes Staffs 46 B12
Four Ashes Suffk 40 H6
Four Cabots Guern 6 d3
Four Crosses Powys 44 G10
Four Crosses Staffs 46 C12
Four Elms Kent 21 S13
Four Foot Somset 17 Q10
Four Forks Somset 16 H9
Four Gates Bolton 55 P5
Four Gotes Cambs 49 Q10
Four Lane End Barns 57 L6
Four Lane Ends Ches W 45 N1
Four Lanes Cnwll 2 H9
Fourlanes End Ches E 45 T2
Four Marks Hants 19 U13
Four Mile Bridge IoA 52 C7
Four Oaks Birm 46 F14
Four Oaks E Susx 12 G11
Four Oaks Gloucs 28 C2
Four Oaks Solhll 36 H4
Fourpenny Highld 109 Q6
Four Points W Berk 19 S5
Four Roads Carmth 25 R9
Four Shire Stone Warwks 29 P1
Fourstones Nthumb 76 H12
Four Throws Kent 12 E10
Four Wents Kent 12 B5
Fovant Wilts 8 E3
Foveran Abers 105 R11
Fowey Cnwll 4 E10
Fowley Common Warrtn 55 Q7
Fowlhall Kent 12 C6
Fowlis Angus 91 M5
Fowlis Wester P & K 90 D7
Fowlmere Cambs 39 P11
Fownhope Herefs 35 N14
Foxbar Rens 89 L13
Foxcombe Devon 5 M3
Fox Corner Surrey 20 G12
Foxcote Gloucs 28 K4
Foxcote Somset 17 T5
Foxdale IoM 60 d7
Foxearth Essex 40 D12
Foxendown Kent 12 B2
Foxfield Cumb 61 N2
Foxham Wilts 18 E5
Fox Hatch Essex 22 E8
Foxhills Hants 9 L6
Foxhole Cnwll 3 P6
Foxholes N York 65 N5
Foxhunt Green E Susx 11 S7
Foxley Nhants 37 R10
Foxley Norfk 50 H9
Foxley Wilts 28 G10
Foxlydiate Worcs 36 D7
Fox Street Essex 23 P2
Foxt Staffs 46 D4
Foxton Cambs 39 P11
Foxton Dur 70 E8
Foxton Leics 37 T3
Foxton N York 70 F13
Foxup N York 62 H4
Foxwist Green Ches W 55 P13
Foxwood Shrops 35 P5
Foy Herefs 28 A2
Foyers Highld 102 E11
Foynesfield Highld 103 N5
Fraddam Cnwll 2 F10
Fraddon Cnwll 3 N5
Fradley Staffs 46 G11
Fradswell Staffs 46 C7
Fraisthorpe E R Yk 65 R7
Framfield E Susx 11 R6
Framingham Earl Norfk 51 N13
Framingham Pigot Norfk 51 N13
Framlingham Suffk 41 N8
Frampton Dorset 7 R5
Frampton Lincs 49 M6
Frampton Cotterell S Glos 28 C11
Frampton Mansell Gloucs 28 H7
Frampton-on-Severn Gloucs 28 D6
Frampton West End Lincs 49 M5
Framsden Suffk 41 L9
Framwellgate Moor Dur 69 S4
Franche Worcs 35 T5
Frandley Ches W 55 P11
Frankaborough Devon 4 K2
Frankby Wirral 54 F9
Frankfort Norfk 51 P9
Franklands Gate Herefs 35 M11
Frankley Worcs 36 C4
Frankley Services Worcs 36 C4
Franksbridge Powys 34 D9
Frankton Warwks 37 M6
Frant E Susx 11 T3
Fraserburgh Abers 105 R2
Frating Essex 23 Q3
Frating Green Essex 23 Q3
Fratton C Port 9 T8
Freathy Cnwll 4 K10
Freckenham Suffk 39 U6
Freckleton Lancs 61 S14
Freebirch Derbys 57 M12
Freeby Leics 48 B9
Freefolk Hants 19 Q11
Freehay Staffs 46 D5
Freeland Oxon 29 T5
Freethorpe Norfk 51 R12
Freethorpe Common Norfk 51 R13
Freiston Lincs 49 N5
Fremington Devon 15 M6
Fremington N York 69 M13
Frenchay S Glos 28 B12
Frenchbeer Devon 5 R3
French Street Kent 21 S12
Frenich P & K 97 N12
Frensham Surrey 10 C2
Freshfield Sefton 54 G5
Freshford Wilts 17 U4
Freshwater IoW 9 L11
Freshwater Bay IoW 9 L11
Freshwater East Pembks 24 H11
Fressingfield Suffk 41 N5
Freston Suffk 41 L13
Freswick Highld 112 J3
Fretherne Gloucs 28 D5
Frettenham Norfk 51 M10
Freuchie Fife 91 L10
Freystrop Pembks 24 G8
Friar Park Sandw 36 D2
Friar's Gate E Susx 11 R4
Friars' Hill N York 64 G2
Friar Waddon Dorset 7 R7

Friday Bridge – Hadrian's Wall 131

Friday Bridge Cambs 49 Q13
Friday Street Suffk 41 M9
Friday Street Suffk 41 P10
Friday Street Suffk 41 Q8
Friday Street Surrey 20 K13
Fridaythorpe E R Yk 64 K8
Friden Derbys 46 G1
Friendly Calder 56 G2
Friern Barnet Gt Lon 21 N4
Friesthorpe Lincs 58 J10
Frieston Lincs 48 D4
Frieth Bucks 20 C4
Friezeland Notts 47 N3
Frilford Oxon 29 T8
Frilsham W Berk 19 R6
Frimley Surrey 20 E11
Frimley Green Surrey 20 E11
Frindsbury Medway 12 D2
Fring Norfk 50 B7
Fringford Oxon 30 D7
Frinsted Kent 12 G4
Frinton-on-Sea Essex 23 T3
Friockheim Angus 91 S2
Friog Gwynd 43 M11
Frisby on the Wreake Leics 47 S10
Friskney Lincs 49 Q2
Friskney Eaudike Lincs 49 Q2
Friston E Susx 11 T11
Friston Suffk 41 R8
Fritchley Derbys 47 L3
Fritham Hants 8 J6
Frith Bank Lincs 49 M4
Frith Common Worcs 35 Q7
Frithelstock Devon 15 L9
Frithelstock Stone Devon 15 L9
Frithend Hants 10 C3
Frithsden Herts 31 M11
Frithville Lincs 49 M3
Frittenden Kent 12 F7
Frittiscombe Devon 5 U12
Fritton Norfk 41 M2
Fritton Norfk 51 S13
Fritwell Oxon 30 B7
Frizinghall C Brad 63 N12
Frizington Cumb 66 F9
Frocester Gloucs 28 E7
Frodesley Shrops 45 M13
Frodsham Ches W 55 M11
Frogden Border 84 K13
Frog End Cambs 39 N11
Frog End Cambs 39 R9
Froggatt Derbys 56 K11
Froghall Staffs 46 D4
Frogham Hants 8 H6
Frogham Kent 13 Q5
Frogmore Devon 5 T12
Frognall Lincs 48 J11
Frogpool Cnwll 2 K8
Frog Pool Worcs 35 T7
Frogwell Cnwll 4 J7
Frolesworth Leics 37 P2
Frome Somset 17 U7
Frome St Quintin Dorset 7 Q4
Fromes Hill Herefs 35 Q11
Fron Denbgs 54 C13
Fron Gwynd 42 G6
Fron Gwynd 52 H12
Fron Powys 44 E14
Fron Powys 44 F13
Froncysyllte Denbgs 44 G5
Fron-goch Gwynd 43 T6
Fron Isaf Wrexhm 44 G5
Frostenden Suffk 41 S4
Frosterley Dur 69 M5
Froxfield C Beds 31 L6
Froxfield Wilts 19 L7
Froxfield Green Hants 9 U3
Fryern Hill Hants 9 N4
Fryerning Essex 22 F7
Fryton N York 64 F5
Fuinary Highld 93 Q9
Fulbeck Lincs 48 D3
Fulbourn Cambs 39 R9
Fulbrook Oxon 29 Q5
Fulflood Hants 9 P2
Fulford C York 64 E10
Fulford Somset 16 H11
Fulford Staffs 46 C6
Fulham Gt Lon 21 N7
Fulking W Susx 11 L8
Fullaford Devon 15 Q5
Fullarton N Ayrs 81 L5
Fuller's End Essex 22 D2
Fuller's Moor Ches W 45 L3
Fuller Street Essex 22 H4
Fuller Street Kent 21 U11
Fullerton Hants 19 N13
Fulletby Lincs 59 N12
Fullready Warwks 36 J11
Full Sutton E R Yk 64 G8
Fullwood E Ayrs 81 N2
Fulmer Bucks 20 G5
Fulmodeston Norfk 50 G7
Fulnetby Lincs 58 J11
Fulney Lincs 49 L9
Fulstone Kirk 56 J5
Fulstow Lincs 59 P7
Fulwell Oxon 29 S3
Fulwell Sundld 77 T14
Fulwood Lancs 61 U13
Fulwood Notts 47 N2
Fulwood Sheff 57 M9
Fulwood Somset 16 H12
Fundenhall Norfk 41 L1
Funtington W Susx 10 C9
Funtley Hants 9 R7
Funtullich P & K 95 V13
Furley Devon 6 J4
Furnace Ag & B 87 U5
Furnace Carmth 25 T10
Furnace Cerdgn 33 N1
Furnace End Warwks 36 H2
Furner's Green E Susx 11 Q5
Furness Vale Derbys 56 F10
Furneux Pelham Herts 22 B2
Further Quarter Kent 12 G8
Furtho Nhants 30 G4
Furzehill Devon 15 R3
Furzehill Dorset 8 E8
Furzehills Lincs 59 N12
Furzeley Corner Hants 9 T6
Furze Platt W & M 20 E6
Furzley Hants 8 K5
Fyfett Somset 6 H2
Fyfield Essex 22 E6
Fyfield Hants 19 L11
Fyfield Oxon 29 T8
Fyfield Wilts 18 H7
Fyfield Wilts 18 J8
Fyfield Bavant Wilts 8 E3
Fylingthorpe N York 71 R12
Fyning W Susx 10 C6
Fyvie Abers 105 M8

G

Gabroc Hill E Ayrs 81 P2
Gaddesby Leics 47 S11
Gaddesden Row Herts 31 N10
Gadfa IoA 52 G5
Gadgirth S Ayrs 81 N8
Gadlas Shrops 44 J6
Gaer Powys 27 M3
Gaerllwyd Mons 27 S8
Gaerwen IoA 52 G8
Gagingwell Oxon 29 T2
Gailes N Ayrs 81 L5
Gailey Staffs 46 B11
Gainford Dur 69 Q9
Gainsborough Lincs 58 D9
Gainsford End Essex 40 B13
Gairloch Highld 107 P9
Gairlochy Highld 94 H2
Gairneybridge P & K 90 H12
Gaisgill Cumb 68 D11
Gaitsgill Cumb 67 N3
Galashiels Border 84 D11
Galgate Lancs 61 T8
Galhampton Somset 17 R11
Gallanachbeg Ag & B 93 U13
Gallanachmore Ag & B 93 U13
Gallantry Bank Ches E 45 M3
Gallatown Fife 91 L13
Galley Common Warwks 36 K2
Galleywood Essex 22 H7
Gallovie Highld 96 H6
Galloway Forest Park 73 L2
Gallowfauld Angus 91 P3
Gallowhill P & K 90 J4
Gallows Green Essex 23 M2
Gallows Green Worcs 36 B8
Gallowstree Common Oxon 19 U4
Galltair Highld 100 h7
Gallt-y-foel Gwynd 52 J10
Gally Hill Hants 20 D12
Gallypot Street E Susx 11 R3
Galmpton Devon 5 R12
Galmpton Torbay 6 A13
Galphay N York 63 R5
Galston E Ayrs 81 Q5
Gamballs Green Staffs 56 F13
Gamblesby Cumb 68 D5
Gambles Green Essex 22 J5
Gamelsby Cumb 67 L2
Gamesley Derbys 56 F8
Gamlingay Cambs 38 K10
Gamlingay Cinques Cambs 38 K10
Gamlingay Great Heath Cambs 38 K10
Gammersgill N York 63 M3
Gamrie Abers 105 M3
Gamston Notts 47 Q6
Gamston Notts 58 B11
Ganarew Herefs 27 U4
Ganavan Bay Ag & B 94 B12
Gang Cnwll 4 J7
Ganllwyd Gwynd 43 P9
Gannachy Angus 98 K9
Ganstead E R Yk 65 Q13
Ganthorpe N York 64 F5
Ganton N York 65 M4
Ganwick Corner Herts 21 N3
Gappah Devon 5 V5
Garbity Moray 104 C5
Garboldisham Norfk 40 H4
Garbole Highld 103 L11
Garchory Abers 104 C13
Garden City Flints 54 H13
Gardeners Green Wokham 20 D9
Garden of England Crematorium Kent 12 G2
Gardenstown Abers 105 N3
Garden Village Sheff 57 L7
Garderhouse Shet 106 t9
Gardham E R Yk 65 M11
Gare Hill Somset 17 U8
Garelochhead Ag & B 88 F7
Garford Oxon 29 T8
Garforth Leeds 63 U13
Gargrave N York 62 J9
Gargunnock Stirlg 89 R7
Garizim Conwy 53 L7
Garlic Street Norfk 41 M4
Garlieston D & G 73 M10
Garlinge Kent 13 R2
Garlinge Green Kent 13 M5
Garlogie Abers 99 P2
Garmond Abers 105 N5
Garmouth Moray 104 C3
Garmston Shrops 45 P12
Garnant Carmth 26 B5
Garn-Dolbenmaen Gwynd 42 J5
Garnett Bridge Cumb 67 R13
Garnfadryn Gwynd 42 E7
Garnkirk N Lans 82 C5
Garnswllt Swans 26 A6
Garn-yr-erw Torfn 27 N6
Garrabost W Isls 106 k5
Garrallan E Ayrs 81 Q9
Garras Cnwll 2 J12
Garreg Gwynd 43 M5
Garrigill Cumb 68 F4
Garriston N York 69 Q14
Garroch D & G 73 P3
Garrochtrie D & G 72 E12
Garrochty Ag & B 80 F2
Garros Highld 100 d3
Garsdale Cumb 62 E2
Garsdale Head Cumb 62 F1
Garsdon Wilts 28 J10
Garshall Green Staffs 46 C7
Garsington Oxon 30 C12
Garstang Lancs 61 T10
Garston Herts 31 P12
Garston Lpool 54 K10
Gartachossan Ag & B 78 E3
Gartcosh N Lans 82 C5
Garth Brdgnd 26 F9
Garth Mons 27 Q9
Garth Powys 33 U11
Garth Powys 34 G6
Garth Wrexhm 44 G5
Garthamlock C Glas 89 Q12
Garthbrengy Powys 34 B14
Gartheli Cerdgn 33 L9
Garthmyl Powys 44 E14
Garthorpe Leics 48 B9
Garthorpe N Linc 58 D3
Garth Row Cumb 67 R13
Garths Cumb 61 U2
Gartly Abers 104 G9
Gartmore Stirlg 89 M6
Gartness N Lans 82 E6
Gartness Stirlg 89 M8
Gartocharn W Duns 88 K8
Garton E R Yk 65 T12
Garton-on-the-Wolds E R Yk 65 M8
Gartymore Highld 109 U2
Garva Bridge Highld 96 G5
Garvald E Loth 84 F4
Garvan Highld 94 D3
Garvard Ag & B 86 F7
Garve Highld 102 C3
Garvellachs Ag & B 87 M3
Garvestone Norfk 50 H12
Garvock Inver 88 G11
Garway Herefs 27 T3
Garway Common Herefs 27 T3
Garway Hill Herefs 27 S2
Garyvard W Isls 106 i7
Gasper Wilts 17 U10
Gastard Wilts 18 C7
Gasthorpe Norfk 40 G4
Gaston Green Essex 22 C4
Gatcombe IoW 9 P11
Gatebeck Cumb 61 U2
Gate Burton Lincs 58 D10
Gateford Notts 57 S10
Gateforth N York 64 D14
Gatehead E Ayrs 81 M5
Gate Helmsley N York 64 F8
Gatehouse Nthumb 76 F8
Gatehouse of Fleet D & G 73 P8
Gateley Norfk 50 G9
Gatenby N York 63 S2
Gatesgarth Cumb 66 J9
Gateshaw Border 76 F1
Gateshead Gatesd 77 R13
Gates Heath Ches W 45 L1
Gateside Angus 91 P3
Gateside E Rens 89 L14
Gateside Fife 90 J10
Gateside N Ayrs 81 M2
Gateslack D & G 74 G5
Gathurst Wigan 55 M5
Gatley Stockp 55 T9
Gatton Surrey 21 N12
Gattonside Border 84 E11
Gatwick Airport W Susx 11 M2
Gaufron Powys 33 U7
Gaulby Leics 47 S13
Gauldry Fife 91 N7
Gauldswell P & K 98 C13
Gaulkthorn Lancs 55 S1
Gaultree Norfk 49 Q12
Gaunton's Bank Ches E 45 N4
Gaunt's Common Dorset 8 E7
Gaunt's End Essex 22 E2
Gautby Lincs 59 L12
Gavinton Border 84 K8
Gawber Barns 57 M5
Gawcott Bucks 30 E6
Gawsworth Ches E 56 C13
Gawthorpe Wakefd 57 L2
Gawthrop Cumb 62 D2
Gawthwaite Cumb 61 P3
Gay Bowers Essex 22 J7
Gaydon Warwks 37 L10
Gayhurst M Keyn 38 B11
Gayle N York 62 H2
Gayles N York 69 P11
Gay Street W Susx 10 H6
Gayton Nhants 37 T10
Gayton Norfk 50 B10
Gayton Staffs 46 C8
Gayton Wirral 54 G10
Gayton le Marsh Lincs 59 R10
Gayton Thorpe Norfk 50 B10
Gaywood Norfk 49 T9
Gazeley Suffk 40 B8
Gear Cnwll 2 J12
Gearraidh Bhaird W Isls 106 i7
Geary Highld 100 b3
Gedding Suffk 40 F9
Geddington Nhants 38 C4
Gedling Notts 47 R5
Gedney Lincs 49 P9
Gedney Broadgate Lincs 49 P9
Gedney Drove End Lincs 49 Q8
Gedney Dyke Lincs 49 P8
Gedney Hill Lincs 49 M11
Gee Cross Tamesd 56 E8
Geeston Rutlnd 48 E13
Geldeston Norfk 41 Q2
Gelli Rhondd 26 H9
Gelli Torfn 27 P9
Gellifor Denbgs 44 D1
Gelligaer Caerph 27 L8
Gelligroes Caerph 27 M9
Gelligron Neath 26 C7
Gellilydan Gwynd 43 N6
Gellinudd Neath 26 C7
Gelly Pembks 24 J7
Gellyburn P & K 90 G4
Gellywen Carmth 25 N6
Gelston D & G 74 E14
Gelston Lincs 48 D4
Gembling E R Yk 65 Q8
Gentleshaw Staffs 46 E11
Georgefield D & G 75 Q7
George Green Bucks 20 G6
Georgeham Devon 15 L5
Georgemas Junction Station Highld 112 E5
George Nympton Devon 15 R8
Georgetown Blae G 27 M6
Georgia Cnwll 2 D9
Georth Ork 106 s17
Gerlan Gwynd 52 K9
Germansweek Devon 5 L2
Germoe Cnwll 2 F11
Gerrans Cnwll 3 M9
Gerrards Cross Bucks 20 H5
Gerrick R & Cl 71 M10
Gestingthorpe Essex 40 D13
Geuffordd Powys 44 F11
Gib Hill Ches W 55 P11
Gibraltar Lincs 49 S2
Gibsmere Notts 47 T4
Giddeahall Wilts 18 C6
Giddy Green Dorset 8 A11
Gidea Park Gt Lon 22 D9
Gidleigh Devon 5 R3
Giffnock E Rens 89 N14
Gifford E Loth 84 E5
Giffordtown Fife 91 L9
Giggleswick N York 62 G7
Gigha Ag & B 79 L6
Gilberdyke E R Yk 64 J14
Gilbert's End Worcs 35 T12
Gilbert Street Hants 9 S2
Gilchriston E Loth 84 D5
Gilcrux Cumb 66 H5
Gildersome Leeds 63 Q14
Gildingwells Rothm 57 S9
Gilesgate Moor Dur 69 S4
Gileston V Glam 16 D3
Gilfach Caerph 27 M8
Gilfach Goch Brdgnd 26 H9
Gilfachrheda Cerdgn 32 H9
Gilgarran Cumb 66 F8
Gill Cumb 67 P7
Gillamoor N York 64 F2
Gillan Cnwll 2 K11
Gillen Highld 100 b4
Gillesbie D & G 75 N7
Gilling East N York 64 E4
Gillingham Dorset 17 V11
Gillingham Medway 12 E2
Gillingham Norfk 41 R2
Gilling West N York 69 Q11
Gillock Highld 112 F5
Gillow Heath Staffs 45 U2
Gills Highld 112 H2
Gill's Green Kent 12 E9
Gilmanscleuch Border 75 R1
Gilmerton C Edin 83 Q5
Gilmerton P & K 90 C7
Gilmonby Dur 69 L10
Gilmorton Leics 37 Q3
Gilroes Crematorium C Leic 47 Q12
Gilsland Nthumb 76 C12
Gilson Warwks 36 G3
Gilstead C Brad 63 N12
Gilston Border 84 C7
Gilston Herts 22 B5
Gilston Park Herts 22 B5
Giltbrook Notts 47 N4
Gilwern Mons 27 N5
Gimingham Norfk 51 N6
Ginclough Ches E 56 E11
Gingers Green E Susx 11 U8
Gipping Suffk 40 J8
Gipsey Bridge Lincs 49 L4
Girdle Toll N Ayrs 81 L4
Girlington C Brad 63 N13
Girlsta Shet 106 u8
Girsby N York 70 E11
Girtford C Beds 38 J11
Girthon D & G 73 Q9
Girton Cambs 39 P8
Girton Notts 58 D13
Girvan S Ayrs 80 H13
Gisburn Lancs 62 G10
Gisleham Suffk 41 T3
Gislingham Suffk 40 J6
Gissing Norfk 40 K3
Gittisham Devon 6 F5
Gladestry Powys 34 F9
Gladsmuir E Loth 84 D4
Glais Swans 26 C7
Glaisdale N York 71 N11
Glamis Angus 91 N2
Glanaber Gwynd 43 M3
Glanafon Pembks 24 G7
Glanaman Carmth 26 B5
Glandford Norfk 50 H5
Glan-Duar Carmth 32 K12
Glandwr Pembks 25 L5
Glan-Dwyfach Gwynd 42 J5
Glandyfi Cerdgn 33 N1
Glangrwyney Powys 27 N4
Glanllynfi Brdgnd 26 F9
Glanmule Powys 34 E2
Glanrhyd Pembks 32 B12
Glan-rhyd Powys 26 D6
Glanton Nthumb 77 M3
Glanton Pike Nthumb 77 M3
Glanvilles Wootton Dorset 7 S3
Glan-y-don Flints 54 E11
Glan-y-llyn Rhondd 27 L11
Glan-y-nant Powys 33 T4
Glan-yr-afon Gwynd 43 T5
Glan-yr-afon Gwynd 44 B5
Glan-yr-afon IoA 52 K6
Glan-yr-afon Swans 26 A6
Glapthorn Nhants 38 F2
Glapwell Derbys 57 Q13
Glasbury Powys 34 E13
Glascoed Denbgs 53 S8
Glascoed Mons 27 Q7
Glascote Staffs 46 H13
Glascwm Powys 34 E10
Glasfryn Conwy 43 T3
Glasgow C Glas 89 N12
Glasgow Airport Rens 89 L12
Glasgow Science Centre C Glas 89 N12
Glasinfryn Gwynd 52 J9
Glasnacardoch Bay Highld 100 f10
Glasnakille Highld 100 e8
Glaspwll Powys 43 P14
Glassenbury Kent 12 E8
Glassford S Lans 82 D9
Glass Houghton Wakefd 57 P2
Glasshouse Gloucs 28 D3
Glasshouse Hill Gloucs 28 D3
Glasshouses N York 63 P7
Glasson Cumb 75 Q13
Glasson Lancs 61 S8
Glassonby Cumb 67 S5
Glasterlaw Angus 98 K13
Glaston Rutlnd 48 C13
Glastonbury Somset 17 P9
Glatton Cambs 38 J3
Glazebrook Warrtn 55 Q8
Glazebury Warrtn 55 Q7
Glazeley Shrops 35 R3
Gleadless Sheff 57 N10
Gleadsmoss Ches E 55 T13
Gleaston Cumb 61 P5
Glebe Highld 102 F12
Gledhow Leeds 63 S12
Gledpark D & G 73 Q9
Gledrid Shrops 44 H6
Glemsford Suffk 40 D11
Glenallachie Moray 104 B7
Glenancross Highld 100 f10
Glenaros House Ag & B 93 P10
Glen Auldyn IoM 60 g4
Glenbarr Ag & B 79 M8
Glenbarry Abers 104 H5
Glenbeg Highld 93 P6
Glenbervie Abers 99 P7
Glenboig N Lans 82 D5
Glenborrodale Highld 93 Q6
Glenbranter Ag & B 88 D6
Glenbreck Border 75 L1
Glenbrittle House Highld 100 d7
Glenbuck E Ayrs 82 D13
Glencally Angus 98 F11
Glencaple D & G 74 J12
Glencarron Lodge Highld 101 R1
Glencarse P & K 90 J7
Glen Clunie Lodge Abers 97 U7
Glencoe Highld 94 G7
Glencothe Border 83 L13
Glencraig Fife 90 J13
Glencrosh D & G 74 E8
Glendale Highld 100 a5
Glendaruel Ag & B 87 T9
Glendevon P & K 90 E11
Glendoe Lodge Highld 96 E2
Glendoick P & K 90 K7
Glenduckie Fife 91 L8
Glenegedale Ag & B 78 E5
Glenelg Highld 100 h8
Glenerney Moray 103 R6
Glenfarg P & K 90 H9
Glenfield Leics 47 P12
Glenfinnan Highld 94 C2
Glenfintaig Lodge Highld 94 J1
Glenfoot P & K 90 J8
Glenfyne Lodge Ag & B 88 F2
Glengarnock N Ayrs 81 L2
Glengolly Highld 112 D3
Glengorm Castle Ag & B 93 L7
Glengrasco Highld 100 d5
Glenholm Border 83 M12
Glenhoul D & G 73 Q2
Glenisla Angus 98 C11
Glenkin Ag & B 88 D9
Glenkindie Abers 104 E13
Glenlivet Moray 103 U10
Glenlochar D & G 74 D13
Glenlomond P & K 90 J11
Glenluce D & G 72 F8
Glenmassen Ag & B 88 D8
Glenmavis N Lans 82 E5
Glen Maye IoM 60 c7
Glen Mona IoM 60 h5
Glenmore Highld 100 d5
Glenmore Lodge Highld 97 R2
Glen Nevis House Highld 94 G4
Glenochil Clacks 90 C12
Glen Parva Leics 47 Q14
Glenquiech Angus 98 G11
Glenralloch Ag & B 87 R12
Glenridding Cumb 67 N9
Glenrothes Fife 91 L11
Glenshero Lodge Highld 96 H5
Glenstriven Ag & B 88 C10
Glentham Lincs 58 H8
Glentrool D & G 72 K4
Glen Trool Lodge D & G 73 L3
Glentruim House Highld 96 K5
Glentworth Lincs 58 F9
Glenuig Highld 93 R3
Glenvarragill Highld 100 d6
Glen Vine IoM 60 e7
Glenwhilly D & G 72 F5
Glespin S Lans 82 F13
Glewstone Herefs 27 V3
Glinton C Pete 48 J12
Glooston Leics 37 U1
Glossop Derbys 56 F8
Gloster Hill Nthumb 77 R5
Gloucester Gloucs 28 F4
Gloucester Crematorium Gloucs 28 G4
Gloucester Services Gloucs 28 F5
Gloucestershire Airport Gloucs 28 G3
Glusburn N York 63 L10
Glutt Lodge Highld 112 B9
Gluvian Cnwll 3 N4
Glympton Oxon 29 T3
Glynarthen Cerdgn 32 F11
Glyn Ceiriog Wrexhm 44 F6
Glyncorrwg Neath 26 F8
Glynde E Susx 11 R9
Glyndebourne E Susx 11 R8
Glyndyfrdwy Denbgs 44 D5
Glynneath Neath 26 F6
Glynn Valley Crematorium Cnwll 3 R3
Glyntaff Rhondd 26 K10
Glyntaff Crematorium Rhondd 26 K10
Glyntawe Powys 26 E4
Glynteg Carmth 25 Q3
Gnosall Staffs 45 T9
Gnosall Heath Staffs 45 T9
Goadby Leics 47 U14
Goadby Marwood Leics 47 U8
Goatacre Wilts 18 F5
Goatham Green E Susx 12 F11
Goathill Dorset 17 S13
Goathland N York 71 P12
Goathurst Somset 16 J10
Goathurst Common Kent 21 S12
Goat Lees Kent 12 K6
Gobowen Shrops 44 H7
Godalming Surrey 10 F2
Goddard's Corner Suffk 41 N7
Goddard's Green Kent 12 F9
Goddards Green W Susx 11 M6
Godden Green Kent 21 U11
Godford Cross Devon 6 F4
Godington Oxon 30 D7
Godley Tamesd 56 E7
Godmanchester Cambs 38 K6
Godmanstone Dorset 7 S5
Godmersham Kent 13 L5
Godney Somset 17 N8
Godolphin Cross Cnwll 2 G10
Godre'r-graig Neath 26 D6
Godshill Hants 8 H5
Godshill IoW 9 Q12
Godstone Staffs 46 D7
Godstone Surrey 21 Q12
Godsworthy Devon 5 N5
Godwinscroft Hants 8 H9
Goetre Mons 27 Q6
Goff's Oak Herts 31 T12
Gogar C Edin 83 N4
Goginan Cerdgn 33 N4
Golan Gwynd 42 K5
Golant Cnwll 4 E10
Golberdon Cnwll 4 J6
Golborne Wigan 55 P7
Golcar Kirk 56 G3
Goldcliff Newpt 27 R11
Golden Cross E Susx 11 S8
Golden Green Kent 12 B6
Golden Grove Carmth 25 U7
Goldenhill C Stke 45 U3
Golden Hill Pembks 24 G10
Golden Pot Hants 19 V12
Golden Valley Derbys 47 M3
Golders Green Gt Lon 21 M5
Golders Green Crematorium Gt Lon 21 N5
Goldfinch Bottom W Berk 19 R8
Goldhanger Essex 23 M6
Gold Hill Cambs 39 R2
Gold Hill Dorset 8 A6
Golding Shrops 45 M13
Goldington Bed 38 G10
Goldsborough N York 63 T8
Goldsborough N York 71 P10
Golds Green Sandw 36 C2
Goldsithney Cnwll 2 E10
Goldstone Kent 13 Q3
Goldstone Shrops 45 R8
Goldsworth Park Surrey 20 G11
Goldthorpe Barns 57 Q6
Goldworthy Devon 14 J8
Golford Kent 12 E8
Golford Green Kent 12 E8
Gollanfield Highld 103 M5
Gollinglith Foot N York 63 N3
Golly Wrexhm 44 H2
Golsoncott Somset 16 D9
Golspie Highld 109 Q4
Gomeldon Wilts 18 J13
Gomersal Kirk 56 K1
Gomshall Surrey 20 J13
Gonalston Notts 47 S4
Gonerby Hill Foot Lincs 48 D6
Gonfirth Shet 106 t7
Goodameavy Devon 5 N8
Good Easter Essex 22 F5
Gooderstone Norfk 50 C13
Goodleigh Devon 15 P6
Goodmanham E R Yk 64 K11
Goodmayes Gt Lon 21 S5
Goodnestone Kent 12 K3
Goodnestone Kent 13 Q5
Goodrich Herefs 27 V4
Goodrington Torbay 6 A13
Goodshaw Lancs 55 T1
Goodshaw Fold Lancs 55 T1
Goodstone Devon 5 T6
Goodwick Pembks 24 F3
Goodworth Clatford Hants 19 N12
Goodyers End Warwks 36 K3
Goole E R Yk 58 B2
Goole Fields E R Yk 58 C2
Goom's Hill Worcs 36 D10
Goonbell Cnwll 2 J7
Goonhavern Cnwll 2 K6
Goonvrea Cnwll 2 J7
Goosecruives Abers 99 P7
Gooseford Devon 5 R2
Goose Green Essex 23 R2
Goose Green Kent 12 B5
Goose Green Kent 12 F8
Goose Green S Glos 28 C13
Goose Green W Susx 10 J7
Goose Green Wigan 55 N6
Gooseham Cnwll 14 F9
Gooseham Mill Cnwll 14 F9
Goosehill Green Worcs 36 B8
Goose Pool Herefs 35 L13
Goosey Oxon 29 S9
Goosnargh Lancs 62 B12
Goostrey Ches E 55 S12
Gordano Services N Som 27 U12
Gorddinog Conwy 53 L8
Gordon Border 84 G10
Gordon Arms Hotel Border 83 R13
Gordonstown Abers 104 H4
Gordonstown Abers 105 L8
Gore Powys 34 G9
Gorebridge Mdloth 83 R6
Gorefield Cambs 49 P11
Gore Pit Essex 23 L4
Gores Wilts 18 H9
Gore Street Kent 13 Q2
Gorey Jersey 7 f3
Goring Oxon 19 T4
Goring-by-Sea W Susx 10 J10
Goring Heath Oxon 19 U5
Gorleston on Sea Norfk 51 T13
Gornal Wood Crematorium Dudley 36 B2
Gorrachie Abers 105 L4
Gorran Churchtown Cnwll 3 P8
Gorran Haven Cnwll 3 Q8
Gorran High Lanes Cnwll 3 P8
Gorrig Cerdgn 32 H12
Gors Cerdgn 33 M5
Gorsedd Flints 54 E11
Gorse Hill Swindn 29 N10
Gorseinon Swans 25 U11
Gorseybank Derbys 46 J3
Gorsgoch Cerdgn 32 J10
Gorslas Carmth 25 U8
Gorsley Gloucs 28 C2
Gorsley Common Herefs 28 C2
Gorstage Ches W 55 P12
Gorstan Highld 102 C3
Gorstella Ches W 44 J1
Gorst Hill Worcs 35 R6
Gorsty Hill Staffs 46 F8
Gorten Ag & B 93 S12
Gorthleck Highld 102 F11
Gorton Manch 56 C7
Gosbeck Suffk 41 L9
Gosberton Lincs 48 K7
Gosberton Clough Lincs 48 J8
Gosfield Essex 22 J2
Gosford Devon 6 F5
Gosford Oxon 29 U5
Gosforth Cumb 66 G12
Gosforth N u Ty 77 Q12
Gosling Street Somset 17 P10
Gosmore Herts 31 Q7
Gospel End Staffs 35 U2
Gospel Green W Susx 10 E4
Gosport Hants 9 S9
Gossard's Green C Beds 31 L4
Gossington Gloucs 28 D7
Goswick Nthumb 85 R10
Gotham Notts 47 P7
Gotherington Gloucs 28 J2
Gotton Somset 16 H11
Goudhurst Kent 12 D8
Goulceby Lincs 59 N11
Gourdas Abers 105 M7
Gourdie C Dund 91 N5
Gourdon Abers 99 Q9
Gourock Inver 88 F10
Govan C Glas 89 M12
Goveton Devon 5 T11
Govilon Mons 27 P5
Gowdall E R Yk 57 T2
Gower Highld 102 F4
Gower Swans 25 T12
Gowerton Swans 25 U11
Gowkhall Fife 90 G14
Gowthorpe E R Yk 64 H9
Goxhill E R Yk 65 R11
Goxhill N Linc 58 K2
Grabhair W Isls 106 i7
Graby Lincs 48 G8
Grade Cnwll 2 J14
Gradeley Green Ches E 45 N3
Graffham W Susx 10 E7
Grafham Cambs 38 J7
Grafham Surrey 10 G2
Grafton Herefs 35 L13
Grafton N York 63 U7
Grafton Oxon 29 Q7
Grafton Shrops 44 K10
Grafton Worcs 35 N8
Grafton Worcs 36 C13
Grafton Flyford Worcs 36 C9
Grafton Regis Nhants 37 U11
Grafton Underwood Nhants 38 D4
Grafty Green Kent 12 G6
Graianrhyd Denbgs 44 F2
Graig Conwy 53 P8
Graig Denbgs 54 C12
Graigfechan Denbgs 44 D3
Grain Medway 23 L12
Grains Bar Oldham 56 E5
Grainsby Lincs 59 N7
Grainthorpe Lincs 59 Q7
Grampound Cnwll 3 N7
Grampound Road Cnwll 3 N6
Gramsdal W Isls 106 d13
Gramsdale W Isls 106 d13
Granborough Bucks 30 G7
Granby Notts 47 U6
Grandborough Warwks 37 N7
Grand Chemins Jersey 7 e3
Grandes Rocques Guern 6 d2
Grandtully P & K 97 Q13
Grange Cumb 67 L9
Grange Medway 12 E2
Grange P & K 91 L6
Grange Wirral 54 F9
Grange Crossroads Moray 104 F5
Grange Hall Moray 103 S3
Grangehall S Lans 82 J10
Grange Hill Essex 21 R4
Grangemill Derbys 46 H2
Grange Moor Kirk 56 K3
Grangemouth Falk 82 H2
Grange of Lindores Fife 91 L8
Grange-over-Sands Cumb 61 S4
Grangepans Falk 82 K2
Grange Park Nhants 37 U9
Grangetown R & Cl 70 H8
Grangetown Sundld 70 F2
Grange Villa Dur 69 R2
Gransmoor E R Yk 65 Q8
Gransmore Green Essex 22 G3
Granston Pembks 24 E4
Grantchester Cambs 39 P9
Grantham Lincs 48 D6
Grantham Crematorium Lincs 48 D6
Granton C Edin 83 P3
Grantown-on-Spey Highld 103 R10
Grantsfield Herefs 35 M8
Grantshouse Border 85 L5
Grappenhall Warrtn 55 P9
Grasby Lincs 58 J6
Grasmere Cumb 67 M11
Grasscroft Oldham 56 E6
Grassendale Lpool 54 J9
Grassgarth Cumb 67 M4
Grass Green Essex 40 B13
Grassington N York 63 L7
Grassmoor Derbys 57 P13
Grassthorpe Notts 58 C13
Grateley Hants 19 L12
Gratwich Staffs 46 D7
Graveley Cambs 39 L8
Graveley Herts 31 R7
Gravelly Hill Birm 36 F2
Gravelsbank Shrops 44 H13
Graveney Kent 13 L3
Gravesend Kent 22 G13
Gravir W Isls 106 i7
Grayingham Lincs 58 F7
Grayrigg Cumb 67 S13
Grays Thurr 22 F12
Grayshott Hants 10 D3
Grayson Green Cumb 66 E7
Grayswood Surrey 10 E4
Graythorpe Hartpl 70 H7
Grazeley Wokham 19 U7
Greasbrough Rothm 57 P7
Greasby Wirral 54 G9
Greasley Notts 47 N4
Great Abington Cambs 39 R11
Great Addington Nhants 38 E5
Great Alne Warwks 36 F9
Great Altcar Lancs 54 H5
Great Amwell Herts 31 U10
Great Asby Cumb 68 E10
Great Ashfield Suffk 40 G7
Great Ayton N York 70 J10
Great Baddow Essex 22 H7
Great Badminton S Glos 28 F11
Great Bardfield Essex 22 G1
Great Barford Bed 38 H10
Great Barr Sandw 36 D1
Great Barrington Gloucs 29 P5
Great Barrow Ches W 55 L13
Great Barton Suffk 40 E7
Great Barugh N York 64 G4
Great Bavington Nthumb 76 K9
Great Bealings Suffk 41 M11
Great Bedwyn Wilts 19 L8
Great Bentley Essex 23 R3
Great Billing Nhants 38 B8
Great Bircham Norfk 50 C7
Great Blakenham Suffk 40 K10
Great Blencow Cumb 67 Q6
Great Bolas Wrekin 45 P9
Great Bookham Surrey 20 K12
Great Bosullow Cnwll 2 C10
Great Bourton Oxon 37 N11
Great Bowden Leics 37 T3
Great Bradley Suffk 39 U10
Great Braxted Essex 23 L5
Great Bricett Suffk 40 H10
Great Brickhill Bucks 30 K6
Great Bridgeford Staffs 45 U8
Great Brington Nhants 37 S7
Great Bromley Essex 23 Q2
Great Broughton Cumb 66 G6
Great Broughton N York 70 H11
Great Budworth Ches W 55 Q11
Great Burdon Darltn 70 D9
Great Burstead Essex 22 G9
Great Busby N York 70 H11
Great Canfield Essex 22 E4
Great Carlton Lincs 59 R9
Great Casterton Rutlnd 48 F12
Great Chalfield Wilts 18 C8
Great Chart Kent 12 J7
Great Chatwell Staffs 45 S11
Great Chell C Stke 45 U3
Great Chesterford Essex 39 R12
Great Cheverell Wilts 18 E10
Great Chishill Cambs 39 P13
Great Clacton Essex 23 S4
Great Cliffe Wakefd 57 M3
Great Clifton Cumb 66 F7
Great Coates NE Lin 59 M5
Great Comberton Worcs 36 C12
Great Comp Kent 12 B4
Great Corby Cumb 67 Q2
Great Cornard Suffk 40 E12
Great Cowden E R Yk 65 S11
Great Coxwell Oxon 29 Q9
Great Cransley Nhants 38 B5
Great Cressingham Norfk 50 E13
Great Crosthwaite Cumb 67 L8
Great Cubley Derbys 46 G6
Great Cumbrae Island N Ayrs 80 H1
Great Dalby Leics 47 T11
Great Denham Bed 38 F11
Great Doddington Nhants 38 C8
Great Doward Herefs 27 U4
Great Dunham Norfk 50 E11
Great Dunmow Essex 22 F3
Great Durnford Wilts 18 H13
Great Easton Essex 22 F2
Great Easton Leics 38 B2
Great Eccleston Lancs 61 S11
Great Edstone N York 64 G3
Great Ellingham Norfk 40 H1
Great Elm Somset 17 T7
Great Everdon Nhants 37 Q9
Great Eversden Cambs 39 N10
Great Fencote N York 69 S14
Greatfield Wilts 29 L10
Great Finborough Suffk 40 H9
Greatford Lincs 48 G11
Great Fransham Norfk 50 E11
Great Gaddesden Herts 31 M10
Greatgate Staffs 46 E6
Great Gidding Cambs 38 H4
Great Givendale E R Yk 64 J9
Great Glemham Suffk 41 P8
Great Glen Leics 47 S14
Great Gonerby Lincs 48 C6
Great Gransden Cambs 39 L9
Great Green Cambs 31 S4
Great Green Norfk 41 N3
Great Green Suffk 40 F7
Great Green Suffk 40 F9
Great Habton N York 64 H4
Great Hale Lincs 48 H5
Great Hallingbury Essex 22 D4
Greatham Hants 10 B4
Greatham Hartpl 70 G7
Greatham W Susx 10 G7
Great Hampden Bucks 30 H12
Great Harrowden Nhants 38 C6
Great Harwood Lancs 62 E13
Great Haseley Oxon 30 D12
Great Hatfield E R Yk 65 R11
Great Haywood Staffs 46 C9
Great Heck N York 57 S2
Great Henny Essex 40 E13
Great Hinton Wilts 18 D9
Great Hockham Norfk 40 G2
Great Holland Essex 23 T4
Great Hollands Br For 20 E9
Great Horkesley Essex 23 N1
Great Hormead Herts 22 B2
Great Horton C Brad 63 N13
Great Horwood Bucks 30 G6
Great Houghton Barns 57 P5
Great Houghton Nhants 37 U9
Great Hucklow Derbys 56 J11
Great Kelk E R Yk 65 Q8
Great Kimble Bucks 30 H11
Great Kingshill Bucks 20 E3
Great Langdale Cumb 67 L11
Great Langton N York 69 S13
Great Leighs Essex 22 H4
Great Limber Lincs 58 K5
Great Linford M Keyn 30 J4
Great Livermere Suffk 40 E6
Great Longstone Derbys 56 K12
Great Lumley Dur 69 S3
Great Lyth Shrops 45 L12
Great Malvern Worcs 35 S11
Great Maplestead Essex 40 D14
Great Marton Bpool 61 Q12
Great Massingham Norfk 50 C9
Great Melton Norfk 50 K12
Great Meols Wirral 54 F8
Great Milton Oxon 30 D12
Great Missenden Bucks 30 J12
Great Mitton Lancs 62 E12
Great Mongeham Kent 13 S5
Great Moulton Norfk 41 L2
Great Munden Herts 31 U8
Great Musgrave Cumb 68 G10
Great Ness Shrops 44 J10
Great Notley Essex 22 H3
Great Oak Mons 27 R5
Great Oakley Essex 23 S2
Great Oakley Nhants 38 C3
Great Offley Herts 31 P7
Great Ormside Cumb 68 F9
Great Orton Cumb 67 M2
Great Ouseburn N York 63 U7
Great Oxendon Nhants 37 T4
Great Oxney Green Essex 22 G6
Great Palgrave Norfk 50 D11
Great Park N u Ty 77 Q11
Great Parndon Essex 22 B6
Great Pattenden Kent 12 D7
Great Paxton Cambs 38 K8
Great Plumpton Lancs 61 R13
Great Plumstead Norfk 51 P11
Great Ponton Lincs 48 D7
Great Potheridge Devon 15 M10
Great Preston Leeds 63 U14
Great Purston Nhants 30 B5
Great Raveley Cambs 39 L4
Great Rissington Gloucs 29 N4
Great Rollright Oxon 29 R1
Great Rudbaxton Pembks 24 G6
Great Ryburgh Norfk 50 G8
Great Ryle Nthumb 77 L3
Great Ryton Shrops 45 L13
Great Saling Essex 22 G2
Great Salkeld Cumb 67 S5
Great Sampford Essex 39 T13
Great Saredon Staffs 46 C12
Great Saughall Ches W 54 J13
Great Saxham Suffk 40 C8
Great Shefford W Berk 19 N5
Great Shelford Cambs 39 Q10
Great Smeaton N York 70 D12
Great Snoring Norfk 50 F7
Great Somerford Wilts 28 J11
Great Soudley Shrops 45 R8
Great Stainton Darltn 70 D8
Great Stambridge Essex 23 L9
Great Staughton Cambs 38 H8
Great Steeping Lincs 59 R14
Great Stoke S Glos 28 B11
Great Stonar Kent 13 R4
Greatstone-on-Sea Kent 13 L11
Great Strickland Cumb 67 S8
Great Stukeley Cambs 38 K6
Great Sturton Lincs 59 M11
Great Sutton Ches W 54 J11
Great Sutton Shrops 35 M4
Great Swinburne Nthumb 76 J10
Great Tew Oxon 29 T2
Great Tey Essex 23 L2
Great Thurlow Suffk 39 U10
Great Torrington Devon 15 L9
Great Tosson Nthumb 77 L5
Great Totham Essex 23 L5
Great Totham Essex 23 L5
Great Tows Lincs 59 M8
Great Urswick Cumb 61 P5
Great Wakering Essex 23 M10
Great Waldingfield Suffk 40 F12
Great Walsingham Norfk 50 F6
Great Waltham Essex 22 G5
Great Warford Ches E 55 T11
Great Warley Essex 22 E9
Great Washbourne Gloucs 36 C14
Great Weeke Devon 5 S3
Great Welnetham Suffk 40 E9
Great Wenham Suffk 40 J13
Great Whittington Nthumb 77 L11
Great Wigborough Essex 23 N4
Great Wilbraham Cambs 39 S9
Great Wilne Derbys 47 M7
Great Wishford Wilts 18 G13
Great Witchingham Norfk 50 K9
Great Witcombe Gloucs 28 H5
Great Witley Worcs 35 S7
Great Wolford Warwks 36 J14
Greatworth Nhants 30 C4
Great Wratting Suffk 39 U11
Great Wymondley Herts 31 R7
Great Wyrley Staffs 46 C12
Great Wytheford Shrops 45 N10
Great Yarmouth Norfk 51 T12
Great Yarmouth Crematorium Norfk 51 T13
Great Yeldham Essex 40 C13
Grebby Lincs 59 R13
Greeba IoM 60 e6
Green Denbgs 54 C13
Green Bank Cumb 61 R3
Greenbottom Cnwll 2 K7
Greenburn W Loth 82 H6
Greencroft Hall Dur 69 Q3
Green Cross Surrey 10 D3
Green Down Somset 17 Q6
Green End Bed 38 F11
Green End Bed 38 G8
Green End Bed 38 H10
Green End Bed 38 H8
Green End Cambs 38 J4
Green End Cambs 38 K6
Green End Cambs 39 N9
Green End Cambs 39 Q7
Green End Cambs 39 Q8
Green End Herts 31 S6
Green End Herts 31 T6
Green End Herts 31 T8
Greenend Oxon 29 R3
Green End Warwks 36 J3
Greenfield Ag & B 88 F7
Greenfield C Beds 31 N6
Greenfield Flints 54 E11
Greenfield Highld 101 U11
Greenfield Oldham 56 E6
Greenfield Oxon 20 B4
Greenford Gt Lon 20 K6
Greengairs N Lans 82 E4
Greengates C Brad 63 P12
Greengill Cumb 66 H5
Greenhalgh Lancs 61 S12
Greenham Somset 16 E12
Greenham W Berk 19 Q7
Green Hammerton N York 64 B8
Greenhaugh Nthumb 76 F8
Green Head Cumb 67 N3
Greenhead Nthumb 76 D12
Green Heath Staffs 46 C11
Greenheys Salfd 55 R6
Greenhill D & G 75 M10
Greenhill Falk 89 T10
Greenhill Herefs 35 R11
Greenhill Kent 13 N2
Greenhill S Lans 82 H12
Green Hill Wilts 29 L10
Greenhillocks Derbys 47 M4
Greenhithe Kent 22 E12
Greenholm E Ayrs 81 Q5
Greenholme Cumb 67 S11
Greenhouse Border 84 F14
Greenhow Hill N York 63 N7
Greenland Highld 112 F3
Greenland Sheff 57 N9
Greenlands Bucks 20 C5
Green Lane Devon 5 T5
Green Lane Worcs 36 E8
Greenlaw Border 84 J9
Greenlea D & G 74 K10
Greenloaning P & K 89 T4
Green Moor Barns 57 L7
Greenmount Bury 55 S4
Green Oak E R Yk 64 J14
Greenock Inver 88 G10
Greenodd Cumb 61 Q3
Green Ore Somset 17 Q6
Green Quarter Cumb 67 Q12
Greensgate Norfk 50 K10
Greenshields S Lans 82 K10
Greenside Gatesd 77 N13
Greenside Kirk 56 J3
Greens Norton Nhants 37 S11
Greenstead Green Essex 22 K2
Greensted Essex 22 D7
Green Street E Susx 12 E13
Green Street Gloucs 28 G4
Green Street Herts 21 L3
Green Street Herts 22 C3
Green Street Worcs 35 U11
Green Street Green Gt Lon 21 S10
Green Street Green Kent 22 E13
Greenstreet Green Suffk 40 H11
Green Tye Herts 22 B4
Greenway Gloucs 35 R14
Greenway Somset 16 K12
Greenway V Glam 26 K13
Greenway Worcs 35 R6
Greenwich Gt Lon 21 Q7
Greenwich Maritime Gt Lon 21 Q7
Greet Gloucs 28 K1
Greete Shrops 35 N6
Greetham Lincs 59 P12
Greetham Rutlnd 48 D11
Greetland Calder 56 G2
Gregson Lane Lancs 55 N1
Greinton Somset 17 M9
Grenaby IoM 60 d8
Grendon Nhants 38 C8
Grendon Warwks 46 J14
Grendon Green Herefs 35 N9
Grendon Underwood Bucks 30 E8
Grenofen Devon 5 M6
Grenoside Sheff 57 M8
Grenoside Crematorium Sheff 57 M8
Greosabhagh W Isls 106 g9
Gresford Wrexhm 44 H3
Gresham Norfk 51 L6
Greshornish House Hotel Highld 100 c4
Gressenhall Norfk 50 G10
Gressenhall Green Norfk 50 G10
Gressingham Lancs 62 B6
Gresty Green Ches E 45 R3
Greta Bridge Dur 69 N10
Gretna D & G 75 R12
Gretna Green D & G 75 R12
Gretna Services D & G 75 R12
Gretton Gloucs 28 K1
Gretton Nhants 38 C2
Gretton Shrops 35 M1
Grewelthorpe N York 63 Q4
Grey Friars Suffk 41 S6
Greygarth N York 63 P5
Grey Green N Linc 58 C5
Greylake Somset 17 L10
Greylees Lincs 48 F5
Greyrigg D & G 75 L8
Greys Green Oxon 20 B6
Greysouthen Cumb 66 G7
Greystoke Cumb 67 P6
Greystone Angus 91 R3
Greywell Hants 20 B12
Gribb Dorset 7 L4
Gribthorpe E R Yk 64 H12
Griff Warwks 37 L3
Griffithstown Torfn 27 P8
Griffydam Leics 47 M10
Griggs Green Hants 10 C4
Grimeford Village Lancs 55 P4
Grimesthorpe Sheff 57 N9
Grimethorpe Barns 57 P5
Grimley Worcs 35 T8
Grimmet S Ayrs 81 L10
Grimoldby Lincs 59 Q9
Grimpo Shrops 44 J8
Grimsargh Lancs 62 B13
Grimsby NE Lin 59 N4
Grimsby Crematorium NE Lin 59 N5
Grimscote Nhants 37 S10
Grimscott Cnwll 14 G11
Grimshader W Isls 106 j6
Grimshaw Bl w D 55 R2
Grimshaw Green Lancs 55 L4
Grimsthorpe Lincs 48 F9
Grimston E R Yk 65 T12
Grimston Leics 47 S9
Grimston Norfk 50 B9
Grimstone Dorset 7 R6
Grimstone End Suffk 40 F7
Grinacombe Moor Devon 5 L2
Grindale E R Yk 65 Q5
Grindle Shrops 45 S13
Grindleford Derbys 56 K11
Grindleton Lancs 62 F10
Grindley Brook Shrops 45 M5
Grindlow Derbys 56 J11
Grindon Nthumb 85 N10
Grindon S on T 70 E7
Grindon Staffs 46 E3
Grindon Hill Nthumb 76 G12
Grindonrigg Nthumb 85 N10
Gringley on the Hill Notts 58 B8
Grinsdale Cumb 75 S14
Grinshill Shrops 45 M9
Grinton N York 69 M13
Griomaisiader W Isls 106 j6
Griomsaigh W Isls 106 d13
Grishipoll Ag & B 92 F7
Grisling Common E Susx 11 Q6
Gristhorpe N York 65 P3
Griston Norfk 50 F14
Gritley Ork 106 u19
Grittenham Wilts 28 K11
Grittleton Wilts 18 C4
Grizebeck Cumb 61 N3
Grizedale Cumb 67 M14
Groby Leics 47 P12
Groes Conwy 53 T10
Groes-faen Rhondd 26 K11
Groesffordd Gwynd 42 E6
Groesffordd Marli Denbgs 53 T8
Groesllwyd Powys 44 F11
Groeslon Gwynd 52 G11
Groeslon Gwynd 52 H10
Groes-Wen Caerph 27 L10
Grogarry W Isls 106 c15
Grogport Ag & B 79 Q7
Groigearraidh W Isls 106 c15
Gromford Suffk 41 Q9
Gronant Flints 54 C10
Groombridge E Susx 11 S3
Grosebay W Isls 106 g9
Grosmont Mons 27 S3
Grosmont N York 71 P11
Groton Suffk 40 G12
Grotton Oldham 56 E6
Grouville Jersey 7 e3
Grove Bucks 30 K8
Grove Dorset 7 S10
Grove Kent 13 P3
Grove Notts 58 B11
Grove Oxon 29 T9
Grove Pembks 24 G10
Grove Green Kent 12 E4
Grovenhurst Kent 12 D7
Grove Park Gt Lon 21 R8
Grovesend S Glos 28 C10
Grovesend Swans 25 U10
Grubb Street Kent 21 U9
Gruinard Highld 107 R7
Gruinart Ag & B 86 D12
Grula Highld 100 c7
Gruline Ag & B 93 N10
Grumbla Cnwll 2 C11
Grundisburgh Suffk 41 M10
Gruting Shet 106 s9
Grutness Shet 106 u12
Gualachulain Highld 94 G9
Guanockgate Lincs 49 N11
Guardbridge Fife 91 Q8
Guarlford Worcs 35 T11
Guay P & K 90 F2
Guernsey Guern 6 d3
Guernsey Airport Guern 6 c3
Guestling Green E Susx 12 G13
Guestling Thorn E Susx 12 G12
Guestwick Norfk 50 J8
Guide Bridge Tamesd 56 D7
Guide Post Nthumb 77 R8
Guilden Morden Cambs 31 S4
Guilden Sutton Ches W 54 K13
Guildford Surrey 20 G13
Guildford Crematorium Surrey 20 G13
Guildstead Kent 12 F3
Guildtown P & K 90 H5
Guilsborough Nhants 37 S6
Guilsfield Powys 44 F11
Guilton Kent 13 Q4
Guiltreehill S Ayrs 81 M10
Guineaford Devon 15 N5
Guisborough R & Cl 70 K9
Guiseley Leeds 63 P11
Guist Norfk 50 H8
Guiting Power Gloucs 29 L3
Gullane E Loth 84 D2
Gulling Green Suffk 40 D9
Gulval Cnwll 2 D10
Gulworthy Devon 5 M6
Gumfreston Pembks 24 K10
Gumley Leics 37 S3
Gummow's Shop Cnwll 3 M5
Gunby E R Yk 64 G12
Gunby Lincs 48 D9
Gunby Lincs 59 S13
Gundleton Hants 9 S2
Gun Green Kent 12 E9
Gun Hill E Susx 11 T8
Gun Hill Warwks 36 J3
Gunn Devon 15 P6
Gunnerside N York 69 L13
Gunnerton Nthumb 76 J11
Gunness N Linc 58 D4
Gunnislake Cnwll 5 L6
Gunnista Shet 106 v9
Gunthorpe C Pete 48 J13
Gunthorpe N Linc 58 D7
Gunthorpe Norfk 50 H7
Gunthorpe Notts 47 S5
Gunton Suffk 41 T1
Gunwalloe Cnwll 2 H12
Gupworthy Somset 16 C10
Gurnard IoW 9 P9
Gurnett Ches E 56 D12
Gurney Slade Somset 17 R7
Gurnos Powys 26 D6
Gushmere Kent 12 K4
Gussage All Saints Dorset 8 E6
Gussage St Andrew Dorset 8 D6
Gussage St Michael Dorset 8 D6
Guston Kent 13 R7
Gutcher Shet 106 v4
Guthrie Angus 98 K13
Guyhirn Cambs 49 P13
Guyhirn Gull Cambs 49 N13
Guy's Marsh Dorset 8 A4
Guyzance Nthumb 77 Q5
Gwaenysgor Flints 54 C10
Gwalchmai IoA 52 E7
Gwastadnant Gwynd 52 K11
Gwaun-Cae-Gurwen Carmth 26 B5
Gwbert on Sea Cerdgn 32 C10
Gwealavellan Cnwll 2 G8
Gweek Cnwll 2 J11
Gwehelog Mons 27 R7
Gwenddwr Powys 34 C12
Gwennap Cnwll 2 J8
Gwennap Mining District Cnwll 2 K8
Gwent Crematorium Mons 27 Q8
Gwenter Cnwll 2 J13
Gwernaffield Flints 54 F13
Gwernesney Mons 27 S7
Gwernogle Carmth 25 T4
Gwernymynydd Flints 44 F1
Gwersyllt Wrexhm 44 H3
Gwespyr Flints 54 D10
Gwindra Cnwll 3 P6
Gwinear Cnwll 2 F9
Gwithian Cnwll 2 F8
Gwredog IoA 52 F5
Gwrhay Caerph 27 M8
Gwyddelwern Denbgs 44 C4
Gwyddgrug Carmth 25 S3
Gwynfryn Wrexhm 44 G3
Gwystre Powys 34 C7
Gwytherin Conwy 53 Q10
Gyfelia Wrexhm 44 H4
Gyrn-gôch Gwynd 42 H4

H

Habberley Shrops 44 J13
Habberley Worcs 35 T5
Habergham Lancs 62 G13
Habertoft Lincs 59 T13
Habin W Susx 10 C6
Habrough NE Lin 58 K4
Hacconby Lincs 48 H8
Haceby Lincs 48 F6
Hacheston Suffk 41 P9
Hackbridge Gt Lon 21 N9
Hackenthorpe Sheff 57 P10
Hackford Norfk 50 J13
Hackforth N York 69 R14
Hack Green Ches E 45 P4
Hackland Ork 106 s17
Hackleton Nhants 38 B9
Hacklinge Kent 13 R5
Hackman's Gate Worcs 35 U5
Hackness N York 65 M1
Hackness Somset 16 K7
Hackney Gt Lon 21 P6
Hackthorn Lincs 58 G10
Hackthorpe Cumb 67 R8
Hacton Gt Lon 22 E10
Hadden Border 84 K11
Haddenham Bucks 30 F11
Haddenham Cambs 39 Q5
Haddington E Loth 84 E4
Haddington Lincs 58 F14
Haddiscoe Norfk 41 R1
Haddo Abers 105 N8
Haddon Cambs 38 H2
Hade Edge Kirk 56 H6
Hadfield Derbys 56 F7
Hadham Cross Herts 22 B4
Hadham Ford Herts 22 B3
Hadleigh Essex 22 K10
Hadleigh Suffk 40 H12
Hadleigh Heath Suffk 40 G12
Hadley Worcs 35 U8
Hadley Wrekin 45 Q11
Hadley End Staffs 46 F9
Hadley Wood Gt Lon 21 N3
Hadlow Kent 12 B5
Hadlow Down E Susx 11 S6
Hadnall Shrops 45 M9
Hadrian's Wall 76 K12

Hodsoll Street – Kingoodie 133

Hodsoll Street Kent 12 B3
Hodson Swindn 18 J4
Hodthorpe Derbys 57 R11
Hoe Hants 9 R5
Hoe Norfk 50 G10
Hoe Benham W Berk 19 P7
Hoe Gate Hants 9 S6
Hoff Cumb 68 E9
Hogben's Hill Kent 12 K4
Hoggards Green Suffk 40 E9
Hoggeston Bucks 30 H8
Hoggrill's End Warwks 36 H2
Hog Hill E Susx 12 G12
Hoghton Lancs 55 P1
Hoghton Bottoms Lancs 55 P1
Hognaston Derbys 46 H3
Hogsthorpe Lincs 59 T12
Holbeach Lincs 49 N9
Holbeach Bank Lincs 49 N8
Holbeach Clough Lincs 49 N8
Holbeach Drove Lincs 49 M11
Holbeach Hurn Lincs 49 N8
Holbeach St Johns Lincs 49 N10
Holbeach St Mark's Lincs 49 N7
Holbeach St Matthew Lincs 49 P7
Holbeck Notts 57 R12
Holbeck Woodhouse Notts 57 R12
Holberrow Green Worcs 36 D9
Holbeton Devon 5 Q10
Holborn Gt Lon 21 P6
Holborough Kent 12 D3
Holbrook Derbys 47 L5
Holbrook Sheff 57 P10
Holbrook Suffk 41 L13
Holbrook Moor Derbys 47 L4
Holbrooks Covtry 36 K4
Holburn Nthumb 85 Q11
Holbury Hants 9 N8
Holcombe Devon 6 C10
Holcombe Somset 17 S7
Holcombe Rogus Devon 16 E13
Holcot Nhants 37 U7
Holden Lancs 62 F10
Holdenby Nhants 37 S7
Holden Gate Calder 56 C2
Holder's Green Essex 22 F2
Holdgate Shrops 35 N3
Holdingham Lincs 48 G4
Holditch Dorset 6 K4
Holdsworth Calder 63 M14
Holehouse Derbys 56 F8
Hole-in-the-Wall Herefs 28 B2
Holemoor Devon 14 K11
Hole Street W Susx 10 J8
Holford Somset 16 G8
Holgate C York 64 D9
Holker Cumb 61 R4
Holkham Norfk 50 E5
Hollacombe Devon 14 J12
Holland Fen Lincs 48 K4
Holland Lees Lancs 55 M5
Holland-on-Sea Essex 23 S4
Hollandstoun Ork 106 w14
Hollee D & G 75 Q12
Hollesley Suffk 41 Q12
Hollicombe Torbay 6 A12
Hollingbourne Kent 12 F4
Hollingbury Br & H 11 N9
Hollingdon Bucks 30 J7
Hollingthorpe Leeds 63 T13
Hollington Derbys 46 H6
Hollington Staffs 46 E6
Hollingworth Tamesd 56 F7
Hollinlane Ches E 55 T10
Hollins Bury 55 T5
Hollins Derbys 57 M12
Hollins Staffs 46 C4
Hollinsclough Staffs 56 G13
Hollins End Sheff 57 N10
Hollins Green Warrtn 55 Q8
Hollins Lane Lancs 61 T9
Hollinswood Wrekin 45 R12
Hollinwood Shrops 45 M6
Hollingrove E Susx 12 C11
Hollocombe Devon 15 P10
Holloway Derbys 46 K2
Holloway Gt Lon 21 P5
Holloway Wilts 8 B2
Hollowell Nhants 37 S6
Hollowmoor Heath Ches W 55 L13
Hollows D & G 75 S10
Hollybush Caerph 27 M7
Hollybush E Ayrs 81 M9
Hollybush Herefs 35 S13
Holly End Norfk 49 Q12
Holly Green Worcs 35 U12
Hollyhurst Ches E 45 N5
Hollym E R Yk 59 P1
Hollywood Worcs 36 E5
Holmbridge Kirk 56 H5
Holmbury St Mary Surrey 10 J2
Holmbush Cnwll 3 Q6
Holmcroft Staffs 46 B9
Holme Cambs 38 J3
Holme Cumb 61 U4
Holme Kirk 56 H5
Holme N Linc 58 F5
Holme N York 63 T3
Holme Notts 48 B2
Holme Chapel Lancs 62 H14
Holme Green N York 64 D11
Holme Hale Norfk 50 E12
Holme Lacy Herefs 35 N13
Holme Marsh Herefs 34 H10
Holme next the Sea Norfk 50 B5
Holme on the Wolds E R Yk 65 M10
Holme Pierrepont Notts 47 R6
Holmer Herefs 35 M12
Holmer Green Bucks 20 F3
Holme St Cuthbert Cumb 66 H3
Holmes Chapel Ches E 55 S13
Holmesfield Derbys 57 M11
Holmes Hill E Susx 11 S8
Holmeswood Lancs 54 K3
Holmethorpe Surrey 21 N12
Holme upon Spalding Moor E R Yk 64 J12
Holmewood Derbys 57 P13
Holmfield Calder 63 M14
Holmfirth Kirk 56 H5
Holmhead E Ayrs 81 R8
Holmpton E R Yk 59 Q2
Holmrook Cumb 66 G13
Holmsford Bridge Crematorium N Ayrs 81 M5
Holmshurst E Susx 12 B10
Holmside Dur 69 R3
Holmwrangle Cumb 67 R3
Holne Devon 5 S7
Holnest Dorset 7 S3
Holnicote Somset 16 B7
Holsworthy Devon 14 H12
Holsworthy Beacon Devon 14 J11
Holt Dorset 8 E8
Holt Norfk 50 J6
Holt Wilts 18 C8
Holt Worcs 35 T8
Holt Wrexhm 44 K3
Holtby C York 64 F9
Holt End Worcs 36 E7
Holt Fleet Worcs 35 T8
Holt Green Lancs 54 J5
Holt Heath Dorset 8 F8
Holt Heath Worcs 35 T8
Holton Oxon 30 D11
Holton Somset 17 S11
Holton Suffk 41 R5
Holton cum Beckering Lincs 58 K10
Holton Heath Dorset 8 C10
Holton Hill E Susx 12 C10
Holton le Clay Lincs 59 N6
Holton le Moor Lincs 58 J7
Holton St Mary Suffk 40 J13
Holt Street Kent 13 Q5
Holtye E Susx 11 R3
Holway Flints 54 E11
Holwell Dorset 7 S2
Holwell Herts 31 Q6
Holwell Leics 47 T9
Holwell Oxon 29 P6
Holwick Dur 68 K7
Holworth Dorset 7 U8
Holybourne Hants 10 A2
Holy Cross Worcs 36 B5
Holyfield Essex 31 U12
Holyhead IoA 52 B6
Holy Island IoA 52 C6
Holy Island Nthumb 85 S10
Holy Island Nthumb 85 S10
Holymoorside Derbys 57 M13
Holyport W & M 20 E7
Holystone Nthumb 76 K5
Holytown N Lans 82 E6
Holytown Crematorium N Lans 82 E6
Holywell C Beds 31 M9
Holywell Cambs 39 M6
Holywell Cnwll 2 K5
Holywell Dorset 7 Q4
Holywell Flints 54 E11
Holywell Nthumb 77 S11
Holywell Warwks 36 H7
Holywell Green Calder 56 G3
Holywell Lake Somset 16 F12
Holywell Row Suffk 40 B5
Holywood D & G 74 H9
Holywood Village D & G 74 J10
Homer Shrops 45 P13
Homer Green Sefton 54 H6
Homersfield Suffk 41 N3
Homescales Cumb 62 B2
Hom Green Herefs 28 A3
Homington Wilts 8 G3
Honeyborough Pembks 24 F9
Honeybourne Worcs 36 F12
Honeychurch Devon 15 P12
Honey Hill Kent 13 M3
Honeystreet Wilts 18 H8
Honey Tye Suffk 40 G13
Honiley Warwks 36 H6
Honing Norfk 51 P8
Honingham Norfk 50 K11
Honington Lincs 48 D5
Honington Suffk 40 F6
Honington Warwks 36 J12
Honiton Devon 6 G4
Honley Kirk 56 H4
Honnington Wrekin 45 R10
Honor Oak Crematorium Gt Lon 21 Q8
Hoo Kent 13 Q3
Hoobrook Worcs 35 T6
Hood Green Barns 57 M6
Hood Hill Rothm 57 N7
Hooe C Plym 5 N10
Hooe E Susx 12 C13
Hoo End Herts 31 Q8
Hoo Green Ches E 55 R10
Hoohill Bpool 61 Q12
Hook Cambs 39 P2
Hook Devon 6 K3
Hook E R Yk 58 C1
Hook Gt Lon 21 L10
Hook Hants 9 Q7
Hook Hants 20 B12
Hook Pembks 24 G8
Hook Wilts 29 L11
Hookagate Shrops 45 L12
Hook Bank Worcs 35 T12
Hooke Dorset 7 P4
Hook End Essex 22 E7
Hookgate Staffs 45 R6
Hook Green Kent 12 C8
Hook Green Kent 22 F13
Hook Norton Oxon 37 L14
Hook Street Gloucs 28 C8
Hook Street Wilts 29 L11
Hookway Devon 15 U13
Hookwood Surrey 11 M2
Hooley Surrey 21 N11
Hooley Bridge Rochdl 56 C4
Hoo Meavy Devon 5 N7
Hoo St Werburgh Medway 22 J13
Hooton Ches W 54 J11
Hooton Levitt Rothm 57 R8
Hooton Pagnell Donc 57 Q5
Hooton Roberts Rothm 57 Q7
Hopcrofts Holt Oxon 29 U2
Hope Derbys 56 J10
Hope Devon 5 R12
Hope Flints 44 H2
Hope Powys 44 G12
Hope Shrops 44 H13
Hope Staffs 46 F3
Hope Bagot Shrops 35 N6
Hope Bowdler Shrops 35 L2
Hope End Green Essex 22 E3
Hopehouse Border 75 Q2
Hopeman Moray 103 T2
Hope Mansell Herefs 28 B4
Hopesay Shrops 34 J4
Hopetown Wakefd 57 N2
Hope under Dinmore Herefs 35 M10
Hopgrove C York 64 E9
Hopperton N York 63 U8
Hop Pole Lincs 48 J11
Hopsford Warwks 37 M4
Hopstone Shrops 35 S2
Hopton Derbys 46 J3
Hopton Shrops 44 J9
Hopton Staffs 46 B8
Hopton Suffk 40 G5
Hopton Cangeford Shrops 35 M4
Hopton Castle Shrops 34 J5
Hoptonheath Shrops 34 J5
Hopton on Sea Norfk 51 T14
Hopton Wafers Shrops 35 P5
Hopwas Staffs 46 G13
Hopwood Rochdl 56 C5
Hopwood Worcs 36 D5
Hopwood Park Services Worcs 36 D6
Horam E Susx 11 T7
Horbling Lincs 48 H6
Horbury Wakefd 57 L3
Horcott Gloucs 29 N7
Horden Dur 70 F4
Horderley Shrops 34 K3
Hordle Hants 8 K9
Hordley Shrops 44 J7
Horeb Carmth 25 S9
Horeb Cerdgn 32 G12
Horfield Bristl 28 A12
Horham Suffk 41 M6
Horkesley Heath Essex 23 N2
Horkstow N Linc 58 G3
Horley Oxon 37 M12
Horley Surrey 11 M2
Hornblotton Green Somset 17 Q10
Hornby Lancs 62 B6
Hornby N York 69 R14
Hornby N York 70 E11
Horncastle Lincs 59 N13
Hornchurch Gt Lon 22 D10
Horncliffe Nthumb 85 N9
Horndean Border 85 N9
Horndean Hants 9 U6
Horndon Devon 5 N4
Horndon on the Hill Thurr 22 G11
Horne Surrey 11 N2
Horner Somset 16 B7
Horne Row Essex 22 J7
Horners Green Suffk 40 G12
Horney Common E Susx 11 R5
Horn Hill Bucks 20 H4
Horning Norfk 51 P10
Horninghold Leics 38 B1
Horninglow Staffs 46 H8
Horningsea Cambs 39 Q8
Horningsham Wilts 18 B12
Horningtoft Norfk 50 F9
Horningtops Cnwll 4 H8
Hornsbury Somset 6 K2
Hornsby Cumb 67 R2
Hornsbygate Cumb 67 R2
Horns Cross Devon 14 J8
Horns Cross E Susx 12 F11
Hornsea E R Yk 65 R10
Hornsey Gt Lon 21 P5
Horn's Green Gt Lon 21 S11
Horn Street Kent 13 N8
Hornton Oxon 37 L11
Horpit Swindn 29 P11
Horra Shet 106 u4
Horrabridge Devon 5 N7
Horringer Suffk 40 D8
Horringford IoW 9 Q11
Horrocks Fold Bolton 55 R4
Horrocksford Lancs 62 F11
Horsacott Devon 15 M6
Horsebridge Devon 5 L5
Horsebridge E Susx 11 T8
Horsebridge Hants 9 L2
Horsebridge Shrops 44 J12
Horsebridge Staffs 46 C3
Horsebrook Staffs 45 U11
Horsecastle N Som 17 M3
Horsedown Cnwll 2 G10
Horsehay Wrekin 45 Q12
Horseheath Cambs 39 T11
Horsehouse N York 63 L3
Horsell Surrey 20 G11
Horseman's Green Wrexhm 44 K5
Horsenden Bucks 30 G12
Horsey Norfk 51 S9
Horsey Somset 16 K9
Horsey Corner Norfk 51 S9
Horsford Norfk 51 L10
Horsforth Leeds 63 Q12
Horsham W Susx 10 K4
Horsham Worcs 35 R9
Horsham St Faith Norfk 51 M10
Horsington Lincs 59 L13
Horsington Somset 17 T12
Horsley Derbys 47 L5
Horsley Gloucs 28 F8
Horsley Nthumb 76 G6
Horsley Nthumb 77 M12
Horsley Cross Essex 23 R2
Horsleycross Street Essex 23 R2
Horsley-Gate Derbys 57 M11
Horsleyhill Border 76 A2
Horsley's Green Bucks 20 C4
Horsley Woodhouse Derbys 47 L5
Horsmonden Kent 12 D7
Horspath Oxon 30 C11
Horstead Norfk 51 N10
Horsted Keynes W Susx 11 P5
Horton Bucks 30 K9
Horton Dorset 8 E7
Horton Lancs 62 H9
Horton Nhants 38 B10
Horton S Glos 28 E11
Horton Shrops 45 L8
Horton Somset 6 K2
Horton Staffs 46 B2
Horton Surrey 21 L10
Horton Swans 25 S13
Horton W & M 20 H7
Horton Wilts 18 F8
Horton Wrekin 45 Q11
Horton Cross Somset 16 K13
Horton-cum-Studley Oxon 30 C10
Horton Green Ches W 45 L4
Horton Heath Hants 9 P5
Horton-in-Ribblesdale N York 62 G5
Horton Kirby Kent 21 U9
Horwich Bolton 55 P4
Horwich End Derbys 56 F10
Horwood Devon 15 M7
Hoscar Lancs 55 L4
Hoscote Border 75 S3
Hose Leics 47 T8
Hosey Hill Kent 21 S12
Hosh P & K 90 C7
Hoswick Shet 106 u11
Hotham E R Yk 64 K13
Hothfield Kent 12 J7
Hoton Leics 47 Q9
Hott Nthumb 76 F8
Hough Ches E 45 R3
Hough Ches E 56 C11
Hougham Lincs 48 C5
Hough End Leeds 63 Q13
Hough Green Halton 55 L9
Hough-on-the-Hill Lincs 48 D4
Houghton Cambs 39 L6
Houghton Cumb 75 T14
Houghton Hants 9 L2
Houghton Nthumb 77 N12
Houghton Pembks 24 G9
Houghton W Susx 10 G8
Houghton Conquest C Beds 31 M4
Houghton Gate Dur 70 D2
Houghton Green E Susx 12 H11
Houghton Green Warrtn 55 P8
Houghton le Side Darltn 69 R8
Houghton-le-Spring Sundld 70 D3
Houghton on the Hill Leics 47 S13
Houghton Regis C Beds 31 M8
Houghton St Giles Norfk 50 F6
Hound Green Hants 20 B11
Houndslow Border 84 G9
Houndsmoor Somset 16 F11
Houndwood Border 85 L6
Hounslow Gt Lon 20 K7
Househill Highld 103 N4
Houses Hill Kirk 56 J3
Housieside Abers 105 P10
Houston Rens 88 K12
Houstry Highld 112 E10
Houton Ork 106 s19
Hove Br & H 11 M10
Hove Edge Calder 56 H2
Hoveringham Notts 47 S4
Hoveton Norfk 51 P10
Hovingham N York 64 F4
Howbrook Barns 57 M7
How Caple Herefs 28 B1
Howden E R Yk 64 C14
Howden-le-Wear Dur 69 Q6
Howe Highld 112 H4
Howe IoM 60 b9
Howe N York 63 T3
Howe Norfk 51 N14
Howe Bridge Wigan 55 Q6
Howe Bridge Crematorium Wigan 55 Q6
Howe Green Essex 22 H7
Howegreen Essex 22 K7
Howell Lincs 48 H4
How End C Beds 31 M4
Howe of Teuchar Abers 105 M6
Howes D & G 75 N12
Howe Street Essex 22 G5
Howe Street Essex 39 U14
Howey Powys 34 C9
Howgate Cumb 66 E8
Howgate Mdloth 83 P7
Howgill Lancs 62 G10
Howick Nthumb 77 R2
Howle Wrekin 45 Q9
Howle Hill Herefs 28 B3
Howlett End Essex 39 S14
Howley Somset 6 J3
How Mill Cumb 67 R1
Howmore W Isls 106 c15
Hownam Border 76 F2
Howrigg Cumb 67 M3
Howsham N Linc 58 H6
Howsham N York 64 G7
Howtel Nthumb 85 M12
Howt Green Kent 12 G2
Howton Herefs 27 S2
Howtown Cumb 67 P9
How Wood Herts 31 P12
Howwood Rens 88 J13
Hoxa Ork 106 t20
Hoxne Suffk 41 L5
Hoy Ork 106 r20
Hoylake Wirral 54 F9
Hoyland Common Barns 57 N6
Hoyland Nether Barns 57 N6
Hoyland Swaine Barns 57 L6
Hoyle W Susx 10 E7
Hoyle Mill Barns 57 N5
Hubberholme N York 62 J4
Hubberston Pembks 24 E9
Hubbert's Bridge Lincs 49 L5
Huby N York 63 R10
Huby N York 64 D6
Huccaby Devon 5 R6
Hucclecote Gloucs 28 G4
Hucking Kent 12 F4
Hucknall Notts 47 P4
Huddersfield Kirk 56 H3
Huddersfield Crematorium Kirk 56 H2
Huddington Worcs 36 B9
Hudnall Herts 31 M10
Hudswell N York 69 P12
Huggate E R Yk 64 K8
Hugglescote Leics 47 M11
Hughenden Valley Bucks 20 E3
Hughley Shrops 45 N14
Hugh Town IoS 2 c2
Huish Devon 15 M10
Huish Wilts 18 H8
Huish Champflower Somset 16 E11
Huish Episcopi Somset 17 M11
Huisinis W Isls 106 e7
Hulcote C Beds 30 K5
Hulcote Nhants 37 T11
Hulcott Bucks 30 J9
Hulham Devon 6 D8
Hulland Derbys 46 H4
Hulland Ward Derbys 46 J4
Hullavington Wilts 18 C4
Hull Bridge E R Yk 65 P11
Hullbridge Essex 22 K8
Hull, Kingston upon C KuH 65 P14
Hulme Manch 55 T7
Hulme Staffs 46 B4
Hulme Warrtn 55 P8
Hulme End Staffs 46 F2
Hulme Walfield Ches E 55 T13
Hulse Heath Ches E 55 R10
Hulton Lane Ends Bolton 55 Q5
Hulverstone IoW 9 M12
Hulver Street Norfk 50 F11
Hulver Street Suffk 41 S3
Humber Devon 6 A9
Humber Herefs 35 M9
Humber Bridge N Linc 58 H2
Humberside Airport N Linc 58 J4
Humberston NE Lin 59 P5
Humberstone C Leic 47 R12
Humberton N York 63 U6
Humbie E Loth 84 D6
Humbleton E R Yk 65 S13
Humbleton Nthumb 85 P13
Humby Lincs 48 F7
Hume Border 84 J10
Humshaugh Nthumb 76 J11
Huna Highld 112 J2
Huncoat Lancs 62 F13
Huncote Leics 47 P14
Hundalee Border 76 C2
Hundall Derbys 57 N11
Hunderthwaite Dur 69 L8
Hundleby Lincs 59 Q13
Hundle Houses Lincs 48 K3
Hundleton Pembks 24 G10
Hundon Suffk 40 B11
Hundred End Lancs 54 K2
Hundred House Powys 34 D10
Hungarton Leics 47 S12
Hungerford Hants 8 H6
Hungerford Somset 16 D8
Hungerford W Berk 19 M7
Hungerford Newtown W Berk 19 N6
Hunger Hill Bolton 55 Q5
Hunger Hill Lancs 55 M4
Hungerstone Herefs 34 K13
Hungerton Lincs 48 C8
Hungryhatton Shrops 45 Q8
Hunmanby N York 65 P4
Hunningham Warwks 37 L7
Hunnington Worcs 36 C4
Hunsbury Hill Nhants 37 T9
Hunsdon Herts 22 B5
Hunsingore N York 63 U9
Hunslet Leeds 63 S13
Hunsonby Cumb 67 S5
Hunstanton Norfk 49 U5
Hunstanworth Dur 68 K3
Hunsterson Ches E 45 Q4
Hunston Suffk 40 G7
Hunston W Susx 10 D10
Hunston Green Suffk 40 G7
Hunstrete BaNES 17 R4
Hunsworth Kirk 56 J1
Hunt End Worcs 36 D8
Hunter's Inn Devon 15 Q3
Hunter's Quay Ag & B 88 E10
Huntham Somset 16 K11
Hunthill Lodge Angus 98 H9
Huntingdon Cambs 38 K6
Huntingfield Suffk 41 P6
Huntingford Dorset 17 V11
Huntington C York 64 E8
Huntington Ches W 54 K14
Huntington E Loth 84 D4
Huntington Herefs 34 G10
Huntington Herefs 35 L12
Huntington Staffs 46 C11
Huntley Gloucs 28 D4
Huntly Abers 104 G8
Hunton Hants 19 Q12
Hunton Kent 12 D6
Hunton N York 63 P1
Hunton Bridge Herts 31 N12
Hunt's Corner Norfk 40 J3
Huntscott Somset 16 B8
Hunt's Cross Lpool 54 K9
Hunts Green Bucks 30 J12
Hunts Green Warwks 36 G1
Huntsham Devon 16 D12
Huntshaw Devon 15 M8
Huntshaw Cross Devon 15 M8
Huntspill Somset 16 K7
Huntstile Somset 16 J10
Huntworth Somset 16 K10
Hunwick Dur 69 Q6
Hunworth Norfk 50 J6
Hurcott Somset 17 L13
Hurdcott Wilts 8 H2
Hurdsfield Ches E 56 D12
Hurley W & M 20 D6
Hurley Warwks 36 H1
Hurley Bottom W & M 20 D6
Hurley Common Warwks 36 H1
Hurlford E Ayrs 81 P5
Hurlston Green Lancs 54 J4
Hurn Dorset 8 G9
Hurn's End Lincs 49 P4
Hursley Hants 9 N3
Hurst Dorset 7 U6
Hurst N York 69 M12
Hurst Somset 17 N13
Hurst Wokham 20 C8
Hurstbourne Priors Hants 19 P11
Hurstbourne Tarrant Hants 19 N10
Hurst Green E Susx 12 D10
Hurst Green Essex 23 Q4
Hurst Green Lancs 62 D12
Hurst Green Surrey 21 R12
Hurst Hill Dudley 36 B2
Hurstley Herefs 34 J11
Hurstpierpoint W Susx 11 M7
Hurst Wickham W Susx 11 M7
Hurstwood Lancs 62 H13
Hurtiso Ork 106 u19
Hurtmore Surrey 20 F13
Hurworth Burn Dur 70 F6
Hurworth-on-Tees Darltn 70 D11
Hurworth Place Darltn 69 S11
Hury Dur 69 L9
Husbands Bosworth Leics 37 R4
Husborne Crawley C Beds 31 L5
Husthwaite N York 64 C5
Hutcherleigh Devon 5 T10
Hutcliffe Wood Crematorium Sheff 57 M10
Hut Green N York 57 S2
Huthwaite Notts 47 N2
Huttoft Lincs 59 T11
Hutton Border 85 N8
Hutton Cumb 67 P7
Hutton E R Yk 65 N9
Hutton Essex 22 F8
Hutton Lancs 55 L1
Hutton N Som 17 L5
Hutton Bonville N York 70 D12
Hutton Buscel N York 65 M3
Hutton Conyers N York 63 S5
Hutton Cranswick E R Yk 65 N9
Hutton End Cumb 67 Q5
Hutton Hang N York 63 P2
Hutton Henry Dur 70 F5
Hutton-le-Hole N York 64 G1
Hutton Lowcross R & Cl 70 J10
Hutton Magna Dur 69 P10
Hutton Mulgrave N York 71 P11
Hutton Roof Cumb 62 B4
Hutton Roof Cumb 67 N6
Hutton Rudby N York 70 G11
Hutton Sessay N York 64 B4
Hutton Wandesley N York 64 C9
Huxham Devon 6 B5
Huxham Green Somset 17 Q9
Huxley Ches W 45 M1
Huyton Knows 54 K8
Hycemoor Cumb 60 K2
Hyde Gloucs 28 G7
Hyde Hants 8 H6
Hyde Tamesd 56 D8
Hyde End Wokham 20 B9
Hyde Heath Bucks 30 K12
Hyde Lea Staffs 46 B10
Hydestile Surrey 10 F2
Hykeham Moor Lincs 58 F13
Hylands House & Park Essex 22 G7
Hyndford Bridge S Lans 82 H10
Hynish Ag & B 92 B11
Hyssington Powys 34 H2
Hystfield Gloucs 28 C8
Hythe Essex 23 P2
Hythe Hants 9 N7
Hythe Kent 13 N9
Hythe Somset 17 M6
Hythe End W & M 20 H8
Hyton Cumb 60 K2

I

Ibberton Dorset 7 U3
Ible Derbys 46 H2
Ibsley Hants 8 H7
Ibstock Leics 47 M12
Ibstone Bucks 20 C4
Ibthorpe Hants 19 N10
Iburndale N York 71 Q11
Ibworth Hants 19 S10
Icelton N Som 17 L3
Ichrachan Ag & B 94 E12
Ickburgh Norfk 40 D1
Ickenham Gt Lon 20 J5
Ickford Bucks 30 D11
Ickham Kent 13 P4
Ickleford Herts 31 Q6
Icklesham E Susx 12 G12
Ickleton Cambs 39 Q12
Icklingham Suffk 40 C6
Ickornshaw N York 62 K11
Ickwell Green C Beds 38 J11
Icomb Gloucs 29 P3
Idbury Oxon 29 P4
Iddesleigh Devon 15 N11
Ide Devon 6 A6
Ideford Devon 6 A9
Ide Hill Kent 21 S12
Iden E Susx 12 H11
Iden Green Kent 12 D8
Iden Green Kent 12 F9
Idle C Brad 63 P12
Idless Cnwll 3 L7
Idlicote Warwks 36 J12
Idmiston Wilts 18 J13
Idole Carmth 25 R7
Idridgehay Derbys 46 J4
Idrigill Highld 100 c3
Idstone Oxon 29 Q11
Iffley Oxon 30 B12
Ifield W Susx 11 M3
Ifold W Susx 10 G4
Iford Bmouth 8 G10
Iford E Susx 11 Q9
Ifton Mons 27 T10
Ifton Heath Shrops 44 H6
Ightfield Shrops 45 N6
Ightham Kent 21 U11
Iken Suffk 41 R9
Ilam Staffs 46 F3
Ilchester Somset 17 P12
Ilderton Nthumb 77 L1
Ilford Gt Lon 21 R5
Ilford Somset 17 L13
Ilfracombe Devon 15 M3
Ilkeston Derbys 47 N5
Ilketshall St Andrew Suffk 41 Q3
Ilketshall St John Suffk 41 Q3
Ilketshall St Lawrence Suffk 41 Q4
Ilketshall St Margaret Suffk 41 P3
Ilkley C Brad 63 N10
Illand Cnwll 4 H5
Illey Dudley 36 C4
Illidge Green Ches E 55 S14
Illingworth Calder 63 M14
Illogan Cnwll 2 H8
Illston on the Hill Leics 47 T14
Ilmer Bucks 30 G11
Ilmington Warwks 36 H12
Ilminster Somset 7 L2
Ilsington Devon 5 T5
Ilsington Dorset 7 U6
Ilston Swans 25 U12
Ilton N York 63 P4
Ilton Somset 17 L13
Imachar N Ayrs 79 R7
Immingham NE Lin 59 L4
Immingham Dock NE Lin 59 L3
Impington Cambs 39 P8
Ince Ches W 55 L11
Ince Blundell Sefton 54 H6
Ince-in-Makerfield Wigan 55 N6
Inchbae Lodge Hotel Highld 108 G11
Inchbare Angus 99 L10
Inchberry Moray 104 C4
Incheril Highld 107 T12
Inchinnan Rens 89 L12
Inchlaggan Highld 101 T11
Inchmichael P & K 90 K6
Inchnacardoch Hotel Highld 102 C13
Inchnadamph Highld 110 F12
Inchture P & K 91 L6
Inchvuilt Highld 101 U4
Inchyra P & K 90 J7
Indian Queens Cnwll 3 N5
Ingate Place Suffk 41 R3
Ingatestone Essex 22 F8
Ingbirchworth Barns 56 K5
Ingerthorpe N York 63 R6
Ingestre Staffs 46 C9
Ingham Lincs 58 F10
Ingham Norfk 51 Q8
Ingham Suffk 40 E6
Ingham Corner Norfk 51 Q8
Ingleborough Norfk 49 Q10
Ingleby Derbys 46 K8
Ingleby Arncliffe N York 70 F12
Ingleby Barwick S on T 70 F10
Ingleby Cross N York 70 G12
Ingleby Greenhow N York 70 J11
Ingleigh Green Devon 15 P11
Inglesbatch BaNES 17 T4
Inglesham Swindn 29 P8
Ingleston D & G 74 J12
Ingleton Dur 69 Q8
Ingleton N York 62 D5
Inglewhite Lancs 61 U12
Ingmanthorpe N York 63 U9
Ingoe Nthumb 77 L11
Ingol Lancs 61 U13
Ingoldisthorpe Norfk 49 U7
Ingoldmells Lincs 59 U13
Ingoldsby Lincs 48 F8
Ingram Nthumb 77 L2
Ingrave Essex 22 F9
Ingrow C Brad 63 M12
Ings Cumb 67 P13
Ingst S Glos 28 A10
Ingthorpe Rutlnd 48 E12
Ingworth Norfk 51 L8
Inkberrow Worcs 36 D9
Inkerman Dur 69 P5
Inkhorn Abers 105 Q8
Inkpen W Berk 19 N8
Inkstack Highld 112 G2
Inmarsh Wilts 18 D8
Innellan Ag & B 88 E11
Innerleithen Border 83 R11
Innerleven Fife 91 N11
Innermessan D & G 72 D7
Innerwick E Loth 84 J4
Innesmill Moray 104 B3
Innsworth Gloucs 28 G3
Insch Abers 104 J10
Insh Highld 97 N3
Inskip Lancs 61 T12
Inskip Moss Side Lancs 61 T12
Instow Devon 15 L6
Insworke Cnwll 5 L10
Intake Sheff 57 N10
Inver Abers 98 C5
Inver Highld 109 R8
Inver P & K 90 F3
Inverailort Highld 93 T2
Inveralligin Highld 107 P13
Inverallochy Abers 105 S2
Inveran Highld 108 K5
Inveraray Ag & B 88 C4
Inverarish Highld 100 e6
Inverarity Angus 91 Q3
Inverarnan Stirlg 88 H2
Inverasdale Highld 107 P8
Inverbeg Ag & B 88 H6
Inverbervie Abers 99 Q9
Inverboyndie Abers 104 K3
Invercreran House Hotel Ag & B 94 E9
Inverdruie Highld 103 N13
Inveresk E Loth 83 R4
Inveresragan Ag & B 94 D11
Inverey Abers 97 T6
Inverfarigaig Highld 102 F11
Inverfolla Ag & B 94 D10
Invergarry Highld 96 C3
Invergeldie P & K 95 U13
Invergloy Highld 101 U14
Invergordon Highld 109 N11
Invergowrie P & K 91 M5
Inverguseran Highld 100 g9
Inverhadden P & K 95 T7
Inverherive Hotel Stirlg 95 M13
Inverie Highld 100 g9
Inverinan Ag & B 87 T2
Inverinate Highld 101 N7
Inverkeilor Angus 91 U2
Inverkeithing Fife 83 M2
Inverkeithny Abers 104 J6
Inverkip Inver 88 F11
Inverkirkaig Highld 110 B13
Inverlael Highld 108 B7
Inverlair Highld 96 C8
Inverliever Lodge Ag & B 87 R4
Inverlochy Ag & B 94 H13
Invermark Angus 98 G7
Invermoriston Highld 102 D12
Invernaver Highld 111 Q4
Inverness Highld 102 J6
Inverness Airport Highld 103 L5
Inverness Crematorium Highld 102 H7
Invernoaden Ag & B 88 D6
Inveroran Hotel Ag & B 94 K10
Inverquharity Angus 98 G12
Inverquhomery Abers 105 S6
Inverroy Highld 96 B7
Inversanda Highld 94 C7
Invershiel Highld 101 N8
Invershin Highld 108 K5
Invershore Highld 112 F9
Inversnaid Hotel Stirlg 88 H4
Inverugie Abers 105 T6
Inveruglas Ag & B 88 H4
Inveruglass Highld 97 N3
Inverurie Abers 105 M11
Inwardleigh Devon 15 N13
Inworth Essex 23 L4
Iona Ag & B 92 H13
Iping W Susx 10 D6
iPort Logistics Park Donc 57 T7
Ipplepen Devon 5 U7
Ipsden Oxon 19 T3
Ipstones Staffs 46 D4
Ipswich Suffk 41 L12
Ipswich Crematorium Suffk 41 L11
Irby Wirral 54 G10
Irby in the Marsh Lincs 59 S14
Irby upon Humber NE Lin 59 L6
Irchester Nhants 38 D7
Ireby Cumb 66 K5
Ireby Lancs 62 D4
Ireland C Beds 31 P4
Ireleth Cumb 61 N4
Ireshopeburn Dur 68 J5
Ireton Wood Derbys 46 J4
Irlam Salfd 55 R8
Irnham Lincs 48 F8
Iron Acton S Glos 28 C11
Iron Bridge Cambs 49 Q14
Ironbridge Wrekin 45 Q13
Ironbridge Gorge Wrekin 45 Q13
Iron Cross Warwks 36 E10
Ironmacannie D & G 73 R4
Irons Bottom Surrey 21 M13
Ironville Derbys 47 M3
Irstead Norfk 51 Q9
Irthington Cumb 75 U13
Irthlingborough Nhants 38 D6
Irton N York 65 N3
Irvine N Ayrs 81 L5
Isauld Highld 112 A3
Isbister Shet 106 t4
Isbister Shet 106 v7
Isfield E Susx 11 Q7
Isham Nhants 38 C6
Isington Hants 10 B2
Islandpool Worcs 35 U4
Islay Ag & B 86 F10
Islay Airport Ag & B 78 E5
Isle Abbotts Somset 17 L12
Isle Brewers Somset 17 L12
Isleham Cambs 39 T6
Isle of Dogs Gt Lon 21 Q7
Isle of Grain Medway 23 L12
Isle of Lewis W Isls 106 i5
Isle of Man IoM 60 f5
Isle of Man Ronaldsway Airport IoM 60 d9
Isle of Mull Ag & B 93 Q11
Isle of Purbeck Dorset 8 E12
Isle of Sheppey Kent 12 J2
Isle of Skye Highld 100 d6
Isle of Thanet Kent 13 R2
Isle of Walney Cumb 61 M6
Isle of Whithorn D & G 73 M12
Isle of Wight IoW 9 Q11
Isle of Wight Crematorium IoW 9 Q10
Isleornsay Highld 100 g8
Isles of Scilly IoS 2 c2
Isles of Scilly St Mary's Airport IoS 2 c2
Islesteps D & G 74 J11
Islet Village Guern 6 e2
Isleworth Gt Lon 21 L7
Isley Walton Leics 47 M9
Islibhig W Isls 106 f6
Islington Gt Lon 21 P6
Islington Crematorium Gt Lon 21 N4
Islip Nhants 38 E5
Islip Oxon 30 B10
Islivig W Isls 106 f6
Isombridge Wrekin 45 P11
Istead Rise Kent 22 F13
Itchen Abbas Hants 9 Q2
Itchen Stoke Hants 9 R2
Itchingfield W Susx 10 J5
Itchington S Glos 28 C10
Itteringham Norfk 50 K7
Itton Devon 15 Q13
Itton Mons 27 T8
Itton Common Mons 27 T8
Ivegill Cumb 67 P4
Ivelet N York 68 K13
Iver Bucks 20 H6
Iver Heath Bucks 20 H6
Iveston Dur 69 P2
Ivinghoe Bucks 30 K9
Ivinghoe Aston Bucks 31 L9
Ivington Herefs 35 L9
Ivington Green Herefs 35 L9
Ivybridge Devon 5 Q9
Ivychurch Kent 12 K10
Ivy Cross Dorset 8 B4
Ivy Hatch Kent 21 U12
Ivy Todd Norfk 50 E12
Iwade Kent 12 H2
Iwerne Courtney Dorset 8 B6
Iwerne Minster Dorset 8 B6
Ixworth Suffk 40 F6
Ixworth Thorpe Suffk 40 F6

J

Jack Green Lancs 55 N1
Jack Hill N York 63 P9
Jack-in-the-Green Devon 6 D5
Jack's Bush Hants 19 L13
Jacksdale Notts 47 M3
Jackson Bridge Kirk 56 J5
Jackton S Lans 81 R2
Jacobstow Cnwll 14 E13
Jacobstowe Devon 15 N12
Jacobs Well Surrey 20 H12
Jameston Pembks 24 J11
Jamestown Highld 102 E4
Jamestown W Duns 88 J9
Janetstown Highld 112 E10
Janetstown Highld 112 J6
Jardine Hall D & G 75 M8
Jarrow S Tyne 77 S13
Jarvis Brook E Susx 11 S5
Jasper's Green Essex 22 H2
Jawcraig Falk 89 T10
Jaywick Essex 23 S5
Jealott's Hill Br For 20 E8
Jeater Houses N York 70 F14
Jedburgh Border 76 C1
Jeffreyston Pembks 24 J9
Jemimaville Highld 102 K2
Jerbourg Guern 6 e4
Jersey Jersey 7 d2
Jersey Airport Jersey 7 b2
Jersey Crematorium Jersey 7 d3
Jersey Marine Neath 26 C9
Jerusalem Lincs 58 F12
Jesmond N u Ty 77 R12
Jevington E Susx 11 T10
Jingle Street Mons 27 T5
Jockey End Herts 31 M10
Jodrell Bank Ches E 55 S12
Johnby Cumb 67 P6
John Lennon Airport Lpool 54 K10
John o' Groats Highld 112 J2
Johns Cross E Susx 12 D11
Johnshaven Abers 99 P10
Johnson Street Norfk 51 Q10
Johnston Pembks 24 F8
Johnstone D & G 75 P5
Johnstone Rens 88 K13
Johnstonebridge D & G 75 M7
Johnstown Carmth 25 Q7
Johnstown Wrexhm 44 H4
Joppa C Edin 83 R4
Joppa Cerdgn 33 L7
Joppa S Ayrs 81 N9
Jordans Bucks 20 G4
Jordanston Pembks 24 F4
Jordanthorpe Sheff 57 N10
Joyden's Wood Kent 22 D13
Jubilee Corner Kent 12 F6
Jump Barns 57 N6
Jumper's Town E Susx 11 R4
Juniper Nthumb 76 J14
Juniper Green C Edin 83 N5
Jura Ag & B 86 J9
Jurassic Coast Devon 6 K7
Jurby IoM 60 f3
Jurston Devon 5 R4

K

Kaber Cumb 68 G10
Kaimend S Lans 82 J9
Kames Ag & B 87 T11
Kames E Ayrs 82 C13
Kea Cnwll 3 L8
Keadby N Linc 58 D4
Keal Cotes Lincs 49 N1
Kearby Town End N York 63 S10
Kearsley Bolton 55 S6
Kearsley Nthumb 77 L10
Kearsney Kent 13 Q7
Kearstwick Cumb 62 C4
Kearton N York 69 L13
Keasden N York 62 E6
Keaton Devon 5 Q10
Keckwick Halton 55 N10
Keddington Lincs 59 P9
Keddington Corner Lincs 59 Q9
Kedington Suffk 40 B11
Kedleston Derbys 46 K5
Keelby Lincs 59 L4
Keele Staffs 45 T4
Keele Services Staffs 45 T5
Keele University Staffs 45 T4
Keeley Green Bed 38 F11
Keelham C Brad 63 M13
Keeres Green Essex 22 E5
Keeston Pembks 24 F7
Keevil Wilts 18 D9
Kegworth Leics 47 N8
Kehelland Cnwll 2 G8
Keig Abers 104 J12
Keighley C Brad 63 M11
Keighley Crematorium C Brad 63 L12
Keilarsbrae Clacks 90 C13
Keillour P & K 90 E6
Keiloch Abers 98 B5
Keils Ag & B 86 J12
Keinton Mandeville Somset 17 P10
Keir Mill D & G 74 G7
Keirsleywell Row Nthumb 68 G2
Keisby Lincs 48 F8
Keisley Cumb 68 F8
Keiss Highld 112 H4
Keith Moray 104 E5
Keithick P & K 90 K4
Keithock Angus 99 L11
Keithtown Highld 102 F4
Kelbrook Lancs 62 J11
Kelby Lincs 48 F5
Keld Cumb 67 S10
Keld N York 68 J12
Keld Head N York 64 H3
Keldholme N York 64 G2
Kelfield N Linc 58 D6
Kelfield N York 64 D12
Kelham Notts 47 U2
Kelhead D & G 75 M12
Kellacott Devon 5 L3
Kellamergh Lancs 61 S14
Kellas Angus 91 Q4
Kellas Moray 103 U5
Kellaton Devon 5 U13
Kelleth Cumb 68 E11
Kelling Norfk 50 J5
Kellington N York 57 S2
Kelloe Dur 70 D5
Kelloholm D & G 74 D3
Kells Cumb 66 E9
Kelly Devon 4 K4
Kelly Bray Cnwll 4 K6
Kelmarsh Nhants 37 T5
Kelmscott Oxon 29 P8
Kelsale Suffk 41 Q7
Kelsall Ches W 55 M13
Kelshall Herts 31 T5
Kelsick Cumb 66 J2
Kelso Border 84 J12
Kelstedge Derbys 57 M14
Kelstern Lincs 59 M9
Kelsterton Flints 54 G12
Kelston BaNES 17 T3
Keltneyburn P & K 95 V9
Kelton D & G 74 J11
Kelty Fife 90 H13
Kelvedon Essex 23 L4
Kelvedon Hatch Essex 22 E8
Kelynack Cnwll 2 B11
Kemacott Devon 15 Q3
Kemback Fife 91 P9
Kemberton Shrops 45 R13
Kemble Gloucs 28 J8
Kemble Wick Gloucs 28 J8
Kemerton Worcs 36 C13
Kemeys Commander Mons 27 Q7
Kemnay Abers 105 L12
Kempe's Corner Kent 12 K6
Kempley Gloucs 28 C2
Kempley Green Gloucs 28 C2
Kempsey Worcs 35 T11
Kempsford Gloucs 29 N8
Kemps Green Warwks 36 F6
Kempshott Hants 19 T10
Kempston Bed 38 F11
Kempston Hardwick Bed 31 M4
Kempton Shrops 34 J4
Kemp Town Br & H 11 N10
Kemsing Kent 21 U11
Kemsley Kent 12 H2
Kemsley Street Kent 12 F3
Kenardington Kent 12 J9
Kenchester Herefs 34 K12
Kencot Oxon 29 Q7
Kendal Cumb 67 R14
Kenderchurch Herefs 27 S2
Kendleshire S Glos 28 C12
Kenfig Brdgnd 26 E11
Kenfig Hill Brdgnd 26 E11
Kenilworth Warwks 36 J6
Kenley Gt Lon 21 P10
Kenley Shrops 45 N13
Kenmore Highld 107 N13
Kenmore P & K 95 V9
Kenn Devon 6 B7
Kenn N Som 17 M3
Kennacraig Ag & B 79 Q3
Kennall Vale Cnwll 2 J9
Kennards House Cnwll 4 H4
Kenneggy Cnwll 2 F11
Kennerleigh Devon 15 T11
Kennessee Green Sefton 54 J6
Kennet Clacks 90 D13
Kennethmont Abers 104 G10
Kennett Cambs 39 U7
Kennford Devon 6 B7
Kenninghall Norfk 40 H3
Kennington Kent 12 K6
Kennington Oxon 30 B12
Kennoway Fife 91 N11
Kenny Somset 16 K13
Kenny Hill Suffk 39 U5
Kennythorpe N York 64 H6
Kenovay Ag & B 92 B9
Kensaleyre Highld 100 d4
Kensington Gt Lon 21 N7
Kensington Palace Gt Lon 21 N6
Kensworth Common C Beds 31 M9
Kentallen Highld 94 E7
Kent and Sussex Crematorium Kent 11 T3
Kentchurch Herefs 27 S2
Kentford Suffk 40 B7
Kent Green Ches E 45 T2
Kentisbeare Devon 6 E3
Kentisbury Devon 15 P4
Kentisbury Ford Devon 15 P4
Kentish Town Gt Lon 21 N6
Kentmere Cumb 67 Q12
Kenton Devon 6 C8
Kenton Gt Lon 21 L5
Kenton N u Ty 77 Q12
Kenton Suffk 41 L7
Kenton Bankfoot N u Ty 77 Q12
Kentra Highld 93 R5
Kents Bank Cumb 61 R4
Kent's Green Gloucs 28 D3
Kent's Oak Hants 9 L4
Kent Street E Susx 12 E12
Kent Street Kent 12 C5
Kenwick Shrops 44 K7
Kenwyn Cnwll 3 L7
Kenyon Warrtn 55 P7
Keoldale Highld 110 H3
Keppoch Highld 101 M7
Kepwick N York 64 B1
Keresley Covtry 36 K4
Kermincham Ches E 55 T13
Kernborough Devon 5 T12
Kerne Bridge Herefs 28 A4
Kerrera Ag & B 93 U13
Kerridge Ches E 56 D11
Kerridge-end Ches E 56 D11
Kerris Cnwll 2 C11
Kerry Powys 34 D2
Kerrycroy Ag & B 88 D13
Kersall Notts 47 T1
Kersbrook Devon 6 E8
Kerscott Devon 15 P7
Kersey Suffk 40 H12
Kersey Tye Suffk 40 G12
Kersey Upland Suffk 40 G12
Kershader W Isls 106 i6
Kershopefoot Cumb 75 U9
Kersoe Worcs 36 C12
Kerswell Devon 6 E3
Kerswell Green Worcs 35 U11
Kerthen Wood Cnwll 2 F10
Kesgrave Suffk 41 M11
Kessingland Suffk 41 T3
Kessingland Beach Suffk 41 T3
Kestle Cnwll 3 P7
Kestle Mill Cnwll 3 L5
Keston Gt Lon 21 R10
Keswick Cumb 67 L8
Keswick Norfk 51 M13
Ketsby Lincs 59 Q11
Kettering Nhants 38 C5
Kettering Crematorium Nhants 38 C5
Ketteringham Norfk 51 L13
Kettins P & K 90 K4
Kettlebaston Suffk 40 G10
Kettlebridge Fife 91 M10
Kettlebrook Staffs 46 H13
Kettleburgh Suffk 41 N8
Kettle Green Herts 22 B4
Kettleholm D & G 75 M10
Kettleness N York 71 P9
Kettleshulme Ches E 56 E11
Kettlesing N York 63 Q8
Kettlesing Bottom N York 63 Q8
Kettlestone Norfk 50 G7
Kettlethorpe Lincs 58 D11
Kettletoft Ork 106 v16
Kettlewell N York 62 K5
Ketton Rutlnd 48 E13
Kew Gt Lon 21 L7
Kew Royal Botanic Gardens Gt Lon 21 L7
Kewstoke N Som 16 K4
Kexbrough Barns 57 M5
Kexby C York 64 G9
Kexby Lincs 58 E9
Key Green Ches E 56 C14
Key Green N York 71 P12
Keyham Leics 47 S12
Keyhaven Hants 9 L10
Keyingham E R Yk 59 M1
Keymer W Susx 11 N7
Keynsham BaNES 17 S3
Keysoe Bed 38 G8
Keysoe Row Bed 38 G8
Keyston Cambs 38 F5
Key Street Kent 12 G3
Keyworth Notts 47 R7
Kibbear Somset 16 H12
Kibblesworth Gatesd 69 R1
Kibworth Beauchamp Leics 37 S2
Kibworth Harcourt Leics 37 S2
Kidbrooke Gt Lon 21 R7
Kidburngill Cumb 66 G8
Kiddemore Green Staffs 45 U12
Kidderminster Worcs 35 T5
Kiddington Oxon 29 T3
Kidd's Moor Norfk 50 K13
Kidlington Oxon 29 U5
Kidmore End Oxon 19 U5
Kidsdale D & G 73 L12
Kidsgrove Staffs 45 T3
Kidstones N York 62 K3
Kidwelly Carmth 25 R9
Kiel Crofts Ag & B 94 C11
Kielder Nthumb 76 C7
Kielder Forest 76 C8
Kiells Ag & B 86 G12
Kilbarchan Rens 88 K13
Kilbeg Highld 100 f9
Kilberry Ag & B 79 N3
Kilbirnie N Ayrs 81 L2
Kilbride Ag & B 87 N10
Kilbride Ag & B 88 B12
Kilbuiack Moray 103 S3
Kilburn Derbys 47 L4
Kilburn Gt Lon 21 M6
Kilburn N York 64 C4
Kilby Leics 37 R1
Kilchamaig Ag & B 79 Q3
Kilchattan Ag & B 80 G2
Kilchattan Ag & B 86 F6
Kilcheran Ag & B 93 U11
Kilchoan Highld 93 M6
Kilchoman Ag & B 78 C3
Kilchrenan Ag & B 94 E14
Kilconquhar Fife 91 Q11
Kilcot Gloucs 28 C2
Kilcoy Highld 102 G5
Kilcreggan Ag & B 88 F9
Kildale N York 70 K11
Kildalloig Ag & B 79 P12
Kildary Highld 109 P10
Kildavaig Ag & B 87 T12
Kildavanan Ag & B 88 B12
Kildonan Highld 111 U12
Kildonan N Ayrs 80 E8
Kildonan Lodge Highld 111 U12
Kildonnan Highld 93 M1
Kildrochet House D & G 72 D8
Kildrummy Abers 104 F12
Kildwick N York 63 L10
Kilfinan Ag & B 87 S10
Kilfinnan Highld 96 B4
Kilford Denbgs 54 C13
Kilgetty Pembks 24 K9
Kilgrammie S Ayrs 80 K12
Kilgwrrwg Common Mons 27 T8
Kilham E R Yk 65 P7
Kilham Nthumb 85 M12
Kilkenneth Ag & B 92 A10
Kilkenzie Ag & B 79 M11
Kilkerran Ag & B 79 N12
Kilkhampton Cnwll 14 G10
Killamarsh Derbys 57 Q10
Killay Swans 25 V12
Killearn Stirlg 89 M8
Killen Highld 102 J4
Killerby Darltn 69 Q9
Killerton Devon 6 C4
Killichonan P & K 95 Q7
Killiechonate Highld 94 J2
Killiechronan Ag & B 93 N10
Killiecrankie P & K 97 Q11
Killilan Highld 101 N5
Killimster Highld 112 H5
Killin Stirlg 95 R12
Killinghall N York 63 R8
Killington Cumb 62 C2
Killington Devon 15 Q3
Killington Lake Services Cumb 62 B1
Killingworth N Tyne 77 R11
Killiow Cnwll 3 L8
Killochyett Border 84 D9
Kilmacolm Inver 88 J11
Kilmahog Stirlg 89 P4
Kilmahumaig Ag & B 87 P7
Kilmaluag Highld 100 d2
Kilmany Fife 91 N7
Kilmarnock E Ayrs 81 N5
Kilmartin Ag & B 87 Q6
Kilmaurs E Ayrs 81 N4
Kilmelford Ag & B 87 R3
Kilmersdon Somset 17 S6
Kilmeston Hants 9 R3
Kilmichael Ag & B 79 M11
Kilmichael Glassary Ag & B 87 R7
Kilmichael of Inverlussa Ag & B 87 P8
Kilmington Devon 6 J5
Kilmington Wilts 17 U9
Kilmington Common Wilts 17 U9
Kilmington Street Wilts 17 U9
Kilmorack Highld 102 E7
Kilmore Ag & B 94 B13
Kilmore Highld 100 f9
Kilmory Ag & B 87 N11
Kilmory Highld 93 N4
Kilmory N Ayrs 80 D8
Kilmuir Highld 100 b5
Kilmuir Highld 100 c2
Kilmuir Highld 102 J6
Kilmuir Highld 109 P10
Kilmun Ag & B 88 E9
Kilnave Ag & B 86 D11
Kilncadzow S Lans 82 G9
Kilndown Kent 12 D8
Kiln Green Wokham 20 D7
Kilnhill Cumb 66 K6
Kilnhouses Ches W 55 P13
Kilnhurst Rothm 57 Q7
Kilninver Ag & B 87 Q1
Kiln Pit Hill Nthumb 69 M1
Kilnsea E R Yk 59 R3
Kilnsey N York 62 K6
Kilnwick E R Yk 65 M10
Kilnwick Percy E R Yk 64 J10
Kiloran Ag & B 86 F6
Kilpatrick N Ayrs 79 S10
Kilpeck Herefs 27 S1
Kilpin E R Yk 58 C1
Kilpin Pike E R Yk 58 C1
Kilrenny Fife 91 S11
Kilsby Nhants 37 Q6
Kilspindie P & K 90 K6
Kilstay D & G 72 E12
Kilsyth N Lans 89 R10
Kiltarlity Highld 102 F7
Kilton R & Cl 71 M9
Kilton Thorpe R & Cl 71 L9
Kilvaxter Highld 100 c3
Kilve Somset 16 F8
Kilvington Notts 48 B5
Kilwinning N Ayrs 81 L4
Kimberley Norfk 50 J13
Kimberley Notts 47 N5
Kimberworth Rothm 57 P8
Kimblesworth Dur 69 S3
Kimble Wick Bucks 30 H11
Kimbolton Cambs 38 H7
Kimbolton Herefs 35 M8
Kimcote Leics 37 Q3
Kimmeridge Dorset 8 C13
Kimmerston Nthumb 85 P11
Kimpton Hants 19 L11
Kimpton Herts 31 Q9
Kimworthy Devon 14 H10
Kinbrace Highld 111 T10
Kinbuck Stirlg 89 S4
Kincaple Fife 91 Q8
Kincardine Fife 90 D14
Kincardine Highld 109 L7
Kincardine Bridge Fife 82 H1
Kincardine O'Neil Abers 98 K4
Kinclaven P & K 90 J4
Kincorth C Aber 99 S3
Kincorth House Moray 103 R3
Kincraig Highld 97 N2
Kincraigie P & K 90 E2
Kindallachan P & K 90 E2
Kinerarach Ag & B 79 M5
Kineton Gloucs 29 L2
Kineton Warwks 36 K10
Kinfauns P & K 90 J7
Kingarth Ag & B 80 F1
Kingcausie Abers 99 R4
Kingcoed Mons 27 S6
Kingerby Lincs 58 J8
Kingford Devon 14 G11
Kingham Oxon 29 Q3
Kingholm Quay D & G 74 J11
Kinghorn Fife 83 Q1
Kinglassie Fife 90 K12
Kingoldrum Angus 98 E12
Kingoodie P & K 91 M6

Littlemore – Mannel 135

Littlemore Oxon 30 B12
Little Musgrave Cumb 68 G10
Little Ness Shrops 44 K10
Little Neston Ches W 54 G11
Little Newcastle Pembks 24 G5
Little Newsham Dur 69 P9
Little Norton Somset 17 N13
Little Oakley Essex 23 T2
Little Oakley Nhants 38 C3
Little Odell Bed 38 E9
Little Offley Herts 31 P7
Little Ormside Cumb 68 F9
Little Orton Cumb 67 N1
Little Ouse Cambs 39 T3
Little Ouseburn N York 63 U7
Littleover C Derb 46 K7
Little Oxendon Nhants 37 T4
Little Packington Warwks 36 H4
Little Pattenden Kent 12 D6
Little Paxton Cambs 38 J8
Little Petherick Cnwll 3 N2
Little Plumpton Lancs 61 R13
Little Plumstead Norfk 51 P11
Little Ponton Lincs 48 D7
Littleport Cambs 39 S3
Littleport Bridge Cambs 39 S3
Little Posbrook Hants 9 Q8
Little Potheridge Devon 15 M10
Little Preston Leeds 63 T13
Little Preston Nhants 37 Q10
Littler Ches W 55 P13
Little Raveley Cambs 39 L5
Little Reedness E R Yk 58 D2
Little Ribston N York 63 T9
Little Rissington Gloucs 29 N4
Little Rollright Oxon 29 Q1
Little Rowsley Derbys 57 L13
Little Ryburgh Norfk 50 G8
Little Ryle Nthumb 77 L3
Little Ryton Shrops 45 L13
Little Salkeld Cumb 67 S5
Little Sampford Essex 39 U14
Little Sandhurst Br For 20 D10
Little Saredon Staffs 46 B12
Little Saughall Ches W 54 J13
Little Saxham Suffk 40 D8
Little Scatwell Highld 102 C4
Little Shelford Cambs 39 Q10
Little Shrewley Warwks 36 H7
Little Silver Devon 6 B3
Little Singleton Lancs 61 R12
Little Skipwith N York 64 F12
Little Smeaton N York 57 R3
Little Snoring Norfk 50 G7
Little Sodbury S Glos 28 E11
Little Sodbury End S Glos 28 D11
Little Somborne Hants 9 M2
Little Somerford Wilts 28 J11
Little Soudley Shrops 45 R8
Little Stainforth N York 62 G6
Little Stainton Darltn 70 D8
Little Stanion Nhants 38 C3
Little Stanney Ches W 54 K12
Little Staughton Bed 38 H8
Little Steeping Lincs 59 R14
Little Stoke Staffs 46 B7
Littlestone-on-Sea Kent 13 L11
Little Stonham Suffk 40 K8
Little Stretton Leics 47 S13
Little Stretton Shrops 34 K2
Little Strickland Cumb 67 S9
Little Stukeley Cambs 38 K5
Little Sugnall Staffs 45 T7
Little Sutton Ches W 54 J11
Little Sutton Shrops 35 M4
Little Swinburne Nthumb 76 J10
Little Sypland D & G 73 S9
Little Tew Oxon 29 S2
Little Tey Essex 23 L3
Little Thetford Cambs 39 R5
Little Thirkleby N York 64 B4
Little Thornage Norfk 50 J6
Little Thornton Lancs 61 R11
Little Thorpe Dur 70 F4
Littlethorpe Leics 37 P1
Littlethorpe N York 63 S6
Little Thurlow Suffk 39 U10
Little Thurlow Green Suffk 39 U10
Little Thurrock Thurr 22 F12
Littleton Angus 98 E13
Littleton BaNES 17 Q4
Littleton Ches W 54 K13
Littleton D & G 73 Q8
Littleton Dorset 8 B8
Littleton Hants 9 P2
Littleton Somset 17 N10
Littleton Surrey 20 G13
Littleton Surrey 20 J9
Littleton Drew Wilts 18 B4
Littleton-on-Severn S Glos 28 A10
Littleton Pannell Wilts 18 F10
Little Torrington Devon 15 L9
Little Totham Essex 23 L5
Little Town Cumb 66 K9
Littletown Dur 70 D4
Little Town Lancs 62 D12
Little Town Warrtn 55 P8
Little Twycross Leics 46 K12
Little Urswick Cumb 61 P5
Little Wakering Essex 23 M10
Little Walden Essex 39 R12
Little Waldingfield Suffk 40 F11
Little Walsingham Norfk 50 F6
Little Waltham Essex 22 H5
Little Warley Essex 22 F9
Little Washbourne Gloucs 36 C14
Little Weighton E R Yk 65 M13
Little Welnetham Suffk 40 E9
Little Welton Lincs 59 P9
Little Wenham Suffk 40 J13
Little Wenlock Wrekin 45 P12
Little Weston Somset 17 R11
Little Whitefield IoW 9 R11
Little Whittingham Green Suffk 41 N5
Little Whittington Nthumb 76 K12
Littlewick Green W & M 20 D7
Little Wilbraham Cambs 39 R9
Littlewindsor Dorset 7 M4
Little Witcombe Gloucs 28 H4
Little Witley Worcs 35 S8
Little Wittenham Oxon 19 S2
Little Wolford Warwks 36 J13
Littlewood Staffs 46 C12
Little Woodcote Gt Lon 21 N10
Littleworth Bucks 30 J8
Littleworth Oxon 29 R8
Littleworth Staffs 46 B9
Littleworth Staffs 46 D11
Littleworth W Susx 10 K6
Littleworth Worcs 35 U10
Littleworth Worcs 36 C8
Littleworth Common Bucks 20 F5
Little Wratting Suffk 39 U11
Little Wymington Bed 38 E8
Little Wymondley Herts 31 R7
Little Wyrley Staffs 46 D12
Little Wytheford Shrops 45 N10
Little Yeldham Essex 40 C13
Littley Green Essex 22 G4
Litton Derbys 56 J11
Litton N York 62 J5
Litton Somset 17 Q6
Litton Cheney Dorset 7 P6
Liurbost W Isls 106 i6
Liverpool Lpool 54 H8
Liverpool Maritime Mercantile City Lpool 54 H9
Liversedge Kirk 56 J2
Liverton Devon 5 U5
Liverton R & Cl 71 M9
Liverton Mines R & Cl 71 M9
Liverton Street Kent 12 G5
Livingston W Loth 83 L5
Livingston Village W Loth 82 K5
Lixwm Flints 54 E12
Lizard Cnwll 2 J14
Llaingoch IoA 52 B6
Llaithddu Powys 34 C4
Llan Powys 43 S13
Llanaber Gwynd 43 M10
Llanaelhaearn Gwynd 42 G5
Llanafan Cerdgn 33 N6
Llanafan-Fawr Powys 33 U9
Llanafan-fechan Powys 33 U10
Llanallgo IoA 52 H5
Llanarmon Gwynd 42 H6
Llanarmon Dyffryn Ceiriog Wrexhm 44 E7
Llanarmon-yn-Ial Denbgs 44 E2
Llanarth Cerdgn 32 H9
Llanarth Mons 27 R5
Llanarthne Carmth 25 T7
Llanasa Flints 54 D10
Llanbabo IoA 52 E5
Llanbadarn Fawr Cerdgn 33 M4
Llanbadarn Fynydd Powys 34 C5
Llanbadarn-y-garreg Powys 34 D11
Llanbadoc Mons 27 R8
Llanbadrig IoA 52 E4
Llanbeder Newpt 27 R9
Llanbedr Gwynd 43 L8
Llanbedr Powys 27 N3
Llanbedr Powys 34 D11
Llanbedr-Dyffryn-Clwyd Denbgs 44 D2
Llanbedrgoch IoA 52 H6
Llanbedrog Gwynd 42 F7
Llanbedr-y-Cennin Conwy 53 N9
Llanberis Gwynd 52 J10
Llanbethêry V Glam 16 D3
Llanbister Powys 34 D6
Llanblethian V Glam 26 H13
Llanboidy Carmth 25 M6
Llanbradach Caerph 27 L9
Llanbrynmair Powys 43 S13
Llancadle V Glam 16 D3
Llancarfan V Glam 16 D2
Llancayo Mons 27 R7
Llancloudy Herefs 27 T3
Llancynfelyn Cerdgn 33 M2
Llandaff Cardif 27 M12
Llandanwg Gwynd 43 L8
Llandarcy Neath 26 C8
Llandawke Carmth 25 N8
Llanddaniel Fab IoA 52 G8
Llanddarog Carmth 25 T7
Llanddeiniol Cerdgn 33 L6
Llanddeiniolen Gwynd 52 H9
Llandderfel Gwynd 43 U6
Llanddeusant Carmth 26 D3
Llanddeusant IoA 52 D5
Llanddew Powys 26 K1
Llanddewi Swans 25 S13
Llanddewi Brefi Cerdgn 33 N9
Llanddewi'r Cwm Powys 34 B11
Llanddewi Rhydderch Mons 27 R5
Llanddewi Velfrey Pembks 24 K7
Llanddewi Ystradenni Powys 34 D7
Llanddoget Conwy 53 P10
Llanddona IoA 52 J7
Llanddowror Carmth 25 N8
Llanddulas Conwy 53 R7
Llanddwywe Gwynd 43 L9
Llanddyfnan IoA 52 H7
Llandecwyn Gwynd 43 M6
Llandefaelog Powys 26 J1
Llandefaelog-Tre'r-Graig Powys 27 L2
Llandefalle Powys 34 D13
Llandegfan IoA 52 J8
Llandegla Denbgs 44 E3
Llandegley Powys 34 D8
Llandegveth Mons 27 Q8
Llandegwning Gwynd 42 E8
Llandeilo Carmth 26 A3
Llandeilo Graban Powys 34 C12
Llandeilo'r Fan Powys 33 S14
Llandeloy Pembks 24 E5
Llandenny Mons 27 S7
Llandevaud Newpt 27 S9
Llandevenny Mons 27 S10
Llandinabo Herefs 27 U2
Llandinam Powys 34 B3
Llandissilio Pembks 24 K6
Llandogo Mons 27 U7
Llandough V Glam 26 H13
Llandough V Glam 27 M13
Llandovery Carmth 33 Q14
Llandow V Glam 26 G13
Llandre Carmth 33 N12
Llandre Cerdgn 33 M3
Llandre Isaf Pembks 24 K5
Llandrillo Denbgs 44 B6
Llandrillo-yn-Rhos Conwy 53 P6
Llandrindod Wells Powys 34 C8
Llandrinio Powys 44 G10
Llandudno Conwy 53 N6
Llandudno Junction Conwy 53 N7
Llandulas Powys 33 S12
Llandwrog Gwynd 52 G11
Llandybie Carmth 25 V7
Llandyfaelog Carmth 25 R8
Llandyfan Carmth 26 A4
Llandyfriog Cerdgn 32 F12
Llandyfrydog IoA 52 F5
Llandygai Gwynd 52 J8
Llandygwydd Cerdgn 32 D12
Llandynan Denbgs 44 E4
Llandyrnog Denbgs 54 D13
Llandyssil Powys 34 E1
Llandysul Cerdgn 32 H12
Llanedeyrn Cardif 27 N11
Llanedi Carmth 25 U9
Llaneglwys Powys 34 C13
Llanegryn Gwynd 43 M12
Llanegwad Carmth 25 T6
Llaneilian IoA 52 G4
Llanelian-yn-Rhôs Conwy 53 Q7
Llanelidan Denbgs 44 D3
Llanelieu Powys 34 E14
Llanellen Mons 27 Q5
Llanelli Carmth 25 T10
Llanelli Crematorium Carmth 25 T10
Llanelltyd Gwynd 43 P10
Llanelly Mons 27 N5
Llanelwedd Powys 34 B10
Llanenddwyn Gwynd 43 L9
Llanengan Gwynd 42 E8
Llanerch Gwynd 43 S10
Llanerch Powys 34 H2
Llanerchymedd IoA 52 F6
Llanerfyl Powys 44 B12
Llanfachraeth IoA 52 D6
Llanfachreth Gwynd 43 Q9
Llanfaelog IoA 52 D8
Llanfaelrhys Gwynd 42 D8
Llanfaenor Mons 27 S4
Llanfaes IoA 52 K7
Llanfaes Powys 26 J2
Llanfaethlu IoA 52 D5
Llanfair Gwynd 43 L8
Llanfair Caereinion Powys 44 D12
Llanfair Clydogau Cerdgn 33 M10
Llanfair Dyffryn Clwyd Denbgs 44 D2
Llanfairfechan Conwy 53 L8
Llanfair Kilgeddin Mons 27 R6
Llanfair-Nant-Gwyn Pembks 25 L3
Llanfairpwllgwyngyll IoA 52 H8
Llanfair Talhaiarn Conwy 53 R8
Llanfair Waterdine Shrops 34 F5
Llanfairynghornwy IoA 52 D4
Llanfair-yn-Neubwll IoA 52 D7
Llanfallteg Carmth 25 L6
Llanfallteg West Carmth 24 K7
Llanfarian Cerdgn 33 L5
Llanfechain Powys 44 E9
Llanfechell IoA 52 E4
Llanferres Denbgs 44 E1
Llanfflewyn IoA 52 E5
Llanfigael IoA 52 D6
Llanfihangel-ar-arth Carmth 25 S3
Llanfihangel Glyn Myfyr Conwy 43 U4
Llanfihangel Nant Bran Powys 33 T14
Llanfihangel-nant-Melan Powys 34 E9
Llanfihangel Rhydithon Powys 34 E7
Llanfihangel Rogiet Mons 27 T10
Llanfihangel Tal-y-llyn Powys 27 L2
Llanfihangel-uwch-Gwili Carmth 25 S6
Llanfihangel-y-Creuddyn Cerdgn 33 N5
Llanfihangel-yng-Ngwynfa Powys 44 C10
Llanfihangel yn Nhowyn IoA 52 D7
Llanfihangel-y-pennant Gwynd 42 K5
Llanfihangel-y-pennant Gwynd 43 N12
Llanfihangel-y-traethau Gwynd 43 L7
Llanfilo Powys 34 D14
Llanfoist Mons 27 P5
Llanfor Gwynd 43 T6
Llanfrechfa Torfn 27 Q9
Llanfrothen Gwynd 43 M5
Llanfrynach Powys 26 K2
Llanfwrog Denbgs 44 D2
Llanfwrog IoA 52 D6
Llanfyllin Powys 44 D10
Llanfynydd Carmth 25 U5
Llanfynydd Flints 44 G2
Llanfyrnach Pembks 25 M4
Llangadfan Powys 44 B11
Llangadog Carmth 25 R9
Llangadog Carmth 26 C2
Llangadwaladr IoA 52 E9
Llangadwaladr Powys 44 E7
Llangaffo IoA 52 F9
Llangain Carmth 25 Q7
Llangammarch Wells Powys 33 T11
Llangan V Glam 26 H12
Llangarron Herefs 27 U3
Llangasty-Talyllyn Powys 27 L2
Llangathen Carmth 25 U6
Llangattock Powys 27 N4
Llangattock Lingoed Mons 27 R3
Llangattock-Vibon-Avel Mons 27 T4
Llangedwyn Powys 44 E9
Llangefni IoA 52 G7
Llangeinor Brdgnd 26 G10
Llangeitho Cerdgn 33 M9
Llangeler Carmth 25 Q3
Llangelynin Gwynd 43 L12
Llangendeirne Carmth 25 S8
Llangennech Carmth 25 U10
Llangennith Swans 25 R12
Llangenny Powys 27 N4
Llangernyw Conwy 53 Q9
Llangian Gwynd 42 E8
Llangiwg Neath 26 C6
Llangloffan Pembks 24 F4
Llanglydwen Carmth 25 L5
Llangoed IoA 52 K7
Llangoedmor Cerdgn 32 D11
Llangollen Denbgs 44 F5
Llangolman Pembks 24 K5
Llangors Powys 27 L2
Llangovan Mons 27 T6
Llangower Gwynd 43 T7
Llangrannog Cerdgn 32 F10
Llangristiolus IoA 52 F8
Llangrove Herefs 27 U4
Llangua Mons 27 R2
Llangunllo Powys 34 F6
Llangunnor Carmth 25 R6
Llangurig Powys 33 T5
Llangwm Conwy 43 U5
Llangwm Mons 27 S8
Llangwm Pembks 24 G9
Llangwnnadl Gwynd 42 D7
Llangwyfan Denbgs 54 D13
Llangwyllog IoA 52 F7
Llangwyryfon Cerdgn 33 L6
Llangybi Cerdgn 33 M10
Llangybi Gwynd 42 H5
Llangybi Mons 27 R8
Llangyfelach Swans 26 A8
Llangynhafal Denbgs 54 D14
Llangynidr Powys 27 M4
Llangynin Carmth 25 N7
Llangynllo Cerdgn 32 G12
Llangynog Carmth 25 P8
Llangynog Powys 44 C8
Llangynwyd Brdgnd 26 F10
Llanhamlach Powys 26 K2
Llanharan Rhondd 26 J11
Llanharry Rhondd 26 J11
Llanhennock Mons 27 R9
Llanhilleth Blae G 27 N7
Llanidan IoA 52 G9
Llanidloes Powys 33 U4
Llaniestyn Gwynd 42 E7
Llanigon Powys 34 F13
Llanilar Cerdgn 33 M5
Llanilid Rhondd 26 H11
Llanina Cerdgn 32 H9
Llanio Cerdgn 33 M9
Llanishen Cardif 27 M11
Llanishen Mons 27 T7
Llanllechid Gwynd 52 K9
Llanlleonfel Powys 33 T10
Llanllowell Mons 27 R8
Llanllugan Powys 44 C13
Llanllwch Carmth 25 Q7
Llanllwchaiarn Powys 34 D2
Llanllwni Carmth 25 S3
Llanllyfni Gwynd 42 J3
Llanmadoc Swans 25 R12
Llanmaes V Glam 16 C3
Llanmartin Newpt 27 R10
Llanmerewig Powys 34 E2
Llanmihangel V Glam 16 C2
Llanmiloe Carmth 25 M9
Llanmorlais Swans 25 T12
Llannefydd Conwy 53 S8
Llannon Carmth 25 T9
Llannor Gwynd 42 G6
Llanon Cerdgn 32 K7
Llanover Mons 27 Q6
Llanpumsaint Carmth 25 R5
Llanrhaeadr-ym-Mochnant Powys 44 D8
Llanrhian Pembks 24 D4
Llanrhidian Swans 25 S12
Llanrhos Conwy 53 N6
Llanrhychwyn Conwy 53 N10
Llanrhyddlad IoA 52 D5
Llanrhystud Cerdgn 32 K7
Llanrothal Herefs 27 T4
Llanrug Gwynd 52 H10
Llanrumney Cardif 27 N11
Llanrwst Conwy 53 P10
Llansadurnen Carmth 25 N8
Llansadwrn Carmth 26 B1
Llansadwrn IoA 52 J7
Llansaint Carmth 25 Q9
Llansamlet Swans 26 B8
Llansanffraid Glan Conwy Conwy 53 P7
Llansannan Conwy 53 R9
Llansannor V Glam 26 H12
Llansantffraed Powys 27 L3
Llansantffraed-Cwmdeuddwr Powys 33 U7
Llansantffraed-in-Elvel Powys 34 C10
Llansantffraid Cerdgn 32 K7
Llansantffraid-ym-Mechain Powys 44 F9
Llansawel Carmth 25 V3
Llansilin Powys 44 F8
Llansoy Mons 27 S7
Llanspyddid Powys 26 J2
Llanstadwell Pembks 24 F10
Llansteffan Carmth 25 Q8
Llanstephan Powys 34 D12
Llantarnam Torfn 27 Q9
Llanteg Pembks 25 L8
Llanthewy Skirrid Mons 27 Q4
Llanthony Mons 27 P2
Llantilio-Crossenny Mons 27 R5
Llantilio Pertholey Mons 27 Q4
Llantood Pembks 32 C12
Llantrisant IoA 52 E6
Llantrisant Mons 27 R8
Llantrisant Rhondd 26 J11
Llantrithyd V Glam 26 J13
Llantwit Fardre Rhondd 26 K10
Llantwit Major V Glam 16 C3
Llantysilio Denbgs 44 E5
Llanuwchllyn Gwynd 43 S7
Llanvaches Newpt 27 S9
Llanvair Discoed Mons 27 S9
Llanvapley Mons 27 R5
Llanvetherine Mons 27 R4
Llanveynoe Herefs 27 Q1
Llanvihangel Crucorney Mons 27 Q3
Llanvihangel Gobion Mons 27 Q6
Llanvihangel-Ystern-Llewern Mons 27 S5
Llanwarne Herefs 27 U2
Llanwddyn Powys 44 B10
Llanwenarth Mons 27 P5
Llanwenog Cerdgn 32 J11
Llanwern Newpt 27 R10
Llanwinio Carmth 25 N5
Llanwnda Gwynd 52 G11
Llanwnda Pembks 24 F3
Llanwnnen Cerdgn 32 K11
Llanwnog Powys 34 B2
Llanwonno Rhondd 26 J8
Llanwrda Carmth 26 C1
Llanwrin Powys 43 Q13
Llanwrthwl Powys 33 U8
Llanwrtyd Powys 33 S11
Llanwrtyd Wells Powys 33 S11
Llanwyddelan Powys 44 C13
Llanyblodwel Shrops 44 F9
Llanybri Carmth 25 P8
Llanybydder Carmth 32 K12
Llanycefn Pembks 24 J6
Llanychaer Pembks 24 G3
Llanycrwys Carmth 33 M11
Llanymawddwy Gwynd 43 T10
Llanymynech Powys 44 G9
Llanynghenedl IoA 52 D6
Llanynys Denbgs 54 D14
Llan-y-pwll Wrexhm 44 J3
Llanyre Powys 34 B8
Llanystumdwy Gwynd 42 J6
Llanywern Powys 27 L2
Llawhaden Pembks 24 J7
Llawnt Shrops 44 F7
Llawryglyn Powys 33 T2
Llay Wrexhm 44 H2
Llechcynfarwy IoA 52 E6
Llechfaen Powys 26 K2
Llechrhyd Caerph 27 L6
Llechryd Cerdgn 32 D12
Llechylched IoA 52 D7
Lledrod Cerdgn 33 M6
Lleyn Peninsula Gwynd 42 F6
Llidiardau Gwynd 43 S6
Llidiartnenog Carmth 25 T3
Llidiart-y-parc Denbgs 44 D5
Llithfaen Gwynd 42 G5
Lloc Flints 54 D11
Llowes Powys 34 E12
Llwydcoed Rhondd 26 H7
Llwydcoed Crematorium Rhondd 26 H6
Llwydiarth Powys 44 B10
Llwyn Denbgs 54 C14
Llwyncelyn Cerdgn 32 H9
Llwyndafydd Cerdgn 32 G9
Llwynderw Powys 44 F13
Llwyn-drain Pembks 25 N4
Llwyn-du Mons 27 P4
Llwyndyrys Gwynd 42 G5
Llwyngwril Gwynd 43 L12
Llwynhendy Carmth 25 T11
Llwynmawr Wrexhm 44 F6
Llwyn-on Myr Td 26 J5
Llwyn-y-brain Carmth 25 L8
Llwyn-y-groes Cerdgn 33 L9
Llwynypia Rhondd 26 H9
Llynclys Shrops 44 G9
Llynfaes IoA 52 F7
Llyn-y-pandy Flints 54 F13
Llysfaen Conwy 53 Q7
Llyswen Cerdgn 32 J8
Llyswen Powys 34 D13
Llysworney V Glam 26 H13
Llys-y-frân Pembks 24 H6
Llywel Powys 26 F1
Load Brook Sheff 57 L9
Loan Falk 82 J3
Loanend Nthumb 85 N8
Loanhead Mdloth 83 Q5
Loaningfoot D & G 66 E1
Loans S Ayrs 81 L6
Lobb Devon 15 L5
Lobhillcross Devon 5 M3
Lochailort Highld 93 T2
Lochaline Highld 93 R10
Lochans D & G 72 D8
Locharbriggs D & G 74 J9
Lochavich Ag & B 87 S2
Lochawe Ag & B 94 G13
Loch Baghasdail W Isls 106 c17
Lochboisdale W Isls 106 c17
Lochbuie Ag & B 93 Q13
Lochcarron Highld 101 M4
Lochdar W Isls 106 c14
Lochdon Ag & B 93 S12
Lochdonhead Ag & B 93 S12
Lochead Ag & B 87 P10
Lochearnhead Stirlg 95 R14
Lochee C Dund 91 N5
Locheilside Station Highld 94 D3
Lochend Highld 102 G8
Locheport W Isls 106 d12
Loch Euphoirt W Isls 106 d12
Lochfoot D & G 74 G11
Lochgair Ag & B 87 S7
Lochgelly Fife 90 J13
Lochgilphead Ag & B 87 R8
Lochgoilhead Ag & B 88 F5
Lochieheads Fife 91 L9
Lochill Moray 104 B3
Lochindorb Lodge Highld 103 Q8
Lochinver Highld 110 B12
Loch Lomond and The Trossachs National Park 88 K3
Lochluichart Highld 102 B3
Lochmaben D & G 75 L9
Lochmaddy W Isls 106 e12
Loch Maree Hotel Highld 107 R10
Loch nam Madadh W Isls 106 e12
Loch Ness Highld 102 F10
Lochore Fife 90 J12
Lochranza N Ayrs 79 S5
Lochside Abers 99 N11
Lochside D & G 74 J10
Lochside Highld 103 M5
Lochslin Highld 109 Q8
Lochton S Ayrs 72 H4
Lochty Angus 98 J11
Lochty Fife 91 R10
Lochuisge Highld 93 T7
Lochwinnoch Rens 88 J14
Lochwood D & G 75 L6
Lockengate Cnwll 3 Q4
Lockerbie D & G 75 M9
Lockeridge Wilts 18 H7
Lockerley Hants 9 L3
Locking N Som 17 L5
Locking Stumps Warrtn 55 P8
Lockington E R Yk 65 M10
Lockington Leics 47 N8
Lockleywood Shrops 45 Q8
Locksbottom Gt Lon 21 R9
Locksgreen IoW 9 N10
Locks Heath Hants 9 Q7
Lockton N York 64 J2
Loddington Leics 47 U13
Loddington Nhants 38 B5
Loddiswell Devon 5 S11
Loddon Norfk 51 Q14
Lode Cambs 39 R8
Lode Heath Solhll 36 G4
Loders Dorset 7 N6
Lodge Hill Crematorium Birm 36 D4
Lodsworth W Susx 10 E6
Lofthouse Leeds 57 M1
Lofthouse N York 63 N5
Lofthouse Gate Wakefd 57 M2
Loftus R & Cl 71 M9
Logan E Ayrs 81 R8
Loganbeck Cumb 61 M1
Loganlea W Loth 82 J6
Loggerheads Staffs 45 R6
Logie Angus 99 M11
Logie Fife 91 P7
Logie Moray 103 R5
Logie Coldstone Abers 98 G3
Logie Newton Abers 104 K8
Logie Pert Angus 99 M11
Logierait P & K 97 R13
Logierieve Abers 105 Q10
Login Carmth 25 L6
Lolworth Cambs 39 N8
Lonbain Highld 107 L14
Londesborough E R Yk 64 K10
London Gt Lon 21 P6
London Apprentice Cnwll 3 Q7
London Beach Kent 12 G8
London Colney Herts 31 Q12
Londonderry N York 63 S2
London End Nhants 38 D7
London Gateway Services Gt Lon 21 L4
Londonthorpe Lincs 48 E6
London Zoo ZSL Gt Lon 21 N6
Londubh Highld 107 Q8
Lonemore Highld 107 N9
Long Ashton N Som 17 P2
Long Bank Worcs 35 S6
Long Bennington Lincs 48 B5
Longbenton N Tyne 77 R12
Longborough Gloucs 29 N2
Long Bredy Dorset 7 Q6
Longbridge Birm 36 D5
Longbridge Warwks 36 J8
Longbridge Deverill Wilts 18 C12
Long Buckby Nhants 37 R7
Longburgh Cumb 75 R14
Longburton Dorset 7 R2
Long Cause Devon 5 T8
Long Clawson Leics 47 T8
Longcliffe Derbys 46 H2
Longcombe Devon 5 U9
Long Common Hants 9 Q6
Long Compton Staffs 45 U9
Long Compton Warwks 36 J14
Longcot Oxon 29 Q9
Long Crendon Bucks 30 E11
Long Crichel Dorset 8 D6
Longcroft Cumb 75 P14
Longcross Surrey 20 G9
Longden Shrops 44 K12
Longden Common Shrops 44 K12
Long Ditton Surrey 21 L9
Longdon Staffs 46 E11
Longdon Worcs 35 T13
Longdon Green Staffs 46 E11
Longdon Heath Worcs 35 T13
Longdon upon Tern Wrekin 45 P10
Longdown Devon 5 V2
Longdowns Cnwll 2 J10
Long Drax N York 64 F14
Long Duckmanton Derbys 57 P12
Long Eaton Derbys 47 N7
Longfield Kent 12 B2
Longford Covtry 37 L4
Longford Derbys 46 H6
Longford Gloucs 28 F3
Longford Gt Lon 20 J7
Longford Kent 21 T11
Longford Shrops 45 P7
Longford Wrekin 45 R10
Longforgan P & K 91 L6
Longformacus Border 84 H7
Longframlington Nthumb 77 N5
Long Green Ches W 55 L12
Long Green Worcs 35 T14
Longham Dorset 8 F9
Longham Norfk 50 F10
Long Hanborough Oxon 29 T5
Longhaven Abers 105 U8
Long Hedges Lincs 49 N4
Longhirst Nthumb 77 Q8
Longhope Gloucs 28 C4
Longhope Ork 106 s20
Longhorsley Nthumb 77 N7
Longhoughton Nthumb 77 Q2
Long Itchington Warwks 37 M7
Longlands Cumb 67 L5
Longlane Derbys 46 H6
Long Lawford Warwks 37 N5
Longleat Safari & Adventure Park Wilts 18 B12
Longlevens Gloucs 28 G4
Longley Calder 56 G2
Longley Kirk 56 H5
Longley Green Worcs 35 R10
Longleys P & K 91 L3
Long Load Somset 17 N12
Longmanhill Abers 105 L3
Long Marston Herts 30 J9
Long Marston N York 64 C9
Long Marston Warwks 36 G11
Long Marton Cumb 68 E8
Long Meadowend Shrops 34 K4
Long Melford Suffk 40 E11
Longmoor Camp Hants 10 B4
Longmorn Moray 104 A4
Longmoss Ches E 56 C12
Long Newnton Gloucs 28 H9
Longnewton Border 84 F13
Long Newton E Loth 84 E6
Longnewton S on T 70 E9
Longney Gloucs 28 E5
Longniddry E Loth 84 C3
Longnor Shrops 45 L13
Longnor Staffs 56 G14
Longparish Hants 19 P11
Longpark Cumb 75 T13
Long Preston N York 62 G8
Longridge Lancs 62 C12
Longridge Staffs 46 B10
Longridge W Loth 82 H6
Longriggend N Lans 82 F4
Long Riston E R Yk 65 Q11
Longrock Cnwll 2 E10
Longsdon Staffs 46 C3
Longshaw Wigan 55 M6
Longside Abers 105 S6
Long Sight Oldham 56 D5
Longslow Shrops 45 Q6
Longstanton Cambs 39 N7
Longstock Hants 19 N13
Longstone Pembks 24 K9
Longstowe Cambs 39 M10
Long Stratton Norfk 41 L2
Long Street M Keyn 37 U11
Longstreet Wilts 18 H10
Long Sutton Hants 20 B13
Long Sutton Lincs 49 P9
Long Sutton Somset 17 N11
Longthorpe C Pete 48 J14
Long Thurlow Suffk 40 H7
Longthwaite Cumb 67 P8
Longton C Stke 46 B5
Longton Lancs 55 L1
Longtown Cumb 75 S12
Longtown Herefs 27 Q2
Longueville Jersey 7 e3
Longville in the Dale Shrops 35 M2
Long Waste Wrekin 45 P10
Long Whatton Leics 47 N9
Longwick Bucks 30 G11
Long Wittenham Oxon 19 R2
Longwitton Nthumb 77 M8
Longwood D & G 73 S7
Longwood Shrops 45 P12
Longworth Oxon 29 S8
Longyester E Loth 84 E5
Lôn-las Swans 26 C8
Lonmay Abers 105 S4
Lonmore Highld 100 b5
Looe Cnwll 4 H10
Loose Kent 12 E5
Loosebeare Devon 15 R11
Loosegate Lincs 49 M8
Loosley Row Bucks 30 H12
Lootcherbrae Abers 104 J5
Lopcombe Corner Wilts 19 L13
Lopen Somset 7 M2
Loppington Shrops 45 L8
Lorbottle Nthumb 77 L4
Lordington W Susx 10 B9
Lordsbridge Norfk 49 S11
Lordshill C Sotn 9 M5
Lords Wood Medway 12 E3
Lornty P & K 90 J2
Loscoe Derbys 47 M4
Loscombe Dorset 7 N5
Lossiemouth Moray 104 A1
Lostford Shrops 45 P7
Lostock Gralam Ches W 55 Q12
Lostock Green Ches W 55 Q12
Lostock Hall Lancs 55 M1
Lostock Hall Fold Bolton 55 Q5
Lostock Junction Bolton 55 Q5
Lostwithiel Cnwll 4 E9
Lothbeg Highld 109 S2
Lothersdale N York 62 K10
Lothmore Highld 109 T2
Loudwater Bucks 20 F4
Loughborough Leics 47 P10
Loughborough Crematorium Leics 47 P10
Loughor Swans 25 U11
Loughton Essex 21 R3
Loughton M Keyn 30 H5
Loughton Shrops 35 P4
Lound Lincs 48 G10
Lound Notts 57 U9
Lound Suffk 51 T14
Lounston Devon 5 T5
Lount Leics 47 L10
Louth Lincs 59 P9
Love Clough Lancs 55 T1
Lovedean Hants 9 T6
Lover Wilts 8 J4
Loversall Donc 57 S7
Loves Green Essex 22 F7
Lovesome Hill N York 70 E13
Loveston Pembks 24 J9
Lovington Somset 17 Q10
Low Ackworth Wakefd 57 Q3
Low Angerton Nthumb 77 M9
Lowbands Gloucs 28 E1
Low Barbeth D & G 72 C6
Low Barlings Lincs 58 J12
Low Bell End N York 71 M13
Low Bentham N York 62 C6
Low Biggins Cumb 62 C4
Low Borrowbridge Cumb 68 D12
Low Bradfield Sheff 57 L8
Low Bradley N York 63 L10
Low Braithwaite Cumb 67 P4
Low Burnham N Linc 58 C6
Low Buston Nthumb 77 Q4
Lowca Cumb 66 E8
Low Catton E R Yk 64 G9
Low Coniscliffe Darltn 69 S10
Low Crosby Cumb 75 T14
Lowdham Notts 47 S4
Low Dinsdale Darltn 70 D10
Lowe Shrops 45 L7
Lowe Hill Staffs 46 C2
Low Ellington N York 63 Q3
Lower Aisholt Somset 16 H9
Lower Ansty Dorset 7 U4
Lower Apperley Gloucs 28 G2
Lower Arncott Oxon 30 D9
Lower Ashton Devon 5 U4
Lower Assendon Oxon 20 B6
Lower Ballam Lancs 61 R13
Lower Bartle Lancs 61 T13
Lower Basildon W Berk 19 T5
Lower Bearwood Herefs 34 J9
Lower Beeding W Susx 11 L5
Lower Benefield Nhants 38 E3
Lower Bentley Worcs 36 C7
Lower Beobridge Shrops 35 S2
Lower Birchwood Derbys 47 M3
Lower Boddington Nhants 37 N10
Lower Boscaswell Cnwll 2 B10
Lower Bourne Surrey 10 C2
Lower Brailes Warwks 36 K13
Lower Breakish Highld 100 f7
Lower Bredbury Stockp 56 D8
Lower Broadheath Worcs 35 T9
Lower Broxwood Herefs 34 J10
Lower Buckenhill Herefs 35 P14
Lower Bullingham Herefs 35 M13
Lower Burgate Hants 8 H5
Lower Burrowton Devon 6 D5
Lower Burton Herefs 34 K9
Lower Caldecote C Beds 38 J11
Lower Cam Gloucs 28 D7
Lower Canada N Som 17 L5
Lower Catesby Nhants 37 P9
Lower Chapel Powys 34 B13
Lower Chicksgrove Wilts 8 D3
Lower Chute Wilts 19 M10
Lower Clapton Gt Lon 21 P5
Lower Clent Worcs 36 B5
Lower Common Hants 20 C10
Lower Creedy Devon 15 T12
Lower Crossings Derbys 56 F10
Lower Cumberworth Kirk 56 K5
Lower Darwen Bl w D 55 Q1
Lower Dean Bed 38 G7
Lower Denby Kirk 56 K5
Lower Diabaig Highld 107 N12
Lower Dicker E Susx 11 T8
Lower Dinchope Shrops 35 L4
Lower Down Shrops 34 H4
Lower Dunsforth N York 63 U7
Lower Egleton Herefs 35 P11
Lower Elkstone Staffs 46 E2
Lower Ellastone Staffs 46 F5
Lower End Bucks 30 E11
Lower End M Keyn 30 K5
Lower End Nhants 38 B9
Lower End Nhants 38 C8
Lower Everleigh Wilts 18 J10
Lower Exbury Hants 9 N9
Lower Eythorne Kent 13 Q6
Lower Failand N Som 27 U13
Lower Farringdon Hants 19 V13
Lower Feltham Gt Lon 20 J8
Lower Fittleworth W Susx 10 G7
Lower Foxdale IoM 60 d7
Lower Frankton Shrops 44 J7
Lower Freystrop Pembks 24 G8
Lower Froyle Hants 10 B2
Lower Gabwell Devon 6 B11
Lower Gledfield Highld 108 K6
Lower Godney Somset 17 N8
Lower Gornal Dudley 36 B2
Lower Gravenhurst C Beds 31 P5
Lower Green Herts 31 Q6
Lower Green Herts 39 P14
Lower Green Kent 11 T2
Lower Green Kent 12 B7
Lower Green Norfk 50 G6
Lower Green Staffs 46 B12
Lower Green Suffk 40 B7
Lower Hacheston Suffk 41 P9
Lower Halliford Surrey 20 J9
Lower Halstock Leigh Dorset 7 P3
Lower Halstow Kent 12 G2
Lower Hamworthy Poole 8 D10
Lower Hardres Kent 13 N5
Lower Harpton Herefs 34 G8
Lower Hartlip Kent 12 F3
Lower Hartshay Derbys 47 L3
Lower Hartwell Bucks 30 G10
Lower Hatton Staffs 45 T6
Lower Hawthwaite Cumb 61 N2
Lower Hergest Herefs 34 G9
Lower Heyford Oxon 29 U3
Lower Heysham Lancs 61 S7
Lower Higham Kent 22 H13
Lower Holbrook Suffk 41 L13
Lower Hordley Shrops 44 J8
Lower Horncroft W Susx 10 G7
Lowerhouse Lancs 62 G13
Lower Houses Kirk 56 J3
Lower Howsell Worcs 35 S11
Lower Irlam Salfd 55 R8
Lower Kilburn Derbys 47 L5
Lower Kilcott Gloucs 28 E10
Lower Killeyan Ag & B 78 D7
Lower Kingcombe Dorset 7 Q5
Lower Kingswood Surrey 21 M12
Lower Kinnerton Ches W 44 H1
Lower Langford N Som 17 N4
Lower Largo Fife 91 P11
Lower Leigh Staffs 46 D6
Lower Lemington Gloucs 36 H14
Lower Llanfadog Powys 33 U7
Lower Lovacott Devon 15 M7
Lower Loxhore Devon 15 P5
Lower Lydbrook Gloucs 28 A4
Lower Lye Herefs 34 K7
Lower Machen Newpt 27 N10
Lower Maes-coed Herefs 27 Q1
Lower Mannington Dorset 8 F8
Lower Marston Somset 17 U8
Lower Meend Gloucs 27 V7
Lower Merridge Somset 16 H10
Lower Middleton Cheney Nhants 30 B4
Lower Milton Somset 17 P7
Lower Moor Worcs 36 C11
Lower Morton S Glos 28 B9
Lower Nazeing Essex 31 U11
Lower Norton Warwks 36 H8
Lower Nyland Dorset 17 U12
Lower Penarth V Glam 16 G3
Lower Penn Staffs 35 U1
Lower Pennington Hants 9 L10
Lower Penwortham Lancs 55 M1
Lower Peover Ches E 55 R12
Lower Place Rochdl 56 D4
Lower Pollicott Bucks 30 F10
Lower Quinton Warwks 36 G11
Lower Rainham Medway 12 F2
Lower Raydon Suffk 40 H13
Lower Roadwater Somset 16 D9
Lower Salter Lancs 62 C7
Lower Seagry Wilts 18 E4
Lower Sheering Essex 22 C5
Lower Shelton C Beds 31 L4
Lower Shiplake Oxon 20 C7
Lower Shuckburgh Warwks 37 N8
Lower Slaughter Gloucs 29 N3
Lower Soothill Kirk 57 L2
Lower Soudley Gloucs 28 C6
Lower Standen Kent 13 P7
Lower Stanton St Quintin Wilts 18 D4
Lower Stoke Medway 22 K12
Lower Stone Gloucs 28 C9
Lower Stonnall Staffs 46 E13
Lower Stow Bedon Norfk 40 G2
Lower Street Dorset 8 A9
Lower Street E Susx 12 D13
Lower Street Norfk 51 N6
Lower Street Suffk 40 C10
Lower Street Suffk 40 K10
Lower Stretton Warrtn 55 P10
Lower Stroud Dorset 7 N5
Lower Sundon C Beds 31 N7
Lower Swanwick Hants 9 P7
Lower Swell Gloucs 29 N2
Lower Tadmarton Oxon 37 M13
Lower Tale Devon 6 E4
Lower Tean Staffs 46 D6
Lower Thurlton Norfk 51 R14
Lower Town Cnwll 2 H11
Lower Town Devon 5 S6
Lower Town Herefs 35 P12
Lower Town Pembks 24 G3
Lower Trebullett Cnwll 4 J5
Lower Treluswell Cnwll 2 K9
Lower Tysoe Warwks 36 K11
Lower Ufford Suffk 41 N10
Lower Upcott Devon 6 A8
Lower Upham Hants 9 Q5
Lower Upnor Medway 22 J13
Lower Vexford Somset 16 F9
Lower Walton Warrtn 55 P9
Lower Waterston Dorset 7 T5
Lower Weare Somset 17 M6
Lower Weedon Nhants 37 R9
Lower Welson Herefs 34 G10
Lower Westmancote Worcs 36 B13
Lower Whatcombe Dorset 8 A8
Lower Whatley Somset 17 T7
Lower Whitley Ches W 55 P11
Lower Wick Gloucs 28 D8
Lower Wick Worcs 35 T10
Lower Wield Hants 19 T12
Lower Willingdon E Susx 11 T10
Lower Withington Ches E 55 T13
Lower Woodend Bucks 20 D5
Lower Woodford Wilts 18 H13
Lower Wraxhall Dorset 7 Q4
Lower Wyche Worcs 35 S12
Lower Wyke C Brad 56 J1
Lowesby Leics 47 T12
Lowestoft Suffk 41 T2
Loweswater Cumb 66 H8
Low Fell Gatesd 77 R14
Lowfield Heath W Susx 11 M3
Low Gartachorrans Stirlg 89 L8
Low Gate Nthumb 76 J13
Low Gettbridge Cumb 75 V14
Lowgill Cumb 68 D13
Lowgill Lancs 62 D7
Low Grantley N York 63 Q5
Low Green N York 63 Q8
Low Habberley Worcs 35 T5
Low Ham Somset 17 M11
Low Harrogate N York 63 R8
Low Hawsker N York 71 R11
Low Hesket Cumb 67 Q3
Low Hutton N York 64 H6
Lowick Cumb 61 P2
Lowick Nhants 38 E4
Lowick Nthumb 85 Q11
Lowick Bridge Cumb 61 P2
Lowick Green Cumb 61 P2
Low Knipe Cumb 67 R9
Low Laithe N York 63 P7
Lowlands Dur 69 P7
Lowlands Torfn 27 P8
Low Langton Lincs 59 L11
Low Leighton Derbys 56 F9
Low Lorton Cumb 66 J7
Low Marishes N York 64 J4
Low Marnham Notts 58 D13
Low Middleton Nthumb 85 S11
Low Mill N York 71 L13
Low Moor C Brad 63 P14
Low Moorsley Sundld 70 D3
Low Moresby Cumb 66 E8
Low Newton Cumb 61 S3
Low Row Cumb 66 J4
Low Row Cumb 67 N5
Low Row Cumb 76 B13
Low Row N York 69 L13
Low Salchrie D & G 72 C6
Low Santon N Linc 58 F4
Lowsonford Warwks 36 G7
Low Street Norfk 51 P9
Low Street Thurr 22 G12
Low Tharston Norfk 41 L1
Lowther Cumb 67 R8
Lowther Castle Cumb 67 R8
Lowthorpe E R Yk 65 P7
Lowton Devon 15 Q12
Lowton Somset 16 G13
Lowton Wigan 55 P7
Lowton Common Wigan 55 P7
Lowton St Mary's Wigan 55 P7
Low Torry Fife 82 K1
Low Toynton Lincs 59 N12
Low Valley Barns 57 P6
Low Wood Cumb 61 Q3
Low Worsall N York 70 E11
Low Wray Cumb 67 N12
Loxbeare Devon 16 B13
Loxhill Surrey 10 G3
Loxhore Devon 15 P5
Loxhore Cott Devon 15 P5
Loxley Warwks 36 J10
Loxley Green Staffs 46 E7
Loxter Herefs 35 R12
Loxton N Som 17 L5
Loxwood W Susx 10 G4
Loyal Lodge Highld 111 N7
Lubenham Leics 37 T3
Lucasgate Lincs 49 P4
Lucas Green Surrey 20 F10
Luccombe Somset 16 B8
Luccombe Village IoW 9 R13
Lucker Nthumb 85 T12
Luckett Cnwll 4 K6
Lucking Street Essex 40 D14
Luckington Wilts 28 F11
Lucklawhill Fife 91 P7
Lucknam Wilts 18 B6
Luckwell Bridge Somset 16 B9
Lucton Herefs 34 K8
Lucy Cross N York 69 R10
Ludag W Isls 106 c17
Ludborough Lincs 59 N7
Ludbrook Devon 5 R10
Ludchurch Pembks 24 K8
Luddenden Calder 56 F1
Luddenden Foot Calder 56 F1
Luddenham Court Kent 12 J3
Luddesdown Kent 12 C2
Luddington N Linc 58 D3
Luddington Warwks 36 G10
Luddington in the Brook Nhants 38 H4
Ludford Lincs 59 L9
Ludford Shrops 35 M6
Ludgershall Bucks 30 E9
Ludgershall Wilts 19 L10
Ludgvan Cnwll 2 E10
Ludham Norfk 51 Q10
Ludlow Shrops 35 M5
Ludney Somset 7 L2
Ludwell Wilts 8 C4
Ludworth Dur 70 E4
Luffenhall Herts 31 S7
Luffincott Devon 4 J2
Luffness E Loth 84 D2
Lugar E Ayrs 81 R8
Luggate Burn E Loth 84 F4
Lugg Green Herefs 34 K8
Luggiebank N Lans 89 S11
Lugton E Ayrs 81 N2
Lugwardine Herefs 35 N12
Luib Highld 100 e7
Luing Ag & B 87 N3
Lulham Herefs 34 K12
Lullington Derbys 46 H11
Lullington E Susx 11 S10
Lullington Somset 17 U6
Lulsgate Bottom N Som 17 P3
Lulsley Worcs 35 R9
Lulworth Camp Dorset 8 A12
Lumb Calder 56 F2
Lumb Lancs 55 T2
Lumbutts Calder 56 E2
Lumby N York 64 B13
Lumloch E Duns 89 P11
Lumphanan Abers 98 K3
Lumphinnans Fife 90 J13
Lumsden Abers 104 F11
Lunan Angus 99 M13
Lunanhead Angus 98 H13
Luncarty P & K 90 G6
Lund E R Yk 65 M10
Lund N York 64 F13
Lundie Angus 91 L4
Lundin Links Fife 91 P11
Lundin Mill Fife 91 P11
Lundy Devon 14 D3
Lundy Green Norfk 41 M2
Lunga Ag & B 87 N4
Lunna Shet 106 u7
Lunsford Kent 12 C4
Lunsford's Cross E Susx 12 D13
Lunt Sefton 54 H6
Luntley Herefs 34 J9
Luppitt Devon 6 G3
Lupridge Devon 5 S10
Lupset Wakefd 57 M3
Lupton Cumb 62 B3
Lurgashall W Susx 10 E5
Lurley Devon 16 B13
Lusby Lincs 59 P13
Luscombe Devon 5 T9
Luson Devon 5 Q10
Luss Ag & B 88 J7
Lussagiven Ag & B 87 L8
Lusta Highld 100 b4
Lustleigh Devon 5 T4
Luston Herefs 35 L8
Luthermuir Abers 99 M10
Luthrie Fife 91 M8
Lutley Dudley 36 B4
Luton Devon 6 B9
Luton Devon 6 E4
Luton Luton 31 N8
Luton Medway 12 E2
Luton Airport Luton 31 P8
Lutterworth Leics 37 P4
Lutton Devon 5 P9
Lutton Devon 5 R8
Lutton Lincs 49 P8
Lutton Nhants 38 H3
Luxborough Somset 16 C9
Luxulyan Cnwll 3 R5
Luxulyan Valley Cnwll 3 R5
Luzley Tamesd 56 E6
Lybster Highld 112 F9
Lydbury North Shrops 34 H3
Lydcott Devon 15 Q5
Lydd Kent 12 K11
Lydd Airport Kent 13 L11
Lydden Kent 13 Q6
Lydden Kent 13 S2
Lyddington Rutlnd 38 C1
Lydeard St Lawrence Somset 16 F10
Lyde Green Hants 20 B11
Lydford Devon 5 N3
Lydford on Fosse Somset 17 Q10
Lydgate Calder 56 D1
Lydgate Rochdl 56 E3
Lydham Shrops 34 H2
Lydiard Green Wilts 29 L10
Lydiard Millicent Wilts 29 L10
Lydiard Tregoze Swindn 29 M11
Lydiate Sefton 54 J6
Lydiate Ash Worcs 36 C5
Lydlinch Dorset 7 T2
Lydney Gloucs 28 B7
Lydstep Pembks 24 J11
Lye Dudley 36 B4
Lye Cross N Som 17 N4
Lye Green Bucks 31 L12
Lye Green E Susx 11 S4
Lye Green Warwks 36 G7
Lye Head Worcs 35 S6
Lye's Green Wilts 18 B11
Lyford Oxon 29 S9
Lymbridge Green Kent 13 M7
Lyme Regis Dorset 6 K6
Lyminge Kent 13 N7
Lymington Hants 9 L9
Lyminster W Susx 10 G10
Lymm Warrtn 55 Q9
Lymm Services Warrtn 55 Q10
Lympne Kent 13 M8
Lympsham Somset 16 K6
Lympstone Devon 6 C8
Lynbridge Devon 15 R3
Lynchat Highld 97 M3
Lynch Green Norfk 51 L12
Lyndhurst Hants 9 L7
Lyndon Rutlnd 48 D13
Lyndon Green Birm 36 F3
Lyne Border 83 P10
Lyne Surrey 20 H9
Lyneal Shrops 44 K7
Lyne Down Herefs 28 B1
Lyneham Devon 5 V5
Lyneham Oxon 29 Q3
Lyneham Wilts 18 F5
Lyneholmford Cumb 75 V11
Lynemouth Nthumb 77 R7
Lyne of Skene Abers 105 M13
Lynesack Dur 69 N7
Lyness Ork 106 s20
Lyng Norfk 50 J10
Lyng Somset 16 K11
Lynmouth Devon 15 R3
Lynn Staffs 46 E13
Lynn Wrekin 45 S10
Lynsted Kent 12 H3
Lynstone Cnwll 14 F11
Lynton Devon 15 R3
Lyon's Gate Dorset 7 S3
Lyonshall Herefs 34 H9
Lytchett Matravers Dorset 8 C9
Lytchett Minster Dorset 8 D10
Lyth Highld 112 G4
Lytham Lancs 54 J1
Lytham St Anne's Lancs 54 H1
Lythbank Shrops 45 L12
Lythe N York 71 P10
Lythmore Highld 112 C3

M

Mabe Burnthouse Cnwll 2 K10
Mablethorpe Lincs 59 T10
Macclesfield Ches E 56 D12
Macclesfield Crematorium Ches E 56 D12
Macduff Abers 105 L3
Macharioch Ag & B 79 N14
Machen Caerph 27 N10
Machrie N Ayrs 79 R9
Machrihanish Ag & B 79 L11
Machrins Ag & B 86 F7
Machynlleth Powys 43 P13
Machynys Carmth 25 T11
Mackworth Derbys 46 K6
Macmerry E Loth 84 C4
Maddaford Devon 5 N2
Madderty P & K 90 E7
Maddington Wilts 18 G12
Maddiston Falk 82 H3
Madehurst W Susx 10 F8
Madeley Staffs 45 S5
Madeley Wrekin 45 Q13
Madeley Heath Staffs 45 S4
Madford Devon 6 F2
Madingley Cambs 39 N8
Madley Herefs 34 K13
Madresfield Worcs 35 T11
Madron Cnwll 2 D10
Maenaddwyn IoA 52 G6
Maenan Conwy 53 N9
Maenclochog Pembks 24 J5
Maendy V Glam 26 J12
Maenporth Cnwll 2 K11
Maentwrog Gwynd 43 N5
Maen-y-groes Cerdgn 32 G9
Maer Cnwll 14 F11
Maer Staffs 45 S6
Maerdy Carmth 26 B2
Maerdy Rhondd 26 H8
Maesbrook Shrops 44 H9
Maesbury Shrops 44 H8
Maesbury Marsh Shrops 44 H8
Maes-glas Newpt 27 P10
Maesgwynne Carmth 25 M6
Maeshafn Denbgs 44 F1
Maesllyn Cerdgn 32 G12
Maesmynis Powys 34 B11
Maesmynis Powys 34 B11
Maesteg Brdgnd 26 F9
Maesybont Carmth 25 U7
Maesycwmmer Caerph 27 M9
Magdalen Laver Essex 22 D6
Maggieknockater Moray 104 C6
Maggots End Essex 22 C2
Magham Down E Susx 11 U8
Maghull Sefton 54 J6
Magna Park Leics 37 P4
Magor Mons 27 S10
Magor Services Mons 27 S10
Maidenbower W Susx 11 M3
Maiden Bradley Wilts 18 B13
Maidencombe Torbay 6 B11
Maidenhayne Devon 6 J5
Maiden Head N Som 17 Q3
Maidenhead W & M 20 E6
Maiden Law Dur 69 Q3
Maiden Newton Dorset 7 Q5
Maidens S Ayrs 80 J11
Maiden's Green Br For 20 F8
Maidenwell Lincs 59 P11
Maiden Wells Pembks 24 G11
Maidford Nhants 37 R10
Maids Moreton Bucks 30 F5
Maidstone Kent 12 E4
Maidstone Services Kent 12 F4
Maidwell Nhants 37 T5
Mail Shet 106 u9
Maindee Newpt 27 Q10
Mainland Ork 106 t19
Mainland Shet 106 u8
Mainsforth Dur 70 D6
Mains of Balhall Angus 98 J11
Mains of Balnakettle Abers 99 L9
Mains of Dalvey Highld 103 T9
Mains of Haulkerton Abers 99 N9
Mains of Lesmoir Abers 104 F10
Mains of Melgunds Angus 98 J12
Mainsriddle D & G 66 D1
Mainstone Shrops 34 G3
Maisemore Gloucs 28 F3
Major's Green Worcs 36 F5
Makeney Derbys 47 L5
Malborough Devon 5 S13
Malcoff Derbys 56 G10
Malden Rushett Gt Lon 21 L10
Maldon Essex 22 L6
Malham N York 62 J7
Maligar Highld 100 d3
Mallaig Highld 100 f10
Mallaigvaig Highld 100 f10
Malleny Mills C Edin 83 N5
Mallows Green Essex 22 C2
Malltraeth IoA 52 F9
Mallwyd Gwynd 43 S11
Malmesbury Wilts 28 H10
Malmsmead Devon 15 S3
Malpas Ches W 45 L4
Malpas Cnwll 3 L8
Malpas Newpt 27 Q9
Malshanger Hants 19 S10
Malswick Gloucs 28 D3
Maltby Lincs 59 P10
Maltby Rothm 57 R8
Maltby S on T 70 G10
Maltby le Marsh Lincs 59 S10
Malting Green Essex 23 N3
Maltman's Hill Kent 12 H7
Malton N York 64 H5
Malvern Worcs 35 S11
Malvern Hills 35 S12
Malvern Link Worcs 35 S11
Malvern Wells Worcs 35 S12
Mamble Worcs 35 Q6
Mamhilad Mons 27 Q7
Manaccan Cnwll 2 K12
Manafon Powys 44 D13
Manais W Isls 106 g10
Manaton Devon 5 T4
Manby Lincs 59 Q9
Mancetter Warwks 36 K1
Manchester Manch 55 T7
Manchester Airport Manch 55 T10
Manchester Crematorium Manch 55 T8
Mancot Flints 54 H13
Mandally Highld 96 B3
Manea Cambs 39 Q3
Maney Birm 36 F1
Manfield N York 69 R10
Mangerton Dorset 7 N5
Mangotsfield S Glos 28 C12
Mangrove Green Herts 31 P8
Manhay Cnwll 2 H10
Manish W Isls 106 g10
Mankinholes Calder 56 E2
Manley Ches W 55 M12
Manmoel Caerph 27 M7
Mannel Ag & B 92 B10

136 Manningford Bohune – Nebo

Manningford Bohune Wilts 18 H9
Manningford Bruce Wilts 18 H9
Manningham C Brad 63 N12
Manning's Heath W Susx 11 L5
Mannington Dorset 8 F7
Manningtree Essex 23 R1
Mannofield C Aber 99 S3
Manorbier Pembks 24 J11
Manorbier Newton Pembks 24 H10
Manordeilo Carmth 26 B2
Manorhill Border 84 H12
Manorowen Pembks 24 F3
Manor Park Gt Lon 21 R5
Manor Park Crematorium Gt Lon 21 R5
Mansell Gamage Herefs 34 J12
Mansell Lacy Herefs 34 K11
Mansergh Cumb 62 C3
Mansfield E Ayrs 81 S10
Mansfield Notts 47 P1
Mansfield & District Crematorium Notts 47 P2
Mansfield Woodhouse Notts 57 R14
Mansriggs Cumb 61 P3
Manston Dorset 17 V13
Manston Kent 13 R2
Manston Leeds 63 T13
Manswood Dorset 8 D7
Manthorpe Lincs 48 D6
Manthorpe Lincs 48 G10
Manton N Linc 58 F6
Manton Notts 57 T11
Manton Rutlnd 48 C13
Manton Wilts 18 J7
Manuden Essex 22 C2
Manwood Green Essex 22 D5
Maperton Somset 17 S11
Maplebeck Notts 47 T1
Maple Cross Herts 20 H4
Mapledurham Oxon 19 U5
Mapledurwell Hants 19 U10
Maplehurst W Susx 10 K6
Maplescombe Kent 21 U10
Mapleton Derbys 46 G4
Mapleton Kent 21 S13
Mapperley Derbys 47 M5
Mapperley Park C Nott 47 Q5
Mapperton Dorset 7 P5
Mappleborough Green Warwks 36 E7
Mappleton E R Yk 65 S11
Mapplewell Barns 57 M4
Mappowder Dorset 7 T3
Marazanvose Cnwll 2 K6
Marazion Cnwll 2 E10
Marbury Ches E 45 N4
March Cambs 39 P1
March S Lans 74 J3
Marcham Oxon 29 U8
Marchamley Shrops 45 N8
Marchamley Wood Shrops 45 N7
Marchington Staffs 46 F7
Marchington Woodlands Staffs 46 F8
Marchros Gwynd 42 F8
Marchwiel Wrexhm 44 J4
Marchwood Hants 9 M6
Marcross V Glam 16 B3
Marden Herefs 35 M11
Marden Kent 12 D7
Marden Wilts 18 G9
Marden Ash Essex 22 E7
Marden Beech Kent 12 D7
Mardens Hill E Susx 11 S4
Marden Thorn Kent 12 E7
Mardlebury Herts 31 S9
Mardy Mons 27 Q4
Marefield Leics 47 T12
Mareham le Fen Lincs 49 L1
Mareham on the Hill Lincs 59 N13
Marehay Derbys 47 L4
Marehill W Susx 10 H7
Maresfield E Susx 11 R6
Marfleet C KuH 65 Q14
Marford Wrexhm 44 J2
Margam Neath 26 D10
Margam Crematorium Neath 26 D10
Margaret Marsh Dorset 17 V13
Margaret Roding Essex 22 E5
Margaretting Essex 22 G7
Margaretting Tye Essex 22 G7
Margate Kent 13 S1
Margnaheglish N Ayrs 80 E6
Margrie D & G 73 P9
Margrove Park R & Cl 71 L9
Marham Norfk 50 B12
Marhamchurch Cnwll 14 F12
Marholm C Pete 48 H13
Marian-glas IoA 52 H6
Mariansleigh Devon 15 R8
Marine Town Kent 23 M13
Marionburgh Abers 99 N2
Marishader Highld 100 d3
Maristow Devon 5 M8
Marjoriebanks D & G 75 L9
Mark Somset 17 L7
Markbeech Kent 11 R2
Markby Lincs 59 S11
Mark Causeway Somset 17 L7
Mark Cross E Susx 11 T4
Markeaton C Derb 46 K6
Markeaton Crematorium C Derb 46 K6
Market Bosworth Leics 47 M13
Market Deeping Lincs 48 H11
Market Drayton Shrops 45 Q7
Market Harborough Leics 37 T3
Market Lavington Wilts 18 F10
Market Overton Rutlnd 48 C10
Market Rasen Lincs 58 K9
Market Stainton Lincs 59 M11
Market Warsop Notts 57 S13
Market Weighton E R Yk 64 K11
Market Weston Suffk 40 G5
Markfield Leics 47 N12
Markham Caerph 27 M7
Markham Moor Notts 58 B12
Markinch Fife 91 L11
Markington N York 63 R6
Markle E Loth 84 F3
Marksbury BaNES 17 S4
Mark's Corner IoW 9 P10
Marks Tey Essex 23 M3
Markwell Cnwll 4 K9
Markyate Herts 31 N9
Marlborough Wilts 18 J7
Marlbrook Herefs 35 M10
Marlbrook Worcs 36 C6
Marlcliff Warwks 36 E10
Marldon Devon 5 V8
Marle Green E Susx 11 T7
Marlesford Suffk 41 P9
Marley Kent 13 N5
Marley Kent 13 R5
Marley Green Ches E 45 N4
Marley Hill Gatesd 77 Q14
Marlingford Norfk 50 K12
Marloes Pembks 24 C9
Marlow Bucks 20 D5
Marlow Herefs 34 K5
Marlow Bottom Bucks 20 D5
Marlpit Hill Kent 21 R13
Marlpits E Susx 11 R5
Marlpits E Susx 12 D13
Marlpool Derbys 47 M4
Marnhull Dorset 17 U13
Marple Stockp 56 E9
Marple Bridge Stockp 56 E9
Marr Donc 57 R5
Marrick N York 69 N13
Marros Carmth 25 M9
Marsden Kirk 56 F4
Marsden S Tyne 77 T13
Marsden Height Lancs 62 H12
Marsett N York 62 J2
Marsh Bucks 30 H11
Marsh C Brad 63 L12
Marsh Devon 6 J2
Marshall's Heath Herts 31 Q10
Marshalswick Herts 31 Q11
Marsham Norfk 51 L9
Marsh Baldon Oxon 30 C13
Marsh Benham W Berk 19 P7
Marshborough Kent 13 R4
Marshbrook Shrops 34 K3
Marshchapel Lincs 59 Q7
Marsh Farm Luton 31 N7
Marshfield Newpt 27 P11
Marshfield S Glos 28 E13
Marshgate Cnwll 4 F2
Marsh Gibbon Bucks 30 D8
Marsh Green Devon 6 D6
Marsh Green Kent 11 Q2
Marsh Green Wrekin 45 P11
Marshland St James Norfk 49 R12
Marsh Lane Derbys 57 P11
Marsh Lane Gloucs 28 A6
Marshside Sefton 54 J3
Marsh Street Somset 16 C8
Marshwood Dorset 7 L5
Marske N York 69 P12
Marske-by-the-Sea R & Cl 70 K8
Marsland Green Wigan 55 Q7
Marston Ches W 55 Q11
Marston Herefs 34 J9
Marston Lincs 48 C5
Marston Oxon 30 B11
Marston Staffs 45 T11
Marston Staffs 46 B8
Marston Warwks 36 H2
Marston Wilts 18 E9
Marston Green Solhll 36 G3
Marston Jabbet Warwks 37 L3
Marston Magna Somset 17 Q12
Marston Meysey Wilts 29 M8
Marston Montgomery Derbys 46 F6
Marston Moretaine C Beds 31 L4
Marston on Dove Derbys 46 H8
Marston St Lawrence Nhants 30 B4
Marston Stannett Herefs 35 N9
Marston Trussell Nhants 37 S3
Marstow Herefs 27 V4
Marsworth Bucks 30 K10
Marten Wilts 19 L8
Marthall Ches E 55 S11
Martham Norfk 51 S10
Martin Hants 8 F5
Martin Kent 13 R6
Martin Lincs 48 H2
Martin Lincs 59 M13
Martindale Cumb 67 P9
Martin Dales Lincs 48 J1
Martin Drove End Hants 8 F4
Martinhoe Devon 15 Q3
Martin Hussingtree Worcs 35 U8
Martinscroft Warrtn 55 Q9
Martinstown Dorset 7 R7
Martlesham Suffk 41 M11
Martlesham Heath Suffk 41 M11
Martletwy Pembks 24 H8
Martley Worcs 35 S8
Martock Somset 17 N13
Marton Ches E 56 C13
Marton Ches W 55 P13
Marton Cumb 61 N4
Marton E R Yk 65 R12
Marton E R Yk 65 S6
Marton Lincs 58 D10
Marton Middsb 70 H9
Marton N York 63 U7
Marton N York 64 G3
Marton Shrops 44 G13
Marton Warwks 37 M7
Marton-le-Moor N York 63 T5
Martyr's Green Surrey 20 J11
Martyr Worthy Hants 9 Q2
Marwell Wildlife Hants 9 Q4
Marwick Ork 106 r17
Marwood Devon 15 M5
Marybank Highld 102 E5
Maryburgh Highld 102 F4
Marygold Border 85 L7
Maryhill C Glas 89 N12
Maryhill Crematorium C Glas 89 N12
Marykirk Abers 99 M10
Maryland Mons 27 U6
Marylebone Gt Lon 21 N6
Marylebone Wigan 55 N5
Marypark Moray 103 U8
Maryport Cumb 66 F5
Maryport D & G 72 E13
Marystow Devon 5 L4
Mary Tavy Devon 5 N5
Maryton Angus 99 M12
Marywell Abers 98 K4
Marywell Abers 99 S4
Marywell Angus 91 U3
Masham N York 63 Q3
Mashbury Essex 22 G5
Mason N u Ty 77 Q11
Masongill N York 62 D4
Masonhill Crematorium S Ayrs 81 M8
Mastin Moor Derbys 57 Q11
Matching Essex 22 D5
Matching Green Essex 22 D5
Matching Tye Essex 22 D5
Matfen Nthumb 77 L11
Matfield Kent 12 C7
Mathern Mons 27 U9
Mathon Herefs 35 R11
Mathry Pembks 24 E4
Matlask Norfk 51 L7
Matlock Derbys 46 K2
Matlock Bank Derbys 46 K1
Matlock Bath Derbys 46 J2
Matlock Dale Derbys 46 J2
Matson Gloucs 28 G4
Matterdale End Cumb 67 N8
Mattersey Notts 57 U9
Mattersey Thorpe Notts 57 U9
Mattingley Hants 20 B11
Mattishall Norfk 50 J11
Mattishall Burgh Norfk 50 J11
Mauchline E Ayrs 81 P7
Maud Abers 105 Q6
Maufant Jersey 7 e2
Maugersbury Gloucs 29 P2
Maughold IoM 60 h4
Mauld Highld 102 D8
Maulden C Beds 31 N5
Maulds Meaburn Cumb 68 D9
Maunby N York 63 T2
Maund Bryan Herefs 35 N10
Maundown Somset 16 E11
Mautby Norfk 51 S11
Mavesyn Ridware Staffs 46 E10
Mavis Enderby Lincs 59 Q13
Mawbray Cumb 66 G3
Mawdesley Lancs 55 L4
Mawdlam Brdgnd 26 E11
Mawgan Cnwll 2 J11
Mawgan Porth Cnwll 3 M3
Maw Green Ches E 45 R2
Mawla Cnwll 2 J7
Mawnan Cnwll 2 K11
Mawnan Smith Cnwll 2 K11
Mawsley Nhants 38 B5
Mawthorpe Lincs 59 S12
Maxey C Pete 48 H12
Maxstoke Warwks 36 H3
Maxted Street Kent 13 M7
Maxton Border 84 G12
Maxton Kent 13 R7
Maxwell Town D & G 74 J10
Maxworthy Cnwll 4 H2
Mayals Swans 25 V13
May Bank Staffs 45 U4
Maybole S Ayrs 80 K11
Maybury Surrey 20 H11
Mayes Green Surrey 10 J3
Mayfield E Susx 11 T5
Mayfield Mdloth 83 S5
Mayfield Staffs 46 G4
Mayford Surrey 20 G11
May Hill Gloucs 28 D3
Mayland Essex 23 M7
Maylandsea Essex 23 M7
Maynard's Green E Susx 11 T7
Maypole Birm 36 E5
Maypole Kent 13 P3
Maypole Mons 27 T4
Maypole Green Norfk 41 R1
Maypole Green Suffk 40 F9
Maypole Green Suffk 41 N7
May's Green Oxon 20 B6
May's Green Surrey 20 J11
Mead Devon 14 F9
Meadgate BaNES 17 S5
Meadle Bucks 30 H11
Meadowfield Dur 69 R5
Meadowtown Shrops 44 H13
Meadwell Devon 5 L4
Meaford Staffs 45 U6
Meal Bank Cumb 67 R13
Mealrigg Cumb 66 H3
Mealsgate Cumb 66 K4
Meanwood Leeds 63 R12
Mearbeck N York 62 G7
Meare Somset 17 N8
Meare Green Somset 16 J12
Meare Green Somset 16 K11
Mearns E Rens 81 Q1
Mears Ashby Nhants 38 B7
Measham Leics 46 K11
Meathop Cumb 61 S3
Meaux E R Yk 65 P12
Meavy Devon 5 N7
Medbourne Leics 38 B2
Meddon Devon 14 G9
Meden Vale Notts 57 S13
Medlam Lincs 49 M2
Medlar Lancs 61 S12
Medmenham Bucks 20 D6
Medomsley Dur 69 P2
Medstead Hants 19 U13
Medway Crematorium Kent 12 D3
Medway Services Medway 12 F3
Meerbrook Staffs 46 C1
Meer Common Herefs 34 J10
Meesden Herts 22 B1
Meeson Wrekin 45 P9
Meeth Devon 15 M11
Meeting Green Suffk 40 B9
Meeting House Hill Norfk 51 P8
Meidrim Carmth 25 N6
Meifod Powys 44 E11
Meigle P & K 91 L3
Meikle Carco D & G 74 E3
Meikle Earnock S Lans 82 D8
Meikle Kilmory Ag & B 88 C13
Meikle Obney P & K 90 F4
Meikleour P & K 90 J4
Meikle Wartle Abers 105 L9
Meinciau Carmth 25 S8
Meir C Stke 46 B5
Meir Heath Staffs 46 B5
Melbourn Cambs 31 U4
Melbourne Derbys 47 L8
Melbourne E R Yk 64 H11
Melbur Cnwll 3 N6
Melbury Devon 14 J9
Melbury Abbas Dorset 8 B4
Melbury Bubb Dorset 7 Q3
Melbury Osmond Dorset 7 Q3
Melbury Sampford Dorset 7 Q3
Melchbourne Bed 38 F7
Melcombe Bingham Dorset 7 U4
Meldon Devon 5 P2
Meldon Nthumb 77 N9
Meldon Park Nthumb 77 N8
Meldreth Cambs 39 N11
Meldrum Stirlg 89 R6
Melfort Ag & B 87 Q3
Meliden Denbgs 54 C10
Melinau Pembks 25 L8
Melin-byrhedyn Powys 43 R14
Melincourt Neath 26 E7
Melin-y-coed Conwy 53 P10
Melin-y-ddol Powys 44 C12
Melin-y-wîg Denbgs 44 B4
Melkinthorpe Cumb 67 S7
Melkridge Nthumb 76 E13
Melksham Wilts 18 D8
Mellangoose Cnwll 2 H11
Mell Green W Berk 19 Q5
Mellguards Cumb 67 P3
Melling Lancs 62 B5
Melling Sefton 54 J6
Melling Mount Sefton 54 K6
Mellis Suffk 40 J6
Mellon Charles Highld 107 P6
Mellon Udrigle Highld 107 Q5
Mellor Lancs 62 D13
Mellor Stockp 56 E9
Mellor Brook Lancs 62 C13
Mells Somset 17 T7
Mells Suffk 41 R5
Melmerby Cumb 68 D5
Melmerby N York 63 M2
Melmerby N York 63 S4
Melness Highld 111 M4
Melon Green Suffk 40 D9
Melplash Dorset 7 N5
Melrose Border 84 E12
Melsetter Ork 106 r21
Melsonby N York 69 Q11
Meltham Kirk 56 H4
Meltham Mills Kirk 56 H4
Melton E R Yk 58 G1
Melton Suffk 41 N10
Meltonby E R Yk 64 H9
Melton Constable Norfk 50 H7
Melton Mowbray Leics 47 U10
Melton Ross N Linc 58 J4
Melvaig Highld 107 M7
Melverley Shrops 44 H10
Melverley Green Shrops 44 H10
Melvich Highld 111 T4
Membury Devon 6 J4
Membury Services W Berk 19 M5
Memsie Abers 105 R3
Memus Angus 98 G12
Menabilly Cnwll 3 R6
Menagissey Cnwll 2 J7
Menai Bridge IoA 52 J8
Mendham Suffk 41 N4
Mendip Crematorium Somset 17 Q8
Mendip Hills 17 P6
Mendlesham Suffk 40 K7
Mendlesham Green Suffk 40 J8
Menheniot Cnwll 4 H8
Menithwood Worcs 35 R7
Menna Cnwll 3 N6
Mennock D & G 74 F4
Menston C Brad 63 P11
Menstrie Clacks 90 C12
Menthorpe N York 64 G13
Mentmore Bucks 30 K9
Meoble Highld 100 g11
Meole Brace Shrops 45 L11
Meonstoke Hants 9 S5
Meopham Kent 12 B2
Meopham Green Kent 12 B2
Meopham Station Kent 12 B2
Mepal Cambs 39 P4
Meppershall C Beds 31 P5
Merbach Herefs 34 H11
Mere Ches E 55 R10
Mere Wilts 17 V10
Mere Brow Lancs 54 K3
Mereclough Lancs 62 H13
Mere Green Birm 46 F14
Mere Green Worcs 36 C8
Mere Heath Ches W 55 Q12
Meresborough Medway 12 F3
Mereworth Kent 12 C5
Meriden Solhll 36 H4
Merkadale Highld 100 c6
Merley Poole 8 E9
Merlin's Bridge Pembks 24 F8
Merrington Shrops 45 L9
Merrion Pembks 24 F11
Merriott Somset 7 M2
Merrivale Devon 5 N5
Merrow Surrey 20 H12
Merry Field Hill Dorset 8 E8
Merry Hill Herts 20 K4
Merryhill Wolves 35 U1
Merry Lees Leics 47 N12
Merrymeet Cnwll 4 H7
Mersea Island Essex 23 P4
Mersey Crossing Halton 55 M10
Mersham Kent 13 L7
Merstham Surrey 21 N12
Merston W Susx 10 D10
Merstone IoW 9 Q11
Merther Cnwll 3 M8
Merthyr Carmth 25 Q6
Merthyr Cynog Powys 33 U13
Merthyr Dyfan V Glam 16 F3
Merthyr Mawr Brdgnd 26 F12
Merthyr Tydfil Myr Td 26 J6
Merthyr Vale Myr Td 26 K8
Merton Devon 15 M10
Merton Gt Lon 21 N8
Merton Norfk 50 F14
Merton Oxon 30 C9
Meshaw Devon 15 S9
Messing Essex 23 L4
Messingham N Linc 58 E6
Metfield Suffk 41 N4
Metherell Cnwll 5 L7
Metheringham Lincs 48 G1
Methil Fife 91 N12
Methilhill Fife 91 N11
Methley Leeds 57 N1
Methley Junction Leeds 57 N1
Methlick Abers 105 P8
Methven P & K 90 F6
Methwold Norfk 40 B2
Methwold Hythe Norfk 40 B2
Mettingham Suffk 41 Q3
Metton Norfk 51 M6
Mevagissey Cnwll 3 Q8
Mexborough Donc 57 Q6
Mey Highld 112 G2
Meyllteyrn Gwynd 42 D7
Meysey Hampton Gloucs 29 M7
Miabhig W Isls 106 f5
Miavaig W Isls 106 f5
Michaelchurch Herefs 27 U2
Michaelchurch Escley Herefs 34 H14
Michaelchurch-on-Arrow Powys 34 F10
Michaelstone-y-Fedw Newpt 27 N11
Michaelston-le-Pit V Glam 27 M13
Michaelstow Cnwll 4 D5
Michaelwood Services Gloucs 28 D8
Michelcombe Devon 5 R7
Micheldever Hants 19 R13
Micheldever Station Hants 19 R12
Michelmersh Hants 9 L3
Mickfield Suffk 40 K8
Micklebring Donc 57 R8
Mickleby N York 71 P10
Micklefield Leeds 63 U13
Micklefield Green Herts 20 H3
Mickleham Surrey 21 L12
Mickleover C Derb 46 K7
Micklethwaite C Brad 63 N11
Micklethwaite Cumb 67 L2
Mickleton Dur 69 L8
Mickleton Gloucs 36 G12
Mickletown Leeds 57 P1
Mickle Trafford Ches W 54 K13
Mickley Derbys 57 M11
Mickley N York 63 R4
Mickley Green Suffk 40 D9
Mickley Square Nthumb 77 M13
Mid Ardlaw Abers 105 Q3
Midbea Ork 106 t15
Mid Beltie Abers 99 L3
Mid Bockhampton Dorset 8 H9
Mid Calder W Loth 83 L5
Mid Clyth Highld 112 G9
Mid Culbeuchly Abers 104 K3
Middle Assendon Oxon 20 B5
Middle Aston Oxon 29 U2
Middle Barton Oxon 29 T2
Middlebie D & G 75 P10
Middlebridge P & K 97 P10
Middle Chinnock Somset 7 N2
Middle Claydon Bucks 30 F7
Middlecliffe Barns 57 P5
Middlecott Devon 5 S3
Middle Duntisbourne Gloucs 28 J6
Middleham N York 63 N2
Middle Handley Derbys 57 P11
Middle Harling Norfk 40 G3
Middlehill Cnwll 4 H7
Middlehill Wilts 18 B7
Middlehope Shrops 35 L3
Middle Kames Ag & B 87 S8
Middle Littleton Worcs 36 E11
Middle Madeley Staffs 45 S4
Middle Maes-coed Herefs 34 H14
Middlemarsh Dorset 7 S3
Middle Mayfield Staffs 46 F5
Middle Mill Pembks 24 D5
Middlemore Devon 5 M6
Middle Quarter Kent 12 G8
Middle Rasen Lincs 58 J9
Middle Rocombe Devon 6 B11
Middle Salter Lancs 62 C7
Middlesbrough Middsb 70 G9
Middlesceugh Cumb 67 P4
Middleshaw Cumb 62 B2
Middlesmoor N York 63 M5
Middle Stoford Somset 16 G12
Middle Stoke Medway 22 K12
Middlestone Dur 69 S6
Middlestone Moor Dur 69 R6
Middle Stoughton Somset 17 M7
Middlestown Wakefd 57 L3
Middle Street Gloucs 28 E7
Middle Taphouse Cnwll 4 F8
Middlethird Border 84 H10
Middleton Ag & B 92 A10
Middleton Cumb 62 C2
Middleton Derbys 46 J2
Middleton Derbys 56 J14
Middleton Essex 40 E13
Middleton Hants 19 P12
Middleton Herefs 35 M7
Middleton Lancs 61 S8
Middleton Leeds 63 S14
Middleton N York 63 N10
Middleton N York 64 H2
Middleton Nhants 38 B3
Middleton Norfk 49 U10
Middleton Nthumb 77 M9
Middleton Nthumb 85 S11
Middleton P & K 90 H10
Middleton Rochdl 56 C5
Middleton Shrops 35 M5
Middleton Shrops 44 H8
Middleton Suffk 41 R7
Middleton Swans 25 R13
Middleton Warwks 46 G14
Middleton Cheney Nhants 37 N12
Middleton Crematorium Rochdl 56 C5
Middleton Green Staffs 46 C6
Middleton Hall Nthumb 85 P13
Middleton-in-Teesdale Dur 68 K7
Middleton Moor Suffk 41 R7
Middleton One Row Darltn 70 E10
Middleton-on-Leven N York 70 G11
Middleton-on-Sea W Susx 10 F10
Middleton on the Hill Herefs 35 M8
Middleton on the Wolds E R Yk 65 L10
Middleton Park C Aber 105 Q13
Middleton Priors Shrops 35 P2
Middleton Quernhow N York 63 S4
Middleton St George Darltn 70 D10
Middleton Scriven Shrops 35 Q3
Middleton Stoney Oxon 30 B8
Middleton Tyas N York 69 R11
Middletown Cumb 66 E11
Middle Town IoS 2 b3
Middletown N Som 17 N2
Middletown Powys 44 H11
Middle Tysoe Warwks 36 K12
Middle Wallop Hants 19 L13
Middlewich Ches E 55 R13
Middle Winterslow Wilts 8 J2
Middlewood Cnwll 4 H5
Middlewood Herefs 34 G12
Middle Woodford Wilts 18 H13
Middlewood Green Suffk 40 J8
Middleyard E Ayrs 81 Q6
Middle Yard Gloucs 28 F7
Middlezoy Somset 17 L10
Middridge Dur 69 R7
Midford BaNES 17 U4
Midge Hall Lancs 55 M2
Midgeholme Cumb 76 C14
Midgham W Berk 19 S7
Midgley Calder 56 F1
Midgley Wakefd 57 L4
Mid Holmwood Surrey 21 L13
Midhopestones Sheff 56 K7
Midhurst W Susx 10 D6
Mid Lavant W Susx 10 D9
Midlem Border 84 E13
Mid Mains Highld 102 D8
Midney Somset 17 N11
Midpark Ag & B 87 U14
Midsomer Norton BaNES 17 S6
Midtown Highld 111 M4
Midville Lincs 49 N2
Mid Warwickshire Crematorium Warwks 36 K9
Midway Ches E 56 D10
Mid Yell Shet 106 v4
Migvie Abers 98 G2
Milborne Port Somset 17 S13
Milborne St Andrew Dorset 7 V5
Milborne Wick Somset 17 S12
Milbourne Nthumb 77 N10
Milbourne Wilts 28 J10
Milburn Cumb 68 E7
Milbury Heath S Glos 28 C9
Milby N York 63 U6
Milcombe Oxon 37 M14
Milden Suffk 40 G11
Mildenhall Suffk 40 B6
Mildenhall Wilts 18 K7
Milebrook Powys 34 H6
Milebush Kent 12 E6
Mile Elm Wilts 18 E7
Mile End Essex 23 N2
Mile End Gloucs 28 A5
Mile End Suffk 41 P3
Mileham Norfk 50 F10
Mile Oak Br & H 11 L9
Mile Oak Kent 12 C7
Mile Oak Staffs 46 G13
Miles Hope Herefs 35 N8
Milesmark Fife 90 G14
Miles Platting Manch 56 C7
Mile Town Kent 23 M13
Milfield Nthumb 85 N12
Milford Derbys 47 L4
Milford Devon 14 F8
Milford Powys 34 C2
Milford Staffs 46 C9
Milford Surrey 10 E2
Milford Haven Pembks 24 F9
Milford on Sea Hants 8 K10
Milkwall Gloucs 28 A6
Millais Jersey 7 a1
Milland W Susx 10 C5
Milland Marsh W Susx 10 C5
Mill Bank Calder 56 F2
Millbeck Cumb 67 L7
Millbreck Abers 105 S7
Millbridge Surrey 10 C2
Millbrook C Beds 31 M5
Millbrook C Sotn 9 M6
Millbrook Cnwll 5 L10
Millbrook Jersey 7 c3
Millbrook Tamesd 56 E7
Mill Brow Stockp 56 E9
Millbuie Abers 99 P2
Millbuie Highld 102 G5
Millcombe Devon 5 U11
Mill Common Norfk 51 P13
Mill Common Suffk 41 R4
Millcorner E Susx 12 F11
Millcraig Highld 109 M10
Mill Cross Devon 5 S8
Milldale Staffs 46 F3
Mill End Bucks 20 C5
Mill End Cambs 39 M4
Millend Gloucs 28 D8
Mill End Herts 31 T6
Millerhill Mdloth 83 R5
Miller's Dale Derbys 56 H12
Millers Green Derbys 46 J3
Miller's Green Essex 22 E6
Millerston C Glas 89 P12
Millgate Lancs 56 C3
Mill Green Cambs 39 T11
Mill Green Essex 22 F7
Mill Green Herts 31 R10
Mill Green Lincs 48 K9
Mill Green Norfk 40 K4
Millgreen Shrops 45 Q8
Mill Green Staffs 46 E13
Mill Green Staffs 46 E9
Mill Green Suffk 40 G12
Mill Green Suffk 40 G9
Mill Green Suffk 40 K8
Mill Green Suffk 41 P8
Millhalf Herefs 34 G11
Millhayes Devon 6 H4
Millhead Lancs 61 T5
Millheugh S Lans 82 D8
Mill Hill E Susx 11 U9
Mill Hill Gt Lon 21 M4
Millhouse Ag & B 87 T11
Millhouse Cumb 67 N5
Millhousebridge D & G 75 M8
Millhouse Green Barns 56 K6
Millhouses Barns 57 P6
Millhouses Sheff 57 M10
Milliken Park Rens 88 K13
Millin Cross Pembks 24 G8
Millington E R Yk 64 J9
Millmeece Staffs 45 T7
Millness Cumb 61 U3
Mill of Drummond P & K 89 T2
Mill of Haldane W Duns 88 J9
Millom Cumb 61 M3
Millook Cnwll 14 E13
Millpool Cnwll 2 F10
Millpool Cnwll 4 E6
Millport N Ayrs 80 H2
Mill Side Cumb 61 S3
Mill Street Kent 12 C4
Mill Street Norfk 50 J10
Mill Street Suffk 40 J6
Millthorpe Derbys 57 M11
Millthrop Cumb 62 D1
Milltimber C Aber 99 R3
Milltown Abers 98 D2
Milltown Abers 104 F12
Milltown Cnwll 4 E9
Milltown D & G 75 R10
Milltown Derbys 47 L1
Milltown Devon 15 N5
Milltown of Auchindoun Moray 104 D7
Milltown of Campfield Abers 99 M3
Milltown of Edinvillie Moray 104 B7
Milltown of Learney Abers 99 L3
Milnathort P & K 90 H11
Milngavie E Duns 89 N11
Milnrow Rochdl 56 D4
Milnthorpe Cumb 61 T3
Milnthorpe Wakefd 57 M3
Milovaig Highld 100 a5
Milson Shrops 35 P6
Milstead Kent 12 H4
Milston Wilts 18 J11
Milthorpe Lincs 48 H7
Milthorpe Nhants 37 Q11
Milton C Stke 46 B3
Milton Cambs 39 Q8
Milton Cumb 76 B13
Milton D & G 72 G9
Milton D & G 74 F11
Milton Derbys 46 K8
Milton Highld 100 g5
Milton Highld 102 E9
Milton Highld 102 G6
Milton Highld 109 P10
Milton Highld 112 H6
Milton Inver 88 J12
Milton Kent 22 G13
Milton Moray 103 U12
Milton Moray 104 G3
Milton N Som 16 K4
Milton Newpt 27 R10
Milton Notts 58 B12
Milton Oxon 29 U9
Milton Oxon 37 N13
Milton P & K 97 T11
Milton Pembks 24 H10
Milton Somset 17 N12
Milton Stirlg 89 M5
Milton W Duns 88 K11
Milton Abbas Dorset 7 V4
Milton Abbot Devon 5 L5
Milton Bridge Mdloth 83 Q6
Milton Bryan C Beds 31 L6
Milton Clevedon Somset 17 S9
Milton Combe Devon 5 M7
Milton Common Oxon 30 E12
Milton Damerel Devon 14 J10
Milton End Gloucs 28 D5
Milton End Gloucs 29 M7
Milton Ernest Bed 38 F9
Milton Green Ches W 45 L2
Milton Hill Oxon 29 U9
Milton Keynes M Keyn 30 J5
Milton Lilbourne Wilts 18 J8
Milton Malsor Nhants 37 T9
Milton Morenish P & K 95 S11
Milton of Auchinhove Abers 98 K3
Milton of Balgonie Fife 91 M11
Milton of Buchanan Stirlg 88 K7
Milton of Campsie E Duns 89 Q10
Milton of Leys Highld 102 J7
Milton of Murtle C Aber 99 R3
Milton of Tullich Abers 98 F4
Milton on Stour Dorset 17 U11
Milton Regis Kent 12 H3
Milton Street E Susx 11 S10
Milton-under-Wychwood Oxon 29 Q4
Milverton Somset 16 F11
Milverton Warwks 36 K7
Milwich Staffs 46 C7
Milwr Flints 54 E12
Minard Ag & B 87 T6
Minchington Dorset 8 D6
Minchinhampton Gloucs 28 G7
Mindrum Nthumb 85 L12
Minehead Somset 16 C7
Minera Wrexhm 44 G3
Minety Wilts 28 K9
Minffordd Gwynd 43 L6
Mingarrypark Highld 93 R5
Miningsby Lincs 59 P14
Minions Cnwll 4 H6
Minishant S Ayrs 81 L10
Minllyn Gwynd 43 S11
Minnigaff D & G 73 L6
Minnonie Abers 105 M3
Minshull Vernon Ches E 45 Q1
Minskip N York 63 T7
Minstead Hants 8 K6
Minsted W Susx 10 D6
Minster Kent 13 R3
Minster Kent 23 N13
Minsterley Shrops 44 J12
Minster Lovell Oxon 29 R5
Minsterworth Gloucs 28 E4
Minterne Magna Dorset 7 S4
Minterne Parva Dorset 7 S4
Minting Lincs 59 L12
Mintlaw Abers 105 R6
Mintlyn Crematorium Norfk 49 U10
Minto Border 76 B1
Minton Shrops 34 K2
Minwear Pembks 24 H8
Minworth Birm 36 G2
Mirehouse Cumb 66 E9
Mireland Highld 112 H4
Mirfield Kirk 56 K3
Miserden Gloucs 28 H6
Miskin Rhondd 26 J11
Miskin Rhondd 26 J8
Misson Notts 57 U8
Misterton Leics 37 Q4
Misterton Notts 58 C8
Misterton Somset 7 N3
Mistley Essex 23 R1
Mistley Heath Essex 23 R1
Mitcham Gt Lon 21 N9
Mitcheldean Gloucs 28 C4
Mitchell Cnwll 3 M6
Mitchellslacks D & G 74 J6
Mitchel Troy Mons 27 T5
Mitford Nthumb 77 P8
Mithian Cnwll 2 J6
Mitton Staffs 45 U10
Mixbury Oxon 30 D6
Mixenden Calder 63 M14
Moats Tye Suffk 40 H9
Mobberley Ches E 55 S11
Mobberley Staffs 46 D5
Moccas Herefs 34 J12
Mochdre Conwy 53 P7
Mochdre Powys 34 C3
Mochrum D & G 72 J10
Mockbeggar Hants 8 H7
Mockbeggar Kent 12 D6
Mockerkin Cumb 66 G8
Modbury Devon 5 R10
Moddershall Staffs 46 B6
Moelfre IoA 52 H5
Moelfre Powys 44 E8
Moel Tryfan Gwynd 52 H11
Moffat D & G 75 L4
Mogador Surrey 21 M12
Moggerhanger C Beds 38 H11
Moira Leics 46 K10
Molash Kent 12 K5
Mol-chlach Highld 100 d8
Mold Flints 54 F14
Moldgreen Kirk 56 J3
Molehill Green Essex 22 E3
Molehill Green Essex 22 H3
Molescroft E R Yk 65 N11
Molesden Nthumb 77 N9
Molesworth Cambs 38 G5
Molland Devon 15 T7
Mollington Ches W 54 J12
Mollington Oxon 37 M11
Mollinsburn N Lans 82 D4
Monachty Cerdgn 32 K8
Mondynes Abers 99 P8
Monewden Suffk 41 M9
Moneydie P & K 90 G6
Moneyrow Green W & M 20 E7
Moniaive D & G 74 E7
Monifieth Angus 91 Q5
Monikie Angus 91 Q4
Monimail Fife 91 L9
Monington Pembks 32 B12
Monk Bretton Barns 57 N5
Monken Hadley Gt Lon 21 M3
Monk Fryston N York 64 C14
Monkhide Herefs 35 P12
Monkhill Cumb 75 R14
Monkhopton Shrops 35 P2
Monkland Herefs 35 L9
Monkleigh Devon 15 L8
Monknash V Glam 16 B2
Monkokehampton Devon 15 N11
Monkseaton N Tyne 77 S11
Monks Eleigh Suffk 40 G11
Monk's Gate W Susx 11 L5
Monks Heath Ches E 55 T12
Monk Sherborne Hants 19 T9
Monks Horton Kent 13 M7
Monksilver Somset 16 E9
Monks Kirby Warwks 37 N4
Monk Soham Suffk 41 M7
Monkspath Solhll 36 F5
Monks Risborough Bucks 30 H12
Monksthorpe Lincs 59 R13
Monk Street Essex 22 F2
Monkswood Mons 27 Q7
Monkton Devon 6 G4
Monkton Kent 13 Q3
Monkton S Ayrs 81 M7
Monkton S Tyne 77 S13
Monkton V Glam 16 B2
Monkton Combe BaNES 17 U4
Monkton Deverill Wilts 18 C13
Monkton Farleigh Wilts 18 B7
Monkton Heathfield Somset 16 J11
Monkton Up Wimborne Dorset 8 E6
Monkton Wyld Dorset 6 K5
Monkwearmouth Sundld 77 T14
Monkwood Hants 9 T2
Monmore Green Wolves 46 B14
Monmouth Mons 27 U5
Monnington on Wye Herefs 34 J12
Monreith D & G 72 K11
Montacute Somset 17 N13
Montcliffe Bolton 55 Q4
Montford Shrops 44 K11
Montford Bridge Shrops 44 K10
Montgarrie Abers 104 H12
Montgomery Powys 34 F1
Monton Salfd 55 S7
Montrose Angus 99 N12
Mont Saint Guern 6 c3
Monxton Hants 19 M12
Monyash Derbys 56 J13
Monymusk Abers 104 K12
Monzie P & K 90 C6
Moodiesburn N Lans 82 C4
Moonzie Fife 91 M8
Moor Allerton Leeds 63 S12
Moorbath Dorset 7 M5
Moorby Lincs 59 N14
Moorcot Herefs 34 J9
Moor Crichel Dorset 8 D7
Moordown Bmouth 8 F10
Moore Halton 55 N10
Moor End C Beds 31 L8
Moor End Calder 63 M14
Moor End Devon 15 Q11
Moorend Gloucs 28 D7
Moor End Lancs 61 R11
Moor End N York 64 E12
Moorends Donc 57 U3
Moorgreen Hants 9 P5
Moor Green Herts 31 T7
Moorgreen Notts 47 N4
Moorhall Derbys 57 M12
Moorhampton Herefs 34 J11
Moorhead C Brad 63 N12
Moor Head Leeds 63 Q14
Moorhouse Cumb 67 L2
Moorhouse Cumb 67 M1
Moorhouse Donc 57 Q4
Moorhouse Notts 58 C13
Moorhouse Bank Surrey 21 R12
Moorland Somset 16 K10
Moorlinch Somset 17 L9
Moor Monkton N York 64 C8
Moor Row Cumb 66 F10
Moor Row Cumb 66 K3
Moorsholm R & Cl 71 L10
Moorside Dorset 17 U13
Moor Side Lancs 61 S13
Moor Side Lancs 61 T12
Moorside Leeds 63 Q12
Moor Side Lincs 49 L2
Moorside Oldham 56 D5
Moorstock Kent 13 M8
Moor Street Birm 36 C4
Moor Street Medway 12 F2
Moorswater Cnwll 4 G8
Moorthorpe Wakefd 57 Q4
Moortown Devon 5 N6
Moortown Hants 8 H8
Moortown IoW 9 N12
Moortown Leeds 63 R12
Moortown Lincs 58 J7
Moortown Wrekin 45 P10
Morangie Highld 109 P8
Morar Highld 100 f10
Moray Crematorium Moray 104 D3
Morborne Cambs 38 H2
Morchard Bishop Devon 15 S11
Morcombelake Dorset 7 M6
Morcott Rutlnd 48 D13
Morda Shrops 44 G8
Morden Dorset 8 C9
Morden Gt Lon 21 N9
Mordiford Herefs 35 N13
Mordon Dur 70 D7
More Shrops 34 H2
Morebath Devon 16 C11
Morebattle Border 84 K14
Morecambe Lancs 61 S7
Moredon Swindn 29 M10
Morefield Highld 107 V5
Morehall Kent 13 P8
Moreleigh Devon 5 T10
Morenish P & K 95 S11
Moresby Parks Cumb 66 E9
Morestead Hants 9 Q3
Moreton Dorset 7 V7
Moreton Essex 22 D6
Moreton Herefs 35 M8
Moreton Oxon 30 E12
Moreton Staffs 45 S10
Moreton Staffs 46 F8
Moreton Wirral 54 G9
Moreton Corbet Shrops 45 N9
Moretonhampstead Devon 5 T3
Moreton-in-Marsh Gloucs 29 P1
Moreton Jeffries Herefs 35 P11
Moretonmill Shrops 45 N9
Moreton Morrell Warwks 36 K9
Moreton on Lugg Herefs 35 M11
Moreton Paddox Warwks 36 K10
Moreton Pinkney Nhants 37 Q11
Moreton Say Shrops 45 P7
Moreton Valence Gloucs 28 E6
Morfa Cerdgn 32 F10
Morfa Bychan Gwynd 42 K6
Morfa Dinlle Gwynd 52 F11
Morfa Glas Neath 26 F6
Morfa Nefyn Gwynd 42 E5
Morganstown Cardif 27 L11
Morgan's Vale Wilts 8 H4
Morham E Loth 84 F4
Moriah Cerdgn 33 M5
Morland Cumb 68 D8
Morley Ches E 55 T10
Morley Derbys 47 L5
Morley Dur 69 P7
Morley Leeds 57 L1
Morley Green Ches E 55 T10
Morley St Botolph Norfk 50 J14
Mornick Cnwll 4 J6
Morningside C Edin 83 P4
Morningside N Lans 82 F7
Morningthorpe Norfk 41 M2
Morpeth Nthumb 77 P8
Morphie Abers 99 N11
Morrey Staffs 46 F10
Morridge Side Staffs 46 D3
Morriston Swans 26 B8
Morston Norfk 50 H5
Mortehoe Devon 15 L3
Morthen Rothm 57 Q9
Mortimer W Berk 19 U8
Mortimer Common W Berk 19 U7
Mortimer's Cross Herefs 34 K8
Mortimer West End Hants 19 T8
Mortlake Gt Lon 21 M7
Mortlake Crematorium Gt Lon 21 L7
Morton Cumb 67 N2
Morton Cumb 67 Q5
Morton Derbys 47 M1
Morton IoW 9 S11
Morton Lincs 48 G9
Morton Lincs 58 D8
Morton Notts 47 T3
Morton Shrops 44 G9
Morton Hall Lincs 58 E14
Mortonhall Crematorium C Edin 83 Q5
Morton-on-Swale N York 63 S1
Morton on the Hill Norfk 50 K10
Morton Tinmouth Dur 69 Q8
Morvah Cnwll 2 C9
Morval Cnwll 4 H9
Morvich Highld 101 P7
Morville Shrops 35 Q2
Morville Heath Shrops 35 Q2
Morwenstow Cnwll 14 F9
Mosborough Sheff 57 P10
Moscow E Ayrs 81 P4
Mose Shrops 35 S2
Mosedale Cumb 67 N6
Moseley Birm 36 E4
Moseley Wolves 46 B14
Moseley Worcs 35 T9
Moses Gate Bolton 55 R5
Moss Ag & B 92 B10
Moss Donc 57 S4
Moss Wrexhm 44 H3
Mossat Abers 104 F12
Mossbank Shet 106 u6
Moss Bank St Hel 55 M7
Mossbay Cumb 66 E7
Mossblown S Ayrs 81 N8
Mossbrow Traffd 55 R9
Mossburnford Border 76 D2
Mossdale D & G 73 R5
Mossdale E Ayrs 81 P12
Moss Edge Lancs 61 S11
Moss End Ches E 55 Q11
Mossend N Lans 82 D6
Mosser Mains Cumb 66 H7
Mossley Ches E 45 U1
Mossley Tamesd 56 E6
Mosspaul Hotel Border 75 S6
Moss Side Cumb 66 J2
Moss-side Highld 103 N4
Moss Side Lancs 61 R13
Moss Side Sefton 54 J6
Mosstodloch Moray 104 C4
Mossyard D & G 73 N9
Mossy Lea Lancs 55 M4
Mosterton Dorset 7 N3
Moston Manch 56 C6
Moston Shrops 45 N8
Moston Green Ches E 45 R1
Mostyn Flints 54 E10
Motcombe Dorset 8 B3
Mothecombe Devon 5 Q11
Motherby Cumb 67 P7
Motherwell N Lans 82 D7
Motspur Park Gt Lon 21 M9
Mottingham Gt Lon 21 R8
Mottisfont Hants 9 L3
Mottisfont Hants 9 L3
Mottistone IoW 9 N12
Mottram in Longdendale Tamesd 56 E7
Mottram St Andrew Ches E 56 C11
Mouilpied Guern 6 d3
Mouldsworth Ches W 55 M12
Moulin P & K 97 Q12
Moulsecoomb Br & H 11 N9
Moulsford Oxon 19 S4
Moulsoe M Keyn 30 K4
Moultavie Highld 109 L10
Moulton Ches W 55 Q13
Moulton Lincs 49 M9
Moulton N York 69 R12
Moulton Nhants 37 U7
Moulton Suffk 39 U8
Moulton V Glam 16 E3
Moulton Chapel Lincs 49 L10
Moulton St Mary Norfk 51 Q12
Moulton Seas End Lincs 49 M8
Mount Cnwll 2 K5
Mount Cnwll 4 E7
Mount Kirk 56 G3
Mountain C Brad 63 M13
Mountain Ash Rhondd 26 J8
Mountain Cross Border 83 N9
Mountain Street Kent 13 L5
Mount Ambrose Cnwll 2 J8
Mount Bures Essex 40 F14
Mountfield E Susx 12 D11
Mountgerald House Highld 102 G3
Mount Hawke Cnwll 2 J7
Mount Hermon Cnwll 2 H13
Mountjoy Cnwll 3 M4
Mount Lothian Mdloth 83 Q7
Mountnessing Essex 22 F8
Mounton Mons 27 U9
Mount Pleasant Ches E 45 T2
Mount Pleasant Derbys 46 J10
Mount Pleasant Derbys 46 K4
Mount Pleasant Dur 69 S6
Mount Pleasant E R Yk 65 T12
Mount Pleasant E Susx 11 Q7
Mount Pleasant Norfk 40 G2
Mount Pleasant Suffk 40 B11
Mount Pleasant Worcs 36 D8
Mountsett Crematorium Dur 69 Q2
Mountsorrel Leics 47 Q11
Mount Sorrel Wilts 8 E4
Mount Tabor Calder 56 G1
Mousehole Cnwll 2 D11
Mouswald D & G 75 L11
Mow Cop Ches E 45 U2
Mowhaugh Border 76 G1
Mowmacre Hill C Leic 47 Q12
Mowsley Leics 37 R3
Moy Highld 96 E7
Moy Highld 103 L9
Moyle Highld 101 M8
Moylegrove Pembks 32 B12
Muasdale Ag & B 79 M7
Muchalls Abers 99 S5
Much Birch Herefs 27 U1
Much Cowarne Herefs 35 P11
Much Dewchurch Herefs 27 T1
Muchelney Somset 17 M12
Muchelney Ham Somset 17 M12
Much Hadham Herts 22 B4
Much Hoole Lancs 55 L2
Much Hoole Town Lancs 55 L2
Muchlarnick Cnwll 4 G9
Much Marcle Herefs 35 Q14
Much Wenlock Shrops 45 P14
Muck Highld 93 L3
Mucking Thurr 22 G11
Muckingford Thurr 22 G12
Muckleburgh Collection Norfk 50 K5
Muckleford Dorset 7 R6
Mucklestone Staffs 45 R6
Muckley Shrops 35 P1
Muckton Lincs 59 Q10
Muddiford Devon 15 N5
Muddles Green E Susx 11 S8
Mudeford Dorset 8 H10
Mudford Somset 17 Q13
Mudford Sock Somset 17 Q13
Mudgley Somset 17 N7
Mud Row Kent 23 P13
Mugdock Stirlg 89 N10
Mugeary Highld 100 d6
Mugginton Derbys 46 J5
Muggintonlane End Derbys 46 J5
Muggleswick Dur 69 M3
Muirden Abers 105 L5
Muirdrum Angus 91 S4
Muiresk Abers 104 K6
Muirhead Angus 91 M5
Muirhead Fife 91 L10
Muirhead N Lans 82 C5
Muirkirk E Ayrs 82 C13
Muirmill Stirlg 89 R9
Muir of Fowlis Abers 104 H13
Muir of Miltonduff Moray 103 U4
Muir of Ord Highld 102 F5
Muirshearlich Highld 94 G2
Muirtack Abers 105 R8
Muirton P & K 90 D9
Muirton Mains Highld 102 E5
Muirton of Ardblair P & K 90 J3
Muker N York 68 K13
Mulbarton Norfk 51 L13
Mulben Moray 104 D5
Mulfra Cnwll 2 D10
Mull Ag & B 93 Q12
Mullacott Cross Devon 15 M4
Mullion Cnwll 2 H13
Mullion Cove Cnwll 2 H13
Mumby Lincs 59 T12
Munderfield Row Herefs 35 P10
Munderfield Stocks Herefs 35 Q10
Mundesley Norfk 51 P6
Mundford Norfk 40 D2
Mundham Norfk 51 P14
Mundon Hill Essex 23 L7
Mundy Bois Kent 12 H6
Mungrisdale Cumb 67 N6
Munlochy Highld 102 H5
Munnoch N Ayrs 80 K3
Munsley Herefs 35 Q12
Munslow Shrops 35 M3
Murchington Devon 5 R3
Murcot Worcs 36 E12
Murcott Oxon 30 C9
Murcott Wilts 28 J9
Murkle Highld 112 E3
Murlaggan Highld 101 Q13
Murrell Green Hants 20 B11
Murroes Angus 91 Q4
Murrow Cambs 49 N12
Mursley Bucks 30 H7
Murston Kent 12 H3
Murthill Angus 98 H12
Murthly P & K 90 H4
Murton C York 64 E9
Murton Cumb 68 F8
Murton Dur 70 E3
Murton N Tyne 77 S11
Murton Nthumb 85 P9
Murton Swans 25 U13
Musbury Devon 6 J6
Muscoates N York 64 F4
Musselburgh E Loth 83 R4
Muston Leics 48 B6
Muston N York 65 P4
Mustow Green Worcs 35 U6
Muswell Hill Gt Lon 21 N5
Mutehill D & G 73 R10
Mutford Suffk 41 S3
Muthill P & K 90 C8
Mutterton Devon 6 D3
Muxton Wrekin 45 R11
Mybster Highld 112 E6
Myddfai Carmth 26 D1
Myddle Shrops 45 L9
Mydroilyn Cerdgn 32 J9
Myerscough Lancs 61 T12
Mylor Cnwll 3 L9
Mylor Bridge Cnwll 3 L9
Mynachlog ddu Pembks 24 K4
Myndd-llan Flints 54 E12
Myndtown Shrops 34 J3
Mynydd-bach Mons 27 T9
Mynydd-Bach Swans 26 B8
Mynydd Buch Cerdgn 33 P5
Mynyddgarreg Carmth 25 R9
Mynydd Isa Flints 54 G14
Mynydd Llandygai Gwynd 52 K9
Mynytho Gwynd 42 F7
Myrebird Abers 99 N4
Myredykes Border 76 B6
Mytchett Surrey 20 E11
Mytholm Calder 56 E1
Mytholmroyd Calder 56 F1
Mythop Lancs 61 R13
Myton-on-Swale N York 63 U6

N

Naast Highld 107 P8
Nab's Head Lancs 62 C14
Na Buirgh W Isls 106 f9
Naburn C York 64 D10
Nab Wood Crematorium C Brad 63 N12
Naccolt Kent 13 L7
Nackington Kent 13 N5
Nacton Suffk 41 M12
Nafferton E R Yk 65 P8
Nag's Head Gloucs 28 G8
Nailbridge Gloucs 28 B4
Nailsbourne Somset 16 H11
Nailsea N Som 17 N2
Nailstone Leics 47 M12
Nailsworth Gloucs 28 F8
Nairn Highld 103 N4
Nalderswood Surrey 21 M13
Nancegollan Cnwll 2 G10
Nancledra Cnwll 2 D9
Nanhoron Gwynd 42 E7
Nannerch Flints 54 E13
Nanpantan Leics 47 P10
Nanpean Cnwll 3 P5
Nanquidno Cnwll 2 B11
Nanstallon Cnwll 3 Q3
Nant-ddu Powys 26 J5
Nanternis Cerdgn 32 G9
Nantgaredig Carmth 25 S6
Nantgarw Rhondd 27 L10
Nant-glas Powys 33 U7
Nantglyn Denbgs 53 T10
Nantgwyn Powys 33 U5
Nant Gwynant Gwynd 43 M3
Nantlle Gwynd 52 H12
Nantmawr Shrops 44 G9
Nantmel Powys 34 B7
Nantmor Gwynd 43 M4
Nant Peris Gwynd 52 K11
Nantwich Ches E 45 Q3
Nant-y-Bwch Blae G 27 L5
Nant-y-caws Carmth 25 S7
Nant-y-derry Mons 27 Q6
Nantyffyllon Brdgnd 26 E9
Nantyglo Blae G 27 M5
Nant-y-gollen Shrops 44 F8
Nant-y-moel Brdgnd 26 G9
Nant-y-pandy Conwy 53 L8
Naphill Bucks 20 D3
Napleton Worcs 35 U11
Nappa N York 62 H9
Napton on the Hill Warwks 37 N8
Narberth Pembks 24 K8
Narborough Leics 37 P1
Narborough Norfk 50 B11
Narkurs Cnwll 4 J9
Nasareth Gwynd 42 J4
Naseby Nhants 37 S5
Nash Bucks 30 G6
Nash Gt Lon 21 R10
Nash Herefs 34 H8
Nash Newpt 27 Q11
Nash Shrops 35 P6
Nash End Worcs 35 S4
Nash Lee Bucks 30 H11
Nash's Green Hants 19 U11
Nash Street Kent 12 B2
Nassington Nhants 38 G1
Nastend Gloucs 28 E6
Nasty Herts 31 U8
Nateby Cumb 68 G11
Nateby Lancs 61 T11
National Memorial Arboretum Staffs 46 G11
National Motor Museum (Beaulieu) Hants 9 M8
National Space Centre C Leic 47 Q12
Natland Cumb 61 U2
Naughton Suffk 40 H11
Naunton Gloucs 29 M3
Naunton Worcs 35 U13
Naunton Beauchamp Worcs 36 C10
Navenby Lincs 48 E2
Navestock Essex 22 D8
Navestock Side Essex 22 E8
Navidale House Hotel Highld 112 B13
Navity Highld 103 L3
Nawton N York 64 F3
Nayland Suffk 40 G14
Nazeing Essex 22 B6
Nazeing Gate Essex 22 B6
Neacroft Hants 8 H9
Neal's Green Warwks 36 K4
Neap Shet 106 v8
Near Cotton Staffs 46 E4
Near Sawrey Cumb 67 N13
Neasden Gt Lon 21 M5
Neasham Darltn 70 D10
Neath Neath 26 D8
Neatham Hants 10 A2
Neatishead Norfk 51 P9
Nebo Cerdgn 32 K7
Nebo Conwy 53 P11
Nebo Gwynd 42 J3
Nebo IoA 52 G4

Necton – Oulton 137

Necton Norfk 50 E12
Nedd Highld 110 C10
Nedderton Nthumb 77 Q9
Nedging Suffk 40 G11
Nedging Tye Suffk 40 H11
Needham Norfk 41 M4
Needham Market Suffk 40 J9
Needham Street Suffk 40 B7
Needingworth Cambs 39 M6
Neen Savage Shrops 35 Q5
Neen Sollars Shrops 35 Q6
Neenton Shrops 35 P3
Nefyn Gwynd 42 F5
Neilston E Rens 81 P1
Nelson Caerph 27 L8
Nelson Lancs 62 H12
Nemphlar S Lans 82 G10
Nempnett Thrubwell BaNES 17 P4
Nenthall Cumb 68 G3
Nenthead Cumb 68 G4
Nenthorn Border 84 H11
Neopardy Devon 15 S13
Nep Town W Susx 11 L7
Nercwys Flints 44 F1
Nereabolls Ag & B 78 C4
Nerston S Lans 81 S1
Nesbit Nthumb 85 P12
Nesfield N York 63 M10
Ness Ches W 54 H11
Nesscliffe Shrops 44 J10
Neston Ches W 54 G11
Neston Wilts 18 C7
Netchwood Shrops 35 P2
Nether Alderley Ches E 55 T11
Netheravon Wilts 18 H11
Nether Blainslie Border 84 E10
Netherbrae Abers 105 M4
Nether Broughton Leics 47 S8
Netherburn S Lans 82 E9
Netherbury Dorset 7 N5
Netherby Cumb 75 S11
Netherby N York 63 S10
Nether Cerne Dorset 7 S5
Nethercleuch D & G 75 M8
Nether Compton Dorset 17 Q13
Nethercote Warwks 37 P8
Nethercott Devon 14 J13
Nethercott Devon 15 L5
Nether Crimond Abers 105 N11
Nether Dallachy Moray 104 D3
Netherend Gloucs 28 A7
Nether Exe Devon 6 B4
Netherfield E Susx 12 D12
Netherfield Leics 47 Q10
Netherfield Notts 47 R5
Nether Fingland S Lans 74 H3
Nethergate N Linc 58 C7
Nethergate Norfk 50 J8
Netherhampton Wilts 8 G3
Nether Handley Derbys 57 P11
Nether Handwick Angus 91 N3
Nether Haugh Rothm 57 P7
Netherhay Dorset 7 M3
Nether Headon Notts 58 B11
Nether Heage Derbys 47 L3
Nether Heyford Nhants 37 S9
Nether Howcleugh S Lans 74 K3
Nether Kellet Lancs 61 U6
Nether Kinmundy Abers 105 T7
Netherland Green Staffs 46 F7
Nether Langwith Notts 57 R12
Netherlaw D & G 73 S11
Netherley Abers 99 R5
Nethermill D & G 74 K8
Nethermuir Abers 105 Q7
Netherne-on-the-Hill Surrey 21 N11
Netheroyd Hill Kirk 56 H3
Nether Padley Derbys 56 K11
Netherplace E Rens 81 Q1
Nether Poppleton C York 64 D9
Nether Row Cumb 67 M5
Netherseal Derbys 46 J11
Nether Silton N York 64 B1
Nether Skyborry Shrops 34 G6
Nether Stowey Somset 16 G9
Nether Street Essex 22 E5
Netherstreet Wilts 18 E8
Netherthong Kirk 56 H5
Netherthorpe Derbys 57 P12
Netherton Angus 98 J12
Netherton Devon 6 A10
Netherton Dudley 36 B3
Netherton Hants 19 N9
Netherton Herefs 27 U2
Netherton Kirk 56 H4
Netherton N Lans 82 E8
Netherton Nthumb 76 K4
Netherton Oxon 29 T8
Netherton P & K 97 U13
Netherton Sefton 54 J7
Netherton Shrops 35 R4
Netherton Stirlg 89 N10
Netherton Wakefd 57 L3
Netherton Worcs 36 C12
Nethertown Cumb 66 E11
Nethertown Highld 112 J1
Nethertown Lancs 62 E12
Nethertown Staffs 46 F10
Netherurd Border 83 M10
Nether Wallop Hants 19 M13
Nether Wasdale Cumb 66 H12
Nether Welton Cumb 67 N3
Nether Westcote Gloucs 29 P3
Nether Whitacre Warwks 36 H2
Nether Whitecleuch S Lans 74 F2
Nether Winchendon Bucks 30 F10
Netherwitton Nthumb 77 M7
Nethy Bridge Highld 103 R11
Netley Hants 9 P7
Netley Marsh Hants 9 L6
Nettlebed Oxon 19 U3
Nettlebridge Somset 17 R7
Nettlecombe Dorset 7 P5
Nettlecombe IoW 9 Q13
Nettleden Herts 31 M10
Nettleham Lincs 58 H11
Nettlestead Kent 12 C5
Nettlestead Green Kent 12 C5
Nettlestone IoW 9 S10
Nettlesworth Dur 69 S3
Nettleton Lincs 58 K6
Nettleton Wilts 18 B5
Nettleton Shrub Wilts 18 B5
Netton Devon 5 P11
Netton Wilts 18 H13
Neuadd Carmth 26 C3
Neuadd-ddu Powys 33 T5
Nevendon Essex 22 J9
Nevern Pembks 32 A12
Nevill Holt Leics 38 B2
New Abbey D & G 74 J12
New Aberdour Abers 105 P3
New Addington Gt Lon 21 Q10
Newall Leeds 63 P10
New Alresford Hants 9 R2
New Alyth P & K 90 K2
Newark C Pete 48 K13
Newark Ork 106 w15
Newark-on-Trent Notts 47 U3
New Arram E R Yk 65 N11
Newarthill N Lans 82 E7
New Ash Green Kent 12 B2
New Balderton Notts 48 B3
New Barn Kent 12 B2
Newbarn Kent 13 N7
New Barnet Gt Lon 21 N3
New Barton Nhants 38 C8
Newbattle Mdloth 83 R5
New Bewick Nthumb 77 M1
Newbie D & G 75 N12
Newbiggin Cumb 61 P6
Newbiggin Cumb 66 G14
Newbiggin Cumb 67 Q7
Newbiggin Cumb 67 S3
Newbiggin Cumb 68 D7
Newbiggin Dur 68 K7
Newbiggin Dur 69 P3
Newbiggin N York 62 K1
Newbiggin N York 63 L2
Newbiggin-by-the-Sea Nthumb 77 S8
Newbigging Angus 91 L3
Newbigging Angus 91 P4
Newbigging Angus 91 Q4
Newbigging S Lans 82 K9
Newbiggin-on-Lune Cumb 68 F12
New Bilton Warwks 37 N5
Newbold Derbys 57 N12
Newbold Leics 47 M10
Newbold on Avon Warwks 37 N5
Newbold on Stour Warwks 36 H11
Newbold Pacey Warwks 36 J9
Newbold Revel Warwks 37 N4
Newbold Verdon Leics 47 M13
New Bolingbroke Lincs 49 M2
Newborough C Pete 48 K12
Newborough IoA 52 F9
Newborough Staffs 46 F8
Newbottle Nhants 30 B5
Newbottle Sundld 70 D2
New Boultham Lincs 58 G12
Newbourne Suffk 41 N12
New Bradwell M Keyn 30 H4
New Brampton Derbys 57 N12
New Brancepeth Dur 69 R4
Newbridge C Edin 83 M4
Newbridge Caerph 27 N8
Newbridge Cerdgn 32 K9
Newbridge Cnwll 2 C10
Newbridge Cnwll 2 K8
Newbridge D & G 74 H10
Newbridge Hants 8 K5
Newbridge IoW 9 N11
New Bridge N York 64 J2
Newbridge Oxon 29 T7
Newbridge Wrexhm 44 G5
Newbridge Green Worcs 35 T13
Newbridge-on-Usk Mons 27 R9
Newbridge-on-Wye Powys 34 B9
New Brighton Flints 54 G13
New Brighton Wirral 54 H8
New Brinsley Notts 47 N3
New Brotton R & Cl 71 L8
Newbrough Nthumb 76 H12
New Broughton Wrexhm 44 H3
New Buckenham Norfk 40 J2
Newbuildings Devon 15 S12
Newburgh Abers 105 R10
Newburgh Abers 105 R4
Newburgh Fife 90 K8
Newburgh Lancs 55 L4
Newburgh Priory N York 64 C4
Newburn N u Ty 77 P12
New Bury Bolton 55 R6
Newbury Somset 17 S7
Newbury W Berk 19 Q7
Newbury Wilts 18 B12
Newbury Park Gt Lon 21 R5
Newby Cumb 67 S8
Newby Lancs 62 G10
Newby N York 62 E6
Newby N York 65 N1
Newby N York 70 H10
Newby Bridge Cumb 61 R2
Newby Cross Cumb 67 N2
Newby East Cumb 75 U14
Newby Head Cumb 67 S8
New Byth Abers 105 N5
Newby West Cumb 67 N2
Newby Wiske N York 63 T2
Newcastle Mons 27 S4
Newcastle Shrops 34 G4
Newcastle Airport Nthumb 77 P11
Newcastle Emlyn Carmth 32 F12
Newcastleton Border 75 U8
Newcastle-under-Lyme Staffs 45 T4
Newcastle upon Tyne N u Ty 77 Q13
Newchapel Pembks 25 M3
Newchapel Staffs 45 U3
Newchapel Surrey 11 P2
Newchurch Blae G 27 M5
Newchurch Herefs 34 J10
Newchurch IoW 9 R11
Newchurch Kent 13 L9
Newchurch Mons 27 T8
Newchurch Powys 34 F10
Newchurch Staffs 46 F9
Newchurch in Pendle Lancs 62 G12
New Costessey Norfk 51 L11
New Cowper Cumb 66 H3
Newcraighall C Edin 83 R4
New Crofton Wakefd 57 N3
New Cross Cerdgn 33 M5
New Cross Gt Lon 21 Q7
New Cross Somset 17 M13
New Cumnock E Ayrs 81 S10
New Cut E Susx 12 F12
New Deer Abers 105 P6
New Delaval Nthumb 77 R10
New Delph Oldham 56 E5
New Denham Bucks 20 H6
Newdigate Surrey 10 K2
New Duston Nhants 37 T8
New Earswick C York 64 E8
New Eastwood Notts 47 N4
New Edlington Donc 57 R7
New Elgin Moray 103 V3
New Ellerby E R Yk 65 R12
Newell Green Br For 20 E8
New Eltham Gt Lon 21 R8
New End Worcs 36 E8
Newenden Kent 12 F10
New England C Pete 48 J13
New England Essex 40 B12
Newent Gloucs 28 D2
New Farnley Leeds 63 R13
New Ferry Wirral 54 H9
Newfield Dur 69 R2
Newfield Dur 69 R6
Newfield Highld 109 P9
New Fletton C Pete 48 J14
New Forest National Park 8 K7
Newfound Hants 19 S10
New Fryston Wakefd 57 Q1
Newgale Pembks 24 E6
New Galloway D & G 73 Q4
Newgate Norfk 50 H5
Newgate Street Herts 31 T11
New Gilston Fife 91 P10
New Grimsby IoS 2 b1
Newhall Ches E 45 P4
Newhall Derbys 46 J9
Newham Nthumb 85 T13
New Hartley Nthumb 77 S10
Newhaven C Edin 83 Q3
Newhaven Derbys 46 G1
Newhaven E Susx 11 Q10
New Haw Surrey 20 J10
New Hedges Pembks 24 K10
New Herrington Sundld 70 D2
Newhey Rochdl 56 D4
New Holkham Norfk 50 E6
New Holland N Linc 58 J2
Newholm N York 71 Q10
New Houghton Derbys 57 Q13
New Houghton Norfk 50 C8
Newhouse N Lans 82 E6
New Houses N York 62 G5
New Houses Wigan 55 N6
New Hutton Cumb 62 B1
New Hythe Kent 12 D4
Newick E Susx 11 Q6
Newingreen Kent 13 M8
Newington Kent 12 G3
Newington Kent 13 N8
Newington Oxon 30 D13
Newington Shrops 34 K4
Newington Bagpath Gloucs 28 F9
New Inn Carmth 25 S3
New Inn Torfn 27 Q8
New Invention Shrops 34 G5
New Lakenham Norfk 51 M12
New Lanark S Lans 82 G10
New Lanark Village S Lans 82 G10
Newland C KuH 65 P13
Newland Cumb 61 Q4
Newland E R Yk 64 J14
Newland Gloucs 27 V6
Newland N York 57 U2
Newland Oxon 29 S6
Newland Somset 15 T5
Newland Worcs 35 S11
Newlandrig Mdloth 83 S6
Newlands Border 75 V7
Newlands Cumb 67 M5
Newlands Nthumb 69 N1
Newlands of Dundurcas Moray 104 B5
New Lane Lancs 54 K4
New Lane End Warrtn 55 P8
New Langholm D & G 75 S9
New Leake Lincs 49 P2
New Leeds Abers 105 R5
New Lodge Barns 57 N5
New Longton Lancs 55 M1
New Luce D & G 72 F7
Newlyn Cnwll 2 D11
Newmachar Abers 105 P12
Newmains N Lans 82 F7
New Malden Gt Lon 21 M9
Newman's End Essex 22 D5
Newman's Green Suffk 40 E12
Newmarket Suffk 39 T8
Newmarket W Isls 106 j5
New Marske R & Cl 70 K8
New Marston Oxon 30 B11
New Marton Shrops 44 H7
New Mill Abers 99 P7
Newmill Border 75 U3
New Mill Cnwll 2 D10
New Mill Herts 30 K10
New Mill Kirk 56 J5
Newmill Moray 104 E5
Newmillerdam Wakefd 57 M3
Newmill of Inshewan Angus 98 G11
Newmills C Edin 83 N5
New Mills Cnwll 3 M6
New Mills Derbys 56 F9
Newmills Fife 82 K1
Newmills Mons 27 U6
New Mills Powys 44 C13
Newmiln P & K 90 H5
Newmilns E Ayrs 81 Q5
New Milton Hants 8 J9
New Mistley Essex 23 R1
New Moat Pembks 24 J5
Newnes Shrops 44 J7
Newney Green Essex 22 G6
Newnham Hants 20 B12
Newnham Herts 31 R5
Newnham Kent 12 J4
Newnham Nhants 37 Q9
Newnham Worcs 35 P7
Newnham on Severn Gloucs 28 C5
New Ollerton Notts 57 U13
New Oscott Birm 36 E2
New Pitsligo Abers 105 P4
New Polzeath Cnwll 4 A5
Newport Cnwll 4 J3
Newport Dorset 8 B9
Newport E R Yk 64 K13
Newport Essex 39 R14
Newport Gloucs 28 D8
Newport Highld 112 D12
Newport IoW 9 Q11
Newport Newpt 27 Q10
Newport Norfk 51 T10
Newport Pembks 24 J3
Newport Wrekin 45 R10
Newport-on-Tay Fife 91 P6
Newport Pagnell M Keyn 30 J4
Newport Pagnell Services M Keyn 30 J4
Newpound Common W Susx 10 H5
New Prestwick S Ayrs 81 L8
New Quay Cerdgn 32 G9
Newquay Cnwll 3 L4
New Quay Essex 23 F3
Newquay Zoo Cnwll 3 L4
New Rackheath Norfk 51 N11
New Radnor Powys 34 F8
New Rent Cumb 67 Q5
New Ridley Nthumb 77 M14
New Road Side N York 62 K11
New Romney Kent 13 L11
New Rossington Donc 57 T7
New Row Cerdgn 33 F6
New Row Lancs 62 C12
New Sauchie Clacks 90 C13
Newsbank Ches E 55 T13
Newseat Abers 105 L9
Newsham Lancs 61 U12
Newsham N York 63 T3
Newsham N York 69 P10
Newsham Nthumb 77 S10
New Sharlston Wakefd 57 N3
Newsholme E R Yk 64 G14
Newsholme Lancs 62 C9
New Shoreston Nthumb 85 T12
New Silksworth Sundld 70 E2
New Skelton R & Cl 71 L9
Newsome Kirk 56 J4
New Somerby Lincs 48 D6
New Southgate Crematorium Gt Lon 21 N4
New Springs Wigan 55 N5
Newstead Border 84 F12
Newstead Notts 47 F3
Newstead Nthumb 85 T13
New Stevenston N Lans 82 E7
New Street Herefs 34 H9
New Swannington Leics 47 M10
Newthorpe N York 64 B13
Newthorpe Notts 47 N4
New Thundersley Essex 22 J10
Newtimber W Susx 11 M8
Newtoft Lincs 58 H9
Newton Ag & B 88 B6
Newton Border 76 C1
Newton Brdgnd 26 E12
Newton C Beds 31 R4
Newton Cambs 39 P11
Newton Cambs 49 P11
Newton Cardif 27 N12
Newton Ches W 45 M2
Newton Ches W 54 K13
Newton Ches W 55 M11
Newton Cumb 61 N5
Newton Derbys 47 M2
Newton Herefs 34 H14
Newton Herefs 34 J7
Newton Herefs 35 M10
Newton Highld 102 C5
Newton Highld 102 K6
Newton Highld 103 L2
Newton Highld 112 H7
Newton Lancs 61 Q12
Newton Lancs 62 B5
Newton Lincs 48 F6
Newton Mdloth 83 R5
Newton Moray 103 U3
Newton Moray 104 C3
Newton N York 64 K5
Newton Nhants 38 C4
Newton Norfk 50 D10
Newton Notts 47 S5
Newton Nthumb 76 J4
Newton Nthumb 77 L13
Newton S Lans 82 H12
Newton S Lans 89 Q13
Newton Sandw 36 D2
Newton Shrops 44 K7
Newton Somset 16 F9
Newton Staffs 46 D8
Newton Suffk 40 F12
Newton W Loth 83 L3
Newton Warwks 37 P5
Newton Wilts 8 J4
Newton Abbot Devon 5 V6
Newton Arlosh Cumb 66 K1
Newton Aycliffe Dur 69 S8
Newton Bewley Hartpl 70 G7
Newton Blossomville M Keyn 38 D10
Newton Bromswold Nhants 38 E7
Newton Burgoland Leics 47 L12
Newton-by-the-Sea Nthumb 85 U13
Newton by Toft Lincs 58 H9
Newton Ferrers Devon 5 P11
Newton Ferry W Isls 106 d11
Newton Flotman Norfk 51 M14
Newtongrange Mdloth 83 R6
Newton Green Mons 27 U9
Newton Harcourt Leics 37 R1
Newton Heath Manch 56 C6
Newtonhill Abers 99 S5
Newton Hill Wakefd 57 M2
Newton-in-Bowland Lancs 62 D9
Newton Kyme N York 64 B11
Newton-le-Willows N York 63 Q2
Newton-le-Willows St Hel 55 N7
Newtonloan Mdloth 83 R6
Newton Longville Bucks 30 H6
Newton Mearns E Rens 81 Q1
Newtonmill Angus 99 L11
Newtonmore Highld 97 L4
Newton Morrell N York 69 R11
Newton Mountain Pembks 24 G9
Newton Mulgrave N York 71 N9
Newton of Balcanquhal P & K 90 J9
Newton of Balcormo Fife 91 R11
Newton-on-Ouse N York 64 C8
Newton-on-Rawcliffe N York 64 J1
Newton on the Hill Shrops 45 L9
Newton-on-the-Moor Nthumb 77 P4
Newton on Trent Lincs 58 D12
Newton Poppleford Devon 6 E7
Newton Purcell Oxon 30 D6
Newton Regis Warwks 46 J12
Newton Reigny Cumb 67 Q6
Newton St Cyres Devon 15 U13
Newton St Faith Norfk 51 M10
Newton St Loe BaNES 17 T4
Newton St Petrock Devon 14 K10
Newton Solney Derbys 46 J8
Newton Stacey Hants 19 P12
Newton Stewart D & G 73 L6
Newton Tony Wilts 18 K12
Newton Tracey Devon 15 M7
Newton under Roseberry R & Cl 70 J10
Newton Underwood Nthumb 77 N8
Newton upon Derwent E R Yk 64 G10
Newton Valence Hants 9 U2
Newton Wamphray D & G 75 M7
Newton with Scales Lancs 61 T13
Newtown Blae G 27 M6
Newtown Ches W 55 M11
Newtown Cnwll 2 F11
Newtown Cnwll 4 H5
Newtown Cumb 66 H3
Newtown Cumb 67 R3
Newtown Cumb 75 S13
Newtown Cumb 75 V13
Newtown D & G 74 E3
Newtown Derbys 56 E10
Newtown Devon 6 E5
Newtown Devon 15 S7
Newtown Dorset 7 N4
New Town Dorset 8 D5
New Town Dorset 8 D5
New Town Dorset 8 D7
New Town E Susx 11 R6
Newtown Gloucs 28 C7
Newtown Hants 8 K6
Newtown Hants 9 S6
Newtown Hants 19 Q8
Newtown Herefs 35 L9
Newtown Herefs 35 M14
Newtown Herefs 35 P11
Newtown Herefs 35 R13
Newtown Highld 96 D3
Newtown IoW 9 N10
Newtown Lancs 55 M3
New Town Nhants 38 E5
Newtown Nthumb 77 L5
Newtown Nthumb 85 P12
Newtown Nthumb 85 Q13
Newtown Poole 8 E10
Newtown Powys 34 D2
Newtown Rhondd 26 K8
Newtown Shrops 44 K9
Newtown Shrops 45 L7
Newtown Somset 6 J2
Newtown Staffs 46 B1
Newtown Staffs 46 C13
Newtown Wigan 55 N6
Newtown Wilts 8 C3
New Town Wilts 19 L6
Newtown Wilts 19 L8
Newtown Worcs 35 U9
Newtown Worcs 36 B5
Newtown-in-St Martin Cnwll 2 J12
Newtown Linford Leics 47 P12
Newtown of Beltrees Rens 88 J14
Newtown St Boswells Border 84 F12
Newtown Unthank Leics 47 N13
New Tredegar Caerph 27 L7
New Trows S Lans 82 F11
New Tupton Derbys 57 N13
Newtyle Angus 91 L3
New Walsoken Cambs 49 Q12
New Waltham NE Lin 59 N6
New Whittington Derbys 57 N11
New Winton E Loth 84 C4
New Yatt Oxon 29 S5
Newyears Green Gt Lon 20 J5
Newyork Ag & B 87 T3
New York Lincs 48 K2
New York N Tyne 77 S11
New York N York 63 P7
Nextend Herefs 34 H9
Neyland Pembks 24 G9
Niarbyl IoM 60 c7
Nibley Gloucs 28 C6
Nibley S Glos 28 C11
Nibley Green Gloucs 28 D8
Nicholashayne Devon 16 F13
Nicholaston Swans 25 T13
Nickies Hill Cumb 76 A12
Nidd N York 63 S7
Nigg C Aber 99 S3
Nigg Highld 109 Q10
Nigg Ferry Highld 109 P11
Nimlet BaNES 17 T2
Ninebanks Nthumb 68 G2
Nine Elms Swindn 29 M10
Nine Wells Pembks 24 C6
Ninfield E Susx 12 D13
Ningwood IoW 9 M11
Nisbet Border 84 H13
Nisbet Hill Border 84 K8
Niton IoW 9 Q13
Nitshill C Glas 89 M13
Noah's Ark Kent 21 U11
Noak Bridge Essex 22 G9
Noak Hill Gt Lon 22 D9
Noblethorpe Barns 57 L5
Nobold Shrops 45 L11
Nobottle Nhants 37 S8
Nocton Lincs 58 J14
Nogdam End Norfk 51 Q13
Noke Oxon 30 B10
Nolton Pembks 24 E7
Nolton Haven Pembks 24 E7
No Man's Heath Ches W 45 M4
No Man's Heath Warwks 46 J12
No Man's Land Cnwll 4 H9
Nomansland Devon 15 T10
Nomansland Wilts 8 K5
Noneley Shrops 45 L8
Nonington Kent 13 Q5
Nook Cumb 61 U3
Nook Cumb 75 U10
Norbiton Gt Lon 21 L9
Norbreck Bpool 61 Q11
Norbridge Herefs 35 R12
Norbury Ches E 45 N4
Norbury Derbys 46 F5
Norbury Gt Lon 21 P9
Norbury Shrops 34 J2
Norbury Staffs 45 S9
Norbury Common Ches E 45 N4
Norbury Junction Staffs 45 S9
Norchard Worcs 35 T7
Norcott Brook Ches W 55 P10
Norcross Lancs 61 Q11
Nordelph Norfk 49 S13
Norden Rochdl 56 C4
Nordley Shrops 35 Q1
Norfolk Broads Norfk 51 S12
Norham Nthumb 85 N9
Norland Town Calder 56 G2
Norley Ches W 55 N12
Norleywood Hants 9 M9
Norlington E Susx 11 Q8
Normanby Lincs 58 G9
Normanby N Linc 58 E3
Normanby N York 64 G3
Normanby R & Cl 70 H9
Normanby le Wold Lincs 58 K7
Norman Cross Cambs 38 J2
Normandy Surrey 20 F12
Normans Bay E Susx 12 C14
Norman's Green Devon 6 E4
Normanton C Derb 46 K7
Normanton Leics 48 B5
Normanton Notts 47 T3
Normanton Rutlnd 48 D12
Normanton Wakefd 57 N2
Normanton Wilts 18 H12
Normanton le Heath Leics 47 L11
Normanton on Cliffe Lincs 48 D4
Normanton on Soar Notts 47 P9
Normanton on the Wolds Notts 47 R7
Normanton on Trent Notts 58 C13
Normoss Lancs 61 Q12
Norney Surrey 10 E2
Norrington Common Wilts 18 C8
Norris Green Cnwll 5 L7
Norris Green Lpool 54 J8
Norris Hill Leics 46 K10
Norristhorpe Kirk 56 K2
Northacre Norfk 50 G14
Northall Bucks 31 L8
Northallerton N York 70 E14
Northall Green Norfk 50 G11
Northam C Sotn 9 N6
Northam Devon 15 L7
Northampton Nhants 37 U8
Northampton Worcs 35 T7
Northampton Services Nhants 37 T9
North Anston Rothm 57 R10
North Ascot Br For 20 F9
North Aston Oxon 29 U2
Northaw Herts 31 S12
Northay Somset 6 J2
North Baddesley Hants 9 M4
North Ballachulish Highld 94 F6
North Barrow Somset 17 R11
North Barsham Norfk 50 F6
North Benfleet Essex 22 J10
North Berwick E Loth 84 E1
North Bitchburn Dur 69 Q6
North Blyth Nthumb 77 S9
North Boarhunt Hants 9 S6
North Bockhampton Dorset 8 H9
Northborough C Pete 48 J12
Northbourne Kent 13 R5
North Bovey Devon 5 S4
North Bradley Wilts 18 C9
North Brentor Devon 5 M4
North Brewham Somset 17 T9
North Bridge Surrey 10 F3
Northbridge Street E Susx 12 D11
Northbrook Hants 19 R13
Northbrook Oxon 29 U3
North Brook End Cambs 31 S4
North Buckland Devon 15 L4
North Burlingham Norfk 51 Q12
North Cadbury Somset 17 R11
North Carlton Lincs 58 F11
North Carlton Notts 57 S10
North Cave E R Yk 64 K13
North Cerney Gloucs 28 K6
North Chailey E Susx 11 P6
Northchapel W Susx 10 F5
North Charford Hants 8 H5
North Charlton Nthumb 85 T14
North Cheam Gt Lon 21 M9
North Cheriton Somset 17 S11
North Chideock Dorset 7 M6
Northchurch Herts 31 L11
North Cliffe E R Yk 64 K12
North Clifton Notts 58 D12
North Close Dur 69 S6
North Cockerington Lincs 59 Q8
North Connel Ag & B 94 C12
North Cornelly Brdgnd 26 E11
North Corner Cnwll 2 K13
North Cotes Lincs 59 P6
Northcott Devon 4 J2
Northcott Devon 6 E2
Northcott Devon 6 F3
North Country Cnwll 2 H8
Northcourt Oxon 29 U8
North Cove Suffk 41 S3
North Cowton N York 69 S12
North Crawley M Keyn 30 K4
North Cray Gt Lon 21 S8
North Creake Norfk 50 E6
North Curry Somset 16 K11
North Dalton E R Yk 65 L9
North Deighton N York 63 T9
North Devon Crematorium Devon 15 M6
Northdown Kent 13 S1
North Downs 12 H4
North Duffield N York 64 F12
North Duntulm Highld 100 d2
North East Surrey Crematorium Gt Lon 21 M9
Northedge Derbys 57 N13
North Elham Kent 13 N7
North Elkington Lincs 59 N8
North Elmham Norfk 50 G9
North Elmsall Wakefd 57 Q4
Northend Bucks 20 B4
North End C Port 9 T8
North End Cumb 75 R14
North End Dorset 8 A3
North End E R Yk 65 R11
North End E R Yk 65 T13
North End Essex 22 G4
North End Hants 8 G5
North End Hants 9 R3
North End Leics 47 Q10
North End Lincs 48 K5
North End Lincs 58 H7
North End Lincs 59 P6
North End Lincs 59 R9
North End N Linc 58 K2
North End N Som 17 M3
North End Nhants 38 E7
North End Norfk 40 G2
North End Nthumb 77 N5
North End Sefton 54 H6
North End W Susx 10 F10
North End W Susx 10 J9
Northend Warwks 37 L10
Northenden Manch 55 T9
Northend Woods Bucks 20 F5
North Erradale Highld 107 M8
North Evington C Leic 47 R13
North Fambridge Essex 23 L8
North Featherstone Wakefd 57 P2
North Ferriby E R Yk 58 G1
Northfield Birm 36 D5
Northfield C Aber 99 S2
Northfield E R Yk 58 H1
Northfields Lincs 48 F12
Northfleet Kent 22 F13
North Frodingham E R Yk 65 Q9
North Gorley Hants 8 H6
North Green Norfk 41 M3
North Green Suffk 41 P8
North Green Suffk 41 Q7
North Greetwell Lincs 58 H12
North Grimston N York 64 J6
North Halling Medway 12 D2
North Haven Shet 106 r11
North Hayling Hants 9 U8
North Hazelrigg Nthumb 85 R12
North Heasley Devon 15 R6
North Heath W Susx 10 H6
North Hele Devon 16 D12
North Hertfordshire Memorial Park & Crematorium Herts 31 Q6
North Hill Cnwll 4 H5
North Hillingdon Gt Lon 20 J6
North Hinksey Village Oxon 29 U6
North Holmwood Surrey 21 L13
North Huish Devon 5 S9
North Hykeham Lincs 58 F13
Northiam E Susx 12 F11
Northill C Beds 38 H11
Northington Gloucs 28 D6
Northington Hants 19 S13
North Kelsey Lincs 58 H6
North Kessock Highld 102 J6
North Killingholme N Linc 58 K3
North Kilvington N York 63 U2
North Kilworth Leics 37 R4
North Kingston Hants 8 H8
North Kyme Lincs 48 J3
North Lancing W Susx 10 K9
North Landing E R Yk 65 S5
Northlands Lincs 49 M3
Northleach Gloucs 29 M5
North Lee Bucks 30 H11
North Lees N York 63 R5
Northleigh Devon 6 G5
Northleigh Devon 15 P6
North Leigh Kent 13 M6
North Leigh Oxon 29 S5
North Leverton with Habblesthorpe Notts 58 C10
Northlew Devon 15 M13
North Littleton Worcs 36 E11
Northload Bridge Somset 17 N9
North Lopham Norfk 40 H4
North Luffenham Rutlnd 48 D13
North Marden W Susx 10 C7
North Marston Bucks 30 G8
North Middleton Mdloth 83 S7
North Middleton Nthumb 85 P14
North Millbrex Abers 105 N7
North Milmain D & G 72 D9
North Molton Devon 15 R7
Northmoor Oxon 29 T7
North Moreton Oxon 19 S3
Northmuir Angus 98 F13
North Mundham W Susx 10 D10
North Muskham Notts 47 U2
North Newbald E R Yk 65 L12
North Newington Oxon 37 M12
North Newnton Wilts 18 H9
North Newton Somset 16 K10
Northney Hants 9 U8
North Nibley Gloucs 28 D8
North Oakley Hants 19 R10
North Ockendon Gt Lon 22 E10
Northolt Gt Lon 20 K6
Northop Flints 54 F13
Northop Hall Flints 54 G13
North Ormesby Middsb 70 H9
North Ormsby Lincs 59 N8
Northorpe Kirk 56 K2
Northorpe Lincs 48 G10
Northorpe Lincs 48 K6
Northorpe Lincs 58 E7
North Otterington N York 63 T2
Northover Somset 17 N9
Northover Somset 17 P12
North Owersby Lincs 58 J8
Northowram Calder 56 H1
North Perrott Somset 7 N3
North Petherton Somset 16 J10
North Petherwin Cnwll 4 H3
North Pickenham Norfk 50 E12
North Piddle Worcs 36 C10
North Poorton Dorset 7 P5
Northport Dorset 8 C11
North Poulner Hants 8 H7
North Queensferry Fife 83 M2
North Radworthy Devon 15 S6
North Rauceby Lincs 48 F4
Northrepps Norfk 51 M6
North Reston Lincs 59 Q10
North Rigton N York 63 R10
North Ripley Hants 8 H9
North Rode Ches E 56 C13
North Ronaldsay Ork 106 w14
North Ronaldsay Airport Ork 106 w14
North Row Cumb 66 K6
North Runcton Norfk 49 T10
North Scale Cumb 61 M6
North Scarle Lincs 58 D13
North Seaton Nthumb 77 R8
North Seaton Colliery Nthumb 77 R8
North Shian Ag & B 94 C10
North Shields N Tyne 77 T12
North Shoebury Sthend 23 M10
North Shore Bpool 61 Q12
North Side C Pete 49 L14
North Side Cumb 66 E7
North Skelton R & Cl 71 L9
North Somercotes Lincs 59 R7
North Stainley N York 63 R4
North Stainmore Cumb 68 H10
North Stifford Thurr 22 F11
North Stoke BaNES 17 T3
North Stoke Oxon 19 T3
North Stoke W Susx 10 G8
Northstowe Cambs 39 P7
North Street Cambs 39 S7
North Street Hants 8 H5
North Street Hants 9 S2
North Street Kent 12 K4
North Street Medway 22 K13
North Street W Berk 19 T6
North Sunderland Nthumb 85 U12
North Tamerton Cnwll 14 H13
North Tawton Devon 15 Q12
North Third Stirlg 89 S8
North Thoresby Lincs 59 N7
North Togston Nthumb 77 Q5
Northton W Isls 106 e10
North Town Devon 15 M11
North Town Somset 17 Q8
North Town W & M 20 E6
North Tuddenham Norfk 50 H11
North Uist W Isls 106 c11
Northumberland National Park Nthumb 76 H5
North Walbottle N u Ty 77 P12
North Walsham Norfk 51 N7
North Waltham Hants 19 S11
North Warnborough Hants 20 B12
Northway Somset 16 F11
North Weald Bassett Essex 22 C7
North Wheatley Notts 58 C9
North Whilborough Devon 5 V7
Northwich Ches W 55 Q12
North Wick BaNES 17 Q3
Northwick S Glos 27 V10
Northwick Somset 17 L7
Northwick Worcs 35 T9
North Widcombe BaNES 17 Q5
North Willingham Lincs 59 L9
North Wingfield Derbys 57 P13
North Witham Lincs 48 D9
Northwold Norfk 40 C1
Northwood C Stke 45 U4
Northwood Derbys 57 L14
Northwood Gt Lon 20 J4
Northwood IoW 9 P10
Northwood Shrops 45 L7
Northwood Green Gloucs 28 D4
North Wootton Dorset 7 S2
North Wootton Norfk 49 T9
North Wootton Somset 17 Q8
North Wraxall Wilts 18 B5
North Wroughton Swindn 18 H4
North York Moors National Park 71 M12
Norton Donc 57 R3
Norton E Susx 11 R10
Norton Gloucs 28 G3
Norton Halton 55 N10
Norton Herts 31 R6
Norton IoW 9 L11
Norton Mons 27 S3
Norton N Som 16 K4
Norton Nhants 37 Q8
Norton Notts 57 S12
Norton Powys 34 H7
Norton S on T 70 F8
Norton Sheff 57 N10
Norton Shrops 35 L4
Norton Shrops 35 P4
Norton Shrops 45 N12
Norton Shrops 45 R13
Norton Suffk 40 G7
Norton Swans 25 V13
Norton W Susx 10 E9
Norton Wilts 28 G11
Norton Worcs 35 U10
Norton Worcs 36 D11
Norton Bavant Wilts 18 D12
Norton Bridge Staffs 45 U7
Norton Canes Staffs 46 D12
Norton Canes Services Staffs 46 D12
Norton Canon Herefs 34 J11
Norton Corner Norfk 50 J8
Norton Disney Lincs 48 C2
Norton Ferris Wilts 17 U9
Norton Fitzwarren Somset 16 G11
Norton Green IoW 9 L11
Norton Hawkfield BaNES 17 Q4
Norton Heath Essex 22 F7
Norton in Hales Shrops 45 R6
Norton in the Moors C Stke 45 U3
Norton-Juxta-Twycross Leics 46 K12
Norton-le-Clay N York 63 U5
Norton Lindsey Warwks 36 H8
Norton Little Green Suffk 40 G7
Norton Malreward BaNES 17 R4
Norton Mandeville Essex 22 E7
Norton-on-Derwent N York 64 H5
Norton St Philip Somset 17 U5
Norton Subcourse Norfk 51 R14
Norton sub Hamdon Somset 17 N13
Norton Wood Herefs 34 J11
Norwell Notts 47 U1
Norwell Woodhouse Notts 58 B14
Norwich Norfk 51 M12
Norwich Airport Norfk 51 M11
Norwich (St Faith) Crematorium Norfk 51 M10
Norwick Shet 106 w2
Norwood Clacks 90 C13
Norwood Derbys 57 Q10
Norwood Kent 13 L9
Norwood End Essex 22 E6
Norwood Green Calder 56 H1
Norwood Green Gt Lon 20 K7
Norwood Hill Surrey 11 L2
Norwoodside Cambs 49 P14
Noseley Leics 47 T14
Noss Mayo Devon 5 P11
Nosterfield N York 63 R3
Nosterfield End Cambs 39 T12
Nostie Highld 101 M6
Notgrove Gloucs 29 M3
Nottage Brdgnd 26 E12
Notter Cnwll 4 K8
Nottingham C Nott 47 Q6
Nottington Dorset 7 S8
Notton Wakefd 57 M4
Notton Wilts 18 D7
Nounsley Essex 22 J5
Noutard's Green Worcs 35 T7
Nowton Suffk 40 E8
Nox Shrops 44 K11
Nuffield Oxon 19 U3
Nunburnholme E R Yk 64 J10
Nuncargate Notts 47 P3
Nunclose Cumb 67 Q3
Nuneaton Warwks 37 L2
Nuneham Courtenay Oxon 30 C13
Nunhead Gt Lon 21 P7
Nunkeeling E R Yk 65 Q10
Nun Monkton N York 64 C8
Nunney Somset 17 T7
Nunney Catch Somset 17 T8
Nunnington Herefs 35 N12
Nunnington N York 64 F4
Nunsthorpe NE Lin 59 N5
Nunthorpe C York 64 E9
Nunthorpe Middsb 70 H10
Nunthorpe Village Middsb 70 H10
Nunton Wilts 8 H3
Nunwick N York 63 S5
Nunwick Nthumb 76 H11
Nupdown S Glos 28 B8
Nup End Bucks 30 J9
Nupend Gloucs 28 E6
Nuptown Br For 20 E8
Nursling Hants 9 M5
Nursted Hants 10 B6
Nursteed Wilts 18 F8
Nurton Staffs 45 T14
Nutbourne W Susx 10 B9
Nutbourne W Susx 10 H7
Nutfield Surrey 21 P12
Nuthall Notts 47 P5
Nuthampstead Herts 39 P14
Nuthurst W Susx 10 K5
Nutley E Susx 11 Q5
Nutley Hants 19 T12
Nuttall Bury 55 S3
Nutwell Donc 57 T6
Nybster Highld 112 J4
Nyetimber W Susx 10 D11
Nyewood W Susx 10 C6
Nymans W Susx 11 M5
Nymet Rowland Devon 15 R11
Nymet Tracey Devon 15 R12
Nympsfield Gloucs 28 F7
Nynehead Somset 16 F12
Nythe Somset 17 M10
Nyton W Susx 10 E9

O

Oadby Leics 47 R13
Oad Street Kent 12 G3
Oakall Green Worcs 35 T8
Oakamoor Staffs 46 D5
Oakbank W Loth 83 L5
Oak Cross Devon 15 M13
Oakdale Caerph 27 M8
Oake Somset 16 G11
Oaken Staffs 45 U13
Oakenclough Lancs 61 U10
Oakengates Wrekin 45 R11
Oakenholt Flints 54 G12
Oakenshaw Dur 69 Q5
Oakenshaw Kirk 63 P14
Oakerthorpe Derbys 47 L3
Oakford Cerdgn 32 J9
Oakford Devon 16 B12
Oakfordbridge Devon 16 B12
Oakgrove Ches E 56 D13
Oakham Rutlnd 48 C12
Oakhanger Ches E 45 S3
Oakhanger Hants 10 B3
Oakhill Somset 17 R7
Oakhurst Kent 21 U12
Oakington Cambs 39 P8
Oaklands Powys 34 B10
Oakle Street Gloucs 28 E4
Oakley Bed 38 F10
Oakley Bucks 30 D10
Oakley Fife 90 F14
Oakley Hants 19 S10
Oakley Oxon 30 G12
Oakley Poole 8 E9
Oakley Suffk 41 L5
Oakley Green W & M 20 F7
Oakley Park Powys 33 U3
Oakridge Lynch Gloucs 28 H7
Oaks Lancs 62 D13
Oaks Shrops 44 K13
Oaksey Wilts 28 J9
Oaks Green Derbys 46 G7
Oakshaw Ford Cumb 75 V10
Oakshott Hants 9 U3
Oakthorpe Leics 46 K11
Oak Tree Darltn 70 E10
Oakwood C Derb 47 L6
Oakwood Nthumb 76 J12
Oakworth C Brad 63 L12
Oare Kent 12 K3
Oare Somset 15 S3
Oare Wilts 18 J8
Oasby Lincs 48 F6
Oath Somset 17 L11
Oathlaw Angus 98 H12
Oatlands Park Surrey 20 J9
Oban Ag & B 94 B13
Oban Airport Ag & B 94 C11
Obley Shrops 34 H5
Obney P & K 90 F4
Oborne Dorset 17 S13
Obthorpe Lincs 48 G11
Occold Suffk 41 L6
Occumster Highld 112 G9
Ochiltree E Ayrs 81 Q8
Ockbrook Derbys 47 M6
Ocker Hill Sandw 36 C2
Ockeridge Worcs 35 S8
Ockham Surrey 20 J11
Ockle Highld 93 P4
Ockley Surrey 10 J2
Ocle Pychard Herefs 35 N11
Octon E R Yk 65 N6
Odcombe Somset 17 P13
Odd Down BaNES 17 T4
Oddendale Cumb 67 S10
Oddingley Worcs 36 B9
Oddington Gloucs 29 P2
Oddington Oxon 30 C9
Odell Bed 38 E9
Odham Devon 15 L12
Odiham Hants 20 B12
Odsal C Brad 63 P14
Odsey Cambs 31 S5
Odstock Wilts 8 G3
Odstone Leics 47 L12
Offchurch Warwks 37 L7
Offenham Worcs 36 E11
Offerton Stockp 56 D9
Offerton Sundld 70 D1
Offham E Susx 11 Q8
Offham Kent 12 C4
Offham W Susx 10 G9
Offleymarsh Staffs 45 S8
Offord Cluny Cambs 38 K7
Offord D'Arcy Cambs 38 K7
Offton Suffk 40 J11
Offwell Devon 6 G5
Ogbourne Maizey Wilts 18 J6
Ogbourne St Andrew Wilts 18 J6
Ogbourne St George Wilts 18 K6
Ogden Calder 63 M13
Ogle Nthumb 77 N10
Oglet Lpool 54 K10
Ogmore V Glam 26 F12
Ogmore-by-Sea V Glam 26 F12
Ogmore Vale Brdgnd 26 G9
Ogwen Bank Gwynd 52 K9
Okeford Fitzpaine Dorset 7 V2
Okehampton Devon 15 N13
Oker Side Derbys 46 J1
Okewood Hill Surrey 10 J3
Olchard Devon 6 A9
Old Nhants 37 U6
Old Aberdeen C Aber 99 S2
Old Alresford Hants 9 R2
Oldany Highld 110 B10
Old Auchenbrack D & G 74 E6
Old Basford C Nott 47 Q5
Old Basing Hants 19 U10
Old Beetley Norfk 50 G10
Oldberrow Warwks 36 F7
Old Bewick Nthumb 77 M1
Old Bolingbroke Lincs 59 Q13
Old Bramhope Leeds 63 Q11
Old Brampton Derbys 57 M12
Old Bridge of Urr D & G 74 E12
Old Buckenham Norfk 40 J2
Old Burghclere Hants 19 Q9
Oldbury Kent 21 U11
Oldbury Sandw 36 C3
Oldbury Shrops 35 R2
Oldbury Warwks 36 K2
Oldbury Naite S Glos 28 B9
Oldbury-on-Severn S Glos 28 B9
Oldbury on the Hill Gloucs 28 F10
Old Byland N York 64 D2
Old Cantley Donc 57 T6
Old Cassop Dur 70 D5
Old Castle Brdgnd 26 G12
Oldcastle Mons 27 Q3
Oldcastle Heath Ches W 45 L4
Old Catton Norfk 51 M11
Old Churchstoke Powys 34 G2
Old Clee NE Lin 59 N5
Old Cleeve Somset 16 D8
Old Colwyn Conwy 53 Q7
Oldcotes Notts 57 S9
Old Dailly S Ayrs 80 J13
Old Dalby Leics 47 S9
Old Dam Derbys 56 H11
Old Deer Abers 105 R6
Old Ditch Somset 17 P7
Old Edlington Donc 57 R7
Old Eldon Dur 69 R7
Old Ellerby E R Yk 65 R12
Old Felixstowe Suffk 41 P13
Oldfield C Brad 63 L12
Oldfield Worcs 35 T8
Old Fletton C Pete 38 J1
Oldford Somset 17 U6
Old Forge Herefs 27 V4
Old Furnace Herefs 27 T3
Old Glossop Derbys 56 F8
Old Goole E R Yk 58 B2
Old Grimsby IoS 2 b1
Old Hall Green Herts 31 U8
Oldhall Green Suffk 40 E9
Old Hall Street Norfk 51 P7
Oldham Oldham 56 D6
Oldham Crematorium Oldham 56 D6
Oldhamstocks E Loth 84 J4
Old Harlow Essex 22 C5
Old Heath Essex 23 P3
Old Hunstanton Norfk 49 U5
Old Hurst Cambs 39 M5
Old Hutton Cumb 62 B2
Old Inns Services N Lans 89 S10
Old Kea Cnwll 3 L8
Old Kilpatrick W Duns 89 L11
Old Knebworth Herts 31 R8
Old Lakenham Norfk 51 M12
Oldland S Glos 17 S2
Old Langho Lancs 62 E12
Old Laxey IoM 60 g6
Old Leake Lincs 49 P3
Old Malton N York 64 H5
Oldmeldrum Abers 105 N10
Oldmill Cnwll 4 K6
Old Milverton Warwks 36 J7
Oldmixon N Som 16 K5
Old Newton Suffk 40 J8
Old Oxted Surrey 21 Q12
Old Portlethen Abers 99 S4
Old Quarrington Dur 70 D5
Old Radford C Nott 47 Q5
Old Radnor Powys 34 G9
Old Rayne Abers 104 K10
Old Romney Kent 12 K11
Old Shoreham W Susx 11 L9
Oldshoremore Highld 110 E5
Old Soar Kent 12 B5
Old Sodbury S Glos 28 E11
Old Somerby Lincs 48 E7
Oldstead N York 64 C4
Old Stratford Nhants 30 G4
Old Struan P & K 97 N10
Old Swarland Nthumb 77 P5
Old Swinford Dudley 36 B4
Old Tebay Cumb 68 D11
Old Thirsk N York 63 U3
Old Town Calder 63 L14
Old Town Cumb 62 B3
Old Town Cumb 67 Q4
Old Town E Susx 11 T11
Old Town IoS 2 c2
Old Trafford Traffd 55 T7
Old Tupton Derbys 57 N13
Oldwall Cumb 75 U13
Oldwalls Swans 25 S12
Old Warden C Beds 31 P4
Oldways End Somset 15 U8
Old Weston Cambs 38 G5
Old Wick Highld 112 J7
Old Windsor W & M 20 G8
Old Wives Lees Kent 13 L5
Old Woking Surrey 20 H11
Old Wolverton M Keyn 30 H4
Old Woodhall Lincs 59 M13
Old Woods Shrops 45 L9
Olgrinmore Highld 112 C6
Olive Green Staffs 46 F10
Oliver's Battery Hants 9 P3
Ollaberry Shet 106 t5
Ollach Highld 100 e6
Ollerton Ches E 55 S11
Ollerton Notts 57 U13
Ollerton Shrops 45 P8
Olmarch Cerdgn 33 M9
Olmstead Green Cambs 39 T12
Olney M Keyn 38 C10
Olrig House Highld 112 E3
Olton Solhll 36 F4
Olveston S Glos 28 B10
Ombersley Worcs 35 T8
Ompton Notts 57 U13
Once Brewed Nthumb 76 E12
Onchan IoM 60 f7
Onecote Staffs 46 D2
Onehouse Suffk 40 H9
Onen Mons 27 S5
Ongar Street Herefs 34 J7
Onibury Shrops 35 L5
Onich Highld 94 E6
Onllwyn Neath 26 E5
Onneley Staffs 45 S5
Onslow Green Essex 22 G4
Onslow Village Surrey 20 G13
Onston Ches W 55 N12
Openwoodgate Derbys 47 L4
Opinan Highld 107 M10
Orbliston Moray 104 C4
Orbost Highld 100 b5
Orby Lincs 59 S13
Orchard Portman Somset 16 H12
Orcheston Wilts 18 G11
Orcop Herefs 27 T2
Orcop Hill Herefs 27 T2
Ord Abers 104 J4
Ordhead Abers 104 K13
Ordie Abers 98 H3
Ordiequish Moray 104 C4
Ordley Nthumb 76 J14
Ordsall Notts 58 B11
Ore E Susx 12 F13
Oreleton Common Herefs 35 L7
Oreton Shrops 35 Q4
Orford Suffk 41 R10
Orford Warrtn 55 P8
Organford Dorset 8 C10
Orgreave Staffs 46 F10
Orkney Islands Ork 106 t19
Orkney Neolithic Ork 106 r18
Orlestone Kent 12 K9
Orleton Herefs 35 L7
Orleton Worcs 35 R7
Orlingbury Nhants 38 C6
Ormathwaite Cumb 67 L7
Ormesby R & Cl 70 H9
Ormesby St Margaret Norfk 51 S11
Ormesby St Michael Norfk 51 S11
Ormiscaig Highld 107 Q6
Ormiston E Loth 83 T5
Ormsaigmore Highld 93 M6
Ormsary Ag & B 87 N11
Ormskirk Lancs 54 K5
Ornsby Hill Dur 69 Q3
Oronsay Ag & B 86 F8
Orphir Ork 106 s19
Orpington Gt Lon 21 S9
Orrell Sefton 54 H7
Orrell Wigan 55 M6
Orrell Post Wigan 55 M5
Orrisdale IoM 60 e4
Orroland D & G 73 T10
Orsett Thurr 22 F11
Orsett Heath Thurr 22 F11
Orslow Staffs 45 T10
Orston Notts 47 U5
Orthwaite Cumb 67 L6
Ortner Lancs 61 U9
Orton Cumb 68 D11
Orton Nhants 38 B5
Orton Staffs 35 U1
Orton Longueville C Pete 38 J1
Orton-on-the-Hill Leics 46 K13
Orton Rigg Cumb 67 M2
Orton Waterville C Pete 38 J1
Orwell Cambs 39 N10
Osbaldeston Lancs 62 C13
Osbaldeston Green Lancs 62 C13
Osbaldwick C York 64 E9
Osbaston Leics 47 M13
Osbaston Shrops 44 H9
Osborne IoW 9 Q10
Osborne House IoW 9 Q10
Osbournby Lincs 48 G6
Oscroft Ches W 55 M13
Ose Highld 100 c5
Osgathorpe Leics 47 M10
Osgodby Lincs 58 J8
Osgodby N York 64 E13
Osgodby N York 65 P3
Oskaig Highld 100 e6
Oskamull Ag & B 93 M10
Osmaston Derbys 46 G5
Osmington Dorset 7 T8
Osmington Mills Dorset 7 T8
Osmondthorpe Leeds 63 S13
Osmotherley N York 70 G13
Osney Oxon 29 U6
Ospringe Kent 12 K3
Ossett Wakefd 57 L2
Ossington Notts 58 C14
Ostend Essex 23 M8
Osterley Gt Lon 21 L7
Oswaldkirk N York 64 E4
Oswaldtwistle Lancs 55 R1
Oswestry Shrops 44 G8
Otford Kent 21 T11
Otham Kent 12 E5
Otham Hole Kent 12 F5
Othery Somset 17 L10
Otley Leeds 63 Q10
Otley Suffk 41 M9
Otley Green Suffk 41 M9
Otterbourne Hants 9 P4
Otterburn N York 62 H8
Otterburn Nthumb 76 H7
Otter Ferry Ag & B 87 S9
Otterham Cnwll 4 F2
Otterhampton Somset 16 H8
Otterham Quay Kent 12 F2
Otterham Station Cnwll 4 F3
Otternish W Isls 106 e11
Ottershaw Surrey 20 H10
Otterswick Shet 106 v5
Otterton Devon 6 E7
Otterwood Hants 9 N8
Ottery St Mary Devon 6 F5
Ottinge Kent 13 N7
Ottringham E R Yk 59 N2
Oughterby Cumb 67 L1
Oughtershaw N York 62 H3
Oughterside Cumb 66 H4
Oughtibridge Sheff 57 M8
Oughtrington Warrtn 55 Q9
Oulston N York 64 C5
Oulton Cumb 66 K2
Oulton Leeds 63 T14
Oulton Norfk 50 K8
Oulton Staffs 45 S9
Oulton Staffs 46 B6
Oulton Suffk 41 T2